e-Business:
organizational and technical foundations

Michael P. Papazoglou
Professor, Tilburg University

Pieter Ribbers
Professor, Tilburg University

John Wiley & Sons, Ltd

Other Wiley Editorial Offices

John Wiley & Sons Inc., 111 River Street, Hoboken, NJ 07030, USA

Jossey-Bass, 989 Market Street, San Francisco, CA 94103-1741, USA

Wiley-VCH Verlag GmbH, Boschstr. 12, D-69469 Weinheim, Germany

John Wiley & Sons Australia Ltd, 42 McDougall Street, Milton, Queensland 4064, Australia

John Wiley & Sons (Asia) Pte Ltd, 2 Clementi Loop #02-01, Jin Xing Distripark, Singapore 129809

John Wiley & Sons Canada Ltd, 22 Worcester Road, Etobicoke, Ontario, Canada M9W 1L1

Wiley also publishes its books in a variety of electronic formats. Some content that appears in print may not be
available in electronic books.

Library of Congress Cataloging-in-Publication Data

Papazoglou, M., 1953-
  E-business : organizational and technical foundations / Mike Papazoglou, Pieter Ribbers.
     p. cm.
  Includes bibliographical references and index.
  ISBN 0-470-84376-4 (pbk. : alk. paper)
  1. Electronic commerce. 2. Electronic commerce–Management. 3. Business enterprises–Computer network
resources. I. Ribbers, Pieter. II. Title.
  HF5548.32.P364 2006
  381 .142 068–dc22   2005019358

British Library Cataloguing in Publication Data

A catalogue record for this book is available from the British Library

ISBN 13 978-0-470-84376-5 (Paper)
ISBN 10 0-470-84376-4 (Paper)

Typeset in 9/11 Baskerville by Thomson Press (India) Limited, Noida, India
Printed and bound in Great Britain by Bell & Bain, Glasgow
This book is printed on acid-free paper responsibly manufactured from sustainable forestry
in which at least two trees are planted for each one used for paper production.

e-Business

7 DAY LOAN

THE UNIVERSITY OF LIVERPOOL
SYDNEY JONES LIBRARY
RESTRICTED LOAN

Please return or renew, on or before the last date below. A fine is payable on late returned items. Items may be recalled after one week for the use of another reader. Items may be renewed by telephone:- 0151 794 - 2678.

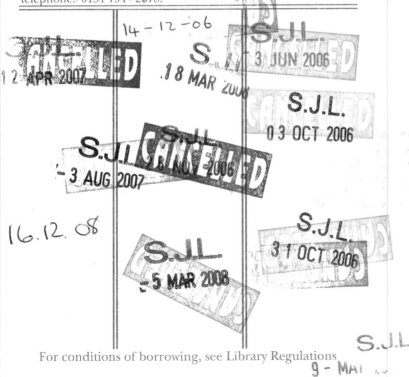

For conditions of borrowing, see Library Regulations

"At last, a book that explains e-Business from all angles. Readers will enjoy a comprehensive presentation of the technological, organizational, and business aspects that combine to create the needs and opportunity of e-business. The breadth of coverage is pleasantly coupled with depth in key aspects of e-business, so that readers interested in either business or technology will find it discussed in a thorough and insightful way."

Fabio Casati, Ph.D.
Senior scientist
Hewlett-Packard Company, Palo Alto, CA

"Mike Papazoglou has been at the forefront of service-oriented computing, distributed systems, information modeling and data engineering for more than fifteen years – developing ideas and technologies to transform businesses into e-Businesses by automating business transactions, information systems and business processes. Working with Pieter Ribbers, Mike has employed that expertise to write a very comprehensive book with case studies and illustrations of e Business foundations – sorting through myriads of emerging technologies, standards and business organization principles."

Asit Dan, Ph.D.
Manager, Autonomic Service Oriented Computing
IBM T.J. Watson Research Center, Hawthorne, NY

"This book represents a shift in our thinking of e-business away from purely technical considerations to a view that embraces business and technical perspectives. The international examples of business applications and technical exercises will be of great value to students".

Professor Christopher P. Holland
Manchester Business School

"Over the past 10 years, e-business has revolutionized the way enterprises conduct business with each other. Yet we are still at the dawn of this revolution because the technology that supports e-business is complex and still being specified. Mike and Piet's book provides the foundation to understand what has been accomplished and to innovate in building the economy of the 21st century."

Jean-Jacques Dubray, Ph.D., Attachmate, Editor of the OASIS ebXML
Business Process Specification v2.0.1

Contents

8. e-Markets   197

18. e-Business Integration   543

19. Loosely Coupled e-Business Solutions   579

About the Authors

Michael P. Papazoglou holds the chair of Computer Science and is director of the INFOLAB at the Univ. of Tilburg in the Netherlands. He is also a honorary professor at the University of Trento in Italy. Prior to this (1991–6), he was full Professor and head of School of Information Systems at the Queensland University of Technology (QUT) in Brisbane, Australia. He also held senior academic positions at the Australian National University, the University of Koblenz, Germany, Fern Universitaet Hagen, Germany, and was principal research scientist at the National German Research Centre for Computer Science (GMD) in St. Augustin from 1983–9.

Papazoglou serves on several international committees and on the editorial board of nine international scientific journals and is co-editor in charge of the MIT book series on Information Systems. He has chaired numerous well-known international scientific conferences in Computer Science. These include the International Conference on Data Engineering (ICDE), International Conference on Distributed Computing Systems (ICDCS), International Conference on Digital Libraries (ICDL), International Conference on Cooperative Information Systems (CoopIS), International Conference on Entity/Relationship Modelling and others. He is the founder of the International Conference on Cooperative Information Systems (CoopIS) and more recently of the International Conference on Service Oriented Computing (ICSOC).

Papazoglou has authored or edited 15 books and approximately 150 scientific journal articles and refereed conference papers. His research was/is funded by the European Commission, the Australian Research Council, the Japanese Society for the Promotion of Science, and Departments of Science and Technology in Europe and Australia. He is a golden core member and a distinguished visitor of the Institute of Electrical & Electronics Engineers (IEEE) Computer Science section.

Pieter M. Ribbers holds the chair of Information Management at Tilburg University, The Netherlands, where he also is head of the Department of Information Systems and Management. From 1991 till 1994 he held a position as affiliated Professor of Information Management at Washington University in St. Louis, Missouri, USA. His interests span management of information technology (in particular questions related to alignment and information economics), inter-organizational systems (in particular electronic commerce), and the strategic and organizational consequences of the use of information technology. He is active as researcher, lecturer and consultant. He has supervised more than 20 PhD theses and has contributed articles in this field to national and international professional journals and has (co)authored several books. He is active at international conferences in information systems (ECIS, HICSS, ICIS) and is a member of the editorial board of *Information and Management – The International Journal of Information Systems Applications*. He has also participated in research programs of the European Commission. As a consultant he has worked with companies such as Brunel, Nolan, Norton & Co., and ING Group especially in outsourcing, scenario development and information economics.

Foreword

Traditionally, students in Management, Computer and Information Sciences are exposed during their undergraduate studies to the theories and practices of business. This includes introduction to organizational principles, as well as analytical and decision-theoretic approaches to business design, supporting technologies, and case studies. The topic of business design is often sub-divided into business-to-business and business-to-consumer commerce.

The world of business is undergoing a radical change that started about a decade ago. Trends in marketplace competition on one hand, and the advent of the Web on the other, have created a brand new landscape within which business is conducted. This is the brave new world of e-Business, wherein enterprises conduct themselves using agile and flexible business models and processes, transform themselves continuously to meet marketplace challenges and opportunities, participate in opportunistic alliances and virtual organizations. This world is founded on information technologies and is built on new economic principles of competitiveness.

This textbook presents a thorough and comprehensive introduction to this new world, focusing on business-to-business commerce. Its scope includes both technological and organizational concepts, tools and techniques. Specifically, the book offers in-depth coverage of the prerequisites, organizational structures, and technological infrastructure for conducting e-Business. It then delves into specific areas of e-Business, such as e-Markets, and e-Procurement. The third part of the book introduces concepts and modelling techniques for topics such as security and reliability, enterprise architectures, Web services and business protocols.

Through this book, the student is assured a comprehensive and state-of-the-art introduction to business-to-business commerce in the new millennium. This introduction is beneficial not only to Management and Computer Science students, but also students in Computer and Industrial Engineering, as well as Information Studies. The book is also useful for practitioners who design software for modern organizations, and researchers who need to make realistic assumptions about the nature of organizations and the trends through which they evolve. After all, most software consists of organizational information systems. Having a solid understanding of the organizational context within which an information system will operate is a critical – and often lacking – requirement for building quality software. For those who believe in this principle, this book is must reading.

John Mylopoulos
Professor, Bell Laboratories Chair in Information Systems
Department of Computer Science
University of Toronto

Toronto, September 2005

Overview

e **-Business is the application of information and telecommunication technologies to conducting business. The phenomenon of e-Business is, on the one hand, the result of competitive drivers which challenge companies in their marketplaces and, on the other hand, the result of new enabling information technologies. Both drivers interact when reshaping the business environment.**

This book focuses on the development of e-Business between enterprises, in other words, business-to-business commerce. In particular, it addresses how enterprises collaborate, what coordination mechanisms are necessary to achieve collaboration and how these two factors are reflected on the technical infrastructure level. The same types of problems concern not only collaborating enterprises but also collaborating business units within an enterprise. The aim is to prepare enterprises to transform their structure and processes in order to embark on an e-Business venture.

Statistics show that in the past this has been and in the future is expected to be the most important growth area for e-Business. Multiple forces contribute to these developments. The average industrial firm spends 58% of every sales dollar on purchases from outside vendors. Every dollar saved in purchasing goes right to the bottom line. As a consequence companies want to reduce transaction costs. The current trend of concentrating on core competencies increases even more the relative amount of goods and services purchased.

Multiple types of relationships with vendors have developed. Accordingly different sorts of collaboration are possible. For instance, products can be designed and developed collaboratively, supply chains can be integrated to produce more added value for the customer, new forms of technology can enable collaborations such as electronic auctions and marketplaces, and so on. Collaborations can be sparse or intense in nature as the market may dictate and this has a direct implication on the technologies used. Moreover, firms try to be flexible when operating in specific markets. Buying processes differ accordingly. These may be lengthy processes involving extensive search and negotiations, quick and efficient spot purchases, or routine procedures. Technology supports and enables these different types of relationships. For example, in the past, Electronic Data Interchange (EDI) traditionally supported more stable relationships between buyers and suppliers; more recently, the Internet and other computer networks support the development of more flexible business scenarios on the Internet.

e-Business contrasts with consumer-oriented e-Commerce on a number of points. Corporations must purchase various goods, products and services, and typically do so under time pressure. Additionally, businesses often purchase parts, components or supplies necessary to create the finished products they sell, while the consumer market typically purchases finished goods. While many consumers pay by credit card, few businesses use this method. For businesses, procedures regulate purchasing. Documents such as purchase requisitions, purchase orders, and invoices follow a constant flow through the enterprise. Understanding the underlying forces of e-Business consequently requires a multi-disciplinary approach in which theories and concepts from business organization, management and technology are brought together and integrated.

Mission and unique features of the book

This book is unique in that it appropriately blends business and technology issues, interrelates them, raises economic concerns and contains an in-depth coverage of both business and technical issues including concepts, definitions, processes, principles and strategy. We firmly believe that e-Business is inseparably about both business and technology, and a solid understanding of the underlying business, organization, management and technology issues is crucial to an understanding of what e-Business is today and how it is going to be shaped in the future.

This is a comprehensive book that introduces and explains the different elements of e-Business and provides a structure that can facilitate the assimilation of new e-Business developments as they occur in the future. We have also included abundant real-world applications to encourage readers to understand and appreciate real-life e-Business applications. Most importantly, the text emphasizes an analytical and critical approach to understanding business issues, decision-making and technology use and development.

The interplay between e-Business technology and business/organizational requirements and strategies is a problem and a challenge, as has been extensively demonstrated by many of the recent dot.com meltdowns. Success of e-Business systems eventually depends on the success of the business ventures in which they have been applied. An infrastructure may be technologically sound but if the fundamentals of the new business models are not right, it will eventually fail. On the other hand, a business model may seem right economically, but fully depend on the technological realization of the required e-Business infrastructure. If business requirements such as full interoperability cannot be met technically, the business venture will not succeed. Consequently, the eventual success of implementation of new e-Business infrastructures depends on the extent to which new technologies are absorbed by new business practices, and vice versa, and so requires a balancing act in adjusting current organizational practices to modern e-Business infrastructures.

The overall purpose of the book is to show how insights of organization theory relate to effects caused by e-Business infrastructures. E-markets will not be used simply because they are there; intermediaries will not be made obsolete just because the Internet exists. However, the management of a company cannot ignore e-Business as an exogenous reality. The economics of it, e.g. reduced transaction costs, may make the company's traditional business model outmoded and will put the company at a competitive disadvantage vis à vis those companies that do adopt e-Business. The concepts, theories, and analyses developed in this book aim at creating a better understanding of the fundamentals of e-Business and the background of e-Business success.

We carried out extensive research for this book and used a large number of references and resources from different fields including information systems and management, organization theory, economics, computer science and engineering. There is a wealth of business issues and technologies that make e-Business possible. Merely choosing which of these to cover and to which depth is mind-boggling. For many of these business and organization issues, a complete treatment requires one or even more books devoted to them. Thus, the question of depth becomes an important concern. We strived to produce a balanced book that provides sufficient depth for readers to have a solid understanding of each issue, its impacts, how they are inter-related and how they fit in the context of the e-Business landscape.

Content and organization

We have already explained how understanding the underlying forces of e-Business requires a multi-disciplinary approach in which theories and concepts from management and technology are integrated. This is why this book offers an in-depth and integrated coverage of both business and technical issues including definitions, principles and strategy. In particular, we focus on the interaction of organizational, managerial and technological concepts. Throughout the book, we provide examples of how e-Business technology affects business practice.

There are a number of issues that we do not cover in this book but which are considered important for an effective implementation of an e-Business strategy. Topics such as legal and ethical aspects of e-Business (how to deal with privacy issues in an international business environment) and the financial aspects of e-Business (how does e-Business affect the financial position of the firm, as a basis for a quantified investment analysis) have been left out of the discussion.

Figure P.1 provides an overview of the overall structure of the book; it may help readers with different interests to navigate through the chapters. The book combines business/organizational aspects of e-Business, with a discussion of the technical foundation necessary for a deployment of an e-Business strategy. This discussion is structured logically in three inter-related parts.

Chapters 1 to 7 cover the relationship between e-Business and business strategy. Fundamental questions are addressed, such as how e-Business relates to business models, to inter-organizational relations with suppliers, customers and other business partners, and how e-Business technologies can affect governance structures. This part ends with a discussion about the technological infrastructure needed to realize e-Business models, and the use of XML as the enabling technology to facilitate communication in an e-Business environment.

- *Chapter 2* sets the strategic context for e-Business. It discusses the relationship between e-Business and strategic business planning. Given a definition of 'e-Business strategy' we consider strategic positioning, at what organizational levels e-Business should be planned, what the business and technology drivers are that trigger e-Business strategies, and how strategic planning processes for e-Business should look. We conclude with a discussion of three theoretical perspectives from which the business effects of e-Business

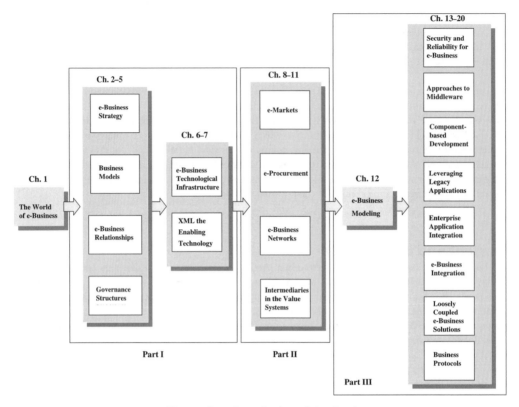

Figure P.1: Organization of the Book

developments can be explained. Finally, we present a case study illustrating how e-Business technology can lead to changing competitive relations within an industry.

- *Chapter 3* considers the concept of 'business model'. What is a business model and why does technology trigger new business models? Traditional business models aimed to create value at the line-of-business level. New business models are customer-centric and create value at the relationship level across products and channels. A new phenomenon is the networked business model. We conclude with examples of two organizations in different industries experimenting with Internet-based networked business models.

- *Chapter 4* discusses characteristics of e-Business relationships and their relevance for the application of e-Business technology. Porter's value chain model and its relevance for e-Business, business process management (BPM) and inter-company relationships are described. Finally, we address how e-Business technology aims at improving the efficiency and effectiveness of inter-organizational transactions and at streamlining business processes. This chapter ends with a case study that illustrates how e-Business technology is changing a hundred-year-old industry.

- *Chapter 5* discusses the topic of governance for e-Business. Governance specifies which parties are involved in a transaction, and what co-ordination mechanisms are used. This chapter explains how advances in information technology and management are affecting choices with regard to in-house production (hierarchy governance), buying (market governance), or longer-term inter-firm collaboration (network governance), from the perspective of transaction-cost economics and the resource-based view. In particular, we pay attention to the 'electronic market hypothesis' and the 'move to the middle' hypothesis.

- *Chapter 6* describes e-Business infrastructure and technologies for e-Business. Defining an adequate e-Business infrastructure to achieve process integration is vital to all companies adopting e-Business. The infrastructure refers to the combination of systems inside an enterprise such as client/servers, the networking facilities used to link an enterprise's internal systems with those of its partners, and the technology used to integrate systems and processes between collaborating enterprises. This chapter acts as a launchpad to discuss a number of key technologies that are pertinent to e-Business. The discussion begins with e-Business challenges on the technology front, and continues with the tenants of the technology stack for e-Business, which include networking facilities, basic infrastructure, such as the client/server architecture and tiered computing models, and collaborative technologies such as workflow systems and EDI.

- *Chapter 7* gives an introduction to XML so that the reader would appreciate its use within the context of e-Business. XML is an extensible markup language used for the description and delivery of marked-up electronic text over the Web. The chapter discusses characteristics and structure in XML documents, presentation, transformation and processing of XML documents, and concludes with an analysis of the relation between XML, EDI and e-Business.

In Chapters 8 to 11, we describe four key topics that companies have to address when designing and deploying an e-Business strategy: e-Markets, e-Procurement, networked organizations and the role of intermediaries in the value system. These key topics relate to the relationships of the focal organization with its transactional environment. In these chapters, we discuss the role and function of e-Markets, the support of the purchasing function by e-Procurement, how to position the focal organization in emerging business networks, and finally the effect of e-Business technology on the configuration of the industry value chain through patterns of intermediation and disintermediation.

- *Chapter 8* discusses definitions, characteristics, and functions of e-Markets. The Internet has the ability to bring buyers and sellers together in a virtual space, in other words, to create electronic markets. However, many initiatives have failed. We analyze differences between traditional and electronic markets and discuss success factors for electronic markets. We conclude with an analysis of four examples of marketplaces.

- *Chapter 9* considers the role of e-Procurement in e-Business. E-Markets enable companies to buy products and services electronically. We start the discussion by positioning the role and importance of the purchasing function in the business organization. Traditional and modern roles of IT, in general, and the Internet, in particular, in procurement are described. The purchasing process is put in the perspective of a broader supply chain context. We conclude with a description of two commercially available e-Procurement solutions.

- *Chapter 10* focuses on network organizations. Collaborative relationships between organizations lead to network organizations. Network organizations are supported and enabled by modern technologies. Different types of network organizations and inter-organizational systems and how they relate to each other are described. A specific class of network organizations, supply chains and their management, is considered. We conclude with two examples of network organizations, one in the finance industry and one in the IT industry.

- *Chapter 11* considers the roles of intermediaries in the value system and how they may be affected by e-Business infrastructures. Information infrastructures are extending to reach individual suppliers, consumers and trading partners, and begin to enable producers to directly interact with consumers. Key questions are to what extent producing organizations will take advantage of direct electronic links with consumers, and whether intermediaries will be eliminated from the value system. Are intermediaries a threatened breed, or is it likely that the mediating function will be present in the electronic marketplace with traditional intermediaries benefiting from network-based transactions to solidify their role in exchanges with new types of network-based entities?

Chapters 12 to 20 concentrate on modeling issues and the technical foundations of e-Business. A key concept for this part of the book is 'interoperability'. Information systems of different organizations need to interact to accomplish the functions of e-Business. Important topics that concern us in this part of the book include the type of requirements that need to be met when addressing business interactions (for example, choosing loose or tight coupling of applications), and how this type of integration affects existing and new applications. In particular, Chapters 17, 18 and 19 address a plethora of important issues that characterize application-to-application integration and business integration.

The discussion starts with modeling and, in particular, process modeling to develop and implement e-Business systems. Next we consider security, middleware, components and e-Business system development, legacy, e-Business integration, Web services and business protocols.

- *Chapter 12* provides readers with an understanding of what is required for modeling e-Business environments and processes. We concentrate on e-Business modeling techniques and methodologies and examine relevant topics associated with the modeling and delivery of e-Business applications based on standardized formal modeling approaches. For this purpose, we first introduce the notions of business modeling and collaborative business processes and then focus on the use of Unified Modeling Language (UML) and standard methodologies, such as the Unified Modeling Methodology (UMM) and the Supply Chain Operations Reference (SCOR) model.

- *Chapter 13* focuses on the role that security plays for e-Business and the specific organizational and technical requirements needed for creating a reliable environment for e-Business communication using the Internet. The security of an enterprise's information systems has become a major management responsibility. e-Business environments impose their own requirements: verification of identities, non-repudiation of agreements and a swarm of other issues often come into play. Alongside such concerns, enterprises making more use of e-Business must protect themselves against a growing number of complex risks. Consequently, quality of service becomes a critical instrument to ensure the enterprise infrastructure delivers the scalability, security, transaction, and content-based requirements of the business.

- *Chapter 14* considers middleware approaches for e-Business. Advanced electronic business strategies try to create a single virtual organization. These systems use middleware, a layer of integration code and functionality that allows multiple diverse and distributed systems to be used as though they were a single system. We first introduce the concepts of messaging, Remote Procedure Calls and Remote Method Invocation and then concentrate on message-oriented middleware. Subsequently, we concentrate on data-access middleware and transaction-oriented middleware. Finally, distributed objects and distributed object middleware platforms, such as CORBA and DCOM, are introduced.

- *Chapter 15* discusses components. Components allow a complex system to be built as a combination of smaller components. The aim with software components is to allow off-the-shelf modules to be quickly assembled into applications with functionality that does not need to be expensively re-implemented for each new system.

- *Chapter 16* focuses on reusing legacy systems and applications in the context of e-Business. Legacy information assets are hindering established enterprises that are trying to get into the e-Business arena. The analysis provides insights into establishing a legacy infrastructure, and overviews strategies and deployment options for managing, modernizing and integrating legacy applications with modern technologies so that they can function without hindrance in the environment surrounding e-Business applications.

- *Chapter 17* considers enterprise application integration (EAI). To be competitive, an organization's core business applications – such as Enterprise Resource Planning (ERP) – must be integrated with customer relationship management (CRM) and Web-based applications to enable connectivity to suppliers, partners, and customers. In Chapters 6 and 14 we presented several technologies and middleware approaches that are used in the context of EAI. In this chapter we shall explain how they can be used in the context of singular or collaborating enterprises to support business integration activities.

- *Chapter 18* provides a detailed introduction to e-Business integration concepts and techniques. Enterprises strive to integrate, automate, and streamline core internal and external business processes to improve their performance in the e-Business environment. A wide range of aspects relating to e-Business integration concepts and techniques are considered, such as standards, e-Business topologies, semantic interoperability, and existing reference models.

- *Chapter 19* discusses how Web services solve integration problems created by multiple parties that want to collaborate in an e-Business environment. Traditional business-to-business connections are usually created virtually point-to-point with human direction at every stage of the process and result in tightly coupled systems. These traditional forms of business-to-business communication have not been able to adequately address the challenges of integrating various customers, suppliers and other strategic partners.

- *Chapter 20* considers how a common understanding of business processes and data to be transferred across existing and future platforms is built with business standards and business protocols. Business standards typically manage the structure for defining form, fit and function of any product or service, regardless of the industry. A business protocol captures the information and exchange requirements that identify the timing, sequence and purpose of each business collaboration and information exchange. A business protocol is associated with business processes and governs the exchange of business information and messages between trading partners across differing enterprise information systems, middleware platforms and organizations. It specifies the structure and semantics of business messages, how to process the messages, and how to route them to appropriate recipients.

Given the wealth of detailed coverage of several business and technical issues, instructors may mix and match concepts to produce the desired coverage, depending on where an e-Business course fits into the curriculum. Instructors may choose to emphasize an appropriate blend of business and technology issues.

Suggested routes through the material for organization and business students

In Figure P.2, we indicate some ways in which the material in this book can be used in educational modules and courses taken by business, information systems and management and/or organization students. These are meant to be purely suggestions.

Suggested routes through the material for technically-oriented students

In Figure P.3, we indicate some ways in which the material in this book can be used in educational modules and courses taken by computer science, information systems and, in general, more technically minded students. Again, these are meant to be purely suggestions.

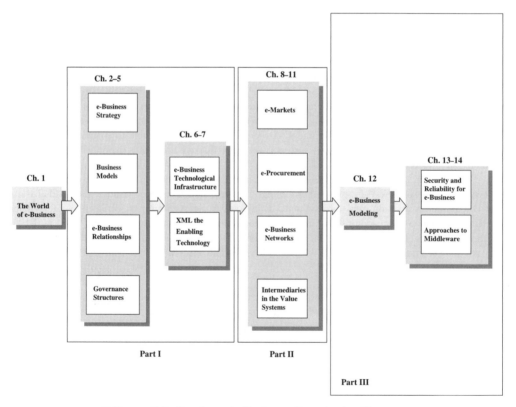

■ **Figure P.2:** Roadmap to Business Organization Chapters

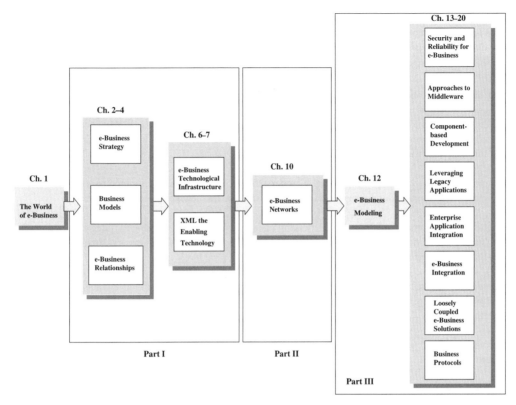

■ **Figure P.3:** Roadmap to Technical Chapters

Audience

Students

This book has mainly been created as a text for advanced undergraduate information systems, information management and computer science students, taking specialist courses or modules which cover e-Business, business process management, information systems strategies, and enterprise integration courses. The course also addresses postgraduate students on specialist masters degrees that require knowledge of e-Business and related topics.

The book targets both business and organization as well as more technically minded students. The reader will learn several aspects of e-Business in depth including strategies and governance structures and will understand how the business and technology issues are applied to the organization context of e-Business.

Researchers

This book can be used as a reference book by researchers who wish to form a solid background in e-Business and a thorough understanding of the interplay between organizational and technology issues. It can, of course, also be used to develop a thorough understanding in either of these two areas in isolation.

We have provided an extensive list of scientific references covering both business and technical issues and open problems that may provide meaningful background and context that could guide researchers with their research work and projects.

Practitioners

This book can also be used by professionals and, in general individuals, who are working, or intending to work, on the area of electronic business. Owing to the widespread use of e-Business systems nowadays, these professionals could come from any company that uses or wishes to use e-Business applications and may have different backgrounds either on business or on technology or even on a mix of both. Professionals that could find this book useful include:

- Senior managers and directors seeking to understand the business and technology issues underpinning e-Business and to develop the right e-Business approach for the benefit of their organization.

- Information systems managers who are developing and implementing e-Business strategies and may wish to acquire more detailed knowledge of the technologies underlying e-Business and their relationship to e-Business strategies.

- Technical managers and developers who may wish to learn more about the technical details of e-Business and may have a limited knowledge of business fundamentals and their relationship to e-Business technology.

- Consultants who wish to find support and a source of information for the solutions they suggest to their customers.

Acknowledgements

Since we have started writing this book, many people have given us invaluable help and have been influential in shaping our thoughts and ideas regarding e-Business and on how to best organize and teach an e-Business course.

From the many who have contributed, it is perhaps invidious to name some and not others. Nevertheless, we would especially like to mention Shahram Dustar, Andy Gravell, Willem Jan van den Heuvel, Chris Holland, Sergey Kostyuchenko, Benedikt Kratz, Shazia Sadiq, Martin Smits, and Martin van Tuyl who have either reviewed several chapters of this book or provided us with useful advice and comments that considerably improved the quality of this book. We are heavily indebted to them for their effort and valuable time.

We would also like to thank our colleagues and PhD students who have contributed directly or indirectly to our insights regarding e-Business. Special thanks also go to our undergraduate students for providing us with valuable comments regarding the parts of this book that we taught in the classroom.

Finally, we wish to thank the entire John Wiley team, who have done an outstanding job. Particular thanks go to Gaynor Redvers-Mutton, our original editor at John Wiley, for her continuous encouragement, perseverance and especially patience with us. This book took considerably more than two years to complete. Our thanks also go to Deborah Egleton at John Wiley, for guiding us throughout the last and most painful hurdles of this book.

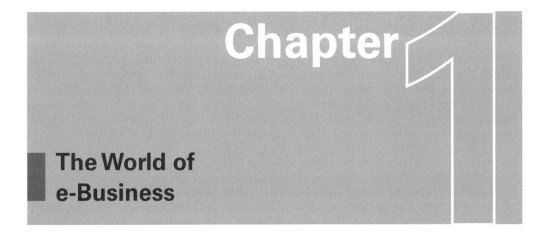

Chapter 1

The World of e-Business

Connectivity to the Internet and the effective exploitation of available Internet service technologies is both the cause and the effect of new ways to conduct business electronically. The potential rewards of doing business over the World Wide Web (the Web) are limitless as companies extend their reach beyond organizational and geographic boundaries to allow the organization to exploit local and global markets.

Harnessing the Internet and the technologies surrounding it has the potential to impact several business drivers such as attracting new customers; retaining customers; streamlining distribution channels, logistics operations and key business processes; attracting new partners; and improving productivity. The power of the Internet to support the sales and marketing of products efficiently has led to incredible levels of Web activity. E-Business is a fast growing area in the new Internet economy and is a critical imperative for business seeking to create or maintain sustained market advantages in the 21st century. The rapid adoption of e-Business models is shaping the future of global businesses and driving deep and profound changes in the structure of business practices of organizations and the interactions between companies.

This chapter explores the use of the Internet and the Web for business purposes. The chapter describes what is meant by the term e-Business and compares and contrasts e-Business with e-Commerce.

1.1 What is e-Business?

IBM was among the first to use e-Business when it launched a thematic campaign built around the term in 1997. Until then, the widely used buzzword was e-Commerce. The shift in terms also meant a shift in paradigm; selling and selling support were the only experiences that companies could reproduce on the Web. Broadening the approach to allow more types of business on the Web created the new term e-Business. E-Business can be defined as the conduct of automated business transactions by means of electronic communications networks (e.g., via the Internet and/or possibly private networks) end-to-end.

The term *end-to-end business transaction* signifies that a succession of automated business processes and information systems of different companies, which are involved in an inter-company business transaction, are successfully integrated. The aim is to provide seamless interoperation and interactive links between all the relevant members of an extended demand and supply chain – ranging from product designers, suppliers and their partners to end-customers. An end-to-end process involves integrating designers, suppliers, and buyers, trading partners, logistics providers and end-customers in the entire planning and execution process. In simple terms, it promotes inter-enterprise business relationships. Note that this definition of e-Business subsumes the term *collaborative business*.

To exemplify the concept of an end-to-end inter-company business transaction, consider the case where the sales department of a large multi-national organization lands a strategic deal. This company needs to quickly update its customer relationship system, the order management system, the billing system, the warehouse management system, and inform its suppliers and its logistics providers that a key order must be filled. All these steps must obviously be carried out in an automated fashion. Similarly, when the marketing department needs to launch a campaign, coinciding with the availability of a new product line that is supported by the sales department armed with new information about this product line, all company resources must be coordinated. In both cases, critical data from multiple sources must be shared across departments (or collaborating enterprises) and seamlessly fused to deliver answers to customers and partners. Accomplishing these types of challenging enterprise business tasks is difficult because of the multiple resources needed and the precise timing required to make a collaborative (intra- or inter-) company network work consistently and effectively. As we shall see throughout this book these are some of the critical questions that must be addressed by companies embarking on e-Business.

1.1.1 e-Business vs e-Commerce

A particular form of e-Business is e-Commerce. E-Commerce is a term that describes a focus on buying and selling products and services on the Internet. This can be conducted from a business-to-business (B2B) or business-to-consumer (B2C) perspective. Compared with e-Commerce, e-Business is a more generic term because it refers not only to information exchanges related to buying and selling but also to servicing customers and collaborating with business partners, distributors and suppliers. E-Business encompasses sophisticated business-to-business interactions and collaboration activities at a level of enterprise applications and business processes, enabling business partners to share in-depth business intelligence, which leads, in turn, to the management and optimization of inter-enterprise processes such as supply chain management [Davydov 2001]. More specifically, electronic business enables companies to link their internal and external processes more efficiently and flexibly, work more closely with suppliers and better satisfy the needs and expectations of their customers. Internal or *back-office processes* include distribution, manufacturing, and accounting while external or *front-office processes* include these processes that connect an organization to its customers and suppliers.

Sometimes people still use the term e-Commerce instead of e-Business. Therefore, before we examine the definition of e-Business any further and deconstruct its meaning, it is useful to understand the differences and similarities between e-Business and e-Commerce.

The meaning of the term electronic commerce has changed over the years. Originally, e-Commerce meant the facilitation of commercial transactions electronically, usually using technology like Electronic Data Interchange (EDI) to send commercial documents like purchase orders or invoices electronically. Today it includes features that may more correctly be termed 'Web Commerce' – the purchase of goods and services over the Web via a secure server with e-shopping carts and electronic pay services, like credit card pay authorizations. We may thus define electronic commerce as the buying and selling of goods and services, and the transfer of funds, through digital communications. This includes on-line display of goods and services, ordering, billing, customer service and all handling of payments and transactions. The selling process may include cataloguing of goods and services, order taking, and billing, however, it does not include key business processes such as Customer Relationship Management (CRM), Supply Chain Management (SCM), and Enterprise Resource Planning (ERP) integration. These terms will be explained in Section 1.3.

As observed above, e-Business is a broader term than e-Commerce. It is usually taken to mean the integration of electronic processes beyond buying and selling activities, e.g. full integration into organizations' ERP (Enterprise Resource Planning) systems or equivalent business tools, to undertake business processes by electronic communications end-to-end. Placing key processes, such as CRM, SCM and ERP, on the Web means that enterprise customers can do far more than simply placing an order and paying for it. They can track the status of an order from placement to delivery, receive prompt support once it has arrived, and easily place follow up and related orders [Boey 1999]. From the enterprise perspective this means that inventory is optimized by directly interfacing with suppliers and customers, partners and suppliers who can transact directly with an enterprise's corporate systems such as inventory, accounting, and purchasing. Transactions can be buying and selling, serving customers, collaborating with business partners, or administrative transactions. Transactions can be internal to a company, e.g., processing a purchase order, and affect the internal supply chain process, or be across firms, affecting external supply chain processes. Business transactions typically generate multiple activities such as credit checks, automated billing, purchase orders, stock updates, and shipping on the back-office systems of an enterprise.

1.1.2 Some critical factors

It is important to reemphasize that e-Business supports business processes along the entire value chain: electronic purchasing ('e-Procurement') and supply chain management, processing orders electronically, customer service and cooperation with business partners. One of the objectives of e-Business is to provide seamless connectivity and integration between business processes and applications external to an enterprise and the enterprise's back office applications, such as billing, order processing, accounting, inventory, receivables, and services focused on total supply chain management and partnership including product development, fulfillment, and distribution. In this respect, e-Business is much more than e-Commerce.

As we explained above, e-Business processes are integrated end-to-end across the company and with key partners, suppliers, and customers; they can respond with flexibility and speed to customer demands and market opportunities. This applies to traditional and virtual organizations. Special technical standards for e-Business facilitate the exchange of messages and combinations of processes between companies.

To succeed in e-Business it is crucial to combine technological developments with corporate strategy that redefines a company's role in the digital economy while taking into account its various stakeholders. It is important to understand the issues, evaluate the options, and develop technology orientation plans. An e-Business strategy helps organizations identify their e-Business concerns, assess their information needs, analyze to what degree existing systems serve these objectives, pinpoint specific improvements, determine the development stages of e-Business solutions and attain concrete and measurable results. It is thus clear that e-Business solutions are not only about technology. They focus on the use of evolutionary technology and reengineered business processes in tandem to develop new applications that are not limited by organizational or geographic boundaries or territorial borders [Adams 2001]. This combination of cutting edge technology and organizational processes supports the emerging set of business strategies and priorities, which include greater speed to market, more flexibility and nimbleness, accelerated global expansion, and tighter integration with one's suppliers and customers. If we take a closer look at the organizational processes involved in e-Business we will discover that they include marketing, manufacturing, and inbound and outbound logistics, while the buy-side transactions with suppliers and the sell-side transactions with customers can be considered to be key business processes.

E-Business solutions support interactivity and transport rich information content, helping customers and businesses redefine concepts such as value, competitiveness, and the very nature of transactions. Moreover, they affect all areas of an organization, fundamentally changing how it buys and sells products; collaborates with customers, suppliers, and distributors; manages its supply chains; and how it designs and launches new products [Adams 2001].

1.2 Characteristics of e-Business

To emphasize, e-Business is not simply buying and selling but encompasses the exchange of many kinds of information, including online commercial transactions. E-Business is about integrating external company processes with an organization's internal business processes; as such, a variety of core business processes could exploit an e-Business infrastructure. These include among other [van de Putte 2001]:

Collaborative product development: this is one of the fastest growing technologies in the engineering-manufacturing market, with some form of the solutions being implemented in a range of industries including automotive, aerospace, office equipment, industrial machinery, agricultural machinery, and construction equipment. Collaborative product development contributes towards making products within a short span of time while maintaining quality and reducing cost. It maximizes the time-to-market benefits of concurrent engineering while maintaining control of product development information. By integrating the design and test cycles of a company's products with the design and test cycles of its suppliers, a company can shorten the complete cycle time of its products. This clearly reduces the total cost of the product cycle, and even more importantly, it reduces the time that is needed to bring products to the marketplace. Collaborative product development solutions offer ERP integration and supply chain management.

Collaborative planning, forecasting and replenishment: this is a process in which manufacturers, distributors, and retailers work together to plan, forecast, and replenish products. In e-Business relationships, collaboration takes the form of sharing information that impacts inventory levels and merchandise flow. Collaboration points include unit sales forecasts, base inventory requirements, manufacturing and logistics lead times, seasonal set schedules, new/remodel store plans, promotional plans to name but a few. The objective behind collaborative planning, forecasting, and replenishment is that the trading partners work from a common forecast or plan in which the retailer, distributor, and manufacturer collect market intelligence on product information, store promotional programs, and share the information in real-time over digital networks. In this way members of a supply chain can lower supply chain cycle times, improve customer service, improve supply chain inventory levels, and lower inventory costs, as well as achieve better control of production planning activities.

Procurement and order management: e-Business has highlighted the importance of procurement as a strategic issue, given that electronic procurement, or e-Procurement, can achieve significant savings and other benefits that impact the customer. To support procurement and order management processes, companies use an integrated electronic ordering process and other online resources to increase efficiencies in their purchasing operations. They achieve cost savings and better service the end-customer by controlling the supply base, negotiating effective buying preferences, and streamlining the entire procurement process.

Operations and logistics: logistics, as defined by the Council of Logistics Management, "is that part of the supply chain process that plans, implements and controls the efficient, effective flow and storage of goods, services and related information from the point of origin to the point of consumption in order to meet customers' requirements." To make this happen, transportation, distribution, warehousing, purchasing, and order management functions must work together. Logistics in the e-Business era is about collaboration – the sharing of critical and timely data on the movement of goods as they flow from raw material all the way to the end- user. Operations and logistics processes are based on open communication between networks of trading partners, where integrated processes and technology are essential for high performance logistics operations. These solutions help manage the logistics process between buyers and suppliers, while eliminating costly discrepancies between purchase order, sales order, and shipping information. By eradicating these variances and inconsistencies improvements in the supply chain may result from the elimination of missed shipments and shipment discrepancies, and the reduction of inventory carrying costs for the customer. At the same time this increases customer satisfaction through improved delivery reliability and improved efficiencies in receiving operations.

1.3 Elements of an e-Business solution

The vision of e-Business is that enterprises will have access to a much broader range of trading partners to interact and collaborate with and not only to buy and sell more efficiently. Also it is expected that e-Business will contribute to the agility of business organizations and with that to reaching higher levels of customization. In this way enterprises can maximize supply chain efficiency, improve service to customers and their profit margin. To accomplish this objective, enterprises must make certain that their mission-critical business information systems such as inventory, accounting, manufacturing and customer support not only can interact with each other but can also become Web-enabled and exposed so that business systems of their partners and customers can interact with them. In addition, in order to optimize their operational efficiency, enterprises need to develop newer distributed applications that extract data and launch business processes across many or all of these systems. An e-Business solution should thus embrace Customer Relationship Management (CRM) systems, Enterprise Resource Planning (ERP) systems, Supply Chain Management (SCM), and vertical product offerings.

Forward-thinking organizations automate, organize, standardize, and stabilize the processes and services offered in order to create and maintain sustainable computer mediated relationships throughout an e-Business life cycle. This is shown in Figure 1.1, which illustrates the typical ingredients found in an e-Business solution. The diagram shows the common topology for conducting e-Business from the point of view of a transacting company. More specifically, it shows how a company interacts with customers, suppliers, distributors, and e-Markets, and sets out the flow of information and materials in an e-Business solution. In the following section. We will concentrate on the basic elements in this e-Business application topology and explain their purpose and functions. Such basic elements in the e-Business topology include:

- *Customer Relationship Management* (CRM) *systems*: these are 'front-office' systems that help the enterprise deal directly with its customers. CRM is the process of creating relationships with customers through

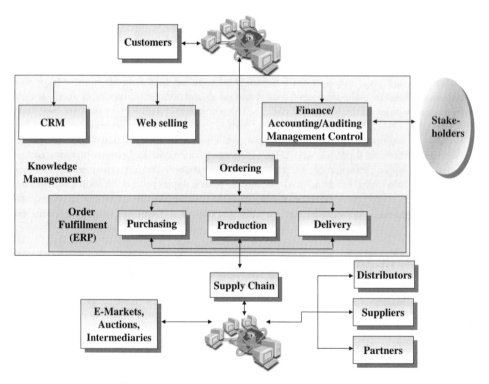

■ **Figure 1.1:** Ingredients of an e-Business Solution

the introduction of reliable service-automated processes, personal information gathering and processing, and self-service throughout the supplying company in order to create value for customers. It attempts to integrate and automate the various customer-serving processes within a company. CRM typically includes three categories of user application: customer-facing applications, sales force-facing applications, and management-facing applications. The customer-facing category includes applications that enable customers to order products and services and obtain customer service and support. The sales force-facing category includes applications that automate some of the company's sales and sales force management functions to deliver effective customer service and support and sell products and services to customers. These applications support the field sales organization with sales-force automation functions and the field service organization with dispatch and logistics functions. The management-facing category includes applications that analyze data gathered by the other applications and provide management reports, including calculations and reports that compute Return on Relationship (ROR) according to a company's business model, competitors, industry trends, and macro-environmental variables. The demands and increased functionality of the Internet and Web-based applications fueled a meteoric growth in demand for CRM. CRM systems are obviously an important element of e-Business.

- *Enterprise Resource Planning systems* (ERP): these are management information systems that integrate and automate many of the business practices associated with the operations or production aspects of a company. These typically include manufacturing, logistics, distribution, inventory, shipping, invoicing, and accounting. Enterprise Resource Planning or ERP software can aid in the control of many business activities, like sales, delivery, billing, production, inventory management, and human resource management. They are often called 'back-office' systems indicating that customers and the general public are not directly involved. This is contrasted with front office systems like customer relationship management systems that deal directly with the customer. The most successful efforts to manage enterprise resources are currently based on ERP systems. These systems grew out of earlier Material Requirements Planning (MRP) and Manufacturing Resource Planning (MRP II) systems of the 1980s. A typical ERP system is designed around four primary business processes:

  - Production: manufacturing resource planning and execution process;
  - Buying a product: procurement process;
  - Sales of products and services: customer order management process;
  - Costing, paying bills, and collecting: financial/management accounting and reporting process.

ERP systems extend beyond the bounds of manufacturing to integrate many functions previously performed by many stand-alone applications for planning, production, asset management, financial control, human resource management, and workflow management. Some of the reasons for this change are that existing heterogeneous systems cannot provide either the data quality (accuracy, currency, etc.) and/or the information availability levels required. ERP can help solve this problem, by combining several critical information systems functions, particularly in the accounting and financial realms. Enterprise resource planning systems are also extending beyond the factory walls to address supply chain integration issues. Supply chain management software can extend the ERP system to include links with suppliers. The most frequently cited benefits of ERP center around process automation and integration, and the availability of data to support business analysis.

- *Supply Chain Management* (SCM): a supply chain is a network of facilities and distribution options that performs the functions of procurement of materials, transformation of these materials into intermediate and finished products, and distribution of these finished products to customers. A supply chain essentially has three main parts: the supply, manufacturing and distribution. The supply side concentrates on how, where from, and when raw materials are procured and supplied to manufacturing. Manufacturing converts these raw materials to finished products, and distribution ensures that these finished products reach the final customers through a network of distributors, warehouses, and retailers. The chain can be said to start with the suppliers of an enterprise's suppliers and to end with the customers of an enterprise's customer. Supply Chain Management deals with the planning and execution issues involved in managing a supply chain. Successful supply chain management allows an enterprise to anticipate demand and deliver the right product to the right place at the right time, at the lowest price to satisfy its customers. Thus the goal of SCM is the creation of value for the supply chain member organizations with a particular emphasis on the end customer in the supply chain. Supply chains and their management are discussed in Chapter 10.

- *Knowledge Management*: this relates to the identification and analysis of available and required knowledge assets and related processes. It embodies organizational processes that seek synergistic combination of data and information processing capacity of information technologies, and the creative and innovative capacity of human beings. Knowledge assets encompass two things, information plus experience. Knowledge assets comprise knowledge regarding markets, products, processes, technologies, and organizations that a business owns or needs to own, and that enable its business processes to generate profits and provide value. Knowledge management also includes the subsequent planning and control of actions to develop both the knowledge assets and the processes to fulfill organizational objectives.

  Knowledge is, besides transaction costs, a strong denominator of a business model. It is the possession of knowledge that determines business competencies, especially when knowledge allied with competence is unique to the business, and so has to be kept in-house. E-Business business models are typically network based, which means that they rely on relationships with external business partners. No core activities are candidates for outsourcing. Economic approaches to business models are discussed in Chapter 3.

- *e-Markets*: an e-Market is an electronic meeting place for multiple buyers and sellers providing many participants with a unified view of sets of goods and services, enabling them to transact using many different mechanisms available in the e-Market. An e-Market uses Internet technology to connect multiple buyers with multiple suppliers so that suppliers, through electronic procurement systems, ERP-based procurement applications, can interact with one another and conduct business transactions. The topic of electronic markets is treated in detail in Chapter 8.

1.4 e-Business roles and their challenges

Typically there are two distinctive sides to any e-Business application: the *buy side* and the *sell side*. The buy side represents organizations that use e-Business facilities for their buying needs, such as spot purchasing and/or addressing their enterprise-wide procurement needs. The sell side, as the name suggests, includes businesses that sell their products via the transaction mechanisms offered in e-Business applications. Sell-side solutions allow a company's customers that are other businesses, or the company's distributors, to purchase goods and services via e-technology. A company can either sell on their own private sell-site or they can connect their e-catalog to a larger marketplace. These two types of e-Business help define two principal roles: *buyers* and *suppliers*. Buyers are organizations that purchase goods and services directly from suppliers. Suppliers are organizations that market and sell goods or services directly to buyers or indirectly through diverse sales channels including Web-based procurement systems and electronic marketplaces. Suppliers typically provide buyers with Web-based services – such as payment, logistics, credit, and shipping – necessary for completing e-Business transactions. Buyers (customers) can thus review product information, receive customer service, ordering services, and customization support facilities, and can submit or modify orders, learn about order status, and make payments. An additional role is that of *market makers* who are third-party organizations that run e-Markets. This role will be described further in Chapter 8 where we introduce the topic of e-Markets. Every participant plays at least one role, and quite often the same participant will play multiple roles.

Each role has distinct business and technical challenges, but they all coalesce around a common point. For buyers as well as for suppliers, the primary challenge is the ability to reach a critical mass of trading partners and transaction volume to sustain their business. In particular, from the supplier's point-of-view, they must be able to support various types of customers that must be served through new electronic methods, along with internal systems that must be integrated and leveraged by their sell-side systems. When looking at all suppliers, there remain several common goals regardless of the complexity or size. These are technology and business considerations and requirements that can help transform traditional suppliers to e-Business enabled suppliers. These include among other things:

- Managing multiple selling channels, based on various technologies, protocols, data formats and standard business processes;

- Having the ability to take multiple types of orders once customers have decided to conduct e-Business-enabled order management through the various selling channels;

- Having the ability to differentiate and customize products and services from other suppliers, and offering them through the various selling channels;

- Having the ability to adapt and grow the e-Business without incurring dramatic technology changes, organizational restructurings, and sweeping changes in their business processes or radical new investments.

To meet the needs of buyers and suppliers, e-Business strategy and solutions should be built around the following basic principles:

> *Empowering suppliers and buyers*: suppliers have unique characteristics yet also have the common goal of reaching customers through many selling channels such as multiple e-Marketplaces, procurement systems, and direct via the Internet. For an e-Business solution to be truly effective for suppliers it must empower them to sell wherever their buyers are located by providing a wide variety of selling channels with relatively low investment. As a result, suppliers can reach far more buyers, increasing their revenue opportunity. Buyers will also have the possibility to choose from many buyers, getting more competitive terms and prices. Buyers must be similarly empowered to pick and choose from a various suppliers at different places in the world by means of different types of selling channels. These selling channels have unique business processes that must be understood to fully leverage them, such as how they send and receive catalog data and orders. In addition, an e-Business solution should also enable interoperation

of a supplier's internal systems with the buyers' and trading and distribution partners' internal systems that are built on a variety of platforms using many different technologies, communication standards, and data formats. To solve this challenge, e-Business technologies utilize XML enterprise application integration (EAI) and Web-service solutions (refer to Chapters 17, 18 and 19) to provide a layer of abstraction between the supplier's internal systems and the different selling channels.

Enabling suppliers of all sizes: an understanding that suppliers of all sizes and levels of complexity exist, from small businesses with relatively low IT capabilities and budget, to the most demanding enterprises with complex products, services, and integration challenges. And as sales grow, and technology needs become more complex, it is important to have a solution that can seamlessly scale with the business. Getting suppliers connected electronically with buyers through flexible solutions is only part of the challenge. When looking at suppliers although they may have differing business sizes, needs or rely on different business process options that require unique technical solutions, there remain several common elements. These include among other things configuration for complex products and services, complex supply-chain integration, advanced analysis capabilities, and management of business processes, sophisticated multi-system back-end system integration using advanced middleware solutions, vertical industry solutions and end-to-end integration of supply chains and e-Business applications.

1.5 e-Business requirements

Enterprises, which desire to conduct business-to-business transactions over the Internet, look to e-Business solutions to improve communications and provide a fast and error-free method of transacting with one another to address their procurement and supply chain processes. However, before enterprises become e-Business enabled and successful users of the techniques they need to address several fundamental business and technology challenges. Typical ones are additional to buy- and sell-side challenges that include the following items that need to be addressed in the sequence indicated below:

1) *Identify/measure quantifiable business objectives*: companies must accurately measure the impact an e-Business initiative has on their business processes to ensure that this initiative is worth pursuing and has sustainable long-term effects.
2) *Ensure organizational/operational flexibility*: however well organized the enterprise was before the deployment of e-Business solutions, the situation will necessarily change because of e-Business initiatives. For instance, business transaction growth, expanded markets, and increased information accessibility constitute major change factors for an enterprise. Enterprises must reposition themselves in their mission, structure and execution to prosper in a substantially more dynamic environment. Such organizational considerations are introduced in Chapters 2, 3, 4 and 5.
3) *Rethink entire company supply chains*: each company in a supply chain must clearly understand the value propositions of other participants. In particular, companies must rethink their entire supply chains to optimize performance and value as they seek to better integrate with suppliers and customers, share information, inter-link processes, and outsource manufacturing logistics systems, on-site engineering, and maintenance activities. Supply chains are discussed along with business networks in Chapter 10.

4) *Transform the company to a process-centric one*: it should be possible for companies to be conceptualized as a set of business processes. Most process-centric companies, like most traditional organizations, still have departments and divisions. Unlike traditional organizations, however, process-centric companies place their primary emphasis on maximizing the efficiency of processes, not on maximizing the efficiency of departmental or functional units. This issue is described in Chapter 4.

5) *Define business processes*: companies must create models of existing processes and interactions, determining the relevant events, time frames, resources and costs associated with business processes. Only in this way will business processes be well defined and measurable. This model can then help streamline and evaluate new business models and processes and serve as a benchmark for determining return on investment. In Chapter 12 we describe how business processes are defined for a simple supply chain.

6) *Understand security requirements*: the breadth of access and interaction representative of e-Business solutions requires the ability to provide controlled and focused access by customers, employees, suppliers, and, in some cases, applications that can interact directly with each other without human intervention. This is described in Chapter 13.

7) *Align business organizations with a flexible IT architecture*: in response to demands for end to end e-Business solutions, companies are expanding their applications to include enhanced integration capabilities. The solutions required reflect the need to integrate business processes at a variety of different levels from applications and data, and finally across (and within) organizations in a way that embraces all possible sources of complexity. This also includes automating business processes that encompass a diverse range of packaged applications and systems within enterprises. The grand challenge is forcing the creation and adoption of new infrastructures and enabling technologies that will be used to facilitate e-Business integration. Assumptions regarding the techniques and technologies used for integrating applications within and across enterprise boundaries can be found in Chapters 17 and 18.

8) *Establish ubiquity within standards*: IT vendors have created many integration technologies that bring value to their customers. However, none of these technologies has achieved complete coverage for the demands of the IT world. Some technologies were proprietary, which required other integration participants to have the same technology. This worked well within an organizational unit, but deteriorated across global enterprises and between separate enterprises. Attempts were made at establishing open standards for interoperability, such as the ones discussed in Chapters 19 and 20.

A number of business and technology-driven requirements are compelling forces that enable successful development and deployment of integrated end-to-end e-Business applications. Success in this environment requires adoption of methods and technologies that support this expanded model of the networked enterprise. These include:

• Efficient business process management technology for modeling and automation of business processes that span business entities;

• Efficient business-to-business communication for secure and reliable exchange of information and transactions with trading partners over public networks such as the Internet;

• Efficient enterprise application integration technology for combining mission-critical legacy systems – throughout the networked enterprise – with new business components.

The above technologies make it possible to support cross-enterprise collaboration at various levels of granularity:

- Supporting discrete, and possibly short-term, activities between small teams working across enterprise boundaries, e.g., participating in isolated business processes;

- Enabling a tactical response, for example at a business unit level, to capture a market opportunity or react to a competitive threat;

- Sustaining long-term, strategic e-Business arrangements that integrate an enterprise's core processes with its supply and value chain and affinity groups, resulting in complex, multifaceted virtual businesses.

These and related issues will be examined and discussed throughout this book.

1.6 Impacts of e-Business

The emergence of e-Business impacts organizations in various ways. Some of the key characteristics of e-Business are the speed at which transactions can occur, the ability to connect multiple parties at the same time, the ability to gather and manipulate information in new ways, and the absence of traditional business tools such as paper forms and face-to-face retail contact. E-Business impacts more than just the sales side of the business. Electronic connectivity not only improves efficiencies across the full value chain, but also has the power to transform the traditional business models entirely.

There is a wide range of potential benefits motivating today's enterprises to undertake e-Business initiatives. In this section we will examine several of these potential benefits and explain their business implications.

Improved operational efficiency and productivity: the most often touted benefit of e-Business is the potential for tremendous improvements in operational efficiency. By using e-Business technologies to interact with trading partners, organizations can streamline their operations and increase their effectiveness at the same time [van Slyke 2003]. By eliminating operational waste and the automation of inefficient business practices, organizations can realize productivity gains.

Reduction in operating costs and costs of goods and services: a major benefit of e-Business is in savings generated by doing common business functions such as the purchase of goods and services, processing purchase orders, order and delivery tracking, and so on, more efficiently but also by enabling collaboration with external partners. Collaboration with suppliers, customers, distributors, and trading partners raises opportunities that range from basic electronic information exchange to facilitating transactional exchanges of information. E-Business technologies help lower the cost of communication and collaboration between trading organizations, in a supply chain. Organizations must communicate and collaborate in connection with the exchange of orders, billing and payment information, shipment dates, sharing product information, forecasting, and demand information, etc. Such collaborative activities can create tighter links among business partners, improving the efficiency of the various support functions involved in bringing products to the market. By connecting directly with suppliers and distributors, organizations can realize more efficient processes that result in reduced unit costs for products or services and, perhaps, lower prices to customers while achieving economies of scale.

Improved competitive position: global reach, rapid growth, efficient reduction of product time to market, and optimization of product distribution channels, all contribute to a superior competitive position. Recent surveys reveal that many companies are adopting e-Business as a key component of their growth strategy. According to these surveys, those companies who already linked their business processes with other companies are showing about 70% higher profitability than those organizations that do not integrate with trading partners.

Penetration into new markets through new channels: for several organizations, e-Business technologies could prove to be the conduit to new markets. E-Business helps companies extend their reach beyond organizational and geographic boundaries and reach markets that were previously considered to be too distant to be practical. With e-Business, location is of no consequence when it comes to reaching customers.

Improved communications, information, and knowledge sharing: the alignment of key supply chain partners with an organization's internal strategies helps exploit their expertise and knowledge in creating value. Collaborative sharing of business information such as forecasting and demand information can better help plan long-term capacity, inventory, and human resource requirements. As an example, consider the case of transportation suppliers in a supply chain. As critical supply chain members, transportation suppliers must be able to function as partners, to produce, share, and manage information, and to provide higher levels of service in terms of speed and reliability. They have to be able to trace and track shipments under their control and make the information readily accessible to customers or supply chain partners. When transportation or logistics services companies can provide real-time information in a customized way, they can become an integral part of their customers' supply chains, creating the opportunity to secure long-term business by embedding their processes in those of their customers, and adding value beyond traditional transportation and logistics offerings.

Harmonization and standardization of processes: to provide simple, transparent, and effective processes for global commerce, it is important not only to exploit advances in information technology, but also adopt new approaches to trade facilitation based on simplification and harmonization of business processes. For this purpose, trading companies in a supply chain analyze the interactive and collaborative roles inherent in performing trade, business and administration activities, define trade, business, and administration information transaction patterns and flows, and document the specific information exchanges (business documents) that flow between the respective roles. A catalog of common business processes is created and reference models are specified according to international, e.g., UN, trade facilitation recommendations, and business process and procedures are defined independent of the resulting implementation technologies. This ensures cross-domain harmonization of business processes with tremendous implications for conduct of transactions across company barriers.

Improved internal information access: quantities and qualitative improvements to internal information access can yield big payoffs for the business. Business areas such as the development of business opportunities and business strategy are particularly rich in this respect.

Improved relationships with suppliers and improved customer service: the Internet is an effective way to maintain relationships with customers and suppliers, and its usefulness for reaching global customers is significant. E-Business enables the sharing of information and business processes across multiple organizations for stronger, more profitable relationships. Consider as an example a typical supply chain. Managing the companies and processes involved in producing and delivering a product involves planning, execution, and control of these processes to deliver products at the lowest cost. At the same time, the need to be responsive to customer demand – just in time delivery, make to order manufacturing systems, and so on – results in the movement of smaller quantities of goods more frequently. The technology of e-Business enables logistics and supply chain managers to meet these demands by integrating systems, collaborating within and across firms, and sharing information throughout the supply chain, enabling supply chain participants to plan and synchronize their processes. The immediate benefits of this procedure are efficient internal processes, improved customer service, and coordination with suppliers, and improved competitive position.

1.7 Inhibitors of e-Business

Counterbalancing the drivers of e-Business adoption is a set of powerful inhibitors. E-Business adoption is closely linked to a company's perception of the importance of trading on the Internet and how it might impact on their business. A key indicator that may influence the adoption of e-Business is the size of the firm (the smaller the firm the less likely it is to use the Internet). It is important to understand that most of the large firms currently developing and implementing e-Business strategies and solutions typically engage Small to Medium Enterprises (SMEs) in their supply chains. For these large firms, the rate at which SMEs adopt e-Business and enhance their capabilities could affect the scope and timing of their e-Business implementation. Alternatively, SMEs that do not keep pace with e-Business may be marginalized as suppliers. Most inhibitors to implementing an e-Business solution include uncertainty of the financial benefits, lack of a clear e-Business strategy, technological concerns, security concerns, privacy and legal issues, suspicion regarding new partnership loyalties, and the high costs of computing technology. Small to medium sized enterprises face the same issues as larger enterprises as they progress through the various stages of adopting information technology and the Internet for business purposes.

We can discern five broad categories of e-Business impediments.

1.7.1 Management/strategy issues

- *E-Business strategy*: the need to develop a strategy is great where e-Business is concerned. The lack of a clearly defined e-Business strategy is a major inhibitor for companies to espouse e-Business-based technological solutions. A sound e-Business strategy constitutes the basic foundation that allows companies of all sizes to move forward and embrace the Internet as a key business tool. Ideally, the e-Business would seamlessly integrate with the business strategy. This would enable the company to set out a critical path to success in e-Business. There is always a need for an e-Business strategy and action plan that has sufficient detail to allow progress to be monitored and measured.

- *Organizational changes required by e-Business*: traditional organizational structures may not be suitable for e-Business as they may fragment customer service, retard market responsiveness, and constrain improvements in process efficiency. Barriers are often erected between departments to inhibit sharing of information – for example, in banking, debt and equity functions are separated to reduce the possibility of conflicts of interest. The e-Business implementation process includes evaluating a company's supply chain, its customer relationship, and an e-Business assessment survey. This enables a company to benchmark e-Business progress against that of similar-sized companies. To identify business opportunities, risks, and process improvements, a company requires good understanding of how suppliers, distributors, retailers, end-users, joint venture partners, and even competitors interrelate. This requires organizational changes so that companies can better integrate with each other. A special challenge in this restructuring is finding new approaches to maintain due diligence while dismantling the old structures.

- *Management attitudes and organizational inflexibility*: these can be more serious in an SME than in a large firm, because of the traditional leadership and organizational forms in many SMEs [USHER 2001]. Firms operating in more traditional sectors also tend to be less innovative. However, this is less of a problem in new companies where management may be more receptive to technology, or it may be central to the activity of the company.

1.7.2 Cost/financing issues

The adoption of e-Business is closely linked to company perceptions regarding the importance of Internet trading, and how they believe it will impact their business in the future. Companies, especially smaller ones, demand clear proof of the Return on Investment (ROI). This implies that e-Business must be proven as essential to the competitiveness of their firm.

- *Costs of implementation of e-Business*: these can be a serious barrier for smaller companies, especially SMEs. The cost of setting up an e-Business includes preliminary planning, procuring hardware and/or software tools (installation, training, and subsequent reorganization), and continuous maintenance, servicing costs, and telecommunications charges. The cost of the initial investment has dropped in recent years.

- *Calculating the Return on Investment (ROI)*: just as it can be difficult to understand the commercial advantages of an e-Business model, it can be difficult to calculate the ROI on an e-Business investment. SMEs often work with limited funding resources and need to see a significant return before they will take a major decision on e-Business.

1.7.3 Security and trust issues

- Security – many companies are afraid to move to electronic trading systems because of the potential for theft of business information and funds, alteration of financial documents, as well as the potential for illicit transactions and concerns over payment security. Potential losses due to inadequate security can be crippling as the entire enterprise network can easily be compromised if appropriate security methods and procedures are not built into the e-Business technology infrastructure. Evolving and thriving as an e-Business entails not only keeping pace with the latest best practices, but also managing and responding to security-related vulnerabilities, risks, and threats. It is essential for enterprises to understand the critical success factors for conducting e-Business securely. To reduce fears of fraud and invasion of privacy, a selling company must provide its customers with a secure, stable, and fraud-proof system for the transfer of their payments and sensitive business-related data. Different kinds of security technology are now available that can effectively support e-Business initiatives. These factors make the topic of e-Business security which is examined in Chapter 13 of this book.

- Trust – one of the most important barriers to the use of e-Business is the level of trust that organizations are willing to place in businesses selling goods and services on the Internet. Trust can be defined as the expectation that the trading party will behave in accordance with its commitments, negotiate honestly, and not take advantage even when the opportunity arises [Hosmer 1995]. Trust is an important commodity in e-Business. In short, if organizations do not trust those companies which provide goods and services, they will not engage in e-Business transactions. Trust is a dynamic concept: the level of trust companies are willing to place in a trading partner may change over time as they become more familiar with the other party through experience or other knowledge [van Slyke 2003].

There is a number of characteristics of e-Business transactions that make trust an important element. First, e-Business transactions occur at a distance where the buyer cannot see the products, unless they are of course digital, and cannot take possession unless it has paid. Because of this the buyer must trust the seller to supply the goods as promised, to ship them correctly and in a timely manner. In addition, the buyer must trust the seller to describe the goods faithfully (for spot buys) and to fairly resolve any disputes that may arise.

- New partnership loyalties – Cooperation rather than competition may be the basis for success in e-Business. E-Business markets may create much larger markets, but can require a great deal of loyalty and trust building in the new partnerships that they create. The emergence of new and unknown online intermediaries addressing aggregations adds to the confusion that many companies feel regarding e-Business. There is recognition by many community and enterprise intermediaries that existing trusted offline relationships, be they a lead company in a business network or a business association, could be important in recruiting companies to online services. The role of the community intermediary is seen as being important in the recruitment of companies to their applications based on their trusted relationship within the e-Market aggregations.

1.7.4 Legal issues

Legal barriers could be defined as a specific legal provision, which prevents enterprises from entering into e-Business. However, the lack of a legal provision may have the same effect, if it is considered as an important condition for e-Business. From an enterprise point of view the concept of legal barriers is a highly subjective concept, reflecting the perception by enterprises of what might constitute a barrier to market access in the wider sense [CEC 2004].

The most important legal issue hampering the growth of e-Business is still a lack of awareness. Few companies are familiar with the rules and regulations that apply to an online environment, leading to much uncertainty for e-Business companies and consumers alike. Many enterprises feel insufficiently informed about legal provisions applicable to e-Business. This lack of awareness may be explained by the large number of new and often unfamiliar rules applicable to e-Business being perceived as too complex and/or too vague by many enterprises. The lack of full harmonization of e-Business legislation, and the resulting divergences between national legislations, has contributed to this negative image [CEC 2004]. In addition, online and offline trade is, in some cases, still treated differently, which further contributes to the confusion. This uncertainty is detrimental to the degree of trust that both companies and consumers have in doing business online. Companies see themselves confronted by an ever increasing number of directives on e-Business. Since these directives all deal with different topics (distance selling, e-signatures, contract law, unsolicited commercial e-mail, etc) it is hard for companies to gain an insightful overview of the situation.

Many differences still exist between national legal provisions applicable to e-Business, which are considered by enterprises as internal market barriers, as they raise legal uncertainties and the cost of compliance with law. Enterprises would favor fully harmonized rules, which would increase legal certainly in e-Business and encourage companies to conduct business electronically across the borders. In particular, in the field of consumer protection, full harmonization would strengthen confidence in the internal market for consumers and business alike [CEC 2004]. Thus, many companies, especially SMEs, are reluctant to engage in cross-border e-Business activities, as they are unfamiliar with e-Business rules and regulations that apply in other countries. The fact that consumers have a strong position when it comes to cross-border disputes exacerbates this problem.

In addition to the above concerns, new trading models, such as business-to-business online auctions, may create new legal challenges, in particular with respect to ensuring fair trade.

1.7.5 Technological concerns

Business-to-business integration means spanning independent businesses, each with its own set of applications and users. Some applications are ERP and SCM packages; others are traditional systems running on a mainframe. In each company, transactions are processed differently. Orders, production scheduling, and other internal processing are also handled differently. Business-to-business integration is about coordinating the flow of information among businesses and their heterogeneous business support systems without being tied to one specific technology. Building integration bridges that span independent organizations and their systems is challenging as it requires linking the elements of business together into a cohesive whole despite different computing platforms, operating systems, database technologies and applications. Business-to-business integration raises various technological requirements including reliable messaging, intra- and inter-enterprise application integration, reusing business logic (no modification of application programs), transformation between heterogeneous platforms and protocols, and information exchange across disparate application domains. All of these and related issues are covered in this book.

1.7.6 Arguments against investment

Uncertainty about the viability of the initial investment and the rising cost of maintenance services may reduce the willingness of enterprises to undertake the necessary investments.

Fear of choosing an incompatible system/application – the SME needs to have a system which is compatible to the systems used by large suppliers or customers who may have resources to implement complex IT solutions. The SME does not have that luxury.

Technology and standardization – more than any other business users, SMEs have a strong interest in standardized and fully compatible ICT solutions that stay relatively stable over time. At present, the complexity and the lack of robustness of many ICT solutions are discouraging many SMEs. Where software or systems prove to be incompatible with those of customers and suppliers, there is a high risk that ICT investment may be lost. SMEs do business with many different clients. Yet they often have to follow the technology and business standards set by major clients, and hence run the risk of becoming 'locked-in' to a specific technology used by one contractor but not by others.

1.8 Chapter summary

E-Business encompasses sophisticated business-to-business interactions and collaboration activities at a level of enterprise applications and business processes, enabling business partners to share in-depth business intelligence, which leads, in turn, to the management and optimization of inter-enterprise processes such as supply chain management. E-business emphasizes end-to-end business transaction in which a succession of automated Business processes and information systems of different companies, which are involved in an inter-company business transaction, are successfully integrated. Transactions can be buying and selling, serving customers, collaborating with business partners, or administrative transactions. Transactions can be internal to a company e.g., processing a purchase order, and affect the internal supply chain process, or be across firms, affecting external supply chain processes. Business transactions typically generate multiple activities such as credit checks, automated billing, purchase orders, stock updates and shipping on the back-office systems of an enterprise. E-Business is about integrating external company processes with an organization's internal business processes and as such a variety of core business processes could exploit an e-Business infrastructure. In simple terms, e-Business promotes inter-enterprise business relationships.

An e-Business solution embraces Customer Relationship Management systems, Enterprise Resource Planning systems, Supply Chain Management and vertical product offerings. Customer Relationship Management systems are 'front-office' systems that help the enterprise deal directly with their customers. Enterprise Resource Planning systems are management information systems that integrate and automate many of the business practices associated with the operations or production aspects of a company. These typically include manufacturing, logistics, distribution, inventory, shipping, invoicing, and accounting. Supply Chain Management deals with the planning and execution issues involved in managing a supply chain. Successful supply chain management allows for an enterprise to anticipate demand and deliver the right product to the right place at the right time, at the lowest price to satisfy its customers.

There are typically two distinctive sides to any e-Business application: the buy side and the sell side. The buy side represents organizations that use e-Business facilities for their buying needs, such as spot purchasing and/or addressing their enterprise-wide procurement needs. The sell side, as the name suggests, includes businesses that sell their products via the transaction mechanisms offered in e-Business applications. Sell-side solutions allow a company's customers that are other businesses, or the company's distributors to purchase goods and services via e-technology. Buy- and sell-side role challenges include managing multiple selling channels, taking multiple types of orders from customers, and adapting to new market demands and growth requirements without incurring dramatic technology changes, e-Business business and technology challenges come in addition to the buy and sell challenges and include a variety of items such as identifying and measuring quantifiable business objectives, ensuring organizational/operational flexibility, rethinking entire company supply chains, transforming the company to a process-centric one, understanding security requirements, aligning business organizations with a flexible IT architecture, and establishing ubiquity within standards.

E-Business is expected to impact organizations in various ways. Potential benefits include improved operational efficiency and productivity, improved competitive position, penetration into new markets, improved communications, information and knowledge sharing, harmonization and standardization of processes, improved internal information access as well as improved relationships with suppliers and improved customer service. However, e-Business is facing a series of serious obstacles including management and strategy issues, cost and financing implications, security and trust problems, legal and technological concerns.

Discussion Questions

- What is e-Business and what are its main characteristics?

- What are the e-Business roles and their challenges? Explain how e-Business helps empower suppliers and buyers and enable suppliers of all sizes.

- Give an illustration to show a typical e-Business architecture for conducting e-Business from the perspective of a transacting company.

- Use this diagram to explain what the main ingredients/features of an e-Business solution are and how they are used in the context of the e-Business architecture you described.

- What are the main e-Business roles and what challenges do they introduce?

- What are the benefits and limitations of e-Business?

Chapter 2

e-Business Strategy

The changes brought about in organizations due to the emergence of direct electronic delivery channels have an obvious impact on industry structure and the general corporate strategy. e-Business has triggered new business models, strategies, and tactics that are made possible by the Internet and related technologies. In order to compete in the marketplace it is essential for organizations to establish strategies for the development of an e-Business. This may include the identification of business opportunities and threats in the external environment, the assessment of internal strengths and weaknesses, and an understanding of the impact of technological change. Such an initiative has to build on the strengths of the organization and take full advantage of the opportunities in the market, meanwhile identifying costly unsuccessful solutions and preventing unwanted market disturbances introduced by carelessly designed e-Business solutions. Understanding the e-Business environment will enable organisations to determine strategic goals and objectives or to identify any changes of direction needed in their current business strategy.

In this chapter we discuss e-Business developments from a strategic perspective. In the first section we define and position the concept of 'e-Business strategy'. We then introduce and explain fundamental principles that companies need to follow to establish strategic positioning. Strategies are developed at different organizational levels. In the next section we discuss three organizational levels, the business unit, corporate and value system levels, which are relevant for e-Business strategies. Then the business and technology drivers for the business strategy are described. We also discuss the strategic planning process and its core components, and the importance of alignment between information technology and business strategy. We conclude the theoretical discussion by presenting three theoretical perspectives from which the effects of e-Business developments can be explained.

Case Study

How e-Business technologies may change competition in an industry

This case study discusses the successful entrance of Tele Flower Auction (TFA) into the flower industry enabled by Information Technology [van Heck 1997, 1998; Ribbers 2002b; Doorduin 2004]. It serves as an illustration of how, for a particular industry, the Internet has impacted competitive relations. Indeed, the development and introduction of TFA is one of the initiatives in response to import restrictions by the traditional Dutch flower auctions. As such the case demonstrates how competitive positions may change due to the enabling power of information technology, particularly the Internet, in a traditional century-old industry.

Industry background The Netherlands is the world's leading producer and distributor of cut flowers and potted plants. In 1997 the Dutch dominated the world export market with a 59% share for cut flowers and 48% share for potted plants. The Dutch flower auctions play a vital role in securing this leadership: these auctions provide efficient centres for price discovery and in transactions between buyers and sellers. The Dutch growers established the auctions as cooperatives. The world's two biggest flower auctions are in two villages, namely Aalsmeer (Flower Auction Aalsmeer) and Naaldwijk/Bleiswijk (Flower Auction Holland). Every day, an average of 30 million flowers – originating not only from the Netherlands but also from other countries such as Israel, Kenya, and Zimbabwe – are traded in 100,000 transactions. There are seven flower auctions in the Netherlands villages of Aalsmeer, Naaldwijk/ Bleiswijk, Rijnsburg, Grubbenvorst, Eelde, Bemmel, and Vleuten.

The Dutch flower auction concept The following auction rules characterize the Dutch flower auction concept. Dutch flower auctions use a clock for price discovery as follows. The computerized auction clock in the room provides the buyers with information on producer, product, unit of currency, quality, and minimum purchase quantity. The flowers are transported through the auction room and shown to the buyers. The clock hand starts at a high price determined by the auctioneer, and drops until a buyer stops the clock by using a button. The auctioneer asks the buyer, by intercom, how many units of the lot he or she will buy. The buyer provides the number of units. The clock is then reset, and the process starts again with the left-over flowers, sometimes introducing a new minimum purchase quantity, until all units of the lot are sold. In the traditional way the buyers must be present in the auction room. In practice, it happens that the Dutch flower auction is a very effective auction mechanism, it can handle a transaction every four seconds.

2.1 What is e-Business strategy?

The concept of strategy carries several connotations [Smits 1997]. In order to position and define e-Business strategy we focus on two of them. One view defines strategy as plans and objectives adopted to achieve higher-level goals: in that sense a strategy is developed to achieve a goal like implementing organizational change, or a large software package such as an ERP-system. Strategy may also relate to plans concerning the long-term position of the firm in its business environment to achieve its organizational goals. In this sense strategic planning, as opposed to tactical and operational planning, has to do with the external positioning of the firm in its competitive environment. *Strategic planning* here comprises a distinct class of decisions (a plan is a set of decisions made for the future) and objectives, and has to be positioned next to *tactical planning* (structuring the resources of the firm) and *operational planning* (maximizing the profitability of current operations) [Ansoff 1968, 1984]. From this perspective, an organization's strategy can best defined as its chosen role and function in its environment [Ansoff 1968,1987; Abell, 1980]. Strategy thus defines the future direction and actions of an organization. Through strategic planning an organization defines its fundamental relationships with key stakeholders, such as customers, competitors, suppliers, stockholders, employees, the government, the general public [Noorderhaven 1995].

Strategy is concerned with changes in the competitive environment that may trigger strategic changes for the individual firm, and so affect its roles and functions in the market. New competitors, development of new products, changing customer preferences and demand patterns may require a company to reassess its strategy. The frequency, dynamics, and predictability of these changes dictate the intensity of the strategic planning activity of the firm. Stable and predictable environments lead to a low to moderate need for strategic planning; a turbulent environment requires frequent changes. We may consequently define *corporate strategy* as: "the direction and scope of an organization over the long term: which achieves advantage for the organization through its configuration of resources within a changing environment to meet the needs of markets and to fulfil stakeholder expectations" [Johnson 1999]

Based on the previous discussion, we can now formulate a definition of e-Business strategy: an *e-Business strategy* is the set of plans and objectives by which applications of internal and external electronically mediated communication contribute to the corporate strategy [Chaffey 2002]. A firm can decide to implement an e-Business strategy for a variety of reasons. The goal of the implementation can be, e.g. purely tactical. This is the case when the effect of the Information Technology applied is to replace existing systems and procedures. For example, instead of sending orders and confirmation through regular mail, traditional EDI (electronic Data Interchange) or more modern Internet-based XML EDI can be used to transfer information about orders and confirmations. The possible effect of this technology is a reduction in cost levels associated with the ordering process and thus an increased efficiency. Usually this type of application also leads to improved data quality which will result in a higher level of effectiveness in the ordering process, e.g., because the information transferred will contain fewer (preferably no) mistakes. This type of application of e-Business technology conforms to the early applications of information technology as generally conceived.

Recent literature stresses the necessity of external motivation to encourage use of IT, or its strategic purpose: leveraging the impact of IT on the strategy of a firm [Parker 1999; Porter 1985b] could help that firm to maintain/improve its market position through the use of computerized information systems. The argument to invest in information technology is not primarily related to cost reduction, but rather to revenue generation or retention and thus to the continued existence of the firm. Given this perspective, the implementation of e-Business may be strategic in nature. The idea then is to create, a preferably sustainable, competitive position for the company, by integrating the Internet and related technologies in its primary processes. In this case adoption of IT may lead to fundamental changes in products and services, markets served, relationships with key stakeholders and business models applied [Venkatraman 1998].

E-Business strategy should support not only corporate strategy objectives but also various functional strategies, like marketing and supply chain management [Chaffey 2002]. This is shown in Figure 2.1, which indicates a possible connection between e-Business and other strategies, such as functional strategies, which encompass supply chain management (SCM), marketing, purchasing and human resources (HR) strategies, and information systems (IS) strategy. Out of functional strategies we especially emphasize SCM and marketing strategies because these are closely related to e-Business. However, one should also bear in mind that other functional domains, such as Human Resources and Finance may have an impact on or may be impacted by e-Business strategies. Double-ended arrows indicate the relationships between strategies and imply that strategies will inform and impact each other.

■ **Figure 2.1:** Relationship Between e-Business and Other Organization Strategies

Supply chain management strategy is based on value chain analysis (see Chapter 4) for decomposing an organization into its individual activities and determining value added at each stage. In this way an organization can assess how efficiently resources are being used at various points within the value chain. The relevance of information technology is that, for each element in the value chain, it may be possible to use IT to increase the efficiency of resources in that area [Chaffey 2002]. Supply chain management strategy also requires an understanding of the procurement process and its impact on cost savings and implementation, e.g., integrated e-Procurement where the aim is to integrate with supplier's systems.

Marketing strategy is a concerted pattern of actions taken in the market environment to create value for the firm by improving its economic performance, as is the case when the firm offers a new product or lowers prices in competition with its rivals. Marketing strategies are often focused on capturing market share or improving profitability through brand building, investment, and efficient contracts. A key factor driving e-Business and marketing strategy objectives concentrates on the current and future projections of customer demand for e-Business services in different marketplace segments. Marketing is based on demand analysis [Chaffey 2002], which examines current and projected customer use of each digital channel within different target markets. It is determined by taking into account factors such as the percentage of customers prepared to use Web-based and e-Business facilities for buying products and considering the barriers to adoption of this technology by customers.

IS strategy is a set of goals and plans with regard to the use of information systems in an organization to support the objectives of that organization in the long run [Galliers 2003]. An IS strategy consists of two components: a demand strategy and a supply strategy [Ward 2002]. The demand strategy defines the requirements or demand for information and information systems from a business point of view. Sometimes this is also called the 'Information Strategy' [Galliers 2003]. In fact, it defines the information systems, application portfolios that the business needs, the benefits that are to be expected from them etc. The supply strategy, sometimes called the 'IT strategy' [Ward 2002] outlines how the company's demand for information systems will be supported by technology, including hardware, software, and networks, also services like software development and user support. It specifies the sourcing of these technologies and services (in-house or outsource) and which capabilities are needed internally to operate those technologies. As we have defined, the *e-Business strategy* relates to electronic communication. As such it is an integral part of IS strategy.

The basic goal of an IS strategy is to ensure the alignment of information systems and technology development with enterprise priorities, and to facilitate the infusion of advanced technology products in the enterprise context. IS strategy helps an organization transform the way it interacts with customers, suppliers, employees, and institutional partners by developing an information technology strategy that integrates a company's business planning initiatives, optimizes current technology investments, incorporates new information management technologies, complies with regulatory reforms, and fosters the reengineering of key business processes. Unlike traditional technology-centric approaches to information management, it focuses on business transformation, to help align the information technology strategy with company business processes, to avoid pitfalls that result from the pursuit of 'fads' and ensure that IT initiatives are focused on the areas of highest 'real value' to the organization, and to address targeted areas of improvement, and strengthen financial results.

The IS strategy and its information technology strategic plan serve as a 'road map' to guide capital investments over a multi-year period. It conducts benchmarking studies of important IT strategy development processes, and also provides a review of the current information technology strategic plan, projects already in the planning stage, and/or perform return on investment analyses.

The strategy of e-Business is based on corporate objectives such as which markets to target and targets for revenue generation from electronic channels such as e-Business. This not only supports corporate strategy, but should also influence or impact it [Chaffey 2002]. There are many alternative ways that Figure 2.1 can be interpreted by different organizations depending on their perception of e-Business. For instance, if a company achieves most of its business in the physical world of manufacturing, supply chain management and marketing strategies are more important than the e-Business strategy. Alternatively, if a company is a services-based one where the nature of the product lends itself to electronic communications to streamline the value chain (see Chapter 3), then Figure 2.1 is more appropriate.

注: strategic positioning 达到 competitive advantage.

2.2 **Strategic positioning**

Companies can become more profitable than the average performer in their industry sector by achieving a sustainable competitive advantage, i.e., by operating at a lower cost, by commanding a premium price, or by doing both. One way of achieving cost and price advantages is through *strategic positioning*. Strategic positioning means that a company is doing things differently from its competitors, in a way that delivers a unique type of value to its customers [Porter 2001]. This may mean offering a different set of products, a different type of services, or different logistical arrangements. The Internet affects strategic positioning in very different ways as it opens new opportunities for achieving or strengthening a distinctive strategic positioning.

Porter suggests six fundamental principles that companies need to follow in order to establish and maintain a distinctive strategic position [Porter 2001]:

1) A company must start with the *right goal*: superior long-term return on investment. Only by grounding strategy in sustained profitability will real economic value be generated. Economic value is created when customers are willing to purchase a product or service that exceeds the cost of producing it.

2) A company's strategy must enable it to deliver a *value proposition*, or set of benefits, different from those that its competitors offer. Strategy defines a way of competing that delivers unique value for a particular set of customers.

3) Company strategy needs to be reflected in a *distinctive value chain*. To establish a sustainable competitive advantage, a company must perform in ways that are different from its rivals or perform similar activities in different ways. A company must configure the way it conducts manufacturing, logistics, service delivery, marketing, human resource management, and so on, differently from its rivals and tailored to its unique value proposition.

4) Robust company strategies involve *trade-offs*. A company may have to abandon or forgo some product features, services, or activities in order to be unique at others. Such trade-offs, in the product and in the value chain, are what make a company truly distinctive.

5) Company strategy defines how all the elements of what a company does fit together. A strategy involves making choices throughout the value chain that are interdependent; all a company's activities must be mutually reinforcing. A company's product design, for example, should reinforce its approach to the manufacturing process, and both should leverage the way it conducts after-sales service. Element fit not only increases competitive advantage but also makes a strategy harder to imitate.

6) Company strategy involves *continuity of direction*. A company must define a distinctive value proposition to which it will abide even if that means forgoing certain opportunities. Without continuity of direction, it is difficult for companies to develop unique skills and assets or build strong reputations with customers.

2.3 **Levels of e-Business strategy**

Strategies will exist at different levels of an organization. Strategic levels of management are concerned with integrating and co-ordinating the many activities of an organization so that the behavior of the whole is optimized and its overall direction is consistent with policies that are identified in its institutional mission.

However, the subjects that are dealt with in strategic plans vary with the corporate level at which they operate.

Ultimately, e-Business is about communication, within business units, between business units of the same enterprise, and between independent organizations. To make electronic communication possible, agreements between the parties that communicate about the information systems used are necessary. In general, the development and implementation of IS strategies, therefore e-Business plans to support the *competitive strategy* of the firm, require action at three levels of strategy [Ward 2002; Laudon 2004]:

- The *supply chain* or *industry value chain* level: e-Business requires a view of the role, added value, and position of the firm in the supply chain (industry value chain). Important issues that need to be addressed here include who are the firm's direct customers, what is the firm's value proposal to those customers, who are the suppliers, and how does the firm add value to those suppliers? What is the current performance of the industry value chain (see Chapter 3 for a definition of value chains) in terms of revenues and profitability, throughput times, inventory levels etc, and, more importantly, what are the required performance levels, and what is the firm's contribution to it? What are current problems in the chain? These are issues that need to be effectively addressed in order to understand the current and future position of the firm in the chain. This analysis gives an impetus to insight in upstream (supplier side) and downstream (customer side) data and information flows, and in the kind of shared IT infrastructure (so-called Inter-Organizational Systems) that is required to enable e-Business developments in the supply chain. This analysis also creates an understanding of how a firm's position in the chain might potentially be affected by new Internet-based technologies. Industry value chains evolve into networks of interrelated organizations. Network organizations and interorganizational systems are discussed in chapter 10.

- The *Line of Business* or *(Strategic) Business Unit* level: understanding the position in the value chain is a starting point for further analysis of how Internet-related technologies could contribute to the competitive strategy of the individual line of business. This is the level where the competitive strategy in a particular market for a particular product, and so the strategic positioning (see Section 2.2), is developed. There are four generic strategies for achieving a profitable business: *differentiation*, *cost*, *scope*, and *focus* [Porter 1980]. We describe each of them briefly. Differentiation strategy refers to all the ways producers can make their products unique and distinguish them from those of competitors. Adopting a strategy for cost competition means that a company primarily competes with low cost: customers are primarily interested in a acquiring a product as inexpensively as possible. Success in such a market usually implies that the company has discovered some unique set of business processes or resources that other firms cannot apply in the marketplace, which make it possible to deliver a product or service at the lowest possible cost. A scope strategy is a strategy to compete in markets worldwide, rather than merely in local, regional or national markets. A focus strategy is a strategy to compete within a narrow market segment or product segment. This is a specialization strategy with the goal of becoming the premier provider in a narrow market.

Critical questions here concern how e-Business plans will contribute to the competitive strategy and organizational performance of the individual Line of Business. How will e-Business processes and technology contribute to the specific value propositions that the line of business has to offer to its customers and suppliers? What are business challenges and problems, how will they be addressed by the deployment of e-Business technologies, and how potentially may e-Business technologies change the business, for instance, by creating a more transparent market, and/or inter- and des-intermediation patterns?

- The *corporate* or *enterprise* level for each firm that encompasses a collection of (strategic) business units. This level addresses the problem of synergy through a firm-wide, available common IT infrastructure. Commonality of e-Business applications is basically needed for two reasons. From an *efficiency* point of view, having different applications for the same functionality in different lines of business is needlessly costly. This calls for central development or acquisition, which may be combined with local deployment that takes into account local differences. From an *effectiveness* point of view there is the need for cross Line of Business communication and share-ability of data. As pointed out earlier, mass customization and individualization put the emphasis in the business plans on the consumer and not on the final product. If an enterprise has structured its activities in business units for each of its different products (e.g. different business units for insurances, banking and stock investments in a financial services organization), focus on the customer requires cross business unit collaboration and information. This can only be realized with an appropriate Enterprise Information Systems (EIS) infrastructure (see Chapter 6 for a definition) in place to support communication and share-ability of data across business units. Definition of business unit processes that need to communicate across different lines of business and common standards to make this possible are also required. These all become subjects of an enterprise-wide e-Business policy.

2.4 The changing competitive agenda: business and technology drivers

Not too long ago, an enterprise could, for the most part, initiate its own agenda of change. If an enterprise decided to expand its market, it did so by making incremental, planned modifications to its organization and strategy. When it modified organizational design, it considered and managed the impact on customers and employees in an attempt to maintain the enterprise equilibrium. Now, however, change is at the top of almost every business agenda. Today, it is the external competitive environment that mandates most internal change [Parker 1999].

Business and technology factors are driving this change in a strategic context. Business drivers are the shift in the balance of power between consumers and corporations, as much by fiercer competition in many industries, also known as hyper competition [D'Aveni, 1994]. Economies are getting transformed from supply oriented to demand oriented. So it is not what a business can deliver but what customers are expecting that becomes the starting point of any business planning. Consumer demand for high quality, customized products determines the performance specification most companies have to comply with to capture and maintain a competitive position. The Internet is even making markets more transparent, helping customers to locate suppliers that best meet their expectations and thus abolishes existing information asymmetries. The technology driver is the enabling power of modern technologies and was caused by the fusion of computer and telecommunication technologies that resulted in networks. Information technologies may trigger new opportunities and threats, like an improved market position, new entrants in the market facilitated by the Internet, new ways of working, new organizational forms, or new business models.

The change from a supplier driven economy to a consumer driven economy, and with that a shift to customer-driven planning, has a large impact on how businesses are managed, which has been widely reported by different authors [Parker 1996, 1999]. Almost a century of management theory focused on the role of standardization as a prerequisite for mass production and mass distribution [Urwick 1943].

In the 1990s the focus changed to customization and customer-driven planning. In a Harvard Business Review editorial, it was observed that modern business involves thinking like a customer, and not like a producer [Kanter 1992]. Moving from a producer focus to a consumer focus causes a shift in the intent of service and quality programs, the impetus for product development, and the structure of the organization itself. It forces a revaluation of the traditional supplier-customer relationship, organizational form and location, market and service requirements, definition of markets and economic base, and structure of distribution channels [Parker 1996, 1999]. Moreover, the business integrates its production and service delivery processes to the feedback it receives from its individual customers. This has led to the development of the concepts of mass customization, and one-to-one marketing [Pine 1993; Peppers 1993, 1997]. *Mass customization* refers to the possibility of delivering products and services that meet the specific needs of individual customers in mass markets. The idea is that if products and services are composed of standardized modules, and if also the assembly and distribution elements of the supply chain are modularized the supply chain can be tailored to the needs of the individual. *One-to-one marketing* means that the collective marketing activities of a firm are being targeted at each individual customer so that each customer gets an individualized product offering. Modern data warehouse technology and the Internet are the key to realizing such marketing strategies.

The Internet has created a highly competitive market environment. Information technology incorporated through the Internet is reducing much of the transaction and coordination costs associated with old economy business operations, and restructuring value chains allowing firms to forwardly integrate and bypass intermediaries. The global nature of the Internet makes competition even fiercer as competitors come across geographic boundaries. Hence, Internet companies operate in an ever more crowded market space, and look for ways to reduce this crowdedness by closing out competition.

As e-Business is introduced into an existing organization, there will be various areas that have to be taken into account when developing a strategy. In addition to elements of traditional strategy approaches, innovative techniques to achieve competitive advantage must be incorporated. One area of particular importance is the strategic impact of IT.

Initially, the role of IT in a business organization was a reactive one. Computer applications supported the existing managerial and operational processes. The view was that investments in IT were replacement investments, for example, replacing manual activities mainly to improve efficiency of information processing operations. Since the mid-1980s, in the literature as in practice, it became clear that IT could fundamentally affect the way a company's business was conducted. This phenomenon was known as the *strategic impact of IT*. Four types of strategic systems can be identified on the basis of several hundreds of examples and case studies of claimed 'strategic systems' [Ward 2002]. These types of strategic systems include:

- Systems that link the company with customers and suppliers and change the nature of the relationship;

- Systems that lead to more effective integration of internal processes of the organization;

- Systems that enable the organization to bring new or improved information based products and services to the market;

- Systems that provide the executives with high quality information to support the development and implementation of strategy.

Specific characteristics make the Internet a technology of interest in respect of potential strategic effects [Ward 2002]. This is affected through its:

- *Pervasiveness* – it supports direct electronic linkages with businesses and end-consumers all day and every day, all over the world, thus enabling totally new ways of doing business.

- *Interactive nature* – this not only enables linear transaction communication, but also all kinds of reciprocal relationships which are characteristic for tasks related to, e.g., problem solving, collaborative planning, and negotiation. Through this technology these relationships become time and location independent.

- *Virtual nature* – this brings business actions from a physical 'marketplace' to a 'market space'. Businesses will have to learn how to deal with the implications of online and screen-based trading for appropriate business models, trust, service delivery, branding, etc.

A lot of the attention that e-Business receives tends to concentrate on the technologies involved. There is no doubt that selecting the right technology, and implementing it well, is crucial. However, the impact those technologies can have on company business processes, relationships, and organization can have much larger ramifications than the technology implementation itself. Inadequately addressing business processes, relationships, and organizational impacts can greatly impede the success of an e-Business program. For e-Business to succeed, the technology and processes must work well together. In some ways, this is similar to the growing recognition throughout the 1990s of the important role that good process design and organizational change management played in successful Enterprise Resource Planning (ERP) implementations. The integrated nature of ERP systems often forced this issue. Now e-Business allows integration across even broader boundaries both within but also outside a company, linking it with customers, suppliers, channel partners, and others. Examples of where process changes may lie are in order management areas, distribution and warehousing, and requisitioning, among many. In addition, entirely new processes and roles may be required, for instance, to create and manage content delivered over the Web, such as product technical information, pricing, and other content. In order to make informed decisions about how to proceed when developing an e-Business strategy, a company needs to understand the impact that various e-Business initiatives will have on its processes, business relationships, and its organization in general. There are several considerations that need to be addressed during the strategy development stage in order to briefly but thoroughly identify major areas of process and relationship impact as well as organizational readiness.

Case Study

How e-Business technologies may change competition in an industry

Business drivers – imports For a long period, imports of cut flowers into the Netherlands have shown an increasing trend. There was a rise of 78% between 1985 and 1990; there was a dramatic increase in the period 1990–1994; finally, from 1996 to 1998 imports through the auctions rose by about 15% per year. There is a growing share of   European Union (EU) countries, Israel, and African countries such as Kenya, Zambia, and Zimbabwe. These increasing imports led to mixed reactions. Dutch growers felt that one of the main consequences of increasing imports was declining prices for all imported and Dutch products. Indeed, a survey in September 1994 showed that 269 out of 433 growers ranked foreign production as the most important threat, and 144 growers ranked auctioning imports as such. Seventy-four percent of the growers stated that imports had a negative effect on prices at Dutch auctions. Dutch producers of roses reacted furiously to the decreasing prices, attributed to the increasing production volumes in Southern Europe and Africa. However, not everybody shared this opinion. Actually, 12% of the growers claimed imports had a positive effect, because they might attract more buyers. The board of directors of Flower Auction Aalsmeer and Flower Auction Holland intended to continue the liberal import policy. Their argument was that Dutch flower auctions should be the center of a global flower market, not a market place for Dutch products only. Nevertheless, in September 1994, the growers (owners) of Flower Auction Aalsmeer and Flower Auction Holland decided to change their import policies, and to impose strict import limitations. They banned the imports during summer completely (between 1 June 1995 and 15 September 1995), determined an upper limit of accepted imports for the rest of the year, and proposed a very tight quality control system for imports. These import restrictions hard three main effects:

- Imports from Africa, Europe, and North-America declined in 1995. The imports via the seven Dutch auctions accounted for 60% of total imports; the remaining 40% were imported directly by wholesalers/exporters and retailers. In 1994 the supply of imported flowers increased by 16.2%. In 1995 it decreased by 1.3% (total of 1.783 billion stems);

- Prices in season 1994/1995 (October-March) decreased, because of unfavourable weather and currency problems ('the strong guilder'). Lower imports should result in higher prices, as was expected by growers; but that impact was not clearly visible. Some growers and buyers had the impression that flower prices were more volatile;

- Importers had to find alternative marketing channels to sell their products.

Technology drivers: reaction to import restrictions – the creation of TFA   One of the biggest importers of cut flowers is East African Flowers (EAF), established in 1984 and located in the Aalsmeer area in the Netherlands. EAF specializes in supply from East Africa (Kenya, Tanzania, and Uganda). EAF takes care of clearance through customs and other formalities. Also they prepare the flowers for auction. The grower pays a fee for these services. For EAF, the effect of the import restrictions was that 30% of their imports could no longer be traded via the Dutch auction clocks during the traditional import season, and in the summer season 100% of their imports could not be traded at all.

EAF retaliated by introducing an electronic alternative to the traditional Dutch auctions, called Tele Flower Auction (TFA). In the TFA, buyers can bid via their personal computers (PCs) or (currently) laptops. Each PC is connected to a fully computerized auction clock. Logistics and price discovery are uncoupled, which leads to faster logistics. Flowers are no longer visible for buyers, and buyers are no longer physically present in the auction room. The PC provides the buyer with information on the next flower lots. On his or her PC the buyer can earmark interesting lots, so at the time those lots are auctioned, the PC will warn the buyer. The PC provides information on the producer, product, unit of currency, quality, and minimum purchase quantity. For each lot, two pictures (photographs made the day before auctioning) are presented on the screen. The auction concept remains the same, as with the Dutch flower auction.

Growers send the flowers to EAF, and EAF stores these flowers in Amstelveen. The distribution of the flowers, after being auctioned, from the Amstelveen area to the buyers' addresses (nearby the traditional auctions of Aalsmeer, Naaldwijk, and Rijnsburg) is done by EAF transporters. Transport costs are paid by EAF.

Developments moved quickly. The creation of TFA was announced in December 1994. In January 1995 the system was tested. On March 24, 1995 TFA started with 70 buyers. In the beginning, TFA was restricted to 15 growers who were the main EAF suppliers. After some months, EAF decided that growers from other countries (for example, Spain, Colombia, France, India, and Israel) were also allowed to use TFA. One year later approximately 160 buyers were connected to TFA. In October 1995, EAF decided that TFA would become a permanent electronic auction market. EAF expected a turnover of 100 million Dutch guilders for the growing season 1995/1996, which is around 3% of the total turnover of the seven traditional Dutch flower auctions. Their turnover in 1998 was estimated at around 160 million Dutch guilders.

2.5 The strategic planning process

Organizations employ strategic planning as a way to move toward their desired future position. Strategic planning is the *process* of developing and implementing plans to reach goals and objectives. Strategic planning, more than anything else, is what gives direction to an organization.

Most strategic planning methodologies are based on a situation, target, and path process:

- Situation – Where a company is right now and how did it get there?

- Target – Where does a company want to be?

- Path – How can it get there?

In general terms, the basic approach to strategic planning requires an industrial organization approach that is based on economic theory and deals with issues such as competitive rivalry, resource allocation, economies of scale. Its basic assumptions focus on rationality, self-interested behavior, and profit maximization. An example of this approach is Porter's five forces model, and Barney's resource model, which are covered in Sections 2.7.1 and 2.7.2.

The *strategic planning process* involves a sequence of steps taken by management to develop new plans, modify existing plans that may require revision, and discontinue plans that are no longer justified functionally or financially [Canzer 2003]. The strategic planning process requires first the establishment and then the maintenance of a plan of action that everyone in the organization is expected to follow.

The *strategic planning process* has four key elements: mission statement, strategic analysis, strategic choice, and strategy implementation [Johnson 1999]. Figure 2.2 illustrates activity flow as new strategic plans are developed and existing plans are monitored, modified, and possibly replaced if they are no longer considered a good match with current conditions or management objectives. After an organization's mission statement is established, analysis of relevant information succeeds and leads to the development of strategic plans and their subsequent implementation by the organization. Feedback links assure the continuous incorporation of new information at all steps of the strategic planning process.

■ **Figure 2.2:** The Strategic Planning Process [Canzer 2003]

The strategic planning process starts with the establishment of the organization's *mission statement,* which is a basic description detailing the fundamental purpose of the organization's existence and encompasses strategy development, including determination of the organization's vision and objectives. It is developed at the highest level of the organization's management and ownership structure, and is fairly stable over longer periods of time, while providing a general sense of direction for all decision making within the firm.

Strategic analysis involves situation analysis, internal resource assessment, and evaluation of stakeholders' expectations. It will include environmental scanning, industry or market research, competitor analysis, analysis of marketplace structure, and relationships with trading partners and suppliers, and customer marketing research. Information is delivered from the analysis of factors that are both internal and external to the firm [Canzer 2003]. These factors are considered important environmental forces acting upon customers, current strategies, and new plans still under development. External factors include socio-cultural, technological, legal and regulatory, political, economic, and competitive forces. Internal factors include the organization's human, material, informational, and financial resources; structure; operational style; culture; and other characteristics that are internal to an organization. Any realistic new plan will have to reflect the reality of both the external world and the internal dynamics of the organization.

Strategic choice is based on the strategic analysis [Johnson 1999] and consists of three parts: Generation of strategic options, highlighting possible courses of action, evaluation of strategic options on their relative merits, and selection of strategy, which is the selection of those options that the organization will pursue. Strategic choice results in *strategic planning,* which is concerned with the organizing and detailing of all the strategies that will be undertaken throughout the organization and their expected target objectives as well as their expected results [Canzer 2003]. Planning includes strategy specification and resource allocation and is organized in a hierarchical top-down fashion. It commences with *corporate-level planning* and objectives that determine the overall direction for the organization. Corporate-level planning drives *division* (or *strategic business unit) level planning* which deals with major areas or groups of related products offered by an organization. Division level plans in turn become the starting point for *operating* (or *functional) level planning,* which involves more local plans within specific departments of the organization.

Implementation relates to the actual tasks that must be executed in order to realize a plan [Canzer 2003] and translates strategy into action. It includes monitoring, adjustment, control as well as a feedback that can direct useful information to the various levels of the organization that are involved ion the ongoing planning process. Control refers to how well an intended objective is likely to be realized, given the current conditions. Feedback refers to the evaluation of activities that are reported back to management decision makers.

The above discussion assumes that strategies are purposefully designed action plans leading to a consistent pattern of actions and so to consistent behavior over time. With this assumption comes the supposition that all (successful) actions today are the result of a purposeful planning activity somewhere in the past, so-called *intended strategies* [Mintzberg 1994]. However, in real life situations, not all realized strategies have been intentional. Some appear simply to have emerged over time, due to a sequence of unanticipated steps: so-called *emergent strategies* (see Figure 2.3) [Mintzberg 1994]. In business practice, strategies are almost always a mix of intended and emergent strategies. The field of information systems and e-Business is particularly one where emergent strategies are important. New technologies that come up are tested in ongoing business processes and, if successful, result in a change of that process.

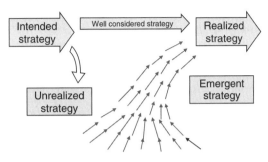

■ **Figure 2.3:** Forms of Strategy [Mintzberg 1994]

Also the literature provides examples of technologies that have been implemented with specific objectives in mind, and, however, turned out to be very successful, in a very different field than the one expected. An early example is the often cited American Airlines case. In the early 1960s, American Airlines invited its travel agents to join a network called SABRE, developed by AA in cooperation with IBM, in order to simplify the reservation systems. Eventually the initiative became so successful that competing airlines were offered the possibility of utilizing the network, of course, at a price. In the end AA realized more profit with making reservations for other airlines than with transporting passengers [Ward 2002]. And today SABRE is one of the leading reservation networks in the US.

2.6 Strategic alignment

In the 1980s the concept of alignment between business and IT was developed [Benson 1985; Parker 1988]. According to this concept it is not only feasible to design and build a technically sophisticated (inter-organizational) infrastructure for e-Business, but also to formulate business strategies that complement and support this infrastructure. If a firm's IT strategic and operational objectives are not in alignment with its business strategies and operations, then this infrastructure is bound to fail. Due to lack of alignment between business and IS strategies, organizations fail to get value out of their IS/IT investments [Ward 2002]. For example, if a firm wants to design an inter-organizational information system that establishes a long-term relationship with its supplier, it needs to provide the supplier with information about requirements, and perhaps even let the supplier monitor its inventory and replenish it periodically.

One of the major issues regarding an enterprise's investment in information technology is whether this is in harmony with its strategic objectives (intent, current strategy, and enterprise goals) and thus building the capabilities necessary to deliver business value. This state of harmony is referred to as *alignment* [IT Governance Institute 2003]. Alignment is complex, multifaceted and almost never completely achieved. It is about continuing to move in the right direction and being better aligned than competitors.

Alignment encompasses more than strategic integration between the (future) information technology organization and the (future) enterprise organization. It is also about whether information technology operations are aligned with the current enterprise operations. Obviously, it is difficult to achieve IT alignment when enterprise units are misaligned.

Any e-Business strategy should articulate an enterprise's intention to use information technology based on business requirements. Linkage to business aims is essential for information technology to deliver recognizable value to the enterprise. When formulating the IT strategy, the enterprise must consider:

- Business objectives and the competitive environment;

- Current and future technologies and the costs, risks, and benefits they can bring to the business;

- The capability of the information technology organization and technology to deliver current and future levels of service to the business, and the extent of change and investment this might imply for the whole enterprise;

- Cost of current information technology, and whether this provides sufficient value to the business;

- Lessons learned from past failures and successes.

Once these issues are clearly understood, the IT strategy can be developed to ensure all elements of the IT environment support the strategic e-Business objectives. This is illustrated in Figure 2.4: Note the existence of a feedback loop. This implies that new developments in the e-Business infrastructure may result in revaluation of the enterprise strategy, business functions, and application architecture.

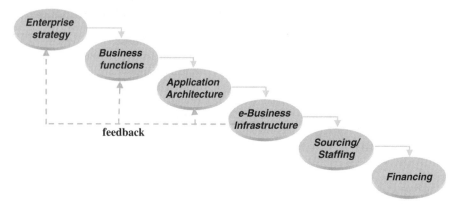

■ **Figure 2.4:** Information Technology Supporting e-Business Strategic Objectives

It is important that the plan for implementing the company strategy be endorsed by all relevant parties. It is also important that the implementation plans be broken down into manageable parts, each with a clear business case incorporating a plan for achieving outcomes, and realizing benefits. Management should ensure that the strategy is reviewed regularly in the light of technological and operational change.

Hence, it should drive business alignment by ensuring that IT strategy is aligned with business strategy and that distributed IT strategies, i.e., e-Business strategy, are consistent and integrated. Management should also ensure that information technology delivers against the strategy on time and within budget, with appropriate functionality, and the intended benefits through clear expectations and measurement. Furthermore, management should ensure that investments between systems that support the enterprise are balanced, and should transform the enterprise or create an infrastructure that enables the business to grow and compete in new arenas.

As information technology becomes more critical for enterprise survival in the e-Business era, in addition to enabling growth, IT strategy committees should not only offer advice on strategy when assisting the management in its IT governance responsibilities, but also should focus on information technology value, risks, and performance [IT Governance Institute 2003].

2.7 The consequences of e-Business: theoretical foundations

The effects of e-Business form the subject of various organization theories. As e-Business is an information technology-enabled organizational phenomenon with economic consequences, economic theories appear to be particularly useful for analyzing the business effects. Several approaches are discussed in the economics literature [Douma 1998].

Strategy is about finding the right (external) fit between organization and environment. Different schools of thought have approached this problem from different angles. Porter's theory on *competitive strategy* is an example of a line of thinking that starts from the positioning of a firm in its competitive environment, and considers how, in the context of external forces, a competitive strategy may result in a sustainable competitive position [Porter 1980, 1985]. However, a firm's strategic position is not only the result of external 'forces' but also the consequence of the expertise and abilities within an organization. The *Resource Based view* [Prahalad 1991] perceives the organization as a collection of competencies, which have to be developed and maintained. According to this view a firm's competitive position is dependent on its competencies that are considered 'core' and also unique. These competencies form the foundation for the position of the firm in the market, and the products and services it develops and brings to the market.

When analyzing the strategic implications of Internet-based business models a third approach prevails. E-Business is about relationships, including transactional relationships, between businesses. It also addresses the problem of how to organize (govern) transactions. The approach dealing with this type of phenomenon is known as *Transaction Cost Economics*, [Coase 1973; Williamson 1975].

In short, when analyzing the business effects of e-Business we will consider the following approaches:

- The theory of competitive strategy;
- The resource-based view;
- The theory of transaction costs.

2.7.1 **Theory of competitive strategy**

According to Porter the structural attractiveness of a firm is determined by five underlying forces of competition [Porter 1997]:

1) The bargaining power of customers;
2) The bargaining power of suppliers;
3) The barriers to entry for new competitors;
4) The threat of new substitute products or services;
5) The competition among existing firms in the industry.

In combination, these forces determine how the economic value created by any product, service technology or way of competing is divided between companies in an industry as well as customers, suppliers, distributors, substitutes, and potential new entrants [Porter 1997].

The bargaining power of customers vis-à-vis a firm could, for instance, depend on the degree of product differentiation, and the size of demand and supply. 'Switching costs' too are very important: they answer the question of how much will it cost the customer to change to another supplier. In cases of high switching costs, the customer may be in a lock- in position. For example, IT through proprietary standards, may exert a lock-in effect. But also improved personalized services, enabled by modern database and data-mining technologies may have a lock-in effect as well. For the customer, moving to another supplier means losing this service.

The bargaining power of suppliers is dependent on a variety of factors, such as relative size, number of suppliers that can deliver a critical resource, and so on. In addition, information technology can lead to lock-in positions and additional switching costs in the specifications of IT suppliers. The Internet causes another specific threat from the perspective of suppliers: they may bypass their customer and directly approach his or her clients. Servicing a final customer directly, and not through an intermediary organization, is an option which may be considered in many industries. Examples include insurance companies, airlines, and tour operators bypassing the intermediary in order to sell directly to the end-customer.

The barriers to entry for new competitors depend on how difficult it is to join the industry. Economic and technology thresholds may prevent outside potential competitors from coming in. Economies of scale, necessary capital, and specialized expertise are important factors in this respect. New Internet-based business models, which do not necessitate investments in 'bricks and mortar' may facilitate an easy entrance and thus create unexpected competitors. As in the case of flower industry, which we discuss in Section 2.4, where an Internet-based auction succeeded in becoming a serious player in the Dutch flower industry within a few months (the former 'bricks' company being pushed out by regulations that fenced off foreign competition) [van Heck 1997].

The threat of substitute products depends on the question of whether other products can deliver added value for consumers instead of current products in the absence of switching costs. For example, the Internet has become a serious threat to the Post Office as e-mail communication takes over regular mail, resulting in a loss of business.

The level of competition among existing firms in the industry will depend on various factors like type of market, existing competitive behavior, and so on. The Internet may affect market competition in a number ways. As explained before, through its pervasiveness it supports direct electronic linkages with businesses and end consumers. Significantly reduced search costs will thus contribute to a much higher market transparency. Profitable market positions based on information asymmetry will be threatened.

Analyzing these five forces of competition clarifies an industry's fundamental attractiveness, exposes the underlying drivers of average industry profitability, and provides insight into how profitability can evolve in the future. The five competitive forces still determine profitability even if suppliers, channels, substitutes, or competitors change [Porter 2001].

Achieving success in any competitive environment in Porter's view depends on a chosen *competitive strategy* which is either based on a firm being a low cost producer (customers buy from you, because you are the most inexpensive supplier) or on a differentiation from competitors in quality offered, as perceived by the customers (customers buy from you because of the quality you offer). These strategies can be pursued either throughout the market or by concentrating on a particular niche.

Various authors, including Porter himself, have applied these concepts to explaining the strategic effects of information technology [Porter 1985a]. More recently, with the help of these models, Porter analyzed the impact of the Internet on industries and individual organizations [Porter 2001]. An examination of a wide range of industries in which the Internet is playing a role revealed some clear trends. Positive trends from the perspective of producers/suppliers include:

- The Internet tends to dampen the bargaining power of channels by providing companies with new, more direct avenues to customers;

- The Internet can also boost an industry's efficiency in various ways, expanding the overall size of the market by improving its position relative to traditional substitutes.

However, the Internet also strengthens the position of customers (both buying companies and end-customers). For instance:

- Internet technology provides buyers with easier access to information about products and suppliers, thus bolstering buyer bargaining power;

- The Internet mitigates the need for such things as an established sales force or access to existing channels, reducing barriers to entry;

- By enabling new approaches to meeting needs and performing functions, the Internet creates new substitutes;

- Because the Internet is an open system, companies have more difficulty maintaining proprietary offerings, thus intensifying the rivalry among competitors;

- The use of the Internet also tends to expand the geographic market, bringing many more companies into competition with one another.

Case Study

How e-Business technologies may change competition in an industry

Porter's competitive forces model The developments in the flower auction industry can be analyzed from the perspective of the Porter competitive forces model. EAF operated as a sales channel for foreign growers, and as such was a direct supplier to the Dutch flower auctions.

Internal competition: at the time of creation of TFA there were seven flower auctions, established as cooperatives by the Dutch growers. Internal industry competition is moderate. Growers have an obligation to auction. By fencing off the market for imported flowers, foreign competition was prevented from entering the market.

Suppliers: there are two categories of suppliers: domestic and foreign. Domestic growers are connected with one of the auctions, and have the obligation to sell their products through that organization. If they sell their flowers via another party, for example, TFA, they lose their rights to utilize the auction. Basically this is a lock in. Foreign growers use different channels to bring their products to the market. EAF acts as an intermediary between African growers and the auctions.

Buyers: buyers are professional traders, mostly (84%) export wholesalers. EAF sells specifically to the wholesale market, those working for the Dutch market and to exporters.

Substitute products: in the flower auction industry two types of substitute may be distinguished: substitute products and substitute sales channels. Other products, like potted plants, may be substituted for flowers. This happens when the economy is slowing down, as potted plants last longer than flowers. Substitute sales channels form a threat to the auctions. Auctions are supply driven, with no possibility for the buyer to plan ahead and exert a direct influence on the products delivered by anonymous suppliers. Alternative trade channels are emerging, like direct contracting between trader and grower, and mediation offices because buyers wish to influence the supply of flowers, in terms of their characteristics and volume. Auctions are reacting to this development by creating 'multi channelling strategies'. In line with this development EAF created 'TFA direct' in 2003, which now accounts for 15% of EAF's total revenue.

New entrants: the industry has a rather closed character and consequently is very stable; few new organizations try to enter the industry. Obstacles for newcomers are the sceptical attitude of the existing organizations in the industry towards 'outsiders' and the obligation to auction for the growers.

In fact TFA by EAF is the only example of a successful new entrant in the industry. As nobody expected that anyone could start a business in this industry, closing the auctions for foreign flowers seemed almost without risks. Who would ever be able to build and run an auction at such a short notice? However, everybody overlooked the possibility of building a digital version of a traditional auction. It took a few months of programming; then EAF moved forward in the flower chain and TFA became a new player in the industry.

Was/is TFA successful? This new entrant's general success may be defined as the ability of a new entrant to build up significant sales volumes with fair prices for the traded products, in a short time frame. EAF announced the creation of TFA in December 1994. In June 1995, the Chief Executive Officer (CEO) of EAF/TFA, Simon van der Burg, stated that the results of TFA were better than expected. Every day, approximately two million stems are auctioned. Buyers were enthusiastic about the quality and the speed of delivery. The prices were on average neither lower, nor higher than in traditional Dutch flower auctions. Growers were also enthusiastic; they benefit from the EAF initiative because they are dependent on EAF's selling power. Also EAF decided that growers not related to EAF could also use TFA as their marketing channel. Compared with the seven traditional Dutch auctions, TFA ranks fourth. TFA has now been in business for 10 years; the turnover in 2002 amounted to 49 million euros.

2.7.2 The resource-based view

According to this theory of economic development, innovation is the source of value creation [Schumpeter 1939]. Technological development is viewed as discontinuous change and disequilibrium resulting from innovation. Several sources of innovation (hence, value creation) are identified including the introduction of new goods or new production methods, the creation of new markets, the discovery of new supply sources, and the reorganization of industries. Innovation emphasizes the importance of technology and considers novel combinations of resources (and the services they provide) as the foundations of new products and production methods. These, in turn, lead to the transformation of markets and industries, and hence to economic development.

Barney's resource-based view (RBV), which builds on the theory of economic development's perspective on value creation, regards a firm as a collection of resources and capabilities [Barney 1991; Amit 2001]. In contrast to theories about company performance, which emphasize external strategic positioning, Barney's resource-based view considers internal resources and competencies as sources of potential competitive advantage, instead of looking at the market and making strategic plans accordingly. The resource-based view looks at available resources first to see how a position in the business environment can be acquired with them. According to this view, a firm can build a strategic position by picking the right resources and building competencies that are unique and difficult to imitate. Resources are considered the raw material for building competencies.

The RBV states that marshalling and uniquely combining a set of complementary and specialized resources and capabilities (which are heterogeneous within an industry, scarce, durable, not easily traded, and difficult to imitate), may lead to value creation [Wernerfelt 1984; Barney 1991; Peteraf 1993; Amit 1993]. The supposition is that, even in equilibrium, firms may differ in terms of the resources and capabilities they control, and that such asymmetric firms may coexist until some exogenous change occurs. Hence, RBV theory postulates that the services rendered by the firm's unique bundle of resources and capabilities may lead to value creation. A firm's resources and core competences are valuable if, and only if, they reduce a firm's costs or increase its revenues compared to what would have been the case if the firm did not possess those resources [Barney 1997].

Core competencies are the 'root system' of an organization 'that provides nourishment, sustenance, and stability; they are the collective learning in the organization of how to coordinate diverse production skills and multiple streams of technology' [Prahalad 1991]. They encompass knowledge bases, skill sets, and service activities that can create a continuing competitive advantage [Quinn 1990].

The concept of core competence plays an important role in analyzing the viability of new Internet-based business models (see Chapter 3). Strategic outsourcing of all activities that are not core competencies potentially allows a company to focus on all those areas, which add most value. Because, by doing so the companies are leaner, they can respond faster to changing environmental demands.

2.7.3 Transaction cost economics

Transaction cost economics attempt to explain firms' choices between internalizing and buying goods and services from the market. According to transaction cost theory [Williamson 1975], exchanges with external firms entail a variety of coordination costs associated with various aspects of inter-firm transactions. These include search costs to find the right trading partner (or supplier of a good or service), as well as negotiation, monitoring, settlement, and various after sales services associated with the exchange. When conditions in the market cause these coordination costs to grow – such as when suppliers are hard to find, or there is a potential for them to behave opportunistically, firms may choose to internalize the production of the needed good or service. Hence, they trade off production costs for coordination costs, using internal management rather than the market as a 'governance' mechanism.

Transaction cost economics theory provides a theoretical framework for discussion of market structures, and addresses the question why necessary resources are obtained either through the market (external procurement) or through internal production (the hierarchy) [Coase 1971; Williamson 1975, 1983]. When a firm decides to bypass a wholesaler or retailer and sell directly to its end-customers, it is internalizing downstream channel services that it formerly acquired from the market.

The central question addressed by transaction cost economics is why firms internalize transactions that might otherwise be conducted in markets. Thus, the two key issues concerning firms are:

1) Which activities should a firm keep within its boundaries, and which activities should it outsource?
2) In which way should a firm manage its relationship with its customers, suppliers and other business partners?

At its core, transaction cost theory is concerned with explaining the choice of the most efficient governance form given a transaction that is embedded in a specific economic context. This choice is explained on the basis of the costs associated with these transactions. According to transaction cost economics, a firm has two options for organizing its economic activities: an internal hierarchical structure where it integrates the activity into its management structure, or a market-like relationship with external firms [Williamson 1975]. When the market mechanism is at work, the flow of materials and services takes the form of external transactions and is coordinated by market forces. Later scholars have extended the scope of transaction cost economics to include quasi-hierarchical and quasi-market structures as alternate governance forms that a firm can opt for [Gulati 1995]. However, the basic concept remains the same: a firm decides to rely on a governance form that is closer to the hierarchical end of the spectrum than the market end when the transaction costs that arise from market coordination outweigh production cost benefits which arise from economies of scale and scope that come with outsourcing to specialized firms. Outside procurement is favored when the sum of external production costs and transaction costs are lower than the sum of internal production and coordination costs.

The design of the organization and the structuring of the industry are to some extent dependent on the two cost components production and transaction cost. Production is the direct cost of producing a given product. Transaction cost includes coordination cost, operations risk, and opportunism risk [Clemons 1993]. Coordination cost includes search cost, negotiation cost, financing cost, and distribution cost. Search cost involves the cost of exchanging information on product details and buyer's needs, along with the cost of finding the right product or service that meets these needs. Negotiation and financing cost involve the cost of determining the appropriate price and payment terms, and identifying suitable financing to pay for the product or service. Distribution cost is the cost of physical transfer of goods to the purchaser's location. Operations risk is the risk that a trading partner may misrepresent or withhold information or under-perform on the contract. Opportunism risk can arise from two sources. One, if the buyer must make an investment with the supplier and this investment is relationship-specific, then the buyer is exposed to the risk that after the investment is made, the supplier reneges on the agreement and attempts to renegotiate the contract or act in other ways detrimental to the interests of the buyer. This investment could be in IT either to coordinate with the supplier or it could be other capital investments such as in production equipment. The second type of opportunism risk is due to small numbers bargaining, where doing business with a supplier creates a situation in which the firm has few alternative sources of supply.

Critical dimensions of transactions influencing the choice of the most efficient governance form are uncertainty, exchange frequency, and the specificity of assets enabling the exchange [Klein 1978; Williamson 1979]. Transaction costs include the costs of planning, adapting, executing, and monitoring task completion [Williamson 1983]. Transaction cost economics identifies transaction efficiency as a major source of value, as enhanced efficiency reduces costs.

A key concept in production is the firm, which is an economic institution that transforms factors of production into consumer goods and services. How an economy operates, which activities are organized through markets, and which through firms depends on various transaction costs involved. Markets reduce transaction costs as people dealing through market mechanisms do not need to negotiate and enforce individual contracts, nor do they need to acquire and process information about alternatives. Generally, the less organized the market, the higher the transaction costs. Transaction cost theory assumes that markets are not perfect, so lead to costs, like search and monitoring costs. This theory assists the understanding of the consequences of Internet Technology for the value system. As Internet technology is expected to significantly reduce transaction costs (and internal coordination costs), this theory provides a basis for assessing the effects of the Internet on new and existing business models. New models are based on choices related to in-house production versus external buying of products and services.

2.8 Success factors for implementation of e-Business strategies

2.8.1 e-Business transformation as an 'ill-structured problem'

Transforming an enterprise (a going concern) from a traditional organization to an e-Business-based organization is a complex endeavor. Its intention is to make a company faster, more efficient, so more competitive throughout the entire value chain. Fundamental questions have to be addressed like what is the impact of the Internet on the business, what is to be considered core to the business, what does really make a difference in an e-business environment? It is essential that *senior management* develops and endorses a broad strategic vision that calls for e-Business transformation.

However once answers have been found to these questions the right implementation strategy has to be chosen. Two approaches prevail: *the top down approach* and *the bottom up approach*.

According to the former, business transformation is *a business-wide* phenomenon that can only be implemented business wide. A stepwise method, starting with the development of the business vision, followed by the identification of processes to be reengineered, identifying opportunities for applying IT and Internet technology in particular, and finally building a prototype is usually applied [Davenport 1993]. However, following this top down trajectory does not guarantee success. A majority of large reengineering projects have not achieved the breakthrough performance improvements that had been expected [Laudon 2004]. Reengineering changes jobs, reporting relationships, patterns of collaboration, and fear of this breeds resistance [Laudon 2004]. When the reengineering effort crosses organization boundaries, which will be the case with transformation to e-business, these failure risks are only amplified.

With a bottom up strategy, business reengineering starts as an experiment in an 'inconspicuous' part of an organization. Lessons are drawn from this experience and the reengineering effort is taken to other and more complex parts of the organization. Essential in this approach is learning from each project, and the transfer of knowledge from one project to another [Caron 1994]. However, unconnected bottom up experiments will only lead to fragmented activities, which cannot lead to a business-wide transformation, based on interoperable systems and processes. Central coordination of the transformation activity is mandatory.

As has already been said, e-Business transformation is complex. The complexity is basically determined by two factors [Schoo 1999]:

- The *number of different parts* of the initial organization and IT environment in which the changes take place;

- The *level of uncertainty* that characterizes the transformation program.

The transformation program *affects multiple interrelated processes and parts of the organization, so*, for example, it will most probably impel purchasing and sales activities onto the Web, which will, as a consequence, involve reengineering of back-office procedures, which in turn may affect HR processes by applying portal technologies to bundle information, services, and applications when interacting with personnel. It may also stimulate computer-supported collaboration between different parts of the organization, a trend toward process orientation which creates interactions between organizational elements that hitherto did not interact. On top of this, if a company has multiple business units, these changes will have to be coordinated across all of them.

Next, both the process and the outcome of transformation activity contain a *high degree of uncertainty*. Nothing is really known at the start of the change program, either about how modern IT and Internet technology will be incorporated into the business model, nor how business processes will exactly change. The level of uncertainty will vary with factors like the number of concurrent change programs in the organization – e.g., the more change programs are running at the same time, the more dependencies have to be taken into account, the degree of necessary customization of information systems, and the availability of adequately trained and experienced project staff on a continued basis. During the transformation process, responsible managers will have to deal with this uncertainty in their decision-making.

Besides the inherent complexity of an e-business transformation program described above there are three other obstacles to success [Schoo 1999]:

- The people involved in the transformation have differing, even conflicting views;

- They would need to have a good shared knowledge and understanding of the current business situation, which is rarely the case;

- There are conflicts and dilemma's arising from the need for changes and the ensuing resistance, like the dilemma between adapting to the information system and adapting the information system itself.

These obstacles turn the goal of having a successful e-business transformation into an 'ill-structured problem'. A problem is ill-structured when the problematic situation shows any one of these components [Schoo 1999]:

- Not all objectives may be known at the outset; multiple objectives exist, and the trade offs of the objectives are largely unknown;

- The identity of all the important variables (both controllable and uncontrollable) that affect the outcomes may not be known at the outset of the decision process;

- The relationship between affecting variables and outcomes are not well known in advance, or they may vary according to different plausible assumptions.

In a complex e-Business transformation project, all three components of an ill-structured problem are present. A consequence of the lack of structure is that one cannot completely model the variables in a transformation project. The lack of a model ensures that there is no ideal single approach to a complex e-Business transformation project.

2.8.2 The need for program management

It follows from the previous discussion that complex e-Business transformation projects consist of a set of sub-projects, which are related regarding contents, resources, and goals, and pursue a common (strategic) goal, for instance, to radically improve the supply chain. Coordination across the projects is essential, otherwise the result would be loss and inefficient use of resources and a fragmented outcome of the total transformation effort. In order to provide for that central coordination, *program management* has to be introduced to the system.

Literature that has focused on the success factors that impact e-business transformations and, e.g., large implementations of ERP is limited [Somers 2001]. Most of it has focused on *project management* and project implementation. Projects are a structured set of activities concerned with delivering a defined capability to an organization based on agreed schedule and budget. E-Business transformation, however, consists of a portfolio of projects, defining a set of related activities for IT and the business side of the organization, which has more or less specified and known goals, and needs to be controlled as a whole. The set of (sub) projects are cast into a *program*. A program has to yield several related results (else it is called a 'project') and has a defined end (to differentiate it from the standing organization) [Schoo 1999; Ribbers 2002a].

Programs are structured, planned and controlled like projects, and have, just like a project has, their own staff. Also program management is in many ways similar to project management; however its overall goals, life cycle, and problem solving processes are different. Compared to single projects with a single result, a program needs [Schoo 1999]:

- A different phase structure, especially in e-Business implementations where initial analysis and piloting may be followed by an extended roll out, consisting of multiple individual implementation projects;

- A more sophisticated progress reporting system, with a focus on overall strategic goals, future delays, and bottlenecks, especially regarding scarce resources and interfaces or dependencies between projects;

- A set of central services to individual projects, regarding process models, methods and tools, communication, experience/know-how databases, supplier contract management;

- A start-up phase in which goals are operationalized, responsibilities defined and priorities assigned;

- A rigorous program and project review mechanism, to introduce learning in ongoing projects, and to elicit experiences from completed phases and projects.

A core part of program management is *multi-project management*, the main objectives of which are to recognize dependencies between projects, share scarce resources in an overall efficient way, and systematically utilize experiences from single projects.

2.8.3 Design characteristics of program management

Program management contains the following key elements [Schoo 1999; Ribbers 2002]:

- Program organization: As the structural organization of a team that plans and controls projects in the program and the related resources;

- Policies: That guide program management to perform within given budgets, required acceptance levels, and goal adherence;

- Plans: That take the implementation goals and drive the projects within the program;

- Communication: As a means of providing information to teams and other staff, to solve problems within and between the teams, and to keep the organization as a whole informed;

- Alignment: The process of adapting information systems to the organization and vice versa, in line with the business direction.

Program organization This reflects in general the complexity of the program to be managed. Coordination is critical in particular with the board, across individual projects, with suppliers, and to achieve overall process efficiency. Teams in complex e-business transformation programs should be structured such that they cover these coordination requirements. The program management team typically contains the following roles:

- The steering committee, which ensures that resources for the program are available. It represents the stakeholders for the overall implementation;

- The program manager, who has to deliver the program results as defined by the business and IT strategies, and within the limits of resource constraints (people, budget, assets);

- Program sponsor, who maintains liaison with the board;

- User representative, who maintains liaison with internal users of the systems;

- Various coordinator roles like coordinator across projects, coordinator with external suppliers, coordinator for an efficient implementation process.

Policies programs are not directed by their project/program managers alone. Senior managers give direction as they sit on steering committees or function as user representatives. Given the strategic direction of the program, their influence is primarily found in setting budgets and deadlines, and restricting these over time. A particular critical question is how to apply budget and time restrictions. A general tendency is to have *a loose budget and time policy in the innovation phase of the project*, during which visioning, software selection, and pilot testing takes place, to ensure that the organization finds and develops the right solution. However, tighter restrictions are applied in the later roll out phase (a so called 'no change policy').

Plans aspects that are particularly relevant in planning an e-Business transformation program are the extent to which implementation projects run in parallel; the technology or organizational emphasis is chosen along the implementation route.

When the number of implementation projects is large, the program manager has to implement them in parallel. A so-called 'big bang' strategy would visit each affected site at once, and introduce all the technical and organizational innovations at once. However once the number of locations exceeds a certain number this approach is not possible. The main reasons are to be found in limited resources to run all projects in parallel, the limited training and knowledge transfer to parallel projects and the overhead entailed for parallel work on system interfaces. The solution is a 'phased' implementation strategy, which introduces limited new functionality first to all sites and later adds remaining functionality, a 'phase based' strategy that brings all functionality to clusters of sites only [Schoo 1999].

For 'phased' implementation strategies, the program manager has to decide which innovations to concentrate on in the first round: the new systems or the new processes and procedures. E-Business transformation programs are characterized by a high degree of innovation and integration of processes and systems, which introduces the need for organizational changes. Especially for a program with a high level of innovation and integration complexity, the organizational changes must be implemented together with the technical changes [Schoo 1999].

Communication is a prerequisite for a shared understanding of the outcomes and goals of a change process. Honest and continuous communication, especially two-way, is proposed to reduce resistance against the impending change. Especially when the program encompasses innovation, program managers have to be aware what the program is asking from the staff. Such communication should answer questions like: 'What will happen'?, 'When'?, and 'How will it affect me'? [Conner 1994]. Communication is also a key condition for emphasizing management sponsorship. Sponsorship should penetrate all levels within an organization. The more locations are affected in the program, and the more they differ, the more difficult it will be for the sponsor to make his or her influence felt, heard, and seen; consequently, the more active sponsorship will be needed.

Alignment as discussed above, continuing alignment between business strategies and IT developments is key. Especially as the roll out comes closer the organization gets more exposed to redesigned processes and new systems. Resistance against foreseeable changes arises and the need for monitoring the alignment becomes apparent. The upcoming resistance is often reflected in a large number of change requests. It is then important that the plan for implementing the company strategy be continuously endorsed by all relevant parties. The program management organization can contribute to this continuing alignment by applying various mechanisms and tools, like program reviews, reviews after each project step, release control, maintaining good informal relationships between IT and the different parts of the organization.

2.8.4 Change agentry

Introducing new IT and redesigning business processes are organizational interventions, which require purposeful change management. Processes, procedures, and information systems can be designed or redesigned and built; however, this cannot ensure that users and managers will apply and use them as intended. Many IT change management projects, whether they are large software implementations, business process redesigns or transforming a traditional organization to an e-Business based organization have resulted in failure [Laudon 2004]. One of the reasons for this is that people see well built IT, which makes it easier for them to work more effectively, as the enabler that will prevent them from working in old, unproductive ways. People stay in their prescribed roles as managers, users, IS specialists etc. with little or no cross-functional collaboration, no real discussion about the reasons for change taking place, and failures will primarily be attributed to the technology.

Leading a change project or business-wide initiative requires people to plan the change and build business-wide support; these are called '*change agents*'. Change agents are part of the program management organization discussed in Section 2.8.3. In principle, everyone involved in a change project can assume the role of a change agent. Different studies have examined the IS specialist's change agent role; three types have been identified [Markus 1996; Binbasioglu 2002]:

- *Traditional*: in the traditional model the IS specialists focus on the delivery of the implementation of technology, without considering the organizational aspects. The assumption is that technology does all the work of organizational change and that change agents only need to change the technology. Consequently the IS specialists become technicians with a narrow area of expertise.

- *Facilitator*: in the facilitator model the central belief is that people, not technologies create change. The change agent brings together all the conditions necessary for the change (ideas, well-built IT, organizational conditions); he facilitates a free change of ideas by creating trust and mutual understanding. In this model the change agent remains neutral, does not 'push', the organization remains responsible for making the change.

- *Advocate*: in this role, change agents focus on inspiring people to adopt the change. As in the facilitator model, the assumption is that people, and not the technology, are creating the change. The facilitator knows clearly what the organization needs and has to do, and shows the people how to do it. He does not remain neutral, but uses any tactic to make the changes accepted (persuasion, manipulation, power etc).

Especially in the case of e-Business transformation, where organizational and IT changes relate to infrastructure and issues of commonality and interoperability, the advocate model seems to be appropriate [Markus 1996]. The benefits of the e-Business infrastructure are primarily felt at an enterprise level, much less at the work group level where people have to adapt their work routines. For this reason, neither persuasion, nor seeking consensus may result in desired organizational outcomes.

2.9 Chapter summary

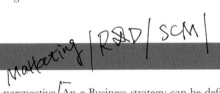

In this chapter e-Business is discussed from a strategic perspective. An e-Business strategy can be defined as the set of plans and objectives by which applications of internal and external electronically mediated communication contribute to the corporate strategy. Besides corporate strategy objectives, the e-Business strategy also supports the various functional strategies, like marketing and supply chain management strategies. The e-Business strategy is also related to the Information Systems strategy: a set of goals, plans with regard to the use of information systems in an organization to support the objectives of the organization in the long run. The basic goal of an IS strategy is to ensure the alignment of information systems, and technology development with enterprise priorities. The e-Business strategy relates to electronic communication; as such it is an integral part of the IS strategy.

Companies can become more profitable than the average performer in their industry sector by achieving a sustainable competitive advantage, i.e., by operating at a lower cost, by commanding a premium price, or by doing both. One way of achieving cost and price advantages is through strategic positioning. Strategic positioning means that a company is doing things differently from competitors, in a way that delivers a unique type of value to its customers. The Internet affects strategic positioning in very different ways as it opens new opportunities for achieving or strengthening a distinctive strategic positioning.

Strategies exist at different levels of an organization: the supply chain or industry value chain level; the Line of Business or (Strategic) Business Unit level; the corporate or enterprise level. The subjects that are dealt with in the strategic plans vary per level. The supply chain level deals with relationships and added value to customers and suppliers; the Business Unit level has to do with issues of competitive strategy; the enterprise level focuses on the synergies between the business units.

There is a two-way relationship between business organizations and IT: the activities of the existing enterprise exert a need for information and information systems; on the other hand IT enables different business models and new business strategies. The latter is called the strategic impact of IT. The Internet has created a highly competitive market environment. Information technology incorporated through the Internet is reducing much of the transaction and coordination costs associated with old economy business operations, and restructuring value chains allowing firms to forward integrate and bypass intermediaries.

Organizations employ strategic planning as a way to move toward their desired future position. Strategic planning is the process of developing and implementing plans to reach goals and objectives. Strategic planning, more than anything else, is what gives direction to an organization. Most strategic planning methodologies are based on a situation, target, and path process. However in real life situations, not all strategies have worked out as intended. Some appear simply to have emerged over time, due to a sequence of not anticipated steps: so-called emergent strategies. In business practice, strategies are almost always a mix of intended and emergent strategies. The field of information systems and e-Business is particularly one where emergent strategies are important.

One of major issues regarding an enterprise's investment in information technology is whether this is in harmony with its strategic objectives (intent, current strategy, and enterprise goals) and thus building the capabilities necessary to deliver business value. If a firm's IT strategic and operational objectives are not in alignment with its business strategies and operations, then this infrastructure is bound to fail.

The effects of e-Business form the subject of various organization theories. Strategy is about finding the right (external) fit between organization and environment. Different schools of thought have approached this problem from different angles. Porter's theory on competitive strategy is an example of a line of thinking that starts from the positioning of a firm in its competitive environment and considers how, in the context of external forces, a competitive strategy may result in a sustainable competitive position. However, a firm's strategic position is not only the result of external forces but also the consequence of the expertise and abilities within an organization. The Resource-Based view perceives the organization as a collection of competencies, which have to be developed and maintained. According to this view, a firm's competitive position is dependent on its competencies that are considered 'core' and also unique. These competencies form the foundation for the position of the firm in the environment and the products and services it develops and brings to the market. When analyzing the strategic implications of Internet based business models a third approach prevails. E-Business is about relationships, including transactional relationships, between businesses. It also addresses the problem of how to organize (govern) transactions. The approach dealing with this type of phenomenon is known as Transaction Cost Economics. According to transaction cost theory, exchanges with external firms entail a variety of coordination costs associated with various aspects of inter-firm transactions. Transaction cost includes coordination cost, operations risk, and opportunism risk.

Transforming an enterprise (a going concern) from a traditional organization to an e-business based organization is a complex endeavor. It is essential that senior management develops and endorses a broad strategic vision. Once the strategy has been determined and approved the implementation strategy has to be chosen. Two approaches prevail: the top down approach and the bottom up approach. According to the former, business transformation is a business-wide phenomenon that can only be implemented business wide. The latter strategy is bottom up. Business reengineering starts as an experiment in an 'inconspicuous' part of the organization. Lessons are drawn from this experience and the reengineering effort is taken to other and more complex parts of the organization. Although the bottom up approach has strong support, especially in the case of innovation, central coordination of the transformation activity is mandatory.

To provide for that central coordination, program management has to be instituted. A core part of program management is multi-project management, the main objectives of which are to recognize dependencies between projects, share scarce resources in an overall efficient way, and systematically utilize experiences from single projects. Program management is characterized by program organization, policies, plans, communication, and alignment.

Leading a change project or business-wide initiative requires persons that plan the change and build business-wide support; these are called 'change agents'. Change agents are part of the program management organization. In principle, everyone involved in a change project can assume the role of a change agent. Three types of change agent roles have been identified: Traditional, Facilitator, Advocate. Especially in the case of e-Business transformation, where organizational and IT changes relate to infrastructure and issues of commonality and interoperability, the advocate model seems to be appropriate

Discussion Questions

- Give a definition of 'e-Business strategy' and describe the components of an e-Business strategy.
- How would you differentiate e-Business-strategy from IS strategy?
- Identify the three levels of strategy that are particularly relevant for IS strategic planning; explain why they are relevant.
- Discuss typical e-Business issues at each level of strategy.
- Describe the different ways in which the Internet can strategically impact an enterprise.
- Describe Porter's competitive forces model and explain how it can be used to identify e-Business strategies.

Assignments

i. Choose one particular company (e.g. using annual reports or business publications like the *Financial Times*, *Business Week*) and analyze it according to Porter's competitive forces model (give at least one example per competitive force).

ii. Imagine that you are the CEO of an Internet retailer that sells books online (like Amazon. com). Like other companies you want to set up a strategic planning process. Using the steps in Figure 2.2, describe a possible strategic planning process for your company.

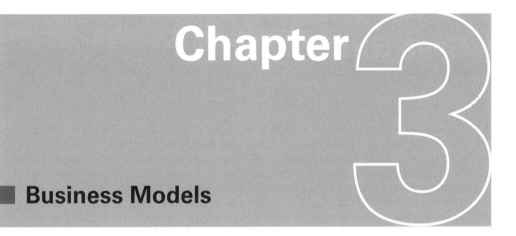

Chapter 3

Business Models

The structure of economic activity within a company is based on a balance struck between the benefits of particular patterns of division of labor and the costs of coordination. The most well-known structure is the vertical bureaucratic structure that is built on the assumption that concentrating similar activities within functions, and thus separating activities which are not similar, would result in economies of scale. Coordinating decisions or standard operating procedures take care of regular coordination problems. According to Transaction Costs Economics (see Chapter 2), the division of economic activity between firms is based on similar considerations and strikes a balance between costs of production and transaction costs.

One economic effect of the Internet and related technologies is that coordination costs and transaction costs are being reduced significantly, bringing about a balance between type of division of labor and coordination changes – both at an intra- and inter-organizational level. New structures that are more coordination intense and are characterized by different groupings of tasks and responsibilities as well as allocation of decision-making authority throughout the organization become now technically and economically feasible. The popular term 'business model' has emerged in the e-Business literature to describe new ways in which companies are doing business.

In this chapter we introduce the concept of 'business model' and present reasons for and an overview of business models targeting e-Business. First the chapter provides an overview and comparison of the various definitions of the concept of a business model. Subsequently, we concentrate on networked business models and present a classification scheme. The chapter also presents two case studies involving two organizations in different industries experimenting with Internet based networked business models.

Case Study

GeneraLife: a virtual insurance company on the Internet

GeneraLife[1] was established in 1995 as a full-service insurance company marketing life and annuity products through brokerage distribution.[2] It was the first virtual – that is, completely Web-enabled – life insurance company in the United States. Its corporate parent, General American Life Insurance Co. of St. Louis, MO, set it up in order to solve a conflict between its in-house sales force and a large group of independent agents. General American decided to spin off its independent-brokerage business into a new company. The Vice President for Brokerage Sales, Michael Conley, was to run the start-up – and to do so cheaply.

The challenge was to start an insurance company from scratch. GeneraLife became a virtual company, using the Internet for application processing, sales support, and general business information. This included working with external third-party administrators who would underwrite the initial contract. Conley knew that life insurers were – as they still are – suffering from declining return on investment, falling sales figures, and increasing overhead and expenses. The problem was, they could not influence mortality rates, nor do much about declining returns on investment. So the only thing that remained was controlling expenses. Conley's plan for reducing costs turned on two strategic moves: outsourcing and automation. Insurance companies had a long history of automating existing procedures, and operated with cumbersome business processes. GeneraLife was in the enviable position of having no such legacy procedures to implement or automate. Despite the inevitable pressure to start business quickly, Conley resisted the temptation to use General American's systems and processes; he insisted on beginning with a clean slate. First, he identified five functions he considered to be of core importance: marketing, operations and compliance monitoring, technological direction, underwriting, and finance. GeneraLife would do those itself. Everything else – from operating Websites to handling payroll – would be outsourced. In addition all functions performed by the company itself would be heavily automated, enabling GeneraLife to accomplish with only 14 people what other companies would need hundreds to do.

Conley was confident that leading-edge technology would enable GeneraLife to realize its innovative business model. What it needed was a company-wide data

[1] This case study is based on *Computer Weekly*, US virtual insurance firm takes on Europe, Company Business and Marketing, Nov 19, 1998; *Inc. Magazine*, William R Pape, Dec 1998, www.inc.com/magazine/19981201/5420.html; *St. Louis Commerce Magazine*, www.stlcommercemagazine.com/w/december2003/; Sharpe G (1999), *Building a Virtual Insurance Company on the Internet*, The Information Management Forum, Atlanta.

[2] www.stlcommercemagazine.com/archives/october2002/insurance.html

warehouse and an e-Commerce solution enabling it to serve its customers, field agents, and internal management better than traditional insurance companies could. G.A. Sullivan was therefore approached, a St Louis-based software enterprise with an excellent reputation for deploying data warehouse and business intelligence technology.[3] First, they designed and built a data warehouse that improved the quality and timeliness of the data distribution to the company's 6000 agents around the US. Then they built GeneraLife's e-Commerce Website, using the data warehouse as a foundation. Next they set up management and agent reporting facilities, provided via the Generalife intranet and extranet.

[3] www.spherecom.com/documents/casestudies/GASullivanCaseStudy_041703.pdf

3.1 Pressures forcing business changes

Today's businesses face unprecedented challenges. Competition is becoming fiercer and more global. Customers, stimulated by competing product and service offerings, become increasingly demanding. Instead of just products they expect complete solutions for their problems and wishes, thus triggering service and product offering integration between value chains. For example, airlines, hotel chains, travel agents, tour operators, and car-rental companies are gradually packaging their offerings to create turnkey products and services. Users who want to book a travel package could use a booking service of an online travel agency, and submit their travel specification to it. The travel agency's booking service would first invoke an airline booking-service to compare different airline offerings and choose the airline ticket best suited to the travel specification (i.e., price range, departure date and time). The travel agency's booking may then dynamically suggest a hotel and car for the same dates. Hotel rooms and rental cars are chosen in a similar fashion by the hotel booking service and car rental service. The car rental service may also call on a GPS-Web-service to provide driving directions inside the rented car. Entertainment, dining and weather services can also be included in the package, if the travel specification calls for it. Such integrated demand requires a close cooperation between the organizations involved, e.g., travel agents, airline companies, and car rental companies. This dynamic assembly of products and services gives the customer real added value and provides enterprises with marketing advantages such as lower costs for acquiring customers and sharing programs for customer loyalty.

Increased competition forces companies to rethink their position in the market place fundamentally. Traditionally, they would themselves execute all necessary activities for the production and delivery of their products and services, unless some would, for specific reasons, be procured from external suppliers. Nowadays, companies tend to think differently: there is no reason to do something oneself unless one is really uniquely good at it. They ask themselves which of their competences are unique and of core importance, which of their resources and functional capabilities really add value, and which might more efficiently be bought externally. Consequently, outsourcing and insourcing movements are expected to cause fundamental changes in the way companies are configured. Uniqueness and value-adding competences are the business drivers of the future. Because of the integration of product and service offerings, and the concentration on core competences, companies' success in today's markets will depend on their ability to set up cross-industry partner networks to provide high-quality, cost-efficient products reflecting the customers' needs.

Such business networking strategies are made possible by the development of modern information technology, including the Internet. Information technology was previously used primarily to supply decision makers with information; today it has become an integral part of companies' organization designs, in which it has several functions. We may, for example, distinguish between strategic networking effects of modern information technology, its electronic communication effects, its electronic brokerage effects, and its electronic integration effects [Malone 1987]. These terms refer respectively to the fact that companies are enabled to set up links amongst themselves in order to achieve joint strategic goals; to the increase in the amount of information that can be transferred per unit of time and the consequent dramatic decrease of communication costs; to a company's ability to bring buyers and sellers together in a virtual market space; and to the support IT gives in setting up joint processes that span at least two separate organizations.

During the past few decades, businesses have had to adapt and transform their organizational structures. A number of change models were introduced and tried. But many of these change strategies involved launching several change initiatives simultaneously, each focused on a specific aspect of the organization. The effect of such a narrowly focused sub-optimal approach was no more than a marginal bottom-line performance improvement. This no longer is enough; certainly not now that constant change is encroaching on many corporations' core, bringing new ways of organizing and doing business. Any initiative to transform or change a company must consider the enterprise as a whole, including its relations with suppliers, business partners, and customers. The role of information technology goes beyond enhancing communication, integration, and decision-making; it has become a key enabler in creating value for the customer.

Case Study

GeneraLife: a virtual insurance company on the Internet

The benefits of this new business model were felt immediately. For example: it took the company only nine days to deliver its first policy, against an industry standard of 35 to 90 days. Since then, turnaround time has only improved. But moving the paperwork online wasn't enough; Conley had a huge sales force to handle, spread across 41 states. A mechanism was needed that would enable agents to help themselves to up-to-date information whenever they needed it. GeneraLife posted daily reports on its Website, providing benchmarks for salespeople to assess their performance. Again, this was an enormous improvement on traditional practice, which was to provide weekly status reports of each agent's customers by regular mail – information that would thus always be out of date. Conley decided that recruitment and management, too, would almost exclusively be run via the Internet. New agent certification suddenly took hours instead of days or weeks, since only one form was needed and it was available on the company Website.

3.2 Business models – definitions

The business literature often uses the concept of a 'business model' in conjunction with e-Commerce. The literature is abundant with e-Commerce business models, and more are being invented frequently. Although many authors maintain that e-Commerce asks for a radical change in business models [Venkatraman 1998], only a few select authors provide clear definitions of the concept of a business model. Despite the abundance of potential models, it is possible to identify major generic types of business models (and variants thereof) that have been developed specifically for e-Commerce and describe their key elements. Existing *business model* definitions can be grouped in three generic categories:

1) Business model definitions that concern themselves with the *participants in a joint business venture*. According to these definitions 'Business models specify the relationships between different participants in a commercial venture, the benefits and costs to each and the flows of revenue. A business model addresses a simple equation (profit = revenue − costs), irrespective of the model [Elliot 2002].' An alternative definition also states that a business model describes how the enterprise produces, delivers and sells products or services, thus showing how it delivers value to the customers and how it creates wealth [Margretta 2002].

2) Business model definitions that concern themselves with the *processes and structure of a business organization*. According to these definitions a business model refers to the structures and processes in place to operationalize the strategy of the business [Peppard 1999]. A more extensive definition that expands on the previous one is also available. According to this definition business models can be described as follows [Timmers 1998]:

   - An architecture for the product, service and information flows;
   - A description of the various business actors and their roles;
   - A description of the potential benefits for the various actors;
   - A description of the sources of revenues.

3) Business model definitions that concern themselves with how business models are *seen from the perspective of a marketplace*: According to these definitions, business models can be analyzed from various perspectives [Chaffey 2002]:

   - Is the company involved in business-to-business activities, business-to-customer activities or both?
   - Which position does the company have in the value chain between customers and suppliers?
   - Which is its value proposition, and which are its target customers?
   - Which are the specific revenue models that will generate its various income streams?
   - How is it represented: by physical shops ('bricks') or online, in the virtual world ('clicks'); or even by a mixture of these two ('bricks and clicks')?

As a general rule, business models do not indicate how the company's business objectives are realized: they should not be confused with *business strategies* (see Chapter 2), which specify how a business model can be applied to differentiate a company from its competitors [Elliot 2002]. Despite the line of thinking that argues for a clear separation between realization of business objectives and strategies, the concept of the *marketing model* was introduced in the literature to encompass both the business model and the strategy of the enterprise under consideration [Timmers 1998].

We may now develop a definition of a *business model* that addresses the requirements of e-Business as described in Chapter 1, and that partially leans on existing definitions that we examined above. One important requirement of such a business model is that it should capture the properties of end-to-end processes and inter-enterprise business relationships. We thus may define a business model from the perspective of e-Business as a descriptive representation of the planned activities of an enterprise (also known as business processes) that involves three integral components, which specify:

1) The internal aspects of a business venture;
2) The type of relationships of the enterprise with its external business environment and its effective knowledge regarding these relationships;
3) How a company's information assets – such as information systems and effective business processes typically grouped in the customer relationship management, supply chain management, and core business operations domains – are embedded in the business venture.

While a conventional business model has as its primary aim to realize the economic and other related objectives of an enterprise, an e-Business model such as the one defined above, in addition to these economic objectives, it also aims to use and leverage the unique qualities and features of Internet-enabled e-Business processes (see Chapter 1) and the World Wide Web in the context of networked organizations.

The business model is at the center of a company's e-Business plan, which consolidates its purpose and goals to outline all kinds of aspects relating to e-Business including: marketing plan, competition, sales strategy, operations plan, management plan. and financial plan.

The business model in any kind of subject area, not just e-Business, must effectively address issues such as: value proposition, revenue model, market opportunity, competitive advantage, market strategy, organizational development, and management [Ghosh 1998]. A *value proposition* defines how a company's products or services fulfil the needs of customers [Kambil 1998a]. A company's *revenue model* describes how the company will earn revenue, generate profits and produce a superior return on invested capital [Laudon 2003]. *Market opportunity* refers to the company's intended marketspace, i.e., area of actual or potential value, and the overall potential financial opportunities available to the company in that marketspace [Laudon 2003]. A company's *competitive environment* refers to other companies selling similar or related products, and operating in the same marketspace. Firms achieve a *competitive advantage* when they can produce a superior product and bring it to the market at lower prices than most or all of their competitors [Porter 1985a]. *Market strategy* is the plan that a company puts together that details its intended approach to penetrate a new market and attract new customers. Companies that hope to prosper in a marketspace need to have a plan for organizational development that describes how the company will organize the work that needs to be performed [Laudon 2003]. Typically, the work is divided into functional departments such as production, shipping, marketing, customer support, and finance, in each of which jobs, job titles and responsibilities are defined. The most important element of a business model is the management, which makes the model work. A strong management team gives a business model credibility to outside investors, immediate market-specific knowledge, and experience in implementing business plans.

The reality behind a business model might be an extremely complex combination of multiple business processes, involving multiple companies, locations, etc. As such, the business model can be viewed as the externalization of the internal business process. These visible aspects are the only things that matter for the customer. The customer can, for instance, even have the experience of a high-quality, rapid, fully automated service, while most of the internal business processes still are handled manually.

As an example, consider the business model for the book retailer Barnes and Noble. This business model is similar to that of most retail establishments: targeted customers' reading needs are satisfied through the business activities of stocking the store shelves with desirable products at affordable prices [Canzer 2003]. How Barnes and Noble specifically carries out its business is detailed in its business plan. Anyone else who wishes to emulate this successful model can study it and adopt it to its own needs. Perhaps instead of books, another retailer might sell clothing or sports equipment.

When taking the internal aspects of a business into account the following elements need to be defined. These include:

1) The *product or service* that a company delivers to its customers. Customers may be end-consumers or businesses that use these products and services as a part of their activity;
2) The *sources of revenue* that indicate how and to what extent a business venture is economically viable;
3) The *activities* according to which a company performs to deliver its products or services and realizes its strategic objectives. Such activities encompass primary and support activities and concern physical activities (like manufacturing) as well as service activities (like coordinating activities by others);
4) The *organization* a company has established to realize its objectives. With organization we mean the company structure (like how tasks are allocated) and the processes (combination of tasks leading to specific outcome, like order acquisition). In particular, processes that may cross the company's boundaries and, maybe, encompass collaborative actions with external business partners (e.g. product development).

When considering the external relationships of a company, the business model defines the *external actors* involved in the business venture. Examples include the customers to whom the products are targeted, external parties who deliver key inputs for the company's operation and with whom important relations exist, and those who fund the operation. As will be argued in Chapter 4, inter-company relationships may exist on an *operational level* (meaning only for the orders placed), but also on a *tactical level* (involving some sharing of planning information and some collaborative planning), and on a *strategic level* (where the companies involved jointly develop their market strategies). In addition, the structure and processes that support the delivery of the final product not only relate to internal structures and processes, but also to those that support relations with customers and suppliers. The business model defines the *potential benefits for the actors* involved and so indicates under what conditions the company can be assured of their continuing support.

The definitions we presented did not explicitly include the role of information technology in the business venture. However, as information technology is to an increasing extent becoming an integral part of business processes and organizational design, we feel that *how information technology is incorporated into the business* venture should also characterize the business model. For instance, whether books are sold through 'bricks and mortar' shops or through a Website radically changes the business model. The use of IT relates to internal processes, e.g., workflow, and relations to external participants, e.g., operational buying and selling relations may be pursued through e-market places.

The effect of the Internet is that it makes new business models possible, in particular through its effect on inter-company relationships. Internet-based business models are more business relationship intense allowing new patterns of inter-company collaboration. A *networked business model* is based on an appropriate technology environment to support electronic linkages (relationships) in the value chain. Networked business models assume the support of interoperable systems. Interoperability can only be achieved with a technology platform that is accepted by all the participants. In other words all the partners in the value chain have to commit to invest in, to adhere to, and to maintain the common platform (see Chapter 10).

Based on the foregoing discussion, we may define an *e-Business model* as the descriptive representation of the fundamental components of a business that operates partially or completely on the Internet [Canzer 2003]. In other words, an e-Business model is a kind of networked business model albeit a more general one. As an example, the e-Business model for Barnes and Noble for its online business activities and operations overlaps somewhat with its traditional bricks and mortar business model. Although there are significant overlaps between the two, business operations in each model are significantly different in many respects. For example, the retail business model is based on selling and distributing a product to customers who walk into the retailer's store, while the e-retail model can accommodate online customers who are dispersed throughout the world by using courier services for delivery and does not operate any real physical stores.

In the next section we discuss the evolution to networked business models, which are the predominant models characterizing most e-Business operations and relationships.

3.3 Classifications of business models

As we have already seen, the emergence of the Internet has had a major impact on the way companies conduct their business. Traditional organization structures were vertical and hierarchical, function-based, product-based, geography-based, or matrix-based. But new information technologies have significantly decreased the costs of sending, storing, and retrieving information, causing coordination costs to drop. And since these costs are a major factor in organizational structures, the effect will be to disrupt traditional business models and to generate new ones. As a result, structures that are more coordination intense have been introduced. Next to hierarchical and procedural coordination, new coordination mechanisms have been developed. In so called team-based structures coordination is achieved through horizontal and lateral relations between employees, empowered to make discretionary decisions, who belong to different departments. These structures can even cross company boundaries, when, for example, the manufacturing departments of a supplying and buying organization collaboratively plan their production activities. Through the Internet and related technologies, it has even become less important to be together in the same location to meet and jointly work in collaborative processes. Consequently, horizontal and network structures are being introduced [Aldrich 1999].

New business models will be based on new views of inter-company relationships and networking: new technologies may make network business models possible and it is the current competitive market that makes it necessary to adopt them. Networking will take place on both intra-organizational and inter-organizational levels, making new working methods possible within and between organizations. Outsourcing non-core activities will unbundle traditional value chains; but on the other hand, combining service and product offerings from multiple organizations will couple previously independent value chains. Most traditional business models used to be seller- or product-driven, aiming to generate value at the product or line-of-business level. Internet-enabled business models, by contrast, are customer-focused: value is generated at the relations level, across products and channels. One important consequence is that various products and services within the same industry will be bundled in order to develop complete solutions. Many companies are now adopting customer-focused business models, becoming more responsive to their customers, and developing deeper relations with them. To establish and maintain such relations with one's suppliers, partners and customers, Internet technology is indispensable; with it, the integration potential is deeper, broader, and more seamless than was ever deemed possible [Papazoglou 2000].

The Internet has spawned many new business models. Of special relevance to this book, however, is the potential of Internet technologies to facilitate the development of new inter-organizational systems, which leads in turn to a new breed of networked-based business models. The need for network structures, such as an integrated value chain, challenges the e-Business to optimize its intellectual assets, and its investments in core business systems in order to deliver its products and services to an unpredictable market. It is this unpredictable nature that challenges the IT organization to deliver the highly scalable and available infrastructure. The unique nature of e-Business and the tight association of the business operations to a technical infrastructure are also challenges. A disciplined and architected approach based on an e-Business (or Internet-centred) model provides the framework needed to build complex business processes and technical infrastructures that the market is increasingly demanding. It is thus not surprising that several Internet-based business models have already been developed – so many that some classification is in order. The literature on e-Business provides various such classifications, the five most important of which we will discuss below: these are the Internet-enabled business models, the value-Web business models, the e-Business-enabled business models, the market participant business models, and the cybermediaries business models. It should be noted that this classification scheme primarily targets the business models that are related to the business model definitions that we examined in Section 3.2. Although this classification scheme is not exhaustive, it encompasses the majority of business models that take into account the unique features of Internet-enabled, e-Business processes and the World Wide Web in the context of networked organizations.

3.3.1 Internet-enabled business models

A number of authors have attempted to categorize the e-Business field based on increasing functionality, innovation, integration, and value, and have defined families of business models that rely on Internet trading technologies [Timmers 1999]. This has resulted in identifying ten different types of business models that are facilitated by the Internet and are based on an analysis of Porter's value chain (value chain deconstruction, value chain reconstruction, and interaction patterns which we introduce in Chapter 4) [Timmers 1999]. All of these elements are relevant for both business-to-business and business-to-consumer environments.

Figure 3.1 illustrates how the Internet-based models are classified according to the degree of innovation and functional integration involved. The first dimension of innovation ranges from basically applying the Internet to replace a traditional way of doing business to more innovative business models. The second dimension of functional integration ranges from business models that encompass one function, such as an e-shop, to a business model that fully integrates multiple functions.

Figure 3.1 is used to execute companies' Internet marketing. Even if a company only has an information Website, this may be considered a basic e-shop. However, companies running such Websites increasingly add facilities for ordering and paying. e-Procurement involves the opposite process: purchasing goods and services through the Web. E-Malls are collections of e-shops under one umbrella (special service or product types, brands, etc.). E-Auctions are Internet bidding mechanisms and can be applied in both business-to-business and business-to-consumer contexts. One of their characteristics is that there is no need to move goods or parties before a deal. Third-party market places are virtual market places where potential suppliers and

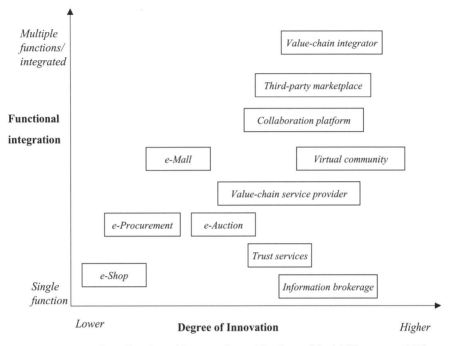

Figure 3.1: Classification of Internet-based Business Model [Timmers 1999]

buyers interact and transact. Virtual communities offer people with a common interest, such as a profession or expertise, facilities to share information; thus they add value for their members and so become important for marketing purposes. Collaboration platforms enable companies and individuals to work together by providing an environment and a set of collaboration tools. Value chain integrators focus on integrating multiple steps of the value chain, and value chain service providers specialize in providing specific functions such as electronic payment services. Finally, information brokers are new, emerging information service providers working for both consumers and businesses; they provide information and help parties generate trust in one another.

3.3.2 Value Web business models

In his doctoral thesis, Selz [Selz 1999] proposes a framework for business models, which he calls the 'value Web' (see Figure 3.2). He states that this framework "…is assuredly not a recipe for success, but a preliminary conception of an emerging form of a fluid and flexible organization". The value Web model consists of several key building blocks: markets, hierarchies, networks, information technology and new-old business models. For the purposes of this chapter we introduce brief definitions of markets, hierarchies, and networks to facilitate understanding of the material that follows. More information on these topics can be found in Chapter 4.

The function of markets is to bring together buyers and sellers, and automate business transactions. This Internet business model has conspicuously emerged during the past years. Traditional large hierarchical

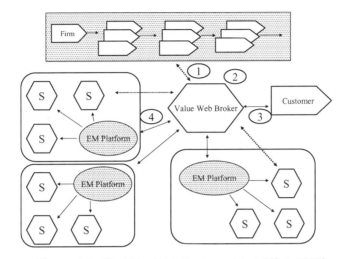

■ Figure 3.2: The Value Web Business Model [Selz 1999]

organizations tended to dominate a market segment and operated through a fixed and predetermined number of suppliers in a 'hub-and spokes' type of network arrangement with all communication lines going through it. Modern companies no longer have traditional, inflexible bureaucratic structures, but flexible, small, adaptive organizations that are able to form and dissolve alliances swiftly in order to exploit specific opportunities. Networks arise because companies move away from the old 'we-do-everything-ourselves-unless' assumption, which meant that customer value was generated by a single organization, to the 'we-do-nothing-ourselves-unless' assumption, which means that value is generated by the network as a whole. Networks are composed of nodes and relations, and none of these nodes can survive without the others. They must all relate to their environment – customers, suppliers, competitors, and regulators – in order to compose the final product. Information technology is a factor the evolution of which is difficult to predict. Finally, Selz [Selz 1999] uses the expression new-old business models because he feels that older business models may still or again be valid. In fact, the value Web model looks much like a specific case of the value chain integrator model, which is part of the Internet-enabled family of business models [Timmers 1998].

According to Selz [Selz 1999], four things will occur (see Figure 3.2). First, is that creative new entrants will cherry-pick among the industry's current value systems. These are traditionally integrated vertically, but the newcomers will choose and configure only those value-adding activities that are meaningful for their targeted customer segment. Subsequently, value Web brokers will emerge. These have the central value Web function of coordinator, integrator, and interface. Third, is when the broker moves to a final position on the Web, with a direct link to its customers and the possibility of establishing loyal relationships. And finally, since brokers are rarely able to provide the entire value proposition by themselves, they make alliances, resorting to third-party component suppliers.

3.3.3 The e-Business-enabled business models

The family of *e-Business-enabled business models* is a classification scheme of business models that is especially valid for business-to-business contexts [Papazoglou 2000]. In it, five representative business model types are distinguished. These are typical of most common modern IT-based business organizations engaging in e-Business. These are the teleworking model, the virtual organization model, the process outsourcing model, the collaborative product development model, and the value chain integration model. This family of e-Business-enabled models considers the degree of integration between collaborating enterprises. A low degree of integration indicates that a small number of core business processes are integrated between networked organizations, while a higher degree of integration indicates that a multitude of core business processes are integrated in a meaningful way and can flow seamlessly between networked organizations. This situation is depicted in Figure 3.3.

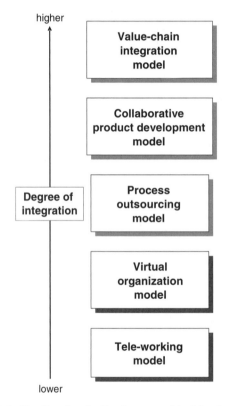

■ **Figure 3.3:** The Family of e-Business-enabled Business Models

Teleworking model: this model involves large numbers of individuals or groups collaborating with the assistance of networking and communication technologies. A classic example is presented by the engineers in multinational companies, who collaborate across the globe on the development of new products and processes. Electronic manufacturing service (EMS) providers who design, assemble, and repair the products of original equipment manufacturers are a typical example of the teleworking model. Several leading original equipment manufacturers are relying on electronic manufacturing service providers such as Solectron Corporation (www.solectron.com) to offer a full range of integrated supply chain solutions. EMS integrated design, manufacturing and after-sales services offer customers competitive outsourcing advantages, such as access to advanced manufacturing technologies, shortened product time-to-market, reduced total cost of ownership and more effective asset utilization. For example, Solectron practices provide collaborative design services using virtual design collaboration techniques, leveraging the latest IT resources, to allow its engineers and customer engineers and manufacturing personnel to concurrently develop specific product technology at any and every stage of the design process as well as service procedures. Once the product is made, it is packaged and shipped to its customers and their end-customers.

Virtual organization model: effective contracting for complementary capabilities through a network of suppliers and subcontractors is a characteristic of the virtual organization model. A virtual organization is a temporary or permanent collection of geographically dispersed individuals, groups and organizational units who are linked electronically in order to complete a collaborative production process; these members do not necessarily belong to the same organization and may even include entire organizations. GeneraL ife, a US-based insurance company, is an example of such a collection. Its core organization, Virtual Life, focuses on its core business: product development and sales. All other functions are outsourced to third party administrators. Its basic infrastructure is the Internet, which is used for sales support towards brokers, for instance, and to enable clients to manage their policies. To GeneraLife's management, the model's main advantages are that it minimizes fixed costs (and thereby significantly increases the variable cost proportion), decreases new product time-to-market, and improves overall flexibility.

Process outsourcing model: this model is the logical consequence of companies beginning to realize they can interact with their customers, partners, and suppliers, and exchange and leverage knowledge in addition to undertaking transactions. Facilities that were once central to the business are now outsourced. Process outsourcing means transferring the responsibility for one or more processes to external suppliers. Typical candidates for such a transfer are companies' human resources, accounting, and logistics functions. An organizational development that often but not necessarily precedes process outsourcing is the set-up of shared service centers (SSCs): a certain process is removed from the company's individual departments and business units and centralized in a shared service center – a move often called 'outsourcing to oneself'. IBM, for example, has merged all its human resource processes into one such center, which operates globally. A critical condition to be met if process outsourcing (including SSCs) is to work, is the smooth coordination and communication between service supplier and service recipient, which among other things means that transaction costs must be low. Therefore, modern IT platforms have become the critical factor without which process outsourcing is impossible.

Collaborative product development model: this model concerns itself with the need to coordinate product development activities that involve multiple companies or organizational units. The Ford Motor Corporation offers a good example of the collaborative product development model that aimed to turn the Ford company into a truly global concern. The need to coordinate disparate product development activities is of central importance to Ford's organization structure and product development processes. This model called for flexible information systems and applications which would make it possible to manage and transmit design documents across various Ford centers around the world.

Value chain integration model: if Internet technology is used to improve communication and collaboration between all supply chain parties, the value chain integration model is followed. Doing so is necessary when vendors must achieve effective coordination between 'upstream' suppliers, internal operations (such as manufacturing), and 'downstream' shippers and customers. Applying this model means that processes once perceived as internal to the company will now span the entire value chain. Effective service providers integrate their operations directly into their customers' processes. Every company in the chain performs a set or sequence of activities contributing to the production of the chain's collaborative products. The links between those activities offer the opportunity to gain competitive advantage, either by being exceptionally efficient or as the result of some form of product differentiation. This chain of partners working in sequence to produce, market and move goods and services grows even more complex when other product and service suppliers join, in order to deliver complete customer 'solutions' that consist of more than single products. On the basis of the intimate trading relations central to the integrated value chain model, modern business partnerships eradicate duplication, irrelevant hand-offs, and rework, thus ensuring that all processes run smoothly and efficiently.

3.3.4 Market participants business model

The *market participants business model* is a more generic classification of Internet-based business models [Applegate 2003] (see Figure 3.4). In this framework, networked business models are defined for companies doing business on the Internet as well as for network infrastructure providers. Starting from the value chain framework, the market participant business model distinguishes two key roles that market participants may assume: that of producer and that of distributor. Producers design and produce products and services, and may market them either via distributors or directly. Examples include the manufacturers of physical products, for whom the effect of going online has been to 'streamline, integrate, coordinate, and control physical channels of production and distribution'. Other producers are engaged in processes of a less physical nature, such as service provisioning, education and consultancy. For them, the Internet and related technologies have a great impact on the production and delivery of their services and products.

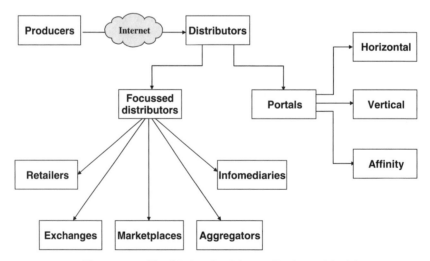

■ **Figure 3.4:** The Market Participants Business Model

The distributors category consists of focused distributors and portals. Focused distributors provide products and services for specific industries. This model distinguishes five types of focused distributors: retailers, marketplaces, aggregators, exchanges, and infomediaries. Retailers sell inventory of which they have assumed control online. Market places facilitate online sales without having physical control over the inventory sold. Aggregators provide information on products or services sold by others in the channel. Exchanges may or may not complete sales online, and may or may not assume control over inventory. Finally, infomediaries are a type of aggregator that brings together the sellers and buyers of information-based products.

Portals are Websites that act as gateways to information and services, including electronic markets, available on the Internet that customize, aggregate and integrate information for specific constituencies, and provide content management, search and categorization capabilities, collaboration, community services, and other related services such as personalized information and news items [Chaffey 2002]. A portal offers a single, secure source for all information, collaborative exchanges, application access, and services provided for an enterprise or value chain. Portals provide access to this mission-critical content based on user preferences, privileges, and activity. In general, portals offer [Marshak 2003]:

- A custom framework for presenting Web pages and components within each page and organizing information for specific constituencies;

- Personalization capabilities for individual users;

- A set of 'portlets' (the components that integrate with data, applications, content, and resources, and actually present information to the portal user);

- A single sign-on to the set of applications accessed via the portal;

- Other features, such as search and collaboration facilities.

Increasing demand for portals derives from the need to deliver personalized, role-based information for employees, partners, customers, and suppliers. There is also a heightened demand for cost-effective communication tools that provide access to information assets. Portals can serve as the application framework for common functions such as presentation, user identification, and personalization. They can also function as the integration mechanism that enables multiple application and content providers to deliver functionality.

Portals can vary in scope and the services they offer. The market participants business model distinguishes between three types of portals: horizontal, vertical and affinity portals. Horizontal portals provide gateway access to a great deal of content and services, often meant for or derived from various industries. Vertical portals are narrowly focused – on one industry, for example, automotive or petrochemical – and provide deep content and information. Finally, affinity portals provide highly specific information, much like vertical portals but targeted on specific interest groups or market segments.

Additional types of portals not described in this business model include geographic portals, marketplaces, and media types. It is apparent that there is an overlap between the different types of portals. Originally, the function of portals was focused on putting through as many visitors, as fast as possible to other relevant sites elsewhere on the Web. Nowadays, more and more portals focus on keeping the visitor on their own site: 'go-through-sites' are becoming 'go-to-sites' [Niks 2000]. Another development is that portals more often have characteristics of communities, as visitors can interact with other visitors through e-mail groups, Web-based discussion forums, or chat. A virtual community can be defined as any group of people who share a common band, yet who are not dependent on physical interaction and a common geographic location in order to sustain their group affinity [Talbott 1995; Millen 2002]. Communities are developed around areas of interest, age, or background.

Case Study

The Agroportal

Our third case study in this chapter is taken from the Dutch agricultural industry and concerns an agricultural portal.

The supply chain in the Dutch agricultural industry is quite complicated – or rather, there is not one single, general chain. Instead, a variety of supply chains can be identified, for dairy, livestock, horticulture, bulbs, and so on, around a core for the primary production of vegetables, ornamental, and livestock products. There are also numerous suppliers, showing a wide diversity. The most common provide propagation materials, foodstuffs, machinery, and credit and financial services, and most are large-scale companies and cooperatives. Recent developments in this industry, including the success of electronic markets, have engendered a number of studies [van Heck 1998; Kambil 1998b]. These show that the introduction of IT-based trading mechanisms has affected the overall structure and flow of the Dutch agriculture supply chains. New intermediary organizations are emerging and traditional positions are affected. These developments may also change the industry's international position.

The Agroportal (www.ziezo.biz) is an example of such a portal for the Dutch agricultural industry. It was launched in the summer of 2002, on the initiative of several large actors in the sector: suppliers of cattle foods, financial service providers (such as Rabobank), farmers' representative organizations (like LTO Nederland), and government-related institutions. They established the Agroportal to support individual farmers and other agricultural entrepreneurs by making relevant agricultural information accessible, and by offering applications to reduce their administrative workload. Dutch farmers are the portal's main customers.

At first the Agroportal offered only limited functionality – information on a few companies, supplies, and products, and interaction between visitors through Web-based discussion forums or chatrooms. Soon extra services were added, such as facilities with which to perform registrations and do one's chemicals administration.

Access to Cowplaza, a mail-order business for trading livestock farming materials, was quickly included too. Via its online, catalog orders can be placed directly. Portal users can personalize the Website by drawing up their own profile, after which the portal will provide them with information only on issues relevant to them. The Agroportal consists of a public section and a closed section accessible only to members. Visitors to the public section can choose one of three perspectives – arable production, horticulture, and livestock – after which only information relevant to the sector selected is displayed. Members may configure detailed interest profiles and receive more specific information about subjects, regions or industrial branches. Thus, the Agroportal can be characterized as a combination of vertical portal with electronic marketplace: it focuses on agriculture, for which it functions as a virtual market space where buyers and sellers meet and do business.

3.3.5 Cybermediaries business model

This category of business models is in disagreement with the widely accepted idea that e-Business will cause industry value systems to be restructured to such an extent that intermediation will no longer be a prominent feature [Sarkar 1995, 1998]. According to the *cybermediaries business models* the trend might just as well be towards an increase in intermediation (see Chapter 11 for more details on intermediation for e-Business). This model does not agree that intermediation will change, and is based on the premise that a new kind of intermediary will emerge: cybermediaries. Cybermediaries are organizations which operate in electronic markets to facilitate exchanges between producers and consumers by meeting the needs of both producers and consumers [Sarkar 1998]. Cybermediaries also increase the efficiency of electronic markets, in a role similar to intermediaries, by aggregating transactions to create economies of scale and scope [Sarkar 1998]. According to the cybermediaries business model it is likely that multi-organization structures will play an important role in emerging electronic markets.

The cybermediaries business model examines the nature of intermediation in electronic markets and its implications for the structure of electronic business; it encompasses a family of eleven business models based on these findings. Each business model is characterized by its functions: directories, search services, malls, virtual resellers, Website evaluators, publishers, auditors, forums, fan clubs and user groups, financial intermediaries, spot market makers and barter networks, and intelligent agents.

Directories or directory service intermediaries help consumers find producers by categorizing Websites and providing structured menus to facilitate navigation. Three types of directory services are distinguished: general directories, commercial directories, and specialized directories. General directories provide a general index of a large variety of different sites; they include, for example, Yahoo and ElNet Galaxy. Commercial directories such as the All-Internet Shopping Directory focus on providing indexes of commercial sites on the Web. They may also provide information about specific commercial areas, as does The Embroidery Directory, and then frequently include companies without Websites of their own. These intermediaries are the Internet equivalent of the publishers of printed industry guides. Finally, specialized directories are topic-oriented, and often consist of nothing more than a single Webpage set up by an individual interested in the subject. An example of such a directory is Jeff Frohwein's ISDN Technical Page. Search services resemble directories, but instead of categorizing and structuring what's on offer they provide facilities with which to conduct keyword searches in extensive databases of Websites and pages. Lycos and Infoseek are typical search service providers.

'Virtual malls' or 'Internet malls' is the usual name given Websites that link to more than two commercial sites. Many of the above commercial directories would fit that description, but Sarkar [Sarkar 1995] and his co-authors explicitly distinguish between them and malls. Directories index external commercial sites, while virtual malls, like their traditional, physical counterparts, provide infrastructures for producers and retailers. Consequently, there is a second key difference: malls derive their income from their renters' fees, while directories (which have no renters) generate theirs from advertising and the like. Virtual resellers in their turn resemble malls, but unlike them, do own the inventory (and not just the infrastructure) and sell products directly to customers.

Website evaluators do what their name implies: they help consumers choose between Websites by offering some form of evaluation, which may help them reduce their risks. Sometimes these evaluations are based on access frequency, but they may also contain explicit Website reviews. Point Communications (which only offers links to what it considers the top 5% Websites) and GNN are examples of this kind of cybermediary. Evaluators generate value by charging either the producers evaluated or the consumers who seek their services. Recently, some directories and search sites have begun introducing evaluations too. Publishers are 'traffic generators': they offer content selections, which they feel consumers will find interesting. As such, they may be considered online newspapers or magazines, as many of their names (*Information Week*, *Wired Magazine*) indicate.

Auditors are not direct intermediaries. They play the same role audience measurement services play with respect to the traditional media, providing advertisers with usage rate information on Internet advertising vehicles, as well as with credible information on audience characteristics. Likewise, forums, fan clubs, and user groups are not necessarily direct intermediaries either. They facilitate customer-producer feedback and support market research. Nevertheless, both kinds of cybermediary play an important role in e-Business, which explains their inclusion in the list.

Spot market makers bring buyers and sellers together. The emergence of such a service is not surprising considering the speed with which electronic networks can distribute information. If buyers and sellers exchange goods rather than pay for them with money, the business model is called a barter network. Basically, these intermediaries are similar to auction houses, flea markets, and commodities exchanges, and the several thriving news groups acting as markets for various products may serve as examples.

Financial intermediaries. Any form of electronic commerce will require some means of making or authorizing payments. Visa and MasterCard provide credit authorization, for example, and Checkfree facilitates the electronic equivalent of writing checks. Digicash makes cash payments possible, and First Virtual facilitates sending secure electronic mail authorizing payments. In an e-Commerce environment, these financial intermediaries may extract fees per transaction in order to absorb some of the risk associated with money flows.

3.4 Towards networked business models

Companies that wish to adopt networked business models must develop an organization view and an information technology view. The organization view concerns their role and position in their value chain:

how will they add value for their customers and those providing the inputs [Ward 2002]? It also establishes their and their partners' willingness to engage in long-term collaboration, as well as the strength of their collaborative links. Are the organizations involved willing to invest in close business relations that will cause the integration of boundary-spanning business processes, or do they wish to retain a maximum flexibility to opt out and choose other partners? From an understanding of these matters follows the analysis of upstream and downstream information flows, that is, to suppliers and customers or intermediaries.

An information technology view shared by all partners is required to set up an appropriate technology environment to support the electronic links between them. Networked business models, which are built on electronic links with other businesses, require common IT platforms in order to enable interoperable systems to support the business collaboration. Such platforms contain a number of components, among which are standards, standard enterprise information systems, applications such as ERP, CRM, and so on (see Section 6.6), standard components with which to build interoperable applications (see Chapter 15), and business protocols (see Chapter 20). Depending on the type of collaboration envisioned various technological solutions will be feasible too, such as enterprise application integration and Web services (see Chapters 17 and 19).

More information on networks can be found in Section 5.2 where networks are examined in the context of e-Business relationships and governance structures.

Case Study

GeneraLife: a virtual insurance company on the internet

The economic consequences of this business model were matchless. Sharpe, GeneraLife's COO, comments: "Rather than being heavily weighed down by on-site back-office fixed expenses that are such a big part of the traditional insurance company, GeneraLife's expenses were largely variable. We outsourced work and incurred expenses only as business grew. While the expenses of insurance companies are usually 80–90% fixed with only a small percentage variable, we were able to flip-flop that." In 1998, Conley could report that since its establishment in 1996 his company had sold $1.6 billion worth of life insurance policies, including $32 million in individual life premiums; the company then worked with 3,800 sales associates. Sharpe commented: "It was about as untraditional as an insurance company could be at that time." And it remained unique, until Basic Life Insurance Co., based in the Netherlands, was set up by the same team: Conley and Sharpe, in collaboration with G.A. Sullivan. They established this second Internet-based company in just four months in 1999. Operating on an annual budget of less than $3 million, Basic Life reached $10 million in premiums in just 18 months. At the time of writing it was the fastest-growing life insurance company in the Netherlands.

E-Business conditions are dynamic. Generalife went back to their parent company, General American Life Insurance Co.[4] The founders went on to form other virtual companies around financial technology. "Conley became so enamored with the virtual insurance company model that he left GeneraLife and started GlobalFT in July 2001. Sharpe and others joined him. By October of last year, the new GlobalFT and G.A. Sullivan were building a term life virtual division for Empire General Life Assurance Company of Kansas City, Mo. Unlike GeneraLife, Empire General sold policies over the Internet." Basic Life[5] is also no longer in operation (since January 2004); their activities have been taken over by other insurance companies.

[4] www.genamerica.com/pubsite/genamweb.nsf/index.htm
[5] www.basic-life.nl

3.5 Chapter summary

The popular term that has emerged in the e-Business literature to capture new ways, in which companies are doing business is referred to as the 'Business Model'. A business model is a descriptive representation of the planned activities of a business that involves three integral components, which specify:

- The internal aspects of a business venture;

- The type of relationships of the enterprise with its external business environment, and its effective knowledge regarding these relationships;

- How a company's information assets are embedded in the business venture.

The effect of the Internet is that it makes new business models possible, in particular through its effect on inter-company relationships. A networked business model is based on an appropriate technology environment to support electronic linkages (relationships) in the value chain. Networked business models assume the support of interoperable systems.

New business models will be based on new views on inter-company relationships and networking: new technologies may make network business models possible and it is the current competitive market that makes it necessary to adopt them. Traditional organizations would themselves execute all necessary activities for the production and delivery of their products and services. Nowadays, companies tend to think differently: there is no reason to do something oneself unless one is really uniquely good at it. Consequently, outsourcing and insourcing are expected to cause fundamental changes in the way companies are configured. Because of the integration of product and service offerings and the concentration on core competences, companies' success in today's markets will depend on their ability to set up cross-industry partner networks.

It is thus not surprising that several Internet-based business models have already been developed – so many that some classification is in order. The literature on e-Business provides various such classifications, the five most important of which we discussed in this chapter:

- Internet-enabled business models: a number of authors have defined families of business models that rely on Internet trading technologies;

- Value Web business models: An emerging form of a fluid and flexible organization, which consists of several key building blocks – markets, hierarchies, networks, information technology, and new-old business models;

- The e-Business-enabled business models: a classification scheme of business models that is particularly valid for business-to-business contexts. In it, five representative business model types are distinguished: the teleworking model, the virtual organization model, the process outsourcing model, the collaborative product development model, and the value chain integration model;

- Market participant business model: a more generic classification of Internet-based business models. Networked business models are defined for companies doing business on the Internet as well as for network infrastructure providers;

- Cybermediaries business model: this model is based on the premise that a new kind of intermediary will emerge: cybermediaries.

Discussion Questions

- Explain the following statement: 'the structure of economic activity within a company is based on a balance stricken between the benefits of particular patterns of division of labor and the costs of coordination'. How does the Internet and related technologies affect that balance? What consequences does this have for the structure of a company?

- Which three categories of elements should be present in a definition of a business model from an e-business perspective? Explain why.

- Why should the way IT is used be a part of the definition of a business model?

- How do you define a portal? What is the difference between a Website and a portal?

- Explain what is meant by an e-mall, a collaboration platform, a virtual community, a third part market place? How do they differ in functional integration and innovation?

- What is the role of a value Web broker in the Selz model?

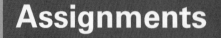

Assignments

i. Visit the Amazon Website. Explain its value proposition and revenue model. Find competing sites in this category and assess how they differ from Amazon. What is Amazon's competitive advantage?

ii. In Section 3 of this chapter, five classifications of business models are discussed. Analyze to what extent they differ and to what extent they overlap.

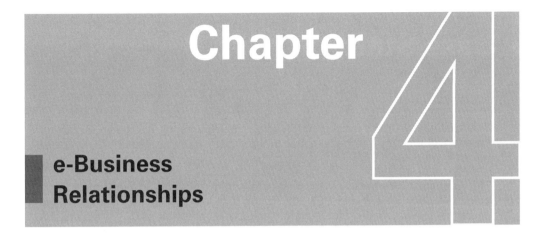

Chapter 4

e-Business Relationships

Relationships in the supply chain can be categorized as either business-to-business (e-Business) or business-to-consumer. Business-to-business relationships concern themselves with inter-company relationships, while business-to-consumer relationships refer to the very last component of the supply chain and its relation to the end customer.

This chapter discusses characteristics of e-Business relationships and their relevance for the application of e-Business technology. In particular, we discuss the value chain model developed by Michael Porter and position e-Business relationships in the business unit and industrial value chain model, introduce the concept of business process and process management, and present specific characteristics of inter-company relationships. We also explain how e-Business technology aims at improving the efficiency and effectiveness of inter-organizational transactions and at streamlining business processes by establishing electronic links.

Case Study

Supply chain integration at Unitech[1]

This case study discusses the supply chain developments at Unitech, a Taiwan-based medium-sized company, active in the design and manufacturing of state of the art IT products.

The company Unitech was established in Taiwan in 1979 and developed in a company of 470 employees and US$ 240 million turnover in 2003.[2] Its product range encompasses automatic identification and data collection (ADC) products, including barcode wedge decoders, scanners, portable and fixed position terminals, as well as application development software. Additionally, Unitech is a reseller of Hewlett-Packard, Apple, and Fuji products for the Taiwanese market. In the mid-1990s, in order to face global competitive pressures, Unitech established partnershiprelationships with local suppliers, and implemented a new organization structure. Three business units were created; one focusing on importing HP, Apple, and Fuji products, for sales, distribution, and services in the Taiwanese market; the second focusing on development, manufacturing, and marketing of own (ADC) products for the international markets; and the third on ADC products for the Taiwanese market. The two latter business units cooperate with third parties in Taiwan to provide total solutions using ADC products for specific industries. For international markets, sales offices were established in the USA (since 1987), China (1998), Europe (1999), and Japan (2001). For the local (Taiwanese) market five branch offices were created.

In 1997 Unitech Europe was set up. Using an outsourcing model, it employed only 15 staff members in 2002. The ADC products in Europe are sold to a variety of industries and include applications for, e.g., inventory control, shipping, warehousing, item tracking, and healthcare. Unitech Europe created opportunities to compete with worldwide large enterprises such as Symbol, Intermec, HHP, and Casio.

The market To operate successfully in the ADC market the company had to deal with specific circumstances. First, the world market is small ($7.6 billion in 2001), volatile (the market contracted in 2001, growth is expected for 2003–2005), and shows considerably different growth rates for the various ADC product types. Second, due to the trend towards open architectures, total solutions can be developed

[1]This case study was prepared by Martin Smits and David Kuo (Tilburg University). Earlier versions have been published as HICSS: Kuo, D and Smits, M: *Performance of Integrated Supply Chains: an international case study in high tech manufacturing*. In Sprague, R.: Proceedings of 32 HICSS, IEEE.

[2]See www.unitech.com.tw

for specific application domains, which contributes to considerably higher profit margins. Third, the required IT skills for an ADC manufacturer result in high entry barriers. Fourth, since the standards and the requirement vary from region to region, domain knowledge and cooperation with local companies are prerequisites to enter local markets over the world. Finally, due to short product life cycles, distributors, systems integrators, and retailers in Europe prefer manufacturing partners with trustable services and a good reputation.

The strategy Before 1998, almost all of the business activities for ADC products took place in Taiwan. Most of the 40 Taiwanese suppliers – with the exception of some large foreign vendors – had long-term and good partnerships with Unitech. They provided the ADC parts like IC circuits, electronics, PC boards, plastic models, and so on. 1997 was the year of a major strategic change. Unitech top management redefined the business goals and the strategy from local to global. The target became Europe: 'to be in the top 10 in PDT (portable data terminals) sales in Europe'. Realizing this strategic goal meant facing the challenge to create a responsive organization. Unitech restructured its business and organization infrastructure and opened branches outside Taiwan, among others in 1999 one in the Netherlands to address requirements in Europe, the Middle East, and Africa. The creation of Unitech Europe resulted in a number of strategic benefits for Unitech Taiwan. The company became visible for large enterprises as a manufacturer of low priced ADC. In return, the acquired knowledge of global ADC needs helped the company to become the primary supplier in the ADC market in Asia.

4.1 Modeling interdependent business activities: the value chain

During the current decade economic realities are demanding that companies become customer-driven organizations that can identify and address customers' needs from a variety of perspectives – at every point in the value chain. Moreover, entire value chains consisting of powerful business alliances are emerging and will compete as single entities for customers.

To help readers understand these business trends we define the concept of value chain and analyze its attributes in this section.

4.1.1 The business unit value chain

To understand and represent how firms developed a competitive position we first need to understand the concept of *value chain* that was proposed by Porter [Porter 1985a, 1990]. Porter states that: "every firm is a collection of activities that are performed to design, produce, market, deliver, and support its products or services. Value chains can only be understood in the context of the business unit". The value chain is a model that describes a series of value-adding activities connecting a company's supply side (raw materials, inbound logistics, and production processes) with its demand side (outbound logistics, marketing, and sales). The value chain model provides managers with a tool to analyze and, if necessary, redesign their internal and external processes to improve efficiency and effectiveness. His classic internal value chain for any firm is shown in Figure 4.1. The actual value chain is different for every organization.

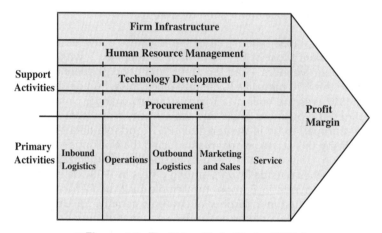

■ Figure 4.1: The Value Chain [Porter 1985a]

A value chain usually describes a major line of business and encompasses two types of activities, *primary activities* and *support activities* (see Figure 4.1). The primary activities are those that have a direct relationship, potential or actual, with the organization's customers. They contribute directly to getting goods and services to the customer, e.g., inbound logistics, including procurement, manufacturing, marketing, and delivery to buyers. Support activities provide the inputs and infrastructure that allows the primary activities to be performed. The primary activities are:

- *Inbound Logistics*: all processes associated with receiving, storing, and disseminating inputs to the production process of the product or service;

- *Operations*: all processes associated with transforming the inputs into outputs;

- *Outbound Logistics*: all activities concerned with distributing the products or services to customers;

- *Marketing & Sales*: activities, which provide opportunities for the potential customer to buy the product or service, and offer inducements to do so. This section of the value chain includes such processes as advertising, pricing, tendering, sales force management, selection of distribution channels, etc.;

- *Service*: all processes concerned with the provision of service as part of the deal struck with customers. They are those activities that enhance or maintain the value of the product or service once the customer has bought it. These activities include repairs, maintenance, spare parts supply, product upgrades, follow-up services, training and installation, and so on.

As Figure 4.1 illustrates the execution of primary activities requires support activities:

- *Firm Infrastructure*: this activity encompasses administration and (general) management for overall planning and control;

- *Human Resource Management*: this function refers to all those activities associated with the recruiting, training, developing, appraising, promoting, and rewarding of personnel;

- *Product / Technology Development*: this function includes all activities that relate to product and process development;

- *Procurement*: this function is responsible for purchasing goods, services, and materials required as inputs for the production process.

The original value chain model is applicable to organizations with a physical goods flow, like manufacturing and trading companies. For service organizations, like banks, insurance companies, tour operators, the original model needs to be adapted to the characteristics of that particular type of company. However, independently of the type of organization under consideration, the basic idea of the model applies: the analysis of how activities add value and the distinction between activities that directly add value to the customer and those that indirectly add value (through the primary activities).

According to Porter, a value chain includes everything that contributes to a major organizational output. By adding up all the costs associated with each activity in a value chain, and subtracting the total from the revenue derived from the output, an organization can determine the profit margin. Enterprises may have from one to few value chains. Organizations typically support from three to fifteen value chains. A financial organization may, for example, support four value chains such as individual checking and savings, business checking and savings, new savings product development, and business loans [Wolf 2003]. This is shown in Figure 4.2.

It is important to notice that Porter includes in his definition of a value chain what we, today, might call supply chain, Customer Relationship Management (CRM), new product development, and all of the support activities required to enable each of these core business processes [Wolf 2003]. Although the topic of supply-chains was briefly mentioned in Chapter 1 and will be covered in considerable length in Chapter 10, we will give here a brief overview to help the reader better understand the material that follows in this chapter.

Supply chain is a network of facilities and distribution options that necessarily performs the functions of procurement and acquisition of material, processing and transformation of the material into intermediate and finished tangible products and finally the physical distribution of the finished tangible products to the customers. Supply chains exist in both manufacturing as well as in service organizations.

A company's supply chain consists of geographically dispersed facilities where raw materials, intermediate products, or finished products are acquired, transformed, stored, or sold, and transportation links connecting the facilities along which products flow. There is a distinction between plants, which are manufacturing

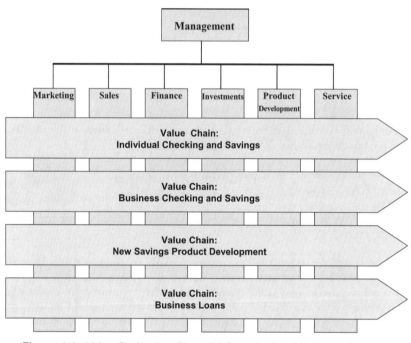

■ **Figure 4.2:** Value Chains in a Financial Organization [Wolf 2003]

facilities where physical product transformations take place, and distribution centers, which are facilities where products are received, sorted, put away in inventory, picked from inventory, and dispatched, but not physically transformed. The company may operate these facilities, or they may be operated by vendors, customers, third-party providers, or other firms with which the company has business arrangements. While, in the past, companies focused primarily on manufacturing and quality improvements within their four walls, now their efforts extend beyond those walls to encompass the entire supply chain.

Value chains are today being seen as a major differentiating factor in a company. According to a research study by Gartner Group, enterprises that implement value chain planning applications with a continuous improvement program are likely to increase ROI by 40% over a five-year lifecycle. Corporations need to continuously ask themselves questions about the organization, designing, and management of efficient processes keeping in mind issues such as shareholder value and returns, competition and margin pressures, mergers and acquisitions, shifts in cost and service structures, new markets and new products, customer requirements and demands, capacity constraints and sourcing and supplier requirements.

4.1.2 Value chain analysis

Porter's value chain framework analyzes value creation at the organization level. It does so by addressing two main questions:

- What activities should a firm perform, and how?

- What is the configuration of the firm's activities that would enable it to add value to the product and to compete in its industry?

Value chain analysis starts by identifying the activities of the firm and then studies the economic implications of those activities. It includes four general steps:

1) Defining the strategic business unit;
2) Identifying critical activities;
3) Defining products;
4) Determining the value of an activity.

Porter defines value as 'the amount buyers are willing to pay for what a firm provides them. Value is measured by total revenue' [Porter 1985a]. Value can be created by differentiation along every step of the value chain, through activities resulting in products and services that lower buyers' costs or raise buyers' performance. Drivers of product differentiation, and hence sources of value creation, are policy choices (what activities to perform and how), linkages (within the value chain or with suppliers and channels), timing (of activities), location, sharing of activities among business units, learning, integration, scale and institutional factors [Porter 1985a]. According to Porter a firm is profitable if the value it commands exceeds the costs involved in creating a specific product.

The analysis of a business unit's value chain in relation to the competitive strategy of the firm helps to understand how enterprise information systems, such ERP, CRM, and SCM, can contribute to the firm's competitive position. Firstly, enterprise information systems may help each activity to be performed well. However, the eventual value generated at the level of the final customer not only depends on the functioning of each individual (functional) activity, it also depends on the coordination of all activities involved. For example, cycle time in production may be reduced; however, if suppliers have unreliable delivery times, the eventual delivery time for the final customer remains long and unreliable. So, secondly, enterprise information systems should also support the – horizontal – flow of information through the business to support overall performance towards the customer [Ward 2002]. However, traditionally, very often, information systems have been set up to satisfy the demands of – vertical – functional departments and much less to support horizontal coordination between departments. The general idea is that for all activities the performance measures and levels set by the market (the customers) drive the way they are executed. It is the alienation from the final market that makes functional departments emphasize internal performance measures, and levels that optimize internal efficiency and effectiveness, losing sight of what the customer really wants.

The relevance of IT and information systems, in particular, is that they create value by supporting differentiation strategies [Porter 1985b]. For each element in the value chain, it may be possible to use information systems to increase the efficiency of resource usage in that particular area. Moreover, information systems can be used between value chain activities to increase organizational efficiency. Porter and Millar [Porter 1985b] propose a five-step process to by which an organization can positively impact on its value chain by investing in new or upgraded information systems, such as enterprise information systems (see Section 6.6 which discusses the role of enterprise information systems in e-Business). The steps in this process are:

1) Assess the information intensity of the value chain. This step assesses the level of information within each value chain and between each level of activity. The higher the level of intensity and/or the higher the reliance on information, the greater the potential impact of new information systems in the value chain;
2) Determine the role of information systems in the industry structure. The role of information systems is different in various industry sectors; for instance, the use of information systems in banking is very different from manufacturing. Additionally, it is important to understand the information linkages between buyers, suppliers within the industry, and how they and competitors might be affected by and react to new information technology;
3) Identify and rank the ways the ways in which information systems might create competitive advantage. Impacting value chain activities or improving linkages between them can achieve this;
4) Investigate how information systems might spawn new business;
5) Develop a plan for taking advantage of information systems. A business-driven rather than a technology-driven plan must be developed. This plan must assign priorities to information systems investments, which should be subjected to cost-benefit analysis.

Finally, value chain analysis can be helpful in examining value creation in virtual markets. A *'virtual' value chain* may include a sequence of gathering, organizing, selecting, synthesizing, and distributing information. While this modification of the value chain concept corresponds better to the realities of virtual markets, and in particular to the importance of information goods [Shapiro 1999], there may still be room to capture the richness of e-Business activity more fully. Value creation opportunities in virtual markets may result from new combinations of information, physical products and services, innovative configurations of transactions, and the reconfiguration and integration of resources, capabilities, roles, and relationships among suppliers, partners, and customers [Amit 2001].

4.1.3 Value stream analysis

Value stream is a concept closely related to the value chain [Womack 1998]. *Value stream analysis* considers how the whole production and delivery process can be made more efficient. To conduct value stream analysis, companies map every activity that occurs in creating new products and delivering products or services to customers, and then categorize them as those that create value as perceived by the customer, those that create no value, and those that do not add value. The last two categories are eliminated.

The *value stream* is the set of all the specific actions required to bring a specific product through the three critical management tasks of any business:

1) Problem-solving (from concept to production launch);
2) Information management (from order-taking to delivery);
3) Physical transformation (from raw materials to finished products delivered to the customer).

It should be noted that tasks 2 and 3 are traditional value chain activities but task 1 is not.

The starting point is that the end customer determines value. This means identifying what the customer is willing to pay for, what creates 'value' for him or her. The whole process of producing and delivering a product should be examined and optimized from the customer's point of view. So once 'value' is defined, we can explore the value stream, being all activities – both value-added and non-value added – that are currently required to bring the product from raw material to end product to the customer.

4.1.4 Unbundling the business unit value chain

Competitive pressures force companies to reconsider their business model. Concentration on what is considered a unique and core competence and outsourcing the rest contributes to a more agile and efficient organization. It is no coincidence that technology companies, with high velocity product cycles and swings, have aggressively embraced outsourcing and specialization; 70% of electronics manufacturing use contract manufacturing [Philips 2000].

As a result of these developments, traditional business unit value chains become unbundled. Primary activities, like logistics, operations, and support activities, and parts of the firm's infrastructure (e.g. accounting, financial services, and human resources) get outsourced. Often, in multi-business-unit firms, a first step to outsourcing is setting up Shared Service Centers for specific activities, like human relations. Outsourced activities have to be procured from one or more external suppliers. *Unbundling of the value chain* contributes to more complex e-Business relationships. Efficiency of the relationship, e.g., through low transaction costs, is or should be an argument when considering the outsourcing movement. It is clear that e-Business technology has an important role to play in this respect.

4.1.5 The industry value chain

Every business unit value chain is part of a larger *industry value chain* (also called the *value system*): a collection of individual business unit value chains that together produce and deliver the goods and services to the final customer. The value system is a model that helps a company to position itself relative to other companies. The idea is to make explicit the role of a company in the overall activity of providing a product to a customer. The value system specifies the suppliers and the immediate customers and defines the sales channels of the given company. It allows understanding of whether all the companies involved in the sales process can potentially collaborate or whether there are conflicts of interests.

How effective (meeting the objectives) and how efficient (meeting the objectives at minimal cost) the industry value chain is able to meet the demands of the final customers, is dependent on both the performance of each individual business unit, and the combined action of all the companies involved in the industry value chain. Availability of supply and demand information at each stage is key for producing the required goods and services as efficiently as possible [Ward 2002]. Typical information exchange in the industry value chain will relate to regular business transactions (orders, order confirmations, invoices, and payments). Basic e-Business technology applications can improve the efficiency of these processes, by just automating the existing procedures or eventually making possible a complete reengineering of the process. Besides information about existing orders, also information about customer demand for the businesses in the chain and available products, services, and production capacity for the intermediate and final customers is challenged by e-Business technology [Rayport 1995; Ward 2002].

As already explained, the value system approach stresses the relative position of a business unit as a part of a larger chain. Related concepts are '*logistics*' and '*supply chain*'. The need to manage an organization as flows of goods, services, and information in contrast to as isolated activities has been recognized by what is called *'logistics'*. Logistics may be defined as the process of planning the flow of goods and related information, including purchasing, storage, transportation, and manufacturing, from suppliers through the organization to final customers. Logistics is an integrative 'planning concept' that develops a system view of the firm to focus on the coordination of material and information flows across the organization to satisfy the needs of end customers at optimal conditions [Christopher 1998]. Logistics aims at avoiding suboptimization that occurs when inventories, purchasing, manufacturing, transportation are being planned as isolated activities. Logistics is closely related to the concept of the 'value chain'.

Whereas logistics focuses on a single firm and its relations to suppliers and customers, the *supply chain* encompasses a more comprehensive view by looking at the collection of firms that are involved in producing and delivering an end product to the final customer. *Supply chain management* is basically an extension of logistics management by adopting a higher-level view when considering all the downstream and upstream relations between the organizations involved in taking a product to the customer. The aim is to do so in optimal conditions from a total supply chain point of view. When individual organizations in the supply chain manage their operations independently of each other, overall supply chain performance, in terms of eventual customer value, will be low. Inventories will be excessive, products will require delivery times etc. By collaborating in the supply chain – which means that the different supply chain members make plans together about manufacturing, inventories, delivery schedules etc – overall supply chain performance can be dramatically improved in terms of value delivered to the customer. The latter process is known as *supply chain integration*. This important topic is elaborated in Section 10.5.

Case Study

Supply chain integration at Unitech

The supply chain: The supply chain has become increasingly complex. Unitech Taiwan buys materials from up to 40, most local, suppliers. Local solution providers in Taiwan helped to meet special customer requirements already before 1997. In Europe, system integrators and value-added providers are involved to deliver total solutions. In 2003, the Unitech Website showed about 45 third parties in 33 countries in Europe, Middle East, and Africa. Unitech Europe manages its own inventory levels, applying its own ordering policies. If Unitech Taiwan has problems in delivering extra orders to Unitech Europe on time, then Unitech Europe can ask other Unitech branches; they become players in the Unitech Europe supply chain. Soon after 2003, it is expected that retailers and distributors around Europe will be able to order and receive products from Unitech Europe to sell to their customers in various sectors.

4.2 Business processes and their management

The focus on the final customer as opposed to the focus on vertical functional activities has led in the 1990s to an increased interest in processes and their management [Davenport 1993]. A *process* is an ordering of activities with a beginning and an end; it has inputs (in terms of resources, materials, and information) and a specified output. We may thus define a process as any sequence of steps that is initiated by an event, transforms information, materials, or business commitments, and produces an output [Harmon 2003c]. Processes can be measured, and different performance measures apply, like cost, quality, time and customer satisfaction. To manage processes properly, new functions and new areas of responsibility have to be introduced, like case managers and process owners.

A *business process* consists of one or more related activities that together respond to a business requirement for action. A (business) process view implies an horizontal view of a business organization, and looks at processes as sets of interdependent activities designed and structured to produce a specific output for a customer or a market. Most analysts use the term *activity* rather informally to refer to a small-scale process that consists of one or a few closely related steps. A process defines the results to be achieved, the context of the activities, the relationships between the activities, and the interactions with other processes and resources. A business process may receive events that alter the state of the process and the sequence of activities. A business process may produce events for input to other systems or processes. It may also invoke applications to perform computational functions, and it may post assignments to human work lists to request actions by human actors.

As a general rule, business processes are the core of an enterprise's identity; they are the steps taken to create a new product, manufacture an item, assemble multiple parts into a finished good, synthesize a raw material for production, answer a customer enquiry, procure supplies, negotiate a partnership, or deliver a product to the market. Each enterprise has unique characteristics that are embedded in its processes. Most enterprises perform a similar set of repeatable routine activities that may include the development of manufacturing products and services, bringing these products and services to market, and satisfying the customers who purchase them. Automated business processes can perform such activities. Although many business processes can be and are automated, others may also require human interaction for performing tasks that are too unstructured to delegate to automated processes, or tasks that require personal interaction with human operators, e.g., customers. Successful enterprises are built on a foundation of business processes that align resources to achieve business goals. Business processes can thus be viewed as unifying threads that bind together the fabric of an enterprise's products, services and value when delivering goods and services to customers, collaborating with partners, coordinating employee efforts, and so on.

An e-Business application is an application that aims at automating some or even all of the tasks involved in the execution of a business process. The various levels of processes are ordered in a process hierarchy. Figure 4.3 shows a business process hierarchy. The largest possible process in an organization is the value chain. The value chain is decomposed into a set of core business processes and support processes necessary to produce a product or product line. These processes are subdivided through various levels of *subprocess*. Subprocesses can be seen as reusable business services. For example in an order entry business process, there will be a step to identify a customer. As input we may have the customer number, and as output the shipping address and other details. The subprocess used to inquire about a customer could be reused in another

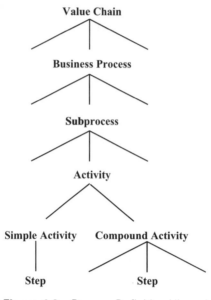

■ **Figure 4.3:** Process Definition Hierarchy

business process, for example, the processing of incoming payments. A subprocess on its own can consist of the integration of multiple applications running on different systems. Subprocesses are in turn divided into activities. Activities span two categories: *simple activities* that only have a single step, and *compound activities*, that include multiple steps [Harmon 2003c]. A simple activity could be 'approve orders', where an office worker picks up an order, reads it, and either approves or rejects it. An example of a compound activity could be 'prepare blueprints', where an architect works through a large number of steps to prepare the blueprints for a house. Activities will inevitably vary greatly from one company to another, and from one business analysis effort to another. A business process activity may invoke another business process in the same or a different business system domain.

At runtime, a business process definition may have multiple instantiations, each operating independently of the other, and each instantiation may have multiple activities that are concurrently active. In general, instances of a process, its current state, and the history of its actions will be visible at runtime and expressed in terms of the business process definition, so that users can determine the status of business activities, and business specialists can monitor the activity and identify potential improvements to the business process definition.

Process views may be adopted at different levels of analysis: e.g., at the level of handling a request for service by a customer, and at the company level when considering the integrated logistics process. Examples of typical processes in manufacturing firms include, among other things, new product development (which cuts across research and development, marketing, and manufacturing), customer order fulfillment (which combines sales, manufacturing, warehousing, transportation, and billing) and financial asset management.

The possibility of designing, structuring, measuring processes, and determining their contribution to customer value, makes them an important starting point for business improvement and innovation initiatives.

As the total process performance depends on coordinated action of a number of activities, information and enterprise information systems play an important role in this respect, of course dependent on the 'information intensity' of the process. For example, the role of IT will differ between insurance companies and healthcare organizations. The process view applies in both, however. IT developments related to process orientation include workflow systems, workflow management systems, and enterprise resource planning systems.

Processes may cross organizational boundaries. Traditional examples are purchasing and sales processes jointly set up by buying and selling organizations, supported by EDI and value added networks. The Internet is now a trigger for the design of new business processes and the redesign of existing ones. For instance, new expectations have arisen from the setting up of *Web services*, which aim at the design of standardized business process based solutions, which act independently of software and harwdare environments (see Chapter 19 for more details).

4.2.1 Business process management

Traditionally, organizations were built around functional departments, attempting to benefit from economies of scale and the specialization of the workforce. However, the concentration of similar activities into one organizational unit has a price: coordination between activities belonging to different organizational units becomes more difficult. This is not a problem when the organization's environment is stable and predictable. The required coordination is tackled by the common hierarchy, which is empowered to make the right decisions, and by formal procedures. The latter are needed to prevent the hierarchy from being flooded by routine questions. However, when the business environment becomes more volatile the combination of coordination by hierarchy and procedures is not sufficient to tackle all the coordination problems.

Besides a structure, an organization, like any biological system, has processes. Processes, like fulfilling a customer order, determine how well an organization functions. Typically, processes are not contained within one functional department. Consequently, the effective execution of a business process is the responsibility of more than one department, and has to deal with differences in functional objectives and priorities. An example of such a situation is the planning of a customer order from the point of view of the sales department and the manufacturing and procurement department. If the sales department imposes its priorities and schedules on the manufacturing department, customers will be satisfied. However, this may probably occur at high manufacturing and procurement costs. On the other hand, when manufacturing imposes its priorities on the sales department and puts the customer on a waiting list, the customer may eventually be lost. Again, under stable conditions the common hierarchy (ultimately the CEO) can handle these differences in points of view effectively.

In a dynamic business environment coordination problems will become apparent and will trigger the need for a more horizontal (as opposed to a vertical functional) view on the organization. Examples are teams, matrix management, networked structures, and so on. However, coordination problems do occur with regard to business processes. For instance, faulty coordination results in low performance of business processes, in terms of quality, flexibility, and throughput time, and threatens directly the competitive position of the company. Implementation of these organizational structures without adopting a process view will probably be in vain. Adopting a Business Process Management (BPM) view involves the explicit planning, organizing, execution, and controlling of business processes as entities.

Typically, processes have internal and external customers and will cross organizational boundaries, both intra-organizational departmental boundaries and inter-organizational company boundaries. The latter are known as *e-Business processes* (see Chapter 18). Processes can be identified by a beginning and an end, and by the organizational units involved; they interface with other processes or deliver to the final customer. It is very important that processes can be measured. Quality of the output, costs caused by the process, throughput time, and flexibility are examples of performance measures, which drive the management of the processes. Typical examples are processing and paying insurance claims, product development, ordering goods and services from suppliers, etc. As will be discussed in Chapter 10, the value chain model helps to identify business processes.

Closely related to business processes are workflows (see Section 6.4). We may define a *workflow* as the sequence of processing steps (execution of business operations, tasks, and transactions), during which information and physical objects are passed from one processing step to the other. Software products that support workflow applications have evolved from various origins like document management systems, image management application systems, and pure workflow software.

4.2.2 Characteristics of business processes

Business processes can be specified by a number of characteristics [Brand 1995] (see Figure 4.4). First, processes exist within an environment, which is both the internal business environment in which the process operates, and the external organizational environment that can trigger the process. It is important to include the environment in the process description. The environment determines the reason for existence of the process, by determining the characteristics of the required output, and the conditions under which it

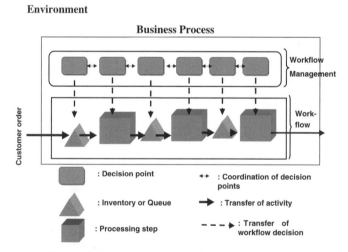

■ **Figure 4.4:** Representation of a Business Process

operates, like degree of stability and predictability. From the environment the processes receive their inputs, such as physical goods, information, energy, etc.

Second, every process has a customer and is initiated by a customer order. The customer may be external, such as the final customer for whom a service or product is produced, or internal, such as another process for which the output of the process under consideration forms an input. Not every process and workflow is directly triggered by a customer order. It is possible that a process is triggered by a standard procedure: e.g., salary payments are triggered by a date in the month, but are eventually meant to satisfy a customer, in particular the employee.

Third, every business process implies processing: a series of activities (processing steps) leading to some form of transformation of data or products for which the process exists. Transformations may be executed manually or in an automated way. A transformation will encompass multiple processing steps. For example, the process 'authorizing invoices' will encompass the steps ' checking whether the invoice has not been paid yet', 'checking the agreed purchasing conditions', 'checking the receiving report', 'checking calculations', and 'checking name, address, and bank account of the creditor'. If and only if all the checkpoints are correct, the invoice will be registered in the accounts payable administration.

By describing the processing steps in a workflow the functionality of the workflow is specified. Especially with regard to data, we may distinguish:

- *Geographic transformation*: documents or other carriers of data are transported from one place to another;

- *Technological transformation*: data are transferred from one carrier to another, e.g., from a physical document to some electronic form;

- *Linguistic transformation*: data are transformed from one language to another, e.g., translated from Dutch to English;

- *Syntactic transformation*: data are transformed from one data structure to another or a standard representation of well-known constructs, e.g., invoice descriptions. Data could also be transformed from one currency or metric sysem, e.g., dollars, to another, e.g., euros;

- *Semantic transformation*: assessments and judgements, mathematical operations leading to some form of decision and/or change in contents of data.

Fourth, communication is an important part of any business process. Communication will take place both within the process and with the environment. There are *planned communication* and *unplanned communication*. The latter may be the result of quality problems with the output of the workflow. Also, the more uncertainty under which the process operates, the more communication there will be. It is important to include a specification of the type of communication and the amount of data involved with it, in the design of the process.

Fifth, workflows have inventories or queues; these are locations where steps in the workflow are waiting to be processed. There are multiple reasons for the existence of queues, for example:

1) Lack of processing capacity;

2) Geographic transformation, which may take time;
3) Availability (or lack of) of all data to accomplish the process.

To some extent allowing queues is a process design decision, e.g., there is a trade off between processing capacity and queuing. Controlling queues requires that, like the process, they are modelled and managed.

Sixth, processes and workflows have decision points. Decisions have to be made with regard to routing and allocation of processing capacity. In a highly predictable and standardized environment, the trajectory in the process of a customer order will be established in advance in a standard way. Only if the process is complex (highly knowledge intense, see Section 2.4) and if the conditions of the process are not predictable, routing decisions have to be made on the spot. In general the customer orders will be split into a category that is highly proceduralized (and thus automated), and a category that is complex and uncertain. Here human experts will be needed and manual processing is the key element in the process. As regards the workflow of the business process, a distinction may be made between the operational and management activities (the decision points). The former is called workflow, while the latter is known as workflow management, (see Section 6.4).

Finally, every process delivers a product, such as a mortgage or an authorized invoice. The extent to which the end product of a process can be specified in advance and standardized impacts the way that processes and their workflows can be structured and automated.

4.2.3 Types of business processes

Business processes and their workflows have several characteristics that impact the way they are structured and the extent to which they can be automated. Characteristics that are particularly important are: type of activity – physical or informational – of the processing steps, the degree of repetition of the process, the expertise required to execute the process, and the level of anticipation of the stimulus that triggers the process [Brand 1995; Platier 1996].

1) First we distinguish between *workflows where information processing supports a physical process* and *workflows where information processing is the process itself*. In a manufacturing environment, handling a customer order requires that physical products have to be produced, picked out of a warehouse, and delivered to the customer. There is a close link between the 'information' component and the physical component of the workflow; e.g. the final and correct delivery on time not only depends on the execution of the 'physical' activities but also on the efficient execution of 'informational' activities. Decisions have to be made, documents will 'flow' from one department to the other, etc. For this type of business processes, workflow systems will basically concern the management of the process. In an insurance company, processing a mortgage application consists basically of processing information about the customer who is applying for the mortgage, about the object (the house) that is to be mortgaged, and about the risks involved. Both the management and the execution of the workflow consist of processing information. Here, workflow systems will typically encompass both.

2) Next the structuring of workflows will differ, depending on the *degree of repetition* and on the level of expertise or knowledge required to execute the process. Workflows that have a low degree of repetition may not have a very fixed structure, may be ad hoc, especially when no particular expertise is required. The required level of expertise determines the type of expert knowledge that is needed to successfully execute the process. For example, to process an insurance claim, the assessment by damage experts

may be needed. The more different types of expertise that are needed, the longer (the more steps) the workflow will be (and consequently the more difficult it will be to manage the workflow). In case of low repetition with a high level of expertise required, processes will be organized as projects around experts. An example is a request by a company to a bank to finance a complex and potentially risky investment. A high degree of repetition will make it economically feasible to implement a structured, formalized workflow. If no specific expertise is required the 'customer order' can be processed as an uninterrupted continuous flow. An example is the processing of routine tax returns by the Internal Revenue Service. If, however, specific expert judgement is required, processes tend to differ with respect to the content. In these situations possibly different experts are needed and again the process is more difficult to manage.

3) A last characteristic concerns *the level of anticipation of the stimulus that triggers the process.* This determines the extent to which an organization can be prepared for the timely execution of a specific process. In particular, in case of highly customized services and products as opposed to standardized services and products, the level of anticipation is low.

Mintzberg [Mintzberg 1983] developed a *typology of organizations* dependent on the complexity and uncertainty of the environment in which they operate. This is illustrated in Figure 4.5.

Environments	*Stable*	*Dynamic*
Complex	Professional Bureaucracy	Adhocracy
Simple	Machine Bureaucracy	Simple Structure

■ **Figure 4.5:** Mintzberg's Typology of Organizations [Mintzberg 1983]

Traditional bureaucratic structures operated under stable and consequently routine conditions and tend to have stable processes with a high degree of repetition. In simple environments, the responsibility for work execution tends to be centralized (machine bureaucracy), and in complex environments the responsibility for work execution is delegated to professionals (professional bureaucracy), see Figure 4.5. The former implies processes for which little specific expertise is needed; the latter on the contrary are organizations with experts, who execute their tasks according to standard professional rules.

Organizations that operate under dynamic conditions abandon the (vertical) bureaucratic structure to adopt (horizontal) organic structures. The execution of business processes will be harder to predict. The responsibility for work execution tends to be centralized in a simple environment and decentralized in a relatively complex environment. In general, the former type of environment tends to be found in entrepreneurial SMEs; the latter are known as 'adhocracies', highly organic structures with little formalization of behavior. They emerge in environments with sophisticated innovation where experts are drawn from different disciplines to form *ad hoc* project teams. As the business environment becomes increasingly dynamic, transactions and their workflows are evolving from predictable and routine to unpredictable and exceptional. Organizations have to become very efficient at handling exceptions.

4.2.4 Role of IT in business processes

IT and business processes have a recursive relationship [Maholtra 1998]. IT supports the process, and business processes are impacted by the capabilities that IT can offer. As for the latter (IT impacts the process), IT may be considered as a key enabler of business process reengineering [Hammer 1990; Davenport 1990] (see Chapter 18).

IT is expected to impact business processes in one or more of the following ways [Davenport 1990]:

1) *Transactional*: with the help of IT unstructured processes can be transformed into highly structured and routinized procedures;
2) *Geographic*: through its electronic communication effect, IT can transport data across large distances swiftly and at low cost, which makes processes independent of any geographic location;
3) *Automated*: IT may replace or reduce human labor in a process;
4) *Analytic*: IT can bring complex analytic tools and methods into a process;
5) *Informational*: IT can bring large amounts of detailed data into a process;
6) *Sequential*: IT can bring about changes in the sequence of steps in a process; tasks that used to be executed sequentially can be worked on simultaneously;
7) *Knowledge management*: IT can allow the capture and dissemination of formal (explicit) knowledge, which can improve the process;
8) *Tracking*: IT allows detailed tracking of status etc of a process;
9) *Disintermediation*: IT can connect two parties in a process who would otherwise work through an intermediary.

To a large extent the effect that IT may have on a process depends on the way that functions are orchestrated to accomplish the outcome of that process. For this purpose we may analyze a process along two dimensions: the degree of mediation and the degree of collaboration [Teng 1994; Maholtra 1998].

The *degree of mediation* refers to the sequential flow of different functions involved in the process. Each function has inputs and outputs, which consist of physical products or of information. The outputs either form inputs to other functions or contribute directly to the final process outcome. A process may encompass a series of steps that are sequentially related to each other and so contribute indirectly to the process outcome, with, of course, the last step contributing directly to the process outcome. Some business processes (such as buying complex products) involve many indirect steps, and are at the high end of the mediation dimension. Business processes may also consist of several functions, which contribute directly to the process outcome, without forming intermediary steps. For example, for accepting a customer order, the manufacturing planning function, the warehouse, and the financial department need to provide inputs. These processes are at the low end of the mediation dimension.

Many business processes have been reengineered from an indirect pattern, with many intermediate steps, to a more direct pattern allowing a set of functions to work independently. IT can be particularly helpful because many input–output relationships are often dictated by the logical sequence of steps and the supporting flow of documents of the process. For example, shared databases, client server technology, and imaging technology have helped to turn many indirect processes into direct ones. When processing loan applications several bank employees can directly work on the digitised image. One employee checks the employee status of the applicant, another works on the credit inquiry, and another performs a credit scoring [Teng 1994].

The *degree of collaboration* indicates the extent of collaboration between functions involved in a particular process. Collaboration involves a reciprocal relation between functions and involves communication and mutual adjustment.

Also this dimension can vary from very low (functions are completely insulated) to extensive (there is a highly collaborative relationship between functions) [Teng 1994]. Contrary to the sequence of input output relations, which is dictated by the process, the degree of collaboration across participants in a process may be at their discretion. Functions may or may not decide to contact each other and make adjustments. Especially in an uncertain environment where planning ahead is difficult, collaboration is necessary react and adjust to current conditions. E-mail and telecommunication-based groupware especially are applications that can stimulate new patterns of collaboration in a process by providing a shared environment for teamwork. It is clear that innovative uses of IT will enable firms to realize new, coordination-intensive structures, making it possible to coordinate activities in ways that were not possible before. As shown in Figure 4.6, that two dimensions can be combined into one framework is exemplified below.

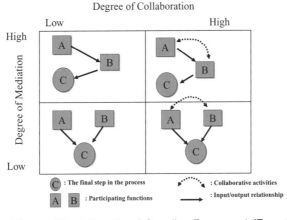

■ **Figure 4.6:** A Functional Coupling Framework [Teng 1994]

In the 'low mediation/low collaboration' side of the quadrant we find functions that directly contribute to the output, with no interaction. Basically the functions can operate independently of each other. The only dependency that exists is a 'time dependency': the delivery of the final outcome depends on the two functions. For Business Process Reengineering this represents the simplest situation, with few possibilities of improvement.

The 'high mediation/high collaboration' side of the quadrant offers the most opportunities for BPR. Functions participate in the process sequentially and with mutual information exchange. A situation like this may be expected under conditions of relatively high uncertainty. An example is the development and manufacturing of a highly customized product, which needs interaction between product development, engineering, and manufacturing.

The 'low mediation/high collaboration' side of the quadrant represents a situation where functions contribute directly to the process outcome (with no sequential relationships) and have an intensive collaboration. Typically, these situations will involve a high level of uncertainty and complexity. A product development with many engineers working on the same product may have these characteristics. The use of CSCW applications, shared databases may offer opportunities for speeding up the process.

In the 'high mediation/low collaboration' side of the quadrant, we find those processes where functions participate in the process sequentially, however, with no mutual exchange of information. These are typically highly proceduralized processes that face by definition very little uncertainty in their execution. These situations often offer opportunities for improvement. An example is the inventory function sending a signal to the purchasing function that a re-order point of some product is reached. Today many companies are trying to improve the efficiency of their procurement activities for MRO products (see Chapter 9).

Under conditions of relative certainty, functions have a good view on what is expected from their output by other functions. These interdependencies can be established in a set of procedures that basically takes care of coordination, without the need of communication. The left side of the framework represents this situation. Under conditions of increasing uncertainty, what functions expect from each other in terms of input and output may be subject to more or less important changes. To achieve a coordinated action between the functions, communication, and mutual adjustment are necessary. Given the increased volatility of the business environment, we may expect that many business processes will move to the right side of the quadrant.

Business processes and collaborations are also the topic of Chapter 12, which deals with modeling the enterprise context.

4.3 Types and characteristics of e-Business relationships

E-Business is about inter-business relationships. Businesses are related to each other as they sell and buy goods and services from each other, and as they may be engaged in different types of collaborative processes, like collaborative planning, joint product design and so on. Products and services sold to the final customer consist of a variety of components or subservices. As we already explained in Chapter 1, and we shall see again in Chapter 10, the collection of companies involved in the chain of activities from the production of basic raw material up to the physical delivery of a product to the final customer is called a supply chain. The structure of the supply chain and the number of participating companies may differ per type of product. For instance, in the petrochemical industry supply chains tend to *diverge*: a few major raw materials result in a large number of end products; in the consumer electronic industry supply chains will *converge*: a very large number of components delivered by about the same number of suppliers result in one end-product. Initially, supply chains were conceived in particular for manufacturing and trade of physical products; the concept however can easily be extended to non-physical products such as financial services, healthcare services, consulting, information services, and so on. Also in these cases different components or services, of which some are externally procured, are being processed, 'manufactured', and assembled into a final 'product' being the particular service offered.

4.3.1 Types of e-Business relationships

In the supply chain, e-Business relationships have been changing in the past decades and became part of the company's longer term planning processes (see Figure 4.7). At first independence prevailed. Companies were buying products, components, piece parts, and services on the basis of current needs and on the expectation that a supplier would exist that could deliver the products and services needed. Products and services offerings to the market were also based on expectations (forecasts) of existing demand. These types of e-Business relationships can be characterized as *operational-level relationships*. Companies decide internally what they need, and next look outside to see who can deliver at the lowest possible price. There exists no sharing of information between the buying and selling organization; the only information exchanged concerns the orders placed.

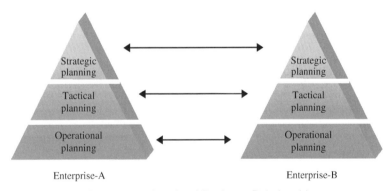

Figure 4.7: Levels of Business Relationship

Independence has its advantages, such as flexibility, possibility to change quickly if a supplier does not perform satisfactorily; however, it also has its price. The price is uncertainty, and therefore the absence of opportunities to plan ahead. Companies deal with uncertainty by imposing long delivery times on their customers, by keeping high inventories, having idle production capacity (so a lower utilization level per production unit), and by selling as standardized a product as possible (as customer specific components can only be ordered after the customer order has been received). When competition put pressure on efficiency, delivery times, and customization of products, a different way of working is needed, and inter-company collaboration based on longer-term relationships is developed. Then the e-Business relationship moves to the *tactical level*. Tactical inter-firm relationships include agreements for some period about amount and type of products to buy (or sell), manufacturing series and reservation of production capacity, moments of delivery, inventories to be kept (and by whom). As a result both organizations benefit from a more stable supplier/buyer relation, reduced uncertainty and so reduced inventory levels (e.g., safety stocks), and improved delivery times. Tactical relationships lead to collaborative planning.

In a subsequent step companies develop relationships on a *strategic level*. They decide to act collaboratively in a specific market where they produce one (or more) specific products. The supplier, by way of specific expertise and skills, develops, designs, and produces specific components for the buying organization. These types of inter-firm collaborative relationships are called *Value Added Partnerships*. With Value Added Partnerships the stability in the relationships increases even further. The collaboration is built around complementarities of competences, and there is a high level of information sharing.

The interplay of operational, tactical and strategic inter-company relationships is shown in Figure 4.7 where it is implied that operational and tactical level processes will be embedded in strategic level relationships between companies. Companies that have a strategic relationship will also be engaged in tactical level planning processes and in operational level processes.

The development of business-to-business relationships outlined previously took place in the last 15 years of the former century. Today all the above types of e-Business relationships can be identified in almost every industry, which means that any company may be engaged in different relationships which are strategic, tactical, and operational. Now that e-Business relationships are included in regular business planning at different planning levels, other recent developments have been impacting the management of the supply chain.

First, there is the *extended scope from a dyadic approach to the full supply chain*. The management focus of e-Business relationships tended to be dyadic in nature: it concerned the relationship between one company and each of its direct suppliers. However, controlling and reducing supply chain costs, sharp reductions of delivery times, customizing products can only be achieved when adopting a full supply chain view. For example, in the car manufacturing industry, when a customer chooses a car (with all the add-ons he/she specifically wants) the order is forwarded to and processed directly by the manufacturing scheduling systems of all the companies in the chain.

Second, companies are constantly reconsidering their business models. Initially most organizations considered in principle keeping all product related activities in house. Today they consider concentrating on those activities that belong to their core competence. Other activities that are considered non-core are preferably procured from external suppliers. This phenomenon is also known as the unbundling of the value chain, (see Section 1.4).

Third, where in our discussion above almost all relationships concerned companies within the same supply chain, increasingly *cross-industry* (and *cross-supply-chain*) *relationships* are developing. Changing customer expectations are the trigger to this development: value propositions to customers need to be solution based (offering a solution to a specific customer problem) rather then product based. Solutions often require coordination of multiple services and products coming from different supply chains. For example, in the case of a customer ordering a car, he/she also needs a financial arrangement, an insurance policy, and if/she is an intensive traveller, easy hotel bookings. This topic is treated in some depth in Chapter 10, which is concerned with e-Business networks.

Fourth, sequential or linear relationships in a supply chain tend to evolve into *reciprocal relationships* between collaborating companies. The specific pattern of collaboration and the companies directly involved may depend on the (highly customized) customer order and will shift swiftly from one company to the other if a new order necessitates this. Supply chains tend to become dynamic value networks, or value Webs, which are stable as far as the 'members' of the network are concerned, but highly flexible as far as the order related collaboration is concerned.

As a result of an extended scope, changing business models, cross supply chain relationships, and dynamic reciprocal relationships modern supply chains are evolving into highly complex business networks (see Chapter 10).

4.3.2 Types of business relationships and information exchange
Different types of relationships – operational, tactical, or strategic – are characterized by differing exchanges of information.

An operational relationship typically concerns direct ordering of specific products or services. Usually quality requirements will be known (unless the order involves some customizing), a price has to be determined, and a delivery schedule has to be agreed upon. A purely operational relationship will start with a selection of the supplier, will incorporate an agreement and will end with the delivery of the order. The transaction can be characterized as *spot* buying and selling. The data exchanged will be typical order related (type, quality specifications, amount, price, delivery moment and location). The operational level of supply chain management is concerned with the very short term decisions made from day to day.

A tactical relationship before the operational stage has a phase of mutual planning, exchange of longer-term planning data, etc. Instead of hoarding this information, which typically would be the case in an operational relationship, there is a sharing of information and joint planning. Typically, procurement and manufacturing planning departments of both organizations will be involved. On the tactical level, medium-term decisions are made, such as weekly demand forecasts, distribution and transportation planning, production planning, and materials requirement planning.

A strategic relationship has a deeper impact on both organizations and may include collaboration between design and development departments, joint decision making on investments, market approach, and so on. After agreeing on type and design of products, tactical planning of necessary resources will follow, eventually leading to an operational relationship. On the strategic level, long-term decisions are made. These in the case of supply-chains are normally related to location, production, inventory, and transportation. Location decisions are concerned with the size, number, and geographic location of the supply chain entities, such as plants, inventories, or distribution centers. The production decisions are meant to determine which products to produce, where to produce them, which suppliers to use, from which plants to supply distribution centers, and so on. Inventory decisions are concerned with the way of managing inventories throughout the supply chain. Transport decisions are made on the modes of transport to use.

Decisions made on the strategic level are of course interrelated. For example decisions on mode of transport are influenced by decisions on geographical placement of plants and warehouses, and inventory policies are influenced by choice of suppliers and production locations. Business modeling and simulation (see

Chapter 12) are frequently used for analyzing these interrelations, and the impact of making strategic level changes in the supply chain.

With differences between types of e-Business relationships also, the technology solutions for supporting these will differ. Relationships, which are purely operational and so highly temporal, require a highly flexible support with little or no relation-specific investments. Tactical relationships, which will be longer term and may even last very long, are tighter, stable, and will justify investments in relation-specific technologies. The EDI solutions in the car manufacturing industry are a traditional example of this. In case of tactical relationships also, technology that supports collaborative planning (CSCW applications) may be implemented. In today's industries – both manufacturing and non-manufacturing – the demands on short delivery and throughput times are such that high requirements are placed on inter-company (and also intra-company) system to system connections. Straight-through processing is only possible with systems that operate seamlessly with each other. This is explained in Chapters 17, 18 and 19 where we describe how systems communicate and inter-work within and between organizations.

Finally, strategic relationships, with as expected the highest degree of stability, next to tactical applications, may include collaborative design platforms. The dynamic value networks, discussed previously, require a type of support, which allows for highly flexible relationships, which are also able to support straight-through processing within a given group of companies. Given the strategic nature of the partnerships, specific investments in technological solutions are to be expected.

4.3.3 Characteristics of e-Business relationships

Relationships in the industry value chain can be categorized as either e-Business or business-to-consumer e-Commerce. Both are quite different from each other and impact the e-Business technology that can be applied differently. In e-Business markets (see Chapter 8), purchasers try to optimize their internal supply chain efficiency by finding the right supplier(s) that are able to deliver the right products, of the right quality, at the right time, at the right place, and at an acceptable price. Buying decisions are the result of a multiphase process. In general, relationships between suppliers and (organizational) buyers are much more complex, long term, contractual, and involve a much larger amount of money [Philips 2000]. In the following sections, we discuss some characteristic differences between e-Business and business-to-consumer e-Commerce trends:

- Economic value per individual company, and per transaction: firms in different industries procure up to 50-60% of their revenues on procurement. The money value per order is high;

- Buying processes: whereas in business-to-consumer e-Commerce markets purchases may be impulse driven and spot transactions, e-Business orders involve many participants and are governed by complex business rules of the buyer and seller. E-Business buyers will compare multiple sources of supply to ensure availability at an acceptable price. Most purchases, after careful selection of a supplier, will be followed by a series of repeat buys;

- Products may be highly customer specific, requiring specific product development activities and tooling;

- Modern logistic concepts, which aim at avoiding inventories, require complex logistic planning;

- Buying expertise: Buyers in e-Business markets are well informed professionals. The complexity of the products, and the processes for which they are needed require often deep industry expertise;

- Pricing: in business-to-consumer e-Commerce markets buyers will often accept a fixed pricing structure. In e-Business markets different price discovery mechanisms exist: fixed price, negotiated prices, sealed bid systems, auctions;

- IT-infrastructure: companies have an IT infrastructure in place which is an impediment for a rapid deployment of new e-Business technology. Restructuring of systems and processes is expected to take years [Philips 2000].

The way that companies interact has led to the following three temporal relationships between companies:

1) A company can buy and sell on a 'spot'-market. This means that products and services are procured and sold *whereas the relationship with the supplier or the customer lasts as long as the transaction*. Although little or no internal information is exchanged, both parties will be very well informed about each other's reputation. Spot market transactions are typically found in markets for basic raw materials and agricultural products.
2) If a company has a regular need for specific products, a relationship may become *longer term*. In general there is a contract, specifying conditions and a delivery volume. Repeat orders are placed within the conditions set by the contract. Exchange of information will be needed for planning purposes.
3) Finally, the relationship may evolve into a *partnership*, where trading partners work together for the longer term and even pursue a joint competitive strategy in their industry. An extensive exchange of information will be the result.

Application of e-Business technology may contribute to increased efficiency in the buyer seller realtionship. In general, there exist three potential problems for which e-Business technology can provide solutions [Philips 2000]:

- Most interactions between businesses are complex and information intensive;

- Supply chains suffer from inefficiencies because of the inability to forecast the right products volumes and mixes;

- Markets are fragmented and lack transparancy.

Every order requires multiple actions at the buyer's side as at the seller's side before it can be completed. Such actions include approval, negotiation, scheduling delivery, backorder information, settlement. These actions are labor and information intensive, and if wrongly organized, lead to waste of resources. e-Business technology has the potential to streamline these activities through reengineering of business processes.

Lack of demand and supply information at various stages in the supply chain, results in uncertainty, which is translated into excess inventories and idle capacity. Each node in the supply chain wants to be prepared for the unexpected, and consequently will keep stocks and will have idle production capacity available. Sharing of information and collaboration, facilitated by e-Business technologies, can contribute to a more efficient supply chain.

Market transparency implies that participants have knowledge about the markets around them. Here we may distiguish four forms of transparency [Philips 2000]:

- Price transparency;

- Availability transparency;

- Supplier transparency;

- Product transparancy.

When market alternatives become transparent participants will change their behavior. Artificially high prices or unusually low quality gets isolated quickly and competitive alternatives eliminate them.

The Internet makes fast communication, irrespective of geographic location, possible at low cost. This potential of collecting and distributing all sorts of information is unprecented. Consequently, one may expect a dramatic improvement of transparency in those markets that are facilitated by the Internet [Philips 2000]. However, we think that the relative impact on the transparency of markets will be bigger in business-to-consumer e-Commerce markets than in e-Business markets. The reason for this is simply that those who operate in e-Business markets are professionals: people who spend a greater part of and possibly an entire career in conducting sales and purchasing operations in particular markets. These professionals are very well informed about suppliers, their product offerings, pricing etc. This is enforced by the fact that many industrial markets are olygopolies (a market with only a limited number of suppliers). Nothwithstanding the fact that, in e-Business markets also, the Internet is an efficient tool for collecting specific information efficiently and quickly. However, it will not have the same impact in terms of transparency improvements as for end consumers who surf the World Wide Web looking for interesting product offerings.

4.4 Electronic links and the value chain

Driven by the ability of information technology to produce cheaper unit costs for coordination, organizations are implementing, increasingly rapidly, new links for relating to each other. These links take many forms, such as electronic data integration, just-in-time manufacturing, electronic markets, strategic alliances, networked organizations, and others. The new links for relating organizations indicate an ongoing transformation of value chains due to technological change [Benjamin 1995].

Several authors examine the potential changes in business unit and industry value chains [Chandler 1979; Williamson 1981b]. Some authors note that every coordinative activity that improves organizational efficiency, speeds up the flow through the system, or permits a more intensive use of the factors of production is likely to improve the performance of the economic system [Chandler 1979]; while others point out that the modern corporation is to be understood as the product of a series of organizational innovations that have had the purpose and effect of economizing on transaction costs [Williamson 1981a]. What has been said about the corporation seems equally applicable to the industry value chain, where Porter notes that competitive advantage is increasingly a function of how well a company can manage this entire system [Porter 1990].

Within a given industry value chain, each business will search for transactions that will provide advantage over its competitors and competitive differentiation to explore the value chain's potentials.

Transportation of physical goods and information are required by e-Business. Transportation of goods requires a physical transportation infrastructure. Electronic links provide a transportation infrastructure for information. It is clear that electronic links make new distribution modes for products that consist of information possible, but they will also impact the distribution of physical products. Electronic links will impact [Benjamin 1995]:

- Producers of information, including computer software, books, movies and music. Using electronic channels these 'information products' can be sold, transported and delivered on demand at almost no (variable) cost;

- Producers of physical goods, including all manufactured goods. The impact of the Internet will not only relate directly to the support of sales processes, but is also expected to affect the level of possible customization of the products and services (see Chapter 5);

- Electronic retailers that use the Internet to offer, represent, and sell products;

- Physical and electronic markets (see Chapter 8);

- Physical distribution networks, which may be simplified by disintermediation effects leading to the movement of products from the manufacturer to the consumer directly, or coordinated by an electronic retailer;

- Access to buyers and sellers through electronic channels; cable providers, telephone, cellular and electric utility industries, all can provide access.

Case Study

Supply chain integration at Unitech

Information systems. Before 1997, the IT architecture of Unitech Taiwan consisted of separate systems for various business functions. Integration of the isolated systems took place in 1997. Web sites were created to prepare the company for e-Commerce and to satisfy the requirements of suppliers with regard to information sharing, online ordering, enquiring inventory status, etc. There were no strong linkages with systems of suppliers, because of the small order quantities, and limited order variation. It was expected that in 2003-2004 a new enterprise resource planning (ERP) system and related systems would be implemented, to fulfill internal and external requirements for more integration and coordination. In April 2002, Unitech contracted Oracle, Anderson Consulting, and a Taiwanese systems integrator to implement Oracle ERP, CRM, and Business Integration. A typical point is that Unitech did not adopt an industrial standard like Rosettanet because of the relatively small scale of the ADC supply chain.

There is no direct link between Unitech Europe and Taiwan; resulting problems still have to be resolved. For example, inventory control and customized demand of Unitech Europe cannot be automatically linked to Unitech Taiwan. Unitech Europe planned to install its ERP software in 2003, to improve internal efficiency and provide online order fulfilment services to regional par tners. Establishing the interfacing between the Unitech Europe ERP system with the Unitech Taiwan ERP system is planned for 2005.

Supply chain performance. Supply chain performance is based on the performance of individual companies and of the network. Unitech Taiwan increased sales from US$ 10 million in 1997 to US$ 24 million in 2002, and managed to reduce significantly labor costs and material cost, and so maintain a profit margin of over 35%. Work in progress improved from 53 days to 21 days. For Unitech Europe sales of ADC products increased from US$ 1.6 million in 1999 to US$ 4.5 million in 2002. The company ranked eighth as ADC vendor in Europe, thus meeting the objective in 1997 of being in the top 10 within five years. However, looking from a network perspective, in 2001 Unitech Europe suffered from unreliable lead-times from Unitech Taiwan factories, resulting in increased (downstream) inventory levels, from products with defects or not meeting the requirements (leading to recalls and higher management and service costs), and delays in time to market of new products.

4.5 Chapter summary

This chapter discusses characteristics of e-Business relationships and their relevance for the application of e-Business technology. The analysis is based on the concepts of the Value Chain, the Value Stream, the Industry Value Chain or Value System, and Business Process.

Value chain

A value chain usually describes a major line of business and encompasses two types of activities, primary activities and support activities. Primary activities describes the activities connecting a company's supply side (raw materials, inbound logistics, and production processes) with its demand side (outbound logistics, marketing, and sales). The value chain model provides managers with a tool to analyze and, if necessary, redesign their internal and external processes to improve efficiency and effectiveness. Value chain analysis includes four general steps:

- Defining the strategic business unit;

- Identifying critical activities;

- Defining products;

- Determining the value of an activity.

Competitive pressures force companies to reconsider their business model and, as a result, traditional business unit value chains become unbundled. Primary activities, like logistics, operations, and support activities, and parts of the firm's infrastructure (e.g., accounting, financial services, and human relations) get outsourced. Unbundling of the value chain contributes to more complex e-Business relationships.

Value stream

Value stream is closely related to the value chain. The value stream is the set of all the specific actions required to bring a specific product through the three critical management tasks of any business: problem-solving (running from concept to production launch); information management (from order-taking to delivery); and physical transformation (from raw materials to finished products delivered to the customer). Value stream analysis considers how the whole production and delivery process can be made more efficient. To conduct value stream analysis, companies map every activity that occurs in creating new products and delivering products or services to customers, and then categorize them as those that create value as perceived by the customer, those that create no value, and those that do not add value. The last two categories are eliminated.

Industry value chain or value system

Every business unit value chain is part of a larger industry value chain (also called the value system): a collection of individual business unit value chains that together produce and deliver the goods and services to the final customer. The value system is a model that helps a company to position itself relative to other companies. The value system specifies the suppliers and the immediate customers, and defines the sales channels of the given company. It allows understanding whether all the companies involved in the sales process can potentially collaborate or whether there are conflict of interests.

Business process

A business process consists of one or more related activities that together respond to a business requirement for action. A (business) process view implies an horizontal view on a business organization, and looks on processes as sets of interdependent activities designed and structured to produce a specific output for a customer or a market. A business process may receive events that alter the state of the process and the sequence of activities. A business process may produce events for input to other systems or processes.

Business processes can be specified by a number of characteristics. First, processes exist within an environment, which is both the internal business environment in which the process operates and the external organizational environment that can trigger the process. Second, every process has a customer and is initiated by a customer order. The customer may be external, like the final customer for whom a service or product is produced, or internal, like another process for which the output of the process under consideration forms an input. Third, every business process implies processing: a series of activities (processing steps) leading to some form of transformation of data or products for which the process exists. Fourth, communication is an important part of any business process. Communication will take place both within the process and with the environment. Fifth, workflows have inventories or queues; these are locations where steps in the workflow are waiting to be processed.

There are different types of business processes. First we distinguish between workflows where information processing supports a physical process, and workflows where information processing is the process itself. Next the structuring of workflows will differ depending on the degree of repetition and level of expertise or knowledge required to execute the process. A last characteristic concerns the level of anticipation of the stimulus that triggers the process.

IT and business processes have a recursive relationship. IT supports the process, and business processes are impacted by the capabilities that IT can offer. As for the latter (IT impacts the process) IT may be considered as a key enabler of Business Process Re-engineering. To a large extent the effect that IT may have on a process depends on the way that functions are orchestrated to accomplish the outcome of that process. For this purpose we may analyze a process along two dimensions: the degree of mediation and the degree of collaboration:

- The degree of mediation refers to the sequential flow of different functions involved in the process;

- The degree of collaboration indicates the extent of collaboration between functions involved in a particular process.

e-Business relationships

E-Business relationships in the supply chain have been changing in the past decades and become part of the company's longer-term planning processes. At first independence prevailed. A relationship lasted no longer than a single transaction. These types of e-Business relationships can be characterized as operational level relationships. Later e-Business relationships moved to the tactical level. Tactical inter-firm relationships include agreements for some period. In a subsequent step companies developed relationships on a strategic level. They decide to act collaboratively in a specific market where they produce one (or more) specific product(s).

Different types of relationships – operational, tactical, or strategic – are characterized by differing exchanges of information. An operational relationship typically concerns direct ordering of specific products or services. A tactical relationship before the operational stage has a phase of mutual planning, exchange of longer-term planning data, etc. A strategic relationship has a deeper impact on both organizations and may include collaboration between design and development departments, joint decision making on investments, market approach, and so on.

Discussion Questions

- Porter developed the concept of the value chain.

- Give a definition of the value chain.

- The value chain is composed of two different types of activities. Give a description and explain differences. Give examples of each type.

- By executing a value chain analysis a company can try to improve its value chain with the help of information systems. A value chain analysis is composed of five steps: describe and explain these five steps.

- What does business process management mean? Why is business process management important, especially in a dynamic environment?

- Describe how market conditions affect business processes, and the extent to which they can be automated.

- Davenport analyses how IT can impact business processes. Discuss and explain these effects.

- What does business process reengineering mean? Which situation in Figure 4.6 would be most interesting from a BPR point of view, which the least interesting? Explain why.

Assignments

i. To enhance his or her business performance, a bank's manager is asking you for help to analyze the value chains in his or her company:

a) Give three examples of a value chain in a bank.
b) One of the objectives of a business unit value chain analysis is to understand how information systems can help a firm to have a better competitive position. Can you give an example of how this analysis can help the bank?

ii. Imagine some company has hired you as a consultant. This company wants to reduce its costs of coordination by implementing various forms of IT. One way to do this is by automating relationships with suppliers and customers. Give an explanation of how e-Business technologies could be implemented to achieve this goal.

iii. Give examples of specific forms of IT and their applicability in specific types of inter-company relations. List possible advantages and disadvantages the company could experience from the application of IT in these relations.

Chapter 5

Governance Structures

Governance is about the organization of transactions and so about inter-organizational relationships. A *governance structure* describes the organizational form, rules, and institutions that structure a certain value exchange. In particular it specifies which parties are involved in a transaction, and which coordination mechanisms are used.

The use of the Internet and related technologies in the coordination of value exchanges impacts the inter-organizational relationships. The Internet provides inexpensive connections for anyone to anyone independent of location, 24 hours a day. As a result, coordination costs are expected to go down, which will affect the choice of the optimal governance structure for a particular value exchange.

This chapter addresses the issue of how advances in information technology and management are affecting organization and market structures. In particular, it explains the 'dichotomy' between market and hierarchy governance and analyzes this topic from two perspectives: transaction cost economics and the resource based view. The chapter introduces a third approach to handling transactions besides market and hierarchy: networks. It discusses the consequences of wide application of information technology on choices in governance and pays particular attention to the 'electronic market hypothesis' and the 'the move to the middle hypothesis'.

5.1 Markets vs. hierarchies: theoretical contributions

Generally speaking economies have two basic mechanisms for coordinating the flow of products and services: markets and hierarchies. On *markets* supply and demand forces regulate the external transactions of material and immaterial goods between individuals and companies, determining design, price, quantity and delivery schedules. Buyers compare the many potential sources and make a choice on the basis of the best combination of these attributes. Suppliers choose their buyers on the basis of the best offer they can get. In the theoretical extreme case of atomic competition there are no relations between buyers and sellers, or among buyers, or among sellers. The relation between a buyer and seller only exists for the duration of a particular transaction.

In *hierarchies*, on the other hand, it is assumed that products and services are produced by the organization that needs them. Production, availability, and delivery are controlled and directed by managerial decisions. It is the higher management strata, rather than market forces, that determine the transaction characteristics. Suppliers are not selected from a group; in fact there is simply only one predetermined supplier, which is the own organization.

Next to market and hierarchies, a third way of coordinating the flow of goods and services has emerged: *network* (see Section 5.2). Networks can be differentiated from pure markets. Coordination with respect to value exchanges in networks is achieved through joint planning and longer-term agreements. Networks can also be differentiated from pure hierarchies. The network consists of legally and economically independent organizations that have agreed to give up, in principle temporarily, their autonomy with respect to a particular value exchange. To what extent autonomy has been given up will differ. Some organizations may be very tightly coupled to each other, some very loosely.

In free market economies one can observe two basic mechanisms for coordinating the flow of materials and services through adjacent steps in the value chain: markets and hierarchies [Malone 1987]. With *markets*, supply and demand forces regulate the external transactions of material and immaterial goods between individuals and companies, determining design, price, quantity, and delivery schedules. Buyers compare the many potential sources and make a choice on the basis of the best combination of these attributes. With *hierarchies*, on the other hand, the flow of products and services is controlled and directed by managerial decisions. It is the higher management strata, rather than market forces, that determine the transaction characteristics. Suppliers are not selected from a group; buyers simply work with a single predetermined supplier. In many cases the hierarchy is simply a firm, while in others it may span two legally separate firms in a close, perhaps electronically mediated, sole supplier relationship. Real-time information exchange, shared data formats and agreed-upon workflows, inevitably increases the degree of cross-business process integration between firms, moving towards electronic hierarchies or private trading networks [Malone 1987]. Moreover, when inter-organizational integration increases further, *trust* between business partners will become a big concern because a significant amount of proprietary and strategic information is shared. Trust deals with the belief, or willingness to believe, that one can rely on the goodness, strength, and ability of somebody (the seller and the buyer), or something (for example, IT innovations). Trust is the expectation that arises within a community of regular, honest, and cooperative behavior, based on commonly shared norms, on the part of other members of that community [Fukuyama 1995].

If market governance is applied, the execution of a value activity is outsourced to another party. Based on the forces of supply and demand, a supplier is chosen that delivers the best combination of design, price, quality, and availability. Co-ordination of market governance mainly exists on acquiring information on aspects regarding design, price, quality, and availability from different sources, listing needs, and selecting a supplier that fits this needs best, for each transaction. If hierarchy governance is applied, the execution of a value activity is then done internally, by the firm itself. Design, price, quality, and availability are not determined by forces of supply and demand, but by managerial decisions. Coordination of hierarchical governance mainly exists on managing the value activity in a way that its outcome fits the requirements of the firm as well as possible.

Firms make decisions on organizational design based on various factors, including which investments have to be made specific to the mechanism for coordinating the flow of materials and services chosen (asset specificity), which activity is critical for effective business performance of the firm, uncertainty in the relationship with partners, and product complexity. Investments specific to the mechanism chosen have as their aim to lock in the supplier and increase the costs of switching to another customer. Demand uncertainty may force a firm to develop a closer relationship with its supplier to better meet market requirements, or alternatively to develop standardized products and have extra inventory to counter the uncertainty.

5.1.1 The transaction cost perspective

In *transaction cost economics*, the fundamental unit of analysis is the transaction. Transactions are the exchanges of goods and services between economic actors inside or outside the organization [Williamson 1983], and take place across markets or within hierarchies. Companies trading products and services incur many different kinds of costs. *Production costs* include the physical or other primary processes necessary to create and distribute the goods or services being produced. *Transaction costs*, also called *coordination costs* [Malone 1987], include the transaction (or governance) costs of all the information processing necessary to coordinate the work of people and machines that perform the primary processes. For example, coordination costs include determining the design, price, quantity, delivery schedule, and similar factors for products transferred between adjacent steps on a value chain. Economic theory and actual market behavior assert that firms will choose transactions that economize on coordination costs.

In transaction cost economics theory, a market transaction simply means that a product is purchased outside the organizational boundaries. The opposite of a market transaction is a hierarchy. It is important to note that the organizational boundaries might be different from the legal firm boundaries. Hierarchy and market are a continuum, so it is necessary to establish exactly what a hierarchy is, to understand what a market is. The defining characteristic of a hierarchy is that, 'hierarchy is its own court of ultimate appeal and the implicit contract law of internal organization is that of forbearance'. [Williamson 1991].

As information technology continues its rapid cost performance improvement, firms will continue to find incentives to coordinate their activities electronically. Coordination costs include the transaction (or governance) costs of all the information processing necessary to coordinate the work of people and computing infrastructure that perform the primary processes. For example, coordination costs include determining the design, price, quantity, delivery schedule, and other similar factors for products transferred between adjacent steps on a value-added chain. Often, coordination takes the form of single-source electronic sales channels (one supplier and many purchasers coordinated through hierarchical transactions) or electronic markets. In markets, this involves selecting suppliers, negotiating contracts, paying bills, and so forth. In hierarchies, this involves managerial decision making, accounting, planning, and control processes.

Electronic markets are more efficient forms of coordination for certain classes of product transactions. Utilizing cheap coordinative transactions, interconnected networks and easily accessible information sources, economic theory predicts that a proportional shift of economic activity from single-source sales channels to electronic markets is likely to occur, as lower coordination costs favor electronic markets. In a market the buyer can compare different possible suppliers and select the one that provides the best combination of characteristics (such as design and price). This results in minimizing production costs for the desired product. One of the obvious benefits of this arrangement is that it allows for pooling the demands of numerous buyers to take advantage of economies of scale and load leveling [Malone 1987]. Trading via markets is, however, expensive because companies face the costs of selecting suppliers, negotiating contracts and administrating payments. Since hierarchies, on the other hand, restrict the procurer's choice of suppliers to one predetermined supplier, production costs are, in general, higher than in the market arrangement. The hierarchical arrangement, however, reduces coordination costs over those incurred in a market by eliminating the buyer's need to gather and analyze a great deal of information about different suppliers. The choice between market and hierarchy procurement influences production and transaction costs differently. Since markets allow buyers to compare the offers of many potential suppliers, sellers are forced to keep their production costs low. But the selection and negotiation process may cost quite a lot of money. Hierarchies, who do business with just one preferred supplier, keep their transaction costs down. On the other hand, their suppliers have little incentive to decrease their production costs, and so these remain relatively high.

In transaction costs economics, the choice for any one way of procuring goods and services is a matter of cost minimization. Transaction costs theory proposes that firms have tried to reduce transaction costs by getting bigger, because they can conduct their internal transactions more efficiently, than transactions with external suppliers. With regard to transaction costs, several aspects of the transactions involved play a vital role here: asset specificity, product complexity and transaction frequency. Also human behavior relating to the transaction is important [Williamson 1975], in particular bounded rationality and opportunism, which we will discuss in the next sections.

5.1.2 Transaction aspects: asset specificity, product complexity, and frequency

Three transaction aspects influence whether a transaction will be carried out in a market or in a hierarchy: asset specificity, product complexity [Malone 1987; Williamson 1991], and transaction frequency [Choudhury 1998].

The *asset specificity* of a transaction refers to the degree to which it is supported by assets that are specific to this transaction alone, and which cannot be used otherwise or elsewhere without incurring a significant reduction of value. If, for example, a power station is located close to a coalmine to minimize transport and inventory costs, then the unlikeliness of these fixed assets being easily moved elsewhere is called *site specificity*. Likewise, *physical asset specificity* occurs when one or both parties invest in equipment that can only be used for this transaction, and that has a low value for alternative uses. *Human capital specificity* refers to employees developing skills that are specific to a particular buyer or customer relation [Douma 1998]. An additional type of asset specificity, *time specificity*, occurs if the value of the product or service depends on its reaching the user within a limited period of time [Malone 1987]. This is the case for perishable products such as cut flowers, or for raw materials needed to prevent manufacturing processes halting at great cost.

Highly specific assets are more likely to be acquired through hierarchical coordination than through a market process. There are several reasons for this. Transactions involving asset specific products often involve long processes of development and adjustment for the supplier to meet the needs of the buyer. Such a process is favored by the continuity of relationships found in a hierarchy. Also, since there are few alternative buyers or suppliers of such highly specific products, both parties are vulnerable. The higher level of control and coordination offered by hierarchies is therefore preferred. For less specific products and services, markets are more appropriate.

Product complexity too plays a role in choosing between hierarchy and market. This is easily understood. Stocks and commodities are simple and standardized; buyers need to know little but their price. They are therefore likely to prefer markets in order to compare the offers of many potential suppliers. Buyers selecting complex products, on the other hand, need much more information. The extra information exchange involved increases the transaction costs. They are, therefore, more likely to work with single suppliers in close, hierarchical relationships.

Finally, setting up specialized governance structures, such as hierarchies employ for their transactions, involves significant expenditures. These costs are only recovered if the transaction volume or *frequency of transactions* is high enough. Hence, low transaction frequencies point to market procurement, high frequencies to acquisition via hierarchies [Douma 1998].

5.1.3 Behavioral assumptions: bounded rationality and opportunism

Bounded rationality is a term used to indicate that the capacity of human beings to formulate and solve complex problems is limited. Decision makers try to optimize the benefit to their outcome, but they do not always succeed. Here, one can draw parallels with the game of chess [Douma 1998]. Chess players have all the information they need for their decisions: the positions of the white and black pieces at the moment a move must be made. However, the total number of alternative sequences of moves and countermoves is too big even for the world's best chess players to think them all through. You may want to make rational decisions, but your capacity to evaluate the consequences of all decisions is limited. The idea of bounded rationality, then, refers to human behavior that is intended to be rational, but in effect is so only to a limited degree.

The limits to human rational capacity present a problem in environments that are characterized by *uncertainty* and/or *complexity*. For example, consider a government that wishes to purchase a new generation fighter plane. Drawing up the contract required is very complicated because it involves defining all product specifications; and there is much uncertainty because the technology to be used may still be in its developmental stage. This means that the costs of the new fighter plane are unknown as well. In such circumstances even drawing up the contract will be expensive. Thus, bounded rationality in conjunction with uncertainty and/or complexity is likely to increase the transaction costs involved.

Human beings not only have a limited capacity for rationality, they also sometimes display opportunistic behavior. *Opportunism* can be described as 'self-interest seeking with guile' and as making 'self-disbelieved statements' [Williamson 1975]. In other words, opportunism is trying to exploit a situation to one's own advantage. This does not mean that everybody behaves opportunistically. But it has to be assumed that some people might do so sometimes, and that it is impossible or difficult (and therefore costly) to distinguish the honest from the dishonest. Suppose you want to buy a second-hand car. You have a choice between cars A and B. You do not see any difference, but car A has been inspected by an independent expert who tells you it has no defects, while in the case of car B you can only take the seller's word for it. Many buyers will prefer car A, even if the inspection has made it a little more expensive. Not that they believe the other seller is lying; they just cannot rule out that possibility and prefer not to take any chances. Therefore, when conducting business, some money is often spent – on contracts, inspections, and the like – just because some people might sometimes behave opportunistically. Now consider a situation in which large numbers of second-hand car sellers and buyers trade with each other on a regular basis.

Buyers who have negative experience with one of the sellers will simply never buy from him or her again but take their business elsewhere. In such a market there is no need for extra inspections, complicated contracts, etc. Opportunism, then, is a problem only if it occurs in conjunction with small numbers of trading partners who do not worry about their reputations because there is no alternative. This is called *small numbers exchange*. It is under circumstances involving the possibility of opportunism and small numbers exchange that transaction costs are likely to increase.

5.1.4 The resource-based perspective

A key to successful IT performance is the optimal investment, use and allocation of IT resources (people, applications, technology, facilities, data) in servicing the needs of the enterprise. Most enterprises fail to maximize the efficiency of their IT assets and optimize the costs relating to these assets. In addition, the biggest challenge in recent years has been to know where and how to outsource, and then to know how to manage the outsourced services in a way that delivers the values promised at an acceptable price.

According to the *resource-based view*, which we covered in some detail in Section 2.7.2, any competitive advantage is based on the possession of certain assets; the extent to which this competitive advantage is sustainable depends on how difficult or costly it is for other companies to obtain the same assets. Sustained competitive advantages derive from resources and capabilities that are valuable, rare, imperfectly imitable, and not substitutable [Barney 2001]. In this framework, resources are defined very broadly, including financial resources, tangible resources (plants, equipment, buildings), and intangible resources (patents, tacit knowledge, brand names, experience, management skills, organizational routines). Some such assets are easily bought and sold on markets. This is true for most financial assets such as marketable securities. Other resources are much more difficult to buy and sell, such as management skills. The resource-based view has a particular impact when one considering networked business models. According to this view outsourcing of particular processes is only an option for those processes that do not belong to the unique core competence of the firm.

The properties a resource must have to satisfy on the basis of a sustainable competitive advantage are as follows [Douma 1998]:

The asset must be difficult to buy. For example, generally, intangible assets such as skills and experience are more difficult to acquire than tangible resources such as equipment. Intangible assets may in turn be subdivided into those with property rights which are well defined (patents, brand names, copyrights) and therefore relatively easily sold and bought, and those whose property rights are ill defined (know-how not protected by patents, organizational routines, management skills, senior management experience). Trading unprotected information is difficult because its value can only be revealed by disclosure, which destroys that value. Interestingly, it is just such unprotected information that can be the basis of a sustainable competitive advantage. Obtaining protection involves (partial) disclosure, after which others may obtain licenses in return for royalties, and then the advantage is no longer sustainable;

The resource must be difficult to replicate. Competitors can copy some resources, such as point-of-sale systems for retailers, fairly easily. On the other hand, highly complex organizational routines are much more difficult to replicate;

It must be difficult to substitute the resource by another asset. For example, pipelines and tankers can both be used to transport oil. Thus, the possession of a pipeline will only offer a sustainable competitive advantage if using tankers is impossible or much more expensive;

Finally, the advantage the resource may yield must not have been competed away by ex-ante competition. Consider a government granting a radio frequency concession for mobile telecommunication services. Surely, this concession is valuable. If, however, the government has allocated it through an auction, the government will have cashed much of this value.

In Chapter 3 we discussed business models, in particular the recently developing Internet- based networked business models. From the foregoing discussion we may conclude that what constitutes a 'right' business model for a specific business venture will depend on a number of factors:

- From the transaction perspective we learn that low transaction costs may contribute to outsourcing specific activities. Reduced transaction costs, e.g. through the effects of Internet technology, may lead to outsourcing and thus reduced size of organizations.

- The resource-based view, stresses that the basis for a sustainable competitive position of the firm is formed by the competencies and the capabilities that it has developed. Competences and resources that are unique and considered core should form an integral part of the business model of any business venture (if a business venture does not have those, the question is how long it will survive). Activities that are considered non-core may be candidates for outsourcing.

5.2 Networks

For some time, increased emphasis has been placed on networks. This development is considered a reaction to the narrow perspective of the original markets-and-hierarchies framework, which seems to suggest that the only choice is between market or horizontal coordination and hierarchical or vertical coordination. New organizational forms are emerging, where independent organizations engage in longer-term relationships. These relationships bear the characteristics of markets: the participants are independent, transactions are governed by contracts in which prices have been agreed, and the participants are able to put an end to the relationship. However, these relationships also bear the characteristics of hierarchies. Multiple coordination mechanisms are applied to improve the efficiency and effectiveness of the transactions. In addition, critical, even confidential, information is shared, participants are engaged in collaborative processes, and coordination occurs through mutual adjustment. The emerging organizational form is called the network organization, made up of more or less equal members who have formal and informal relationships with one another. *Inter-company networks* (or simply *networks*) are complex arrays of relationships between companies, which establish these relationships by interacting with each other [Jarillo 1988]. The basis of these relationships is trust [Douma 1998]. The companies' interactions imply making investments to build their mutual relationships, thus consolidating the network; caring for the company's relationships becomes a management priority. Competing is a matter of positioning one's company in the network rather than of attacking the environment.

In Chapter 4 we distinguished between three types of e-Business relationships: operational, tactical, and strategic. Typical of tactical and strategic types of relationships is an increased commitment to each other. The relation on an operational level exists for the duration of a single order; on a tactical level it may have the scope of a year or longer (e.g., needing a sharing of planning information). Managers or entrepreneurs can use networks to move their companies into stronger competitive positions. That is why these are called *strategic* networks: long-term, purposeful arrangements among distinct but related profit-oriented organizations that allow their participants to gain or sustain competitive advantages over their competitors outside the network [Jarillo 1988]. The participating companies remain independent in that they do not depend on each other completely; but their relationships are essential to their competitive position. Networks are a mode of organization that is neither based strictly on the price mechanism nor on hierarchical decision-making, but on coordination through adaptation. An essential component of the strategic network concept is the *hub company* (or *server company* [Hinterhuber 1994]): the company that sets up the network and actively takes care of it.

Stability of inter-company networks presupposes that the long-term gain to be accrued from participating is considered superior to that obtained by going it alone [Jarillo 1988]. This can be achieved only if two conditions are met: participation must result in a superior performance and the network's sharing mechanisms must be fair. Therefore, trust is important. Lack of trust (a reaction to the possibility of opportunism) has been defined as the essential cause of transaction costs [Williamson 1981b]. Thus, being able to generate trust is the fundamental entrepreneurial skill. Trust is needed to lower those costs and render the network economically feasible. It also contributes to efficient problem solving: if the decision-makers feel no need to protect themselves from the others' opportunistic behavior, information is exchanged freely and more solutions are explored. For such trust to develop, the emphasis on long-term relationships is essential because this shows that the relationships themselves are considered valuable.

The thrust of the previous discussion is that the activities necessary to produce a good or service can be carried out either by an integrated company or by a network of companies. However, if an arrangement is found in which companies keep to themselves those activities in which they have a comparative advantage while outsourcing other activities to the most efficient supplier, and if they manage to lower transaction costs, then a superior mode of organization emerges: the strategic network. Strategic networks share some characteristics with markets and some with hierarchies. They are economically feasible because their participants' specialization lowers the final total costs. They are sustainable because long-term relationships generate trust and thus lower transaction costs. Sharing fairness achieves added value, and problems are easily solved, because there is trust and because the relationships themselves are valued.

According to another perspective of strategic networks, the organization of international business has moved from an uncontrolled chaos of atomic competition to diversified conglomerates, and then on to focused business units [Hinterhuber 1994]. Nowadays, the most successful organizations are moving on again, reorganizing themselves into collections of units each with its own *core competence*. Thus, networks of strategically structured business cells are created. A similar movement can be observed among smaller companies. They naturally focus on their own specific competence and are building strategic networks with each other. Time is of overwhelming strategic importance for such initiatives [Hinterhuber 1994]. When facing increasing dynamics and uncertainty in their environment, what becomes critical for organizations is how fast they are able to react with an adequate response. Rethinking established business processes, and rebuilding one's organization in the form of smaller units with clear goals and benchmarks, can achieve a time advantage. These units must be free to operate with a large degree of independence, and they must be linked with each other to form a flexible network. Unlike the Strategic Business Units of the past, these entities are focused on their specific core competence, and a collection of them forms the strategic structure of the company or an industrial cluster.

Naturally, neither the fact that companies outsource some activities nor the development of focus and the creation of strategic business units is a new phenomenon in itself. What is interesting, though, is that is has become clear that only an extremely focused unit functioning in a network more or less loosely coordinated by a *server company* can be quick and flexible enough to survive and prosper. An intelligently set up network of small or medium-sized companies may very well be superior to a large competitor for several reasons, including the following:

- Each participant stays small and thus remains lean, fast and flexible;

- The network is large and thus offers economies of scale like those of a large company;

- The ability to correct, adjust, and change the network constantly keeps it superior in the long term;

- Building from small components is much easier than breaking up a large whole into small units.

5.3 A supply chain perspective: value-adding partnerships

Value-adding partnerships are sets of independent companies that work closely together to manage the flow of goods and services along their entire value chain [Johnston 1988]. It is this focus on the value chain that distinguishes value-adding partnerships from strategic networks. Most historians agree that the development of cheap centralized power and efficient but costly production machinery tipped the scales of competitive advantage in favor of large companies that could achieve economies of scale. Today, however, low-cost computing and communication technology seem to be tipping them back in favor of partnerships of smaller companies, each of which performs one part of the value chain and coordinates its activities with the rest of the chain. Such value-adding partnerships are not necessarily technology driven, though. They may emerge as the result of computerized links between companies, but they may also exist before such links have been made. What they depend on is the attitudes and practices of the participating managers. Computers simply make it easier to communicate, share information, and respond quickly to shifts in demand.

A case study may serve as an example to highlight aspects of value-adding partnerships [Johnston 1988]. McKesson Corporation used to be a conventional distributor of drugs, healthcare products and other consumer goods. It always found itself squeezed by vertically integrated chain stores. Then using innovative information technology to improve customer service and cut order-entry costs, it transformed itself into the hub company of a large value-adding partnership that can hold its own against the chains. McKesson's managers began with an order entry system at one of its warehouses. This dramatically cut the costs of order processing by expediting the steps in checking inventory, and calling in, recording, and eventually packing and shipping orders. The system also specifies how orders should be packed to match the arrangement of the customers' shelves, which improves the efficiency of their restocking processes. McKesson soon realized that the data gathered could be processed in order to help customers set prices and design store layouts, to perform accounting services, and to warn consumers of potentially harmful drug combinations by tracking prescription histories. McKesson thus offered independent drugstores the many advantages of automated services via computerized systems that no store could afford by itself. Nevertheless, the drugstores maintained their autonomy so they could be responsive to the needs of their local communities. The next step was selling up-to-date sales information to McKesson's suppliers, for whose consumer goods product managers such information proved to be of immense value. They use it to improve the timing of their shipments to McKesson in much the same way McKesson uses it for its shipments to the drugstores. It also enables them to plan their production more efficiently and to streamline their inventories. Another McKesson innovation is to use its computerized system to help process insurance claim applications for prescription compensation, thus strengthening the ties among insurance companies. As a result, McKesson's network includes the entire value chain, from manufacturers through distributors and retailers to consumers, and even including third-party insurance suppliers.

5.4 The effects of information technology on governance

Recent advances in computing and communications technology have affected the costs of coordination, so have had a dramatic impact on the risks associated with inter-company coordination. This has changed the balance between markets and hierarchies, contributing to the rise of new strategies and structures, for individual companies and entire industries [Clemons 1993; Gurbaxani 1991].

5.4.1 The electronic market hypothesis

By bringing buyers and sellers together online, electronic markets play the role of digital intermediaries, for instance, they aggregate and disseminate demand and supply information thus matching buyers and sellers. To achieve this, markets aggregate suppliers' product offerings, and help buyers search for desired products and discover attractive prices. After buyers and sellers agree on a deal, facilitating mechanisms for transaction settlement also can be provided so that logistics and payment can be arranged. Moreover, industry-specific expertise is an important capability that electronic market intermediaries are able to leverage. When the business process or the product selection procedure is complex, expert advice can save buyer time and effort spent on purchasing. Both market facilitation and expert services become integral parts of the offerings associated with the new electronic market business models leveraging the Web [Dai 2002].

Information technology is leveraged to perform the above and other essential market functions more efficiently and effectively. More than a decade ago, Malone, Yates and Benjamin [Malone 1987] formulated the *electronic market hypothesis*, and offered the prediction that electronic markets would become the favored mechanisms for coordinating material and information flows among organizations in the presence of electronic communication technologies. The basic argument is that IT reduces the coordination costs between firms involved in supplier selection, price discovery, delivery scheduling and other activities associated with business transactions, enabling buyers to compare purchase alternatives at lower search costs, and to transact with business partners more efficiently. [Malone 1987]. This leads to an overall shift toward proportionately more use of markets – rather than hierarchies – to coordinate economic activity [Malone 1987]. This development was expected because information technology would lessen the importance of asset specificity and product complexity (traditionally elements pointing in the direction of hierarchies) and because it would make *electronic communication*, *brokerage* and *integration* a realistic possibility. We can also observe that within a value chain any of its participants might be the initiator or market maker of its electronic market, from the producer to the procurer, plus any intermediary such as financial service providers, distributors, and IT vendors. Since both buyers and sellers should benefit from electronic market development, all should be prepared to pay the market maker for his or her services.

We have seen in Section 5.1.2 that high asset specificity and product complexity increase transaction costs. Thus, hierarchies would be better equipped to organize the flow of goods and services under these circumstances, since they lower those expenditures. But information technology significantly decreases the costs of the coordination needed in situations of high asset specificity. For example, in the case of Computer Aided Manufacturing (CAM) production, technology can easily be reconfigured to match changing manufacturing requirements. Information technology also allows the effective and efficient transfer and handling of very complex product information, making product complexity much less of a difficulty. (What used to be highly complex relative to handling capacity is now handled quite easily.) With the introduction of Internet-based electronic markets, it has become much quicker and more convenient for buyers to screen suppliers and product offers using the *electronic communication* and information sharing capabilities of the World Wide Web [Berghel 2000]. Thus, with the focus shifting back from transaction costs to production costs, markets are increasingly attractive as a means of organizing economic activity.

Electronic communication basically is to the advantage of both markets and hierarchies; both benefit if communication costs decrease. But *electronic brokerage*, in which buyers and suppliers are electronically connected, works rather more to the advantage of markets. The need for expensive intermediaries is removed because the electronic market makes it so much easier to compare the offers of many potential suppliers. And by increasing the number of alternatives, the quality of the option eventually selected is improved too. The electronic brokerage effect is a basis for the so-called 'Threatened Intermediary Hypothesis', which will be discussed in Chapter 11. *Electronic integration* goes one step further. Suppliers and procurers use information technology to create joint, interpenetrating processes between them, thus tightening their cooperation. Time is saved and errors are avoided – this can be attested by the wide use of CAD/CAM and Just in Time (JIT) systems. Again, coordination is made easier and more reliable, and transaction costs are lowered (see Section 5.3). Many reasons to organize the economic process into hierarchies are removed.

According to the electronic market hypothesis, the development that electronic markets are expected to go through would involve a complete change in the way the value chain's activities are carried out [Malone 1987]. The first electronic markets are expected to be *biased markets*: markets that favor certain buyers or sellers. Competitive or legal forces would then make these biased markets reduce or remove their bias. They would then become *unbiased markets*, open to all parties but favoring none. Such unbiased markets, however, would overwhelm their buyers with the alternatives offered. There would simply be too many offers for most buyers to be able to make a rational selection. So the markets would develop personalized decision aids, leading to the emergence of *personalized markets*.

Several researchers have tested the validity of the electronic market hypothesis. It is worth noting the position of Daniel and Klimis [Daniel 1999] who consider it essentially valid. They investigated the financial services and the music industries, and indeed found evidence for a reduction of the importance of asset specificity and product complexity due to the use of information technology in retail. They expect that the impact of the shift from hierarchies to markets will be so great it will totally disrupt the conventional practices in many value chain activities. For the two industries they researched, they propose three modifications to electronic market hypothesis:

1) In the financial services industry, the need for confidence between suppliers and buyers will lead to the emergence of *regionalized personalized markets*. Buyers probably won't want to deposit savings with suppliers who are located far away and whose credibility is consequently unknown. Laws and regulations will

contribute to keeping this industry regionalized as well. Other industries in which trust and regulations are important will probably develop in a similar way.

2) In the music industry, on the other hand, trust and regulation are not so relevant. Also the industry is dominated by a few large global players. Therefore, for music and other such low-risk products and services, truly *global personalized markets* are expected to evolve.

3) Finally, market power – currently on the suppliers' side – will increasingly move to the buyers. Online services will give them access to more information. And, very important, electronic chat-areas and bulletin boards will bring them into contact with other consumers so that they can learn from each other's experience. This shift will eventually cause the rise of *reverse markets*: buyers publish their requirements for goods and services through the electronic market medium; suppliers must then bid to win their business, either by virtue of their prices or because of their product and service features.

5.4.2 The move-to-the-middle hypothesis

Although information technology enables firms to do business with more sellers, researchers have found that inter-organizational information systems (see Sections 5.3.3 and 10.3.3) do not necessarily create unbiased electronic markets where firms source their procurement from a lot of participants in the markets. For instance, a study conducted in the home mortgage industry showed that computerized loan origination systems failed to develop into electronic markets as predicted by the electronic markets hypothesis [Hess 1994]. Among a variety of possible reasons, one explanation is the need for a limited number of suppliers to maintain suppliers' incentives to participate in a trading network. Accordingly, numerous authors have independently suggested alternative views on how information technology will affect market structures. In particular, they argue that the introduction of information technology may result in fewer, rather than more, suppliers, despite the reduction in transaction costs [Hess 1994].

When considering the impact information technology will have on the organization of economic activity it is expected that industrial restructuring will be characterized by a *move-to-the-middle hypothesis* (MMH) [Clemons 1993]. More specifically, the move-to-the-middle hypothesis that was proposed by Clemons, Redi, and Raw suggests that:

1) There will be a greater degree of outsourcing: as IT increases information availability and processing capacity, coordination costs, operations risk, and opportunism risk are all reduced. The results are a reduced need for ownership and more outsourcing due to lower transaction costs (that is, a move away from ownership and vertical integration). However, reducing the transaction costs will lead to more explicit coordination, which generates highly integrated inter-organizational relationships involving significant investment in human relationships and organizational processes.

2) Companies will favor developing long-term value-adding partnerships with a small group of suppliers: companies will rely on fewer suppliers than before, with whom they will have close and long-term relationships and with whom they will cooperate and coordinate closely (that is, when outsourcing they move away from the market in the direction of intermediate governance structures – a kind of 'middle' position).

There are several factors that need to be examined in the context of the two hypotheses listed above. In line with transaction cost theory, first consider the total costs companies will want to minimize to be the sum of their production costs and their transaction costs. Subsequently, break down transaction costs into coordination costs, operations risk costs, and opportunism risk costs. *Coordination costs* are the expenditures made for coordinating production units; both in terms of machines and people. These costs include the costs of exchanging product information such as characteristics, prices, availability, and demand. *Operations risk costs* are made to cover the risk that other parties in the transaction might intentionally misrepresent a situation, withhold information, or under-perform in connection with agreed-upon responsibilities. These costs originate from the differences in objectives between the parties and are sustained by any information asymmetry between them. *Opportunism risk costs* are the consequence of a lack of bargaining power, or the loss of it, as a direct result of the execution of a relationship. Curiously, while the economics literature has often focused on the risk of opportunism, and while the information technology community has spent much effort on reducing coordination costs, operations risk costs are a subject rarely made explicit even though they are not covered by either of the other cost categories.

The first hypothesis (information technology will increase the degree of outsourcing) raises the question of how to determine whether the production of goods or services should be outsourced. The costs of in-house production normally balance the costs of outside procurement. Outside procurement generates a product cost advantage, but it increases the operations and opportunism risk costs. In-house production reduces operations and opportunism risk costs, but raises the product costs. It is, however, expected that information technology will reduce the sum total of coordination, operations risk, and opportunism risk costs due to the following reasons:

- Information technology reduces the unit costs of communicating and of handling information, thus resulting in significant reductions of the costs of coordination;

- Information technology increases both the availability of and the processing capacity for information, thus allowing a reduction of the operations risk costs by improving both parties' monitoring of the activities;

- Information technology investments are less relationship-specific than traditional investments in coordination, such as manufacturing equipment and dedicated staff, so the opportunism risk costs are reduced.

The second hypothesis consists of two elements: there will be fewer suppliers because of the use of information technology, and relationships with them will be long term and close. Having fewer suppliers is attractive for three reasons:

1) Outsourcing involves significant fixed investments in human relationships and business processes; these are more easily recovered by the economies of scale inherent in having only a small number of suppliers.
2) If a company buys specific commodities from a limited set of suppliers, the latter will recover their investments more quickly because they have a greater share of the business. This serves as an incentive for them to invest in services beyond the specifics of the contract, such as electronic data interchange systems, which are to the advantage of the buying company.
3) Suppliers are not evaluated on the basis of their prices only, but on lead times, flexibility, reliability, innovation, and value-added services as well; since these service characteristics are more difficult to specify, having to compare the offers of a large number of suppliers is difficult and thus expensive.

The prediction that information technology will lead to the development of long-term, close relationships between buyers and sellers is based on three arguments as well:

- Long-term relationships allow outsourcing companies to recoup their investments in human relationships and organizational processes; they also provide their suppliers with an incentive to make the investments required;

- The degree to which information technology reduces coordination costs and facilitates monitoring depends on the duration of the relationship (it takes time to coordinate one's activities); long-term contracts allow both partners the benefits of a learning curve;

- Long-term partnerships will motivate suppliers to charge fair or even relatively low prices, and to deliver better-quality, low-cost products and services.

As a result of the above argument we may conclude that information technology investments will cause a shift toward more outsourcing and long-term relationships between buyers and sellers [Clemons 1993]. Information technology enables outsourcing companies to achieve a level of coordination normally associated with in-house production, without the offsetting increase in operations and opportunism risk costs that used to accompany it.

5.4.3 A supply chain perspective

An alternative description of how information technology affects market structures can be formulated on the basis of the impact of *inter-organizational information systems* on the structure and management of supply chains [Holland 1995].

Inter-organizational information systems link companies to their suppliers, distributors, and customers, and allow the movement of information across organizational boundaries. These are implemented in all kinds of industries to establish electronic links between separately owned organizations. In their simplest form, inter-organizational information systems may be basic electronic data interchange systems for purchase orders, delivery notes, and invoices. They may also involve much more complex interactions, as do integrated cash management systems or shared technical databases. The phenomenon of shared information systems has a profound effect on business relationships, market structure, and competition. Inter-organizational information systems are revisited in Chapter 10 in the context of supply chains.

Not only can inter-organizational information systems improve internal operations to an organization, they can also improve the performance of the value chain through the transformation of inter-organizational business processes. The key features of these innovative inter-company processes are increased interdependence and expanded coordination between participating organizations enabled by IT. For example, in the retail industry, EDI systems are deployed to create a continuous replenishment process between manufacturers and retailers. This kind of process is made possible by the increased coordination and interdependence that EDI systems promote, often resulting in 50% to 100% higher inventory turns than are achieved before the deployment of continuous replenishment [Clark 2000].

An investigation conducted on current competitive strategies in the textile industry and a subsequent analysis regarding the communication patterns associated with them concluded that a move towards cooperative relationships is intended to make the supply chain as a whole more competitive [Holland 1995]. The resulting market structure is an electronic hierarchy in which inter-organizational information systems are used to integrate business processes across organizational boundaries. Cooperation is a significant element of the strategies employed by the companies in this case study. Companies use inter-organizational information systems to support their relationships, which are characterized by mutual adaptation and a reduction of competition in terms of open tendering. The effect of these individual strategies is to move the organizations closer together, resulting in vertical integration but without ownership. One might also say each 'owns' a small part of its supply chain partners (without necessarily realizing that it is 'owned' by its partners too), except that this ownership is not expressed in equity terms, but in influence and shared responsibility. In effect, it is inherent in the strategies of such companies to arrange themselves into hierarchies.

The interplay between business strategies and inter-organizational information systems leads to the emergence of product group supply chains consisting of integrated business processes across organizational boundaries. The cooperation between their component organizations, intended to allow the effective management of their logistic, financial, technical and design interdependencies, causes supply chains to behave as single units. Cycle times are reduced, quality is improved, and costs are reduced. Gradually, cooperation turns to integration, both organizationally and technically. Competition between individual organizations is replaced by competition between supply chains. The structures that result from this process are referred to as *virtual hierarchies* [Holland 1995].

5.5 Chapter summary

A governance structure describes the organizational form, the rules, institutions, which structure a certain value exchange. In particular it specifies which parties are involved in a transaction, and what co-ordination mechanisms are used. Generally speaking economies have two basic mechanisms for coordinating the flow of products and services: markets and hierarchies. This chapter addresses the issue of how advances in information technology and management are affecting organization and market structures. In particular, it explains the 'dichotomy' between market and hierarchy governance, and analyzes this topic from two perspectives: transaction cost economics and the resource-based view. In *markets*, supply and demand forces regulate the external transactions of material and immaterial goods between individuals and companies, determining design, price, quantity and delivery schedules. In *hierarchies*, on the other hand, it is assumed that products and services are produced by the organization that needs them. Production, availability, and delivery are controlled and directed by managerial decisions. Next to market and hierarchies, a third way of coordinating the flow of goods and services has emerged: *network*.

In *transaction cost economics*, the fundamental unit of analysis is the transaction. *Transaction costs*, also called coordination costs, include the transaction (or governance) costs of all the information processing necessary to coordinate the work of people and machines that perform the primary processes. Three transaction aspects influence whether a transaction will be carried out in a market or in a hierarchy: asset specificity, product complexity, and transaction frequency. The *asset specificity* of a transaction refers to the extent to which assets that are specific to this transaction alone, and which cannot be used otherwise or elsewhere without incurring a significant reduction of their value, support it. For less specific products and services, markets are more appropriate. *Product complexity* too plays a role. Buyers selecting complex products need much more information. The extra information exchange involved increases the transaction costs. Finally, setting up specialized governance structures such as hierarchies employ for their transactions, involves significant expenditures. These costs are only recovered if the transaction volume or *frequency* is high enough.

Also behavioral assumptions regarding bounded rationality and opportunism affect the choice between markets and hierarchies. Bounded rationality is a term used to indicate that the capacity of human beings to formulate and solve complex problems is limited. The limits to human rational capacity present a problem in environments that are characterized by uncertainty and/or complexity. Human beings not only have a limited capacity for rationality, they also sometimes display opportunistic behavior. Opportunism can be described as 'self-interest seeking with guile' and as making 'self-disbelieved statements'.

A key to successful IT performance is the optimal investment, use, and allocation of IT resources (people, applications, technology, facilities, data) in servicing the needs of the enterprise. According to the resource-based theory, any competitive advantage is based on the possession of certain assets, and the extent to which this competitive advantage is sustainable depends on how difficult or costly it is for other companies to obtain the same assets.

For some time, increased emphasis has been placed on networks. New organizational forms are emerging, where independent organizations engage in longer-term relationships. *Inter-company networks* (or simply *networks*) are complex arrays of relationships between companies, who establish these relationships by interacting with each other [Jarillo 1998]. The basis of these relationships is trust [Douma 1998]. Trust is needed to lower costs and render the network economically feasible.

According to the *electronic markets hypothesis*, electronic markets would become the favored mechanisms for coordinating material and information flows among organizations in the presence of electronic communication technologies. The basic argument is that IT reduces coordination costs. As Information technology significantly decreases the costs of coordination needed in situations of high asset specificity, and allows the effective and efficient transfer and handling of very complex product information, making product complexity much less of a difficulty, markets are increasingly attractive as a means of organizing economic activity.

In fact, electronic communication basically is to the advantage of both markets and hierarchies; both benefit if communication costs decrease. But *electronic brokerage*, in which buyers and suppliers are electronically connected, works rather more to the advantage of markets. The need for expensive intermediaries is removed because the electronic market makes it so much easier to compare the offers of many potential suppliers. And by increasing the number of alternatives, the quality of the option eventually selected is improved too. *Electronic integration* goes one step further. Suppliers and procurers use information technology to create joint, interpenetrating processes between them, thus tightening their cooperation; time is saved and errors are avoided. This can be attested by the wide use of CAD/CAM and Just in Time (JIT) systems. Again, coordination is made easier and more reliable, and transaction costs are lowered.

Although information technology enables firms to do business with more sellers, researchers have found that inter-organizational information systems do not necessarily create unbiased electronic markets where firms source their procurement from a lot of participants in the market. More specifically, the move-to-the middle hypothesis suggests that:

- There will be a greater degree of outsourcing;

- Companies will favor developing long-term value-adding partnerships with a small group of suppliers with whom they will cooperate and coordinate closely.

Discussion Questions

- Generally speaking economies have two basic mechanisms for coordinating the flow of products and services: markets and hierarchies. Explain both mechanisms and also name three advantages for both mechanisms.

- Describe the specific effects of the 'move to the middle hypothesis', and explain what Clemons, Redi, and Raw mean by 'moving to the middle'.

- Explain from a procurement perspective why a firm would 'move to the middle'.

- How would you apply the marketeers' 20/80 rule to the move-to-the-middle effect?

- The 'Electronic communication effect' works as an advantage for both markets and hierarchies; however, the 'electronic brokerage effect' does not. Define the 'electronic brokerage effect' and explain whether and how it works to the advantage of either markets or hierarchies.

- Explain how bounded rationality and opportunism influence transaction costs.

Assignments

i. Select a company described in a business publication like the *Financial Times*, the *Wall Street Journal*, or other and visit the Website of that company to find out additional information about that company. Find out what products and services it produces and delivers, and where, and when the two traditional coordination mechanisms are used. To what extent can you recognize the emergence of the network coordination mechanism due to IT progress?

ii. The chapter states that recent advances in information technology have affected the costs of coordination and that, as a result, new strategies and structures for markets and hierarchies have come up (the electronic market hypothesis, the move-to-the- middle hypothesis or the supply chain perspective). Does the company you selected for the above assignment apply one or more of these new strategies and structures and explain why or why not?

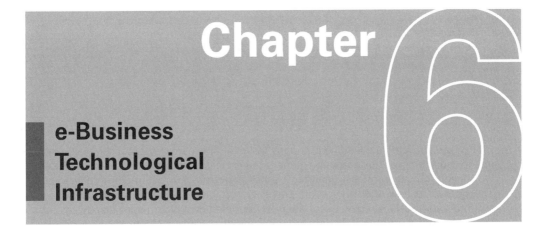

Chapter 6

e-Business Technological Infrastructure

Defining an adequate e-Business infrastructure to achieve process integration is vital to all companies adopting e-Business. The infrastructure refers to the combination of systems inside an enterprise such as client/servers, the networking facilities used to link an enterprise's internal systems with those of its partners, and the technology used to integrate systems and processes between collaborating enterprises. The infrastructure directly affects the quality of the service experienced by end customers.

This chapter acts as a launching pad to discuss, in future chapters, a number of key technologies that are pertinent to e-Business. In particular, this chapter introduces the material that is necessary to understand more advanced chapters that employ this technical infrastructure including Chapters 14, 17, and 18. The discussion begins with e-Business challenges on the technology front (Section 6.1), and continues with the tenants of the technology stack for e-Business, which includes networking facilities, basic infrastructure, such as the client/server architecture and tiered computing models, and collaborative technologies such as workflow systems and Electronic Data Interchange (EDI).

Case Study

Embedding workflow management technology in travel intelligence

iJET (www.ijet.com) is a leading company in travel risk management technology and integrated solutions. This company gathers travel-related information from over 8000 worldwide sources, verifies it, analyzes it, and transforms it into actionable intelligence. The goal is to help travellers avoid travel disruptions. Its online service provides corporate decision makers with continuously updated destination-specific advice and intelligence for more than 450 destinations worldwide, pushes real-time travel alerts and advice to users, and provides access to iJET's country security assessment ratings. iJET also provides risk management services for corporations and their traveling employees, including traveler tracking and communications capabilities, and round-the-clock access to emergency medical and security response services.

Key components of iJET's Collection and Processing System include a source catalog – a register of a large number of sources that have been vetted and rated by human collection specialists who process thousands of messages every day from news wires and weather, transportation, financial and many other automated feeds. These feeds are augmented by automated Web search and monitoring systems that alert iJET to updated content on selected Web sites. This information is processed through a dictionary scan to categorize it by geography and intelligence category. Special watch words and phrased trigger information such as 'strike action' or 'hurricane' immediately alerts Watch Operations.

iJET's Global Travel Intelligence Database is the central, integrated repository of all travel intelligence created and maintained by iJET. This database consists of tens of thousands of pieces of intelligence. A typical traveler's report will carry dozens or hundreds of items, uniquely assembled based on a personal profile and itinerary.

iJET developed a solution based on BEA's WebLogic application server and Fujitsu's I-Flow embedded workflow (process mangement) technology. iJET embedded its workflow system to streamline and automate its intelligent travel processing, ensuring that all editorial and approval guidelines are followed, and that the final TravelWatch product can help customers avoid travel problems [Negron 2002]. Intelligence objects are routed through the processes managed by the workflow mangement engine. Intelligence objects consist of meta-data mapped to itinerary and personal profile data including such items as the traveler's contact information, age, gender, and medical condition. This mapping enables iJET's software to determine when and where intelligence might affect travelers.

> The combination of iJET's software and the workflow engine enables a continuous stream of updates that provide up-to-the-second travel intelligence gleaned from more than 5000 sources, worldwide, on topics ranging from health, security, and transportation to entry/exit rules and communications.

6.1 Technical e-Business challenges

e-Business means automating business processes across an extended enterprise. In an e-Business environment both inter-organizational and intra-organizational relations are supported by modern information technologies. As a result, in an e-Business environment, businesses will reconsider their position in the market. They will place their focus on core competencies; possibly outsource all non-core aspects of their business to others, such as suppliers, distributors, and even customers (for order placement). As discussed in Chapters 2 and 3, this approach comes in contrast to enterprises with a self-sufficient, 'closed box' approach, in which they perform all end-to-end processes through the value chain. Key management issues in an e-Business environment are coordination, collaboration, and integration; both with respect to business processes (for example, leading to e-Business process management) and taking information systems into account. By inter-firm coordination, collaboration, and integration, an extended, virtual enterprise is created. As we have already explained in Chapter 5 where we discussed e-Business strategy, successful enterprises of tomorrow will be those that embrace the opportunities presented by the Internet to define new markets, create new revenue opportunities, and achieve higher levels of efficiency. This has led to the development of sophisticated trading networks where e-Business relationships (see Chapter 3) are formed dynamically as required and to the introduction of new e-Business models such as electronic marketplaces, private and public exchanges, trading hubs, and so on (see Chapters 2, 8, and 10).

Business process integration is what is widely regarded as the ultimate objective of e-Business. With business process integration, interactions between enterprises are achieved electronically according to some predefined process which ensures that the business transaction is both meaningful and reliable. Typically, an e-Business transaction such as transmitting an electronic purchase order, requires both interacting partners' public processes (the external processes that take place between enterprises) to be closely coordinated, together with a detailed exchange of messages in an agreed format. These public processes are typically developed by either a detailed agreement between the trading partners, or codified on the basis of a business standard, such as Electronic Data Interchange described in Section 6.4.1, or RosettaNet described in Chapter 20. As we explained in Chapter 4 business relations may differ; for example, they may be stable or dynamic, tight or loose, and so differ in flexibility, and, depending on the information exchange, they may be thick or thin. With those differences the type of business process integration will differ, and so consequently will the technological infrastructure supporting the relation. For example, in a dynamic business network, the participants and the inter-company relations will typically change over time. A situation like this will be found in project-based industries, like the construction industry. Products, types of orders, number of orders, etc. will change per project. This situation is quite different from a well established relationship between a supplier and a buyer, where there is a high volume flow of standardized products according to agreed planning schedules, as, for instance, in the automotive industry.

Providing end-to-end process integration is not an easy undertaking. A major effort is required to leverage public processes to back-end applications, such as procurement, customer service, order processing and fulfillment, payroll processing, financial accounting (accounts payable/receivable), delivery, and so on. Most enterprises do not have this type of environment. Until the advent of e-Business, the resulting inefficiencies, inaccuracies, and inflexibilities did not matter. Customers had few options, and all competitors were equally inept. However, with the advent of e-Business, end-to-end process integration becomes of paramount importance. Consider, for example, the case of an automotive manufacturer where public processes do not communicate with private processes and back-end systems. An automotive manufacturer may swap forecast and inventory information with its key part suppliers to ensure that parts availability can meet production demand. Assume now that the manufacturing department's manager may still need to update the internal material requirements planning system, which enables the company to predict, track and manage the constituent parts of automobiles, manually. In this way there is no visibility into a large pending order being quoted on the sales system, or a billing problem that could hold up delivery. This may have major financial implications for this manufacturer. If all systems where integrated end-to-end, under a managed process, any issues would become immediately visible and appropriate action could be taken.

This chapter describes the status of some of the most important underlying technologies and infrastructure for e-Business. These are shown in Figure 6.1. In particular, this figure summarizes how the different technologies examined in this chapter relate to each other. These technologies can be seen as different layers that built upon each other. The bottom layer includes networking topologies, the Internet, and protocols such as the Transmission Control Protocol/Internet Protocol (TCP/IP). Internet protocols define, in general, the standards by which the different components in a distributed system communicate with each other and with remote components. Internet protocols, just like other conventional protocols, define the format and the order of messages exchanged between two or more communication entities, as well as the actions taken

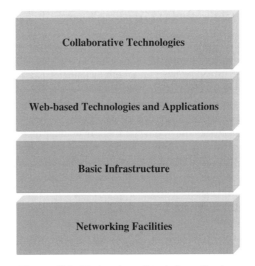

■ **Figure 6.1:** Technology Stack for e-Business

on the transmission and/or receipt of a message or event. Networking facilities are not covered in this book any further. A good source for this type of technology infrastructure is [Kurose 2003].

The layer above the networking facilities is called the basic infrastructure layer and contains such as client/ server and tiered architectures. The layer above the basic infrastructure is called the Web technologies and applications layer, and contains the technologies that are required to develop Web-based applications. Finally, the top layer contains collaborative technologies such as workflow systems and EDI.

6.2 Basic infrastructure: client/server technology

Distributed computing has evolved significantly over the past decades in self-contained and distinct stages. Each stage introduced new architectural modes and new sets of protocols.

Initially, time sharing systems were introduced to support daily business operations by means of a central, high performance host computer and database servers. With such mainframe architectures, user interaction could be accomplished using PCs or Unix workstations. Mainframe architectures promoted a *single-tier* approach whereby the code that implements the business rules (see Chapter 12 for a definition of business rules) in an application, and automates business processes was lumped together with user interface and data access functions in a single, large, monolithic application. These monolithic applications did not easily support graphical user interfaces or access to multiple databases from geographically dispersed sites. The file sharing architectures that followed the mainframe architectures solved some of the problems mainframes had with GUI support, but also introduced a lot of limitations of their own. Their main problems were that they could only work with low volumes of shared usage, low update contention, and low data transfer volumes.

Computers in networks with distributed processing have replaced standalone computers with centralized processing. Centralized processing accomplishes all processing in one central computer; in distributed processing, the processing work is executed by different computers, like mainframes, midrange computers, and PCs linked together. A widely applied form of distributed processing is client/server computing. The client/server architecture is one of the common solutions to the conundrum of how to handle the need for both centralized data control and widespread data accessibility. *Client/server* is a computational architecture that involves client processes (service consumers) requesting service from server processes (service providers). For instance, a client can be some computer that requests a service such as a data on the stock in an inventory, Web page or printing a file, while a server is a computer that carries out the service request. In the previous example we can differentiate between three types of servers that can service client requests: file servers (for the file printing client request), database servers (for the data retrieval request), and Web server (servicing the request that references a Web page). As can be deduced from these examples, client/server computing does not emphasize hardware distinctions; it rather focuses on the applications themselves. This means that the same device may function as both client and server. For example, there is no reason why a Web server – which contains large amounts of memory and disk space cannot function as both client and server when local browser sessions are run there. Furthermore, servers can be clients of other servers. For example, a Web server is often a client of a local file server that maintains and manages the files in which the Web pages are stored.

Although the client/server concept can be used by applications within a single computer, as already explained above, it is far more important in a network. In a network the client/server model provides a typical way to interconnect programs that are distributed across different locations. There are different ways in which processing tasks can be divided between the client and the server. Possible arrangements range from thin clients, with heavy servers to servers that only contain common data with all the processing executed at the level of the client. Database transactions using the client/server model are very common. In practice solutions chosen will depend on specific requirements of each application, such as local vs. central control, number of users, processing needs etc. Figure 6.2 provides a high-level view of a simple client/server model.

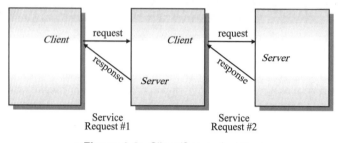

■ **Figure 6.2:** Client/Server Architecture

The basic features of the client/server model can be summarized as follows:

1) Clients and servers are functional modules with well defined interfaces, i.e., they hide internal information. The functions performed by a client and a server can be implemented by a set of software modules, hardware components, or any combination.
2) Each client/server relationship is established between two functional modules, where one module, the client, initiates service requests and the other module, the server, responds to these requests.
3) Information exchange between clients and servers, i.e., requests and responses, are strictly through messages.
4) Message exchange is typically interactive.
5) Clients and servers may run on separate dedicated machines connected through a network.

Client/server applications provide a reasonable mechanism for organizations to design applications that fit their business needs. For example, an order application can be implemented using the client/server model by keeping the order processing databases (dealing with such information as customers, products, and bills) at the corporate office and developing/customizing the order processing logic and user interfaces for different stores that initiate the orders. In this case, store computers accommodate the order processing clients.

Client/server applications use architectures that are dictated by the tools employed in their construction. As a result, most of the conventional applications use a *two-tier client/server architecture*. The tiers in a client/server application refer to the number of executable elements into which the application is partitioned, not the number of platforms where the executables are deployed. Thus the tiers into which an application is partitioned are commonly referred to as the *logical partitioning* of an application as opposed to the *physical partitioning* which refers to the number of platforms where the application executables are deployed. The tiers are connected network-based protocols such as the TCP/IP which has become the de facto standard for enterprise networks and the Internet. The main design goal of TCP/IP was to build an interconnection of networks that provided universal communication services over heterogeneous physical networks. The clear benefit of such an interconnected network is the enabling of communication between hosts on different networks typically separated by large geographic areas.

The most typical variant of the two-tier client/server architecture performs most of the code that implements the graphical user interface and business application logic, and rules on the client-side of the tier, while it implements the database access mechanisms on the server tier (see Figure 6.3). 'Logic' in the server might include simple constraints, such as foreign key constraints, or non-null constraints. These database constraints disallow operations that would cause obvious data integrity problems.

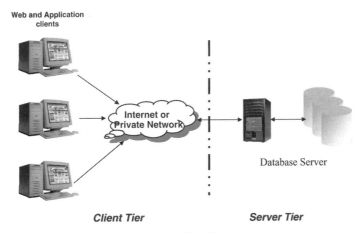

Figure 6.3: Two-Tier Client/Server Architecture

The client in such a two-tier system is known as 'fat client' while the server is commonly referred to as the database server. Such systems are still very common and constitute a flexible solution since the client/server conversation occurs at the level of the server's database language. In this type of architecture, a properly designed client can be modified to reflect new business rules and conditions without modifying the server, as long as the server has access to the database schema needed to perform these transactions.

Although the introduction of client/server computing consisted of a significant advancement over the host-based, centralized computing models, the level of integration remained insignificant. Client front-ends provided a friendlier user interface, but actual access data, data flow, and the effectiveness of applications showed little improvement. The two-tier architecture has several drawbacks, which are especially problematic for large and distributed applications. These include:

1) *Scalability problems*: a key concern with the two-tier model is scalability. Application performance can degrade rapidly when the number of concurrent users reaches a threshold between a few hundred and one thousand users. This is true even for large database servers.

2) *Poor business logic sharing*: in a client/server architecture business logic is kept on the client. When business logic is in the client it is usually very difficult to re-use it between applications and amongst tools. Since the business rules are tightly integrated with the user interface code, the code implementing the business logic and rules must be deployed on the same platforms as the user interface. This means that the entire workstation-resident portion of the application m ust be redeployed when either a business rule or the user interface changes.

3) *Client reliance on the database structure*: applications that access the database server become dependent on the existing database schemas and structure. This makes it more difficult to redesign the database since other applications are intimate with the actual database schemas and structure.

4) *Limited interoperability*: the two-tier architecture uses stored procedures to implement complex processing logic, such as managing distributed database integrity. These procedures are normally implemented using a commercial database management system's proprietary language. This means that processing modifications and interoperation with more than one DBMS cannot happen unless applications are rewritten.

5) *High-maintenance costs*: if the number of workstations in typical client/server architecture is high, or the workstations are geographically dispersed, the maintenance costs for two-tier applications escalate rapidly. Application changes have to be distributed to each client. When there are a large number of users, this entails considerable administrative overhead.

The *three-tier architecture* (see Figure 6.4) emerged to overcome the limitations inherent in the two-tier architecture. In the three-tier architecture, a middle tier is introduced between the user system interface client environment and the database management server environment. Hence, the application is partitioned into three logical tiers: the *presentation tier,* the *processing tier* (or middle tier), and the *data tier.* Figure 6.4 shows a three-tier architecture. If the processing tier is to be implemented in one or more layers or distributed in one or more places, this architecture is referred to as *multi-tier architecture* (see Section 6.3.2).

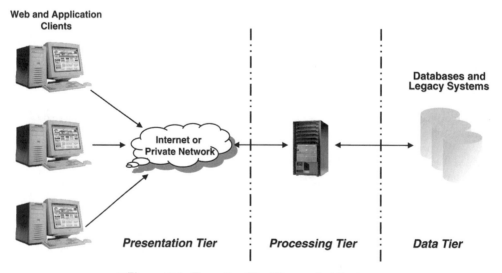

■ **Figure 6.4:** Three-tier Client/Server Architecture

The *presentation tier* is responsible for the graphical user interface (GUI) layer usually in the form of a Web browser. The *processing tier* contains the business logic and is responsible for the processing associated with the applications supported. Finally, the *data tier* holds the permanent data associated with the applications supported. This layer contains various Enterprise Information Systems (see Section 6.5), including modern and legacy application databases and transaction management applications, and will interpret requests from a client and route them to a suitable data resource.

The processing tier enables developers to isolate the main part of an application that can change over time: data and relationships inherent in the data. In this tier, we can find business objects that correspond to entities in the business domain such as sales orders, invoices, products and sales notes, and so on. This tier has the effect of logically and physically decoupling business logic from the presentation and database functions. The ramifications for application development and maintenance are compelling. Customized code can be replaced with standardized APIs to interface business logic with presentation code and database access protocols. When properly implemented, the hardware and software for each of the three layers can be scaled and upgraded independently.

There are a variety of ways of implementing this middle tier, such as transaction processing monitors, message servers, or application servers (see sections 14.7.1 and 14.7.2). In addition, the middle tier adds scheduling and prioritization for work in progress. In many systems, a middle tier serves as a link between clients and back-end services. By using a middle tier, a lot of processing can be off-loaded from clients (making them lighter and faster) and servers (allowing them to focus on their mission).

When compared to the two-tier approach, the three-tier client/server architecture provides improved performance for groups with a large number of users, and increases interoperability, flexibility, maintainability, reusability, security, and scalability. At the same time, it hides the complexity of distributed processing from client applications.

The topology used for e-Business application integration must leverage an enterprise's existing resources and provide a common infrastructure to enable systems integration and connectivity to external applications originating from customers, suppliers or trading partners. The three-tier topology examined above improves the functionality of distributed computing, and can be used as a basis for developing and deploying e-Business applications. More specifically, the partitioning introduced by the three-tier application architecture makes it easier to integrate new applications in the environment. Application code no longer has to be re-created when a new user interface is added, or when a transaction is linked with another application. We shall examine further the three-tier architecture in connection with middleware, enterprise application, and e-Business integration technologies in Chapter 14 (middleware approaches) and Chapters 17 and 18 (EAI and e-Business Integration).

6.3 Web technologies and applications

Technically speaking, the World Wide Web (Web) is a collection of middleware services that operates on top of TCP/IP networks, i.e., the Internet. Conceptually, the Web can be viewed as a vast information system consisting of software applications or processes that exchange information and that act on behalf of a user or another application. Identification, data formats, and protocols are the main technical components of Web architecture [Jacobs 2002]. This architecture consists of:

- Identifiers. A single specification to identify objects in the system: the Uniform Resource Identifier (URI) [Berners-Lee 1998].

- Formats. A non-exclusive set of data format specifications designed for interchange between agents in the system. This includes several data formats used in isolation or in combination (e.g., HTML [Raggett 1999], XHTML [Pemberton 2000], Xlink [DeRose 2001], RDF, and so on), as well as technologies for designing new data formats (XML schemas and namespaces).

- Protocols. A small and non-exclusive set of protocol specifications for interchanging information between agents, including HTTP [Gettys 1999], SMTP, and others. Several of these protocols share a reliance on the Multipurpose Internet Mail Extensions (MIME) Media Type, a metadata/packaging system [Freed 1996].

The Web is a universe of resources. A resource is defined to be anything that has identity. Examples include documents, files, menu items, machines, and services, as well as people, organizations, and concepts [Berners-Lee 1998]. A Web architecture starts with a uniform syntax for resource identifiers, so that one can refer to resources, access them, describe them, and share them. The *Uniform Resource Identifier* (URI) is the basis for locating resources on the Web. A URI consists of a string of characters that uniquely identifies a resource. The W3C uses the newer and broader term URI to describe network resources rather than the familiar but narrower term, the Uniform Resource Locator (URL). URI is all-inclusive, referring to Internet resource-addressing strings that use any of the present or future addressing schemes [Berners-Lee 1998]. URIs include URLs, which use traditional addressing schemes such as http and ftp, and Uniform Resource Names (URNs), a newer Internet addressing scheme. URNs address Internet resources in a location-independent manner; unlike URLs, they are stable over time.

The Web organizes inter-linked pages of information residing on sites throughout the world. Web pages rely on markup languages to tag text files for display at Web browsers. Hypertext Markup Language (HTML) defines the display characteristics of those Web pages, and the HTTP protocol delivers pages between servers and client applications [Raggett 1999]. Hyperlinks within document pages provide a path from one document to another. The hyperlinks contain URLs for the needed resources. Interwoven pages can simply be traversed by following hyperlinks. An HTML document comprises elements and tags. The elements are the HTML encoding that specifies how a document or part of a document should be formatted and arranged on the display screen. HTML also uses tag encodings that indicate where an HTML element should start and where it ends to define elements.

The Web is designed to create the large-scale effect of a shared information space that scales well and behaves predictably. Hypertext Transfer Protocol (HTTP) is an application-level protocol specially designed for Web users. HTTP is a text-based protocol intended for collaborative, distributed, hypermedia information systems [Gettys 1999]. HTTP uses an extremely simple request/response model that establishes connection with the Web server specified in the URI, requests a specific Web page, retrieves the needed content (document), and closes the connection. After the requesting application (client) establishes connection with a receiving application (server), it sends a request message to the server. The request message contains the URI identifying the resource in question, a request method, protocol version, request modifiers, client information, and possible body contents [Gettys 1999]. The request method is the most important element of the message as it shows the type of operation that needs to be performed. HTTP offers a variety of ways to interact with a resource, including GET, POST, PUT, and DELETE.

6.3.1 Web-based applications

Web sites provide the content that is accessed by Web users. For example, Web sites provide the commercial presence for each of the content providers doing business over the Internet. Conceptually, a Web site is a catalog of information for each content provider over the Web. In reality, a Web site consists of three types of components:

1) A Web server;
2) Content files (Web pages);
3) And/or gateways (programs that access non-Web content such as databases).

A Web server is an application (technically a server process) that receives calls from Web clients and retrieves Web pages and/or receives information from gateways.

Web browsers are the clients that typically use graphical user interfaces to wander through the Websites. At present, Web browsers such as Netscape and Internet Explorer provide an intuitive view of information where hyperlinks appear as underlined items or highlighted text/images. If a user points and clicks on the highlighted text/images, then the Web browser uses HTTP to fetch the requested document from an appropriate Website through its underlying Web server. A user can connect to resources by typing the URL in a browser window or by clicking on a hyperlink that implicitly invokes a URL. Eventually, the requested document is fetched, transferred to, and displayed at the Web browser.

Web-based applications are applications that leverage Web clients, such as Web browsers, Web application servers, and standard Internet protocols. They also typically leverage existing applications and data from external sources. The major elements involved in a Web application topology are the following [Nartovich 2001]:

• Web clients (typically browsers but also Web applications) through which users communicate with Web application servers – using Internet protocols such as TCP/IP, and HTML – to access business data and logic. The primary function of the client is to accept and validate user input, and present the results received from the Web application server to the user.

• Web application servers that administer the entire information content intended for publication on the Web and dispense files that contain Web pages, images, sound and video clips, and other media. The main function of the Web application server is to process requests from the clients by orchestrating access to business logic and data and returning Web pages composed of static and dynamic content back to the user or client application. The Web application server provides a wide range of programming, data access, and application integration services for developing the business logic part of Web-based business applications. We shall describe these services in some detail when we discuss issues relating to Enterprise Application Integration and application server-based topologies in Chapter 17.

• Infrastructure services that equip the Web application server with caching, directory and security services. Included in these services are firewalls that protect an organization's network and resources from being compromised.

• External services that consist of existing (non-Web) mission-critical applications and data internal to an enterprise as well as external partner services, e.g., financial services, payment services, information services, and so on, and external partner business applications. Most of these existing services control an enterprise's core business processes.

Types of Web applications

There are many types of Web documents that are displayed on a Web site. These include not only HTML pages but also other content types such as GIF and JPEG format images, MPEG-format video, and so on. Usually these document types are presented to the user as subsidiary parts of the HTML page. However, from the server's perspective, all Web documents are equal in that they require the server to respond to a unique request. The server may handle that request by delivering a file, e.g., an HTML page stored in the file system, which is found on the server system, or by executing another program to dynamically generate the requested resource. The distinction between the documents found on a file, and are known as *static documents*, and documents that have an interactive and usually time-sensitive nature, and are known as *dynamic documents*, is important.

Static documents are delivered from the file system of the Web server, which locates the file in the filing system and delivers it to the client application. Static documents present information that is unlikely to change, or information that needs to be updated by hand. Static documents cannot accept complex input from the user, but can contain links to other documents. This capability delivers a simple form of interactivity. It can be even used to explore databases only when the Web page author has anticipated possible ways in which the user may wish to explore the database and has provided links to that effect [Boutell 1996]. This approach can be effective, only the databases are very small. However, such systems tend to grow fast, and they get quickly overwhelmed by the maintenance efforts, e.g., cost-intensive editing, that are required to keep them up-to-date. Eventually, these types of static documents are converted to documents that can be automatically modified and generated dynamically by interacting with large databases.

Dynamic documents, unlike static documents require the server to generate the document on the fly. While static documents can be read from an existing file, dynamic documents may not exist on a disk at all. For example, dynamic documents can be generated from databases, video capture systems, and from scientific instruments such as weather monitoring systems [Boutell 1996]. Such documents are generated by the server and often transmitted directly to the client as soon as they are created, without being stored in the server's file system.

Construction of Web applications

Purely dynamic documents are generated when the Web server invokes gateway programs, see Figure 6.5. The Web gateway receives user input associated with the document and generates the document along with any important information that identifies it. Web gateways are used as a means to generate Web content, i.e., HTML pages, and provide access to non-Web content such as databases. In general, Web gateways to non-Web resources are mechanisms used to bridge the gap between Web browsers and the corporate applications and databases. Web gateways are used for accessing information from heterogeneous data sources (e.g., relational databases, indexed files, and legacy information sources) and can be used to handle resources that are not designed with an HTML interface. The gateways are used to provide access to non-HTML information and convert it to HTML format for display at a Web browser.

The traditional way of adding functionality to a Web server is the Common Gateway Interface (CGI), a language-independent interface that allows a server to start an external process on behalf of the client. This

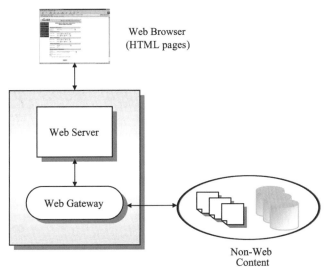

Figure 6.5: Generating Dynamic Web Documents

external process gets information about a request through environment variables, the command line, and its standard input stream, and writes response data to its standard output stream. Most scripts generate a new Web page as output, which is then returned to the client.

CGI is the earliest and most basic attempt to create dynamic page effects by executing programs entirely on the application server side, and, as a result, this approach has several limitations:

• For high-volume sites, performance is one of the most serious CGI limitations. In a traditional CGI environment, the Web server spawns a new process every time a client requests a CGI application, loading and executing a Perl interpreter for each request. This can cause severe performance problems for the server if many users submit requests concurrently and also makes it cumbersome to manage persistent data.

• A CGI program does not get stored in memory between requests. Thus, a CGI program needs to be loaded and started for each CGI request.

• The CGI interface is supported on a wide variety of Web servers. However, CGI programs themselves are not inherently portable across platforms, so careful design is required to construct portable CGI applications.

The limitations of CGI are addressed by newer Web approaches which dynamically generate content for Web pages, such as, for example, JavaServer Pages and PHP. As we shall see in Section 6.3.2, JavaServer Pages avoid this limitation. Each program is compiled once, remaining in memory for subsequent requests.

6.3.2 Architectural features of Web-based applications

Web-enabled applications are a special case of client-server applications where the client is a standard Web browser like Netscape Communicator or Microsoft Internet Explorer. Modern Web-enabled applications leverage the three-tier architecture that we discussed earlier in this book. With Web-enabled applications the middle tier in the three-tier architecture is divided into two units with different functions. The reason is that clients in Web-enabled applications are typically used to generate Web pages and dynamic content using HTML and XML [Pemberton 2000], while application servers are written in C++ or Java. Hence, the gap between these thin clients, which contain almost no application logic, and the application servers is too big to link them together. To remedy this situation the classical presentation tier of the three-tier architecture is subdivided into a client tier and a new presentation tier. The needs of this new presentation tier are addressed by an infrastructure known as a *Web server* (see Figure 6.6). The Web server is implemented in a scripting language and its function is to receive requests from client applications and generate HTML using the services provided by the business (processing) tier. This additional tier provides further isolation between the application layout and the application logic.

As Figure 6.6 illustrates, a customer, business partner, or service provider may send a requests from a Web browser. This could be using a workstation or PC-based browser or some other means such as a WAP phone or PDA. The request is sent to the Web server via the relevant network medium, which could be the Internet, an intranet, or extranet via HTTP and other Internet-related protocols, e.g., SOAP. The Web server receives the request from the network and handles requests for traditional static pages while it passes any requests for other types of processing (such as dynamic pages) to the application server. The application server extracts information from a variety of back-end data sources in line with business rules. The results are finally sent back to the Web-server for passing on to the client application.

The client tier of a Web application is implemented as a Web browser running on the user's client machine. Its function in a Web-based application is to display data and let the users and client applications enter/update data. The client may also perform some limited dynamic HTML functions, such as hiding fields no

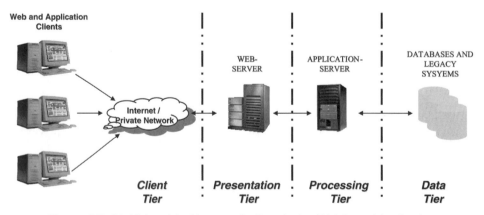

Figure 6.6: Multi-tiered Architecture for Developing Web-based Applications

longer applicable fields due to earlier selections, rebuilding selection lists according to data entered earlier in the form, and so on, using JavaScript or other browser scripting languages. The client tier may use a variety of clients, such as Web browsers, client-applications, e.g., Java applications, and even hand held devices.

The presentation tier generates Web pages in which it includes dynamic content. It supports different types of clients such as pure HTML and Java-capable clients. The dynamic content typically originates from a database, for instance, a list of matching products, a list of transaction conducted over a specific time period, and so on. The other task that a Web-server needs to perform is to find the client application or user-entered data in Web pages coming back from the client and forward it to the business logic tier. The Web server provides different ways to forward a request to an application server and to forward a modified or new Web page to the user. These approaches include the Common Getaway Interface, Microsoft's Active Server Page, servlets and the Java Server Page.

One advantage of this type of middle tier processing is simply connection management. A set of servlets could handle connections with hundreds of clients, if not thousands, while recycling a pool of expensive connections to database servers. The presentation tier is generally implemented inside a Web server such as Apache WebServer, IBM Websphere, or Microsoft IIS.

As expected most of the application logic is written in the processing or business logic tier. *Business logic* includes performing all required calculations and validations, managing workflow and all data access for the presentation tier. An application server is typically a component-based product that resides in the middle tier of a server centric architecture. It provides middleware services for security and state maintenance, along with data access and persistence. The application server handles the network connections, protocol negotiation, class loading, and other advanced functionality such as transaction management, security, database connection, pooling and so on. Isolating the business logic from these 'house-keeping' activities allows developers to focus on building application logic while application server vendors differentiate their products based on manageability, security, reliability, scalability, and tools support.

In modern Web applications, business logic is frequently built using Enterprise JavaBeans (EJB), which conveys several benefits in terms of distribution, transaction processing capabilities, and persistence. Another technology to use for building business logic based applications is ASP.NET, which is the unified Web development platform that provides the services necessary for developers to build enterprise-class Web applications. Applications can be coded in a .NET compatible language, e.g., ASP.NET Visual Basic.NET, or C#. The languages can be used to develop .NET business objects that are the building blocks for multi-tiered Web applications, such as those with a layer for data access or common application rules. The business logic tier is generally implemented inside an application server like IBM Websphere, Microsoft MTS, Oracle Application Server, and so on.

The data tier is responsible for managing the data. The data tier provides the business logic tier with required data when needed and to store data when requested. In a simple case, a data tier may include relational databases. However, it may also include data access procedures to other data sources such as enterprise application programs, ERP applications, legacy databases, and legacy applications.

Client-side programming

There are two types of programming approach associated with the development of Web applications: *client-side programming* and *server-side programming*. The former involves associating program code with Web pages that are downloaded into a client running a Web browser, with the code being run on the client installation. The latter involves code being stored on the Web server and being executed when a particular event as, for instance, a Web page being demanded, occurs.

In this section we will describe client-side programming approaches to Web applications, while in the next section we will concentrate on server-side programming approaches. The two most popular approaches for client-side programming of Web applications are applets and JavaScript [Ince 2002].

Applets

The main mechanism for client-side programming in Java is the applet. Applets are snippets of Java code that are firmly anchored in a Web document and run on the client side. An applet can be sent with a Web page to a user. As soon as an applet-supporting browser loads the Web document, the applet displays the results in a pre-assigned position in the document. The execution then is done through the client, which must be Java-enabled. Java applets can perform interactive animations, immediate calculations, or other simple tasks without having to send a user request back to the server because of security problems, applets loaded over the Internet are prevented from reading and writing files on the client file system, and from making network connections except to the originating host. In addition, applets loaded over the net are prevented from starting other programs on the client, and also not allowed to load libraries, or to define native method calls.

Developing applets is rather different from developing code that implements other containers, such as frames. The main difference is that applets do not have constructors: an applet is created by the browser and by constructors found in the program code [Ince 2002].

JavaScript

JavaScript statements are directly embedded in the HTML code. This code interacts with the browser. This is in contrast to the applets approach where the code is found on the server, referenced in the HTML, downloaded onto the client, and executed.

JavaScript has a number of features including conventional data types and operators, arrays, control structures, functions, and the ability – using a technology known as dynamic HTML (DHTML) – to interact with the elements that make up a Web page [Raggett 1999]. In this way, we can access the elements of an HTML form, or change the look of a textual element.

Server-side programming

Several technologies have been developed to alleviate the problems with CGI programming. The main approaches for server-side programming include Java servlets and JavaServer Pages.

Servlets

These are modules of Java code that run in a server application to answer client requests [Java servlets]. A servlet is a Java component that can be plugged into a Java-enabled Web server to provide server extensions in the form of customized services. Such services include the development of new features, runtime changes to information content, and presentation, the inclusion of new standard protocols (such as FTP), and new custom protocols.

Similar to a GCI program, servlets can receive client requests, handle them, and send a response. If a servlet is called through HTTP, the response is typically an HTML flow. Unlike CGI programs that are loaded in memory each time a client makes a request, a servlet is loaded in memory once by the application server, and can serve multiple requests in parallel using threads. By using servlets as a server-side programming model, developers have access to the full range of Java APIs. In addition servlets perform better than CGI programs (because they are preloaded and initialized), do not run in separate processes (this avoids creating a new process for each request as is the case for CGI programs), are more scalable (unlike CGI, servlets are multithreaded), and portable.

As already noted, servlets are designed to work within a request/response processing model. In a request/response model, a client sends a request message to a server and the server responds by sending back a reply message. Requests can come in the form of HTTP, URI, FTP or a custom protocol. Typical uses for servlets include [Java servlets]:

- Processing and/or storing data submitted by an HTML form;

- Providing dynamic content, e.g., returning the results of a database query to the client application;

- Managing state information on top of the stateless HTTP. Normally, the state of the client/server connection cannot be maintained across different request/response pairs. However, session information is maintainable with servlets, e.g. for an online shopping cart system which manages shopping carts for many concurrent customers and maps every request to the right customer.

Servlets provide Web developers with a simple, component-based, platform-independent mechanism for extending the functionality of a Web server, and for accessing existing business systems without the performance limitations of CGI programs. Servlets are not tied to a specific client-server protocol but they are most commonly used with HTTP. Unlike proprietary server extension mechanisms (such as the Netscape Server API or Apache modules), servlets are server- and platform-independent. Servlets involve no platform-specific consideration or modifications; they are Java application components that are downloaded, on demand, to the part of the system that needs them.

Servlets are a popular choice for building interactive Web applications. The Java Servlet API includes several Java interfaces, and fully defines the link between a hosting server and servlets. Servlets have access to the entire family of Java APIs, including the JDBC API to access enterprise databases, and can also access a library of HTTP-specific calls. More importantly, because servlets plug into an existing server, they leverage a lot of existing code and technology. When servlets run on the Web server, they act as a middle tier between a request coming from a Web client (browser) or other HTTP client and databases, and applications hosted on the back-end server (see Figure 6.7). As servlets are located at the middle tier, they are positioned to add a lot of value and flexibility to a Web-enabled system.

Third-party servlet containers are available for Apache Web Server, Sun ONE Web Server, Microsoft IIS, and others. Servlet containers can also be integrated with Web-enabled application servers, such as BEA WebLogic Application Server, IBM WebSphere, Sun ONE Application Server, and others.

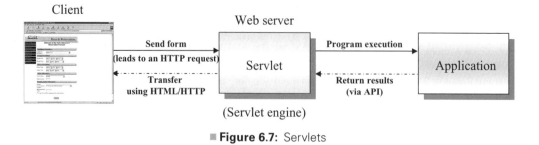

■ **Figure 6.7:** Servlets

Because of their power and flexibility, servlets can play a significant role in a business system architecture. They can perform the application processing assigned to the middle tier, act as a proxy for a client, and even augment the features of the middle tier by adding support for new protocols or other features.

JavaServer Pages

JavaServer Pages (JSP) technology is an extension of the servlet technology created to support authoring of HTML and XML pages [JSP]. JSP technology enables rapid development of Web-based applications that are platform independent and makes it easier to combine fixed or static template data with dynamic content. It allows Java code to be embedded into Web pages to carry out the display of information dynamically on as and when needed basis. The full JSP syntax lets developers insert complex Java code fragments in HTML, declare variables, create methods, or influence the code generated by the JSP compiler.

Many Web pages that are built by CGI programs are primarily static, with the parts that change limited to a few small locations. For example, the initial page at most online stores is the same for all visitors, except for a small welcome message giving the visitor's name if it is known. Almost all CGI variations, including servlets, generate the entire page even though most of it is always the same [Hall 2001]. In contrast to these approaches, JSP component can be viewed as a template for the HTML result page, with 'holes' for the dynamic data that may vary on each request. These holes are filled at runtime with dynamic data coming from the servlet. The servlet may, for example, query dynamic data and pass to the JSP component. A Java bean (a reusable Java component, see Section 12.8.2) is used as a contract between the servlet and a JSP component, see Figure 6.8. The servlet stores dynamic data in a bean instance and places the bean instance in a place that the JSP component can access it. The JSP component retrieves the bean instance and inserts the dynamic data (typically bean properties) into the HTML page using special JSP tags.

JSP technology allows Web developers and designers to rapidly develop and easily maintain, information-rich, dynamic Web pages that leverage existing business systems [JSP]. As JSP technology separates the user interface from content generation it enables designers to change the overall page layout without altering the underlying dynamic content.

JavaServer Pages technology uses XML-like tags to encapsulate the logic that generates the content for the page. Additionally, the application logic can reside in server-based resources (such as JavaBeans component architecture) that the page accesses with these tags. When a Web page is first requested, JSP is parsed into a Java source file which is then compiled into a servlet class. Formatting, e.g., HTML or XML, tags are passed directly back to the response page. By separating the page logic from its design and display

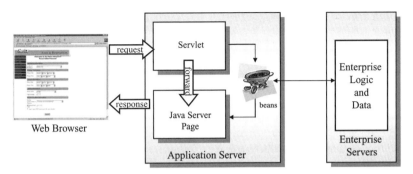

Figure 6.8: JavaServer Pages

and supporting a reusable component-based design, JSP technology makes it faster and easier to build Web-based applications.

JSP enables developers to mix regular static HTML pages with dynamic content generated from servlets. The code is executed on the server and the result is a dynamic page that is returned to the client browser. Although JSPs are simple to build they have at their disposal the full power of Java and the Java Server API. JSPs make heavy use of JavaBeans, which are classes that follow a standard pattern of a no-argument constructor (required in JSPs) and public GET and SET methods.

6.4 Collaborative technologies

The objective of collaborative technologies is to eliminate the manual trading processes by allowing internal applications of different companies to directly exchange information and documents. In traditional commerce, both customers and vendors may be automated internally, but their systems are usually isolated from an ability to communicate with each other. Therefore, trading partners must traverse the gulf between each system by manual processes such as mail, e-mail, fax, meetings, and phone calls. The objective of collaborative technologies is to minimize this manual gulf between trading partners.

Business transactions have many parties which are interested in products or services, payments arrangements, or monitoring and control, and all have in common the need for information for their decisions, their actions, and for the synchronization of these actions. It is the purpose of collaborative technologies such as Electronic Data Interchange and workflows that we will examine in this section to facilitate information flows within and across enterprise boundaries. The purpose of such collaborative technologies is to provide and manage smooth and efficient flows of goods and payments, detect any inaccuracies and errors in the information flow, and report disturbances or exceptional situations, for instance, in production or transport, to the consignees automatically.

6.4.1 Electronic Data Interchange (EDI)

International trade transactions involve many transacting parties – some twenty parties to a transaction are not uncommon. The interest of these parties in the transactions may be the products or services, payments arrangements, or monitoring and control, but they all have in common the need to use information for their decisions, their actions and for the synchronization of these actions. While the physical transport and handling of goods constitute a flow made up of a straightforward series of activities, the corresponding information flow shows a more varied and complex pattern.

The purpose of the information flow is to provide and manage smooth and efficient flows of goods and payments [Kubler 1999]. To this end, the information in each step has to be accurate and reliable. It has to meet the needs of each recipient and be presented in an appropriate form and in a timely manner. Any inaccuracies and errors in the information flow may have immediate consequences for the recipient's ability to proceed with his or her part of the trade transaction. This may, for instance, result in enhancements in goods movement in the various ways modern integrated logistics chains are organized. These chains normally involve several parties, as in the manufacturing, assembly or sales of commodities. Together they develop sophisticated goods flows to keep inventory and buffers in production low. Examples of such strategies include Just-in-time (JIT) manufacturing and Quick Response (QR). These logistics methods use carefully streamlined procedures for the exchange of information. They presuppose close partnership, standardization and, to a certain level, integration of applications. At transacting corporations, these streamlined procedures regulate purchasing. On the documentation side, business documents define the transactions conducted between trading partners. Examples of such documents include purchase requisitions, purchase orders, invoices, remittance advice, and so on. These documents contain the information exchanged between the parties to the trade transaction, and may thus be legally binding to trading partners, and follow a consistent flow between the trading enterprises (see Figure 6.9).

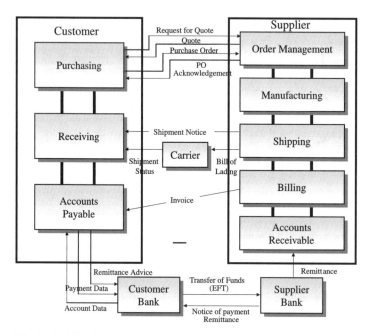

■ **Figure 6.9:** Typical Business Documents Exchanged During a Simple EDI Application

Exchanging data in a standard format has long been the goal of e-Business. In the mid-1970s, Universal Product Codes were used to assign unique identifiers to each product and assist companies in the retail supply chain to exchange data and to help keep industrial inventories under control [Kubler 1999]. In the early 80s the need for interaction among companies and their trading partners led to the development of Electronic Data Interchange, which has been for many years the fastest and most dependable way for companies to exchange business-to-business documents. EDI is commonly defined as the application-to-application transfer of structured trading data or documents by agreed message standards between computing systems. Structured data is precise, recognized and accepted method of assembling data. EDI is a fast, cost effective, and safe method of sending purchase orders, invoices, shipping notices, and other frequently used business data and documents between transacting partners.

In essence, EDI is a means of paperless trading and was a natural evolution from paper documents as data carriers, to computer and telecommunication systems as automatic carriers and processors of data. In traditional business processes, such as ordering and invoicing, paper documents contain structured information in various 'boxes'. In EDI this information is mapped into a structured electronic message. In operation, EDI is the interchange of these agreed messages between trading partners to ensure speed and certainty, and better business practice in the supply chain.

The development of EDI was motivated by the realization that simple cross-organization business processes such as purchasing, shipment tracking, and inventory queries were tremendously inefficient. Two business partners were likely to each have enterprise systems that provided internal support for these processes. Yet, when it came to make a purchase order, the order itself and all associated documents would be transmitted and processed using inefficient manual processes and slow delivery mechanisms such as postal mail.

EDI thus focused initially on producing electronic versions of traditional business documents such as purchase orders and invoices, and then enabling automated processing and transmission of those documents. By introducing EDI systems, organizations were able to transform processes that could take as much as a week and perform them in hours.

There are two key elements in basic EDI. Firstly, electronic documents replace their paper counterparts. Secondly, the exchange of documents takes place in a standardized format. Using these two basic concepts, enterprises can enter the world of EDI and begin taking advantage of electronic business.

In a typical EDI application to support purchasing, an EDI system is integrated with the existing purchasing system at the customer side (see Figure 6.9). When a customer enters a new purchase request into the purchasing system, a corresponding request is received by the sender's EDI system, which then constructs an electronic purchase order document and transmits it to the supplying company. Originally, all EDI transactions were sent over dedicated communications channels, which meant that such channels had to be set up between any pair of organizations wishing to use EDI between themselves. To alleviate this bottleneck, third-party organizations have emerged offering value-added networks (VANs). These VANs take care of the transmission details between subscribers. Thus, a company can subscribe to a single VAN, and require all its partners to subscribe to that VAN. In this way, the company does not need to set up dedicated networking connections to each of its partners. EDI transactions can also be delivered over the Internet.

When the purchase order is received at the supplying company, over a dedicated connection, via a VAN, or via the Internet, it is processed by the receiver's EDI system. This system transforms the message as required and inputs it into the receiver's enterprise system. Once in that system, the new order is handled just as any other order would be.

This example illustrates that any two partner organizations need to agree on the exact formats of documents exchanged between them. The EDI standards provide definitions of common business documents. Standards are of the utmost importance to EDI. Without pre-defined, agreed standards EDI is of little value. By using standard messages, organizations can exchange information between many different trading partners and be sure of common understanding throughout the supply chain. EDI formats the structured trading information into a commonly recognized standard, published and maintained by a standards body such as ANSI X12 and the United Nation's UN/EDIFACT, or Tradacoms. The UN/EDIFACT standard (United Nations Electronic Data Interchange for Administration, Commerce and Transport), which was extended beyond international trade, is the most important format.

EDI uses document standards and maps rather than markup languages. With EDI, each enterprise that wishes to participate in an automated document exchange must first map their documents, such as invoices, purchase orders, ship notices, and so on, to EDI-conformant document standards. EDI standards define the electronic documents sent between trading partners, called *transaction sets* by the ANSI X12 (or messages by EDIFACT). Transaction sets reflect the agreement by companies on certain predefined transactions that are routine and repetitive for a certain industry sector. Transaction sets serve as electronic equivalents of hardcopy business documents, and, in most cases, use names such as purchase order, dispatch advice, invoice, payment order, remittance advice, shipping notice, or healthcare claim. The standards groups design transaction sets broadly, building in many features to address as many industries and business needs as possible. In operation, EDI is the interchange of these agreed transaction sets between trading partners, to ensure speed and reliability, and better business practice in the supply chain.

EDI itself began in the transportation industry, where the Transportation Data Coordinating Committee (TDCC) created transaction sets for vendors to follow in order to enable electronic processing of purchase orders and bills. The TDCC established a suite of electronic documents for retail, motor, ocean and airfreight. Nowadays, the EDIFAT standard is used in several industry sectors, including transport, customs, finance, construction, insurance, tourism, healthcare, social, and public administration.

Transaction sets define a set of fields (e.g., a contact field that includes the name of a company, its address, main telephone and fax number and so on), the order and length of fields along with business rules that accompany the fields. To implement the EDI, trading partners would have to follow the following steps [Goldfarb 2001]:

1) Trading partners enter into an agreement, called a trade arrangement.
2) They select a *value-added network* (VAN). This is a common communications network that provides value-added services such as data validation, logging for audit trails, accountability, error detection and/or faster response time, and allows trading partners to use these services for a substantial fee.
3) The trading partners typically either contract for, or build themselves, custom software that maps between the two formats that are used between the trading partners. With EDI, each company that wishes to participate in automated document exchange must first map its documents (invoices, purchase orders, ship notices) to EDI document standards. Once everyone has mapped specific document types to standard document formats, the documents themselves flow easily between applications without human intervention. When using EDI, it is not necessary that trading partners have identical document

processing systems. When the sender sends a document, the EDI translation software converts the proprietary format into an agreed upon standard. When a recipient receives a document, the recipient's EDI translation software automatically changes the standard format into the proprietary format of the recipient's document processing software.

4) Each time a new trading partner is added, new software has to be written to translate the sender's data for the recipient.

Transaction sets are typically transmitted over expensive proprietary networks, e.g., VANs, which generally base charges on a mixture of fixed fees and message lengths. These fees can become substantial, but are typically overshadowed by the cost of building and maintaining the translation software.

It is important to note that EDI is not simply a mechanism for exporting data from one system to another, but a bi-directional mechanism for interaction between systems. Because these disparate systems typically employ different file formats (data notations), schemas, data exchange protocol, and so on, the process of exchanging data is very cumbersome [Goldfarb 2001].

Figure 6.10 shows typical EDI components involved in an exchange of transaction sets between two companies. This figure shows that a source application prepares an electronic business document, e.g., a purchase order, which is being sent must be translated and structured according to the EDI format, e.g., ANSI X12 or EDIFAC, that is understood by the target application. The translation software translates the document into an EDI standard, formats it, and performs all necessary administrative, audit, and control

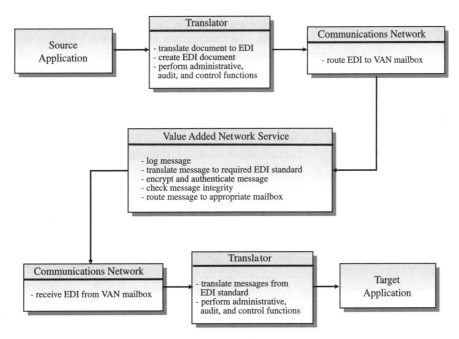

■ **Figure 6.10:** EDI Transaction Set

functions. Rather than directly connecting to a trading partner the target application forwards the ensuing transaction set to a VAN service via a dedicated communications network. The transaction set is received by a target application, e.g., an order-to-cash process, and is also encrypted and authenticated by the VAN service, also checked for integrity, i.e., completeness and authorization.

EDI has evolved significantly since the 1980s. The first stage of EDI focused on document automation [Laudon 2003]. Procurement agents would create purchase orders electronically and send them to trading partners, who in turn would ship order fulfillment and shipping notices electronically back to the purchaser (see Figure 6.9). Invoices, payments, and other documents would follow.

In the early 1990s the new methods of production called for greater flexibility in scheduling, shipping, and financing of supplies. Thus EDI evolved and in its second stage concentrated on the automation of internal industrial processes, and movement toward just-in-time production and continuous production. To support the new automated production processes used by manufacturers, EDI was used to eliminate purchase orders and order documents entirely, replacing them with production schedules and inventory balances [Laudon 2003]. Supplier firms were sent monthly statements of production requirements and precise scheduled delivery times, and orders would be fulfilled continuously, with inventory and payments being adjusted at the end of each month.

In the third stage of EDI, suppliers were provided with online access to selected parts of a purchasing firm's production and delivery schedules. Movement towards this continuous access model of EDI was spurred in the mid 1990s by large manufacturing firms, such as oil and chemical companies, which were implementing ERP systems. These systems required standardization of processes, and resulted in the automation of production, logistics, and many financial processes. These new processes required closer collaboration with suppliers, and relied on more precise delivery schedules and flexible inventory management systems. This third stage of EDI introduced an era of continuous replenishment [Laudon 2003]. For instance, manufacturers provided their suppliers with access to their store inventories, and suppliers were expected to keep stock of products on the shelf within pre-specified targets.

Currently, EDI still accounts for the bulk of e-Business transactions, and has proved to be very reliable and capable for specific processes in a wide range of industries, including automotive, retail, and grocery. EDI has been successful in reducing the supply chain costs of large enterprises by automating the batch processing of information related to orders, invoices and deliveries. Thus EDI is widely used by large enterprises for sending purchase orders, invoices, shipping notices, and other frequently used business documents. Although traditional EDI is able to automate many fundamental business transactions, such as purchase orders and invoices; it is still predominantly message centric, i.e., uses standardized message formats. However, electronic messaging and transaction transmission are insufficient for e-Business transactions that require automation of complicated business process flows and interactions.

Traditional EDI suffers from many problems that have limited its growth. These include the following:

- **Fixed transaction sets** One of the most significant problems of EDI is the fact that it based on the transfer of fixed transaction sets. This rigidity makes it extremely difficult to deal with the normal evolution necessary for companies introducing new products and services, or evolving computing infrastructure, or improving business processes. Transaction sets cover a wide range of business scenarios, thus they are of generic nature. Transactions that do not fit into the strict model of EDI transactions can either be negotiated as a new transaction type (if transactions will recur frequently to warrant the work involved) or be handled as exceptions. As a result, industries (and even individual enterprises) have found transaction sets not to be practical for daily business use. Thus they have developed their own implementation guidelines by picking and choosing among the data segments, elements, and codes in the generic standards that apply to them. Some guidelines also added specific industry codes for use in industry transaction sets. Although this process gives trading partners structured and predictable electronic business messages, it also means each industry and sometimes companies in the same industry use EDI differently. Therefore, connecting new partners using EDI becomes a challenging issue as enterprises must first agree which part of the standard they are using.

- **Resilience to change** EDI standards are defined by standards bodies that are structurally ill equipped to keep up with the rapid pace of change in the various business sectors they impact. The current process of defining standards for transaction sets may take years [Goldfarb 2001]. This requires that, in many cases, suppliers implement costly one-off solutions for each trading partner. Because of the informational needs of companies, it is impractical to assume that EDI standards can be a one-size-fits-all proposition. The variables of company size, focus, industry, infrastructure, etc., will continue to create needs that are unique to each company.

- **Reliance on proprietary communications networks** EDI messages are mainly carried on proprietary communications networks that are relatively expensive and that have compatibility problems when communicating across networks. The initial deployment costs, inflexibility, and ongoing network charges for EDI are comparatively high. As a result, enterprises that use EDI are combining the structure and integrity of their existing infrastructure with the Internet to take advantage of a more cost effective solution. Traditional EDI is considered too expensive and complex for smaller organizations to implement, especially in the case of small to medium enterprises.

- **Encapsulation of business rules in transaction sets** Business rules are encapsulated in the definition of transaction sets as implementation guidelines. However, business rules cannot be legislated easily and thus they can be rigid. Business rules that apply to large organizations may be completely inappropriate for an SME. Business rules will also vary between different industry/business sectors. Even companies of the same size and in the same industry will implement different business rules. What is also important to note is that business rules will change with time. One of the biggest problems of EDI, is that it considers processes as an integral part of the transaction set. Unlike new technologies such as XML, it does not separate processes or business rules from the content and structure of the data. Achieving this separation is critical to the widespread adoption of EDI.

EDI still continues to play an important role in business in traditional supply chain relationships between trading partners. Large organizations that have invested heavily in large and sophisticated EDI systems are unlikely to reengineer their business processes overnight and reinvest in new systems to facilitate new technologies such as XML. Common practise nowadays is that companies install XML-EDI translators on Web servers to allow EDI and XML to work together.

Another notable trend is the change of focus within the UN/EDIFACT Working Group (EWG). Traditionally the group has focused solely on the development and maintenance of the UN/EDIFACT standard and Directories. There has been a shift in thinking within the EWG to incorporate the emerging trends and technologies surrounding the area of structured data transfer, such as business process modeling and XML.

The Technical Assessment Group, for example, has agreed that it will only accept Data Maintenance Requests (DMRs) (requests for changes to the UN/EDIFACT Directories) for new messages with a business model represented in Unified Modeling Language (UML). This has a major impact on the future of EDI, specifically UN/EDIFACT, as it indicates a change of approach from data-centric bottom-up to business-process top-down approach. The intention, within EWG, is to incorporate new developments in the areas of business process modeling and XML.

In Chapter 7 we introduce XML and in Section 7.6 we discuss the use of XML and EDI in the context of e-Business.

6.4.2 Workflow systems

A company's operational performance depends heavily on its business processes (see Chapter 4). The execution of business processes determines how effective and efficient a company reacts to specific situations like service requests, and customer orders. Due to a poor organization, inefficient paperwork and procedures, business processes can be slow, cumbersome and costly. Inefficient business processes eventually threaten the competitive position of a firm.

Through the application of new information systems, organizations can significantly contribute to improved performance. In particular, the focus on reengineering business processes, in combination with the enabling power of IT, has the potential to achieve significant improvements in costs, throughput time, quality, etc. Business process reengineering aims at analyzing, simplifying, and optimizing business processes (see Section 18.2). It reorganizes workflows by cutting, splitting, and combining information intensive tasks. Documents play an important role in this (see Section 7.2). The creation of virtual documents, for example, makes it possible for different people to work simultaneously on the same 'case' or document, resulting in a shorter delivery time. Also electronic storage and retrieval of documents largely contributes to an increased efficiency and a less error-prone process.

A workflow system automates a business process, in whole or in part, during which documents, information, or tasks are passed from one participant to another for action, according to a set of procedural rules [WfMC 1999a]. Workflows are based on document lifecycles and forms-based information processing, so generally they support well-defined, static, 'clerical' processes. They provide transparency, since business processes are clearly articulated in the software, and they are agile because they produce definitions that are fast to deploy and change.

A workflow normally comprises a number of logical steps, each of which is known as an *activity*. As Figure 6.11 illustrates, an activity may involve manual interaction with a user or workflow participant, or might be executed using diverse resources such as application programs or databases. A *work item* or data set is created, processed, and changed in stages at a number of processing or decision points (steps in Figure 6.11) to meet specific business goals. Most workflow engines can handle a very complex series of processes.

A workflow can depict various aspects of a business process including automated and manual activities, decision points, and business rules, parallel and sequential work routes, and how to manage exceptions to the normal business process. A workflow can have logical *decision points* that determine which branch of the flow a work item may take in the event of alternative paths. Every alternate path within the flow is identified and controlled through a bounded set of logical decision points. An instantiation of a workflow to support a work item includes all possible paths from beginning to end. Business rules at each decision point

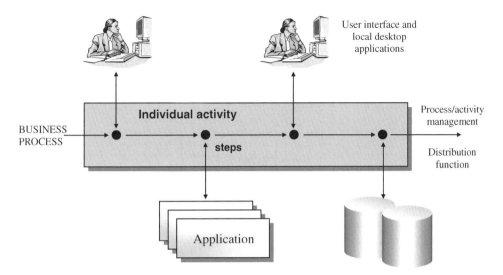

User interface and local desktop applications

Process/activity management

Distribution function

■ **Figure 6.11:** The Workflow Management Coalition Diagram of Process Flow Across Applications

determine how workflow-related data are to be processed, routed, tracked, and controlled. For instance, one rule might generate e-mail notifications when a condition has been met, while another rule might implement conditional routing of documents and tasks.

Workflow technology enables developers to describe full intra- or inter-organizational business processes with dependencies, sequencing selection, and iteration. It effectively enables the developers to describe the complex rules for processing in a business process, such as merging, selection based on field content, time-based delivery of messages, and so on. Moreover, it not only streamlines and accelerates business processes but also allows people to be deployed more productively within an organization. It is a major ingredient that, when combined with middleware, provides an enabling infrastructure for e-Business applications.

These days, workflow systems are increasingly migrating from departmental server-based architectures to more powerful EAI, and e-Business messaging-based architectures espousing the business process-modeling paradigm of BPM. Modern workflow products extend their functionality into the domain of both enterprise and e-Business integration by automating business processes whose structure is well-defined and stable over time. They achieve this by integrating middleware, process sequencing and orchestration mechanisms as well as transaction processing capabilities. A business activity, such as a submission of an order, invoicing, triggering a business transaction, and so on forms part of a business process with which a workflow is associated. This is irrespective whether the issue is the management of a logistics chain, supply chain planning, or simply the exchange of documents between trading partners.

Figure 6.12 illustrates a simple process-based workflow involving the submission of an order. The workflow is made up of tasks that follow routes, with checkpoints represented by business rules, e.g., 'pause for a credit approval' (not shown in this figure). Such business process rules govern the overall processing of activities, including the routing of requests, the assignment or distribution of requests to designated roles, the passing of workflow data

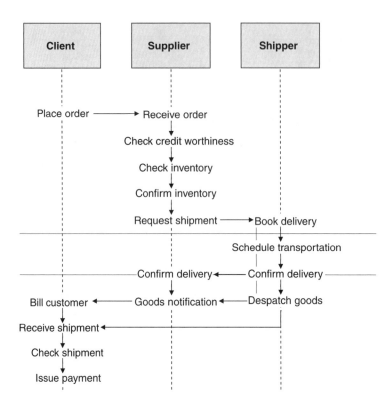

■ **Figure 6.12:** Simplified Workflow for Processing a Client Initiated Order

from activity to activity, and the dependencies and relationships between business process activities. The process-based workflow is shown to include actors (such as a client, a supplier and a shipper), sequencing of activities, parallel paths, and logical decision points, e.g., 'if deliver is confirmed by shipper', that determine which branch of the flow a work item may take, e.g., 'confirm delivery to supplier', and 'dispatch goods'.

The definition, creation and management of the execution of workflows are achieved by a *workflow management system* running on one or more workflow engines. A workflow management system (WMS) is capable of interpreting the process and activity definitions, interact with workflow participants and, where required, invoke the use of software-enabled tools and applications (see Figure 6.11). It is important to note that while this definition covers the spectrum of workflow systems, it excludes simple relational database systems and e-mail systems with programmable delivery mechanisms.

Most WMSs integrate with other systems used by an enterprise, such as document management systems, databases, e-mail systems, office automation products, geographic information systems, production applications, and so on. This integration provides structure to a process that employs a number of otherwise independent systems. It can also provide methods, e.g., a project folder, for organizing documents and data from diverse sources. As an application of workflow, consider the domain of banking and the automation of the steps in a loan approval business process. A customer applying for a loan could access a digital form from the bank's Web site, fill out the loan request, and submit it electronically. When this form arrives at the bank, the WMS would direct the loan request to a credit-scoring system, receive the results, initiate funding requests, receive the approval decision, update databases, and merge loan information, e.g., terms and conditions, rates, payment terms, consumer information, etc., into a personalized loan document. The WMS would then create an e-mail message to the loan applicant with the loan documents as an attachment. The WMS can also drive applications to create the rejection or acceptance letters and loan contracts, supervise the approval process, and drive other applications to dispatch the documents electronically by fax or by e-mail.

The business loan granting process describes how a banking institution grants a loan. An instance of this process is actually granting a loan to a specific client. The process comprises activity instances that include the work items that are passed to a workflow participant, or to another process, for action. For example, in the loan granting process a client may receive all mortgage related documents for a specific property, and may be asked to approve or reject the proposed loan.

In the previous example, the business loan granting process is divided into sub-processes such as reviewing the application for completeness and accuracy, executing a credit check, creating a new loan contract, sending it to the client, checking the form on its return, set-up of payment schedule, and finally issuing the check.

The WMS may synchronize and execute many of the aforementioned sub-processes in parallel, thus reducing the time taken to handle each application and improving customer service. Consequently, workflow implementations could reduce work times substantially.

As a final remark, the ability to distribute tasks and information between participants is a major distinguishing feature of workflow runtime infrastructure. The distribution function, illustrated in Figure 6.11, may operate at a variety of levels (cross to inter- to intra-organization) depending upon the scope of the workflows; it may use a variety of underlying communications mechanisms such as e-mail, messaging passing, Web services, and so on.

Characteristics of workflow systems

Each workflow management system can be viewed at the highest level as providing support for three functional areas:

- Build time functions: these are concerned with defining, modeling and analyzing workflow processes and related activities;

- Runtime process control functions: these are concerned with managing the sequencing and execution of workflow processes;

- Runtime interactions: these are concerned with supporting interactions with human users and applications, and tools for processing activity steps in workflow processes.

Build-time functions are used to define business processes in a way that can be interpreted and executed by the workflow management system. A workflow design solution incorporates two basic phases: mapping and modeling. *Mapping* is the first stage in the adoption of a workflow solution and involves the crucial task of revealing and recording all of the manual and automated internal business processes of an enterprise. Based on the outcomes of the mapping phase, the enterprise develops a *model* that helps to streamline internal processes irrespective of whether they are based on a person-to-person, person-to-application, or application-to-application interaction. The process model (or definition) has to comprise all required information for the execution of a process. This includes starting and finishing conditions, constituent activities, rules defining the execution, and so on. Some workflow management systems have the ability to allow dynamic changes to process definitions at run-time, as indicated in Figure 6.13, which describes the architecture of a typical workflow system.

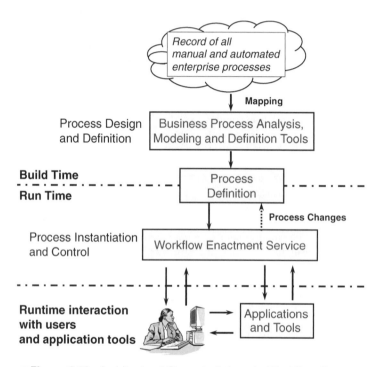

■ **Figure 6.13:** Architectural Characteristics of a Workflow System

In Figure 6.13 the process definition may be given in textual or graphical form, or in a formal process definition language depending on the implementation of the definition tool of a specific product. Once the business process model has been developed, it is ready to be seamlessly integrated across the enterprise. Thus, the result of the build-time function, the process definition, is identified as one of standardization to enable interchange of process definition data between different build-time tools and runtime processes [Hollinsworth 1995].

The core component in runtime process control functions is the basic workflow management control software (or 'engine'). Modeled process definitions are passed to the engine for enactment. A workflow engine provides the runtime execution of business processes and is responsible for process creation and deletion, control of the activity scheduling within an operational process, and interaction with application tools or human resources. It is the process engine that executes the facets of the process model, such as rules based routing and work assignment, prioritization, and time rules for management of deadlines and responses. During the execution of a work item, people, systems, and applications within the business environment, interact with the process engine.

The workflow enactment software is often distributed across a number of computer platforms to cope with processes, which operate over a wide geographic area.

Individual activities, defined as steps in a process, are human- or computer-oriented and usually require the use of particular tools, e.g., form filling functions, or application programs to operate on some defined information, e.g., updating an orders database with a new record. These facilities could also enable management to better forecast and manage their projects and personnel, resulting in a more efficient and effective organization. Interaction with the process control software is necessary to transfer control between activities, to determine the operational status of processes, to invoke application tools and pass the appropriate data, and so on.

There are several benefits in having a standardized framework for supporting this type of interaction, including the use of a consistent interface to multiple workflow systems, and the ability to develop common application tools to work with different workflow products [Hollinsworth 1995].

Types of workflow

Over the years, there had been several attempts to classify workflow products based on the role implemented processes plays in the enterprise. Most analysts have classified workflow products into production, administrative, ad hoc, and collaborative. These days with processes spanning organizations and playing a major role in an e-Business environment, this classification scheme is inadequate. However, this classification is useful to understand the characteristics of and differences between various workflow systems.

Production workflow: Production workflow systems make up the traditional part of the workflow market [Leymann 2000]. They have evolved from the first systems on the market and route folders consisting of one or more forms or different types of documents through the organization. They typically store documents in a central repository and provide check-in, check-out, and version control mechanisms for those documents.

The key goal of production workflow is to manage large numbers of similar core tasks and to optimize productivity in an enterprise. Thus, this type of workflow is characterized by a high business value and a high repetition rate. A production workflow could be completely pre-defined and prioritized, or follow a general procedure, with additional steps or processes added as required [Plesmus 2002]. It thus supports high volumes of work. Production workflow is optimized to attain high levels of quality and accuracy by executing highly repetitive tasks, usually in a non-stop manner [Allen 2001b]. The events that require human contribution are minimized, as is the duration and complexity of that intervention. Human input is required only to manage exceptions — those work items that fall outside pre-determined process tolerances. For example, settling a car accident claim has some generic steps that are part of most claims, e.g., identifying parties, confirming policy coverage, ordering copies of accident reports, etc. However, there may be additional more specialized tasks or workflows added to the overall process, e.g., settle property damage, handle bodily injury, etc.

Production workflows can manage hugely complex processes, and can be tightly integrated with existing (legacy) systems. Production workflow systems are available in two distinct categories [Allen 2001b]:

- *Autonomous workflow management systems* that are separate pieces of application software providing the entire workflow functionality. An autonomous workflow management system is operational without any additional application software, with the exception of database management systems and message queuing middleware. For the deployment of an autonomous workflow solution, application systems that are external to the workflow management system are invoked at runtime, and workflow-relevant data are passed between the workflow participants.

- *Embedded workflow management systems* that are operational only if they are employed by their surrounding (embedding) system – such as, for instance, an Enterprise Resource Planning system, a payment or a settlement system. The functionality of embedded workflow management systems is exhibited by their surrounding software. Workflow components are used to control the sequence of the application's functions and to assist with exception processing. As an example of embedded workflow management systems, we have seen in the case study at the outset of this chapter how iJET embedded its workflow system to create streamline and automate its intelligent travel process, ensuring that all editorial and approval guidelines are followed, and that its travel services can help customers avoid travel problems.

Administrative workflow: Administrative workflows exhibit low business value, however, their repetition rate is quite high. This workflow is a cross between ad hoc and production workflows and concentrates on typical administrative processes such as purchase orders or expense accounts. The flow is predefined, such as, for instance, the steps required to place an order or approve an expense report. Sometimes the flow can be reviewed or even altered, e.g., add a note to ask a supervisor to endorse any exceptional expenses incurred.

The most important feature of an administrative workflow system is the ease of defining the process. Normally, there are many definitions running concurrently, and they tend to involve a large number of users – typically, employees. Process definitions are usually created using forms. Flexibility is more important than productivity, and these systems handle one or two orders of magnitude lower numbers of instances per hour than production workflow systems [Allen 2001b].

Ad-hoc workflow: Ad-hoc workflow systems allow users to create and amend processes. They exhibit a low business value and low repetition rate, and have no predefined structure; the user usually determines the next step in a process. Each business process is constructed individually; process definitions change frequently and easily to address new circumstances as they arise. Ad-hoc workflow is normally characterized by negotiation and a new workflow is defined for each use. Therefore, it is possible to have almost as many process definitions as there are instances of the definitions. This type of workflow is flexible and provides good control of the process, e.g., what is the status of each step?, who did what and when?, where is the work now?, and so on. Ad-hoc workflows are usually built on top of an e-mail platform and use e-mail to deliver the work [Plesmus 2002].

Ad-hoc workflow maximizes flexibility in areas where throughput and security are not major concerns [Allen 2001b]. Whereas in production workflow the enterprise owns the process, ad-hoc workflow users are in possession of their own processes.

Collaborative workflow: Collaborative workflow is characterized by a high business value but infrequent execution. Collaborative workflow focuses on teams of people working together towards common goals. Groups can vary from small, project-oriented teams, to widely dispersed teams of people that share common interests. The processes that fall under this category may be associated with designing and building an automobile, creating technical documentation for a software product and so on. Effective use of collaborative workflow to support team working is now considered a vital element in enterprises of all kinds.

With collaborative workflows, throughput is not an important consideration; process definitions are not rigid and can be amended frequently [Allen 2001b]. Collaborative workflow is sometimes called Groupware. However, there are certain types of groupware that are not workflow products, for example, bulletin boards or videoconferencing.

Workflow reference model

The Workflow Management Coalition (WfMC) was founded in August 1993 with a mission to promote the use of workflow through the establishment of standards for terminology, interoperability, and connectivity between workflow products. The Coalition is a non-profit organization representing users, vendors, analysts, and university/research groups.

All workflow systems contain a number of generic components that interact in a defined set of ways; different products will typically exhibit different levels of capability within each of these generic components. Therefore, one of the early tasks of the WfMC was to propose a *reference model* that was developed from the generic workflow application structure by identifying the interfaces within this structure that enable products to interoperate at a variety of levels. To achieve interoperability between workflow products a standardized set of interfaces and data interchange formats between such components is necessary. The architecture identifies the major workflow components and interfaces. These are considered in turn in the following sections.

Components of workflow systems: As illustrated in Figure 6.14, one of the essential elements in the workflow reference model is the enactment service. The workflow enactment service is the workflow runtime environment in which process instantiation and activation occur. This component may utilize multiple workflow management engines that create, manage, and execute multiple workflow instances related to business processes, and interact with the external resources necessary to process the various activities. Applications may interface with this service via the workflow application-programming interface (WAPI).

The WfMC model provides for the logical separation between *process* and *activity* control logic. Process logic is embedded within the workflow enactment service; activity logic concerns the end-user processing and application tools associated with individual activities. This separation allows the integration of other business applications and third-party workflow clients with a particular workflow application.

The reference model supports the notion that the workflow enactment service can be either centralized or distributed. Where the enactment service is distributed, several workflow engines – each of them controlling a part of the process enactment – interact with a different sub-set of users and application tools responsible for the enactment of a sub-set of a business process. Such an enactment service is considered to have common naming and administrative scope so that process definitions, or their subsets, and application names are handled consistently [Hollinsworth 1995].

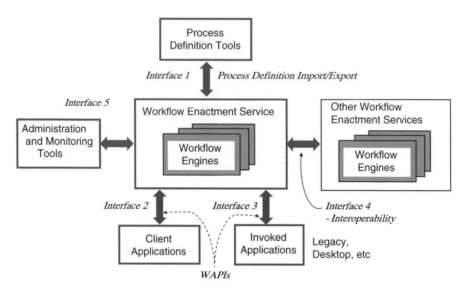

■ **Figure 6.14:** Components and Interfaces of the WfMC Reference Model

A workflow engine is the software service or 'engine' that provides the runtime execution environment for a process instance. A workflow engine typically executes the following functions [Hollinsworth 1995]:

- Interprets process definitions;

- Controls process instance states such as creation, activation, suspension, termination, and so on;

- Provides facilities for navigating between process activities that may involve sequential or parallel operations, deadline scheduling, interpretation of workflow relevant data, and so on;

- Signs on and signs off specific participants;

- Identifies work items for user attention and provides an interface to support user interactions;

- Maintains workflow control data and workflow relevant data, and passes workflow relevant data to/from applications or users;

- Provides an interface to invoke external applications and link any workflow-relevant data;

- Supports supervisory actions for control, administration, and audit purposes.

A workflow engine may be responsible for the whole runtime environment but also for only part of it. In an enactment service consisting of multiple workflow engines, there is a partitioning of process execution across the constituent engines. This may be by process type, with a particular engine controlling a particular process type in its entirety, by functional distribution, with a particular engine controlling those parts of a process requiring user or resource allocation within its own control domain, or some other partitioning mechanism [Hollinsworth 1995].

Workflow interfaces: The reference model architecture specifies five interfaces that let different compliant workflow products and other applications interoperate on several levels. This is illustrated in Figure 6.14. The five interfaces collectively provide an interface to the Workflow Enactment Service by means of the Workflow API and Interchange formats (WAPI). The WAPI is a set of constructs by which the services of the workflow system may be accessed and which regulate the interactions between clients and invoked applications with workflow management products [WfMC 1998].

The process definition interface: process definition tools are software tools that are used by process designers to create a representation of a business process, including all process related data, which can be interpreted by a workflow enactment service later [WfMC 1999b]. Process definition tools have different levels of sophistication; in addition to modeling they may include services for the definition and analysis of process models. The process definition tools interface deals with passing process definitions from external tools to the workflow engine where they are enacted.

Tools that find their origin in the Computer-Aided Software Engineering (CASE) and Business Process Reengineering fields usually cannot interact directly with workflow systems; those versions developed by workflow vendors tend to be specific to their own application and application area. To address these shortcomings, the WfMC proposes a common interchange format that allows such tools to share process definitions and exchange information. The process definition interface, also called Interface 1 in the workflow reference model, covers standard definitions and the interchange of such information as:

• Process start and termination conditions;

• Identification of activities within a process, including associated applications and workflow relevant data;

• Identification of data types and access paths;

• Definition of transition conditions and flow rules.

The workflow process definition (import/export) interface defines a common interchange format, which supports the transfer of workflow process definitions between separate products. This interface also defines a formal separation between the development and runtime workflow management software. It thus, helps to separate process modeling and process execution responsibilities. It also enables a process definition, generated by one modeling tool, to be used as input to a number of different workflow runtime products.

To provide a common method to access and describe workflow definitions, the WfMC has recently introduced the XML Process Definition Language (XPDL). XPDL is a workflow process definition meta-data model that identifies commonly used entities within a process definition. A variety of attributes describe the characteristics of this limited set of entities. Consequently, the process definition interface provides a framework for implementing business process management and workflow engines, and for designing, analyzing, and exchanging business processes. Based on this model, vendor specific tools can transfer models via a common exchange format.

One of the key elements of the XPDL is its extensibility to handle information used by a variety of different tools. This approach needs two operations to be provided by a vendor: (1) import a workflow definition from XPDL; (2) export a workflow definition from the vendor's internal representation to XPDL. The specification uses XML as the mechanism for process definition interchange. XPDL forms a common interchange standard that enables products to continue to support arbitrary internal representations of process definitions with an import/export function to map to/from the standard at the product boundary.

The workflow client application interface: A workflow client application is an application which interacts with a workflow engine, requesting facilities and services from the engine. Client applications may interact with a workflow engine for a variety of reasons. Client applications may perform some common functions such as work-list handling, process instance initiation, and process state control functions (e.g., suspend, resume, etc.), retrieval and manipulation of process definition data and various system administration functions (e.g., suspending the use of certain process definitions [WfMC 1999a].

The workflow client application interface, which is also called Interface 2 in the workflow reference model, enables the access from a workflow client application to the workflow engine and work-list in a product independent manner. This interface defines standards for workflow engines to maintain work items that the workflow client presents to the user. The workflow client presents the user with work items, and may also invoke appropriate applications to present the task and data associated with it. Once the user has completed the task, the work item is returned to the workflow enactment service. Workflow clients may be provided as part of a complete workflow management system or a third-party product or application. For example, it should be possible within the framework of the reference model for vendors of ERP/MRP applications to provide compliant workflow clients written specifically for their application.

The invoked application interface: an invoked application is a workflow application that is invoked by the workflow management system to carry out an activity by an application, fully or partly, or to support a workflow participant in processing a work item [WfMC 1999a]. The invoked applications interface, also called Interface 3 in the workflow reference model, defines a standard interface allowing a workflow engine to invoke a wide variety of applications. It is defined as a set of APIs that enable the cooperation of a workflow enactment service and tools or workflow enabled applications.

The reference model envisages a set of APIs that would allow application developers to workflow-enable their applications. These could then be integrated seamlessly in the business process and invoked directly by the workflow engine. Workflow-enabled applications are applications that can interact with the workflow enactment service by using standardized APIs.

WAPIs combine the workflow client application and invoked application interfaces. The support of these interfaces in workflow management products allows the implementation of front-end applications that need to access workflow management engine functions (workflow services). Integration between workflow and other desktop tasks (calendar, mail, reminders, etc) is often a common target, and the WAPIs allow workflow task integration into a common desktop.

WAPIs allow a workflow systems integrator to have a single end-user interface and functions set, regardless of the number of workflow management products existing in an installation. Whereas previously many workflow projects required development of a user interface most, though not all, workflow management systems now provide a user interface to facilitate human interaction with workflow processes. The interface can range from simple browsers to allow for work browsing, selection, and completion, to more complex interfaces that provide a flexible environment through user configuration and forms definition.

The workflow interoperability interface: the WfMC defines workflow interoperability as, "the ability of two or more workflow engines to communicate and interoperate in order to coordinate and execute workflow process instances across those engines" [WfMC 1999a]. Interoperability levels may range from supporting simple passing of tasks between different systems to supporting complete sharing and transferring of process definitions, and adoption of a common look and feel. A number of APIs have been defined to support this concept.

The interoperability interface addresses a key concern of the reference architecture, that is, the issue of defining standards that allow workflow systems developed by different vendors to pass work items between one another across a network. This network can be a LAN, WAN or Internet/Intranet.

Thus the interoperability interface defines the mechanisms that workflow product vendors are required to implement so that one workflow engine may make requests of another to effect the selection, instantiation, and enactment of known process definitions by that other engine. The requesting workflow engine is also able to pass context data (workflow relevant or application data), and receive back status information, and the results of the enactment of the process definition, in a manner that is transparent to the user.

To support the interaction and data transfer between compatible and incompatible workflow process engines the WfMC has also defined an interoperability abstract specification (Wf-XML) [WfMC 2000]. Wf-XML is an XML-based variant of the WfMC interoperability interface that can work with HTTP or a number of other transport mechanisms, including e-mail and direct TCP/IP connection, or MOM (Message Oriented Middleware).

One of the goals for Wf-XML is to provide an interoperability interface between multiple workflow systems. This means enabling organizations to communicate with other enterprises via their respective automated workflow systems. This is important in many e-Business environments where several enterprises need to communicate with each other. Wf-XML supplies the interoperability interface that the workflow systems use to communicate.

Wf-XML can be used to implement chained workflows, nested workflows, and parallel-synchronized workflows [WfMC 2000]. Wf-XML supports these three types of interchanges both synchronously and asynchronously, and allows messages to be exchanged individually or in batch operations. It also supports enhanced parallel-synchronized processing by allowing the notification of arbitrary events as they occur in the lifecycle of a business process.

The administration and monitoring tools interface: The administration and monitoring interface enables several workflow services to share a range of common administration and monitoring functions, also analysis of a consistent audit data across heterogeneous workflow products. This interface defines a standard that allows one vendor's task status monitoring application to work with another vendor's workflow enactment service. This will allow a complete view of the status of work throughout the organization and extended enterprise, irrespective of which workflow system is currently controlling the work.

During the initialization and execution of a process instance, multiple events occur which are of interest to a business, including WAPI events, internal workflow management engine operations, and other system and application functions. With this information, a business can determine what has occurred in the business operations managed by workflow. To achieve this the administration and monitoring interface may support the following types of operations [Hollinsworth 1995]: user management operations, role management operations, audit management operations, resource control, and process supervisory operations, as well as process status functions.

6.5 The role of enterprise information systems in e-Business

Before closing this chapter, it is useful to understand how Enterprise Information Systems (EIS) function within the context of e-Business. We shall start with a definition of an EIS first. An EIS encompasses the business processes and information technology infrastructure used within enterprises, and delivers the information infrastructure internal to an enterprise [Sharma 2001b]. An EIS exposes a set of services to its users. These can be at differing levels of abstraction – including data level, function level, business object, or process level. Many different applications and systems qualify collectively as EIS. These include among other things the following components:

- Enterprise applications that have been developed by an enterprise to meet specific business needs. These are developed using different programming languages, such as C, C++ or Java, and are considered to be custom applications. They may also fall under the banner of legacy systems, depending on which technologies are used.

- Legacy systems and applications that manage mission critical data to the business processes within an enterprise (see Chapter 16).

- Enterprise Resource Planning (ERP) systems that provide a unified, organization-wide view of business processes and associated information thus supporting the e-Business effort of the enterprise and being part of the whole value and supply chain (see also Section 1.2). EIS also include applications that are part of an ERP suite possibly augmented with special-purpose modules for procurement, customer relationship management (CRM), and so on. These are at the heart of EIS and often include modules that cover everything from accounting to quality management plant maintenance, and human resource and project management.

- CRM is the essential functionality that encompasses an organization's end-to-end engagement with its customers over the lifetime of its relationship with them. CRM systems achieve their functionality by accessing and analyzing data from disparate databases within the enterprise, drawing heavily on data already available in ERP systems (see also Section 1.2).

- Transaction processing systems and applications (see Section 14.7).

6.6 Chapter summary

Key management issues in an e-Business environment are coordination, collaboration and integration, with respect to business processes (for example, leading to e-Business process management) and to information systems.

The most important technologies and infrastructure underlying e-Business can be seen as different layers that are built upon each other. The bottom layer includes networking topologies, the Internet, and protocols such as TCP/IP. The layer above that is called the basic infrastructure layer and contains such as client/server and tiered architectures. The layer above the basic infrastructure is called the Web technologies and applications layer, and contains the technologies that are required to develop Web-based applications. Finally, the top layer contains collaborative technologies such as Electronic Data Interchange and workflow technologies.

Mainframe architectures promoted a single-tier approach whereby the code that implements the business rules in an application and automates business processes was lumped together with user interface and data access functions in a single large monolithic application. Client/server is the successor of mainframe architectures where client processes (service consumers) request service from server processes (service providers). Client/server applications use a two-tier client/server architecture in which tiers refer to the number of executable elements into which the application is partitioned. Two-tiered architectures provide a reasonable mechanism for organizations to design applications that fit their business needs. However, they present several drawbacks including poor business logic sharing and limited interoperability. The three-tier architecture emerged to overcome the limitations inherent in the two-tier architecture. In the three-tier architecture, a middle tier is introduced between the user system interface client environment and the database management server environment. Hence, the application is partitioned into three logical tiers: the presentation tier, the processing tier (or middle tier), and the data tier.

Web-based applications are applications that leverage Web clients, such as Web browsers, Web application servers, and standard Internet protocols. With Web-enabled applications the middle tier in the three-tier architecture is divided into two units with different functions. The reason is that the gap between thin clients used to generate Web pages and dynamic content using HTML and XML (which contain almost no application logic), and the application servers is too big to link them together. To remedy this situation, the classical presentation tier of the three-tier architecture is subdivided into a client tier and a new presentation tier addressed by an infrastructure known as a Web-server.

Collaborative technologies attempt to eliminate manual trading processes by allowing internal applications of different companies to directly exchange information and documents. The purpose of collaborative technologies such as Electronic Data Interchange and workflows is, in particular, to facilitate information flows within and across enterprise boundaries. EDI is commonly defined as the application-to-application transfer of structured trading data or documents by agreed message standards between computing systems. Structuring data is a precise, recognized, and accepted method of assembling data. Workflow systems automate a business process, in whole or in part, during which documents, information, or tasks are passed from one participant to another for action, according to a set of procedural rules. They are based on document lifecycles and forms-based information processing, so generally they support well-defined, static, 'clerical' processes, and provide transparency, since business processes are clearly articulated in the software, and are agile because they produce definitions that are fast to deploy and change.

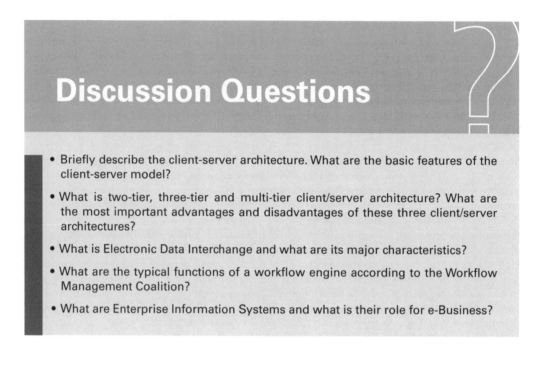

Discussion Questions

- Briefly describe the client-server architecture. What are the basic features of the client-server model?

- What is two-tier, three-tier and multi-tier client/server architecture? What are the most important advantages and disadvantages of these three client/server architectures?

- What is Electronic Data Interchange and what are its major characteristics?

- What are the typical functions of a workflow engine according to the Workflow Management Coalition?

- What are Enterprise Information Systems and what is their role for e-Business?

Assignments

i. A company uses electronic mail to send notification of shipments of material to its customers. Design an EDI solution for this company on the basis of the diagram in Figure 6.9.

ii. Develop a workflow solution for the above problem. Use as a basis the diagram in Figure 6.12 and extend it with appropriate symbols to explicitly represent decision points, alternatives, and parallel paths. Compare and contrast the EDI and the workflow solution.

Chapter

7

XML the Enabling Technology for e-Business

T
he Extensible Markup Language was defined by the XML Working Group of the World Wide Web Consortium (W3C) and is widely used for the definition of device and system-independent methods of storing and processing texts in electronic form. One of the main uses of XML in e-Business is the representation of the various business transactions that occur on a regular basis between trading partners. This includes purchase orders, invoices, shipping, bills of lading, and warehousing information. In addition, to the actual transactions themselves, XML helps standardize the process by which these messages are exchanged between trading partners. XML is also making a major impact in a number of areas, such as payment for services and security specification for e-Business, ranging from encryption and authorization to privacy.

The present chapter attempts to give an informal introduction to XML so that the reader would appreciate its use within the context of e-Business. Several aspects of XML are discussed in future chapters that cover a number of key technologies pertinent to e-Business, such as Enterprise Application Integration (Chapter 17), e-Business Integration (Chapter 18), and especially Web Services (Chapter 19), which rely heavily on XML-based standards and infrastructure.

The next few pages provide a brief overview of XML, discuss the characteristics of electronic documents, define structure in XML documents, and discuss presentation, transformation, and the processing of XML documents. The chapter also compares and contrasts XML and EDI in the context of e-Business. As the nature of this chapter is purely introductory, interested readers should also consult a number excellent introductory textbooks or Web sites now available on the subject.

7.1 Brief overview of XML

The Extensible Markup Language (XML) is an extensible language used for the description and delivery of marked-up electronic text over the Web, just like HTML (Hypertext Markup Language), which has been the standard language used to create Web pages. The word *markup* is used to describe annotations or special marks (codes) inserted into electronic texts to govern text formatting, printing, or other processing. The term is taken to mean making explicit the interpretation of a text. A *markup language* denotes a set of conventions used together for encoding texts. It must specify what markup is allowed, what is required, what it means, and how it is to be distinguished from text.

XML is a *meta-language*, that is, it provides a means of formally describing a language, in this case, a markup language. Unlike HTML, which is a predefined language, XML does not have predetermined tags but allows the definition of new tags and languages (in fact, there is an HTML version in XML). While the predefined tags of HTML are used to specify the visual aspects of the document, in XML they are used to structure the document, to define its contents, and to describe the data.

Three important characteristics of XML distinguish it from other markup languages:

1) Emphasis on *descriptive* rather than prescriptive (or procedural) markup;
2) Document type concept;
3) Portability.

In a descriptive markup system, the markup annotations simply categorize parts of a document. Markup codes such as <para> in HTML simply identify a portion of a document and assert of it that 'the following item is a paragraph'. By contrast, a prescriptive or procedural markup system defines what processing needs to be carried out at particular points in a document, e.g., 'move the left margin 0.2cm left, skip down one line, and go to the new left margin', etc.

In XML, the instructions needed to process a document for some specific purpose, e.g., to format it, are sharply distinguished from the descriptive markup, which occurs within the actual XML document. Formatting instructions are collected outside the document in separate procedures or programs, and are usually expressed in a distinct document called a *stylesheet*. With descriptive instead of procedural markup, the same document can be processed readily in many different ways, using only those parts of it that are considered relevant.

A second important aspect of XML is its notion of a *document type*. XML documents are regarded as having types. Its constituent parts and their structure formally define the type of document. The definition of a 'technical report', for example, might be that it consisted of a 'title' and possibly an 'author', followed by an 'abstract', and a sequence of 'sections'. Anything lacking a title, according to this formal definition, would not formally be considered as a technical report. Once an XML parser is provided with an unambiguous definition of a document's type, it can check that any document claiming to be of a particular type does in fact conform to the specification. For instance, an XML parser can check that only elements specified for a particular document type are present, that they are combined in appropriate ways, correctly ordered, and so on.

Finally, a basic design goal of XML is to ensure that documents are portable between different hardware and software environments. All XML documents, whatever language or writing system they employ, use the same underlying character encoding scheme. This encoding scheme is defined by an international standard, which is implemented by a universal character set maintained by an industry group called the Unicode Consortium, and is known as Unicode (Unicode World Wide Character Standard). Unicode is a standard encoding system that supports characters of the diverse natural languages.

The markup language with which XML is most frequently compared is HTML, the language in which Web pages had always been written until XML began to replace it. Compared with HTML, XML has some other important characteristics:

- XML is extensible as it does not contain a fixed set of tags;

- XML focuses on the meaning of data rather than on its presentation;

- XML documents must be well-formed according to a defined syntax, and may be formally validated.

XML is used in cases where documents cannot be adequately described by HTML. This includes documents that do not consist of typical HTML components (headings, paragraphs, lists, tables and so on); are used to describe customized database information, such as product descriptions, sorted according to price, delivery destination, etc; need to be organized in a tree-like hierarchical fashion such as, for example, describing the parts of a product and their subparts.

7.2 Characteristics of XML documents

Documents are vital for organizations. They perform various critical functions. Through documents, much of the formal communication within an organization and between organizations is executed. Documents provide legitimacy, which is the possibility of demonstrating that procedures have been executed in accordance with laws, (company) rules, and good practice. Documents safeguard accountability, which is the possibility of accounting for actions, and the way these actions have been performed. For example, a supplier's invoice communicates the amount of money that has to be paid by the buyer, certifies that the amount is based on agreed terms and conditions, and accounts for payments that the receiver has to make.

A document may be defined, irrespective of its form, as a reproducible collection of interrelated data, carried as a unity, reproduced or communicated by means of a storage medium [Clark 1999]. Documents are characterized by contents, structure, and presentation. Documents can have two appearances: physical or non-virtual and virtual. Non-virtual documents exist in a physical shape, or occur as a (digital) substitute (which means, not the same storage medium, but identical data and form). In a non-virtual document the data relate to each other by way of a fixed connection. Document imaging systems convert physical documents into a digital representation so that they can be stored and accessed by a computer [Laudon 2004]. Virtual documents are those documents that do not have a physical shape, but, however, can get this physical shape as copy or print. The data aren't bound to the specific documents in which they are used; they can be used in more than one document.

Documents are an essential component of business processes. Business processes generate and manipulate information like records and documents, and often their end products consist of 'items of information'. The efficiency of individual business processes, and of sequences of related business processes, depends largely on the efficiency with which documents are processed and exchanged. In fact, one might say that the flow of a business process is defined by the flow of documents [Davenport 1993].

One of the most common problems that enterprises face today is the exchange of documents between different organizational units of the same company rather than different companies: each program stores its data in one or more proprietary formats that are difficult to exchange with and understand by other programs. XML has been designed to facilitate the exchange of documents between different kinds of applications. In this way, XML facilitates developing an infrastructure that helps eradicate manual processes and enables seamless data and document flows both within and between enterprises.

For an XML document to be easily interpreted, it must contain three distinct parts as shown in Figure 7.1. These parts are the *content* or document data (normally text) that makes up the information contained within the document; the *definition* of the structure and organization of document elements using XML DTDs or Schema; the *presentation* of a document's visual aspects, e.g., its style defined by means of Stylesheets.

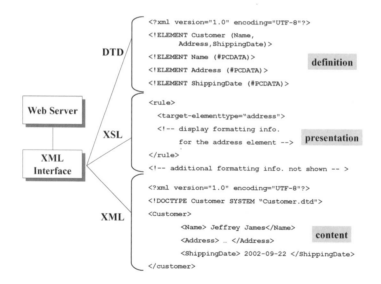

■ **Figure 7.1:** The Three Parts of an XML Document

For the moment we shall concentrate on the content of XML documents, while in subsequent sections we shall cover its definition (structure) and the presentation of the visual aspects of XML documents.

In XML, text represents the content of the document. The text in an XML document consists of intermingled markup and character data. The term markup is used to signify delimited text that describes the storage layout and logical structure of a document. In XML, all that is included between angled brackets ('<' and '>'), is considered markup, and is called a *tag*; for example, the construct <name> is a tag. Markups are demarcated text that describes the storage layout and logical structure of a document. Typical kinds of markup supported by XML include element start and end tags, empty element tags, comments, document type declarations, processing instructions, XML declarations, text declarations, CDATA section delimiters, entity references, character references, and any white space that is at the top level of the document.

An XML document is typically a computer file the contents of which meet the requirements laid out in the XML specification. However, XML documents may also be generated on the fly, e.g., an XML document may be dynamically compiled from information contained in a database.

A typical XML document consists of two main parts: the XML declaration or prologue and the document element (or root element). The prologue consists of an XML declaration, possibly followed by a document type declaration. The body is made up of a single root element, possibly with some comments and/or processing instructions, see Figure 7.2.

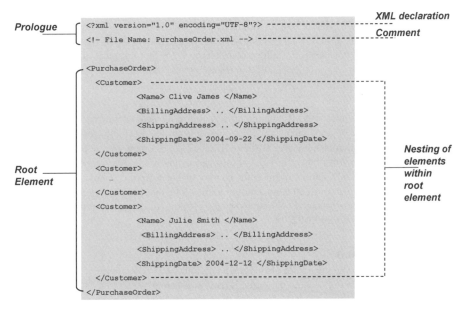

■ **Figure 7.2:** Layout of Typical XML Document

7.2.1 XML declaration

The first few characters of an XML document must make up an XML declaration. The XML processing software uses the declaration to determine how to deal with the subsequent XML content. A typical XML declaration begins with a prologue that contains a declaration of conformity to version 1.0 of the XML standard and to the UTF-8 encoding standard: **<?xml version="1.0" encoding="UTF-8"?>**

The encoding of a document is particularly important, as XML processors will default to UTF-8 when reading an 8-bit-per-character document. XML processing applications can also handle 16-bit-per-character documents in the Unicode encoding, which makes XML a truly international format, able to handle most modern languages.

7.2.2 Element

The second main part of an XML document is a single element known as the document or root element. The technical term used in XML for a textual unit, viewed as a structural component, is *element*. The elements in an XML document indicate the logical structure of the document and contain the information content of the document (which in the example that follows is customer information, such as names, addresses, street names, and numbers, shipping dates, and so on).

A typical element consists of a start tag, the content of the element, and an end tag, as follows: **<my_tag> the text data </my_tag>**. The content of an element can be character data, other nested elements or a combination of both. Most usually, elements of one type are embedded within elements of another type.

Different types of elements are given different names, but XML provides no way of expressing the meaning of a particular type of element, other than its relationship to other element types. For instance, all one can say about an element called (for instance) <address> in Figure 7.2 is that instances of it may (or may not) occur within elements of type <customer>, and that it may (or may not) be decomposed into elements of type <street name> and <street-number>.

Another way of putting data into an XML document is by adding *attributes* to start tags. Attributes are used to better specify the content of an element on which they appear. The attributes for a given element are serialized inside the tag for that element. An attribute specification is a name–value pair that is associated with an element. Attribute names have the same construction rules as element names. The value of the attribute is usually intended to be data relevant to the content of the current element. An element can have any number of attributes, which must all have different names. The following is an example of an element declaration using an attribute to specify the shipping date for a hypothetical customer: **<Customer name= "Marion" shippingdate = "2003-02-03">**.

7.2.3 XML namespaces

XML allows designers to choose the names of their own tags and, as a consequence, it is possible that name clashes (that is, situations where the same tag name is used in different contexts) occur when two or more document designers choose the same tag names for their elements. XML namespaces provide a way to distinguish between elements that use the same local name, but are, in fact, different, thus avoiding name clashes. For instance, a namespace can identify whether an address is a postal address, an e-mail address, or an IP address. Tag names within a namespace must be unique.

Namespaces in XML provide a facility for associating the elements and/or attributes in all or part of a document with a particular schema or DTD. All namespace declarations have a scope, i.e., all the elements to which they apply. A namespace declaration is in scope for the element on which it is declared, and of that element's children. The namespace name and the local name of the element together form a globally unique name known as a *qualified name* [Skonnard 2002].

A namespace declaration is indicated by a URI denoting the namespace name. Recall from Section 3.2 that the key aspect of the URI is that it is unique. The URI may be mapped to a prefix that can then be used in front of tag and attribute names, separated by a colon. If not mapped to a prefix, the URI sets the default schema for the current element and all of its children. If no default namespace declarations are in scope, then elements are not in any namespace. Elements not in any namespace are known as *unqualified elements* [Skonnard 2002].

There are three possible parts of a namespace used to declare XML document namespaces. These are [Valentine 2002]:

1) The `xmlns` attribute that identifies the values as an XML namespace;
2) The `:prefix` identifier that is used to identify a namespace. It is used only in the case where a namespace is declared;
3) The unique identifier `namespaceURI`. The values of this identifier do not necessarily have to point to the Web; it is simply a symbolic identifier.

There are two different ways to declare a namespace [Valentine 2002]:

1) Default namespace. This declares a namespace using the `xmlns` attribute without a prefix. All descendant attributes are assumed to belong to the defined namespace;
2) Prefixed namespace. This declares a namespace using the `xmlns` attribute with a prefix. When the prefix is associated with a particular element, then this element is assumed to belong to that namespace.

Listings 7.1, 7.2, and 7.3 illustrate examples of simple qualified and unqualified elements following the previous conventions.

Listing 7.1 shows an element with the local name of `Customer` and a prefix of `cust` that is mapped to the namespace name urn:sample-org:Customers. The element has children with local names of `name` and `shippingdate`. Both these child elements are unqualified, i.e., they are not in any namespace.

```
<cust:Customer xmlns:cust= 'urn:sample-org:Customers'>
    <name> Marion </name>
    <shippingdate > 2003-02-03 </shippingdate>
</cust:Customer>
```

■ **Listing 7.1:** Example of Qualified and Unqualified Elements

Listing 7.2 shows an element with the local name of `Customer` and a prefix of `cust`. The element is in the scope of the namespace urn:sample-org:Customers. The element has children with local names of `name` and `shippingdate`. Both these child elements are qualified as they have a prefix of `cust` that is mapped to the namespace name urn:sample-org:Customers.

```
<cust:Customer xmlns:cust= 'urn:sample-org:Customers'>
    <cust:name> Marion </cust:name>
<cust:shippingdate> 2003-02-03 </cust:shippingdate >
</cust:Customer>
```

■ **Listing 7.2:** Example of Qualified Elements

```
<Customer xmlns:cust= 'urn:sample-org:Customers'>
    <name> Marion </name>
    < shippingdate > 2003-02-03  </ shippingdate >
<Customer>
```

■ **Listing 7.3:** Example of Qualified Elements using a Default Namespace

Listing 7.3 shows an element with the local name of Customer and no prefix. The element is in the scope of the namespace urn:sample-org:Customers by virtue of an in-scope default namespace declaration for that URI. The element has children with local names of name and shippingdate. Both these child elements are qualified as they are under the namespace name urn:sample-org:Customers. This example is identical to that in Listing 7.2.

7.2.4 Well formed and valid documents

An XML document must be *well formed,* that is, one in which, in addition to all the constructs in the XML being syntactically correct, there is exactly one top element, with all open tags having corresponding closing tags or, using the empty element shorthand syntax, and all tags are correctly nested [Skonnard 2002]. In addition, all attributes of an element must have different names. If the attributes are namespace qualified, then the name space name and local name must be different.

A well-formed XML document consists of two main parts: a prologue and a document element (the root element). In addition, following the document element, a well-formed XML document may include comments, processing instructions, and white space such as spaces, tabs, or line breaks.

Although the property of well-formedness is a matter of making certain that the XML document complies with syntactical rules, document validity is a different issue. A well-formed XML document is considered *valid* only if it contains proper document type declarations and if the document obeys the constraints of those declarations. In most cases, type declarations and constraints will be expressed either by document type declarations (DTDs), or by an XML schema (both described in Section 7.3). Well-formed XML documents are designed for use without any constraints, while valid XML documents require constraint mechanisms expressed by either DTD or XML schema constructs. In addition to constraining the possible elements and the ordering of those elements in a document, valid XML documents can take advantage of advanced features including data typing, linking mechanisms, value and range bounding. These mechanisms are absent from well-formed documents due to lack of support by DTD or XML schema.

The use of valid documents can greatly improve the quality of document processes. Valid XML documents allow users to take advantage of content management, e-business transactions, enterprise integration, and all other kinds of business processes that require the exchange of meaningful and constrained XML documents.

7.3 Defining structure in XML documents

As already explained, the ability to perform validation is one of the key advantages of using XML. To carry this out, some way of formally stating the criteria for successful validation is necessary: in XML this formal statement may be provided by an additional document known as a document type declaration, or by an XML schema.

When an XML document declares a document type as declaration, a validating parser, for instance, a parser that supports validation using DTDs, reads the DTD, and uses it to check the XML document. If the XML document does not conform to the DTD it is said to be invalid and the parser should generate an error message.

7.3.1 Document Type Definition (DTD)

The Document Type Definition is a special form of document definition that defines a content model and document elements, such as including rules governing element content and properties, for some specific document. In a document definition (or a schema), the content model expresses what forms a document's structure may take.

The DTD contains the definition rules of tags; it denotes the elements and their order inside the XML document. Other than defining the elements, the DTD defines the syntax and the relations among elements, and is required to verify the validity and congruence of the document. The structure of an XML document is seen as a tree in which elements represent the nodes. Listing 7.4 represents the structure of a hypothetical list of customers.

The DTD is declared in the XML document's prologue using the `!DOCTYPE` tag. The `DOCTYPE` declaration is placed at the top of an XML document and is the container for all other DTD declarations. By convention the name of a DTD corresponds to that of the root element (in our example 'customer'). The DTD can be internal or external to the XML document. A DTD can be internal or external to the XML document; generally it is written in one or more separate documents.

If the DTD is internal to the XML document, the DTD starts with a DOCTYPE declaration: `<!DOCTYPE root_element [element, attribute, entity, notation]>`. This declaration must be made inside the XML document. The previous declaration identifies the four distinct components that make up an XML DTD, namely element type declarations, attribute-list declarations, notation declarations, and entity declarations. If the DTD is external to the document, then the document must reference the external file containing the declaration of the DTD. If the DTD of the customer document is in a separate file, say customer.dtd, then the XML document would include the statement: `<!DOCTYPE library SYSTEM "customer.dtd">`

```
<!DOCTYPE PurchaseOrder [
<!ELEMENT PurchaseOrder (customer+)>
<!ELEMENT customer (name, address, shippingdate)>
<!ATTLIST customer_id ID #REQUIRED>
<!ELEMENT name (first_name, last_name)>
<!ELEMENT address (street, city, state, zip)>
<!ELEMENT shippingdate (#PCDATA)>
<!ELEMENT first_name (#PCDATA)>
<!ELEMENT last_name (#PCDATA)>
<!ELEMENT street (#PCDATA)>
<!ELEMENT city (#PCDATA)>
<!ELEMENT state (#PCDATA)>
<!ELEMENT zip (#PCDATA)>
]>
```

■ **Listing 7.4:** A Sample Purchase order DTD

Listing 7.4 shows a sample DTD, `PurchaseOrder.dtd`, representing the structure of XML Purchase-Order documents.

Examining the declaration of the PurchaseOrder element, we note that it comprises one or more `customer` elements. Each `customer` element contains elements such as `name`, `address`, and `shippingdate`. These elements are separated by a comma and thus must be present in that exact order in the `PurchaseOrder.xml` file (see Figure 7.3). This figure depicts a simplified version of the DTD in Listing 7.4 and associates it with an XML document instance.

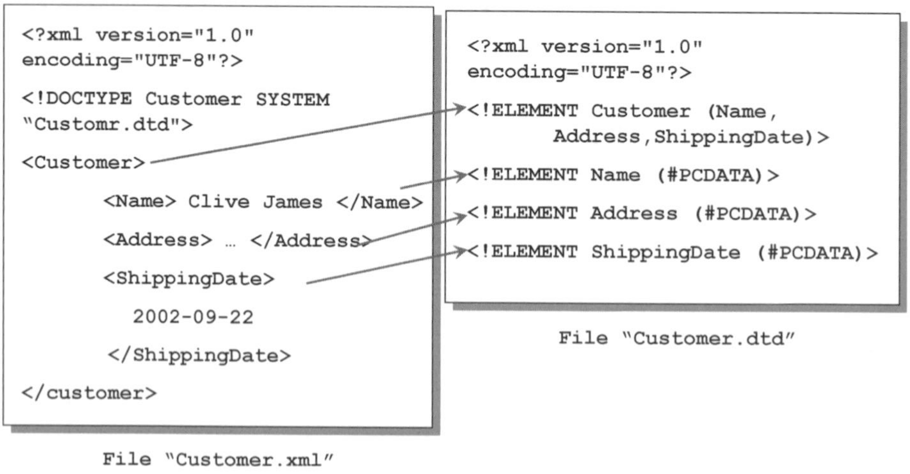

■ **Figure 7.3:** Connecting a DTD Specification to an XML Instance Document

In Listing 7.4 the declaration `<!ELEMENT name (first_name, last_name)>` signifies that the element `name` contains two subelements, namely `first_name` and `last_name`. A declaration such as `<!ELEMENT first_name (#PCDATA)>` means that the `first_name` element can be composed by any characters (only text) except for markup strings or special characters like , & or]. The `PCDATA` means parsed character data.

As we explained in Section 7.2.2, attributes are used generally as specifications of elements, to provide meta-information to an element content. In this case, we can consider attributes as metadata. In addition, attributes are also used to exercise control over values. This implies that we declare attributes as an enumeration of tokens forcing them to take values from a list of predefined enumerated values, very much in the same way that *enumerated types* do in programming languages such as C.

Attribute types can be CDATA (character data), ID, or a list of values (enumerated type) and are declared in this way: `<!ATTLIST element_name attribute_name attribute_type default_value>`. In the sample DTD illustrated in Listing 7.4, the ATTLIST declaration defines the set of attributes that is allowed on a specific element, e.g., `customer` element. In particular this construct specifies through the ID data type an attribute value (`customer_id`) that must be an XM name that is unique within a document instance. The default value of an attribute is compulsory when the option #REQUIRED is specified (in our example the customer element is compulsory). It can be optional if the data type #IMPLIED is specified, or may have a specified fixed value of the data type #FIXED is specified.

A DTD, such as the `PurchaseOrder` DTD, is what gives XML data its portability. If an application is sent a `PurchaseOrder` document in XML format, and has the `PurchaseOrder` DTD, it can process the document according to the rules specified in the DTD. For example, given the `PurchaseOrder` DTD, a parser will know the structure and type of content for any XML document based on that DTD. If the parser is a validating parser, it will know that the document is not valid if it contains an element not included in the DTD, such as `<customer>`, or if the `address` element precedes the `<name>` element.

In addition to elements and attributes, the DTD can contain notations and entities.

Notations are used to identify non-XML data and to provide instructions on how to process that data [Valentine 2002]. For example, a reference to a Graphics Interchange Format (GIF) image, the image is not only referenced, but also the XML processor is told how to handle it. In this particular example, the processor could be instructed to pass it to a GF viewer.

Consider the following DTD, where the `img` attribute is an entity that points to `mxhtml.gif`, and then the notation declaration for this image is defined.

```
<cover img="mxhtml">
<!NOTATION gif SYSTEM "image/gif">
```

If the processor is to handle this image, then in addition to defining a notation for it, an entity that references the external file containing the image should also be defined [Valentine 2002].

An XML document can be composed by elements referencing other objects; these objects are called entities. An *entity* is a placeholder for content. Entities serve several useful functions, such as, for instance, defining data that can be used in multiple places in a document. The following example shows a reference to non-XML data by means of an entity that can be further used from within attribute values:

```
<!NOTATION gif SYSTEM "image/gif">
<!ENTITY mxhtml SYSTEM  "graphics/mxhtml.gif" NDATA gif>
```

Other features also contribute to the popularity of XML as a method for data interchange. For one thing, it is written in a text format, which is readable by both human beings and text-editing software. Applications can parse and process XML documents, and human beings can also read them in case there is an error in processing. Another feature is that because an XML document does not include formatting instructions, it can be displayed in various ways. Keeping data separate from formatting instructions means that the same data can be published in different media.

7.3.2 Overview of XML schema

While the DTD model serves to define document-focused pages in XML, it suffers from a number of limitations that make it inadequate for advanced Web and e-Business applications. The DTD weaknesses include:

- The DTD model is not powerful or precise enough to express rich, extensible, or derived data types. The only basic data type supported by DTDs is character data. Applications requiring other data types, such as date or numeric, are forced to perform data type conversions.

- DTDs paradoxically use a syntax that is substantially different from XML. They are based on an approach that was originally defined in SGML (the pre-Web compound document markup language standard), and were carried forward to XML. This means that they cannot be processed with a standard XML parser.

- DTDs are not context-sensitive and do not support modularity. This issue stems from the fact that DTD specifications are linear (non-hierarchical), and DTDs do not support namespaces. This fact forces designers to come up with new names for similar elements in different settings. Moreover, DTDs do not support cross-DTD references, making thus reuse and refinement of existing DTDs an extremely challenging issue.

Another way to define XML tags and structure is with schemas. Schemas can be used in place of DTDs and provide many more capabilities for expressing XML documents. Because DTDs are not written using XML syntax, they have some inherent limitations which schemas can help overcome. The term *schema* is commonly used in the area of databases to refer to the logical structure of a database. When the term is used in the XML community, it refers to a document that defines the content of, and structure of, a class of XML documents. More specifically, *XML schema* describes the elements and attributes that may be contained in a schema-conforming document and the ways that the elements may be arranged within a document structure. The schema itself is a special kind of XML document written according to the rules of the XML Schema Definition Language (XSDL) recommended by the W3C.

Schemas are more powerful when validating an XML document because of their ability to clarify data types stored within the XML document. Because schemas can more clearly define the types of data that are to be contained in an XML document, schemas allow for a closer check on the accuracy of XML documents. As the purpose of a schema is to define a class of XML documents, the term *instance document* is often used to describe an XML document that conforms to a particular schema. Figure 7.4 illustrates an XML schema for a customer, which corresponds to the DTD, and a conforming instance document.

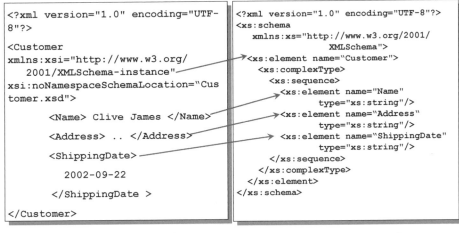

              File "Customer.xml"   File "Customer.xsd"

■ **Figure 7.4:** Connecting a Schema Specification to an XML document Instance

It is obvious from what has been previously stated that an XML schema is a meta-model in the sense that it can describe business models. To exemplify this, consider the customer schema in Figure 7.4 again. A customer schema can be considered as a type of grammar or set of rules that describes all possible customers (schema instances) that might be created. A schema language, in turn, can be considered as the tool to describe schemas.

The XSDL provides a very powerful and flexible way in which to validate XML documents. It includes facilities for declaring elements and attributes, reusing elements from other schemas, defining complex element definitions, and for defining restrictions for even the simplest of data types. This gives the XML schema developer explicit control over specifying a valid construction for an XML document. For instance, a document definition can specify the data type of the contents of an element, the range of values for elements, the minimum as well as maximum number of times an element may occur, annotations to schemas, and much more.

An XML schema is made up of *schema components*. These are building blocks that make up the abstract data model. Element and attribute declarations, complex and simple type definitions, and notifications are all examples of schema components. Schema components can be used to assess the validity of well-formed element and attribute information items, and, furthermore, may specify augmentations to those items and their descendants. XML schema components include the following [Valentine 2002]:

- Data types: these include both simple and complex/composite and extensible data types. For example, XML schema offers simple data types such as string, Boolean, float, date, time, binary, and so on. It also offers the possibility of defining complex data types. For instance, customer in Figure 7.4 is an example of a composite type composed of name, address type, and shipping date elements. Elements such as addresses could also be complex in their own right.

- Element type and attribute declarations: elements are the basic building blocks of XML documents; they may contain content, other elements, or attributes. XML elements are used to describe entities and attributes in logical data modeling terms.

- Constraints: these are declarative rules for data types and elements, such as enumerated types, min/max values, default values, and formatting conventions.

- Relationships: these express associations between elements. For instance, a purchase order may be associated with multiple order products. Inheritance can also be provided as an extension or restriction of base types. Such derived data types can originate from existing data types known as *base types*. Base types can be primitive types or even other derived types.

- Namespaces and import/include options: these support modularity as they make it possible to include externally managed XML schemas. As an example, an application may decide to use and extend a business partner's purchase order rather than defining its own.

Listing 7.5 depicts a purchase order for various items and Listing 7.6 illustrates an instance document conforming to this schema. The remainder of this section is devoted understanding the XML schema for the XML document shown in Listing 7.5. This document allows one customer to receive the shipment of the goods and an entirely different individual to pay for the purchase. This document also contains specific information about the products ordered, such as how much each product cost, how many were ordered, and so on. This simple XML schema was derived on the basis of similar schema specifications found in [Schmelzer 2002]. The purchase order schema consists of a schema element and a variety of sub-elements, most notably element, `complexType` and `simpleType` that determine the appearance of elements and their content in instance documents. We will briefly explain these components in the following.

```
<xsd:schema xmlns:xsd="http://www.w3.org/2001/XMLSchema">

  <xsd:annotation>
    <xsd:documentation>
        Purchase Order schema for an online store.
    </xsd:documentation>
  </xsd:annotation>

  <xsd:element name="PurchaseOrder" type="PurchaseOrderType"/>

  <xsd:complexType name="PurchaseOrderType">
```

```xml
  <xsd:all>
    <xsd:element name="ShippingInformation" type="Customer"
      minOccurs="1" maxOccurs="1"/>
    <xsd:element name="BillingInformation" type="Customer" minOccurs="1"
      maxOccurs="1"/>
    <xsd:element name="Order" type="OrderType" minOccurs= „1"
      maxOccurs="1"/>
  </xsd:all>
  <xsd:attribute name="Tax">
    <xsd:simpleType>
      <xsd:restriction base="xsd:decimal">
        <xsd:fractionDigits value="2"/>
      </xsd:restriction>
    </xsd:simpleType>
  </xsd:attribute>
  <xsd:attribute name="Total">
    <xsd:simpleType>
      <xsd:restriction base="xsd:decimal">
        <xsd:fractionDigits value="2"/>
      </xsd:restriction>
    </xsd:simpleType>
  </xsd:attribute>
</xsd:complexType>

<xsd:complexType name="Customer">
  <xsd:sequence>
    <xsd:element name="Name" minOccurs="1" maxOccurs="1">
      <xsd:simpleType>
        <xsd:restriction base="xsd:string"/>
      </xsd:simpleType>
    </xsd:element>
    <xsd:element name="Address" type="AddressType" minOccurs= "1"
      maxOccurs="1"/>
      <xsd:choice minOccurs="1" maxOccurs="1">
      <xsd:element name="BillingDate"  type=" xsd:date „/>
      <xsd:element name="ShippingDate" type=" xsd:date „/>
    </xsd:choice>
  </xsd:sequence>
</xsd:complexType>

<xsd:complexType name="AddressType">
  <xsd:sequence>
    <xsd:element name="Street" type="xsd:string">
    <xsd:element name="City"   type="xsd:string">
    <xsd:element name="State"  type="xsd:string">
    <xsd:element name="Zip"    type="xsd:decimal">
```

```
    <xsd:sequence>
  </xsd:complexType>

  <xsd:complexType name="OrderType">
    <xsd:sequence>
      <xsd:element name="Product" type="ProductType" minOccurs= „1"
        maxOccurs="unbounded"/>
    </xsd:sequence>
    <xsd:attribute name="SubTotal">
      <xsd:simpleType>
        <xsd:restriction base="xsd:decimal">
          <xsd:fractionDigits value="2"/>
        </xsd:restriction>
      </xsd:simpleType>
    </xsd:attribute>
    <xsd:attribute name="ItemsSold" type="xsd:positiveInteger"/>
  </xsd:complexType>

  <xsd:complexType name="ProductType">
    <xsd:attribute name="Name" type="xsd:string"/>
    <xsd:attribute name="Price">
      <xsd:simpleType>
        <xsd:restriction base="xsd:decimal">
          <xsd:fractionDigits value="2"/>
        </xsd:restriction>
      </xsd:simpleType>
    </xsd:attribute>
    <xsd:attribute name="Quantity" type="xsd:positiveInteger"/>
  </xsd:complexType>

</xsd:schema>
```

 **Listing 7.5:** A Sample Purchase Order Schema

```
<PurchaseOrder Tax="5.77" Total="75.77">
 <ShippingInformation>
  <Name> Clive James </Name>
  <Address>
   <Street>158 Anne st.</Street>
   <City> Sydney </City>
   <State> NSW </State>
   <Zip> 2055 </Zip>
  </Address>
```

```
  <ShippingDate> 2002-09-22 </ShippingDate>
</ShippingInformation>

<BillingInformation>
  <Name> Jenny James</Name>
  <Address>
   <Street>158 Anne st. </Street>
   <City> Sydney</City>
   <State> NSW </State>
   <Zip> 2055 </Zip>
  </Address>
  <BillingDate> 2002-09-15 </BillingDate>
</BillingInformation>

<Order SubTotal="70.00" ItemsSold="2">
  <Product Name="USB Drive" Price="50.00"
  Quantity="1"/>
  <Product Name="Mac Software" Price="20.00"
  Quantity="1"/>
</Order>
</PurchaseOrder>
```

■ **Listing 7.6:** An XML Instance Document Conforming to the Schema in Listing 7.7

Type definitions, element and attribute declarations

The XSDL differentiates between *complex types*, which define their content in terms of elements that may consist of further elements and attributes, and *simple types*, which define their content in terms of elements and attributes that can contain only data. The XSDL also introduces a sharp distinction between *definitions* that create new types (both simple and complex), and *declarations* that enable elements and attributes with specific names and types (both simple and complex) to appear in document instances. To *declare* an element or attribute in a schema means to allow an element or attribute with a specified name, type, and other features to appear in a particular context within a conforming XML document.

In this section, we focus first on declaring elements and attributes, and then on defining simple and complex types that include them.

Declaring elements and attributes

Elements are the primary ingredients of an XML schema and can be declared using the `<xsd:element>` element from the XSDL. The element declaration defines the element name, content model, and allowable attributes and data types for each element type. The `<xsd:element>` element either denotes an element declaration, defining a named element and associating that element with a type, or it is a reference to such a declaration [Skonnard 2002]. The location at which an element is defined, determines certain characteristics about its availability within the schema. The element declarations that appear as immediate descendants of the `<xsd:schema>` element are known as *global element declarations* and can be referenced from anywhere within the schema document or from other schemas. For example, the `PurchaseOrderType` in Listing 7.5 is defined globally and in fact constitutes the root element in this schema. Global element declarations describe elements that are always part of the target namespace of the schema. Element declarations that appear as part of complex type definitions, either directly or indirectly – through a group reference – are known as *local element declarations*. These include elements such as `Customer` and `Order`.

The basic components of an element declaration include: `type`, `ref`, `minOccurs`, `maxOccurs`, `abstract`, `substitutionGroup`, `block`, `default`, `fixed`, and `nillable` [Skonnard 2002]. These are explained briefly in the following.

The `type` attribute defines the type of the element being declared. This attribute is a reference to a simple or complex type. The `ref` attribute specifies a reference to a global element declaration. Two attributes control occurrence behavior (constraints). These are: `minOccurs` and `maxOccurs`. The `minOccurs` and `maxOccurs` attributes specify the minimum and maximum number of times this element may appear within the context where it is declared in a valid XML document. In general, an element is required to appear when the value of `minOccurs` is 1 or more. The default value for both the `minOccurs` and the `maxOccurs` attributes is 1.

The `abstract` attribute indicates whether the element being declared may show up directly within the XML document. An abstract `element` may not show up directly in an instance document; rather, an element in this element's `substitution` group must appear instead. The XML `substitution` mechanisms allow for one group of element to be replaced by another group of elements. If, for example, we need to have multiple elements that share the same basic values specified for the attributes on the `<element>` element, rather than defining and setting those attribute values for each element, we can declare an abstract element, set the values once, and substitute the abstract element definition as needed.

The `block` attribute specifies what substitution mechanisms are prohibited for the element being declared. The `block` attribute may assume any of the following values: `#all`, `extension`, `restriction`, `substitution`. If the value `#all` is specified within the `block` attribute, no elements derived from this element declaration may appear in place of this element. A value of `extension` prevents any element whose definition has been derived by extension from appearing in place on this element. If a value of `restriction` is assigned, an element derived by restriction from this element declaration is prevented from appearing in place of this element. Finally, a value of `substitution` indicates that an element derived through substitution cannot be used in place of this element.

The `final` attribute specifies what derivation mechanisms are prohibited for the element being declared. The block attribute may assume any of the following values: `#all`, `extension`, `restriction`, `substitution`. If `extension` is specified then elements in the substitution group of this element may not be of a type derived by extension, either directly or indirectly, from the type of this element. If `restriction` is specified then elements in the substitution group of this element may not be of a type derived by restriction, either directly or indirectly, from the type of this element. If the value `#all` is specified, then both of the above cases apply.

The `default` attribute may be specified only for an element based on a `simpleType` or an element whose content is text only. This attribute assigns a default value to that element. The fixed attribute specifies that the element has a constant, predetermined value. The fixed and default attributes are mutually exclusive.

The `nillable` attribute indicates whether an explicit NULL value can be assigned to the element. If this particular attribute is omitted, it is assumed to be false. If this attribute has a value of true, the nil attribute for the element will be true.

When working with content models, a schema designer can specify reusable model groups, occurrence behavior, and different types of element content. An element that declares an element content may use composition components to define and constrain the behavior of child elements. There are three types of composition components that can be used within XML schemas. These are `sequence, choice` and `all`. The construct `sequence` requires that content models follow the element sequence defined. The construct `choice` requires that the document designer makes a choice between a number of defined options. Finally, the construct `all` requires that all the elements in a group may appear once or not at all, and may appear in any order.

Attributes in an XML document are contained by elements. To indicate that a complex element has an attribute, we use the `<attribute>` element of the XSDL. For instance, from Listing 7.5 we observe that, when declaring an attribute, e.g., `Tax` or `Total`, we must specify its type. This type must be one of the simple types: Boolean, byte, date, dateTime, decimal, double, duration, float, integer, language, long, short, string, time, token, etc.

Apart from defining the type of an attribute, the `<attribute>` element within the XSDL contains a use attribute to assist in defining when an attribute is `optional, required, or prohibited`, whether its value is fixed, whether there is a `reference` to this attribute, and what its `default` value is [Schmelzer 2002].

If the use attribute is set to `required`, the parent element must have the attribute; otherwise the document will be considered invalid. A value of `optional` indicates the attribute may or may not occur in the document, and the attribute may contain any value. By assigning a value of `prohibited` to the use attribute, a schema developer can indicate that the attribute may not appear at all within the parent element. Specifying a value for the `default` attribute indicates that if the attribute does not appear within the specified element of the XML document, it is assumed to have the default value. A value within the fixed attribute indicates the attribute has a constant value.

The `ref` attribute for the `<attribute>` element indicates that the attribute declaration exists somewhere else within the schema. This allows complex attribute declarations to be defined once and referenced when necessary. If, for instance, one reuses element and attribute declarations from another schema within the current schema, this would provide the perfect opportunity to take advantage of the ref attribute. Just as attributes can be defined, based on the simple data types included in the XSDL, they can also be defined based on `<simpleType>` elements.

Simple types

The `<simpleType>` element of the XSDL is used to define new types based on existing simple types. These simple type elements are used to define all attributes and elements that contain only text, and do not have attributes associated with them. When defining simple types by means of the `<xsd:simpletype>` element, the developer can use XSDL data types to restrict the text contained by an element or attribute. Some of these simple types, such as string and decimal, are built into the XSDL while others are derived from the built in types. For instance, one can require an attribute value to be a date or an integer. In addition, this integer can be further restricted to assume a limited range of values, e.g., from 0–100.

Derived data types are derived from an existing data type known as the *base type*. New derived types can originate from either a primitive type or another derived type. The `base` attribute type may contain any simple XML data type or any `simpleType` declared within the schema. Specifying the value of this attribute determines the type of data it may contain. A `simpleType` may contain only a value, but not any other elements or attributes, and can be derived by restricting an existing simple type. We use the `restriction` element to indicate the existing (base) type, and to identify the 'facets' that constrain the range of values. This is probably the most common method in which to declare types, and it helps to set more stringent boundaries on the values an element or attribute based on this type definition may hold. For example, Listing 7.5 indicates that the values of the simple element `Name` in `Customer` are restricted to only string values. Moreover, this Listing specifies that each of the simple attributes `Name`, `BillingDate`, and `ShippingDate` must appear exactly once as a child of the `Customer` element. By the same token, Listing 7.5 indicates that simple attribute types like `Tax`, `SubTotal`, `Total`, and `Price` are restricted to decimal values only with two digits allowed to the right of the decimal point.

Complex types

The `<complexType>` element is used to define structured types. An element is considered to be a complex type if it contains child elements (which could be simple or complex) and/or attributes. Complex type definitions appear as children of an `<xsd:schema>` element and can be referenced from elsewhere in the schema, and from other schemas. Complex types typically contain a set of element declarations, element references, and attribute declarations. The declarations are not themselves types, but rather an association between a name and the constraints that govern the appearance of that name in documents governed by the associated schema. Elements are declared using the `<element>` element, and attributes are declared using the `<attribute>` element.

An example of a complex type in Figure 7.5 is `PurchaseOrderType`. This particular element contains three child elements – `ShippingInformation`, `BillingInformation`, and `Order` – as well as two attributes, namely `Tax` and `Total`. The use of the `maxOccurs` and `minOccurs` attributes on the element declarations with a value of 1 for these attributes, indicates that the element declarations specify that they must occur only once within the PurchaseOrderType element.

The basic syntax for the `<complexType>` element is as follows [Skonnard 2002]: `abstract`, `block`, `final`, `mixed`.

The `abstract` attribute indicates whether an element may define its content directly from this type definition or from a type derived from this type definition. An abstract type may not appear in an instance document; rather, a derived type must appear in its place, e.g., through the use of substitution groups. The `block` attribute indicates what types of substitution mechanisms are prevented for this element definition. This attribute can contain any of the following values: `#all`, `extension`, `restriction`. A value of `extension` prevents complex type definitions derived through extension from being used in place of this type definition. Assigning a value of `restriction` prevents a complex type definition derived through restriction from being used instead. A value of #all prevents all complex types derived from this type definition by both extension and restriction from being used in place of this type definition. The `final` attribute specifies which derivation mechanisms are prohibited for type definitions that reference this type as their base type. The `mixed` attribute indicates that the content model of the complex type may contain text and element children.

An element declared with a content model can contain one or more child elements of the specified type or types, as well as attributes. To declare an element with element content, a schema developer must define the element type using the `<complexType>` element and include within a content model that describes all permissible child elements, the arrangement of these elements, and rules for their occurrences. In the XSDL the following elements: `all`, `choice`, `sequence`, or a combination of these elements can be used for this purpose. As an example, notice the use of the `<xsd:sequence>` and `<xsd:choice>` elements in Figure 7.5. The `<xsd:sequence>` element is used to indicate when a group of elements or attributes is declared within a `<xsd:sequence>` schema element, they must appear in the exact order listed. This the case with the `street`, `city`, `state`, and `zip` attributes in the complex type `AddressType`. The `<xsd:choice>` element is used to indicate when a group of elements or attributes is declared within an `<xsd:choice>` schema element, any one, but not all, of the child elements may appear in the context of the parent element. This the case with the `BillingDate` and `ShippingDate` attributes in the complex type `Customer`.

7.4 Document presentation and transformation

A key feature of XML is that it allows document developers to decouple the structure of a document from its presentation (appearance). An XML document does not include formatting instructions and can be displayed in various ways. Keeping document data separate from formatting instructions means that different media, such as a browser or a hand-held device, can display the same document.

XML presentation facilities provide a modular way to display document content on a variety of devices such as Web browsers, WAP browsers, VoiceXML browsers (for speech-enabled applications), and in various formats, e.g., HTML for Web display, Wireless Markup Language (WML) for display on WAP devices, voice form for VoiceXML browsers, and alternate XML dialects (protocols) for e-Business data transfer.

It is important to realise that when we think about document styling and representation for display on different devices and formats, two distinct processes are involved. Firstly, we must transform document information from the organization and structure used when it was created into the organization and structure required for consumption. Secondly, when rendering document information we must express, whatever the medium chosen, aspects of the appearance of the reorganized document information. To address this issue, the W3C has introduced the *Extensible Stylesheet Language* (XSL) for XML documents. XSL comprises two parts:

1) A transformation sub-language called XSLT (*XSL Transformations*), which is a language for transforming source (input) XML documents into target (output) languages, such as HTML, dialects of XML, or any text representation language, including programming languages.
2) A formatting sub-language called Extensible Stylesheet Language Formatting Objects (XSL-FO) is used to specify the document styling, i.e., how the data are to be displayed, and representation in a way that is suitable for display.

A requirement for an expression sub-language to select parts of a document for transformation was identified while XSLT was being developed. This resulted in the W3C defining the XPath sub-language [Gardner 2002]. *XPath* is used to define search expressions that locate document elements to be used in the process of transformation. XPath is an abstract language that defines a tree model that codifies the logical structure of an XML document against which all expressions are evaluated. The logical structure for the instance document defined in Listing 7.6 can be found in Figure 7.5.

7.4.1 Using XSL to display documents

To perform document transformation, a document developer usually needs to supply a style sheet, which is written in XSL. The *style sheet* specifies how the XML data will be displayed. XSLT uses the formatting instructions in the style sheet to perform the transformation. The converted document can be another XML document or a document in another format, such as HTML, that can be displayed on a browser. Formatting languages, such as XSLT and XSL, can access only the elements of a document that are defined by the document structure, e.g., XML schema.

The style sheet describes how an XML data stream is to be rendered or converted. XSL does not only determine the style or presentation of the XML document, but also the medium on which it is presented, such as a browser or a hand-held device. An XSL style sheet contains a series of pattern-action rules, called *templates*, each of which specifies a pattern to be matched in the *source document*, and a set of actions to be taken when the pattern is matched. A *pattern* is a restricted XPath location path that associates a template with a set of nodes in the source document. The results of the actions become the body of the *target document*. One starts with a source document, applies the style sheet actions, and generates the target document. The selection of target elements can be qualified in a number of ways. For example, XSL allows different rules to be applied to the same element type dependent on what its ancestors, siblings, or contents are. In addition, processing rules can be specified for application when particular attribute values have been associated with an element, or when the element has specific contents.

The XSL style sheet pattern-action rules allow document developers precisely to select the XML data that they wish to display, to present those data in any order or arrangement, and to freely modify or add information. XSL provides document designers with access to XML components such as elements, attributes, comments, and processing instructions; while at the same time allowing them to sort and filter XML data. In addition, it offers facilities that allow document designers to include loop and conditional structures, and use variables very much as in programming languages as well as a set of built-in functions.

The power of style sheets is that the formatting information is completely independent of the XML data. Because of that independence, one style sheet can apply to many XML documents, or conversely, several style sheets can apply to one XML document so as to present the XML data in a variety of ways. The advantage of this is that once a standard type of style sheet has been developed, such as those for

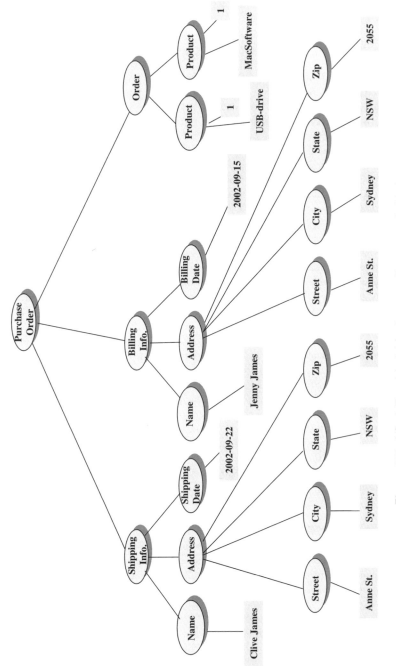

■ **Figure 7.5:** XPath Tree Model for Instance Document in Listing 7.7

presenting XML documents in a certain browser format, it can be reused several times on many different XML documents. In addition, enhancements that are made to existing style sheets are easy to apply to XML documents.

7.4.2 Using XSLT to transform documents

A feature that contributes to the popularity of XML is its use as a method for data interchange. Since XML is written in a text format, which is readable by text-editing software, applications can parse and process XML documents. An XSL schema, such as the `PurchaseOrderType`, is what gives XML data its portability. If an application is sent a `PurchaseOrderType` document in XML format, and has the `PurchaseOrderType` schema, it can process the document according to the rules specified in the schema. For example, given the `PurchaseOrderType` schema, a parser will know the structure and type of content for any XML document based on that schema. If the parser is a validating parser, it will know that the document is not valid if it contains elements not included in the schema, or if the structure or order of elements is not correct.

XSLT is a data-driven specification that allows the conversion of an XML document into another XML document, or into any other type of document. An XSLT style sheet or script contains instructions that tell the transformation processor how to process a source document to produce a target document. This makes XSLT transformations very useful for e-Business applications. Consider, for example, XML documents generated and used internally by an enterprise that may need to be transformed into an equivalent format that customers or service providers of this enterprise are more familiar with. This can help to transfer information easily to and from an enterprise's partners.

XLST transformations are usually applied to XML documents in one of three ways:

1) The transformation takes place on the server side, whereby the template is applied before the data are sent to the client, and only the resultant style sheet is displayed on the client side.
2) The transformation may take place at the client side, whereby both the source XML document and the template driving the transformation are sent to the client. The client then applies the template and displays the resultant style sheet.
3) Some third-party software transforms the XML document, and both client and server see only the transformed document.

XSLT version 1.0 defines an XML-based programming language for transforming documents into other text formats. The most common use of XSLT is for transforming documents in one XML dialect into another XML dialect. It is also common to use XSLT for transforming XML documents into HTML, or some other presentation-oriented format [Skonnard 2002]. In addition, XSLT can be used to transform XML documents to other types of text format, such as programming languages like C++/Java source files.

XSLT transformations occur through a series of tests that compare parts of an XML document against templates (pattern-action rules) that are defined in a style sheet, which is written in XSL. The XSL style sheet specifies how XML data will be displayed. XSLT uses formatting instructions in the style sheet to perform the transformation. The style sheet templates act like rules that are matched against the specification of a style sheet. When a match is detected, XSL reads the target XML file and then constructs an XPath tree of the objects of the document. It transforms the original tree into a resultant tree for the target document by applying transformation rules and, subsequently, formats the target document. This means that a common understanding of the same contents of a document is possible even when it is formatted or structured differently.

Figure 7.6 illustrates the process of transforming between two different XML versions of Customer documents. Both XML fragments are clearly expressing the name and address of a customer. To relate the first to the second fragment, we need to assign the values of Name related attributes in the first fragment to the values of Name related elements in the second fragment, the values of Address elements in the first fragment to the values of Address related elements in the second fragment, dropping the ShippingDate element entirely.

Notice that when we speak of transforming data, we are not talking about converting data from one representation into something entirely different. Rather, we have the problem of translating between two dissimilar but related XML applications. These applications are related in the sense that they are representing the same entities, i.e., customers and addresses.

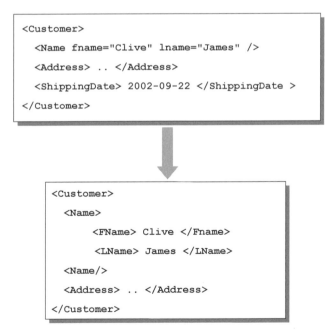

■ **Figure 7.6:** Transforming between two Different Versions of Customer Documents

7.5 Processing XML documents

Programmatic access to XML is provided by means of specialized software processors known as XML *parsers* or XML *processors*. XML parsers read XML documents, validate document syntax against a DTD or XML schema, and then allow programmatic access to a document's contents depending on application needs. XML parsers can perform both validation and processing. If during validation an XML document is found not to be well-formed, the parser reports errors.

There are two major document parsing and processing alternatives in the XML world: the Simple API for XML (SAX) and the Document Object Model (DOM). These XML parsers use languages such a Java or Python for accessing a document's content programmatically.

SAX is a set of abstract programmatic interfaces designed for the Java programming language that project an XML document onto a stream of well-known method calls. SAX provides a streaming model that can be used to process XML documents as well as produce XML documents. Developers implement the SAX interface to process XML documents, and invoke the SAX interfaces to produce XML documents.

SAX defines an API for an *event-based* parser. Being event-based means that the parser reads an XML document from beginning to end, and each time it recognizes a syntax construction, such as elements, attributes, comments, etc, it generates an *event* that notifies the application that is running it. These events return data from the XML document. Software programs can 'listen' for events and obtain data from the XML document.

SAX interfaces are amenable to pipeline-style processing. With pipeline-style processing an implementation of a SAX interface, such as `ContentHandler` that models the core information of an XML document as an ordered sequence of method calls, can intercept items it recognizes but pass along unrecognized items to a downstream processor that also implements the same interface [Skonnard 2002]. In this way, SAX supports filter chains that may be used to construct event-processing pipelines. Filter chains are useful when building complex XML applications that can be partitioned into tasks modeled as simple SAX components [Coyle 2002].

A DOM parser builds a hierarchical model of the parsed XML document (known as the 'document object model'), with each of the important locations in the document, the various element and attribute containers, and characteristics of that model being represented as *nodes*. The DOM is a set of abstract programmatic interfaces that project an XML document onto a tree structure. The DOM API provides a generic object model to represent the structure of documents, and a standard set of interfaces for traversing and manipulating them. The DOM API provides a platform and language-independent interface to allow developers to programmatically access and modify the content of tree-structured documents, such as HTML or XML [Coyle 2002]. Due to the fact that DOM is language independent developers can use for scripting languages or programming languages such as Java to process XML.

DOM falls under the category of tree-based APIs that are useful for a variety of applications, but strain memory when processing large documents. A DOM-based parser builds a tree structure in memory that contains the XML document's data and allows multiple passes through a document. In addition, because DOM is language neutral, it introduces undesirable complexities when translating from DOM interfaces to language-specific data structures of strongly typed languages such as Java.

Because SAX offers a streaming model, it is often preferred over the DOM when performance becomes an issue. The SAX approach uses less memory and is more efficient for messaging and transformation. However, SAX parsers place more processing burden on the application program for the logic and navigation. Developers working with SAX must build their own data structures to help keep track of where they are in a document. This means that they must maintain document state as they process XML using SAX. This can make application programs complex and more difficult to maintain.

The choice between XML parsers often depends on application needs. If an application requires parsing an XML document only for performing a single specific task, e.g., for mapping it to an existing program or database application, SAX is then the preferable choice. However, if the document is used as a continuing source, or data, or requires frequent interaction, DOM makes more sense.

7.6 XML, EDI and e-Business

Though many enterprises are announcing strategies on how they are going to take advantage of the rich capabilities provided in XML, this markup language is still not in mainstream use. Most enterprises view XML as a robust technology to exchange information between disparate applications, irrespective of whether these applications reside within the enterprise or across the value chain. For the most part, these companies use Electronic Data Interchange as a means to exchange this information today. As we have already explained at the outset of this book, in essence EDI is a means of paperless trading (see Section 6.4.1). With EDI, the standards define the syntax for exchanging data and the business semantics.

EDI has traditionally been regarded as a specialized solution, optimized for 'heavy' data volume performance between larger enterprises that have the resources to implement it. While traditional EDI has proved the feasibility and efficiencies possible when using e-Business transactions, its limitations have been found to be the cost of integration, deployment, and maintenance by smaller business partners. EDI involves complex and costly mapping and reengineering procedures each time a new partner enters the chain. It also involves tremendous operational costs, and requires dedicated services, which, apart from installation costs, consume considerable repeat expenditure by way of maintenance. These facts have meant that EDI has become the preserve of large organizations, and has resulted in EDI being adopted by over 90% of *Fortune* 100 companies, but it has only a meager 2% adoption rate among SMEs (Small to Medium Enterprises). As a result, EDI often cannot provide the agility enterprises need to respond to new business opportunities or integrate with their business partners.

By contrast, XML can be perceived as a dynamic trading language that enables diverse applications to flexibly and cost effectively exchange information. XML allows the inclusion of tags pertinent to the contextual meaning of data. These tags make possible precise machine-interpretation of data, fine-tuning the entire process of information exchange between trading enterprises. In addition, the ability of the XML schema to reuse and refine the data model of other schema architectures enables reuse and extension of components and reduces the development cycle and promotes interoperability. This technique is contrary to that of traditional EDI where the whole is standardized rather than the individual parts.

Other positive aspects of XML include the ease with which XML-coded files become stored repositories. By storing data in the clearly defined format provided by XML, data can be transferable to a wide range of hardware and software environments. XML clearly permits options for exchanging data not easily implemented via the use of EDI. Highly interactive information exchange that tends to be human interface-intensive lends itself much more to XML technologies than to traditional EDI. Moreover, unlike traditional EDI solutions, where information movement between companies is predominantly through batch transfers (to optimize huge transactional costs), XML fosters cost-effective, real-time information exchange.

The technical implications for e-Business information exchange technology are that it must be flexible, in a way that will accommodate the dynamic information requirements between disparate trading partners. An additional requirement is an ability to embrace open standards, which are essential to allow rapid establishment of business information exchange and interoperability. XML is ideally suited to these requirements as it can be used to encode complex business information. For example, XML is well suited to transactional processing in a heterogeneous, asynchronous, open, and distributed architecture that is built upon open standard technologies, such as parsers and interfaces. Not only does this apply to e-Business integration with trading partners, but also in terms of EAI.

For all the above reasons, XML holds the promise of realizing the original goals of EDI, making it simpler to implement with a relative lower cost of entry, and easier to exchange electronic documents over the Internet.

The ideal modus operandi would be not to replace EDI with XML, but to continue benefiting from existing EDI integrated network partnerships and, at the same time, using an EDI-XML hybrid to reach out to small/mid-size enterprises with a more flexible technology. The EDI–XML gap can be effectively bridged, by translation software that allows bi-directional XML/EDI conversion.

Several XML developers have already turned to standard EDI messages that they map to XML to provide better descriptions and definitions of business operations. This mapping has been perceived as a very attractive and effective solution. However, it negates the point of using XML. Simply mapping standard EDI messages to XML perpetuates the problem of non-aligned implementations.

To align differing business processes successfully and reliably requires agreements on how to transmit an XML message, the meaning of its elements, how to identify and name elements, and which elements various business processes require, e.g., when placing an order. In order to use XML for e-Business means finding a way for industries and even individual enterprises to use their own codified business language, but at the same time, be able to trade with partners that use other languages.

The electronic business XML (ebXML) initiative (see Chapter 20) that strives to create a single global electronic marketplace where enterprises of any size and in any geographical location can meet and conduct business with each other through the exchange of XML-based messages, tackles this problem at two levels:

1) At a high level, ebXML identifies common cross-industry business processes that characterize business transactions, and define a structure of those processes that enables development of a Business Process Specification Schema (BPSS). Business processes identify the parties conducting business, their specific roles, the interactions among the parties, the flow of messages in those interactions, and major pieces of data carried in those messages.
2) At a more detailed level, ebXML developed core components with perhaps the most potential impact on e-Business applications. Core components address semantic interoperability (see section 18.7) at the level of individual data items, seeking a way to bridge the individual industry terminologies, much as ebXML business processes work at a high level.

In a recent interesting development, the standards bodies behind EDI and ebXML (the Accredited Standards Committee X12, UN/EDIFACT Working Group, UN/CEFACT and OASIS) have jointly affirmed that the two technologies ought to identify areas of convergence. As the first crucial step towards a complementary standardization strategy, the groups have taken upon themselves to identify a set of core business process components that would benefit from a standard integration framework. This would make possible the concept of `Business Process Integration' that aims at providing comprehensive integration capability to an organization, and fosters varied process transactions across multiple industries.

7.7 Chapter summary

XML is an extensible markup language used for the description and delivery of marked-up electronic text over the Web. The word markup is used to describe annotations or special marks (codes) inserted into electronic texts to govern text formatting, printing, or other processing, while the term markup language denotes a set of markup conventions used together for encoding texts.

Important characteristics of XML are its emphasis on descriptive rather than prescriptive (or procedural) markup, its document type concept, and its portability. In XML, the instructions needed to process a document for some specific purpose, e.g., to format it, are sharply distinguished from the descriptive markup, which occurs within the actual XML document. Formatting instructions are collected outside the document in separate procedures or programs, and are usually expressed in a distinct document called a stylesheet. With descriptive instead of procedural markup, the same document can readily be processed in many different ways, using only those parts of it that are considered relevant. Another important aspect of XML is its notion of a document type. XML documents are regarded as having types. Its constituent parts and their structure formally define the type of a document. In XML, text represents the content of the document. The text in an XML document consists of intermingled markup and character data.

A typical XML document consists of two main parts: the XML declaration or prologue and the document element (or root element). The prologue consists of an XML declaration, possibly followed by a document type declaration. The elements in an XML document indicate the logical structure of the document and contain its information.

An XML document must be well formed. If it is, in addition to all the constructs in the XML being syntactically correct, there will be only one top element, all open tags will have corresponding closing tags or use the empty element short hand syntax, and all tags will be correctly nested. A well-formed XML document is considered valid only if it contains proper document type declarations, and if the document obeys the constraints of those declarations. Type declarations and constraints will be expressed either by document type declarations or by an XML schema.

The Document Type Definition is a special way of defining a content model and document elements, such as including rules governing element content and properties, for some specific document. While the DTD model serves to define document-focused pages in XML, it suffers from a number of limitations that make it inadequate for advanced Web and e-Business applications. These limitations are addressed by XML schema. XML schema describes the elements and attributes that may be contained in a schema-conforming document, and the ways that the elements may be arranged within a document structure. The schema itself is a special kind of XML document written according to the rules of the XML Schema Definition Language recommended by the W3C. Schemas are more powerful when validating an XML document because of their ability to clarify data types stored within the XML document.

Elements are the primary ingredients of an XML schema and can be declared using the <xsd:element> construct. The <simpleType> element of the XSDL is used to define new types based on existing simple types. These simple type elements are used to define all attributes and elements that contain only text and do not have attributes associated with them. The <complexType> element is used to define structured types. An element is considered to be a complex type if it contains child elements (simple or complex) and/or attributes. Complex type definitions can be referenced from elsewhere in the schema and from other schemas. Complex types typically contain a set of element declarations, element references, and attribute declarations.

A key feature of XML is that it allows document developers to decouple the structure of a document from its presentation (appearance). An XML document does not include formatting instructions and can be displayed in various ways. Keeping document data separate from formatting instructions means that different media, such as a browser or a hand-held device, can display the same document. The Extensible Stylesheet Language for XML documents is used for this purpose. XSL has two parts. A transformation sub-language called XSLT (XSL Transformations), which is a language for transforming source (input) XML documents into target (output) languages, and a formatting sub-language called Extensible Stylesheet Language Formatting-Objects (XSL-FO) which is used to specify the document styling.

EDI has traditionally been regarded as a specialized solution for e-Business applications. However, it is optimized for 'heavy' data volume performance between larger enterprises that have the resources to implement it. While traditional EDI had proved the feasibility and efficiencies possible when using e-Business transactions, the limitations were found to be the cost of integration, deployment, and maintenance by the smaller business partners. In contrast, XML can be perceived as a dynamic trading language that enables diverse applications to flexibly and cost-effectively exchange information. XML holds the promise of realizing the original goals of EDI, making it simpler to implement with a relative lower cost of entry, and more ease of exchanging electronic documents over the Internet.

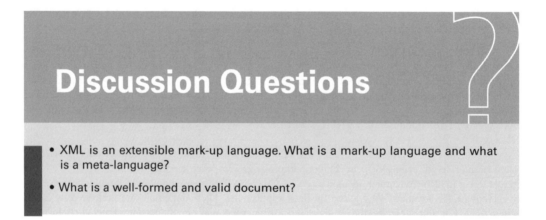

Discussion Questions

- XML is an extensible mark-up language. What is a mark-up language and what is a meta-language?
- What is a well-formed and valid document?

- What are simple and complex types? What is the relationship between them? Describe a situation in which a complex type can be used and a simple type cannot.

- What is the purpose of the abstract language XPath?

- Describe the two approaches that XML parsers or XML processors use to provide.

- Discuss some of the impacts of XML for e-Business.

Assignments

i. Listing 7.5 defines a complex type `AddressType`. Use the XML `complexContent` element to derive a new complex type from `AddressType`. This type should be able to represent an international address format, say Australian or European addresses, by adding the element country to the complex type `AddressType` definition in Figure 7.7. Complex content extensions allow reusing type definitions as they are by adding more fields to the end of the content model of the base type. One can add attributes, but cannot modify or remove existing attributes.

ii. XML is well suited as a method for describing transactions. Transaction-oriented content can serve a number of purposes but often represents the content of an exchange between applications or the data captured from a Web server. Transactions tend to include granular collections of data elements. Extend the purchase order schema in Listing 7.5 to describe the case of an enterprise that sells products to its customers by accepting only credit cards as a payment medium. A simple order-processing transaction should contain basic customer, order, and product type information as well as payment information, including fields for credit card number, expiration date, and payment amount. Show how this purchase order schema can import the address schema that you develop for Web assignment 3.

Chapter 8

◼ e-Markets

The Internet has a powerful effect on transaction costs. As a consequence, businesses are expected to consider buying goods and services they need instead of producing them themselves. One of the effects of the Internet is the electronic brokerage effect: the ability to bring buyers and sellers together in a virtual space, in other words, to create electronic markets.

Electronic markets are commerce sites on the public Internet that allow large numbers of buyers and suppliers to meet and trade with each other. They are also known as electronic market places, online markets, e-hubs, or business-to-business markets. At its most basic, an electronic market is a Website where many companies can buy from and sell to each other using a common technology platform. Many electronic markets also offer additional services, such as payment or logistics services that help members complete a transaction. They may also support community activities, like distributing industry news, sponsoring online discussions, and providing research on customer demand or industry forecasts for components and raw materials. Theoretically, electronic markets present ideal structures for commercial exchange, because of the market efficiency attained by tightening and automating the relations between sellers and buyers of services and products. Many different market mechanisms are made available to e-Markets' participants, and the markets' flexibility may thus be customized to serve any industry's full supply chain.

Although e-Markets have not taken off as expected, they are still likely to be an important channel for e-Business connecting buyers and suppliers. e-Markets agglomerate their member companies into trading communities united by common business interests, thus improving speed and efficiency. They offer both buyers and sellers forums to reduce transaction costs, to enhance sales, to streamline distribution processes, to deliver and consume value-added services, and to streamline customer management.

In this chapter we present an analysis of e-Markets. In particular, we define and describe characteristics of e-Markets, discuss functions performed by e-Markets, and analyze the differences between traditional markets and electronic markets. Subsequently, we explain the specific effects of trading through an e-Market, and discuss critical success factors for electronic markets.

Case Studies
Four electronic markets[1]

MetalSite
MetalSite was an electronic market operating in the metal industry, which was recently shut down [Nooteboom 2001]. It was created for companies that produce, sell, and use metal, in order to reduce the supply chain inefficiencies associated with the metal industry. It grew from the Website by which manufacturer Weirton Steel sold secondary and excess metal products.

ChemConnect
ChemConnect is an electronic market for worldwide buyers and sellers of chemicals, plastics, and industrial gases. Its buyers are medium-size to large companies, either in the chemistry business or in the manufacturing of paper, paints, household products, etc., for the production of which chemicals are needed. Its sellers, too, are medium-size to large companies, such as DSM and Akzo Nobel. ChemConnect has been created to increase the efficiency of the heavily fragmented market of industrial chemicals. While sellers may be disadvantaged by ChemConnect's lower prices (compared to offline markets), the e-Market's reduction in transaction time and costs is favorable to buyers and sellers.

CheMatch
CheMatch is an electronic market for bulk commodity chemicals, polymers, feedstocks, and fuel products. Fred Cook, a former Dow Chemical employee, founded it in 1997, supported by Dewitt Consulting, with whom he shared a vision of facilitating the buying and selling of bulk commodity chemicals via the Internet. Their primary sources of revenue are the commissions charged per transaction on their exchange, the fees charged per transaction through their auction, and subscription fees for the general use of CheMatch. Electronic markets like CheMatch need large transaction volumes to generate enough revenue to be viable.

[1]These case studies were developed by A. Nooteboom as part of his Master's thesis at Tilburg University.

Eumedix

Eumedix is an electronic market operating in the medical industry which was recently shut down. Three persons who had all been working for companies which supply medical products to hospitals, a very inefficient market in which buyers switch suppliers only very infrequently, founded Eumedix. Eumedix facilitated the trade of medical products, from disposables such as needles and gloves to high-value

products such as CT-scanners. Hospitals also used it to procure non-industry-specific MRO-goods, such as printers and computers. As an electronic market, Eumedix cast its net wide. It focused on the worldwide procurement of medical products, depending for its revenue on the fees paid per transaction; it needed volume to survive.

8.1 Electronic markets defined

Every market, whether online or not, represents a complex assembly of buyers and suppliers united by intricate lines of power and dependency. Although supply and demand control the business flow, each market carries a built-in measure of inefficiency. Electronic markets minimize that inefficiency by tightening the relationships between supplier and buyer, promoting price transparency and spending aggregation, reducing supply chain costs, and increasing the reach of suppliers. If they attain enough liquidity, electronic markets offer the closest approximation to a perfectly efficient trading system developed so far.

An e-Business electronic market (or simply *e-Market*) can be defined as a virtual online market, i.e., a network of company interactions and relationships, where buyers, suppliers, distributors, and sellers find and exchange information, conduct trade, and collaborate with each other via an aggregation of content from multiple suppliers, trading exchanges, and member communications supported by collaboration tools. E-Markets typically offer a wide variety of ancillary services required by the members of the trading community, such as authenticating buyers and sellers, and streamlining procurement workflows, risk management, settlement services, conflict resolution services, and logistics services. This is illustrated in Figure 8.1 where the central box represents the marketplace software and the two 'wings' represent the buyer and seller business processes surrounding the marketplace.

The e-Market brings all interconnections to a single point – the trading hub. A trading hub takes content from different suppliers, rationalizes it, and makes it usable by all buyers. E-Business markets serve three particular functions:

1) They act as an exchange for business transactions – not only purchasing but also for checking prices and stock availability, invoicing, and order chasing;
2) They manage catalog content, converting product information into a common format understood by all parties (see Section 8.5.3);
3) They provide additional services to support the trading process, from shipping, payment, and tax to online auctions, tendering, and vetting a company's financial status.

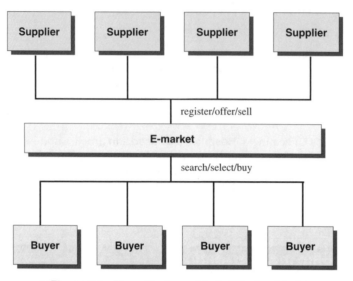

■ Figure 8.1: The e-Business Market Trading Model

E-Markets are having such an impact on business-to-business operations because they provide a more efficient and cost-effective means of conducting trade. E-Markets automate and streamline multiple steps in the buying process and, therefore, have evolved as new channels for corporate purchasing. For example, buyers can save significant time and money on simplified product searches through content-rich online catalogs. They can create online requests for proposals to solicit service providers, and these providers can respond to potential buyers rapidly and at a low cost. They also provide open transaction networks where a large number of potential buyers and sellers are able to participate without the restrictions of time and space. Automated transactions save on communication and people costs, and result in fewer ordering errors. Moreover, e-Markets assist order tracking, payments, and collections as well as easy reordering and product replenishment. Leading e-Markets are building integrated sets of value-added services, including logistics, financial services (for example, credit checks, escrow, and electronic payments), content management and analytics, and forecasting, to address more sophisticated needs in ways that create competitive advantages for participants.

The central role of conventional markets is to facilitate the exchange of information, goods, services and payments [Bakos 1998]. These basic market functions are also a necessary part of e-Business electronic markets, which generally support the whole transaction process by electronic means, including information search, price discovery,. and transaction settlement. Through aggregation, e-Business e-Markets compile product information from many suppliers so that buyers can do one-stop shopping on the Internet [Bailey 1997]. Electronic cataloging is the common mechanism that electronic markets use to aggregate supplier offerings. The topic of electronic cataloging is treated in Section 9.5.3.

An electronic marketplace will not thrive without a critical mass of buyers and sellers. For a buyer, the more suppliers in an electronic market, the more purchase alternatives it can consider, and the more benefits it can extract from the low operating and search costs provided by Internet technologies. For a supplier, the more buyers in an e-Market, the more reach its products achieve, and thus the better are the firm's chance of increasing sales. The organizational adoption of electronic markets must take into account the installed base of participants (buyers from the point of view of a seller, and sellers from the point of view of a buyer). The greater the installed base of market participants the greater will be the business value of a specific electronic market [Dai 2002]. However, the number of market participants is not the only criterion. It is also important that the electronic marketplace creates for its participants significant added value, and not just minor savings in transaction costs. Buyers need enough pricing and product information to be able to make a buying decision. Buyers need high-quality content – not just product information content, but the ability to mix related content with regulations, hazardous materials information, product reviews, and editorial content, etc. Matching that will provide a richer mix of information. Value-added content such as industry news, expert advice, or detailed product specification sheets can make a marketplace much more compelling. Offering services such as financing, logistics, back-end system integration, and procurement management helps strengthen e-Market ties with market participants.

8.1.1 How electronic markets work

In a typical e-Market, groups of buyers and sellers in a particular industry are linked together. In the most common scenario, organizations establish a marketplace system to provide an electronic catalog service that features the products and services of many suppliers in an industry sector. Sellers register their product and service offerings with the e-Market's electronic catalog. Buyers use their browsers to search for and review product offerings, fill electronic forms, and generate their orders. The orders are passed to the messaging system, which interprets messages, sends the orders to appropriate suppliers, and communicates other order-status tracking documents. This is depicted in Figure 8.2. This figure depicts two key elements:

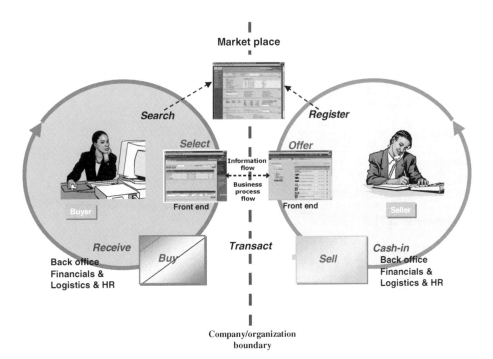

■ **Figure 8.2:** Typical Functions in an e-Market

1) An enterprise portal that provides users with a personalized, Web-browser-based work environment that offers everything they need to do their work;

2) E-Market (marketplace), an open electronic business-to-business hub that enables inter-company relationships for buying, selling, communicating, and acquiring information by employing Web services.

Companies operating marketplaces are referred to as intermediaries or market makers. They may themselves be participants in the market – buyers or sellers – or independent third parties, financial services providers, IT vendors, or multiform consortia. E-Markets provide mechanisms to facilitate finding buyers for sellers and suppliers for buyers, matching what is wanted with what is offered in the market. In e-Business e-Markets, such matching is implemented through dynamic trading processes, or electronic auctions. In addition to aggregation and matching facilities that enable firms to identify products and discover prices, e-Business e-Markets usually provide facilitation services that help companies conduct business transactions. Financial services and logistics arrangements are two of the most important facilitation functions that should be activated once buyers and sellers agree on a deal. The fact that electronic markets provide online facilities that ease transactions between buyers and sellers, means that they potentially provide support for every step of the order fulfillment process [Strader 1997; Daniel 1999].

Market makers provide a comprehensive range of services surrounding trade, and thus offer a strong value proposition, improve customer retention, and expand their own potential revenue. Some of the value market makers may provide to an e-Market include:

• Industry expertise and content;

• Catalog aggregation;

• Transaction negotiation and facilitation;

• Shipping/logistics services;

• Internationalization;

• Procurement workflow;

• Financial settlement or financing;

• Quality assurance and rating services;

• Business intelligence;

• Customer service.

It is interesting to note that e-Business electronic markets leverage their information processing, storage capacity, and communication networks to satisfy management needs in business transactions [Dai 2002]. Procurement knowledge is derived from the vast quantity of data generated from online transactions as firms analyze purchase patterns. In addition, product information and purchase expertise can be made available for better sourcing decisions. Such procurement expertise and knowledge will greatly help management in strategic sourcing activities.

By bringing buyers and sellers together online, electronic markets play the role of digital intermediaries [Bailey 1997; Bakos 1998]. For example, demand and supply information can be aggregated and disseminated, and buyers and sellers can be matched in electronic markets. To achieve this, markets aggregate suppliers' product offerings, and help buyers search for desired products and discover attractive prices. After buyers and sellers agree on a deal, facilitating mechanisms for transaction settlement also can be provided so that logistics and payment can be arranged.

E-Markets also provide the possibility of forward and reverse auctions. The forward auction brings together many buyers and one seller. By the nature of this model, the price can only increase. It is most beneficial to companies that are looking to unload surplus inventory. The reverse auction model, on the other hand, brings together many sellers and few buyers. The buyer drives the price so in this model prices are naturally driven downward.

8.1.2 Functional characteristics of business-to-business e-Markets

Although business-to-business e-Markets show different levels of functional sophistication, the typical exchange combines the four core enterprise applications: Enterprise Recourse Planning (ERP), Supply Chain Management (SCM), Customer Relationship Management (CRM), and Electronic Procurement (see Figure 8.3).

ERP systems are normally used to run financial and accounting activities; thus, when e-Market participants engage in online transactions, the ERP system automates the order fulfillment process, from creating a customer to tracking the order through shipping and billing in the case of an e-Market seller (see Section 6.6). In the case of an e-Market buyer, the ERP software may be used to issue purchase orders, and track and manage inventory. Integration with a back-office accounting system is also established through that software package.

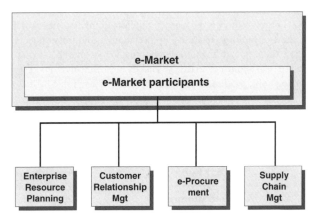

■ **Figure 8.3:** Core Applications in an e-Market

Supply chain management software is essentially a decision support application that uses complex mathematical algorithms that balance multiple, often competing, constraints in the supply chain. These constraints include available and alternative inventory and finished goods, transportation, and manufacturing capacity. Supply chain management identifies the most economic trade off between these constraints. It focuses on reducing inventory and optimizing manufacturing in order to take costs out of the whole extended production system, and should provide the e-Market participant with the ability to conduct real time and iterative decision making. The topic of supply chains and supply chain management is introduced in Chapter 10.

Customer Relationship Management (CRM) solutions reach across and into an enterprise, affecting anybody who interacts with a customer (see Section 1.3). Typically, CRM focuses on automating interactions with clients, typically in sales and support functions. CRM applications are also important in e-Market processes, as e-Market sellers are interested in optimizing their service, support, and marketing functions.

E-Procurement is the buying and selling of goods and services (business to business) in a digital environment by means of software applications that are Web or Internet based. An e-Procurement network provides a secure market place, sales platform, and transaction tracking system for buyers and sellers. Buying application software allows an organization to carry out purchasing processes. Depending on the sophistication of the software, e-Procurement allows buyers to perform some or all of the following functions: access supplier information, including catalogs, generate requisitions, obtain approvals in accordance with the business rules of the organization, send purchase orders to suppliers, receive invoices, and process payment. E-Procurement is treated in detail in Chapter 9.

8.1.3 Classification of electronic markets

To understand electronic markets, it is useful to understand what merchandise businesses purchase and how they acquire it. Generally speaking, businesses buy two types of products: *operating inputs* and *manufacturing inputs* [Kaplan 2000]. Operating inputs are also called maintenance, repair, and operating (MRO) goods. They may include non-production materials such as software, printers, hardware, office equipment, and so on, and are not specific to the industry in which the business buying them operates. *Manufacturing inputs* are raw materials (wood, plastic, chemicals, etc.), needed for the company's' processes or products, and therefore usually specific to its industry. Both kinds of purchases may be made in two ways. Many businesses have negotiated, usually long-term contracts with qualified suppliers with whom they develop close relations. This is called *systematic sourcing*. The alternative is *spot sourcing*: fulfilling immediate needs at the lowest cost possible. This generally involves short-term, loose relations; in fact, many spot market buyers don't know who their supplier is. By combining these two distinctions, operating versus manufacturing goods and systematic versus spot sourcing, we arrive at a four-cell matrix to classify electronic markets according to four economic models: MRO hubs, catalog hubs, yield managers, and exchanges (see Table 8.1 below).

	Products bought	
Buying method	Operating inputs	Manufacturing inputs
Systematic sourcing	**MRO hub**	**catalog hub**
Spot sourcing	**yield manager**	**exchange**

■ **Table 8.1:** Four Types of Electronic Market [Kaplan 2000]

- The systematic sourcing of low-cost operating inputs often involves high transaction costs. *MRO hubs* lower these costs (for buyers and sellers) by disintermediating, that is, bypassing middlemen. *MRO hubs* are business providers of horizontal markets that enable systematic sourcing of operating inputs. Operating inputs tend to be low-value goods with relatively high transaction costs, so these electronic hubs provide value largely by improving efficiencies in the purchasing process. Many of the best known players in this area, such as Ariba and Commerce One, started out by licensing 'buy-side' software for e-Procurement to large companies which used the software on their own intranets. Now, instead of licensing their software to individual companies, MRO hubs are hosting it on their own servers to provide an open market. These markets give buyers access to consolidated MRO catalogs from a wide variety of suppliers.

- *Yield managers* create spot markets for common operating resources with a high degree of price and demand volatility, such as manufacturing capacity, labor, and advertising, which allow companies to expand or contract their operations at short notice. This type of electronic hub adds the most value in situations with high price and demand volatility, such as those found in utilities markets, or with huge fixed-cost assets that cannot be liquidated or acquired quickly, such as person power and manufacturing capacity. Examples of yield managers are Employease and Elance for human resources, CapacityWeb.com for manufacturing capacity, and Youtilities for utilities.

- *Exchanges* are electronic markets closely related to traditional commodity exchanges that enable the spot sourcing of manufacturing inputs. They are essentially online exchanges that facilitate the trade of commodities and near-commodities needed for production, such as steel or paper, thus allowing purchasing managers to smooth out the peaks and valleys in demand and supply by rapidly exchanging one commodity for another. The exchange maintains relationships with buyers and sellers, making it easy for them to conduct business without negotiating contracts or otherwise hammering out the terms of relationships. Examples of exchanges include e-Steel for the steel industry, Paper Exchange.com for paper, and Altra Energy for energy.

- Catalog *hubs* facilitate the systematic sourcing of non-commodity manufacturing inputs, such as plastics and chemicals, and create value by reducing transaction costs. Like MRO hubs, catalog hubs bring together many suppliers. The only difference is that unlike MRO hubs they are industry specific. They can also be buyer-focused or seller-focused. Because their products tend to be specialized, catalog hubs often work closely with distributors to ensure safe and reliable deliveries. Examples of catalog hubs include PlasticsNet.com in the plastics industry, Chemdex in the specialty chemicals industry, and SciQuest.com in the life-science industry.

Since exchanges and catalog hubs facilitate the trade of industry-specific products, they are often called *vertical* electronic markets. These are also known as industry consortia, and are industry-owned vertical marketplaces that serve specific industries. Likewise, MRO hubs and yield managers establish the trade of non-industry-specific products, and are therefore referred to as *horizontal* electronic markets. In contrast to vertical marketplaces, *horizontal* marketplaces sell specific products and services to a wide range of companies. This introduces a useful categorization scheme that can be built upon the scope of an e-Market, and its position in the value chain. At the highest level, e-Markets can thus be categorized in two groups:

1) Vertical e-Markets: this variation of an e-Market provides value by efficiently managing interactions between buyers and sellers in a specific industry sector and tries to offer all the inputs, strategic and non-strategic, that are required to operate in this industry. Vertical e-Markets are typically very

industry specific and deal with a set of specialized goods or services, e.g., in domains such as aerospace, chemicals, healthcare, floral industries, construction, automotive industries, and so on. This variation mainly addresses the supply chain processes of businesses. Typical examples would be Covisint for the automotive industry and Petroleumplace.com for the petrochemical industry. General Motors, Ford, Renault, and Daimler Chrysler created a marketplace for the automotive industry, called Covisint, by providing procurement, supply-chain, and product development functionality. The objective of Covisint is to assist the automobile industry in dramatically increasing the efficiency of the supply chain by both creating digital markets and increasing coordination among buyers and suppliers. A similar consortium, Petroleumplace.com is a marketplace that provides equipment and services that are largely specific to the oil industry. There are, however, also multi-industry vertical marketplaces which seek to create trading communities in several industries. An example would be Freemarkets.

2) *Horizontal e-Markets*: this variation of an e-Market has a product focus, e.g., indirect goods, and shipping, and takes shape around a supply market that cuts across several industries. Examples include the many marketplaces being set up to buy and sell MRO (materials, repair, and operations) goods, such as safety supplies, hand tools, and janitorial services, which are consumed on the plant floor but do not become part of the final product. This variation mainly addresses the spot purchasing needs of different types of businesses; its main value proposition is the delivery of goods and services at reduced prices. Examples would be the maintenance, repair, and operations (MRO) exchange Grainger.com or the office supplies provider Staples.com.

E-Markets are usually tilted toward a supplier, a buyer, or a neutral third party thus giving rise to three general ownership-based market models:

1) *Buyer-dominated marketplace*: these are markets that are set up by large buyers, often in conjunction with technology partners. This is a many-to-one model where many companies sell products and services to one company via an intranet-based procurement system. The buyer's intranet is outfitted with a custom-assembled catalog that aggregates many supplier catalogs into a single catalog, while purchases are linked to back end ERP and legacy purchasing systems, so avoiding potential bookkeeping errors. An example would be the Covisint, a joint venture between General Motors, Ford, DaimlerChrysler, Renault, Nissan, Oracle, and i2.

2) *Supplier-dominated marketplace*: this is a one-to-many model where one company sells products and services over its Website to many other companies by displaying its catalog on its Website. These markets are set up by suppliers, such as UTC, Honeywell, and their technology partner i2, who developed a marketplace for aerospace equipment (MyAircraft.com).

3) *Neutral marketplace*: this is a many-to-many model where many companies sell products and services to many other companies via an online marketplace. Sellers' catalogs are aggregated for the benefit of any buyer visiting the marketplace. It primarily suits fairly static prices and commodity purchases. Buyers and sellers can find each other and execute transactions online. This model has the potential to radically reduce buyers' costs, and allow sellers to reach out to new customers by providing many-to-many liquidity. Examples of this type of model are companies like MetalSite and eSteel, both of which facilitate the sale of excess steel inventory, and have multiple steel sellers and multiple steel buyers transacting business over their sites.

E-Business electronic markets are generally considered as a potential source of significant efficiency gains. They generate efficiencies in three ways. First, they put a downward pressure on purchasing prices. Secondly, they decrease informational costs and expand everyone's market reach by removing the geographic barriers to buyers and sellers efficiently discovering each other. Thirdly, they allow a reduction in transaction costs and an improvement of inventory management [Lucking 2001].

8.1.4 Market-making mechanisms

A closer look reveals that systematic sourcing requires a different market-making mechanism from that of spot sourcing. Electronic markets for systematic sourcing use an *aggregation mechanism*, in which large numbers of buyers and sellers are brought together under one virtual roof. This reduces transaction costs by providing one-stop shopping. The aggregation mechanism is static in nature because the parties involved pre-negotiate their prices. An important characteristic of this mechanism is that adding another buyer to the electronic market benefits only the sellers and vice versa.

The *matching mechanism*, on the other hand, brings together buyers and sellers to negotiate prices on a dynamic and real-time basis. This is required for spot sourcing situations, in which prices are determined at the moment the purchase is made. This means that spot sourcing may become an auction. The matching mechanism involves interchangeable players' roles: buyers can be sellers and vice versa. Therefore, adding new members increases the market's liquidity and thus benefits both buyers and sellers.

8.1.5 Biased or unbiased markets

One other important characteristic of electronic markets must be mentioned here: their bias. Electronic markets can be either unbiased or biased. *Unbiased* or neutral electronic markets are operated by independent third parties, and do not favor buyers over sellers or vice versa. Their benefit is that they are true market makers, because they bring buyers and sellers together [Kaplan 1999]. Their problem is that buyers will only participate if there is a sufficient number of sellers, and sellers will only participate if there are enough buyers.Electronic markets that favor either buyers or sellers are called *biased*. Of these, *forward aggregators* favor sellers by bringing them together and negotiating for them under an aggregation mechanism. *Forward auctioneers* do so under a matching mechanism. The term 'forward' in this sense indicates that the process follows the traditional supply chain model, with the supplier at the start and the buyer at the end. Likewise, *reverse aggregators* and *reverse auctioneers* attract large numbers of buyers, and then bargain with suppliers on their behalf. [Kaplan 2000]. Table 8.2 summarizes the foregoing discussion.

Type of product	Manufacturing inputs	Operating inputs	
Type of contract	Systematic sourcing	Spot sourcing	
Market-making mechanism	Matching	Aggregation	
Bias	Buyer-centered	Seller-centered	Neutral

■ **Table 8.2:** The Dimensions of Electronic Markets

8.2 The functions of electronic markets

Markets play a central role in the economy, and the electronic economy in particular will play an important role by facilitating the exchange of information, goods, services, and payments. In the process, they create economic value for buyers, sellers, market intermediaries, and for society at large. Both traditional and electronic markets have three main functions:

1) Matching buyers and sellers;
2) Facilitating the exchange of information, goods, services, and the payment associated with market transactions;
3) Providing an institutional infrastructure, such as a legal and regulatory framework, that makes the efficient functioning of the market possible.

Traditionally, intermediaries provide the first two functions, while the institutional infrastructure is typically the area with which governments concern themselves. Electronic markets employ information technology to perform all three functions, increasing effectiveness and reducing transaction costs, thus resulting in more efficient, so-called friction-free markets [Bakos 1998].

Matching buyers and sellers

Markets operate by matching demand and supply. The behavior of buyers, sellers, and intermediaries in markets is motivated by the desire to maximize benefits. When markets function well, the available productive resources are efficiently allocated. Thus, markets function as both the engine and the steering system of our economy. The process of matching buyers' demands with sellers' product offerings has three main components.

1) *Determining product offerings*: markets provide sellers with demanded information that allows them to employ inputs such as capital, technology, and labor, and develop products with characteristics that match the buyers' needs. Sellers determine a product offering's schedule that they expect will maximize their profits.
2) *Searching*: buyers select their purchases from the available product offerings after considering factors such as price, product characteristics, and delivery time. Obtaining and processing this information involves making search costs. These include the opportunity costs for the time spent searching, as well as associated costs for traveling, making telephone calls, and magazine subscriptions. Typically, sellers exploit these search costs by raising their prices, and thus enjoy higher profits. But sellers may face search costs too, for locating qualified buyers for their products: market research, advertising, and sales calls, for example.
3) *Discovering prices*: a key function of markets is the process of determining the prices at which demand and supply meet and trade occurs. A number of mechanisms for price discovery is available. On financial markets, for instance, several types of auctions are used. Other markets, such as the traditional auto dealership, employ negotiation between buyers and sellers until a price is reached. In department stores, merchants make firm offers that customers can either take or leave.

Facilitating the exchange

The markets' matching function establishes relationships between buyers and sellers. To facilitate the exchange of information, goods, services, and payments, four aspects have to be considered to establish these relations correctly:

1) *settlement*: the payments of the buyer must be transferred to the seller. For example, when a travel agent uses an airline reservations system to book a flight, the system will generate the ticket and process a credit card payment;
2) *logistics*: after a transaction is agreed upon, the product sold must be transported to the buyer;
3) *trust*: market transactions require the establishment of a certain level of trust, which protects buyers, sellers, and intermediaries from the opportunistic behavior of other market participants. This trust role may include banks issuing letters of credit, credit reporting bureaus, or trusted third parties;
4) *physical infrastructure*: markets provide the physical infrastructure that allows transactions between buyers and sellers to take place. This includes real assets such as physical structures, trading floors, computers, communication networks, transportation systems, and cash dispensers.

Institutional infrastructure

The *institutional infrastructure* specifies the *laws*, *rules*, and *regulations* that govern market transactions. This involves contract law, dispute resolution, and intellectual property protection, for instance, and provides mechanisms for their enforcement. As electronic markets can provide large economies of scale in the field of distribution – a single online retailer or intermediary serving a very large market, for example – certain antitrust issues may be involved as well.

8.3 How do electronic markets differ from traditional markets?

Electronic markets have a major impact on the way in which markets function. Several trends are emerging that distinguish electronic markets from their traditional counterparts.

8.3.1 Personalization and customization

Consumer-tracking technology allows the identification of individual buyers: information about them, such as demographics, consumer profiles, and comparisons with the known preferences of similar consumers, can be used to discover or estimate their preferences. In addition, information-rich products lend themselves to cost-effective customization. For instance, delivering electronic newspapers tailored to the interests of individual readers is not necessarily more expensive than delivering the same copy to all subscribers. Such 'one-to-one marketing' is based on the supplier's knowledge of individual customers, distilled from the feedback and experiences of other consumers with similar preference profiles. Establishing a dialogue and a sense of community among customers will create value by enabling them to share their experiences, problems, and solutions, but it also allows the collection of important information about individual customers. The ultimate objective behind personalization and customization is to provide customized services according to individual preferences, whether expressed or inferred. Increased selling effectiveness comes from being able to design the appropriate products to address the needs of individual consumers, and from being able to identify the moment when a customer's purchasing decision is most likely to occur – and to be prepared for that moment, one step ahead of the competition. An example: Amazon.com not only provides individuals with information about the book they might like to buy, but also offers reviews by previous buyers and personal recommendations on other books one might be interested in.

Product bundling

When determining their product mix, sellers must decide which product components or features will be included in each product, and whether they will be marketed and priced individually or as a package. These decisions are driven by the costs of different product bundles, which include:

- production costs: the costs of producing additional features for inclusion in the bundle, including the storage, processing, and communications costs incurred in the process;

- transaction and distribution costs: the costs of distributing a bundle of goods and administering the transactions involved, such as arranging for payment;

- binding costs: the costs of binding the component goods together for distribution as a bundle;

- menu costs: the costs of administering multiple prices. If a mixed bundling strategy is pursued, in which the components available are offered in different combinations, numerous prices will have to be administered.

In electronic markets, these costs impose fewer constraints than in traditional markets; new types of intermediaries arise who create value by bundling services and products that used to be offered by separate industries. For example, a consumer looking for a new car may select a make and model, agree on the price, order it and then arrange financing and purchase insurance through a single Internet intermediary. All he or she must do is go to the car dealer for is the actual, physical test drive. *Intermediaries* are emerging in many areas, such as travel services and real estate transactions (intermediaries are discussed more extensively in Chapter 11).

8.3.2 Information goods

The Internet allows the almost costless creation and distribution of perfect copies of digital information goods, such as news articles, digital images, and music. Thus, the marginal production and distribution costs of such products are dramatically reduced. Meanwhile, electronic-payment technology reduces the transaction costs for their commercial exchange. This creates new opportunities for repackaging content by bundling, site licensing, subscriptions, rentals, differential pricing, per-use fees, etc. Many information goods are bundled solely to save on transaction, distribution, and menu costs, yet these costs are much lower on the Internet. Bundling information goods can be a surprisingly profitable strategy in a situation of low marginal costs, and a homogeneous consumer population [Bakos 1999].

8.3.3 Search

Electronic markets lower the costs buyers face for obtaining information about prices and product features, as well as the costs sellers face for advertising such information. By lowering buyers' search costs, electronic markets increase economic efficiency. Not only are the costs reduced even when many more product offerings are considered, e-Markets also enable buyers to identify and purchase a better match. Multiple Internet-based technologies assist buyers during their search process: search engines, hierarchical directories, or tools specially designed for specific markets (such as Pricewatch for computers and components). Lower search costs also stimulate the emergence of new markets. For example, consider buying second-hand vehicles. In conventional markets, the costs of carrying out a thorough search are almost prohibitively high, but on the Internet they are insignificant. Thus, new markets for second-hand vehicles develop. Similarly, product information, recommendation, and personalization, as well as comparative seller information, are increasingly provided.

Case Study

ChemConnect

ChemConnect is an electronic market for worldwide buyers and sellers of chemicals, plastics, and industrial gases. In the chemistry business, the buyer and seller sides of the market are both very fragmented. Therefore, in 1995 ChemConnect was created, to increase the market's efficiency. It started as a bulletin board, migrating to the Internet in 1998. ChemConnect has a membership of 18,000 from 125 countries, of which 30% are located in the US, 30% in Europe, and 40% in the rest of the world.

8.3.4 Transaction mechanisms

In any e-Market there are four main transaction mechanisms. These are [Moore 2000]:

1) *Standard price offerings*: these are predetermined prices for a given set of goods or services. This transaction model is in some ways similar to the typical B2C catalog pricing system. In e-Markets, standard price offerings are further broken down to two sub-models:

   a. Fixed price: fixed price offerings as the name suggests are offerings that have a fixed price associated with a particular set of goods or services;
   b. Contract: contracts are results of offline negotiations between buying and selling organizations. Contracts typically are entered into the system with special pricing, expiration rules, and termination rules. Contracts can also be generated as result of a Request for Quote (RFQ) process.

2) *Auctions*: these are used in e-Markets to allow rapid inventory turnover, while providing goods and services to buyers at a reduced price. Several different styles of auctions, such as open cry, sealed bid, and Dutch auctions, are available.

3) *Requests for Quote (RFQs)*: buyers can create RFQs in the e-Market if the product they are interested in does not exist there, or if they would like to solicit the selling organizations for a better price for an existing product. Selling organizations view the RFQs in the e-Market, and respond to the ones they are interested in. The buying organization that initiated the RFQ, reviews the responses and selects a possible winner. The winning RFQs can be used to create a fixed price order, or to establish a contract. Due to the opposite behavior of RFQs compared to auctions, RFQs are sometimes referred to as reverse auctions. For more information on auctions and reverse auctions refer to Sections 8.6 and 8.7.

4) *Exchanges*: these utilize sets of predefined rules to fulfill the buying and selling needs of e-Market members. Exchanges match bid offers with ask offers based on e-Market rules, and inform the parties involved of the potential match. E-Markets and exchanges are not interchangeable. The former tend to offer a range of differentiated products allowing buyers to compare features and prices offered by individual suppliers. Exchanges tend to be Internet-based industry spot markets for commodity products with a dynamic market setting supply, and demand prices in the fashion of existing exchanges. The general idea is very similar to the procedures in stock market exchanges. Exchanges are the most complicated way of conducting transactions in an e-Market.

The success of an e-Market depends on many factors, one of which is the ease of performing a transaction. To provide an easy and quick method of accessing products and offerings available, the e-Market uses an aggregated catalog. Buyers interact with an aggregated catalog to view the products with real-time pricing, descriptions, and comparisons between different vendors. The general idea is to consolidate products from multiple vendors with all possible existing transaction mechanisms in a single catalog and allow the buyers to be more efficient in purchasing goods and services.

8.3.5 Price discovery

Electronic markets allow new price discovery mechanisms to be employed. For example, some airlines auction lat-minute unsold seats to the highest bidder. There are intermediaries who, on the basis of their buyers' product and price requirements, make offers to their sellers, thus reversing traditional retail market mechanisms. The degree of product customization now possible, combined with the substantial amount of prospective buyer information (demographics, preferences, past shopping behavior) that becomes available, greatly improves sellers' ability to price discriminate: charging different customers different prices. This is a powerful tool. It allows sellers to increase their profits by reducing the consumer surplus enjoyed by buyers. It also enables sellers to service customers that would otherwise decline to buy because of the price level. The ability to implement different price discovery mechanisms may result in more efficient markets, benefiting buyers, and forcing suppliers to be efficient. As menu costs decrease, sellers will move away from fixed pricing. More prices will become negotiable. Economic theory predicts that buyers with more bargaining power, typically the more affluent ones, will be better off in this situation [Bakos 1998].

8.3.6 Facilitation

The yearly costs of transporting products from sellers to buyers have been estimated at more than 10% of the gross national products of most western countries. Electronic markets improve information sharing between buyers and sellers, which helps lower logistics costs and promotes quick, just-in-time delivery which in turn leads to reduced inventories. The distribution of information goods such as newspapers, music, videos, and software is likely to be completely transformed, as the information infrastructure will replace physical distribution systems. Sellers in electronic markets have taken charge of the delivery of physical products as well. Increasingly they contract with third-party providers for direct delivery from the manufacturer to the final customer, reducing costs and time-to-delivery. Delivery providers such as FedEx and UPS emerge as major Internet intermediaries because of their logistics expertise, and their economies of scale in distribution.

8.3.7 Electronic invoicing and payment

Recall from Chapter 1 that compared to business to consumer e-Commerce transactions, e-Business transactions are very complex and so is e-Business invoicing. e-Business transactions typically include procurement, contract administration, fulfillment, financing, credit ratings, shipment validation, order matching, payment authorization, remittance matching and general ledger accounting [Fairchild 2003]. Each of these steps may be governed by complex business rules. For example, trading partners may require multiple invoice accounts per customer, with a separate workflow process for each. Moreover e-Business transactions will involve irregular products like manufactured goods or materials. Services and products delivered are different each time, and payments are requested using itemized invoices. These invoices are difficult to recognize for an accounts payable department, so it is necessary to identify who was responsible for ordering the goods, to check the accuracy of the invoice, and then to match it with delivery reports and purchase orders.

It is no surprise that e-Business invoicing and payment is a cumbersome and costly process; it was estimated to have cost US companies $90 billion dollars in 1999 [Young 2002]. As a result, companies are moving more invoices and payments to the Internet. Streamlining accounts receivable and accounts payable processes, and cost cutting, are, however, not the only reasons for companies adopting electronic invoicing and payment systems. A faster invoicing and payment process also leads to faster payments, improved working capital, and reduction of Days Sales Outstanding (DSO); so faster cash flow is the other business driver behind the introduction of electronic invoicing and payment systems [Gartner 2001; GTNews 2003].

Currently, companies are supporting a variety of invoice distribution methods, including paper, EDI, XML, flat-files, and customer spreadsheets. A large majority of invoices and payments is processed in a manual, paper intensive environment. Financial Electronic Data Interchange only provides a limited solution. It has all the disadvantages of traditional EDI. Due to the cost involved, it is generally only applicable for large corporates. Fixed links have to be created between established trading partners. It has a limited functionality because it does not allow an interactive exchange of data. This means that organizations using financial EDI have to supplement this with paper-based invoicing for many of its customers and suppliers.

A solution for the complex invoicing and payments needs of companies in an e-Business environment is Electronic Invoice Presentment and Payment (EIPP). It allows the electronic delivery of complex business invoices while accommodating highly variable billing data. It offers an interactive system to support online dispute resolution, automatically matches invoices to purchase orders, creates internal audit trails, accepts payments over the Internet, and posts the results to the accounting systems. In the future, it is expected to make it possible for suppliers and buyers, regardless of size, to send and receive invoices online to and from their entire customer and supplier base in a many-to-many environment. At present EIPP is still geared more to the corporate world [Fairchild 2003, 2004]. EIPP solutions are offered by specialist EIPP suppliers and traditional financial institutions, and can be integrated with e-Markets.

Currently three EIPP models are used in industry today [Fairchild 2003, 2004; NACHA 2001]

- Seller Direct: the seller controls the EIPP application. This model comprises a one-to-many relationship linking the seller to multiple buyers. It is typically used when a trade relationship already exists between a seller and its buyers, where payment requirements and credit terms have been established;

- Buyer Direct: the buyer controls the EIPP application. Also this model comprises a one-to-many relationship – with one buyer providing an interface for many sellers. A buyer deploys this model by requiring that its sellers put invoices into the buyer EIPP system;

- EIPP Consolidator: the consolidator controls the EIPP application. This model comprises a many-to-many relationship – providing an interface between multiple sellers and buyers. The consolidator acts as an intermediary, and eliminates the necessity for point-to-point connections.

8.4 What are the effects of electronic markets?

8.4.1 The impact of the emergence of electronic markets

Microeconomic models typically assume that price and product information can be acquired without costs. However, there is little disagreement that this costless-ness is an unrealistic assumption. In real-world markets, the evident variability of prices, and the emphasis on the dissemination of information through advertising and other media, suggest that the costs and availability of price and product information are important determinants of economic behavior. They introduce inefficiencies into market-intermediated transactions, lessening the markets' ability to provide an optimal allocation of resources.

Electronic markets reduce the costs of acquiring price and product information. Economic theory suggests that this reduction in search costs significantly influences market efficiency and competitive behavior. It results in direct efficiency gains from reduced intermediation costs, and in indirect but possibly larger gains in the allocation efficiency of better-informed buyers. Thus, the market power of both suppliers and customers is increased.

Let us take a look at five characteristics of electronic markets and their impact on market structure and efficiency [Bakos 1991].

1) *Cost reduction*: electronic markets reduce the costs of obtaining information on the prices and products of alternative suppliers. They also reduce the costs of advertising price and product information to additional customers.
2) *Network externalities*: the benefits for individual participants in electronic markets increase as more businesses join their interorganizational information systems. Electronic markets with large numbers of buyers and sellers create more value for their participants, who are provided with a wider selection of potential suppliers and customers. These network externalities may also generate an early mover advantage because early movers have more time to attract buyers and sellers.
3) *Switching costs*: electronic markets may require sizeable investments from their participants, for hardware, software, employee training, and organizational transformations. Such investments may become worthless should the participant decide to join a different system, or revert to the previous mode of operation.
4) *Economies of scale and scope*: electronic markets typically require large capital investments and offer substantial economies of scale and scope. Intermediaries usually incur large system development and maintenance costs. But then they face relatively small incremental costs for additional transactions until the capacity of the system is approached, resulting in substantial economies of scale. Furthermore, it may be possible to transfer the technological and organizational resources and expertise acquired during the development and operation of one system to other systems. This, too, results in economies of scale.
5) *Technological uncertainty*: potential participants of electronic markets face substantial uncertainty regarding the actual benefits of joining such a system. (Occasionally this uncertainty remains even after they have joined.) This may affect the behavior of buyers, sellers, and potential intermediaries, who may adopt a

'wait and see' attitude: delaying the introduction of a system, or waiting before they join, hoping they will learn from the experience of other organizations.

8.4.2 Stakeholders: buyers, suppliers, investors and service suppliers

With respect to electronic markets, stakeholders may be described as participants who affect or are affected by the market's development and implementation. This description includes *buyers, sellers, investors, and service providers*. Generally speaking, 'electronic markets arise when exchange costs are lower than in traditional markets' [Dominique 1998]. This means that electronic markets will be used if they generate an advantage for buyers and sellers that is larger than their traditional, offline counterpart. Electronic markets themselves assume their role of intermediary primarily because of the profits and revenues expected.

Buyers and sellers are institutions or organizations that use the electronic market to buy or sell goods or services. For instance, BASF might use ChemConnect, an electronic market for chemical products, to buy the chemicals it needs for its videotape production from BP Amoco. In a similar manner, FedEx might sell its delivery services to Dell through the National Transportation Exchange.

Investors are institutions or organizations that have invested financial or human resources in electronic markets. Companies that intend to make money by receiving dividend and by ultimately selling their shares with a profit are called external investors. For example, the Internet Capital Group has invested in several electronic markets such as Paperexchange, CommerceX, and Logistics.com. Companies likely to trade on the electronic market they invest in are called internal investors or partners. Procter & Gamble, Unilever, Heinz, and Danone, for instance, have invested in Transora, an electronic market for packaged consumer goods. Their goal is to achieve efficiency by using electronic markets for their procurement and selling processes.

Case Study

Chematch

In the summer of 1999, thirteen large companies provided substantial funds. Since then, CheMatch has attracted buyers and sellers from 750 medium-size to large companies in the chemistry business, like DuPont, General Electric, and Exxon, as well as several from other industries, such as Proctor & Gamble, Samsung, and BF.

Service providers are institutions or organizations that supply third-party services. For example, Ariba supplies technology and infrastructure, PriceWaterhouseCoopers has know-how and consultancy skills, American Express offers credits, DHL delivers logistic services. Electronic markets may use other electronic markets as providers of complementary products or services. Transora, for example, has relations with The WorldWideRetailExchange, an e-Market for procurers of packaged consumer goods such as retailers.

8.5 Electronic market success factors

Discussing success factors for electronic markets raises the question under what conditions a market place can be considered successful. Success will depend on whether the market is able to meet the objectives of the key stakeholders. Investors expect a return on their investment; buyers and sellers expect success in their trading processes. An important criterion for success is *critical mass*. Critical mass may be defined as 'the minimal number of users of an interactive innovation for the further rate of adoption to be self-sustaining' [Schoder 2000a]. The importance of the establishment of critical mass for electronic markets has also been illustrated by the observation that the benefits realized by individual participants in electronic market systems increase as more organizations join the system [Lee 1996].

Reaching critical mass is closely related to the alignment of stakeholders' motives, since this directly influences the number of participants. And the simultaneous adoption and use of an electronic market by all stakeholders involved is necessary for it to achieve critical mass [Damsgaard 1998], as the benefits a user has from utilization of a network's services increases with the number of users utilizing it [Castelli 1993]. This phenomenon is known as 'network externalities': a quality of certain goods and services is such that they become more valuable to a user as the number of users increases' [Economides 1991]. In fact, if critical mass is reached, the initial joining motives, such as a decrease in transaction costs, may not only be confirmed but also even reinforced. Subsequently, buyers and sellers profit from a further reduction in transaction costs, and the market itself profits from a further increase in revenue. Such a confirmation of initial joining motives increases the convergence of stakeholders' motives, and may thus increase the number of e-Market's participants. The importance of reaching critical mass can be summed up as follows [Lee 1996]: 'The benefits realized by individual participants in an electronic market system increase as more organizations join the system. Without a critical mass of users, an electronic market system is unlikely to spread its usage and may be extinguished'.

Factors that potentially contribute to the success of an electronic market place, and so to its critical mass, are related to the electronic market's context and to its processes [Nooteboom 2001; Fairchild 2004a]. *Context-related success factors* are the conditions under which the electronic market operates; generally, these are beyond the control of the market maker but they do affect the market's potential success. *Process-related success factors* are the characteristics of the trading processes on the market; the market maker generally controls them. Context-related success factors are:

- stakeholder motives;

- products traded, and in particular:
  - complexity of product description;
  - asset specificity.

Process-related success factors are:

- Functionality and support;

- Learning costs;

- Trust;

- Quality of information;

- Information security;

- Geographic location;

- Partnerships.

8.5.1 Context-related success factors
Stakeholder motives

Case Study

MetalSite

Differences at MetalSite between the buyers' and the sellers' motives became apparent, and they led to MetalSite's failure. Ryerson Cole only used MetalSite to sell its short-term, excess inventories. It probably did not want to jeopardize its long-term customer relations. And while the lower prices paid for its excess materials (the result of price erosion caused by the pricing information included in MetalSite's offerings) were no problem since Ryerson did not make any opportunity costs for them, such price erosion was not acceptable for its main products. Meanwhile, MetalSite's buyers didn't get enough additional value and functionality, so they only used it for short-term spot purchasing. So the trade volume was too small for the electronic market to survive: the transaction cost benefits buyers and sellers could realize were insufficient, and so was the revenue generated for its investors.

Eumedix

Also Eumedix was not successful at this point. Here, too, the divergence between the motives of the parties involved was simply too great. In the first place, in most hospitals it isn't the purchasing staff who takes the real purchasing decisions. It is the medical staff who decides which products they want. And they are usually perfectly happy using the products they have been using for sometimes more than twenty years already. Besides, the reversed auction mechanism offered by Eumedix meant they might have to do without the perks involved in their longstanding relations with their suppliers. Purchasing staff, for their part, are often held accountable not for the financial benefits they realize but for the speediness with which they satisfy the demands of the medical staff.

Different stakeholders will often pursue different, and sometimes conflicting, goals. Generally speaking, their decision to enter an electronic market will be based on its perceived contribution to their individual goals. As said, stakeholders are buyers, sellers, and investors. 'In the exchange of goods and services, buyers, and sellers are primarily interested in price, quality, amount, and timeliness of delivery' [van Heck 1998]. Buyers' and sellers' main motive for using electronic markets is the decrease in transaction and logistic costs. Especially buyers and sellers may have opposite motives in deciding whether to join a marketplace or not. Buyers are typically interested in low(er) prices. Sellers, however, fear price erosion. Strong opposite motives of key stakeholder groups is a serious threat for an electronic market place.

Investigations of electronic markets in the financial industry have found that several financial intermediaries had been threatened by the introduction of the electronic market and that in some cases, opposition had been mounted against the electronic market [Hess 1994]. Consequently, these investigations conclude that 'the need to align the incentives of the parties in the market has been perceived as one of the potential remedies for the failure of electronic markets' [Hess 1994]. In addition, it has been established that the match of the market structure implemented and the market structure demanded is most critical for the success of an electronic trading system [Reck 1998]. In this context, market structure is defined as the description of traders' needs.

An investigation conducted on Traxon, an electronic market in Hong Kong's air cargo industry, has revealed that it was essential that all parties see the benefits from the arrangement and decide to participate [Damsgaard 1998]. Traxon, therefore, designed its system to accommodate the needs of the airlines, forwarders, and air cargo terminals, but also carefully preserved the sensitive distribution of power and responsibilities between them. Furthermore, the Traxon system did not carry any information about prices or discounts. This left the market opaque for outsiders, and preserves the roles and power balances between airlines, freight forwarders, and shippers [Damsgaard 1998].

Research was also conducted on the failure of a similar initiative in the Dutch air cargo industry [Christiaanse 1995]. According to this research, the system failed due to a misfit of interests between stakeholders, which was ignored by the initiators. Because the electronic market provided price transparency to its participants, it eliminated the function of the freight forwarders who normally coordinate this market. This induced them to withdraw their support and eventually led to the e-Market's failure.

Firms that are affected adversely by an electronic market can be expected to fight the system [Lee 1996]. Therefore the electronic market has to develop a strategy to deal with potential retaliations. For example, a system that includes just product information and not prices is unlikely to create price wars, but, instead, should allow sellers to respond more effectively to market demand and supply levels [Choudhury 1998].

Products
Complexity of product description: Highly complex product descriptions require more information exchange and thus increase the coordination cost advantage of hierarchies over markets. Consequently, items with simple product descriptions are expected to be more suitable for (electronic) markets [Malone 1987]. As can be illustrated by one of our case examples, Eumedix failed as a market place because its initiators underestimated the complexity of products sold (e.g., medical gloves used in hospitals).

Case Study

Eumedix

Eumedix is a marketplace for supplying medical products to hospitals, a very inefficient market in which buyers switch suppliers only infrequently. Suppliers can easily fix prices, which are therefore relatively high. And since hospitals so often stick to their relations with their suppliers, new entrants are in a difficult position. Such a reluctance to switch suppliers is explained by the complexity inherent in medical products. For example, it takes more than thirty attributes to describe the characteristics and quality of surgical gloves. It is too difficult and costly to make frequent comparisons between different suppliers; most hospitals prefer to stay where they are.

Together, these factors made it difficult to acquire sufficiently large buyer and seller bases. But, in the meantime, it took a great effort to specify the enormous number of hospital demand product attributes, both objective and subjective. For these reasons Eumedix was discontinued.

Asset specificity: transactions involving asset-specific products often involve long processes of development and adjustment for the supplier to meet the needs of the buyer, a process that favors the continuity of relations found in a hierarchy. Therefore, (electronic) markets are probably best suited to source goods with a low asset specificity [Malone 1987].

8.5.2 Process-related success factors
Functionality and support
It has been suggested that a final stage in the evolution of electronic markets would be the development of those providing personalized decision aids to help individual buyers make a selection from various alternatives [Malone 1987]. A study that has examined several electronic markets for logistics services, has concluded that the market maker in the role of intermediary should seek a win-win relationship with sellers and innovate services to meet the needs of the buyer. A specific type of decision aid that could provide value-added functionality is transaction mechanisms that assist buyers and sellers in making improved selling or purchasing decisions, opposed to merely aggregating supply and demand [Nunes 2000]. Being able to offer multiple transaction approaches, allows electronic markets to win a larger share of existing customers' business as well as bring new types of buyers into the fold.

The functionality offered by a market place must match the process requirements of the users. Especially in e-Business markets, where long established relationships between buyers and sellers exist, collaboration may be as or even more important than competition. As a consequence, successful e-Markets, which support systematic sourcing, should support collaborative processes through computer supported collaborative work applications (CSCW).

Learning costs

The reluctance of traders to adopt new technologies and embark on a new round of organizational learning may serve as a barrier to the successful implementation of electronic markets. Technology that differs too much from current trading practice will serve as barriers to a successful implementation [Damsgaard 1998; van Heck 1998; Fong 1998; Lee 1996].

Trust

In electronic markets, in which the only contact between buyers and sellers is through the market's databases and telecommunication network, trading partners may be exposed to opportunistic behavior. Trust is an essential element for the functioning of the electronic market place. Various factors contribute to trust.

Quality of information

The availability of correct information on products, trading partners, and contracts is considered a success factor for electronic markets. Accurate and objective product description is crucial [Fong 1998]. Moreover, if market-making firms fail to ensure that product information properly reflects the original products, or if they are not equipped to protect buyers from misinformation, buyers will resist the new system [Lee 1996]. There are two crucial features for reducing the uncertainties involved in product descriptions in electronic markets: (1) create certain standards for product ratings, and (2) establish a trusted third party to carry out inspections. As to the specification of product quality, 'if markets fail to assure the quality of products, buyers are not likely to adopt the new online trading services' [Lee 1998]. For example, an investigation regarding the adoption of an electronic auction system for livestock has revealed that a certain degree of standards for product ratings, and the presence of a trusted third party for product evaluations, are essential elements for the successful development of electronic markets [Atkins 1998].

It has also been argued that *authenticity* (identity of buyers and sellers), *integrity* (verifiability and completeness of product and price information), and *non-repudiation* (the ability to hold a buyer or seller to the terms of the transaction they are committed to) are the three key features that will fuel the growth of e-Commerce [Alba 1997].

It is important that, in order to preserve the efficiency and participation of sellers, an electronic market must have a verification mechanism to check for genuineness of bookings [Beach 1999]. Furthermore, in a global market, a reliable and generic way of contracting is crucial [Schmid 1997]. Therefore, a successful electronic market architecture grants mechanisms for the automated production of electronic contracts which are reliable for the customer and the supplier, giving security and guarantees, even in case of failure of one or the other sort.

Information security

The integrity and confidentiality of information (especially personal and financial data) should always be safeguarded, not only by instituting robust and secure encryption algorithms, but also by ensuring that the service providers observe the highest level of ethical standards in the handling and storage of such information [Asuncion 1997]. Moreover, it is imperative that any transaction in an electronic market be secure and its integrity upheld.

Geographic location

Several studies suggest that perceived risks associated with the physical, geographic location of an e-Market, may contribute to the confidence of (potential) participants. An investigation conducted on an electronic market in the financial industry found that due to the need for any financial service to be based on confidence between the buyer and the supplier, more localized, personalized markets will evolve [Daniel 1999]. Research on Traxon, which we discussed earlier in this chapter, found that the focus on several localized rollouts contributed to its success. Thus, the locally-based Cathay Pacific was in charge of the rollout in Hong Kong, while in Japan it was Japan Airlines. A similar approach was applied in Europe' [Damsgaard 1998].

Partnerships

Partnerships with industry leaders and domain experts can contribute to perceived trust in the viability of the market place. The relationship with acknowledged industry domain experts allows acquiring extensive industry knowledge that contributes to the credibility of the marketplace in the industry. Also, when large well-known companies are willing to invest in the market place, it may be expected that these companies will bring their buyers and suppliers to the electronic market, which may contribute to a more rapid achievement of a critical mass.

Case Study

ChemConnect

The general strategy ChemConnect uses to attract buyers and sellers involved a combination of direct marketing and a sales force. Furthermore, it has attracted a total of 33 companies in the chemistry business to invest in ChemConnect as a means of obtaining industry credibility and to attract more buyers and sellers.

8.6 e-Market technology solutions

The marketplace-based solution aims to facilitate direct integration with trading partners. Typical solutions will be hosted, either directly by the market maker organization, or via an Application Service Provider (ASP) model. Trading partners can then connect to the e-Market. The marketplace will then manage the transformation routing and delivery of messages in much the same way as an internal broker joins disparate

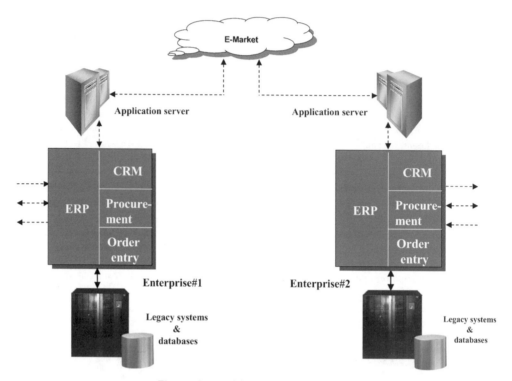

■ Figure 8.4: e-Market Technical Solution

applications. Figure 8.4 illustrates the interaction between the e-Market and the supplier's business system, as well as that between the buyer's procurement system and the business functions of the e-Market, where the interaction is governed by a well defined and executable contract. This figure also shows how the EISs of two or more enterprises (supplier and buyer) can interact within an electronic market. Dotted arrows refer to electronic flows, e.g., purchase orders. Since e-Market solutions are based on Web technologies, they rely directly upon an application server. For this reason solutions must be as open as possible to be supported by most application servers on the market. There are two important categories of ways in which this interaction can occur. The first is the potential for various electronic markets to serve as new intermediaries (see Chapter 11). Second is the potential for enterprises to use the Internet to bypass a segment of the supply chain, either via an intermediary or directly. This phenomenon is known as disintermediation (see Chapter 11).

e-Market solutions can also be realized by using novel technologies such as Web services which are said to be the next generation of application integration technology, with the potential to radically change e-Business. As we shall explain in Chapter 19, Web services are self-contained, modular applications that can be described, published, located, and invoked over a network. Any piece of code can be transformed into a Web service. Services can be legacy functions or new software. Any application component deployed on a system can become a Web service.

The automation of maintenance, repair, and operations (MRO) procurement (see Section 1.3) is a good example of applying Web services technology to e-Market solutions. MRO procurement allows a company to make available to every employee on the company intranet a catalog of all the non-production maintenance, repair, and operations goods that can be purchased, such as office supplies and equipment. Employees order their own goods; the system collects these orders and sends those that need approval to the proper individual, then forwards the consolidated orders to the proper vendors for fulfillment.

MRO procurement was, until recently, a paper transaction process with heavy human input. Web-services technology can automate most of this process (except the approvals part that requires human intervention). Using a Web services powered marketplace, employees can leverage the Internet for better prices, more choices, and efficiency of logistics management.

8.7 Chapter summary

An e-Business electronic market (or simply *e-Market*) can be defined as a virtual online market, i.e., a network of company interactions and relationships, where buyers, suppliers, distributors, and sellers find and exchange information, conduct trade, and collaborate with each other via an aggregation of content from multiple suppliers, trading exchanges, and member communications supported by collaboration tools. E-Markets typically offer a wide variety of ancillary services required by the members of the trading community, such as authenticating buyers and sellers, and streamlining procurement workflows, risk management, settlement services., conflict resolution services, and logistics services.

In a typical e-Market, entire groups of buyers and sellers in a particular industry are linked together. Companies operating marketplaces are referred to as *intermediaries* or *market makers*. They may themselves be participants in the market – buyers or sellers – or independent third parties, financial services providers, IT vendors, or multiform consortia.

E-Business markets serve three particular functions:

1) They act as an exchange for business transactions – not only mere purchasing but also for checking prices and stock availability, invoicing, and order chasing;
2) They manage catalog content, converting product information into a common format understood by all parties;
3) They provide additional services to support the trading process, from shipping, payment, and tax to online auctions, tendering, and vetting a company's financial status.

Although business-to-business e-Markets show different levels of functional sophistication, the typical exchange combines the four core enterprise applications, Enterprise Recourse Planning (ERP), Supply Chain Management (SCM), Customer Relationship Management (CRM), and Electronic Procurement.

Various classifications of electronic markets exist:

- MRO hubs lower the transaction costs of low-cost operating inputs by disintermediating, that is, bypassing middlemen;

- *Yield managers* create spot markets for common operating resources with a high degree of price and demand volatility;

- *Exchanges* are electronic markets closely related to traditional commodity exchanges that enable the spot sourcing of manufacturing inputs;

- Catalog *hubs* facilitate the systematic sourcing of non-commodity manufacturing inputs, such as plastics and chemicals, and create value by reducing transaction costs.

Since exchanges and catalog hubs facilitate the trade of industry specific products, they are often called vertical electronic markets. These are also known as industry consortia and are industry-owned vertical marketplaces that serve specific industries. Likewise, MRO hubs and yield managers establish the trade of non-industry specific products, and are therefore referred to as horizontal electronic markets.

e-Markets are usually tilted toward a supplier, a buyer, or a neutral third party thus giving rise to three general ownership-based market models:

1) Buyer-dominated marketplace;
2) Supplier-dominated marketplace;
3) Neutral marketplace.

Both traditional and electronic markets have three main functions:

1) Matching buyers and sellers by offering support for determining product offerings, search, and price discovery;
2) Facilitating the exchange of information, goods, services, and the payment associated with market transactions; four aspects have to be considered to establish these relations correctly: settlement, logistics, trust, physical infrastructure;
3) Providing an institutional infrastructure, such as a legal and regulatory framework, that makes the efficient functioning of the market possible: the laws, rules, and regulations that govern market transactions.

Electronic markets differ from traditional markets with respect to:

- The possibilities of personalization and customization;

- The trade of information goods;

- Search possibilities;

- Available transaction mechanisms;

- Price discovery;

- Facilitation;

- Electronic invoicing and payment.

Typical economic effects of e-markets include:

• Cost reduction;

• Network externalities. The benefits for individual participants in electronic markets increase as more businesses join their interorganizational information systems;

• Switching costs. Electronic markets may require sizeable investments from their participants, for hardware, software, employee training, and organizational transformations;

• Economies of scale and scope. Electronic markets typically require large capital investments and offer substantial economies of scale and scope;

• Technological uncertainty. Potential participants in electronic markets face substantial uncertainty regarding the actual benefits of joining such a system.

Whether an e-market is successful depends on the willingness of the stakeholders to join it. Stakeholders are typically buyers, suppliers, investors, and service suppliers. This means that electronic markets will be used if they generate an advantage for both buyers and sellers that is larger than their traditional, offline counterpart. Electronic markets themselves assume their role of intermediary, primarily because of the profits and revenues expected, so must generate a sufficient ROI for investors to be interested.

Factors that potentially contribute to the success of an electronic market place, so to its critical mass, are related to the electronic market's context and processes. *Context-related success factors* are the conditions under which the electronic market operates; generally, these are beyond the control of the market maker, but they do affect the market's potential success. They include the motives of the stakeholders and the characteristics of the products traded, in particular the complexity of product description and their asset specificity. *Process-related success factors* are the characteristics of the trading processes on the market; the market maker generally controls them. They include the functionality and support offered, the learning costs needed, the trust created, quality and security of information, geographic location of the head quarters of the e-Market place, and the partnerships with companies having a high reputation.

Discussion Questions

• What is an e-Market?
• Name four core enterprise applications and explain their function with respect to e-Markets.

- Explain the difference between a vertical and a horizontal e-Market. Give an example of both types and explain why they are vertical or horizontal.

- Two types of sourcing are distinguished in the book: systematic- and spot sourcing. For which one is the electronic market place the most suitable environment; explain why, and give an example of both types of sourcing.

- Give the motives of the three stakeholders that act in an e-Market to use the e-Market. Why are these motives at the same time a threat to the success of e-Markets?

- Name the two business drivers behind the introduction of electronic invoicing and payment systems, and name the three EIPP models.

Assignments

i. Visit www.alibaba.com/aboutalibaba/overview.html. Explain what type of e-Market Alibaba is in terms of:

- Spot or Systematic sourcing;
- Market making mechanism;
- Transaction mechanism;
- Functionality and support.

ii. Visit www.usedcars.com/equityInvestors.shtml. The writers of 'about us' make us think that the company is doing very well. Is that true, based on the figures in the article? Explain your answer.

Chapter 9

e-Procurement

No company is self-sufficient. Every company depends on suppliers and contractors to meet a variety of organizational needs: manufacturing, support, and management processes require materials, components, goods, equipment, supplies, merchandise, and specialist services. Consequently, purchasing is a function every company requires. The changes in competitive environments of the past two decades have made it even more important. One of the major strategic implications of these changes has been a strategic reorientation on the degree of vertical integration. Business strategy is moving away from in-house manufacturing towards an increasing dependence on suppliers and subcontractors [van Stekelenborg 1997].

Economically speaking, a company's profitability depends to a large extent on its ability to procure necessary goods and services at competitive conditions. This contribution of the purchasing function, not only relates to the availability of goods and services, it also concerns the efficient (internal) organization of buying processes. In this chapter, we discuss how the Internet potentially impacts the total purchasing process, and how it may improve the efficiency of traditional IT support. For this purpose we define *e-Procurement* as the application of Internet technology to the buying and selling of goods and services. An e-Procurement network provides a secure market place, sales platform, and transaction tracking system to buyers and sellers.

The following pages review the role and importance of the purchasing function in the business organization. Subsequently, we discuss the purchasing process, recent developments affecting the purchasing process, the roles of IT and the Internet, e-Procurement models and catalog systems, auctions and reverse auctions.

Case Study

Commerce One and Ariba, two popular e-Procurement solutions

Commerce One brings buyers and sellers together over the internet. With almost half of revenues being spent on purchasing activities, one of the ways to deliver fast bottom line results is to reduce purchasing costs and increase the efficiencies of the purchasing process. Commerce One contributes to increased efficiency in the purchasing processes of their clients by increasing control over the spend cycle. Its supplier relation management (SRM) solution aims at automating, integrating, and optimizing the entire source-to-pay process; it covers all the steps in the traditional spend cycle. Since 1996 Commerce One's services have been used by Boeing, Deutsche Telekom, Eastman Chemical, and Schlumberger, among others.[1]

Ariba focuses on achieving significant improvements in the spend management of their clients. While most organizations recognize the need for a cohesive spend management strategy, many of them do not realize the expected bottom line results. The Ariba Spend Management Solution helps organizations to develop a cohesive spend management program through a comprehensive suite of applications and services, such as the Ariba Procurement Solution, which delivers flexible applications and services to support every phase of the procurement process. Ariba Buyer automates the full buying cycle. In addition to restricting uncontrolled buying by forcing compliance with negotiated contracts, Ariba Buyer increases the efficiency of the procurement process from requisition to payment.[2]

[1] www.commerceone.com
[2] www.ariba.com

9.1 Introduction

Purchasing is the external acquisition at optimum conditions of goods, services, and materials (including machinery, tooling) that are needed for production, sales, and maintenance. This implies optimizing not only the costs of the goods and services themselves, but of the organization involved as well. In doing so the purchasing function contributes to the company's profit potential. The responsibilities of those involved in purchasing therefore include the goods flow planning – in terms of on-time availability – of materials and services, as well as guaranteeing the current, uninterrupted continuity of the goods flow by ensuring the availability of goods and services to be purchased. The general objectives of the purchasing function are traditionally expressed as the *five rights:* acquiring materials and services of the right quality, in the right quantity, at the right time, at the right price, and from the right supplier. The right supplier is mentioned explicitly because it must not only fulfill the first four objectives but also be able to deliver the right services in order to secure the optimum supply and utilization of materials under all conditions.

The purchasing function's economic importance is considerable. The average industrial company in the United States spends around 56% of its sales income on purchases from outside sources. This percentage varies from 35% for instrument manufacturers to 90% in the petroleum and coal industry. It is evident that, on average, purchases of materials and services substantially exceed the expenditures for any other category [Dobler 1990]. The tendency to outsource activities that are not considered core business will only increase these numbers. In addition, every dollar saved in purchasing goes straight to the bottom line. Companies making a 10% profit margin, for example, must generate extra sales to a value of ten times the amount of money saved on purchasing, if these sales are to yield the same extra profit.

Companies generally buy many different kinds of products and services. Industrial purchasing activities focus on several categories of goods:

- Natural and chemical raw materials, including ferrous and non-ferrous metals and plastics, but also energy, water, etc.;

- Components, that is elements used directly for assembling;

- Semi-finished products (which require one or more extra processing steps), either standard or customer-specific;

- Capital goods such as buildings, land and machinery;

- Non-production materials such as office supplies, computer equipment;

- MRO supplies (maintenance, repair, and operating or office goods);

- Finished products, to be sold unchanged as an addition to one's own assortment;

- Services, such as market research, financial services, and consulting.

The kinds of goods companies buy depend to a large extent on their position in the value chain. Production companies close to the final customer, such as manufacturers of cars or household appliances, buy a large variety of finished products from a large number of suppliers, which they assemble into their own products. Companies at the other end of the value chain, as in the chemical and oil industries, buy a limited number of essential raw materials, which they process into many different products. For almost every company, however, the *Pareto Analysis* holds: a small number of important articles represents a major share of the value purchased, while a large number of articles represents only a small part of this value. Often, three classes of articles are defined [Christopher 1998] (see Figure 9.1):

1) Class A articles: a small number of articles (say, 20% of the total) representing a major share (say, 80%) of the company's purchasing budget;

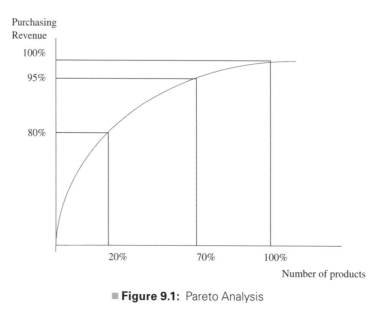

Purchasing
Revenue

■ **Figure 9.1:** Pareto Analysis

2) Class B articles: the next 50%, representing 15% of the value purchased;
3) Class C articles: a large number of articles (30%) representing only 5% of the purchasing budget.

These different categories and classes of goods and services each require their own specific procurement processes. MRO supplies, for example, are generally considered routine Products, and thus candidates for automated buying processes. Class C articles may represent little stock value, but the costs of their ordering and administration are substantial; reducing those costs by efficient ordering systems is very important, therefore. Each product category and class thus generates its own specific management issues.

9.2 The purchasing process

Purchasing activity is the result of a decision-making process. In their classic study, Webster and Wind define *organizational buying behavior* as the decision-making process by which formal organizations establish the need for purchased products and services, and identify, evaluate, and choose among alternative brands and suppliers [Webster 1972]. This *purchasing process* is initiated by a current or, preferably, anticipated purchasing problem – in other words, there is a need that can be fulfilled by externally acquiring goods or services. Such processes consist of a number of logical subsequent steps, such as adequately defining the purchasing problem, performing market research into suppliers and products, coming to an agreement on purchasing conditions, and, finally, the purchasing decision itself. Implementing the decision includes placing orders, receiving and checking deliveries, checking and paying invoices. Finally the supplier's performance has to be evaluated. Depending on the newness of the purchasing problem, preparing purchasing decisions either involves simple routine procedures or a complex set of activities. Especially when the goods involved are of essential importance to the company, purchasing will be a strategic activity characterized by extensive preparations, and negotiations with multiple suppliers. Depending on the size of the company, representatives from a number of departments (manufacturing, product development, finance, etc.) are then involved in the process. Routine decisions, on the other hand, are of a repetitive nature and are handled in a proceduralized way.

9.2.1 Modeling the purchasing process

Different models have been proposed to describe the organizational buying process. We shall first introduce the buy-grid model [Robinson 1967] and then the Purchasing Portfolio [Kraljic 1983]. The *buy-grid model* is based on an early descriptive study by the Marketing Science Institute, which concluded that a division into eight stages best describes the organizational buying process:

1) Anticipating or recognizing a problem (need) and proposing a general solution;
2) Determining the characteristics and the quantity of the item needed;
3) Describing the characteristics and the quantity of the item needed;
4) Searching for and qualifying potential sources;
5) Acquiring and analyzing proposals;
6) Evaluating proposals and selecting suppliers;
7) Selecting an order routine;
8) Performance feedback and evaluation.

As one moves through stages 1 to 8, a process occurs that is called 'creeping commitment': at first a maximum of alternative products, qualities, and suppliers is available, but as you go further, conditions are increasingly fixed. This means that new potential suppliers are less and less likely to be introduced into the process. A subsequent analysis revealed that the eight stages of organizational buying processes can be reduced to the following three [Zenz 1994]:

1) Information: prospective buyers identify their needs and evaluate potential sources to fulfill them, gathering information about market conditions, products, and sellers;
2) Negotiation: the business partners start to interact, determining the prices and the availability of the goods and services, as well as delivery conditions; successful negotiations are finalized with a contract;
3) Settlement: the terms of the contract are carried out and the goods and services are transferred in exchange for money or other forms of compensation.

The buy-grid model combined the division of the organizational buying process into stages with three classes of buying situation that are determined by its newness. The Marketing Science Institute also conducted this study to understand the organizational setting of buying processes. In this context a 'new task' buying situation is defined as one in which the company buys for the first time, perhaps even seeking solutions for new product functions. 'New task' buying situations naturally evolve into 'straight rebuy' situations: proceduralized situations in which everything (quality specifications, prices and conditions, suppliers) is fixed except the quantities needed and the delivery schedule. In their turn 'straight rebuy' situations typically evolve into 'modified rebuy' situations. Then all parameters are reevaluated, which generally also involves investigation of alternative suppliers. The combination of buying process stages and buying situations provides a grid, which was called the Buygrid (see Figure 9.2). Naturally, the most complex circumstances are found in that part of the grid representing the first of several stages of the process, and the 'new task' buying situation (see shaded area B in Figure 9.2). Then the largest number of decision makers and buying

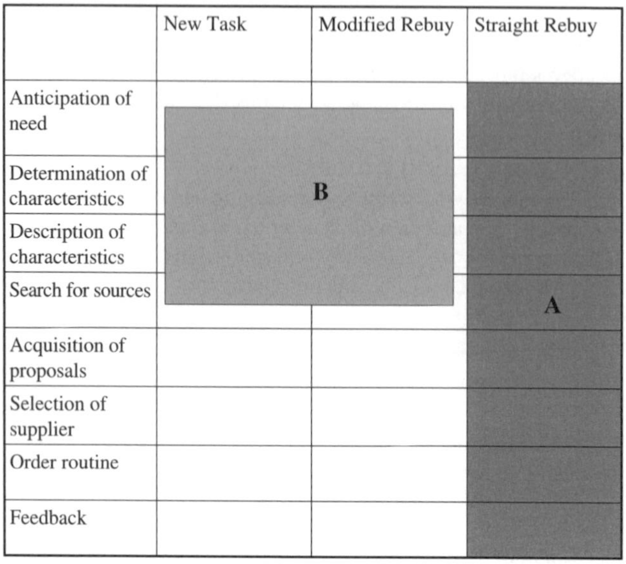

	New Task	Modified Rebuy	Straight Rebuy
Anticipation of need			
Determination of characteristics		**B**	
Description of characteristics			
Search for sources			**A**
Acquisition of proposals			
Selection of supplier			
Order routine			
Feedback			

■ **Figure 9.2:** The Buy-grid Framework [Webster 1972]

influences is involved. A 'straight rebuy' situation, by contrast, is an almost automatic process (see shaded area A in Figure 9.2).

One of the major drawbacks of the buy-grid model is that the importance of the goods and services bought, and the potential consequences of the buying situation, are left undifferentiated. The *Purchasing Portfolio* is another purchasing model [Kraljic 1983] that addresses this aspect. It introduces two variables:

1) The company's strategic vulnerability with respect to the purchase, expressed in criteria such as added value and the percentage of the company's products' cost price, determined by the goods purchased;
2) The complexity of the supplying market (determining the difficulty with which the purchase is made), expressed in criteria such as scarcity and entry barriers.

Combining these two variables, a matrix is formed that offers insight into the company's position in the buying market. This is illustrated in Figure 9.3. Corresponding to the matrix cells, four kinds of items are defined that companies can buy:

1) Strategic items, characterized by high buying risks and a major profit impact;
2) Bottleneck items, characterized by high buying risks, but a small profit impact;
3) Leverage items, characterized by low buying risks, but a major profit impact;
4) Routine items, characterized by low buying risks and a small profit impact.

According to the purchasing portfolio model, each of these four categories requires a distinctive purchasing approach [Kraljic 1983]. Buying strategic items involves extensive purchasing processes, in which the

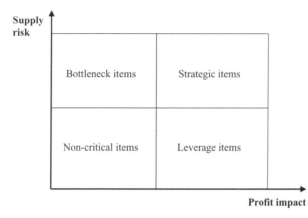

■ **Figure 9.3:** A Purchasing Portfolio Model [Kraljic 1983]

decisions are taken at executive management level. Decisions concerning less critically important items, on the other hand, are generally taken at operational management levels. Finally, the purchasing portfolio model suggests that a purchasing portfolio must be updated regularly, since the goods and services companies buy more from one category than another as a result of economic and other changes.

An example of how an approach like that of the purchasing portfolio model works is presented by Shell's 'procurement targeting approach', an element of its 'procurement business strategy' [van Stekelenborg 1997]. It was devised to enhance the added value generated by the company's purchasing processes. For routine items, the aim is to minimize the cost of acquisition by standardization, automation and, wherever practical, contracting out the purchasing process itself. When purchasing leverage items, the company's business units aim at maximizing their commercial advantage. In the bottleneck category of goods and services, the key requirement is to ensure supply continuity. And, finally, purchasing strategic items requires considerable time and effort with respect to quality assurance, supply continuity, and overall costs.

9.2.2 Purchasing as part of supply chain management

Purchasing is increasingly considered a part of logistics management, the ultimate goal of which is to manage the flow of goods and services from raw materials to final product delivery [Christopher 1998]. Customer demands for on time delivery of customized products and services, are met by coordinating material and information flows that extend from the market place, through the company, and beyond to its suppliers. This requires a tight coordination between marketing, manufacturing, and purchasing. Logistics aims for a system-wide view of the company (see Section 10.4.1 for details on the role of logistics in the supply-chain). Fundamentally, it is a planning concept that seeks to establish a framework in terms of which the needs of the market can be translated into manufacturing strategies and plans, which in turn are linked to procurement strategies and plans. Ideally, businesses should strive for the replacement of the conventional, separate, stand-alone plans of their marketing, distribution, production, and procurement departments by an integrated business plan.

Traditionally most companies view themselves as entities which exist independently from others and which must, indeed, compete with them to survive. However, from the point of view of modern performance measures – like customization, shortening delivery times, keeping inventories low – focusing on competing instead of cooperating can be self-defeating. Hence the rise of supply chain integration (see Chapter 10). The idea here is that buyer-supplier relations should be partnerships. Buying companies increasingly discover the advantages to be gained by aiming at mutually beneficial, long-term relations with suppliers. From the supplier's point of view, such partnerships are formidable entry barriers to competitors: the more the processes between a supplier and its customer are linked, the higher will be their mutual dependence, hence the more difficult it is for competitors to gain a foothold. Supply chain management by definition concerns the management of relations in complex networks of companies, which, while legally independent, are in reality interdependent. Those supply chains will be successful which are governed by a constant search for win-win solutions based on mutuality and trust.

9.3 Developments in purchasing

It was only in the latter half of the twentieth century that the importance of purchasing was widely recognized. During the 1973 oil crisis, senior managers began taking an active interest in the consistency of suppliers' performance, and purchasing started to evolve into more than a clerical function. Many authors note that during the past few years purchasing has begun to play an even more important role in companies' strategies. During the past decade the purchasing function won a reputation in many executive boardrooms as a powerful tool for improving profitability [Monczka 2000]. There are three reasons for this:

1) The purchasing function offers great cost savings potential;
2) The goods and services bought have a major impact on the quality of one's own products and services;
3) Purchasing influences a company's technology development and the improvement of product and process designs.

Consequently, buyers no longer simply process requisition and order forms. They are increasingly active in strategic areas such as supplier development and improvement, early supplier involvement, cross-functional teams, full-service suppliers, total cost supplier selection, and integrated information systems providing links with suppliers.

As purchasing decisions became more important, so did the considerations and arguments underlying these decisions. Because of the increased attention paid by executive managers, purchasing managers are now confronted with questions concerning the rational justification of their decisions, and they are held responsible for the performance changes resulting from these decisions. This demand for well-considered purchasing decisions has made purchasing decision-making more complex, whereas earlier purchasing decisions were often justified on the basis of a single criterion (often price); now multiple criteria play a role, many of which are 'soft'.

The increased importance of purchasing has also generated a significant shift in the way   purchasing decisions are made. From its traditional operational, clerical role, the purchasing function evolved to supply management. Its managers now participate in decisions concerning supply chain management and supply alternatives, as well as in strategy formulation processes [Cavinato 1992]. Purchasing increasingly has to take into account companies' logistics, product development, and manufacturing functions.

9.4 IT and purchasing

Purchasing is a classic source of inefficiency [Gebauer 1998]. Policies and forms are among the most common instruments to standardize and control the purchasing process, but to cover the wide range of potential situations, companies usually apply a large numbers of rules, and the resulting procedures are often complex, slow, and expensive. Especially in the case of class C products, the costs of the buying process are often higher than those of the goods and services purchased. With buying processes typically involving a large amount of information processing and communication, procurement is well suited for IT support and automation, in every stage. However, before the advent of the Internet, IT systems available often supported only the information stage (electronic catalogs), or they were used to automate operational activities during the settlement stage – including payment, especially in cases in which high volumes and frequencies justified setting up electronic data interchange (EDI) systems. The companies using them often owned these systems, and they were not interactive. Generally, little IT support was provided for the negotiation stage, or for capital and maverick buying. Maverick buying relates to a situation where employees directly buy products, possibly bypassing existing central contracts with suppliers. In these areas most processes were still mainly paper-based and manual [Segev 1997].

The first application of IT to purchasing processes was the use of CDs to record and transfer product and supplier information, which saved time during the selection stage. But all suppliers had their own way of offering information, which made comparing them difficult. E-Procurement implementations started out by placing orders with suppliers through fax and e-mail, and EDI (Electronic Data Interchange). EDI systems helped to improve the efficiency and speed of the contracting and ordering stages, which was especially practical for companies which regularly ordered large quantities of the same goods, since it improved transaction efficiency and speed. EDI systems, however, are only worthwhile for long-term supplier-client relations since they involve significant investments. Subsequently, most solutions have added XML (extensible Markup Language) and access to online catalogs as a means of placing orders. These allowed buyers to compare products and offerings.

9.5 e-Procurement

Procurement is an important element in any business. It is involved in almost every link in the supply chain where physical products and information flow from suppliers to end customers. Procurement can be both driven by long run production plans and short-term needs with little predictability. Procurement can be classified as *direct procurement* and *indirect procurement* based on the nature of an organization's products [Baron 2000]. Direct procurement deals with items that are required for the direct production of an organization's products, while indirect procurement deals with items that support the production. Items that are used in the production of an organization's products – direct items – are typically planned and predictable and

have high value of MRO orders. In contrast, items that are used in processes that support production –
indirect items – are often less planned and, thus, less predictable with the value of MRO orders being
much smaller than that of direct items. As a result, direct procurement is well planned and predictable,
while indirect procurement often happens on an ad hoc basis and is much less predictable. Although the
value of indirect item orders is much smaller than that of direct items, the cost to process each is roughly
the same, and this can result in the classic case of an item that costs more to order than it does to pay for
[Baron 2000].

Global competition, pricing pressures, and difficult financial markets are forcing organizations to develop
new strategies for achieving improvements in productivity and costs. As a result, the ability to control costs
and coordinate activities across the supply chain is rapidly emerging as a primary source of competitive
differentiation within every industry. Automating procurement offers the greatest opportunity to improve
processes, increase productivity, and reduce costs across the supply chain. Purchased products and services
are the single largest expense at most organizations, accounting for around \$.50–.55 of every dollar earned
in revenue [Aberdeen 2001].

E-Procurement leverages Internet technology to electronically enable corporate purchasing processes [van
Weele 1994]. It is the electronic purchase and sale of supplies and services over the Internet. The Internet
has virtually eliminated traditional procurement barriers, providing instant access to thousands of buyers,
suppliers, and marketplaces around the world. E-Procurement covers the entire purchasing process, from
gathering information to delivery. Consequently, the process includes inbound logistics such as transportation,
goods-in, and warehousing before an ordered item is used. E-Procurement utilizes electronic catalogs,
automatic routing of an electronic requisition through approval process, and electronic transmission of the
completed purchase order to the vendor.

E-Procurement is characterized by the purchase of supplies and services over the Internet. Its software
applications and services are employee self-service solutions that streamline and support the purchase of
non-production materials like office supplies, computer equipment, and maintenance, repair, and operating
(MRO) provisions. These items can account for 30% to 60% of a company's total expenditure, yet they
remain poorly controlled and costly to process at most organizations. The services of e-Procurement include
consolidation, control, and automation of purchasing processes. Typically, e-Procurement systems allow
qualified and registered users to look for buyers or sellers of goods and services. Depending on the approach,
buyers or sellers may specify prices or invite bids. Transactions can be initiated and completed. Ongoing
purchases may qualify customers for volume discounts or special offers. The possibility of an end-to-end
integration of the purchasing cycle is created by e-Procurement. Buyers can look into their supplier's systems
to check inventory before ordering, configuring products, scheduling production and receiving, optimizing
logistics, and coordinating and planning supply chain activities.

Systems of e-Procurement may make it possible to automate some buying and selling processes. Companies
participating expect to be able to control procurement process more effectively, reduce purchasing agent
overhead, and improve manufacturing cycles. Appropriate e-Procurement application software allows an
organization to carry out purchasing processes. Depending on the sophistication of the software, it allows
buyers to perform some or all of the following functions: access supplier information, including catalogs,
generate requisitions, obtain approvals in accordance with the business rules of the organization, send
purchase orders to suppliers, receive invoices, and process payment. Handling all these steps electronically
allows better control, quicker transactions, and a reduction of the amount of paper used.

E-Procurement solutions provide increasing support for unplanned purchases, which can represent between 30% and 40% of all indirect procurement [Aberdeen 2001]. Spot buys involve a frontline employee requesting that the purchasing department source or acquire an item or service that is not currently represented in the organization's existing contracts. Typically managed through a mix of phone calls and 'paper pushing', the spot-buy process is inefficient and time consuming. Automating the request and sourcing process reduces the cycle time and costs associated with spot buys.

The three main types of e-Procurement schemes are *online catalogs, auctions* and *reverse auctions.* Online catalogs are management-selected purchasing catalogs that enable various departments in the purchasing company to buy items directly out of this catalog. Online catalogs reduce the purchasing costs of a company as the lengthy authorization processes, for instance, stationary procurement, is eliminated, because employees can buy the required stationary directly over the Web. In addition, smaller participants in an e-Market are allowed to join the pricing contracts of the large companies on the exchange and thus profit from their purchasing leverage.

Users of e-Procurement systems participate in auctions to acquire new goods or dispose of excess inventory or assets. *Reverse auctions* let organizations set a price they are willing to pay for goods or services, which suppliers then can bid to fulfill. Forward auctions enable buyers to efficiently disburse excess assets and inventories. In addition, some systems offer support for vendor selection and enablement, in the form of sourcing capabilities. These are important features of e-Procurement functionality, as they give users more flexibility in product selection and pricing, and open the procurement space up to e-Business activities other than straight purchasing.

An e-Procurement solution offers the following key advantages:

• Reduced costs: e-Procurement empowers aggregated, cross-enterprise spending, resulting in lower prices through higher-volume purchasing;

• Improved process efficiency: e-Procurement makes it easier for companies to increase purchasing control and work with preferred suppliers;

• Increased control: e-Procurement provides a consistent method for handling all purchasing needs;

• Global reach: e-Procurement provides access to a global supplier base, allowing companies to work with suppliers who better fit their needs and reduce material costs by strengthening existing supplier relationships.

Figure 9.4 shows a simplified e-Procurement system, with a purchasing officer using an e-Procurement system to search an electronic catalog containing product information from preferred suppliers at negotiated prices, and then to place an order for approval. Electronic catalogs could, for example, be in-house catalogs that aggregate supplier data for the use of company purchasing officers (see Section 9.5.1 on e-Procurement models for more details on this subject). The electronic requisition is automatically routed, e.g., via e-mail, to a budget manager (approver) who is authorized to approve such orders. Approvers review and approve the requisition online. Approved orders are sent directly to the relevant supplier. A requisitioner places the order on behalf of the buying organization. The requisitioner can at all times check its status. In addition, the company's accounting department is also kept up-to-date regarding the order. These key procurement activities and their associated information flows are shown in Figure 9.4.

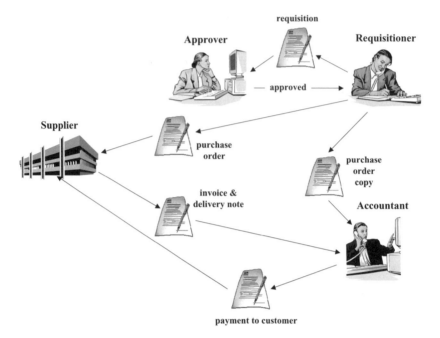

■ **Figure 9.4:** Key Procurement Activities Within an Organization

Internet technology has had a major impact on the purchasing process and on automating e-Procurement solutions. Not only does it allow better support of the process' several stages – for many different goods and services and for all three buying situations – it also improves the efficiency of traditional IT support. Several tools have been developed to this end [Gebauer 1998]:

- *Search engines* – using keywords, buyers find the items they look for; thus the information stage is supported, in particular when buyers look for new sources to fulfill unexpected requirements;

- *e-catalogs* – these allow buying companies to browse, search, and place orders online; they combine and extend many features of the current channels (content, searching capabilities, ordering);

- *Internet EDI links* – potentially less costly than leased lines and VANs; VANs are third-party-managed data networks that a number of organizations use on a subscription basis [Laudon 2004].

- *Online auctions and bidding systems* – these support the negotiation stage by providing simple negotiation mechanisms.

The most exciting current developments are probably found in the area of MRO procurement, in which numerous companies launch initiatives, trying to be the first to present viable business models and software. The systems they present allow buyers to combine catalogs from several suppliers, check the availability of the items they need, place orders then track their fulfillment, and initiate payment. All this is done through the Internet. There seems to be a general development [Gebauer 1998] towards a change in the roles played by end users and purchasing departments, in this respect. New procurement systems, into which companies' purchasing and approval rules have been integrated, allow end users to place individual orders. Their handling is fully automated, thus allowing purchasing departments to concentrate on strategic and managerial tasks, while still maintaining control over the purchasing process. Other areas of development from which major gains are expected include automated negotiations and electronic auctions.

9.5.1 e-Procurement models

Three basic architecture models have evolved over a number of years; they can be broadly described as buyer-centric, seller-centric, and e-marketplace [USHER 2002]. These electronic procurement models take a 'hub and spokes' approach (the hub being the organization at the centre of the system, while the buyers and/or suppliers who interact with the system are at the ends of the spokes).

From a buying organization's perspective, the key differences between e-Procurement models in the market today lie where the buying application software and electronic catalog(s) reside. In a *buyer-centric* or *buyer-managed purchasing model,* the buying organization implements software to support its procurement processes, obtains catalog data from its contracted suppliers, and aggregates the catalog data into a single internal catalog for the use of its purchasing officers [USHER 2002]. With this model, the buyer is at the hub with suppliers connected at the end of the spokes.

The main advantages of this model are that it offers tight control over the procurement software, catalog, and other procurement data and processes, and makes it easier for procurement solutions to be fully integrated into a company's financial management system. In addition, the costs of participating in a buyer-centric purchasing system are generally low as they do not involve any transaction fees, and require fairly low investment from suppliers to participate.

In contrast to the buyer-centric purchasing model, in a *seller-centric procurement model* the seller is at the centre of the hub, with buying organizations connected at the spokes. Buyers use the supplier's system, accessible over the Internet, to browse the supplier's catalog and place orders. This space in the marketplace has been largely the domain of business-to-consumer selling, although increasingly business-to-business trading is occurring on these sites [USHER 2002].

The main advantages of this model are that, from the supplier's point of view, it is very attractive in terms of control, cost, maintenance, and functionality. For the buyer, these solutions generally offer the lowest investment cost; however, customers need to know where to find these systems so their use may be limited. To address this problem some sites are being aggregated into virtual e-Malls to reduce the need to search many different sites.

The main disadvantages are that suppliers' sites provide only limited support for the buyer's purchasing process, typically only the ability to browse catalogs and place orders. Moreover, buyers have no control over catalog data and must access each supplying organization's system individually, and only one supplier's catalog can be accessed at a time. Integration into financial management systems at the buyer's end is also very difficult to achieve.

The final model is the *e-Marketplace model,* in which a third party is at the hub, with buying and selling organizations trading with each other through the common marketplace. The marketplace hosts supplier catalogs, and provides electronic transaction capabilities of varying sophistication to buyers and suppliers.

The main advantages of this model are that e-Marketplaces allow extended trading between many organizations – buyers and sellers of different sizes. E-Marketplace solutions are usually least expensive, in terms of overall initial costs, from the combined perspective of buyers and sellers.

On the downside, e-Marketplaces have the highest ongoing costs (subscriptions, maintenance, and/or transaction fees). Although e-Marketplaces allow extended trading to access buyers and suppliers linked to the e-Marketplace, companies need to subscribe to the e-Marketplace.

The procurement models we examined above generally involve 'closed' communities and systems, limiting the flexibility of those on the periphery. They are also based on one dominant party, which establishes the trading rules for the system, and this limits other participants' flexibility. There is therefore an emerging trend towards a more open trading environment, based on open standards, which is intended to overcome the limitations of these closed systems.

An open trading environment allows buyers and sellers to establish systems that meet their requirements, without imposing them on their trading partners. Under an open trading model, buyers implement software that allows them to establish and maintain local internal catalogs, but also to access e-Marketplaces and suppliers' stand-alone catalogs. Suppliers are free to choose whether to host their own catalogs or use marketplaces. These arrangements benefit both buyers and suppliers. Buyers benefit from flexibility in accessing supplier catalogs, regardless of where the catalogs are hosted, while suppliers are able to make their catalogs visible to the widest possible market, regardless of the e-Procurement arrangements individual buyers have implemented.

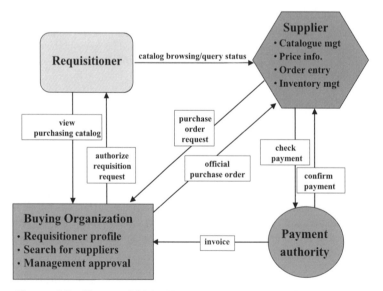

■ **Figure 9.5:** Abstract OBI Architecture: Entities and Information Flows

Open trading arrangements of this kind, however, require a commitment to open standards on the part of buyers, suppliers, and e-Marketplace providers. Currently two potential standards are available, XML/EDI and Open Buying on the Internet (OBI). *XML/EDI* is a standardized framework in which EDI-based business documents and messages are described using XML syntax. XML/EDI is briefly discussed in Chapter 7. We will consider OBI in the remainder of this section.

OBI is a common set of business requirements built for e-Business applications. It includes a supporting architecture, technical specifications, and guidelines. Adoption of the standard provides companies with a secure, common, and easy to use method for conducting business online. OBI provides interoperability among purchasing systems to allow companies to conduct business-to-business electronic purchasing independent of technology.

The OBI architecture is based on the premise that process 'owners' should be responsible for information associated with their business processes. For example, buying organizations are responsible for requisitioner profile information, account codes, tax status, and approvals. Selling organizations are responsible for electronic catalogs and the associated price, order entry, and inventory mechanisms.

At an abstract level, the OBI architecture can be viewed as the interaction of the four entities, shown in Figure 9.5 and described below.

1) Requisitioner: is the person who actually places the order. The requisitioner is assumed to have a digital certificate, issued by a trusted certificate authority (see Chapter 13);
2) Buying Organization: represents the purchasing management and the information systems which support purchasing;
3) Selling Organization: maintains an electronic catalog that presents accurate product and price information – information which can be tailored, based on the organizational affiliation of the requisitioner as specified in a digital certificate. Product and price information reflects the contract with a buying organization. The selling organization's catalog must be integrated effectively with inventory and order management systems, and an OBI server for sending OBI Order Requests and receiving OBI Orders. Selling organizations must be able to authorize certain transaction types with the appropriate payment authority;
4) Payment Authority: provides authorization for the payment presented by the requisitioner. Payment authorities must provide payments to selling organizations with a timely invoice, or debit to the buying organization.

9.5.2 The components of e-Procurement systems

Improved integration technology is the reason e-Procurement is on the rise. Business software vendors are building better application programming interfaces for connecting systems, and builders are developing better tools, which translate into shorter implementation cycles and lower costs.

E-Procurement systems generally consist of four components [Pettinga 1998]: content management, requisition management, transaction management, and connectivity management.

Content management is the core component of e-Procurement systems and includes managing the data involved in e-Procurement processes, e.g., supplier and product information, as well as availability. This type of data originates from many different suppliers. Content is an e-Procurement system's information-technological heart, and therefore cannot be missed: the data entered must be up-to-date, and it has to be possible to standardize, integrate, and enrich it – actions which are often the system's bottleneck. There are two aspects to content management:

1) Content – all product and supplier information must be up-to-date, so guidelines are required with respect to making changes;
2) Technology – this concerns the functionality of the system, for which order approval authority must be established, among other things.

The importance of content management lies in the fact that e-Procurement systems allow every individual purchasing officer to place orders directly from an electronic catalog into which the contract terms involved, and the company's purchasing rules, have been integrated. The potential impact of such centralization is significant. It reduces the number of suppliers, which leverages the buying power of the company as a whole, so leads to better buying conditions, and possibly to a higher degree of standardization of products bought. Standardization contributes to stock optimization, and centralized control over the buying process allows procurement on the basis of skeleton agreements, so restricts maverick buying. Online spend analysis allows better control of the overall purchasing performance of the company. However, to achieve this, one's data must be managed properly. Therefore, content management is one of e-Procurement's critical success factors.

The remaining three components play more supporting roles; their potential impact concerns a reduced administrative workload. *Requisition management* involves enabling end users to place and transact orders. Selecting a product or service from a digital catalog is the first step, but workflow transactions are part of requisition management too. Workflow support, routes the order via the managers whose authorization is needed, and manages the budget limits per user or department.

The *transaction management* component of e-Procurement systems transfers the order to the relevant supplier using open standards, e.g., XML/EDI or OBI. Finally, *connectivity management* ensures coupling with the supplier's systems and the company's own internal financial, and logistic systems (ERP – Enterprise Resource Planning system). To this end interfaces are required that allow the unhindered, fully automated exchange of data of whatever format or structure. Using these interfaces, e-Procurement systems are connected to the suppliers' systems – to, e.g., transfer orders and order confirmations – and to internal enterprise resource planning (ERP) systems, to facilitate budget control, order registration, accounting procedures, and payment for orders.

9.5.3 Internet-based e-Catalog systems

Successful e-Procurement depends upon large numbers of requisitioners, buying the products and services they need, from approved suppliers, at the negotiated prices. Effective supplier enablement, which is about buyers working collaboratively with their suppliers so that they are integrated into an e-Procurement solution, is essential to this process. Content management is the first step in the wider scope of supplier enablement. In the same way that buyers are looking to take out significant cost from purchase transaction processing through automation, these same benefits are available to suppliers as sales transaction efficiencies, e.g., through back-office/ERP integration.

Catalogs play an important role in day-to-day procurement. Hundreds of millions of dollars are transacted between companies on the basis of catalogs. However, using physical catalogs involves significant difficulties and is rather inefficient [Gartner 2001]. They are cumbersome, they require much storage room; search and comparison activities are very difficult to do, they are outdated soon after publication (everybody always seems uncertain of whether they have the latest edition), and half the time you cannot find them at all. Catalogs recorded on CD are generally user-friendlier, but they too are soon out of date and they still require physical storage and some means of remote access or control. Buying on the basis of catalogs is often inefficient and slow. Checking availability and placing orders take time; notification of receipt, billing, and paying require manual intervention. From the supplier's point of view, physical catalogs have disadvantages too. Printing them is a huge task. It can only be done periodically, say once a year, thus freezing products and prices for a long time. And suppliers face high order processing costs, because their clients will use all available means of communication to place their orders, e.g., fax, mail, or the telephone.

Internet or Web-based electronic catalogs offer significant advantages. Displaying merchandise for sale, i.e., content, through an online catalog is a key factor in the success of e-Procurement both from the buyer and supplier perspective. Moving the physical catalog online makes it dynamic: suppliers do not have to wait for the next printing of a paper catalog to change products and prices.

Case Study

Commerce One

Commerce Chain is an example of an online catalog, since it can also be used to keep one's catalog content up-to-date.

Electronic catalogs may be defined [Baron 2000] as electronic representations of information on the products and services a company offers, and they are a means by which buyers view their suppliers' information and interact with it. Their chief advantages are the ease with which they are kept up-to-date and adapted, and the simplified search processes they offer. Internet-based e-Catalogs do not have to be stored physically, locating the latest version is easy, and buyers have the benefit of computer-assisted search facilities. This makes locating and evaluating products and offers much easier and more effective. Selection and ordering facilities, which are usually included as well, make life even easier; and since they feed their information back to the client, the buying company has a management tool for understanding and controlling expenditure. From the supplier's point of view, the advantages of Internet-based e-Catalogs include their greater flexibility for changing the range of goods and prices offered, and the potential to personalize their content. Also, telephones, faxes, and physical mail are replaced by communication through a standardizing interface, which allows the processing of structured messages at significantly lower costs. Since the costs of coordination, data gathering, and analysis are reduced as well as those of processing, suppliers can expand their market to include a broader range of products and clients.

Introducing electronic catalogs does, of course, involve some costs. Suppliers will encounter expenditures for integrating their order processing systems with the e-Procurement systems of their customers. Apart from system integration costs, suppliers' fulfillment costs may also rise, for example, if all their customers' employees have access to their catalog system so that order placement is widely distributed instead of centralized as before.

Essentially, three approaches are available to buying companies which have to deal with a large number of catalog suppliers: *supplier-managed catalogs, buyer-managed catalogs,* and *third-party-managed catalogs*. The first two of these approaches are peer-to-peer methods, in which buyer and seller interact directly; the third approach involves the services of the company managing the catalog.

In the *supplier-managed model*, the supplier hosts the content and usually the selection or configuration application that is delivered over the Internet to the requisitioner. With supplier-hosted model, the supplier will be responsible for providing buyer-specific content, and is responsible for the cost and effort of maintaining the catalog, but can exert a high control over how this is presented. This model can be used to support all catalog types from simple line items through to complex, configurable items. Working with supplier-managed catalogs, buyers use catalogs provided by individual suppliers. This works particularly well when catalogs include special features, such as search and ordering facilities tailored to the specifics of their goods and services. This model is also a means by which suppliers can integrate e-Procurement directly with their own supply chain and financial systems, while buyers will need controls around content, for example, when a price or specification changes.

With the *buyer-managed e-Catalog* model, data must be supplied, or massaged, into the exact format required to load correctly into the target application. This model gives the buying organization a high degree of control over content and pricing, and can be used to ensure that only correct contracted items and prices are available to the requisitioner base. Buyers who wish to set up buyer-managed catalogs must fill these with the content provided by their suppliers. From the buying company's perspective this approach has merits since it then controls the catalog, but making and maintaining large aggregated catalogs is neither simple nor cheap [Gartner 2001]. It requires specialist tools, processes, and people.

Third-party-managed catalogs (also called market-managed catalogs or commerce network-managed catalogs) are aggregated catalogs containing the data of many suppliers, which is made available to buying companies on a commercial basis. These are suitable for very large catalogs (e.g., some MRO categories), for producing buyer-specific views of a catalog and allow suppliers to potentially gain access to many buyers. The market-managed e-Catalog model is geared towards providing a scalable content management model and is managed by an electronic market (see Chapter 8).

There are two primary models of third-party-managed catalogs: public and personalized. The public model involves an intermediary who sets up a single catalog with aggregated content from many suppliers, and makes it available to many buyers. In the personalized model, these catalogs contain additional data, provided by suppliers along with their content, which selects the information to which individual buying companies are given access. Thus special prices, product range restrictions, etc. are reflected in the offer presented to each individual user. It has been observed that a new class of service providers seems to be emerging [Gartner 2001]: catalog management intermediaries. These provide hosted environments, presenting suppliers with a single point of product maintenance and allowing the export of content to buyers or electronic markets. Thus, technical issues revolve around data security, and how to restrict buyer-specific views.

Different e-Procurement system vendors provide solutions for the buyer-centric and third-party-managed types of e-Catalog models. For example, Ariba, Commerce One, Requisite Technology, TCN, and Aspect

Development sell technologies that help companies aggregate catalogs from their suppliers and add proprietary content.

The kind of catalog chosen will depend on the buyer's business. Small enterprises are most likely to use a single third-party-managed catalog in order to satisfy their buying needs. For medium-sized companies, these might not be enough, and they will complement them with seller- and buyer-managed catalogs. Large companies, established on different locations, will have to use many catalogs, of all three kinds.

9.5.4 Catalog aggregation

With the buyer-centric and third-party-managed types of e-Catalog models, companies are part of an interconnected, trading-partner network. Within this network, purchasing companies and marketplaces play the role of catalog aggregators, while suppliers and distributors play the role of catalog providers. Aggregators gather disparate and fragmented e-catalog information from their supply chains, and generate unified, consistent, market-wide e-Catalogs that can be presented to end users.

Catalog aggregation is a one-to-many, buyer-focused model. Sellers' catalogs are aggregated at the e-Business exchange, e.g., e-Market, for the benefit of any buyer visiting the site. It primarily suits fairly static prices and commodity purchases. Buyers and sellers can find each other and execute transactions online.

In the catalog aggregation model, suppliers and distributors would much rather create e-Catalogs once, disseminate them inexpensively through their distribution channels, and update them automatically when the need occurs. However, the reality is that in such networks where each organization must deal with numerous other organizations, data providers, who are also owners for product information, need to provide their e-Catalogs selectively to their trading partners. The fact that different purchasing companies and marketplaces require the catalogs to be in different formats, and maintain them in different ways, makes the aggregation process particularly cumbersome.

9.6 Auctions

Auctions can be of three types: open, completely anonymous, and closed, or in any combination between the two extremes. Companies are in general pre-registered with auctions, and are given a window of time to bid. Companies can bid more than once, and can see the bids coming from their competitors, though the names are not usually disclosed. In auctions, the nature of the product or service being auctioned must be clearly described, so that the price is the only criterion for uptake of bids.

The duration of auctions is normally limited. Also, in normal cases the highest bid must be accepted (the 'English outcry auction'), which is only possible if the auctioned article can be described in as much detail as possible. The added value created by the operator of the service is first and foremost the choice of a suitable auction format, and the selection of information to be made available to the participants in the auction [Statham 2001]. Here anonymity is often requested, because, for example, a sale of products may permit inferences about surplus capacity and a purchase inference about shortages. On the other hand, the realization that a non-anonymous major player is taking part in an auction may influence the judgment of the other market participants, and make them offer higher bids. Striking the balance between providing enough information to realize the best (highest) price, but not so much as to give away business secrets, the greatest challenge for the operator of a marketplace of this kind.

The advantages and disadvantages of auction sites for buyers and sellers largely correspond to those of exchange services. In addition, auctions also offer a good way to discover market prices or, for example, to establish the value of a brand, by offering the same product once anonymously and once under the brand name.

The reverse auction adopts a one-to-many model and is buyer-centric. A purchaser engages several qualified sellers who compete in an auction with dynamic downward pricing. The purchaser usually sends out so-called requests for quotations, which list the specifications of the commodity or component it wishes to procure. Companies are pre-registered and again given a time frame in which to bid. Contracts go to the lowest bidder. This model most benefits the buyer by enabling purchase at the lowest price offered.

As with the conventional auction model, the exchange may support public and private reverse auctions [Statham 2001]. Qualified sellers approved by the exchange, and who meet the conditions stipulated by the buyer for any particular auction, can compete in a public reverse auction. In this, such conditions could relate, for example, to a geographic region, production capacity, availability, quality, shipping, and payment. In a private reverse auction, the buyer specifically invites an established base of suppliers to take part. Offers to sell, matching of buy-sell orders, and the execution of transactions may occur either in real time or over a longer time frame. FreeMarkets is one example. Its exchanges utilize a trading engine that offers real-time pricing and order matching for short-term reverse auctions

9.7 e-Procurement solutions

To fully deliver on its promise, e-Procurement must integrate on the buyer's back-end with financial systems for invoice processing and accounts payable, including Enterprise Resource Planning (ERP) systems to tie procurement in with the rest of an organization's business processes. It should in addition provide better integration with suppliers' existing back-office systems to help streamline the order processes and automate suppliers' activities. E-Procurement solutions support the full spectrum of supplier enablement capabilities, from full EDI to XML-based integration, and to the suppliers' order management systems.

E-Procurement systems provide a complete purchasing management solution that offers a seamless connection between buyers and suppliers for the purchase of direct and indirect goods and services within a framework of predefined business rules. They enable automated enterprise-wide requisitioning for inventory items, by generating inventory demand signals from approved requisitions. To achieve this, back-office purchasing systems leverage the e-Procurement workflow and electronic order transmission capabilities, features not typically found in ERP purchasing modules. Typical abilities of modern e-Procurement solutions include:

- Performing catalog aggregation functions and managing content from multiple suppliers in disparate formats;

- Providing customized access to purchasing requirements;

- Maintaining role-based custom item catalogs that enable requesters to order from item categories that are relevant to their role in the organization;

- Matching validation between receipts, purchase orders, and invoices, and automatically generating debit memos;

- Providing requisition management and tracking, e.g., they view resulting purchase order details and track the full business cycle of requests;

- Providing budget checking and commitment control.

The concept of *approvals workflow* is an essential element in the establishment of a system of e-Procurement. It typically uses workflow technology to create sophisticated workflow rules for approval or notification within an organization – graphically and without coding – from a browser. In particular they:

- Use serial and parallel approval paths that can be triggered from any requisition business data;

- Control requisition authorizations through workflow-enabled approvals;

- Look at a graphical bird's-eye-view for quick status checking;

- Provide 'on behalf of' approvals for requests from a third individual;

- Take advantage of comprehensive escalation processing.

According to a study published by purchasing.com [Hannon 2002], the use made of e-Sourcing tools is slowly increasing (see Table 9.1), but not to the levels that most sourcing technology providers would like. Online collaboration with suppliers is growing most rapidly, jumping from 10% to 21% in less than two years. Extranet use seems to be on the decline.

9.8 Chapter summary

Every company depends on suppliers and contractors to meet a variety of organizational needs: manufacturing, support, and management processes require materials, components, goods, equipment, supplies, merchandise, and specialist services. Consequently, purchasing is a function every company requires. The purchasing function's economic importance is considerable. The average industrial company in the United States spends around 56% of its sales income on purchases from outside sources. The contribution of the purchasing function to the organization's effectiveness, however, not only regards the availability of goods and services, it also concerns the efficient (internal) organization of buying processes.

For almost every company, the Pareto Analysis holds: a small number of important articles (class A articles) represents a major share of the value purchased, while a large number of articles (class C articles) represents only a small part of this value. These different categories and classes of goods and services each require their own specific procurement processes.

Tools	2002 (%)	2000 (%)
tools for supply base and strategic sourcing research	60	66
supplier directories and databases	74	73
commerce-enabled extranets with selected suppliers	23	25
demand aggregation with other companies	9	6
E-RFQs[3]	34	30
electronic data interchange systems (EDI)	38	32
e-Matching (nasdaq-style)	8	4
e-Auctions (reverse: buyer-controlled)	15	6
e-Auctions (forward: seller-controlled)	8	6
e-Auctions (real time)	11	9
e-Auctions (not real time)	6	4
e-Collaboration with suppliers	21	10
supplier-hosted Internet storefronts	57	56

■ **Table 9.1:** The Use of e-Sourcing Tools, 2002 vs. 2000 [Hannon 2002]

Different models have been proposed to describe the organizational buying process. We discussed the buy-grid model and Kraljic's purchasing portfolio model.

The buy-grid model combines the division of the organizational buying process into stages (information, negotiation, and settlement) with three classes of buying situations that are determined by the newness of the buying situation: new task, straight rebuy, and modified rebuy. A 'new task' buying situation is defined as one in which the company buys for the first time, perhaps even seeking solutions for new product functions. 'New task' buying situations naturally evolve into 'straight rebuy' situations: proceduralized situations in which everything (quality specifications, prices and conditions, suppliers) is fixed except for the quantities needed and the delivery schedule. In their turn, 'straight rebuy' situations typically evolve into 'modified rebuy' situations. Then all parameters are reevaluated, which generally also involves investigating alternative suppliers.

One of the major drawbacks of the buy-grid model is that the importance of the goods and services bought, and the potential consequences of the buying situation, are left undifferentiated. The Purchasing Portfolio is another purchasing model that addresses this aspect. For this purpose it introduces two variables:

- The company's strategic vulnerability with respect to the purchase, expressed in criteria such as added value, and the percentage of the company's products' cost price determined by the goods purchased;

- The complexity of the supplying market (determining the difficulty with which the purchase is made), expressed in criteria such as scarcity and entry barriers.

Corresponding to these variables a matrix is formed with four cells, representing four kinds of items that companies can buy:

1) Strategic items, characterized by high buying risks and a major profit impact;
2) Bottleneck items, characterized by high buying risks but a small profit impact;
3) Leverage items, characterized by low buying risks but a major profit impact;
4) Routine items, characterized by low buying risks and a small profit impact.

The relevance of these models for automation of the purchasing process is clear. For straight rebuy situations and routine items, the aim is to minimize the cost of acquisition by standardization, automation, and, wherever practical, contracting out the purchasing process itself.

Purchasing is a classic source of inefficiency. Especially in the case of class C products, the costs of the buying process are often higher than those of the goods and services purchased. With buying processes typically involving a large amount of information processing and communication, procurement is well suited for IT support and automation, at every stage. The first application of IT to purchasing processes was the use of CDs to record and transfer product and supplier information, which saved time during the selection stage. But all suppliers had their own way of offering information, which made comparing them difficult.

For the purpose of this chapter we defined e-Procurement as the application of Internet technology to the buying and selling of goods and services. E-Procurement creates the possibility of an end-to-end integration of the purchasing cycle. Buyers can look into their supplier's systems to check inventory before ordering, configuring products, scheduling production and receiving, optimizing logistics, and coordinating and planning supply chain activities. E-procurement systems generally consist of four components: *content management, requisition management, transaction management, and connectivity management.*

Several tools have been developed to this end:

- Search engines;

- E-Catalogs;

- Internet EDI links;

- Online auctions and bidding systems.

From a buying organization's perspective, the key differences between e-Procurement models in the market today, lie in where the buying application software and electronic catalog(s) reside. In a buyer-centric purchasing model, the buying organization implements software to support its procurement processes, obtains catalog data from its contracted suppliers, and aggregates the catalog data into a single internal catalog for the use of its purchasing officers. With a seller-centric procurement model, the seller is at the centre of the hub, with buying organizations connected at the spokes. Buyers use the supplier's system, accessible over the Internet, to browse the supplier's catalog and place orders. The final model is the e-Marketplace model, in which a third party is at the hub, with buying and selling organizations trading with each other through the common marketplace.

The procurement models we examined above generally involve 'closed' communities and systems, limiting the flexibility of those on the periphery. An open trading environment, however, allows buyers and sellers to establish systems that meet their requirements, without imposing these on their trading partners. Open trading arrangements of this kind, however, require a commitment to open standards on the part of buyers, suppliers, and e-Marketplace providers. Currently, two potential standards are available, XML/EDI and Open Buying on the Internet (OBI).

Discussion Questions

- What are the five general objectives of the purchasing function (the 5 Rights)?
- How does the purchasing portfolio model differ from the buy grid model?
- Discuss traditional applications of IT to the purchasing process.
- Discuss and explain the Open Buying on the Internet (OBI) Architecture.
- Explain what is meant by 'e-Procurement creates the possibility of an end-to-end integration of the purchasing cycle'.
- Name and explain the four components of an e-Procurement system according to [Pettinga 1998].

Assignments

i. In 'the buy grid framework' [Robinson 1967] the organizational buying process consists of eight stages. In general, the first stages are the most complex. The 'purchasing portfolio' [Kraljic 1983] differentiates products by complexity and profitability. Find examples of products in each segment of the purchasing portfolio, and define the critical steps in the buy grid framework for that product.

ii. Give some advantages and disadvantages of third-party-managed, supplier- managed, and buyer-managed catalogs. Find some examples of each kind of catalog. Give some advantages and disadvantages of third-party-managed, supplier-managed and buyer-managed catalogs. Find some examples of each kind of catalog.

Chapter 10

e-Business Networks

As explained in Chapter 2 Transaction Cost Economics suggests that companies may decide to acquire the necessary inputs for their primary processes in two fundamentally different ways: either by producing the required services and products themselves (which in TCE terminology is called 'hierarchy'), or by buying them from other – independent – organizations ('market'). Obviously, this choice has consequences for the transaction costs incurred. Producing products and services increases one's internal coordination costs (for planning, meetings, etc.), while outside procurement drives up the search, settlement, contract, and monitoring costs. The reduction of transaction costs made possible by the introduction of the Internet and similar technologies will, then, lead to a more 'market'-like approach: it will trigger companies to buy their inputs instead of producing them. In Chapter 8 we argued that electronic markets might play an important role in this process. However, several authors [Clemons 1993] feel that this dichotomy is too simplistic. They suggest a third way of procuring the necessary products and services. Companies may engage in partnerships in which they maintain their economic and legal independence, but restrict their short-term freedom of action by agreeing to collaborate in regard to specific issues for a specific period. Such collaboration patterns are called 'networks'. Networks are typically designed to handle environments and tasks that demand flexibility. They consist of internal and external links for specific purposes, which may be dismantled and replaced by other links when those purposes have been achieved [Baker 1993]. Networks may differ in respect to the goals pursued, the type of collaboration, their structure, and the information systems and information technologies used to support them.

This chapter focuses on network organizations. It builds on the analysis of networks that we presented in Section 5.2; its purpose is to analyze different types of network organizations, of interorganizational systems, and how they relate to each other. In particular, we position the relationship between network organizations and information systems, define network organizations, and develop a typology on the basis of management objectives for networking. Subsequently, the chapter defines interorganizational systems and develops a classification of interorganizational systems based on their objectives, and examines a specific class of network organizations: supply chains and their management.

Case Study

Business network redesign at Robeco

Robeco Group is one of Europe's largest asset management organizations, managing around US$90 billion of assets. In managing mutual funds, the Robeco Group executes hundreds of thousands of financial securities transactions all over the world [Toppen 1998a, 1998b, 1999]. Until about 1994, the entire transaction process was mainly paper based. Both internal transaction information and settlement instructions were created manually and sent to the receiving organization by regular mail. Communication with stakeholders was based on telex and facsimile; information had to be rekeyed into different systems and instructions to stakeholders had to be generated manually several times. Needless to say, there was a need for tight and extensive checks and control measures because the entire process was prone to errors.

Analysis of the transaction processes showed that problems occurred in 23% of all transactions. There were internal problems consisting of incorrect or not timely information related to the transactions. Robeco Group therefore decided to reengineer its business processes and to transform the inter-company network.

The Robeco Group case is a practical example of what might be achieved in applying business process redesign theories in a network organization. Business process redesign has been fundamental to Robeco's growth between 1994 and 1998 from about US$4 25 billion to US$85 billion in assets under management, from about 100,000 to 500,000 transactions a year, and from 500 to 1500 accounts.

10.1 Introduction

Traditional forms of inter-company collaboration include buying and selling as well as subcontracting and joint product design. They may also involve less direct collaboration, via intermediaries. Nowadays, however, inter-company collaboration is changing because of the widespread proliferation of IT applications, and new partnership forms are developed on the basis of extended enterprising and networking as well as new market processes. Organizational boundaries blur as companies participate in supply chains and virtual networks, and as IT is used to cooperate faster, more effectively, and in completely new ways. Such collaboration will be coordinated and organized in IT-based networks, in which IT serves two purposes: facilitating the desaggregation of productive processes into activities performed in supply chains or networks, and providing the information and coordination instruments required for this process. Thus, information technology's potential for flexibility and agility is fully exploited.

Information technology makes the development of new business and trading processes and relations possible. Therefore, it is the basis of these new forms of network (also called distributed) organizations. The productivity and value creation potential inherent in these business processes and relations is still largely unexploited. We may, however, give some examples of their implications for organizational and interorganizational structures and processes:

- Emergence of open standards for communication fosters cross-functional teams, helps replace traditional hierarchical structures with networks of 'agile', flexible organizational forms;

- Open standards (such as Web-services and e-Business protocols that we introduce later in this book), and the presence of high-performance IT networks support the unbundling and reconfiguration of traditional value chains;

- Diminishing importance of distance in service cost structures will facilitate new forms of work organization (e.g. on the basis of time zone structures), and therefore new opportunities for worldwide service delivery as well;

- Importance of location will diminish, since it is increasingly determined by other factors than communication costs (that is, productivity, wage levels, education infrastructure, and the availability of knowledge);

- Company size will become less important, because information technology enables small companies to initiate and manage supply chains on a worldwide scale;

- New kinds of communities will arise, such as specialists' knowledge networks, virtual communities, agile enterprises, and new trading forms;

- A tendency towards self-organization and decentralization will require new forms of loyalty, trust, liability, responsibility, privacy, and contra ctual arrangements.

Generally speaking, IT infrastructures, organizational structures, and business processes must be attuned to allow the realization of the productivity and value creation potential that network organizations offer. To achieve this attunement, flexible IT systems must be designed, but one must also be able to restructure organizations and to reengineer business processes towards innovative, flexible, and effective structures, including the management and coordination mechanisms required. Several bottlenecks may be encountered, including inflexible organizational designs and enterprise information infrastructures. To deal with such difficulties, the conditions under which IT-based network organizations can work effectively must be understood better, and methods and approaches with which to analyze benchmarks and bottlenecks are needed, as well as methods for the improved design and integration of IT systems in networked organizational environments.

Of course, IT does more than support internal business processes. It plays a role in connecting organizations with each other through automated business processes (that is, selling, buying, trading, production, and logistics), which increasingly form the interfaces between organizations, teams, and persons. Links between internal business organizations and networked exchange-oriented business processes are therefore of prime importance. IT affects internal processes and their coordination, as well as organizational exchange processes, on the basis of its potential to combine office automation, business process redesign, workflow management, and electronic markets.

Essentially, effective, flexible network organizations are based on the triple interplay of information technology, organizational and interorganizational structures, and business processes:

- IT facilitates new business processes and strategies, helps set up and supports new exchange forms, and stretches organizations' boundaries;

- New business processes, strategies, and exchange forms require new organizational and interorganizational forms and governing structures;

- Organizational forms, governing structures and strategies require IT solutions for their information exchange and coordination.

10.2 Network organizations

The term *network* is most generally used to describe a structure of ties among actors in a social system – actors being roles, individuals, organizations, industries, or even nation states [Nohria 1992]. These ties can be based on anything that generates relationships, such as business conversations, authority, or economic exchanges. In this book we are particularly interested in networks in business settings. These networks may be intraorganizational as well as interorganizational in nature. Although we will focus on interorganizational networks, the IT support needed to coordinate network nodes is similar for both. In the following we shall first provide a brief overview of definitions developed by different authors, and will conclude with a list of components that would constitute a definition of inter-company networks.

The literature on *network organizations* provides a variety of definitions. Networked organizations could be defined as virtual partnerships formed by separate companies to enable them to operate as integral elements of a greater organization while retaining their own authority in major budgeting and pricing matters. According to this definition, the term network organization is synonymous with modular organization, virtual corporation, organic network, value-adding partnership, and interorganizational configuration. Networks can be perceived as intermediary organizational forms between markets and hierarchies [Sydow 1993]. Corporate networks are a long-term arrangement among distinct, but related, for-profit organizations. As such, they are an organizational form between markets and hierarchies. Compared to markets, a network has more structure, produces more interaction among the network organizations, provides 'thicker' information channels, demands more loyalty, exhibits more trust, prefers voice to exit, and puts less emphasis on prices [Sydow 1993]. Compared to hierarchies, a network is somewhat underorganized, due to the loose coupling of the network organizations, and the open boundary of the network itself. Finally, we can define inter-company networks as the relationships between a defined set of distinct organizations (the network structure) and their interactions (the network process) [Klein 1996]. Inter-company networks exhibit the following characteristics:

- Links between network participants are based on various types of exchange (e.g., economic goods, money, information, and knowledge);

- Networks have a distinct boundary with their environments;

- Network participants pursue a common goal;

- All network participants have, nevertheless, their own diverse, specific goals;

- Networks consist of relationships characterized by mutual investments or interdependences (that is, not just simple transactional links).

Based on previous definitions, we can now deduce a list of desirable features that must characterize inter-company networks:

- Networks consist of nodes and relations; their nodes are the independent organizations that participate, and the relationships between these participants are based on specific exchanges of goods, information, and knowledge;

- Inter-company networks are an organizational form to manage interdependence between companies; they differ from mergers, collecting organizations into a single company, as well as from coordination through market signals (such as pricing) only; they are based on purposeful collaboration and specific communication patterns;

- Inter-company networks vary with respect to their goals, boundaries, structures, processes, and other attributes.

There is a large poten tial variety of structures that may constitute network organizations. Consequently, it is difficult to fit the concept into one single definition. Some authors [Douma 1998] even deny that inter-company networks represent a third way of organizing transactions (beside markets and hierarchies); they believe they are simply another way to organize a market by new coordination mechanisms, if its price mechanism fails. Because the concept is so elusive, and because network organizations differ in size, structure, processes, relations etc., general statements about network organizations are hard to make. Nevertheless, several attempts have been made. Authors have proposed classifications on the basis of various network characteristics.

10.2.1 Classifying networks

In this book, network organizations are discussed in the context of information technology. For this purpose, we consider inter-company networks to be the result of sets of management decisions, and set up with specific business objectives in mind. There may be several reasons to set up or join a network organization: combining competences, benefiting from economies of scale, achieving overall supply chain benefits, sharing know-how, combining power, etc. The type of network organization set up depends on the participants' objectives. We therefore need a classification on the basis of networking business objectives. Such a classification scheme needs to distinguish between *strategic networks* and *operative networks* [Kubicek 1992]. In strategic networks, companies in different parts of the value chain or the world agree on cooperation mainly with respect to research and development, production and marketing. The objective is to gain competitive advantage. Operative networks are sets of contractual relations covering common agreements on electronic exchanges; their main objective is not competitive advantage but the rationalization of information exchange with respect to routine operations.

We use the above broad classification scheme to identify additional properties of inter-company networks. These properties are formed on the basis of the functionality of the network.

Network types may be distinguished on the basis of whether they focus on operational coordination (operational networks), on joint decision making (collaborative networks), on innovation (innovative networks), or on defending specific interests of participants (interest group networks):

- *Operational networks* focus on short-term collaboration between various companies (suppliers, producers, transporters, traders, etc.) on an operational and tactical level, aiming at efficiency and effectiveness improvements by lowering inventory levels, reducing cycle times, improving products and service quality levels, and the like;

- *Collaborative networks* involve long-term collaboration on a strategic level, in order to win business and strengthen market positions by focusing on core competences;

- *Innovative networks* aim to reduce their participants' risks and costs by joining their research and development activities and sharing knowledge and know-how;

- *Interest group networks* try to defend their participants' interests and help them gain a stronger position; they may be considered power groups, in which even competitors may join forces to gain a stronger position with respect to, for example, the government.

Regardless of their purpose, inter-company networks may have specific characteristics, which are relevant to the systems that support them. Several classification schemes have been proposed on the basis of specific features characterizing inter-company networks. The most important features include the state of the network, the intensity of relationships in a network, the structure of the network, and so on. Here we provide a brief overview.

Networks between independent companies distinguish between *stable networks* and *dynamic networks* [Miles 1992]. In stable networks there are long-term, stable relationships between limited numbers of carefully selected suppliers, producers, and distributors. They are designed to serve mostly predictable markets by linking independently owned specialized organizations along given product or service value chains. Stable networks are typically based on partial outsourcing and strive to introduce flexibility into the overall value chain. Often, they consist of sets of vendors nestled around a large 'core' company, whose inputs they provide and whose outputs they distribute.

The main idea of dynamic networks is to form temporary alliances between organizations in order to respond to actual market forces. Thus, companies along the value chain of a specific product, or belonging to two different industry value chains, are coupled contractually for perhaps no more than a single project or customer order. The lead companies of such networks typically rely on a core skill such as marketing, innovation, manufacturing, or even pure brokering. Other services are contracted for the one specific product or project, and then uncoupled to become part of other business ventures. Dynamic networks, too, may use brokers in order to locate the functions needed.

Internal networks could also be set up within companies in order to make them more flexible and entrepreneurial in spirit [Miles 1986]. It is a move away from hierarchical structures, in the direction of market structures, but within the boundaries of a single organization. It entails stimulating the company's departments and divisions to buy and sell products and services both within and without the company, against market prices. The basic logic of internal networks is that if a company's departments and divisions are exposed to market discipline, instead of being able to work with artificial transfer prices, they will become more innovative and will seek performance improvements. To locate functions that are needed, but cannot be sourced from within the company, broker companies may be used.

Networks can also be classified on the basis of the intensity of their relationships. A *thick network* typically involves intensive relationships and communication patterns, and presupposes close collaboration. The notion of *thin networks* arose as a consequence of the potential offered by electronic communication: they are composed of companies that communicate extensively, but they involve much less integration over multiple types of socially important relationships.

Finally, we may also classify networks on the basis of their structure. This gives rise to *tightly coupled* and *loosely coupled* networks [Weick 1976; van den Heuvel 2002]. Tightly coupled networks are relatively stable networks of trading partners with shared planning and control cycles. This entails organizing business activities along a virtual value chain to attain a shared goal. They may involve predefined interaction patterns, such as trading protocols requiring detailed agreements on cross-organizational business processes; some flexibility must prevail, however, to enable the participants to respond to ad-hoc requests. In loosely coupled networks, trading partners preserve their independence. They can unilaterally decide to change their internal business processes and information systems, without influencing one another to the extent that the collaboration is disabled.

It is obvious that these classifications, which are based on properties of networks, can be combined with our classification scheme on network types. Each of the types of network we distinguished may be stable or dynamic, loosely or tightly coupled, and thick or thin. This results in a matrix associating the types of network with properties of networks as shown in Table 10.1. Network properties are situation dependent, and will impact the enterprise information systems and interorganizational information systems that support them. This means that even within the same organization, one may have different types of networks at the same time, depending on business requirements and objectives. It is the business requirements and objectives that determine which properties a given network may exhibit. One specific network may exhibit the characteristics of more than one type of networks. It may be an operational network when exchanging orders and information on products with customers or external partners. In another situation, it may be a collaborative network when trading companies are making joint production plans for future years. It may exhibit the characteristics of an innovative network when trading companies are involved in collaborative product design, while finally it may become an interest group when trading

Networks Properties Types of networks	Stable/Dynamic	Tightly/Loosely coupled	Thick/Thin
Operational NW			
Collaborative NW			
Innovative NW			
Interest group NW			

■ **Table 10.1:** Classification Scheme for Business Networks

companies exchange knowledge and information about their own products, business processes, and markets. Each type of network may be supported by different enterprise information systems. Below, we present a few examples relating to the previous discussion and the classification scheme presented in Table 10.1.

Operational networks may be stable, tightly coupled, and thick. In some industries, suppliers have long-established relationships with their customers, serving together a relatively predictable market: their relationships are stable. To optimize their supply chain, they will collaborate to plan production batches, order quantities, and making capacity reservations to deal with uncertainties in demand, etc.; optimizing their supply chains requires close coordination of business processes leading to tightly coupled networks. These collaborative planning activities may be at different planning levels – for example, at a strategic planning level, where product development issues are being discussed and coordinated, at a tactical planning level, when considering production schedules for the coming period, and at an operational planning level when planning the production batches for the coming week. The operational level arrangements result in routine ordering activities. The information exchanged between these organizations will result in a 'thick' relationship. Typically these relationships are supported by tightly coupled information systems like EDI and extranets. The expected duration of the relationship justifies a high investment in coupling between processes and information systems. Moving out of such networks will consequently entail high switching costs (caused by the business processes and information systems that have to be uncoupled, and the new couplings that have to be established with other companies).

Where operational relations are changing and becoming highly temporal, operational networks may become dynamic and loosely coupled. For example, different customer orders may require different products and different suppliers. Here, there is loose coupling between the organizations, and maintaining flexibility is mandatory. Where the willingness to invest in combined processes and information systems is minimal, the expected duration of the relation will probably be too short to allow for a payback of high investments. Internet- based technologies may support these types of relationships. A similar situation may exist with innovative networks, for example, aiming at the development of a new product or process. The network may only exist for the duration of one project and will be dismantled after completion. The relationships within the network are determined by different collaborative relationships instead of simply ordering products. These networks require a more flexible IT environment with a specific support for different collaborative processes.

It is clear that organizations may be part of different networks simultaneously. For example, we may expect that relatively stable relationships exist with a smaller number of 'trading partners': these relationships will be stable, tightly coupled, and probably 'thick', allowing for a relatively high investment in supporting technologies. At the same time, with other organizations, the company can be engaged in various temporary operational networks, requiring a highly flexible platform, which can connect and disconnect parties in a highly efficient way.

10.3 Interorganizational information systems and network organizations

Interorganizational information systems are a specific class of information systems that automate the flow of information across organizational boundaries and enterprise information systems, and link an organization to suppliers, customers, and possibly other organizations (like, for instance, the government) [Laudon 2004]. *Interorganizational information systems (IOSs)* are extensions of multilayered architecture for developing Web-based applications (see Section 6.3.2), where application servers are interconnected in order to integrate e-Business applications and their underlying enterprise information systems. IOSs also encompass other technologies like EDI. In this book, however, we focus on Web-based systems to support flexible network organizations. We describe the technical characteristics of these systems in depth in Chapter 18.

10.3.1 System integration and business benefits

Information technology is a basic tenant of the new forms of networked organizations discussed above, as interorganizational information systems make intercompany communication, transactions, and various kinds of collaborative processes possible. The effects of Information Technology on network organizations are two fold:

1) IT supports current structure by improving its efficiency and effectiveness;
2) IT enables new working methods, new structures, and so on.

Using interorganizational information systems, networked organizations can plan, organize, execute, and monitor relevant processes, like manufacturing processes, as if they were all carried out in one company (e.g., the 'virtual enterprise'). Thus, with up-to-date customer and resource availability information always at hand, customer orders can be executed with minimal inventory and delivery time. Such an ideal situation requires prompt communication between the network's participants.

The most well-known framework for analyzing the impact of IT on the way organizations structure and coordinate their operational processes, proposes distinguishing between five levels of *IT-induced business transformation* [Venkatraman 1991, 1994] These consider issues that are both internal to an organization as well as interorganizational factors. The five levels include:

1) *Localized exploitation*: this refers to information systems used within departmental or group boundaries; these systems are specifically designed to meet the needs of that department or group;

2) *Internal integration*: this involves the interdepartmental integration of information systems and the use of these for the company's entire internal business process;

3) *Business process redesign*: this means combining the integration between departments with the reorganization and optimization of their processes, using the possibilities information technology offers;

4) *Business network redesign*: this includes the internal business processes of other companies as well, in order to establish interorganizational business processes;

5) *Business scope redefinition*: which means identifying organizations that are evaluating the use of existing situations in order to benefit from new situations in which parallel value chains might be integrated.

The first two levels, which are intraorganizational, can be identified as evolutionary [Venkatraman 1991, 1994]: the current situation is one's point of reference. The third level is also intraorganizational, but revolutionary in nature: it changes internal business processes radically. The last two levels are interorganizational in nature, and considered revolutionary, since they require radical changes in business practice.

To cater for e-Business integration, a business integration level should be interposed between the third and fourth levels. This happens because integrated networks of redesigned business processes can exist without requiring that the entire intercompany network be redesigned. This would lead to a six level framework instead of the conventional five level framework that has been used so far to analyze operational processes of large organizations (see Figure 10.1).

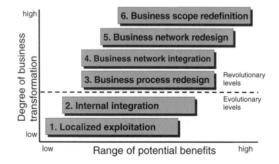

■ **Figure 10.1:** IT-Induced Business Reconfiguration [Toppen 1998, after Venkatraman 1994]

The basic idea of such a framework is that the transition from lower to higher levels of IT-induced business transformation, result in higher potential benefit levels. This view has found support from several authors who either propose a framework that focuses on the merging of technological and process innovations in order to achieve the potential to transform both organizations and interorganizational processes and relations [Clark 1996], or argue that the benefits, especially cost savings, of electronic data interchange (EDI) can only be realized when one's basic organizational structures and work processes are redesigned [Benjamin 1990].

Case Study

Robeco

Following the IT-induced transformation model, and its extension to e-Business settings, six forms of IT enabled business transformation can be identified at Robeco Group [Toppen 1998a]:

1) *Localized exploitation*: some of the processes are supported by local information systems; spreadsheets used to generate, for instance, transaction sheets, or settlement instructions to be printed in a standard format. The information systems are not linked to other systems in the organization, or to information systems in other organizations.

2) *Internal integration*: based on the previous step, Internal integration links several local applications to enable a more integrated support by information systems of (parts of) the internal processes. An example of this situation is the use of a database in which a broker code corresponds to a total set of settlement instructions that are no longer derived from paper sheets, but are automatically retrieved from the database based on the broker code and currency code of the transaction. Here, the transaction information system is linked to the settlement instruction information system.

3) *Business process redesign*: by linking local applications, redesign opportunities are generated and organizations following redesign principles build an internally integrated information system supporting the entire internal processes. At the Robeco Group, this has resulted in a newly built information system in which the trader enters the transaction details only once. Afterwards, the data are used in automated processes in other departments to generate settlement instructions. Data are also used in processes that cross the organizational boundaries (phase 5). Some control processes or checks are no longer necessary because the controls are carried out by the system (risk controls), or have become obsolete (no more re-keying).

4) *Business network integration*: the business process redesign phase can include processes that involve other organizations. At the Robeco Group, this phase involved changing the way transaction confirmations were received (switch from fax/telex to Electronic Trade Confirmation Systems), and the way settlement instructions were sent (switch from fax/telex to SWIFT). Sending instructions electronically by mid- 1996 reduced the error rate by 25%, because fewer errors occurred after the receiving organization did not need to rekey the settlement information into their own system. Next to this, the costs of processing of settlement instructions were reduced from around US$60 to around US$35.

5) *Business network redesign*: in the financial securities sector, the business network redesign phase includes the straight through processing concept. This concept focuses on achieving process throughput without manual intervention. As soon as an error occurs, the process is stopped because the error needs to be investigated. Involving the process characteristics of the receiving organizations in the process of generating settlement instructions, improves the straight through processing rate. This has resulted in the costs of settlement instructions being further reduced to around US$20.

6) *Business scope redefinition*: integration of parallel value chains is perhaps the most difficult phase to achieve. On the other hand, disintermediation can be seen as an example of this phase.

10.3.2 Interoperability: a matter of standards

Interorganizational information systems can only work if they are able to communicate and work with other such systems and interact with people. This requirement is called *interoperability*, and it can only be met if communication standards are applied [Aldrich 1999]. A standards-based technology platform allows partners to execute a traditional business function in a digitally enhanced way [Aldrich 1999]. A common information systems platform, then, basically is a set of standards that allows network participants to communicate and conduct business processes electronically.

Interoperability requires standardization in four dimensions: technology, syntax, semantics, and pragmatics. *Technology standards* concern middleware, network protocols, security protocols, and the like. *Syntax standardization* means that the network organization has to agree on how to integrate heterogeneous applications based on the structure or 'language' of the messages exchanged. Normally, commonly acceptable data structures are chosen to represent well-known constructs, e.g., invoice descriptions. *Semantic standards* constitute agreements in extension to syntactic agreements on the meanings of the terms used for an enterprise's information systems to communicate with and understand the messages of another enterprise's information systems. This may be rather difficult to achieve. For instance, consider the immense variety of components and parts in an automotive industry supply chain, for most of which many companies, e.g., suppliers, distributors, etc, may have their own names and possibly different meanings. All these names must be standardized if the supply chain's support is to be fully automated. Semantic interoperability is of major importance to e-Business integration and therefore is treated in some detail in Section 18.6. *Pragmatic standards*, finally, are agreements on practices and protocols triggered by specific messages, such as orders and delivery notifications.

The first two interoperability standards, technology and syntax, are of a technical nature, and are therefore relatively easily addressed. The latter two standards relate to business practice and industry culture, which may differ widely from industry to industry, and from country to country. They can therefore be difficult to agree upon, causing the network organization's electronic communication to be hampered by a lack of interoperability. The degree to which this difficulty becomes a problem partly depends on the kind of communication needed.

Here, we distinguish between two types of IT supported communication: *system-to-system communication* and *person-to-system communication*. In the case of system-to-system communication, there is no human intervention.

The former is generally used for operational networks, that is, operational supply chain applications in business-to-business settings, in which orders are transmitted from buying organizations to suppliers. The latter type of communication encompasses a vast array of applications. Among these are situations in which customers contact a company's Website and manually place an order and an inventory reservation, and the support of online collaborative design processes with CSCW applications connecting engineers in various laboratories in various places in the world. If system-to-system communication is required, full standardization is needed in all four areas. If people are involved in the communication process, however, applying technology and syntax standards may suffice because of the Internet's free-format communication possibilities and direct human involvement.

Obviously, standards are needed both within companies and for their outside communication. Of these two, interorganizational interoperability is the more difficult to achieve since there is then no central authority (such as a CEO) who can force network members to adhere to the standards. We will not in this book discuss how, and under which circumstances, standards are adopted (by power, mutual agreement, government stimulation, etc.), but we must stress that without agreements on standards, network organizations will benefit very little from the enabling possibilities of information technology.

Case Study

Robeco

Analysis of the communication with external stakeholders made clear that electronic integration – e.g., using standard SWIFT messages, and integrating messaging systems with existing information systems – would make human intervention superfluous and lead to more efficient processing.

More efficient processing was necessary to meet the challenge of increased competition from ABN-AMRO, Fidelity, Fleming, and others. To keep up with market requirements, in May 1996, Robeco Group decided to reengineer its processes, by making use of the SWIFT network for all settlement instructions, around 300,000 per year. First, the project focused on substitution of the instructions sent by telex, which used to be the majority. The project also analyzed the straight through processing concept, defined as 'immediate transaction processing, without manual intervention, processing information by the receiving organization' [Toppen 1999].

10.3.3 Classifying interorganizational information systems

There are many different types of interorganizational systems, which make it difficult to present a single all-encompassing definition. It is more reasonable to classify IOSs on the basis of their functionality [Sheombar

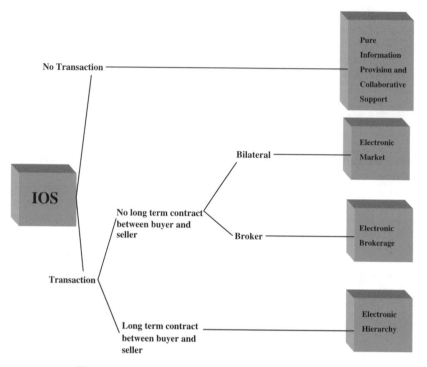

■ Figure 10.2: Functionalities of IOSs [Sheombar 1995]

1995]. This is shown in Figure 10.2, where we may distinguish between systems that are transaction oriented, and those that are not [Benjamin 1990].

Transaction-oriented systems focus on facilitating transactions. E-Business and e-Procurement applications (ERP, XML/EDI, workflow) are typical examples of such systems: e-Procurement applications support transactions with suppliers, while e-Business applications support effective order placement, order status information provision, and customer interaction for after-sales service purposes. This category may be further divided into 'bilateral forms of integration' and 'multilateral situations' [Bakos 1991]. The former involves buyers and sellers with long-term relations; the latter are used to establish new buyer-seller relations, after which a third party may be introduced to differentiate still further between pure markets and brokerages.

Non-transaction-oriented systems facilitate communication and other coordinative processes. These systems include databases, e-mail software, video conferencing, groupware, CAD, expert communities, and so on. This category may be subdivided into systems purely for information provision, and systems intended for collaboration purposes.

Five functionality classes for interorganizational information systems may be distinguished on the basis of these criteria. To transaction-oriented systems belong those systems that offer electronic markets, electronic brokerages and support electronic hierarchies. To non-transaction-oriented systems belong those systems that support electronic collaboration and pure information provision.

Electronic markets (see Chapter 8) involve bilateral transactions but no long-term relationships, and are infrastructures provided by third parties acting as facilitators without interfering. In this type of interorganizational information system, the transactions between buyers and sellers are structured by business communication protocols. Having industry-wide standards for messages and for settlement processes, price discovery methods, etc., is a prerequisite for the viability of electronic markets, because of the wide variety of potential buyer-seller pairs.

Electronic brokerage implies that transactions are carried out via an intermediate third party, the electronic broker. Its function is to collect supply and demand data and make this information available to clients, the buyers and sellers. Just as in the case of electronic markets, no long-term relationships are established between buyers and sellers.

An *electronic hierarchy* (see Chapter 4) is formed when the organizations involved have long-term contracts or partnerships with each other, and they use the interorganizational information system to align their internal processes with those of their partners. Communication, that is, message transfer, takes place without human intervention (system-to-system communication). Usually some form of EDI (XML/EDI) is used. Depending on the degree of process alignment, the parties may decide to use proprietary message standards, since the official standardization institutes cannot oversee all the process intricacies about which parties may wish to exchange messages, and may therefore not be able to provide a proper standard.

Relationships between organizations often involve more than the traditional arm's length market transactions. When joint decision-making is facilitated by Internet technology, this is called an *electronic collaboration* [Lee 2001]. This includes 'person-to-system' communication. It may involve sharing information and knowledge that used to be considered private or strategic and was consequently hoarded: sales data, market forecasts, inventory statuses, production schedules, etc. Organizations may also engage in collaborative planning, for instance, by planning and monitoring their supply chain together in order to increase customer responsiveness while maintaining cost efficiency. And then there is the possibility of joint product development, in which geographically dispersed partners may collaborate by setting up communications between their engineers, architects, suppliers, and auditors.

Pure information provision systems store data in a central database and make it available to the participating companies [Sheombar 1995]. Nielsen Marketing Data and Reuter's Financial Information are examples of such systems. Various types of systems are conceivable, which may facilitate, depending on what is needed, remote database access and file transfer (person-to-system communication), or periodic update messages that are sent by an information provider, and that automatically update the receiver's database (system-to-system communication).

In Section 10.2 we developed a classification scheme for networked organizations on the basis of the business objectives for which they are set up. A question that arises is whether there is a relationship between a type of network organization and the types of interorganizational information system used.

In operational networks all functionality types may be potentially applied:

- Transaction-oriented functionalities support the operational relations between networked companies. In case of a close relationship, information systems will facilitate the integration of business processes through e-hierarchy-type functionality. For other, less close, buyer-seller situations, for example, in the case of a request for quotation, or an auction for invited business partners, e-markets and e-brokerage types of functionality apply and are often used.

- Since companies in operational networks must collaborate, it is to be expected that the e-collaboration type of functionality will also be applied.

As there are no transactions in collaboration, innovation, and interest group type networks, the interorganizational information systems used in these settings will belong to the e-collaboration and information provision types.

10.3.4 Limits to the reach of network organizations

How many companies may be encompassed by a network organization? As has been suggested in the Information Systems literature, this obviously depends on the kind of information exchanged. Grouping activities within organizations typically make possible the exchange of rich information among a narrow, internal group of participants [Evans 1997]. Markets enable their participants to exchange information among a large, external group, whose information, however, is proposed to be 'thinner'. *The trade-off between richness and reach* is increasingly affected by modern information technology, which will make 'higher' combinations of richness and reach possible. Vertically integrated value chains are likely to be deconstructed, resulting in network organizations in which information collection and provision are separated from the products. This is likely to have enormous consequences for many aspects, such as task division within the network, coordination mechanisms, and intermediation and disintermediation processes.

Similar deliberations can be made with respect to the information technology infrastructure employed in business networks [Weill 1998]. Here two aspects can be identified: *IT infrastructure reach* and *range* [Keen 1991]. Reach refers to the locations and people whom the infrastructure is capable of connecting. Range refers to the functionality of information systems in terms of business activities that can be completed and shared automatically and seamlessly across each level of reach. In Figure 10.3 the dimensions of IT infrastructure range and reach are shown.

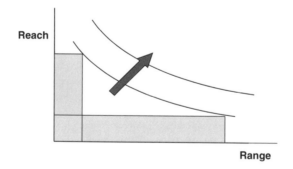

■ **Figure 10.3:** Reach and Range of the e-Business Infrastructure [Adapted from Weill 1998]

These two models are quite similar. They show that, since information sharing isn't effortless, there are limits to the reach that can be attained when information is shared – and the richer the information, the more limited the reach, whereas 'thin' information can potentially be shared on a global scale. This brings us back to our discussion of information standards. The richer the information to be exchanged, the more difficult it is to agree on standardization. The consequence is that network organizations are limited in size, and the character of the exchanges in the network determines how large or small the group of companies may be. In practice, relationships can only be very intense if the number of participants is restricted. In networks with many members, relationships are generally much more superficial. This is shown in Figure 10.3. In other words: 'thick' corresponds with tightly coupled, 'thin' with loosely coupled networks. The question of how many organizations are allowed to maintain 'thick' relationships within a network requires a management decision that is of great importance to the effectiveness of the network as a whole. However, as a consequence of the spread of modern Internet-based technologies, these limits will supposedly be relaxed gradually.

10.4 Supply chains

Until recently, most organizations focused on their direct customers and internal functions, and placed relatively little emphasis on other organizations within the context of their supply chain. Before the emergence of the concept of supply chain, many manufacturers routinely competed for suppliers of raw materials on price alone, without looking at the longer-term implications of quality, or considering critical factors such as shipping. Enterprises that wish to engage in e-Business, find that they must be involved in managing the network of all upstream companies (supplier side) that provide input directly or indirectly, as well as the network of all downstream companies (customer side) that are responsible for delivery and aftermarket service of a particular product to the customer [Handfield 2002]. Essentially, a supply chain is a network of interlinked suppliers and customers, where each customer is, in turn, a supplier to the next down-stream organization until a complete product reaches the end customer.

We may define a *supply chain* as the network that encompasses all the organizations and activities associated with the flow and transformation of goods from the raw materials stage, through to the end user, as well as the associated information flows [Handfield 2002; Christopher 1998]. The supply chain includes all of the capabilities and functions required to design, fabricate, distribute sell, support, use and recycle, dispose of a product, as well as the associated information that flows up and down the chain. In this definition, material and information flow both up and down the supply chain, while the supply chain manages enterprise information systems, sourcing and procurement, production scheduling, order processing, inventory management, warehousing, customer service, and after-market disposition of packaging and materials. Supply chains are typically comprised of geographically dispersed facilities and capabilities, including sources of raw materials, product design, and engineering organizations, manufacturing plants, distribution centers, retail outlets, and customers, as well as the transportation and communication links between them.

Figure 10.4 illustrates an individual enterprise within the context of a supply chain and includes its *upstream supplier network*, its *internal functions*, as well as its *downstream distribution channels*:

- The *upstream supplier network* consists of all organizations that provide inputs, either directly or indirectly to the focal company. If, for instance, we consider the case of an automotive company's supplier network, then this includes a large number of firms that provide items ranging from raw materials, such as steel and plastics, to complex assemblies and subassemblies, such as electronic transmissions, gearboxes, and brakes. The supplier network may include internal divisions of the company as well as external suppliers. A given

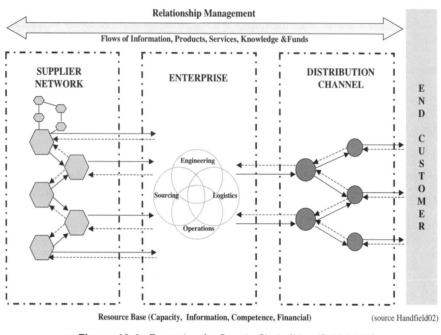

■ Figure 10.4: Example of a Supply Chain [Handfield 2002]

material may pass through multiple processes within multiple suppliers (who in their turn may have their own suppliers) before it can be assembled into a vehicle.

- A company's *internal functions* include the different processes used in transforming the inputs provided by the supplier network. In the case of an automotive company, this includes all of its parts manufacturing, e.g., power train and components, that need to be brought together in actual automobiles. Coordinating and scheduling these internal flows is a challenging undertaking. For instance, order-processing managers are responsible for translating customer requirements into actual orders that are put into the system. In the case of an automotive company, these order-processing managers work with an extensive dealer network to ensure that the right mix of vehicles and service parts is available so that dealers can meet the demands of their customers. Order processing may also involve extensive customer interaction, including quoting prices, agreeing on delivery dates, conditions and shipment requirements, and after-market service.

- Finally, a company's *downstream distribution channels* contain all downstream organizations, processes, and functions that the product passes through on its way to the end customer, such as distributors, transport providers (e.g., shipping companies), and retailers. In the case of an automotive company's distribution network, this includes its finished goods and pipeline inventory, warehouses, dealer network, and sales o perations. Within the downstream distribution channel, the logistics function is responsible for moving materials between locations. Logistics activities typically include packaging, warehousing, transportation, materials handling, and finished goods inventory management.

Suppliers and distributors mediate the value chain between manufacturers and consumers, and all parties simultaneously have concerns of both suppliers and consumers. Because members in a supply/value/demand chain may play multiple roles, supply chain management requires a holistic approach.

To have an effective supply chain means that companies need to consider their business processes in terms of all of the organizations involved in the production, marketing/sales, and distribution of the products or services in the supply chain. Sending goods from a supplier to a customer entails sending information about those goods (called a ship notice) for the customer to receive, store, and eventually pay for them. This flow of data and information occurs as part of a larger set of interactions in the supply chain. Companies have discovered that the management of the information flow among trading partners can make or break the trading partners. The supply chain can significantly affect a manufacturing project based on its ability to deliver materials in a timely and efficient manner. Several surveys have shown that the supply chain-related problems, such as material shortage and late delivery, are the highly ranked causes of delay in a construction project. Because of the long information lead-time and lack of coordination, it is difficult for members in a chain to have appropriate information to make sure that all materials and equipments arrive on site in time to allow an orderly progression of work. As a simple example, consider a ship notice that does not reference a purchase order or other documentation authorizing the shipment. No receiving manager will accept this ship notice.

If the flow of material and information is entangled across a supply chain, and each of the process segments is not tightly coupled, information lead-time will increase. This happens by making the flow of information stagnated in some points of a supply chain.

The first step in developing an efficient supply chain is to improve the efficiency of disparate internal systems and processes (logistics control, for example) responsible for managing and coordinating the interactions in the value chain (see the Venkatraman framework discussed in Section 10.3.1, especially the transition from the *'localized exploitation'* stage to the *'internal integration'* stage). This requirement explains the rapid growth of packaged ERP applications, which help integrate and streamline internal systems. In addition, companies are increasingly concerned with trying to conceptualize and manage supply chain processes as integrated wholes. They have already achieved significant improvements, but most are only beginning to realize the opportunities to create truly efficient supply chains. Most large scale companies today are focused on improving supply chain systems by traditional means – reorganizing processes to function more efficiently, buying new specialized hardware that speeds the physical processing of products, and training employees. At the same time, they are thinking about how they might automate their supply chain processes in the future. To achieve supply chain management and improvement, companies may rely on the Supply Chain Council Operations Reference (SCOR) methodology that provides supply chain managers with a nearly ideal approach for analyzing and improving existing supply chains. This methodology is covered along with business modeling techniques in Chapter 12.

10.4.1 Logistics – flow and network perspectives

Supply chains exist in all industries and sectors. Physical manufacturing activities offer typical examples of supply chains. But arranging activities in a particular order and coping with problems of queuing, capacity utilization, delivery times, etc. are phenomena common to all sectors, whether it is healthcare, education, financial services, or anything else. These are therefore called supply chain problems.

The discipline that studies this process is called *logistics*. This was originally a military term, referring to the provision of armies on the march with the materials they need (food, ammunition, clothes). In a business setting, it refers to the (material and information) flows involved in supplying an end customer with a product or service, all the way from the acquisition of raw materials to the product's or service's delivery [Christopher 1998].

There are two basically differ ent forms of logistics. One optimizes a *steady flow* of material through a network of transportation links and storage nodes. The other coordinates a sequence of resources to carry out some *project*:

- *Steady-state flow systems* are usually optimized for one of several goals: avoiding shortages of the product, minimizing transportation cost, minimum time to obtain an object, or minimum total storage (time and amount) of objects (to minimize the interest losses of in-storage inventory). A recent trend in large distribution chains is to assign these goals to individual stock items, rather than optimizing the entire system for one goal. This is possible because the plans usually describe stock amounts to be stored at particular locations, and these vary depending on the strategy.

- As for *projects*, logistics experts discover the sequence in which a project will use particular resources. They then arrange to send the resources so that they will arrive when needed.

Logistic management means considering the interdependence between all decisions concerning goods, services, and information flows. In a business setting, logistics management is about satisfying customers by coordinating goods and information flows, from raw materials through manufacturing and other operations to the delivery of the final product. 'Getting the logistics right' has for decades been acknowledged as a major task facing companies that wish to acquire and maintain a competitive position. The role logistics are perceived to play in companies' competitive strategies has gradually changed, however.

As already explained, logistics is about flows – of goods, of services, of information, and of money. Operations management didn't always focus on flows, however. Divisions, departments, and business units used to specialize, optimizing internally. Consequently, additional costs were acquired when products and services were transferred to the next stage. These were the result of having to keep stocks, of long delivery times and delays, of manufacturing capacity standing idle, etc. Supply and demand uncertainties as well as diversity used to make logistics expensive. Competitive pressures then forced companies to take a closer look at these costs, and therefore at organizational relations too. Their first move was to integrate companies' internal tasks. Materials manager positions were set up to plan and monitor the flow of goods from purchasing, through inventory and manufacturing, to sales and warehousing. Sometimes a physical distribution manager was appointed as well, but with two such positions an integrated view on the company's logistics was difficult to attain, so both tasks were combined into one logistics manager position. Then new concepts, such as just-in-time logistics, became popular, aimed at getting products at the right place neither too early nor too late but exactly on time, and thus allowing for zero inventory.

Internal integration took care of avoidable logistic costs made within the company. Sourcing one's supplies, both goods and services, might still be difficult, though – certainly if one worked with suppliers who lacked such logistic discipline. And there was still the uncertainty of customer demand, so inventory costs, longer delivery times, etc. could not altogether be avoided. The next move was the 'dyad': one-on-one relations with direct suppliers and clients in business-to-business markets, involving shared forecast and planning information in order to plan one's production and delivery activities better. It was Forrester [Forrester 1961] who then showed that a comprehensive look at the whole chain of activities was needed, from customer demand to raw material purchasing. Because there was little insight into real demand evolution, small demand increases perceived by the chain's customer-side might cause enormous, unnecessary production and capacity increases at the other end (the Forrester or *bullwhip effect*).

The latest logistic challenge is caused by strategic changes in the market. The traditional focus on products, manufactured by a single company or business unit, is being replaced by a customer focus. Customers are perceived to be looking for solutions (for their problems or needs) rather than for individual producs. Selling and maintaining cars, for instance, is not really about cars; it is about realizing the customer's mobility – under all circumstances. This includes minimizing the inconvenience customers experience when cars break down or when they have an accident, and it thus presupposes links with rental companies, hotel chains, healthcare services, insurance services, etc. This customer focus causes offerings to be made that are composed of a great variety of products and services, requiring links *across different value systems.*

10.4.2 Supply chain management

Supply chain management may be defined as the management of upstream and downstream relations with suppliers and customers to deliver superior value at less cost to the supply chain as a whole [Christopher 1998]. Essentially, supply chain management is the integration and management of organizations and activities through cooperative organizational relationships, effective business processes, and high-levels of information sharing in order to create high-performing value systems that provide the organizations in a supply chain with a sustainable competitive advantage [Handfield 2002].

Supply chain management is characterized by two models: the push and pull model or a combined push-pull approach:

- In the *push model*, production, assembly and distributions are based on forecasts. It helps to plan inventories, production, assembly, and distribution in optimal batches. However, forecasts are often wrong and cannot be used for highly customized products. Conventional IT support for the push model focuses on the use of independent data management activities for enterprise information systems, by supply chain members as well as limited use of XML/EDI.

- In the *pull model*, products are built in response to customer orders. Actual customer demand (the customer order) drives the planning of production and distribution. Here the supply chain is constructed to deliver value to the customer by reducing costs and increasing service quality. In the pull model, there needs to be much closer links between the members of the supply chain through the use of technology such as XML/EDI to minimize document transfer and reuse.

Several techniques to implement supply chain management have been identified in the literature [Higginson 1997]. These include:

- Maintaining long-term relationships with supply chain members [Buzzel 1995];

- Working cooperatively with fewer suppliers to reduce chain-wide inventory levels and cycle times [Davis 1993; Inge 1995];

- Information sharing with supply chain members [Sandelands 1994].

Although these approaches seem to take different strategies, they emphasize a basic common principle: the importance of communication and collaboration between the members in a supply chain.

In this context, information sharing is a fundamental approach, which seeks the goals of the other approaches at the same time. The coordination and integration of information flows within and across companies, are critical for an effective supply chain management. Sharing information is a key component for tight integration to optimize the chain-wide performance, and it has been facilitated due to recent advances in information technology.

As we explained in the previous section, the scope of logistics changed, and so did the perception of supply chain management's effect on organizational and strategic effectiveness. The first improvements made to logistics organization focused on cost containment. Reducing inventory costs and improving the efficiency of production capacity utilization were the main targets in the 1970s and 1980s. However, in a changing competitive arena, these 'tactical' improvements proved not to be enough. The economy changed from a supplier's economy into a customer's economy. It is no longer the standardized and common needs of a large group of customers that drive companies' activities, but the individualized needs of single customers. Companies must compete on the basis of individualized product offerings, and still serve all their customers with very short delivery times and at low cost. Mass customization is a serious challenge for modern manufacturing and service industries. With that, logistics and supply chain management have become a core element of companies' competitive performance. Apart from inventory level control and production capacity efficiency, it now involves setting up a responsive and cost-efficient organizational setting able to react swiftly to uncertain customer demand. This includes deciding which competences are unique and of core value, and which are less important and may thus be outsourced. It also entails establishing partnership arrangements with preferred suppliers and customers, and setting up collaborative processes with partners, for planning and other purposes. Arms-length relationships with many suppliers are increasingly replaced by 'value-added partnerships' with fewer suppliers, networks of organizations that collaboratively compete in a market, and jointly plan and monitor the flow of goods and services to that market. In such a network, partners may be located in various parts of the world; globalization makes logistic management even more complex. The flexibility that is required of logistic chains adds further complexity and necessitates the formation of dynamic business networks.

As a consequence of these changes, a new supply chain concept is emerging, which includes many more aspects than did the traditional concept: the *integrated supply chain*.

10.4.3 Technology solutions for supply chains

The Internet has added a new twist to collaborative technologies – making geographic and commercial boundaries disappear. In the early days of linking supply chain member organisations, *EDI* was successful in reducing the supply chain costs of large enterprises by automating the batch processing of information related to orders, invoices, and deliveries. As explained in Section 6.5, EDI is widely used by large enterprises for sending purchase orders, invoices, shipping notices, and other frequently used business documents. By using standard EDI messages, organizations can exchange information between many different trading partners and be sure of common understanding throughout the supply chain. Although EDI is able to automate many fundamental business transactions, such as purchase orders, invoices, and so on, it has limited ability to enable value chain interactions as it is predominantly message centric, i.e., uses standardized message formats. Electronic messaging and transaction transmission are insufficient for e-Business transactions that require automation of complicated business process flows and interactions. To achieve increased integration between member organisations and their internal systems in a supply chain, a full commitment must be made to deploying e-Business applications across the supply chain structure. Any technology that automates trading partner interactions in a supply chain must also represent the business processes and vocabulary of its respective industry to have any chance of working.

Many enterprise technology systems, such as SAP, JD Edwards, PeopleSoft, etc, use Web-enabled front-ends or back-ends to leverage Internet's ability to link value chain constituents together for faster, more seamless communication. In fact, many current SCM solutions have been developed as 'bolt ons' to ERP systems. However, although ERP systems may be very good candidates for integrating internal business processes, they are often not capable of linking suppliers and customers in the supply chain. Conventional ERP systems lack the advanced functionality required for the following types of supply chain processes: advanced order management, transportation planning, and electronic procurement.

Figure 10.5 shows a typical distributed computing solution that integrates data sources and computing capacity across a supply chain involving manufacturers, suppliers, and customers. This solution involves highly scalable application servers to support portals, and collaboration services that let partners, suppliers, and customers communicate and share resources, e.g., enterprise information systems, such as ERP, CRM and SRM, to deliver applications such as procurement, demand forecasting, planning, manufacturing, distribution, and transportation management. It also involves Web servers and communication servers to manage access to enterprise information systems, maintain connectivity, and handle data representation. Note that, in Figure 10.5, a shared data repository is used to enable collaboration through end-to-end order and inventory visibility.

Nowadays, to achieve increased integration, the trend is towards the combination of an IT architecture featuring loosely coupled and decentralized Web services, with standard (industry-specific) business processes that closely reflect the interactions among trading partners in a supply chain. Each Web service is a building block that enables the sharing of software functionality with other applications residing outside the Web service's native environment. A function deployed as a Web service uses common protocols to communicate with other Web services, and systems that can receive XML-based data. Web services could be used for aspects of supply chain integration. For example, a Web service could be harnessed to [Hernacki 2003]:

- Check inventory levels in various databases on the supply network;

- Compare that with orders for product that use that inventory;

- Check orders already placed with the supplier to replenish existing inventory;

- Determine the difference;

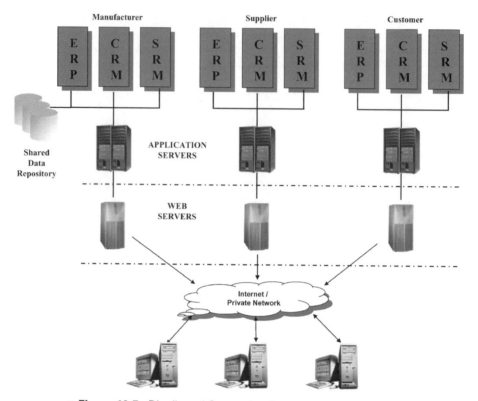

■ **Figure 10.5:** Distributed Computing Solutions for Supply Chains

- Automatically place orders directly with the supplier's systems. This becomes a purely automatic function, ensuring that inventory for production is always at sufficient levels.

The Web services approach, which is covered in Chapter 19, offers the possibility for companies to conduct their business functions uninterrupted (e.g., production, marketing, sales, etc), yet still enable their enterprise information systems to adjust quickly to new business relationships.

An early good example of how to enable enterprise information systems to adjust quickly to new business relationships is a practice that began in the automotive industry during the 1990s called evaluated receipts settlements. The automotive companies discovered they could combine the data from EDI ship notices and corresponding receiving advice messages exchanged with suppliers, along with the purchase orders indicating desired quantities and negotiated prices, and eliminate having to send invoices to most of their suppliers. By providing the data from these transactions, the companies could empower the receiving managers to authorize payment on the spot, or indicate exceptions if the shipments did not meet the requirements spelled out in the order. The results were lower costs and faster payments, two highly desirable conditions in any business.

10.5 Integrated supply chains

A company rarely interacts only within a single supply chain, but rather must connect with several supply chains as product offerings and business dictate. As a consequence, businesses increasingly integrate their value chains by redesigning their structures to move from hierarchical – with a focus on management control – to horizontal organizations – built around business processes, teamwork, and empowerment. This development along with the emergence and greater acceptance of higher-order collaborative interorganizational relationships, has fostered the emergence of the concept of an *integrated supply chain*. By coordinating, collaborating, and integrating with other suppliers, customers, and business partners, companies create an extended virtual enterprise. Company value chains are thus transformed into integrated value chains to support the requirements of the new extended enterprises.

Supply chain integration may be defined as the process by which multiple enterprises within a shared market segment collaboratively plan, implement, and monitor the flow of goods, services, and information along the value system in a way that increases customer-perceived value and optimizes the efficiency of the chain [Dobbs 1998]. Company value chains are transformed into integrated value systems, if they are redesigned to act as '*extended enterprises*', generating and enhancing customer-perceived value by means of cross-enterprise collaboration. With the emergence of such networks, the focus of competition has shifted, from individual companies to business networks [Holland 1995], and thus from individual company performance to supply chain performance. There is now an emphasis on continuous improvement in the entire network. This has presented new challenges to business managers charged with company and supply chain performance improvement, or with the management of effective interorganizational systems and relations.

The concept of integrated value system is expected to have major impact, allowing companies, and ultimately customers, to benefit from reduced inventories, cost savings, improved value-added goods and services to customers, and tighter links with business partners. In these settings, enterprise information systems can no longer be confined to internal processes, applications, and data repositories, rather they span networks of enterprises, incorporating systems of trading- and distribution-partners as well as customers.

Figure 10.6 shows an extended value chain involving complex interactions between multiple partners, e.g., manufacturers, distributors, suppliers, etc, that includes the exchange of forecasts, inventory, orders, product data, pricing, batch management, shipment planning, shipping notifications, invoicing, payment, proof of delivery, and so on.

The aim of extended (or integrated) supply chains is to integrate isolated enterprise value chain environments to create a superior collaborative commerce infrastructure. Successfully implemented, extended value chain applications can be linked with other systems to extend isolated solutions into enterprise channel-wide value grids that supply information about market demand and customer interest. This results in virtual enterprises that appear to the outside observer almost edgeless, with permeable and continuously changing interfaces between company supplier and customer [Davidow 1992]. Such a virtual enterprise is characterized by the following features [Kraut 1998]:

- Processes transcend the boundaries of a single form and are not controlled by a single organization;

- Production processes are flexible with different parties involved at different times;

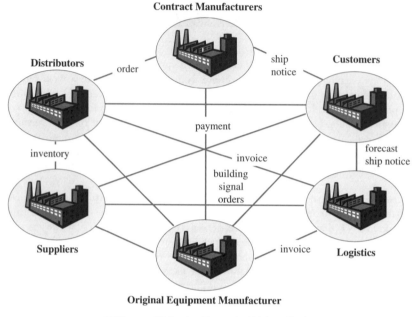

Figure 10.6: An Extended Value Chain

- Parties involved in the production of a single product are often geographically dispersed;

- Given the geographic dispersion of parties in an integrated supply chain (virtual enterprise), coordination is heavily dependent on suitable information technology infrastructure and telecommunications networks.

10.5.1 Essential requirements of integrated value chains

Once the movement of information extends beyond the confines of a single organization, it requires the introduction of changes to the modeling of business activities manifested in the introduction of new improved business models. Moreover, it requires interoperable technology that allows business processes to cross organizational, computing, and geographic boundaries.

e-Business-enabling business models

Enterprises can only become an effective link in a leading value chain by reconceptualizing the company as a collection of business operations and processes, by reshaping corporate structures around modern business processes, and by making their internal processes align with and support the integrated value chain. This requires that business models be created to offer a new way to deliver value to customers. *Business modeling* is the practice of abstracting and representing a business in a way that illuminates particular aspects for better understanding and communication (see Chapters 2 and 12). Models can represent enterprise or business areas, markets, resource supplies, demographics, and so on. Models also represent business processes or data, such as business process reengineering (BPR) process models.

Over the past two decades, businesses had to adapt and transform their organizations. A number of change models have been introduced and tried during that time, but at best, they produced only incremental improvements on the 'fringes' with marginal bottom line results. Many involved change strategies that launched several initiatives within the organization simultaneously, each narrowly focused on specific aspects of the organization, with little or no preplanning and coordination. Such an approach tries to change the organization's parts, but ultimately results in suboptimizing the whole system for marginal bottom line performance. Any initiative to transform or change an enterprise must consider how that particular enterprise operates as an integrated whole, and its relationships with its suppliers, business partners, and customers.

Most traditional seller- or product-driven businesses create value primarily at the product or line-of-business level. In contrast to this, the integrated value chain business model is customer-centric, where value is created at the relationship level across products and channels, rather than at the individual product level. Value-chain integration is necessary if vendors are to coordinate between upstream suppliers, internal operations (e.g., manufacturing processes), downstream distributors and shippers as well as customers effectively. With this model, processes once perceived as internal to the company, now span the entire value chain. Effective service providers integrate their operations directly into the processes of their customers. With this model, every company in the chain performs a set or sequence of activities to produce its products. The links between those activities provide a prime opportunity for competitive advantage, whether due to exceptional efficiency or some form of product differentiation. This chain of partners that work in sequence to create, market, and move goods and services grows ever more complex. For example, take SouthWest Airlines value chains which have as strategic partners not only the Boeing Co., with all of its aircraft, but also General Electric Co., which makes the engines that Boeing uses. In addition, the airline has partners including jet fuel makers, travel agents, long-distance vendors, and computer hardware and software markets in its value chain.

End-to-end integration of processes and e-Business applications

Another important requirement is that integrated value-chains take advantage of existing and emerging technologies and systems that can be used to link and enable the entire value chain. The foundation of this barrier-free environment is interoperability (see Section 10.3.2). Value-chain integration means that an organization's enterprise information systems can no longer be confined to internal processes, programs, and data repositories. For example, although ordering and distribution of goods can be fast, the supporting accounting and inventory information, payment, and actual funds transfer – which require communication of business processes with enterprise information systems – tends to lag by a substantial amount of time. Classical examples of enterprise information systems and applications, which typically rely on database support, are an accounts receivable system that keeps track of invoices sent and payments received. The time-lag and the decoupling of accounting and payment information systems from the ordering and delivery of goods and service (business) processes, increases the transaction's credit risks. Moreover, it may often introduce discrepancies between various information sources, requiring expensive and time-consuming reconciliations. Ideally, an e-Business solution should eliminate the gaps between ordering, distribution, and payment, concentrating the development of interoperable links on record-keeping and accounting information systems.

End-to-end e-Business integration and interoperation require that structural and semantic system incompatibilities be overcome, and that business processes and information systems not only harmonize but are also combined with legacy assets to accommodate a broader range of business process variability and evolution.

End-to-end e-Business integration should rely on accepted open standards for interoperability, that employ a standard terminology and business processes to formally describe business interactions between organizations, and a standard terminology to combat semantic interoperability problems. Many vertical industries provide data and business process definitions, including relationships and cross-references, and a business terminology organized on a per industry domain basis. Industry standards groups, such as the automotive industry, financial services industry, the insurance and travel industries, and so on use are examples of industries working on domain-specific XML standards. This results in an industry-wide universal foundation for conducting global electronic business, ensuring the integrity of fast, clean business transactions, guaranteeing common semantics and data integrity across the Internet, backed with the industry representation. More information on this topic can be found in Section 18.8 and Chapter 20.

In an enterprise framework, there is a pressing demand to integrate 'new generation' business processes with legacy perspectives, processes, and applications. Legacy systems are systems that are critical for the day-to-day functioning of an organization; they normally comprise monolithic applications that consist of millions of lines of code in older programming languages (e.g., COBOL), are technically obsolete with a poor performance, and hard to adapt and maintain [Umar 1997; Brodie 1995]. Few businesses can afford to completely abandon their existing information systems to implement new ones. Beyond the volumes of data collected in those systems, there are key features and functions that need to be continuously used even when new systems are introduced. Thus, in addition to improved business modeling and interoperability, the challenges include achieving integration without having to significantly change existing applications; solving the issues of handling transaction-based data; dealing with issues of performance through leveraging middle-tier services; and using standards-based technologies to aggregate information and data from legacy sources into a coherent, customized view of an e-Business application scenario. More details on this topic can be found in Chapter 16.

It is our conviction that the widespread end-to-end integration of supply chain processes will probably be delayed until some of the emerging technology for loose coupling, such as Web-services (see Chapter 19), matures.

10.6 Concluding remarks

There are some key recurring themes and options that permeate this chapter, and the following points should be carried forward.

The gradual application of various information-based technologies has been both the cause and the effect of new ways of doing business. The five-level (or six-level) framework (Section 10.3.1) nicely characterizes this process. The first computer systems were exploited locally: automating basic clerical operations made efficiency improvements possible, along with the ability to process large amounts of data supported decision-making using management information systems as well as the application of statistical and mathematical methods to logistic planning. In the 1980s, IT made internal integration possible by speeding up companies' internal business processes. This in turn led to companies redesigning business processes, enabling them to realize new concepts such as just-in-time logistics. At the same time, the rise of electronic data interchange (EDI) systems made links with external parties within the supply chain possible, facilitating the exchange of orders without human intervention. The result was the next stage, network integration. Again efficiency benefits were realized, but, more importantly, it also allowed for a new focus on strategic objectives.

Current Internet-based technologies allow organizations to extend their collaborative relations to other functions, such as marketing, research, and development, introducing the next stages of business network redesign and business scope redefinition. The convergence of IT and telecommunications, and the availability of bandwidth, make new organizational designs (network organizations, links of supply chain partners, alliances exploitin g uniquely grouped core competences) possible and support for them. From a technology perspective, integrated value systems require fully integrated frameworks and infrastructure support to provide them with access throughout the chain. As we saw in Section 10.3.2, the foundation of such a barrier-free environment is interoperability, the ability of one system to process information from and to another at a syntactic and semantic level without requiring either system to make changes to accommodate the other, as well as the ability to integrate end-to-end e-Business processes. Thus, redesigned interorganizational business processes and interoperability are core requirements, of critical importance to the success of integrated supply chains.

We may now combine our network and information system classifications with our analysis of supply chains and their development. The rise of long-term collaboration patterns in supply chains allows us to categorize supply chains as operational networks. When network participants collaborate in areas such as logistic planning and market strategies, they can be classed as collaborative networks, requiring e-collaboration functionalities. And when supply chain partners engage in product and process innovation together, their collaboration has the characteristics of an innovative network. Supply chains consequently will utilize interorganizational systems with transaction and non-transaction types of functionality. Their operational level activities will require interorganizational information systems with an e-Hierarchy type of functionality. Developing contacts with (new) partners will be supported by e-Brokerage and e-Market types of functionality. Collaborative planning will require e-collaboration type of functionality. Updating partners with various kinds of information, such as actual demand and supply statuses, is supported by a pure information provision-type of functionality.

10.7 Chapter summary

10.7.1 Network organizations and their IOSs

This chapter focuses on networked organizations; its purpose is to analyse different types of network organizations, of interorganizational systems, and how they relate to each other. Subsequently, the chapter defines interorganizational systems and develops a classification of them based on their objectives, and examines a specific class of network organizations: supply chains and their management.

Networked organizations could be defined as virtual partnerships formed by separate companies to enable them to operate as integral elements of a greater organization while retaining their own authority in major budgeting and pricing matters. According to this definition, the term network organization is synonymous with modular organization, virtual corporation, organic network, value-adding partnership, and interorganizational configuration. Networks can be perceived as intermediary organizational forms between markets and hierarchies.

Different classifications of network organizations exist:

- Network types may be distinguished on the basis of whether their objective is operational coordination (operational networks), joint decision-making (collaborative networks), innovation (innovative networks), or defending specific interests of their participants (interest group networks).

- Networks between independent companies distinguish between *stable networks* and *dynamic networks*. Stable networks involve long-term, stable relationships between limited numbers of carefully selected partners. Dynamic networks are temporary alliances between organizations in order to respond to actual market forces.

- *Internal networks* (versus *external networks*) could be set up within companies to make them more flexible and entrepreneurial in spirit.

- Networks can be classified on the basis of the intensity of their relationships. A *thick network* typically involves intensive relationships and communication patterns, and presupposes close collaboration. The notion of *thin networks* arose as a consequence of the potential offered by electronic communication: they are composed of companies that communicate extensively, but they involve much less integration.

- Finally, we may also classify networks on the basis of their structure: *tightly coupled* and *loosely coupled* networks. Tightly coupled networks are relatively stable networks of trading partners with shared planning and control cycles. In loosely coupled networks, trading partners preserve their independence.

Network organizations are supported/enabled by Interorganizational information systems (IOSs). IOSs are a specific class of information systems that automate the flow of information across organizational boundaries and enterprise information systems, and link an organization to suppliers, customers, and possibly other organizations (like, for instance, the government). Venkatraman [Venkatraman 1991] developed a framework for analyzing the impact of IT (including IOSs) on the way organizations structure and coordinate their operational processes. The framework proposes to distinguish between five levels of IT-induced business transformation: localized exploitation, internal integration, business process redesign, business network redesign, and business scope redefinition. Higher levels of business transformation assume higher levels of potential benefits.

Interorganizational information systems can work only if they are able to communicate and work with other such systems and interact with people. This requirement is called *interoperability*, and it can only be met if communication standards are applied. Interoperability requires standardization in four dimensions: technology, syntax, semantics, and pragmatics. Technology standards concern middleware, network protocols, security protocols, and the like. Syntax standardization means that the network organization has to agree on how to integrate heterogeneous applications based on the structure or 'language' of the messages exchanged. Semantic standards constitute agreements on the meanings of the terms used for one enterprise's information systems to communicate with and understand the messages of another's. Pragmatic standards are agreements on practices and protocols triggered by specific messages, such as orders and delivery notifications.

Lack of interoperability impedes communication. The degree to which this difficulty becomes a problem partly depends on the kind of communication needed: system-to-system communication or person-to-system communication. In the case of system-to-system communication there is no human intervention.

IT is generally used for operational networks, that is, operational supply chain applications in business-to-business settings, in which orders are transmitted from buying organizations to suppliers. The latter type of communication encompasses a vast array of applications.

IOSs may be classified into *transaction oriented* and *non-transaction-oriented systems. Transaction-oriented systems* focus on facilitating transactions. E-Business and e-Procurement applications (ERP, XML/EDI, workflow) are typical examples of such systems. This category may be further divided into 'bilateral forms of integration' and 'multilateral situations'. The former involves buyers and sellers with long-term relationships (electronic hierarchies); the latter are used to establish new buyer-seller relationships, and then a third party may be introduced to differentiate still further, between pure markets and brokerages. *Non-transaction-oriented systems* facilitate communication and other coordinative processes. These systems include databases, e-mail software, video conferencing, groupware, CAD, expert communities, and so on. This category may be subdivided into systems purely for information provision and those intended for collaboration purposes.

A relationship can be established between types of network organization and types of IOSs used. In operational networks all functionality types may be potentially applied. As there are no transactions in collaboration, innovation, and interest group type networks, the interorganizational information systems used in these settings will belong to the e-Collaboration and information provision types.

There are limits to the reach of network organizations. As has been suggested in the Information Systems literature, this depends on the kind of information exchanged. Grouping activities within organizations typically makes possible the exchange of rich information among a narrow, internal group of participants. Markets enable their participants to exchange information among a large, external group, which information, however, is said to be 'thinner'. The trade-off between richness and reach is increasingly affected by modern information technology, which enables 'higher' combinations of richness and reach.

10.7.2 Supply chains

A supply chain is a network of inter-linked suppliers and customers, where each customer is, in turn, a supplier to the next down-stream organization until a complete product reaches the end customer. Supply chain management may be defined as the management of upstream and downstream relations with suppliers and customers to deliver superior value at less cost to the supply chain as a whole, and deals with the management of materials, information, and financial flows in the network.

Supply chain management is characterized by two models: the *push* and *pull* varieties or a combined push-pull approach. A manufacturer who develops a product, and then identifies a suitable target market for it, can depict the push model. Conventional IT support for the push model focuses on the use of independent data management activities for enterprise information systems by supply chain members, as well as limited use of XML/EDI. The pull model targets the customer's needs and starts with an analysis of his of her requirements through market research and close cooperation with customers and suppliers in the development of a new product. There are much closer links between the members of the supply chain through the use of technology, such as XML/EDI, to minimize document transfer and reuse.

Sharing information is a key for supply chain management. Different technology solutions exist. By using standard EDI messages, organizations can exchange information between many different trading partners.

EDI, however, has limited ability to enable value chain interactions, as it is predominantly message centric, i.e., uses standardized message formats. To achieve increased integration between member organizations and their internal systems in a supply chain, a full commitment must be made to deploying e-Business applications across the supply chain structure. Any technology that automates trading partner interactions in a supply chain, must also represent the business processes and vocabulary of its respective industry to have any chance of working.

Many enterprise technology systems, such as SAP, JD Edwards, PeopleSoft, etc., use Web-enabled front-ends or back-ends to leverage Internet's ability to link value chain constituents together for faster, more seamless communication. However, although ERP systems may be very good candidates for integrating internal business processes, they are often not capable of linking suppliers and customers in the supply chain. Conventional ERP systems lack the advanced functionality required for the following types of supply chain processes: advanced order management, transportation planning, and electronic procurement.

The emergence and greater acceptance of higher-order collaborative interorganizational relationships has fostered the emergence of the concept of an integrated supply chain management approach. By coordinating, collaborating, and integrating with other suppliers, customers and business partners, enterprises create an extended virtual enterprise. Supply chain integration may be defined as the process by which multiple enterprises within a shared market segment collaboratively plan, implement, and monitor the flow of goods, services, and information along the value system in a way that increases customer-perceived value and optimizes the efficiency of the chain. Essential requirements for integrated supply chains are e-Business-enabling business models and end-to-end integration of processes and e-Business applications.

Discussion Questions

- Governance through network organizations is often positioned between governance through markets and governance through a hierarchy.
  - Discuss key characteristics of a network organization.
  - Discuss differences between network and hierarchy type of governance.
  - Discuss differences between network and market type of governance.

- Interorganizational information systems can be classified in two broad categories. Discuss these two categories.

- What is the definition of a supply chain? What are the most important flows within the supply chain?

- What is the definition of supply chain management?

- What potential benefits could the use of Internet-based technologies bring to the supply chain?

- The aim of extended supply chains is to integrate isolated enterprise value chain environments, to create a superior collaborative commerce infrastructure. What are the four key characteristics of an integrated supply chain (also called a virtual enterprise)?

Assignments

i. In this chapter, five types of organizational networks have been distinguished.

    a. Describe their properties.
    b. Give an example of each type (e.g., from business publications, or published case studies) and describe objectives, participants, type of relationships, and supporting technologies.

ii. Analyze how a supply chain collaboration between a company and its suppliers can reduce inventory costs; how could the use of IT networks contribute to a further decrease of inventory costs?

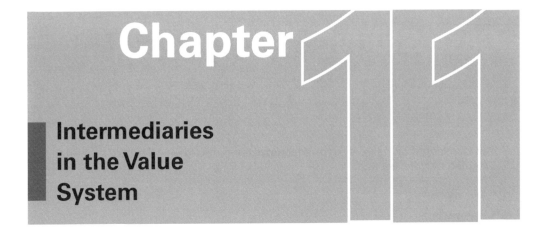

Chapter 11

Intermediaries in the Value System

The increasing popularity of the Internet has generated significant interest in the development of electronic retail commerce. As we already explained in Chapter 8, the Internet has the potential to evolve into an interconnected marketplace, facilitating the exchange of a wide variety of products and services. The development of such electronic marketplaces implies that there will be significant changes in the economics of marketing channels and the organizational structure of distribution, which will lead to a redefinition of industry value systems.

Today, information infrastructures are extending to reach individual suppliers, consumers and trading partners. The potential for transformations in the value systems of many firms is thus far greater now than it has been in the past, as technology begins to enable producers to directly interact with consumers. This chapter focuses on a key set of issues concerning the role of intermediaries in the value system. Namely it examines how an interconnected data network infrastructure affects the role of the intermediary in the exchange process between producers and consumers. One fundamental question that needs to be addressed in this context is to what extent producing organizations would take advantage of direct electronic links with consumers and whether, in the process, intermediaries would be eliminated from the value system. Consequently, this chapter also concentrates on the issue of whether intermediaries are a threatened breed, or is it likely that the mediating function will be present in the electronic marketplace with traditional intermediaries benefiting from network-based transactions to solidify their role in exchanges with new types of network-based entities.

This chapter presents different views on how the Internet will affect intermediaries, defines and classifies intermediaries while analyzing possible dynamics involving intermediaries in the value chain, caused by the Internet.

Case Study

Successful intermediation by Internet-based intermediaries in the transportation value system[1]

The transportation value system encompasses the following functions generally executed by different parties:

- the shipper
- the forwarder
- the logistic service provider
- the carrier

Shippers are initiators of distribution and transport. Their manufacturing and trading activities create a need for transportation. The forwarder plans and controls the shipping orders received from the shipper and is responsible for selecting the transport modes, for passing orders to the transport companies and for monitoring the adequate execution of the transportation. In some cases the shipper may execute these functions. The services offered by the logistic service providers include activities when the goods do not move, like storage, (re) packaging and even small assembly operations; typically these activities are performed in distribution centers, warehouses etc. The carrier is responsible for the physical movement of goods from one place to the other. Different modes of transport are available, such as road, rail, air, inward shipping and sea. Combinations of modes may be used, called multimodal transport. The most dominant mode is road transport.

The transportation industry is under pressure. Logistic concepts such as JIT result in the production of smaller batches and translate into integral logistic planning, more frequent deliveries and the requirement for an increasing efficiency and flexibility of distribution. The transport industry itself is highly fragmented with small market shares: in Europe there are an estimated 450 000 trucking companies; 85% own less than 10 trucks. The industry suffers from overcapacity with, as a result, low loading factors; price competition strongly limits profitability. Transportation companies attempted to respond in two ways. First by offering fixed line schedules in a permanent network and by building long-term relationships with shippers, both in

[1]This case description is based on H. Krcmar, B. Schwarzer (eds) (1995) *The Impact of Information Technology on the European Transport Sector,* Gabler Edition Wissenschaft, Deutsche UniversitaetsVerlag; F. Cruijssen (2004) "A Survey on European Inter-organizational Data Sharing Implementations in Transportation". Klict.

the region of origin and in the region of destination. Second by executing irregular transport, especially as return cargo. However, the competition in this segment is very strong and prices are under pressure. The need for cost cutting on the shipper's side and for higher load factors on the carrier's side helped infomediaries to develop. In the period 1999–2001 an estimated 200 players emerged in the European market [Cruijssen 2004]. We present two examples: Informore/LogicLogistics and Teleroute.

Informore/LogicLogistics

The distribution process of materials is very information intense. The amounts of data and the numbers of documents that have to be exchanged are tremendous; moreover, correctness of data is a particularly critical precondition for smooth operations. As a result, in the 1990s, intermediary organizations which only provided information (systems) services, emerged. One example is Informore (www.informore.com) that started in April 1992 and has been successful ever since. Its original objective was to unite small and medium-sized transport companies under one 'EDI-umbrella' and to connect them to shippers. Also any shipper may join the system and take along his preferred carrier(s).

Informore launched LogicLogistics (www.logistics.nl), a logistics execution platform for those who act as supply chain coordinators. Through the platform, the coordinator has access to data from other supply chain parties. Logistic execution scenarios, meaning the plans for how shipments are transported from the pick-up address to the delivery address, encompassing e.g. modes of transportation, carriers' names, tariffs, transit time etc. are stored in a central database, called a datahub. LogicLogistics takes care of the system integration between customers and the datahub by means of EDI, XML, FTP, or HTTP. The supply-chain coordinator defines the access that parties have to information in the database. Standard services of LogicLogistics include tracking and tracing, management reports, mode selection, automatic invoicing, exception alerts, route planning, and shipment execution planning.

Teleroute

Assuring return freights is essential for the profitability of a transport organization and so, although most of the relationships with clients are based on long-term contracts, almost every transport company is at least partially dependent on ad hoc offerings. In this market segment the Wolters Kluwer Publishing company introduced Teleroute (www.teleroute.com), an electronic marketplace for transport capacity for forwarders and carriers (not for shippers). It started as a videotext application and is now available on the Internet. Forwarders and carriers are connected to the central Teleroute computer. The database is accessible 24 hours a day and gives a picture of freight and vehicle availability across Europe. Teleroute is established in 16 countries across Europe. Daily 35 000 carriers and forwarders trade on Teleroute and execute more than 56 000 transactions; on a yearly basis 7 million freights are sold on Teleroute.

11.1 Introduction

Intermediation refers to something or somebody going 'in between'. In a broad sense the telephones we use to communicate with one another could be called intermediaries. In this chapter, however, we will look at intermediation from an economic point of view: a process in which independent organizations take up positions between other organizations (or individuals), while focusing on their own 'utility curves' and their own revenue and profit objectives [Van Tuijl 2002]. Such intermediating organizations act as agents for those other organizations (or individuals), who may be buyers as well as sellers, and use their 'middleman' position to foster their clients' communications with other parties with the ultimate aim of generating transactions between them.

Ever since the Internet emerged, people have discussed the consequences of its rise for intermediary roles and functions – and thus for the viability of intermediary companies. More than a decade and a half ago, it was pointed out that the disintermediating effect of the 'future perfect' market forces would change business fundamentally: "In a complex industrial economy, for example, a tremendous amount of space in the marketplace is taken up by intermediation... finding ways to disintermediate is a way to create space for new opportunities" [Davies 1987]. And in 1996 business strategist Don Tapscott identified disintermediation as one among 12 overlapping themes in the new economy: "Middleman functions between producers and consumers are being eliminated through digital networks" [Tapscott 1996].

Many, on the other hand, have expressed more balanced opinions on the disappearance or continued existence of the intermediary function. In 1995, when the Internet was still in its early stages of development, Bill Gates recognized the fact that intermediaries will remain important: "Industry after industry will be changed by the development of the information highway, and change is unsettling. Some middlemen who handle information or product distribution will find they no longer add value and change fields, whereas others will rise to the competitive challenge" [Gates 1995]. In his 1999 book *Business @ the Speed of Light* Bill Gates devoted an entire chapter, called 'The middleman must add value', to intermediaries' prospects. In it he developed his ideas on the way in which they may continue to add value. "Now that customers can deal directly with manufacturers and service providers, there is little value added in simply transferring goods or information. Various commentators have predicted the 'death of the middleman'. Certainly the value of 'pass-through' middlemen is quickly falling to zero. In the future travel agents will need to do more than book tickets. If you are a middleman, the Internet's promise of cheaper prices and faster service can 'disintermediate' you, eliminate your role of assisting the transaction between the producer and the consumer." [Gates 1999]

11.2 Definition and classification of intermediaries

Before we look more closely at the *intermediary* function, the concept of *intermediation* must be clearly defined first. The trouble is that intermediaries can play many different roles, each of which serves to add value. They may provide physical infrastructures for transportation and storage, or they may help generate economies of scale. Some intermediaries provide human interaction, including sales staff, which can be very useful when physical goods and services are sold and distributed. Others transfer information to suppliers, about demand patterns for example, which helps their clients improve their inventory management and production scheduling processes.

Therefore, some researchers use very broad definitions indeed. For instance a recent definition states that "any person or institution in the entire value system – from raw input to final consumption – is an intermediary" [Singh 2002]. That leaves out very few businesses, effectively only those companies active in the mining industry and other producers of basic raw materials. Even Dell, for example, which buys hardware and software components directly from suppliers and assembles them into ready-to-use computers, must then be considered an intermediary – while it is usually mentioned as an example of disintermediation [Evans 1999]. For the purposes of our discussion we therefore will need a definition with somewhat narrower and well-defined boundaries. Thus, we adopt the following definition: "an intermediary is an economic agent that buys from suppliers in order to resell to customers, or that helps consumers and suppliers to meet and transact" [Spulber 1996].

11.2.1 Transactional intermediaries or infomediaries

However, even within the above definition of intermediaries, there are still two major kinds of intermediaries:

- Transactional intermediaries: those who move, store and deliver physical goods

- Infomediaries: those who provide information and information services, usually relating to those physical goods and services

Many of the companies who handle physical goods and services are intermediaries of the kind that Bill Gates calls "pass-through middlemen". Their value-adding potential decreases now that customers can contact their suppliers directly using the Internet. For a limited number of such enterprises there will remain significant opportunities, however, if they manage to exploit the economies of scale inherent in logistic specialization. Such economies of scale will shorten and narrow the supply chains involved – an effect predicted by many as the major result of the increasing importance of the Internet.

The information business is a different issue altogether. It involves capturing and manipulating information in such a way that value is added for one's clients, who include buyers as well as sellers. As said previously, such intermediaries are often called infomediaries, and their line of business is the transaction channel [Cort 1999; Porter 1999]. Infomediaries never own the products and services involved; these are still shipped directly from supplier to customer. But they do bring buyers and sellers together, thus revealing potential transactions; they also help them make deals, transfer titles and arrange and make payments (all of which include providing access to the resources needed); and they assist in setting up after-sales relations management. Stockbrokerage and market making are examples of such activities. Effectively, these activities are new products and services and they generate value because of their low costs.

If the original product is information (that is, books, CDs, software etc.) infomediaries may deliver as well as intermediate. Forrester Research [Forrester 2000] has predicted that the digital delivery of custom-printed books, textbooks and e-books, for instance, will account for a total of 7.8 billion dollars by 2005, or 17.5% of the publishing industry's revenues. Thus, publishing companies are being forced to restructure their processes and technologies drastically. The same effect is taking place in many other industries.

Case Study

Informore/LogicLogistics

As Informore focuses on the information aspect of transportation, it has a good insight into current transportation schedules, which enables it to suggest possible combinations of freights of different accounts and returning freights. This contributes to higher loading factors.

Infomediary revenue is generally collected on the supplier side, from seller membership fees, for example, or customer-finding fees. Doing so requires a wide and always increasing range of knowledge and capabilities in order to gather, interpret and use the information needed about customers and suppliers. Clients and offerings must be matched, advice must be given and – not least important – privacy must be protected. And once customers realize that suppliers target their exact needs, they will demand even more precision. Thus, specialization is stimulated, which lengthens and widens supply chains – exactly the opposite of the trend expected by those who think the Internet will eliminate all intermediaries [Cort 1999].

11.2.2 Added value and functions

Business literature furnishes several lists of intermediaries' value-adding functions. For example, intermediaries' *value-adding functions* may be grouped according to their economic implications into four broad categories: pricing, inventory holding, transaction coordinating and performance monitoring [Spulber 1996].

Theoretically, in a perfectly competitive market, companies only react to prices. In reality many companies have at least some influence on prices because they can influence the transportation and transaction costs involved, and even the switching costs. Intermediaries, in fact, set prices according to demand and supply, thus coordinating and even stimulating transactions between suppliers and customers. Suppose, for example, demand falls. Intermediaries will then generally lower the asking prices in order to stimulate demand while at the same time decreasing the bidding prices to discourage supply. Likewise, in a market hit by a supply decrease, intermediaries will react by raising the asking prices in an attempt to ration demand, simultaneously raising the bidding prices to encourage supply. Thus, intermediaries manipulate price levels so that their markets clear at a lower or higher trade volume.

Inventories basically serve to smooth away demand and supply fluctuations. Many intermediaries, therefore, assume an inventory holder's role. They keep stocks to be able to sell immediately, and they keep money reserves to be able to buy immediately. Thus they render what are called immediacy services. These are provided in financial markets, in which intermediaries provide liquidity by being available to buy and sell stocks, as well as in retail and wholesale markets, where they are ready to buy and sell commodities.

Market intermediaries coordinate the transactions of buyers and sellers, reducing or even eliminating the uncertainty associated with making a perfect match. Doing so involves adding to the number of potential trading partners, which increases the chance of finding the right trading partner and reduces search costs. Centralized search and negotiation activities by intermediaries are generally more efficient than those carried out by customers and suppliers seeking each other and negotiating terms and conditions themselves. Customer needs and supplier needs, however, do not always coincide [Sarkar 1996, 1998]. Therefore, in a competitive environment successful integrated intermediaries must provide bundles of services which balance the needs of clients and producers and are acceptable to both. An example will serve to explain how this may be done. The ideal market for consumers is one in which they are given complete, objective product information. However, producers prefer to influence their clients' purchase decisions, so they like markets in which they can provide biased information. And since providing information is a costly affair, the question arises of whose needs it should serve. Sometimes this is determined by law. But it is mostly retail intermediaries who, through their displays and packaging, strike a balance between the two, ensuring that both are adequately satisfied. Only companies who do so successfully will flourish in competitive markets for intermediary services; otherwise, they stand to lose clients at both ends.

As this example also shows, market information is usually asymmetrically distributed over the market's participants. Sellers are not aware of all their buyers' characteristics; buyers do not know all product characteristics such as quality, durability and safety. Intermediaries can solve this problem by collecting such information and making it available. Thus, transactions may result that the information asymmetry would otherwise have prohibited, and the intermediaries profit along with their clients. Furthermore, intermediaries are likely to generate economies of scale in the production and distribution of information, and they can even warrant its accuracy, backing it up by their own reputations or by means of binding contracts with their providers.

Case Study

Informore/LogicLogistics

As an intermediary, Informore has been successful in reducing administrative and logistic expenses in the transportation value system.

In this way, intermediaries bundle information with products and services. That sounds more complicated than it is. What happens is, for example, that retailers test products and inform their clients about their features. Likewise, wholesalers provide their suppliers with information about market demand and customer requirements. Taken one step further, intermediaries may also play the role of performance monitors. Buyers always face costs for monitoring whether their suppliers – be they lawyers or bicycle repairers - really serve their interests. If this can be delegated, benefits from economies of scale and scope as well as learning curves are to be expected. Essentially, this is what happens when you hire a contractor to build you a house:

they will locate carpenters, plumbers, electricians and masons as subcontractors and monitor their work. Since the contractor is more capable in this field than you are, your house will be built better and cost less than if you do all that yourself.

11.2.3 Services

The coordinating role intermediaries play in the exchange process in fact consists of many different functions. Electronic services provided through the Internet have different consequences for each of these functions. Network-based services may facilitate product search, but they are less well equipped to offer product distribution (except of course in the case of information and software products). So the Internet does not influence all intermediary services to an equal extent or in the same way. For infomediaries, several *services* have been suggested as specifically well-suited [Bakos 1998; Chircu 1999a; Grover 2001]. These include the following:

- *search and complexity services* – infomediaries simplify the searching process by providing information, guiding buyers to an informed choice

- *matching services* – advances in information technology, such as agent technology, are used to assists one's clients

- *content services* – this involves infomediaries providing product content, such as independent evaluations, directory services for alternative suppliers etc. on their websites (see Chapter 8)

- *community services* – by generating a certain 'stickiness' between their sites and their clients, infomediaries set up communities of buyers with similar interests

- *informational services* – these include dynamic pricing, notification services, and so on

- *privacy protection services* – privacy is an immediate concern for all participants on the Internet, who will value infomediary services which include protection of their privacy

- *infrastructure services* – these include facilities for conducting secure transactions via the Internet.

Case Study

Informore/LogicLogistics

LogicLogistics performs a few of these services. LogicLogistics takes care of the system integration between customers and the datahub by means of EDI, XML, FTP, or HTTP. The supply chain coordinator defines the access that parties have to information in the database.

11.3 **Dynamics in the value system**

Information Systems' researchers have from the outset looked into the evolution of intermediary roles and positions as a consequence of the Internet's emergence and growth. Basically, the literature in which they reported their findings and expectations presented the same views as those advertised by Internet gurus and business reporters. At first, the electronic market hypothesis was predominant (see Section 5.4.1). Electronic marketplaces would arise, which would have strong disintermediating effects. Subsequently, the move-to-the-middle hypothesis emerged (see Section 5.4.2): companies would use information technology to build strong long-term relations with limited numbers of suppliers. Evidently, this would endanger the position of intermediaries as well, at least in business-to-business e-Commerce.

Originally it was believed that electronic markets would cause massive disintermediation and this was shown by the findings of an economic study [Kaufmann 2001]. According to economic theory the costs for buyers to obtain information on pricing and product offerings are a major determinant of market efficiency and competitive behavior. Traditional intermediaries could exist because they lowered such costs in comparison with direct client–producer exchange, meanwhile generating revenue by taking a slice of the difference for themselves. It was also argued that electronic marketplaces would be likely to reduce buyers' search costs considerably [Bakos 1991]. Lower transaction costs, and lower search costs in particular, would thus eliminate the need for intermediaries, while at the same time allowing efficiency improvements resulting from a greater degree of outsourcing. And worse, electronic markets are more than just meeting places for supply and demand: they also facilitate the integration of additional functionality and services such as contracting, insurance, logistics, and general transaction support. Thus, other 'middlemen' might be endangered as well. In addition to this came the move-to-the-middle hypothesis [Clemons 1993]. Using information technology, companies would establish long-term collaboration relations with only a few of their suppliers. Such relations would be preferred to short-term market arrangements since they would allow the companies to enjoy the benefits of their investments for a longer period. And indeed, a 'move to the middle' was then shown to take place in supply chain and outsourcing relations facilitated by electronic data interchange (EDI) systems. In business-to-business markets the hypothesis received much support as the positions of many intermediaries were indeed weakened.

11.3.1 **Disintermediation**

Disintermediation has been defined [Wigand 1997] as "the displacement or elimination of market intermediaries, enabling direct trade with buyers and consumers without agents."

In economics, disintermediation is the removal of intermediaries in a supply chain. Disintermediation is often the result of high market transparency, in that buyers are aware of supply prices direct from the manufacturer. As a result, buyers will bypass the middlemen (wholesalers and retailers) in order to buy directly from the manufacturer and thereby pay less. Buyers can alternatively elect to purchase from wholesalers. For instance, a business-to-consumer intermediary often functions as the bridge between buyer and manufacturer. To illustrate this concept, a typical business-to-consumer supply chain is composed of four or five entities (in order):

- supplier

- manufacturer

- wholesaler

- retailer

- buyer

It has been argued that the Internet modifies the supply chain to the following three entities owing to market transparency:

- supplier

- manufacturer

- buyer

Although the scope of disintermediation is greater in the case of information products, it may also occur in the supply of physical goods. In this case the supplier may still have significant shipping and handling costs so it will need to find significant cost savings elsewhere [Chen 2001]. An example of disintermediation is Dell Computers, which has managed to link its online ordering with innovations in the supply chain to allow reduced stockholding costs as well as customized assembly of PCs. In the non-Internet world, disintermediation has played an important part for many big box retailers, such as Walmart, which attempt to reduce prices by reducing the number of intermediaries between the supplier and the buyer. Disintermediation is also closely associated with the idea of just-in-time manufacturing as the removal of the need for inventory removes one function of an intermediary.

Disintermediation has occurred less frequently as a result of the Internet than many expected. Retailers and wholesalers provide functions such as the extension of credit, aggregation of products from different suppliers, and processing of returns. In addition, shipping goods to and from the manufacturer can in many cases be far less efficient than shipping them to a store where the consumer can pick them up. This issue is elaborated further in the following section.

11.3.2 Are intermediaries threatened?

Transaction costs theory was introduced in Chapter 2 section 7.3 and arguments for disintermediation are often based on transaction costs. Lower transaction costs using a direct electronic link, it is argued, will favor direct marketing over transactions via an intermediary [Chen 2001]. This situation is depicted in Figure 11.1.

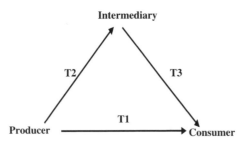

■ **Figure 11.1:** Potential Transactions Between Producers, Consumers, and Intermediaries

In 1987 Malone, Yates, and Benjamin [Malone 1987] were among the first to link transaction costs theory to electronic communication, illustrating how electronic networks could lower the costs of transactions and influence the formation of both electronic markets and electronic hierarchies. "More efficient transactions help firms reduce the costs of coordination, which are defined as the transaction costs of all the information processing necessary to coordinate the work of people and machines that perform the primary processes...[and] take into account the costs of gathering information, negotiating contracts and protecting against the risks of opportunistic bargaining" [Malone 1987]. This hypothesis was later espoused by several scholars who made predictions about the end of intermediaries in the earliest days of electronic commerce over the Web [Wigand 1995; Hoffman 1995]. In particular, Wigand and Benjamin [Wigand 1995] point out that a network infrastructure connecting both businesses and end consumers allows producers to internalize activities that were traditionally performed by intermediaries. Businesses can sell directly to end customers at a higher than wholesale price, therefore capturing more of the value in their goods. Both producers and consumers will benefit because the markup in price caused by intermediaries disappears. Thus, the producers retain more of the profits that are generated by the value system, while the consumers benefit from expanded choice and lower prices. In other words, the network's ability to efficiently support direct exchanges will increase both producer and consumer welfare. According to this logic, a trend was predicted towards producers selling directly to consumers, and consumers preferring to buy directly from producers.

Sarkar *et al.* [Sarkar 1996] refer to predictions about the bypass of intermediaries in business value systems as the *Threatened Intermediaries Hypothesis* (TIH). This argues that that online consumers will interact directly with online suppliers and, hence, prices will decrease owing to the disappearance of margins calculated by intermediaries. Information Systems' researchers pointed out that the Internet encourages such disintermediation, precisely because it reduces many of the transaction costs associated with market exchanges. On a simple level, the consumer can merely point their browser to a producer's site and purchase goods directly. These goods might be manufactured on demand, or maintained in a central inventory. Courier services then become the downstream channel for physical goods, while the Internet itself is the downstream channel for information goods. Through electronic brokerage the network itself minimizes buyers' search costs by finding the best supplier according to specified criteria [Malone 1987]. Through the network, negotiation, monitoring, settlement and after-sales service can also be handled at lower costs, enabling producers to avoid contracting with external providers of downstream distribution services.

The flaws in the disintermediation scenario presented above were first elaborated by Sarkar *et al.* [Sarkar 1996, 1998]. They considered a simple situation, focusing on the possible transactions between a producer, a consumer, and an intermediary (Figure 11.1) and the associated transaction costs involved (T1, T2 and T3) and pointed out that using the same transaction costs' argument can lead to exactly the opposite conclusion – greater rather than lesser use of intermediaries. They challenged the following two key assumptions that govern the disintermediation scenario:

1. The Internet will make all transaction costs insignificant.
2. Transactions are atomic, and not further decomposable into smaller units.

We elaborate on these two assumptions below.

According to Sarkar *et al.*, the first assumption is difficult to accept. For many goods, the costs of transferring from producer to consumer are not likely to decrease dramatically. Therefore, they proposed to modify the first assumption as follows: "The availability of the Internet will force all transaction costs to approach a non-zero minimum."

Let T1, T2, and T3 denote pre-Internet transaction costs, while T1 , T2 and T3 indicate transaction costs after the arrival of the Internet (see Figure 11.1). One can then explain the TIH as follows.

Prior to the Internet, transactions were intermediated and a competitive market for intermediary services entails:

$$T1 > T2 + T3$$

After the arrival of the Internet, all transaction costs reach the theoretical minimum. Consequently:

$$T1^* = T2^* = T3^* = T^*$$

and the costs of direct exchange are equal to:

$$T1 = T^*$$

whereas the costs of intermediated (indirect) exchange (from producer to consumer) are equal to:

$$T2^* + T3^* = 2T^*$$

Therefore, after the arrival of the Internet, removing intermediaries undoubtedly savescosts, since:

$$T1^* < T2^* + T3^*$$

These cost savings will be passed on to at least one of the market participants, i.e., either the producer or consumer or even both. This outcome seems to confirm the TIH. However, Sarkar *et al.* argue that it is not likely that all transaction costs will approach the same minimum T*. Relaxing this crucial assumption, so that different types of transactions are affected in different ways, causes every type of transaction cost (producer–consumer, producer–intermediary and intermediary–consumer) to reach its own minimum. They denote this as the modified Assumption 1. According to this modified assumption the four outcomes depicted in Figure 11.2 are possible in the post-Internet world.

Desintermediation is the only one of the possibilities predicted on the basis of the modified assumption. A good example of this is traditional travel agents, and traditional life/auto-insurance agents, and underperforming existing channels. Other possibilities are:

1. The internet-supplemented direct market: If it was formerly less expensive to sell directly to consumers, using such techniques as call centres, printed catalogs and/or customer service representatives, then the Internet can reinforce this by offering a direct supplemented sales approach. A good example of this is Dell Computers, which formerly relied on a direct sales approach, and now uses the Internet to supplement its activities.
2. Cyberintermediaries: these use the Internet to reduce producer to intermediary or intermediary to consumer transaction costs. Cyberintermediaries are simply intermediaries that take advantage of the

Post-Internet	Pre-Internet	
	$T1 < T2 + T3$ Direct \$ < Indirect \$	$T1 > T2 + T3$ Direct \$ > Indirect \$
$T1' < T2' + T3'$ Direct \$ < Indirect \$	Supplemented Direct Market	Threatened Intermediaries
$T1' > T2' + T3'$ Direct \$ > Indirect \$	Cybermediaries	Supplemented Intermediaries

■ **Figure 11.2:** Possible Impacts of the Internet on Intermediaries [Sarkar 1996, 1998]

Internet to create these economies of scale and scope by aggregating transactions. The best example here is Amazon.com, which quickly exploited its Internet skills and knowledge to capture business from traditional booksellers. Another example is Expedia.com.

Case Study

Teleroute

An example of a cybermediary is Teleroute. The way Teleroute works is as follows. Forwarders enter their delivery orders into the system, specifying the quantities involved, pick-up dates and destinations. Carriers can search this information on the basis of four criteria: geographical zone of departure, type of goods, sizes and weights. If a transportation company is interested in a specific order, it contacts the forwarder. Prices are negotiated by telephone. Teleroute is successful because it helps carriers to increase their loading factors, especially for the return trips, and it provides forwarders with transport capacity at a lower price than they are used to. The increased transparency of the market, caused by the electronic marketplace, leads to lower prices. Although carriers of course do not like the latter, they all use Teleroute to get their share of return freights.

3. And finally, Sarkar *et al.*, [Sarkar 1996, 1998] point to the situation where network-based transactions reinforce an existing channel structure when firms use electronic commerce to supplement the economies of scale, scope and knowledge that arise as a result of the technologies involved. This may also arise when the network permits existing intermediaries to create economies of scale, scope, and knowledge that arise for supporting information or risk management services (*internet supplemented intermediaries*). For example, book publishers still use intermediaries such as Barnes and Noble, a traditional book retailer, which found that its ability to reach consumers was strengthened by setting up an Internet shop (Barnesandnoble. com). Another example includes credit card companies which might use the Internet to offer money-back guarantees for purchases made over the Internet.

In the supplemented direct market and supplemented intermediaries scenarios, the Internet reinforces existing direct market or intermediated structures, respectively. These possibilities had previously not been considered explicitly in the literature.

The most interesting scenario, in the opinion of Sarkar *et al.* [Sarkar 1996] is cyberintermediaries. In this case new, Internet-based intermediaries (which they call cybermediaries, (see Chapter 2 on business models for further details on this topic) would be more cost-effective than direct markets. Such cybermediaries would do so by developing economies of scale and scope, resulting in lower producer–intermediary and intermediary–consumer transaction costs. And indeed, many examples of cybermediaries now operate on the Internet: directory services (general directories, commercial directories and specialized directories) and search services; malls and virtual resellers; publishers and financial intermediaries; spot market makers and barter networks; website evaluators, auditors and forums, fan clubs and user groups; and, finally, intelligent agents. In Chapter 2 we discussed a classification of 11 business models for cybermediaries based on the function they perform.

Assumption 2, which characterizes the roles of intermediaries generally as coordinators, is also problematic as it underestimates the services provided by an intermediary. The main fallacy of the Threatened Intermediaries Hypothesis here is its interpretation of intermediation as a single service rather than a number of different services. Therefore, the effects of the diffusion of electronic commerce on each of the intermediation services have to be studied before one can draw conclusions about e-Commerce and the structure of intermediation based on their relative importance.

Intermediaries provide many functions that may be difficult for producers to replicate. For consumers, intermediaries select and evaluate the products they carry, assess buyers' needs and suggest products that meet them, absorb some of the risk (e.g. by offering to handle returns of flawed merchandise), and distribute the product to the buyer by maintaining an inventory of delivery capability. For sellers, they help disseminate product information, influence the purchase of products, provide marketing information about buyers' tastes and demands, and absorb risks such as faulty payments [Sarkar 1996]. Because they typically carry the products of several producers, they can aggregate transactions and benefit from economies of scope not available to a single producer attempting to sell directly to consumers. And their product advice is not necessarily viewed as biased, as would be the case with a firm that only was selling their own products. Taking this multifunctional perspective further illustrates the fallacy of simplistic assumptions about intermediary bypass, and explains their continued presence in the new electronic commerce environment.

Sarkar *et al.* also point out the institutional, social and subjective factors that might influence the extent to which producers can impose the channel structures they desire. First, established intermediaries may derive considerable power from their relations with consumers. Therefore, producers frequently do not attempt to circumvent them completely, as they fear channel conflicts and retaliation. Second, intermediaries satisfy a number of different customer wishes. When there are many manufacturers, customers appreciate intermediary services to help them make a choice: intermediaries who represent several producers are generally less biased than producers, even though sellers may vary their relative profit margins in order to manipulate the intermediaries. And, quite apart from financial and quality arguments, traditional shopping provides social interaction and entertainment.

Finally, social relations influence the patterns of economic exchange [Granovetter 1985]. Therefore, companies may engage in trading relations that seem economically inefficient but are inevitable given the norms of the community. In some cultures, for example, it may be common for members of the same family which owns the production unit to own the intermediaries as well. Such trading relations may in fact yield long-term benefits. They may imply a high degree of trust, reducing transaction costs since contractual and legal expenses to control opportunistic behavior can be avoided [Zucker 1986].

The validity of the Threatened Intermediary Hypothesis has been also questioned by other researchers, who feel it is far too simplistic [Schmitz 2000]. They point out three services that intermediaries provide but which have been much neglected in Information Systems publications: inventory holding for immediacy service purposes; reducing information asymmetry; and gathering, organizing and evaluating dispersed information. The continuity of these three services is probably more important to market participants than cost reduction on simple order-processing services. In the opinion of these researchers e-Business has no systematic effect on the arrival rates of buying and selling orders, nor is e-Business likely to affect individual risk preferences. First therefore, the demand for immediacy and insurance against systematic valuation risks is not expected to fall, and intermediaries holding inventories to provide such services will continue to prosper. Second, the number of participants in any single market will probably rise as electronic markets grow. The probability that one frequently trades with the same partner will consequently decrease, lessening the need to establish a solid reputation. The demand for services which alleviate information asymmetry thus rises. Monitoring the performance of parties with an informational advantage is increasingly delegated to specialized intermediaries. And third, since the knowledge of particular circumstances of time and space is dispersed in society, such information will still have to be gathered, organized and evaluated. e-Business is unlikely to reduce the demand for this particular intermediation service. Accordingly, the informational efficiency of intermediation is expected to prevail, rendering the complete centralization of information gathering, organizing, and evaluating highly implausible [Schmitz 2000].

11.3.3 The intermediation–disintermediation–reintermediation cycle

The *intermediation-disintermediation-reintermediation (IDR) cycle* is an approach that describes traditional industry structures by e-Business [Chircu 1999a, 1999b, 2000a, 2000b]. This approach comprises the following three steps:

1. Internet-based intermediaries interject themselves among buyers and suppliers, and possibly among other intermediaries as well (intermediation).
2. Established 'middlemen' are pushed out of their market niche (disintermediation).
3. Finally, these disenfranchised players recapture their position by combining leveragable specialized assets with technological innovation (reintermediation).

This shows that the long-term effects that e-Business has on market structures are different from what happens within a shorter period. And what is more, this cycle is permanently repeated because innovation is a continuous process.

In order to establish the strategies available to electronic intermediaries, a number of miniature case studies, studying the IDR cycle in the fields of financial services, retail (books, CDs and cars), real estate, and collector goods, were considered [Chircu 2000b]. These identified four major competitive strategies:

1. Partnering for application development – This involves electronic intermediaries forming alliances with established industry participants. The right combination of industry expertise and technology may generate a sustainable competitive advantage. Moreover, it facilitates risk management for the development of large and complex Internet applications. This strategy may be applied to new services, for which there are as yet no intermediaries.
2. Partnering for access – Electronic intermediaries contract for exclusivity agreements with high-traffic websites. The choice of partner is of crucial importance to this strategy's success. Since it can easily be imitated, it is unlikely that this strategy will lead to a sustainable competitive advantage.
3. Partnering for content – To do so, electronic intermediaries must become aggregators of products and information. For example, AutoByTel maintains large databases of available cars, a 'virtual' product variety that increases every dealer's chances of selling cars. Automobile dealers then pay AutoByTel fees to be listed on their website and when they receive orders through such listings. Such aggregation is a typical first mover strategy. It is so easily imitated that no sustainable competitive advantage can be expected to be derived from it.
4. Technology licensing – This involves providing technology services to other agents. Amazon.com, for example, allows external websites to open bookstores using Amazon technology. The licensed website simply links to Amazon.com, which charges fees for the purchase requests generated for downstream vendors.

Each of these strategies obviously requires a different mix of capabilities and environmental conditions. And another thing these strategy descriptions show is that e-Business innovations generally do not yield sustainable competitive advantages. Success requires vision, marketing skills, operational and corporate finance capabilities, as well as the luck of doing things in the right place and at the right time. However, information technology may help companies use their critical resources to generate sustainable competitive advantages. Furthermore, achieving long-term competitiveness in e-Commerce requires that companies either develop the relevant complementary assets or gain control over them, which these strategies may help them do. Finally, digital intermediaries must continually update their organizational skills, resources and functional competence. If they do not, they are in danger of losing the advantages they have gained [Teece 1997], and therefore continuous updating must become part of the company culture.

The major contribution of the IDR cycle, however, is the identification of three factors, which generally cause reintermediation to fail:

1. Strategic uncertainty, because of the company's inability to determine its key mission in the presence of rapid technological change – Traditional companies are often unwilling to commit themselves to new, technology-enabled business models. They often doubt their applicability both to their customers' needs and to their own current strategy. This attitude is reinforced by uncertainty about the new market and future profits.
2. The transformation of value creation - In the retail brokerage industry, for example, customer demand has been unbundled. No longer do all brokerage customers consider 'advice' a necessary ingredient of

their consumption bundle; many want only transaction processing. Intermediaries who still focus on their traditional qualities no longer add value like they used to.

3. The forces of digital convergence – In many industries, companies' converging capabilities are a strategic market imperative in an era dominated by innovations based on information technology [Prahalad 1998]. The market effects of technological innovation are beginning to overlap. Therefore, many re-intermediating companies will probably be unable to anticipate the next strategic challenge, because they do not know from which angle to expect it. Challenges can come from technology providers, from generic e-Business-only companies or from other large traditional participants without experience of a specific product or marketplace.

11.4 Chapter summary

This chapter presents different views on how the Internet will affect intermediaries, defines and classifies intermediaries and analyzes possible dynamics involving intermediaries in the value chain caused by the Internet. Following Spulber [Spulber 1996] we define an intermediary as an economic agent that buys from suppliers in order to resell to customers, or that helps consumers and suppliers to meet and transact.

Within the above definition of intermediaries, there are two major kinds of intermediaries: those who move, store and deliver physical goods and services, and those who provide information and information services, usually relating to those physical goods and services. The information business is a different issue altogether. It involves capturing and manipulating information in such a way that value is added for one's clients, who include buyers as well as sellers. Such intermediaries are often called *infomediaries*, and their line of business is the transaction channel. Stockbrokerage and market making are examples of such activities.

Business literature furnishes several lists of intermediaries' value-adding functions. According to their economic implications they may be grouped into four broad categories: pricing, inventory holding, transaction coordinating and performance monitoring. The coordinating role intermediaries play in the exchange process consists of many different functions. Electronic services provided through the Internet have different consequences for each of these functions. For example, network-based services may facilitate product search, but they are less well equipped to offer product distribution (except of course in the case of information and software products). So the Internet does not influence all intermediary services to an equal extent or in the same way. For infomediaries, several services have been suggested as specifically well suited, such as search, matching, informational services etc.

Originally it was believed that electronic markets would cause massive disintermediation; displacement or elimination of market intermediaries, enabling direct trade between suppliers and buyers. However disintermediation is only one possibility; others are the internet-supplemented direct market, cyberintermediaries, and the internet-supplemented intermediaries. Also the fact that intermediaries offer multiple services instead of one single service has been underestimated. Therefore, the effects of the diffusion of electronic commerce on each of the intermediation services have to be studied before one can draw conclusions about e-Commerce and the structure of intermediation based on their relative importance.

The intermediation–disintermediation–reintermediation (IDR) cycle is an approach that stresses the dynamics in the development of industry structures. This approach comprises the following three steps:

1. Internet-based intermediaries interject themselves among buyers and suppliers, and possibly among other intermediaries as well (intermediation).
2. Established 'middlemen' are pushed out of their market niche (disintermediation).
3. Finally, these disenfranchised players recapture their position by combining leveragable specialized assets with technological innovation (reintermediation).

The IDR cycle shows that the long-term effects that e-Business has on market structures are different from what happens within a shorter period. And what is more, this cycle is permanently repeated because innovation is a continuous process.

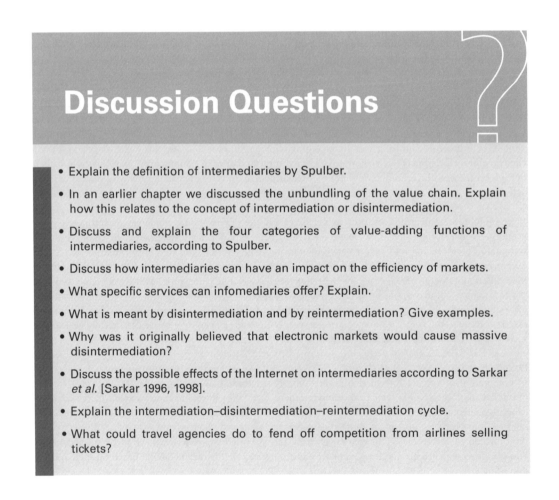

Discussion Questions

- Explain the definition of intermediaries by Spulber.

- In an earlier chapter we discussed the unbundling of the value chain. Explain how this relates to the concept of intermediation or disintermediation.

- Discuss and explain the four categories of value-adding functions of intermediaries, according to Spulber.

- Discuss how intermediaries can have an impact on the efficiency of markets.

- What specific services can infomediaries offer? Explain.

- What is meant by disintermediation and by reintermediation? Give examples.

- Why was it originally believed that electronic markets would cause massive disintermediation?

- Discuss the possible effects of the Internet on intermediaries according to Sarkar *et al.* [Sarkar 1996, 1998].

- Explain the intermediation–disintermediation–reintermediation cycle.

- What could travel agencies do to fend off competition from airlines selling tickets?

Assignments

i. Analyze the supply chain of the music industry (CDs etc). Find information using the Internet and business publications:

- Describe its configuration.
- List the intermediaries.
- How do new Internet-based intermediaries add value to both their customers and their suppliers?

ii. Select a 'physical goods' supply chain (e.g. automotive) and analyze it according to the questions under (1). What differences do you notice compared to (1)?

iii. An insurance company active on the b2b market (especially SMEs) considers selling products online and/or through intermediaries. Discuss the major arguments for both alternatives. Should the insurance company choose one channel (e.g. online selling) or can it use both channels?

iv. Analyze the supply chain of the publishing industry (in particular: scientific journals). Find information using the Internet and business publications:

- Describe its configuration.
- List the intermediaries.
- How do new Internet-based intermediaries add value to both their customers and their suppliers?

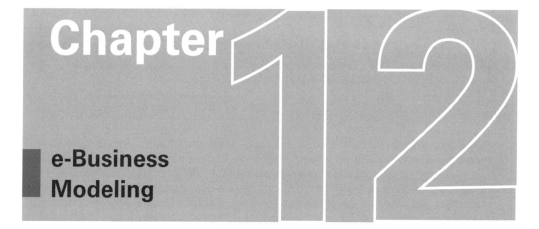

Chapter 12

e-Business Modeling

e-Business initiatives expose enterprise key processes beyond the boundary of the corporation itself into an ever-wider audience – customers, suppliers, partners, brokers, and competitors – on a global scale. This has resulted in considerable progress being made in building and deploying complex systems for business process automation. One of the most important decisions that application developers need to make is deploying the right system for the right type of business work. Very often solutions are quickly sketched (if at all) before they are designed and implemented, and once deployed they solve only a limited and specific type of problem. Understanding where systems are being deployed, how they need to integrate with other existing systems and what types of business tasks they automate is crucial to the success of e-Business. This is usually accomplished by *business modeling*, which is a technique to model the characteristics and behavior of business processes. The world of e-Business represents a serious opportunity to rethink the traditional application software modeling and development processes. In particular, this should include careful validation of business requirements through formal modeling techniques.

The primary purpose of this chapter is to equip readers with an understanding of what is required for modeling e-Business environments and processes. We shall concentrate on e-Business modeling techniques and methodologies and examine the various relevant topics associated with the modeling and delivery of e-Business applications based on standardized formal modeling techniques. For this purpose we first introduce the notions of business modeling and collaborative business processes and then focus on the use of the Unified Modeling Language (UML)to address business process modeling. We also present standard business methodologies, such as the UN/CEFACT Modeling Methodology, the Supply-Chain Operations Reference model and the Business Process Modeling Notation to model e-Business processes and supply-chain applications.

Case Study

Intel – Experience with the supply-chain operations reference model

SCOR (see Section 12.5) is a cross-industry, standardized supply-chain reference model for analyzing and improving supply-chain operations. Intel applied SCOR methodology on supply-chain projects within specific Intel business groups, in the process evolving a SCOR best known method (BKM) [Intel 2002]. Intel noticed that in several cases its supply chains were not as cost effective and/or customer responsive as required for a growing, high-volume business. Intel's traditional business model did not always support certain new segment needs and some of the current 'work around' processes are not efficient or robust. Hence, Intel launched its first SCOR project to identify areas for improvement in customer service and internal supply-chain efficiency. The intent of the project was to pilot the use of SCOR methodology and tool(s) within Intel and to establish guidelines for its use.

The pilot project's deliverables included documenting the business's supply chain and the supply-chain process improvement efforts that were in place, identifying short-term improvements, getting the appropriate level of support and identifying owners for long-term improvements. Additional deliverables included a summary of the project's findings and what was learned from using SCOR methodology and tools, along with guiding principles for applying SCOR to similar businesses.

The models employed to support the SCOR methodology were not classical process decomposition models, but archetypical models representing supply-chain process patterns that can be applied to configure and reconfigure the supply chain. Using SCOR as a reference model provided a balanced, horizontal view across all of the operation's processes. At the highest level, the SCOR methodology assumed material flow between entities within the supply chain, which requires modeling of organizations by geography and function, relative to components within product hierarchies. At its lowest level, the SCOR model facilitated representation of the process context for information flow between roles in inter- and intra-enterprise transactions, which is dependant on role-based organizational models to support the process modeling.

The application of the SCOR model resulted in providing a mechanism for Intel to benchmark across its industry and a standard means for identifying performance improvements. It also helped with aligning performance metrics at both a strategic and operational level and establishing a standard for communicating internal and external supply-chain requirements. Finally, the SCOR model equipped Intel with a structured way for diagnosing the supply chain and identifying supply-chain improvements.

Using SCOR in this case resulted in recommendations supported by a quantifiable business case. As a result, management endorsed some key programs that were at that time under way and authorized 'Go do' actions.

Intel's experience in SCOR modeling encouraged it to extend supply-chain modeling that was based on SCOR to modeling the e-Business scenarios that were recommended as high-priority improvement projects.

12.1 Business modeling

Developers and business analysts who build complex structures or systems have been creating models of what they build. The term *model* could be defined as an abstract representation of the real world that reduces complexity and represents only the details necessary for a specific purpose. Developing enterprise-wide models prior to coding applications provides a conceptual 'blueprint' that ensures that business users and software developers have a common understanding of the systems to be developed. Enterprises model complex software applications for the same reason that they hire architects to design buildings before actually having them built. In the long run a detailed blueprint saves time and money. Modeling allows developers to consider alternatives, select the best option, work out details, and achieve agreement before application developers start building an application.

Modeling is the designing of software applications before coding. Modeling is an essential part of any large software project, as it plays the analogous role in software development that blueprints and other plans (site maps, elevations, physical models) play in the construction of an office building. Using a model, software developers can assure themselves that business functionality is complete and correct, end-user needs are met, and program design supports requirements for scalability, robustness, security, extendibility, before implementation in code renders changes difficult and expensive to make.

Modeling the enterprise uses a systems approach. Generally, a system is defined as a set of elements, characterized by interrelations, with a common objective. Following the systems approach modeling first requires a definition of the system boundaries, which answers the questions about what is considered to be internal to the system that has to be modeled, and what is considered as the environment. Next the components of the system (the subsystems) and their interrelationships have to be determined. This is called decomposition of the system. Decomposition reduces complexity and results in a workable overview (model) of the system. Interrelationships between subsystems may be physical, e.g. exchange of goods from one production unit to another, or informational, e.g. decisions or general information passed from one decision unit to another. Exchange of data between subsystems can be modeled as communication (exchange of messages). Also the relationship between the focal system and its environment consists of physical and/or information exchanges, which form either an input to the system or an output from the system to the environment.

The systems approach helps to move from higher to lower levels of analysis, which is necessary to develop a good understanding of the reality that is being modeled. Following two principles reduces real-life complexity: subsystems are considered as black boxes and modeling follows a top-down pattern. Treating subsystems as black boxes helps us to concentrate on relations between subsystems, and not be confused by the internal specifics of each subsystem. Following the top-down approach, once higher level subsystems and their relations have been identified, allows the further decomposition of each subsystem to lower levels of analysis.

Business process models define how business processes are described. Business processes represent the artifacts of electronic business and can be represented using *modeling tools*. The specification for business process definition enables an enterprise to express its business processes so that they are understandable by other enterprises. Business process models specify business processes that allow business partners to collaborate. This enables the integration of business processes within an enterprise or between enterprises.

Depending on the type of activity and the industry in which they operate, business organizations will differ or share specific characteristics. For example viewed on an organizational level a hospital is different from a manufacturing company and differs from a financial institute. Viewed on a process level (or activity level) a buying or ordering process is typically present in almost any type of organization, like manufacturing, trade or municipal organizations. Similarities between organizations can be used to improve the efficiency of the modeling activity by creating so-called *reference models*. Reference models are representations of particular types of organizations that help to decompose organizations into subsystems and to identify critical information systems.

A *modeling methodology* sets out a procedure that should be followed to ensure consistent production and delivery of results. It specifies activities to be performed, roles of participants, techniques to be used and deliverables to be produced. Its use is normally supported by the use of computer-aided tools. A methodology is used to enable e-Business application users and developer groups to adopt a common approach to specification of business requirements and data so that they can be shared within an enterprise and provided externally in a consistent manner.

Business modeling is a modeling methodology for business processes. Business process models provide a means of expressing business processes in terms of business activities and collaborative behavior. Business modeling involves designing processes at both the enterprise level and across entire supply chains to take advantage of Internet connectivity.

Business models come in two main flavors: descriptive (or non-normative) and normative. Descriptive models are models where the real world is simply 'described'. A *descriptive model* limits the types of objects, relationships and properties to be identified and modeled, but does not limit the modeler in how they go about mapping these concepts to the domain of investigation. In short, the descriptive modeler can freely choose and name the objects perceived, their relationships and which properties to capture. As such, descriptive models offer a great deal of freedom and flexibility to the modeler. In contrast, a *normative model* restricts how the system being examined can be represented. A normative model forces modelers to select from a prespecified set of constructs and essentially map the perceived system into this prespecified set. This substantially reduces the flexibility and freedom (and variety) of models produced. However, it yields models that are rigorous, improves consistency and reduces representational complexity. In this chapter we shall introduce several normative models for e-Business including the Unified Modeling Language, the UN/CEFACT modeling methodology, the Supply-Chain Operations Reference model and the Business Process Modeling Notation.

In addition to normative models, visual modeling becomes essential in the face of increasingly complex systems for e-Business applications. As the complexity of a system increases, so does the importance of good modeling techniques. Visual (or graphical) models allow different stakeholders to view the system from different angles and communicate their perspectives with each other [RUP 2001]. Using a rigorous modeling language standard is one essential ingredient for the success of a modeling technique. In this chapter we illustrate how to effectively use the Unified Modeling Language, the Supply-Chain Operations Reference model and the Business Process Modeling Notation to develop business models that reflect activities in integrated value chains and thus span multiple enterprises.

12.2 Business processes and collaborations

In Chapter 4 we introduced the concept of business processes and argued that the ability to rationalize and streamline business processes – especially those concerned with customer service, product management, order processing, and supply-chain management – creates opportunities to improve customer service and reduce costs. Process improvement and rationalization is particularly necessary prior to implementation of e-Business solutions. For instance, it could be a very important element in the case of sales and service, participation in marketplace exchanges, or supply-chain integration with trading partners. This requires collaboration between otherwise independent business processes.

Collaborative processes span multiple enterprises. A business collaboration activity is a predefined set of activities and/or processes of partners that is initiated by a partner to accomplish an explicitly shared business goal and terminated upon recognition of one of the agreed conclusions by all the involved partners. Business information is gathered for the purpose of specifying business collaboration activities in terms of goals, requirements, and constraints: for instance, supply-chain management extending across several layers of an industry or customer relationship management mobilizing a broad range of specialized third parties to support the customer.

Collaboration between processes is related to strategic relationships (Section 4.3.2) and has far-reaching implications regarding collaboration between diverse departments and organizations and implies joint decision making. Business modeling is frequently used for analyzing process interrelations, and the impact of making strategic-level changes regarding collaborative processes in the supply chain.

A *collaborative process* is a process that is implicit in the behavior and interaction between multiple business entities described as having different roles. A business entity may perform more than one role, but these will typically represent different business function responsibilities within the entity, e.g. an entity might have the role of both seller and creditor. The collaborative process is controlled only by the intentional conformance of the independent entities to an agreed-upon exchange of messages. Business goals, requirements and constraints are expressed in formal representations that can be understood and confirmed by the business environment experts. Business collaboration activities can be specified by a business process analyst as use cases, requirements and business object flow graphs that define the choreography of business processes. This is explained in the following section.

The activities of a collaborative process are the actions performed by the participating business entities in response to messages they receive from other participating entities. For example, a collaborative process definition might specify the exchange of messages between two entities to perform the purchase of a product and arrange for payment and shipping. A collaborative process activity will normally be implemented by activities of a private business process. The order message is received by an activity in the seller's internal (private) business process. This activity may then cause other activities and potentially subprocesses to take appropriate action on the order. An internal business process might implement the order processing of the seller to cause the order to be validated, payment terms to be accepted, the product to be produced, packaged and shipped, and the invoice to be generated. The negotiation of payment terms could involve another collaborative process with a financial institution. When the seller's process has determined that the order is acceptable and assigned a price and delivery date, another activity will send a response message. The sending activity is then complete and may cause another activity to wait for the buyer's acceptance of the price and date. Similar actions may occur for each activity in the collaborative process.

12.3 Business modeling with UML

The Unified Modeling Language defines a standard language and graphical notation for creating models of business and technical systems. UML defines model types that span a range from functional requirements and activity workflow models to class structure design and component diagrams. These models, and a development process that uses them, improve and simplify communication among an application's many diverse stakeholders. Modeling e-Business applications with UML reveals how to create complex Web applications and achieve business-to-business application integration.

UML allows an application model to be constructed, viewed, developed, and manipulated in a standard way at analysis and design time. Just as blueprints represent the design for an office building, UML models represent the design for an application, allowing business functionality and behavior to be represented clearly by business experts at the first stage of development in an environment undistorted by computing technology.

In the following section we will present several UML constructs that help develop business process models. This section is not intended to teach UML to the reader, it simply provides a high-level introduction to the most widely used diagrams in UML as used throughout this book. For a comprehensive coverage of UML we direct the interested reader to [Booch 1998]. This section assumes that you have a rudimentary understanding of object-oriented design. Readers who need a little assistance with object-oriented concepts might find the Sun brief tutorial on Object-Oriented Programming quite useful.

(http://java.sun.com/docs/books/tutorial/java/concepts/)

UML diagrams, which are often proposed for business process modeling, are the Class diagrams, Activity diagrams, Use Case diagrams, Sequence diagrams and Deployment diagrams. A Class diagram describes the static structure in a business. A Use Case diagram describes the business context and shows processes in a non-sequential representation. An Activity diagram describes the behavior of the business, or business workflows, in a manner similar to a flowchart. A Sequence diagram describes the dynamic interactions between employees and the items they manipulate. Consequently, it indicates how the behaviors described in activity diagrams are realized. Finally, the Deployment diagram shows how a system will be physically deployed in its implementation environment.

In the following we shall utilize a high-level definition of a supply-chain management application in the domain of manufacturing to exemplify the above constructs. This example was adapted from [WS-I 2002].

The application being modeled is that of a computer manufacturer offering computer devices to consumers via its Website, a typical business to consumer model. To fulfill orders the manufacturer interacts with several subcontractors, which each specialize in the production of specific computer-related devices (e.g. computer chips, keyboards, monitors). When an order comes in, the manufacturer contacts the relevant subcontractors to order the component parts. The manufacturer itself does not manage stock in warehouses; rather, parts are ordered in a just-in-time fashion (a typical e-Business model) and assembled upon receipt. In order to fulfill the manufacturer's request a subcontractor may have to execute a production run to build the component part(s). This is the case when the ordered part(s) are not currently in stock or the stock levels fall below a certain threshold. In both scenarios the subcontractor ships the ordered computer part(s) to the manufacturer once they are available. Subsequently, the manufacturer assembles the parts in its factory and the end product, the computer, is shipped to the customer.

12.3.1 Class diagrams

The purpose of the *class diagram* is to show the static structure of the system being modeled. The diagram specifically shows the entities in the system together with each entity's internal structure and its relationships with other entities in the system. Because class diagrams only model the static structure of a system, only types of entities are shown on a class diagram; specific instances are not shown. Class diagrams are particularly useful for business modeling. Business analysts can use class diagrams to model a business's current assets and resources, such as account ledgers, products, or geographic hierarchy.

A UML class diagram can be constructed to represent the elements, relationships, and constraints of an XML vocabulary visually. Class diagrams allow complex vocabularies to be shared with non-technical business stakeholders. In the following we summarize the primary elements of a UML class diagram to facilitate understanding of the examples that follow:

- Class: a class represents an aggregation of structural features and defines a namespace for those feature names. The class diagram for the computer manufacturer system in Figure 12.1 defines 10 classes.

- Attribute: each class may optionally define a set of attributes. Each attribute has a type; in the class diagram for the computer manufacturer system in Figure 12.1, string, double, integer and non-negative integer refer to the built-in data types as defined by the XML Schema specification.

- Operation: operations define what can be done to objects of the class, in addition to defining the structure of the data for these objects.

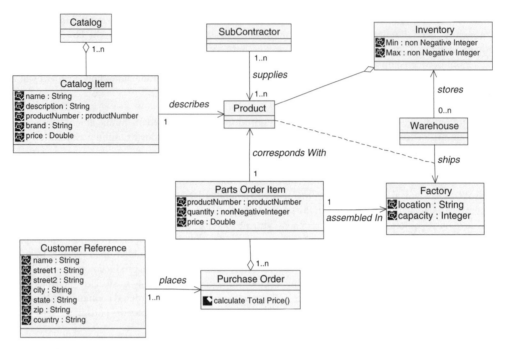

Figure 12.1: Class Diagram for the Computer Manufacturer System

- Association: an association relates two or more classes in a model. If an association has an arrow on one end, it means that the association is usually navigated in one direction and provides a hint to the design and implementation of this vocabulary.

- Role and Multiplicity: the end of an association may specify the role of the class. This is conventional for a bidirectional association and is indicated by a solid line between the two classes. At either end of the line, we place a role name, e.g. describes, places, stores, ships, etc., in Figure 12.1, and a multiplicity value.

- Inheritance: this refers to the ability of one class (child class) to inherit the identical functionality of another class (super class), and then add new functionality of its own. To model inheritance on a class diagram, a solid line is drawn from the child class (the class inheriting the behavior) with a closed arrowhead (or triangle) pointing to the super class.

- Aggregation: this is a special type of relationship used to model a 'whole to its parts' relationship. In basic aggregation relationships, the lifecycle of a part class is independent from the whole class's lifecycle. To represent an aggregation relationship, one draws a solid line from the parent class to the subordinate class, and an unfilled diamond shape on the parent class's association end.

The class diagram in Figure 12.1 describes the different types of objects and data elements involved in the computer manufacturer system and the relationships that exist among them. It serves to define the vocabulary of the system and helps to define the schemas. The class diagram in Figure 12.1 is a conceptual diagram and is not meant to impose any structure on implementations.

This diagram distinguishes 10 classes for the computer manufacturer system. For instance, the class 'Customer Reference' describes the data structure for customer reference objects, consisting of attributes like 'name', 'street1' and 'country'. An example of an operation can be found in the class 'Purchase Order', where the operation 'calculateTotalPrice' determines the overall price of the order based upon the prices of the ordered parts. The diagram also illustrates several associations, for example between 'Catalog Item' and 'Product' expressing that each catalog item describes exactly one product (i.e. the multiplicity of the association is 1). An aggregation relationship exists between 'Catalog' and 'Catalog Item'. This depicts that a catalog consists of catalog items. An interesting association exists between 'Warehouse' and 'Factory', where class 'Product' is associated with the association between these two classes. Here 'Product' functions as an association class, expressing the fact that the warehouse of the SubContractor ships products to the factory of the Manufacturer.

12.3.2 Activity diagrams

The purpose of the *activity diagram* is to model the procedural flow of actions that are part of a larger activity. In projects in which use cases are present, activity diagrams can model a specific use case at a more detailed level. However, activity diagrams can be used independently of use cases for modeling a business-level function, such as buying electronic goods or ordering a product. Activity diagrams can also be used to model system-level functions, such as how a ticket reservation data mart populates a corporate sales system's data warehouse. Because it models procedural flow, the activity diagram focuses on the action sequence of execution and the conditions that trigger or guard those actions. The activity diagram is also focused only on the activity's internal actions and not on the actions that call the activity in their process flow or that trigger the activity according to some event [Bell 2003].

The activity diagram in Figure 12.2 checks inventory, ships orders and updates the inventory or manufactures parts (use case UC4 in Figure 12.3) for the SubContractor. This activity diagram is based on a high-level definition of a Supply-Chain Management application in the form of a set of use cases proposed by Web Services-Interoperability Organization (www.ws-i.org) to demonstrate the use of scenarios in the Web Services-Interoperability Basic Profile [Anderson 2003].

In Figure 12.2, upon receipt the order is first validated. If it is incorrect, then a fault is reported and the system exits. Otherwise, the SubContractor checks for the ordered part and its current inventory level to determine whether it can fulfill the order. If not, a production order is issued and the SubContractor waits until production has been completed. Once this is the case, then the SubContractor ships all the finished goods to the Manufacturer's factory and sends the factory a shipping notification. Finally, the SubContractor updates its parts' inventory level based on the quantity being shipped. If the quantity of goods is found to be below the minimum threshold, then more are manufactured.

12.3.3 Use case diagrams

A use case illustrates a unit of functionality provided by the system. The main purpose of the *use case diagram* is to help development teams visualize the functional requirements of a system, including the relationship of 'actors' (human beings who will interact with the system) to essential processes, as well as the relationships among different use cases. Use case diagrams generally show groups of use cases – either all use cases for the

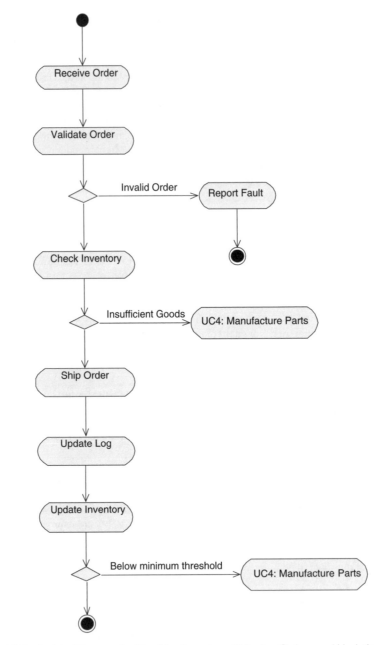

■ **Figure 12.2:** Activity Diagram for Checking Inventory, Shipping Orders and Updating the Inventory

complete system, or a breakout of a particular group of use cases with related functionality (e.g. all security administration-related use cases).

Figure 12.3 shows a number of use cases for the computer manufacturer system. As can be seen from this figure, there are three actors involved: the Customer, the Manufacturer and the SubContractor. The Customer and Manufacturer interact in use cases UC1 and UC2 for the purchasing and delivery of goods. In UC3 the Manufacturer interacts with the SubContractor to order the necessary computer parts. These are subsequently produced by the SubContractor in UC4, the manufacturing of parts, and shipped to the Manufacturer in UC5.

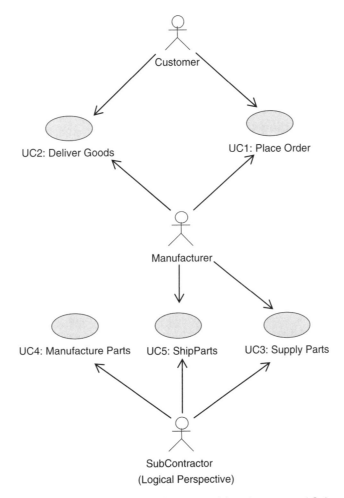

■ **Figure 12.3:** Use Case Diagram of Customer, Manufacturer and Subcontractor

12.3.4 Sequence diagrams

Sequence diagrams show a detailed flow for a specific use case or even just part of a specific use case. They show the calls between the different objects in their sequence and can show, at a detailed level, different calls to different objects. A sequence diagram has two dimensions: The vertical dimension shows the sequence of messages/calls in the time order that they occur, while the horizontal dimension shows the object instances to which the messages are sent.

Figure 12.4 shows a possible sequence of interactions between the Manufacturer and the SubContractor for use case UC3, the supplying of parts. The Manufacturer initiates the interaction by sending a 'partsOrder'. In response the SubContractor validates the order and, once it is correct, orders its Warehouse to ship the ordered part(s). Subsequently, the Warehouse checks its inventory, gathers the requested part(s) and sends them to the Factory of the Manufacturer. The Factory then confirms shipment to the Warehouse and to the Manufacturer. Finally, the Warehouse relays this response to the SubContractor in the form of a 'shipPartsResponse' statement. Observe that the diagram could be much more complex, for instance, by including the possibility that the parts are not currently in stock, as expressed by the activity diagram in Figure 12.2. In that case a number of interactions would take place between the SubContractor and the Warehouse to produce these parts.

12.3.5 Deployment diagram

A deployment diagram shows how a system will be physically deployed in the target environment. Its purpose is to show where the different components of the system will physically run and how they will communicate with each other.

The deployment diagram in Figure 12.5 depicts a conceptual view of an example implementation of the computer manufacturer system. As the figure shows, the major functions of each actor in the system have been represented as component services. An example is the factory service in the Manufacturer System. This service interacts with the SubContractor System, to be precise with the Warehouse Service, representing the interaction between the Computer Manufacturer and the SubContractor regarding the delivery of ordered computer part(s).

12.3.6 Business process modeling with UML 2.0

Owing to recent advances in component-based development for enterprise applications, the propagation of environments such as J2EE and .NET and the common use of more mature modeling languages, such as the Specification and Description Language [IEC 2000] and the Real-Time Object-Oriented Modeling language [Selic 1994], to specify components and system architectures for real-time applications, UML has lately undergone a major revision advancing from version 1.4 to version 2.0 [OMG 2004].

The major improvements to UML 2.0 include, but are not limited to, support for component-based development via composite structures; hierarchical decomposition of structure and behavior; cross-integration of structure and behavior; integration of action semantics with behavioral constructs; and a layered architecture to facilitate incremental implementation and compliance testing [Kobryn 2004]. Cumulatively these improvements increase the precision and expressiveness of UML so that it can be effectively used to model large, complex architectures and business processes. In the following, we shall confine ourselves to the description of UML 2.0 constructs which can be used in the context of enterprise modeling and in particular of modeling business process interactions. Interested readers can refer to [OMG 2004] for a full description of the UML 2.0 specification.

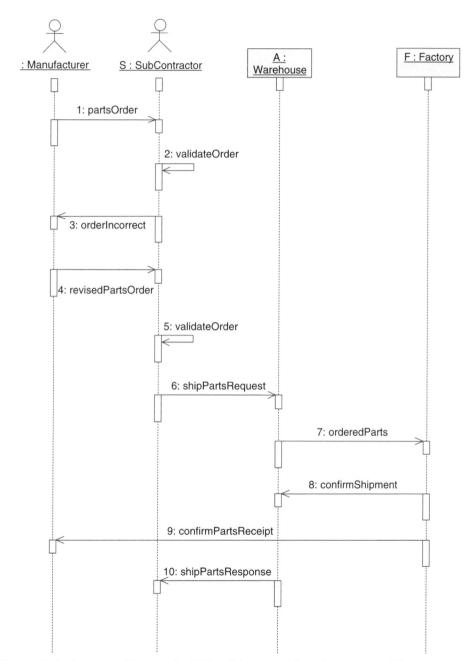

■ **Figure 12.4:** Sequence Diagram for UC5 – Shipment of Parts between the Manufacturer and the SubContractor

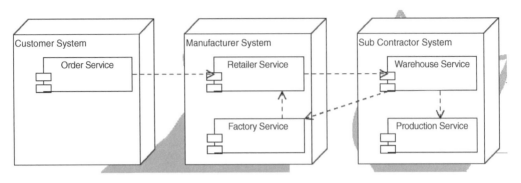

■ **Figure 12.5:** Computer Manufacturer System Deployment Diagram

One of the most important improvements in UML 2.0, which is of particular importance to e-Business modeling, is that it specifies dynamic behavioral constructs, such as activities, actions, interactions and state machines that can used in various behavioral diagrams, such as activity diagrams, sequence diagrams, and state machine diagrams. Such behavioral constructs are of prime importance when modeling business processes.

An *action* is the fundamental unit of behavior specification. An action takes a set of inputs and converts them into a set of outputs. In addition, some actions modify the state of the system in which the action executes. The values that are the inputs to an action may be obtained from the results of other actions using the activity flow model or they may be described by value specifications. The outputs of the action may be provided as inputs to other actions using the activity flow model.

Actions are contained in activities, which provide their context. *Activities* provide control and data sequencing constraints among actions as well as nested structuring mechanisms for control and scope. An action execution corresponds to the execution of a particular action within an activity. Each action in an activity may execute zero, one, or more times for each activity execution.

Activity modeling emphasizes the sequence and conditions for coordinating lower level behaviors, rather than which structural constructs, such as classes or components, own those behaviors. These are commonly called control flow and object flow models. The actions coordinated by activity models can be initiated because other actions finish executing, objects and data become available, or events occur external to the flow. Consequently, an activity diagram depicts behavior using control and data-flow modeling constructs.

The UML 2 activity models follow traditional control and data-flow approaches by initiating sub-behaviors according to when others finish and when inputs are available. The approach of UML 2 to behavioral semantics is to define abstract virtual machines based on the routing of control and data through a graph of nodes connected by directed edges [Bock 2003]. Each node and edge defines when control and data values move through it. These token movement rules can be combined to predict the behavior of the entire graph.

There are three kinds of node in activity models [Bock 2003]:

1. An action node, which operates on control and data values it receives, and provides control and data to other actions.
2. A control node, which is an activity node used to coordinate the flows between other nodes. It comprises an initial node, a final node, a fork node, a join node, a decision node and a merge node. Control nodes route control and data tokens through the graph. These include constructs for choosing between alternative flows (decision points), for proceeding along multiple flows in parallel (forks), and so on.
3. An object node that holds data tokens temporarily as they wait to move through the graph.

Figure 12.6 illustrates the following kinds of activity node: action nodes (e.g. Receive Order, Fill Order), object nodes (Invoice), and control nodes (the initial node before Receive Order, the decision node after Receive Order, and the fork node and join node around Ship Order, merge node before Close Order, and activity final node after Close Order). Decision nodes and merge nodes in this figure are represented using a diamond-shaped symbol, while forks and joins are represented by vertical bars. Edges in this figure represent control flow. The entry into a flow is depicted by a solid black circle; whereas, the final node of a flow is depicted as usual as a solid circle within a hollow circle (bull's eye). Each edge can be annotated with a guard condition, which must be satisfied in order for the transition to take place.

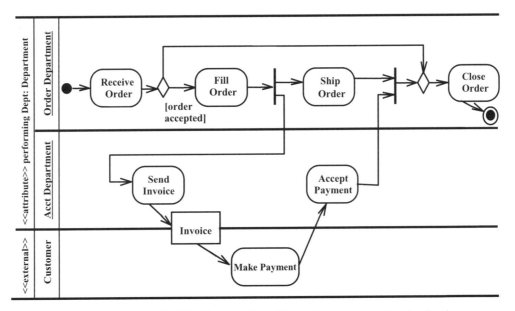

■ **Figure 12.6:** An Activity Diagram for a Simple Order-processing Application

The execution semantics of action and control nodes in a UML 2.0 activity diagram are summarized as follows.

An action node can execute when a control token arrives at one of its incoming edges. In other words an action node possesses XOR semantics. It places a control token on its single outgoing edge, which has a guard condition that is always true.

A decision node can execute when a control token arrives at its single incoming edge. It places a control token on exactly one of its outgoing edges (XOR semantics), namely, the one edge whose guard condition is satisfied. This semantics assumes the guard conditions of all outgoing edges of a decision node are mutually exclusive and exhaustive.

A merge node is a control node that brings together multiple alternate flows. It is not used to synchronize concurrent flows but to accept one among several alternate flows. Thus its execution semantics are the same as in the case of an action node.

A fork node is a control node (is a workflow construct) that splits a flow into multiple concurrent flows. A fork node has one incoming edge and multiple outgoing edges. It can execute after a token arrives on its single incoming edge. It places control tokens on all of its outgoing edges (AND semantics) and thereby starts parallel executions of flows. We assume that outgoing edges of forks are only annotated with guard conditions that are true.

A join node is a control node (is a workflow construct) that synchronizes multiple flows. A join node has multiple incoming edges and one outgoing edge. It can execute when control tokens arrive on all of its incoming edges (AND semantics). It places a control token on its single outgoing edge.

Based on the execution semantics that we examined previously, we can now interpret the context of the activity diagram depicted in Figure 12.6. An initial node, shown in the upper left of this figure, triggers the Receive Order action. A decision node after Receive Order illustrates branching based on order rejected or order accepted conditions. Fill Order is followed by a fork node which passes control both to Send Invoice and Ship Order. The join node indicates that control will be passed to the merge when both Ship Order and Accept Payment are completed. Since a merge will just pass the token along, Close Order activity will be invoked (control is also passed to Close Order whenever an order is rejected). When Close Order is completed, control passes to an activity final.

UML 2.0 activity and use case diagrams can be used to model business processes and facilitate the representation of the process context for information flow between roles in inter- and intra-enterprise transactions, such as the ones involved in the Intel case study that we examined at the outset of this chapter.

12.4 Business process modeling methodologies

A *process-centric company* is an organization whose managers conceptualize it as a set of business processes. Most process-centric companies, like most traditional organizations, still have departments and divisions. Unlike traditional organizations, however, process-centric companies place their primary emphasis on maximizing the efficiency of processes, and not on maximizing the efficiency of departmental or functional units [Harmon 2003a]. In effect, departments or functions contribute employees, knowledge and management skills to processes. Departments perform activities or even manage entire subprocesses. They also maintain functional standards and evaluate employees. The sales department, for example, hires sales people and manages and evaluates their performance. Ultimately, however, the core business processes are managed and evaluated as wholes, and departments are rewarded for their effective contributions to successful processes.

Modeling the processes of an enterprise captures corporate knowledge. To be stored, maintained and exploited, this kind of knowledge needs to be structured and formatted. A business process model is a powerful tool for structuring and formatting enterprise-related information. Process models are the cornerstones for the modeling and eventual development of e-Business applications. Such models can be used to define amongst other things standardized operating procedures, to analyze the structuring of value chains, to create a shared understanding of how a business functions, or even just to test assumptions. Detailed business process models allow analysts to visualize, analyze and improve processes, so that e-Business workflow implementations are tested before design and implementation. Virtually all enterprises are using process modeling techniques before making actual investments in e-Business application or system implementations. A major advantage of a formalized business process model is the guarantee that processes will be executed in a repeatable, consistent and precise way. Errors are avoided and customers do not get frustrated. Every process instance follows the same rules of execution.

One immediate advantage of business process models is the visibility of the business rules, which makes it easier to adapt them to changing market conditions, and a shared understanding of what functions are supported by the enterprise, and how these are supported. *Business rules* are precise statements that describe, constrain and control the structure, operations and strategies of an enterprise. Most of them take the natural form of if [conditions] then [actions] that can be easily created and understood. Business rules are found everywhere in the enterprise as they express its peculiarities, its originality and its values. Business rules can express pricing and billing policies, quality of service, process flow – where they describe routing decisions, actor assignment policies, etc. – regulations, and so on. Business rules define what must be done within an organization in general and they include among other things typical business situations such as escalation 'send this document to a supervisor for approval', managing exceptions 'this loan is more than $250K, send it to the CFO', and progression assurance 'make sure that we deal with this within 30 mins or as specified in the customer's service-level agreement'. For instance, an online hotel reservation service may entail an availability notification message that is often sent in conjunction with two other messages: a message that communicates the rates that apply to the availability, and a message that communicates the restrictions that apply to the availability and rates. These messages include a complex set of controls that indicate whether the hotel has available inventory, i.e. closed or open for booking. In addition, booking restrictions that apply to each individual rate, such as a minimum length of stay, must also be communicated to the booking agent so that the hotel guest is informed of all the regulations that govern their reservation.

Historically, the definition of e-Business applications and constructs to support information exchange between enterprises has been severely hampered by the fact that these are tightly tied to the process model that the individual enterprise supports and the technology syntax used to describe it. This has hampered the migration of existing, working inter-organization information exchanges to new technologies. In the conventional methodologies the syntax is so tightly intertwined with the business semantics that it is not easy to retain the semantics (and business knowledge from which they derived) as one attempts to move to new syntaxes such as XML [UMM 2003]. To this end, methodologies and supporting components are called to capture business process knowledge, independent of the underlying implemented technology so that the business acumen is retained and usable over generations of implemented technology.

The sheer diversity of e-Business applications shows that there is a need to follow a series of meaningful steps to ensure consistent production and delivery of real technical implementations from high-level problem descriptions. This methodology is independent of the middleware platform and tools used to develop the e-Business applications. The following items are useful tools when taking these steps [Chappell 2001]:

1. A modeling language to precisely model the business processes that the e-Business application or system automates and the activities that are performed in these processes. The e-Business community is following the software engineering community in standardizing on UML, which we covered in the preceding section.
2. A standardized methodology to organize the e-Business project activities needed to develop the process models.
3. Schema languages to model the business information that is exchanged in e-Business messaging on the basis of XML (see Chapter 20).

Consistency in modeling techniques and methodologies not only forces discipline on analysts and produces better analysis, but also produces analysis in a form that can be more easily validated by subject matter experts and used by software developers. In addition, in the classical software development model the analysis is kept distinctly separate from architecture or design. In addition to making both the analysis and design more understandable by not mixing them up, this allows the consideration of several different implementations that might satisfy the most important functional and nonfunctional (quality of service) requirements.

12.4.1 The unified software development process

Standardized software development processes can be used to produce generic characteristics, which can then be specialized to construct tailor-made types of software development processes. The designers of UML developed a Unified Software Development Process [Jacobson 1997] that builds on UML and is complementary to it. This methodology describes the key concepts, the core workflows and the overall management required for the development of generic software development processes.

The *Unified Software Development Process* defines a 'process framework' for different kinds of software systems, domains, and organizations. The main characteristics of this process are that it is 'use case driven' and 'architecture-centric', while at the same time defining iterative and incremental process phases. The overall Unified Software Development Process development life cycle is divided into four main phases (*inception, elaboration, construction* and *transition*) and consists of a sequence of iterations. The definition of the phases reflects the main focus of the iterations, each conducted at certain stages of product development. Like UML, the Unified Software Development Process is generic, which means that it can be specialized for specific types of software development projects. These specializations retain the general characteristics of the Unified Software Development Process, which are as follows [Chappell 2001]:

- Iterative development: software systems can be developed and delivered incrementally to be able to validate architectural assumptions and requirements early in the software analysis, and to adapt the system architecture as requirements evolve and as complications and risks are better understood.

- Use case driven: the software development project should take the desired functionality of the application or system that is to be delivered as a starting point for requirements specification, analysis, design, and construction. A use case is the specification of the behavior of a system (or part of a system), and a use case diagram is an appropriate way to visualize a use case.

- Requirements and change management: in an e-Business development project assumptions made at an early stage should be constantly checked so that they remain valid throughout the project. Furthermore, a procedure should be in place to manage requests for change or functionality extensions.

- Model based: standard visual models facilitate communication in an e-Business project involving teams of analysts/developers. They are easier to maintain than other forms of documentation. Visual tools based on UML help express models that can support configurations of operational systems that implement a business scenario from graphical descriptions.

- Component based: the architecture of an Internet-based system should be based on component-based development (see Chapter 15).

These characteristics of the Unified Software Development Process are inherited and further specialized for use in specific application areas. Figure 12.7 shows the relationship between the Unified Software Development Process and the software development methodologies covered in this chapter.

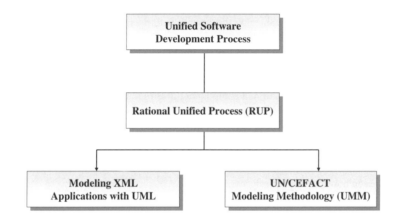

■ **Figure 12.7:** Relationships between Software Development Methodologies

12.4.2 The Rational Unified Process (RUP)

The *Rational Unified Process*, or RUP, is a configurable software development process platform that delivers proven best practices and a configurable architecture that enables software developers to select and deploy only the process components needed for each stage of a large-scale software development project. Proven best practices for the RUP are based on the Capability Maturity Model (CMM) [Paulk 1993], which is a framework that describes the elements of an effective software process. The CMM describes an evolutionary improvement path from an ad hoc, immature process to a mature, disciplined process. Essentially RUP is a Web-enabled software engineering process that enhances team productivity and delivers software best practices to all team members. It makes processes practical by providing extensive guidelines, templates, and examples for all critical e-development activities. RUP also includes e-Business-specific extensions that provide explicit guidance in areas such as business modeling, Web architectures and testing for the Web. The Rational Unified Process is designed and documented using the Unified Modeling Language. An underlying object model, the Unified Software Process Model (USPM), provides a coherent backbone to the process.

The Rational Unified Process describes how to effectively deploy commonly used 'best practices' in industry to software development for software development teams. The RUP provides each team member with the guidelines, templates and tool mentors necessary for the entire team to take full advantage of among others the following [Kruchten 2004, RUP 2001]:

1. Develop Software Iteratively: For the development of process-based software an iterative approach is required that enables an increasing understanding of the problem through successive refinements, and an incrementally grown effective solution over multiple iterations. RUP supports an iterative approach to development that addresses the highest risk items at every stage in the lifecycle, significantly reducing a project's risk profile. An iterative approach also makes it easier to accommodate tactical changes in requirements, features or schedules [Boehm 1996].
2. Manage Requirements: The Rational Unified Process describes how to elicit, organize, and document required functionality and constraints; track and document tradeoffs and decisions; and easily capture and communicate business requirements. The notions of use case and scenarios proscribed in the process provide coherent and traceable threads through both the development and the delivered system [Jacobson 1997].
3. Use Component-based Architectures: The RUP supports component-based software development. Components are non-trivial modules, subsystems that fulfill a clear function. It provides a systematic approach to defining an architecture using new and existing components. These are assembled in a well-defined architecture, either ad hoc, or in a component infrastructure such as the Internet, CORBA, and COM (see Section 14.8 and Section 15.1).
4. Visually Model Software: Visual abstractions help developers communicate different aspects of the software they develop; see how the elements of the system fit together; make sure that the building blocks are consistent with their code; maintain consistency between a design and its implementation; and promote unambiguous communication. RUP uses the visual notation of UML and provides developers with guidelines on how to use UML effectively.
5. Verify Software Quality: RUP assists in the planning, design, implementation, execution, and evaluation of system reliability, functionality, application performance and system performance. Quality assessment is built into the process, in all activities, involving all participants, using objective measurements and criteria, and not treated as an afterthought or a separate activity performed by a separate group.
6. Control Changes to Software: RUP describes how to control, track and monitor changes to enable successful iterative development of software. It also guides developers in how to establish secure workspaces by providing isolation from changes made in other workspaces and by controlling changes of all software artifacts (e.g. models, code, documents, etc.). And it brings a team together to work as a single unit by describing how to automate integration and build management.

The overall architecture of the Rational Unified Process has two dimensions [Kruchten 2004]:

- The *horizontal dimension* represents time and shows the lifecycle aspects of the process as it unfolds.

- The *vertical dimension* represents core process disciplines (or workflows), which logically group software engineering activities by their nature.

The first (horizontal) dimension represents the dynamic aspect of the process expressed in terms of cycles, phases, iterations, and milestones. In the RUP, a software product is designed and built in a succession of incremental iterations. This allows testing and validation of design ideas, as well as risk mitigation, to occur earlier in the lifecycle. The second (vertical) dimension represents the static aspect of the process described in terms of process components: activities, disciplines, artifacts, and roles.

Business Modeling is an optional discipline in RUP that looks at the broader scope of the business. It is used to understand the current business processes to determine how they can be improved. Identifying opportunities for automation is one way in which business processes can be improved. Business Modeling can be performed before system development efforts to better understand the dependencies between business and information system development models [Kruchten 2004].

RUP is also a process framework that can be adapted and extended to suit the needs of an enterprise that uses it. It is general and comprehensive enough to be used 'as is' by many small-to-medium software development organizations, especially those that do not have a very strong process culture. But the adopting organization can also modify, adjust, and expand the Rational Unified Process to accommodate the specific needs, characteristics, constraints, and history of its organization, culture, and domain.

12.4.3 The UN/CEFACT modeling methodology

A business environment may be large and complex. Any basic understanding of this environment begins with information and documentation provided by business experts. Business experts provide a categorization and decomposition of the business environment into business areas, process areas and business processes. The United Nations Centre for Trade Facilitation and Electronic Business (*UN/CEFACT*) *Modeling Methodology* (UMM) is a methodology for business process and information modeling [UMM 2003]. The UMM is based on the Open EDI Reference Model, as defined by the ISO standard 14662 [ISO 1997]. This reference model outlines a different approach to EDI based on business scenarios rather than the conventional EDI concept of individual transaction sets or messages. The business scenarios cover much of the interaction between companies, and as a result the extended period and lengthy development cycle needed to establish an e-Business relationship can be reduced significantly [Kotok 2002].

UMM has been developed as a specialization of a modified subset of the RUP. It is intended as a framework for modeling business processes using UML for application in e-Business projects. The subset covers the first two phases recognized by the RUP [Chappell 2001]. UMM is in fact an extension of UML in that it comprises a UML profile that is used to describe the UMM components needed to specify business domain-specific stereotyping that supports a complete business process and associated information definition model.

UMM is an incremental business process and information model construction methodology that provides levels of specification granularity that are suitable for communicating the model to business practitioners, business application integrators and network application solution providers. UMM provides the conceptual framework to communicate common concepts and provides a common underlying metamodel (the model that defines the UMM modeling language) that represents the concepts, process semantics and relationships that are inherent in a process specification. Before we concentrate on the characteristics and functions of the UMM it is useful to briefly examine the concept of a metamodel.

A *metamodel* is an explicit specification of a set of concepts and relations, which are used to define and constrain models. In other words, a metamodel is an explicit model of the constructs and rules needed to build specific models within a domain of interest. A metamodel is used as a consensual abstraction filter in a particular modeling activity. It defines a description language for a specific domain of interest (platform or business). For example UML describes the artifacts of an object-oriented software system. Some other metamodels may address other domains like process, organization, test, quality of service, etc. They correspond to highly specialized identified domains (platform or end-user). They are defined as separate components and many relationships exist between them. A metamodel can be viewed from three different perspectives:

1. as a set of building blocks and rules used to build models;
2. as a model of a domain of interest;
3. as an instance of another model.

Model engineering considers metamodels as first-class entities with low granularity and high abstraction.

UMM prescribes a specific way to perform business process and information modeling for electronic business while the UMM metamodel is a description of business semantics that allows trading partners to capture the details for a specific business scenario (a business process) using a consistent modeling methodology. A commercial trading agreement is modeled as a business collaboration model according to the UMM metamodel. The UMM metamodel is defined as an extension of the UML stereotype syntax and semantics with the syntax and semantics of the business collaboration domain. This allows for continued development of notation and graphical techniques based on UML to support process definition activities.

The process methodology used in UMM recognizes that any software engineering or e-Business project passes through a series of general phases over the course of time. These phases are:

- Inception: where the project focuses on the requirements specification and determining the scope and vision of the overall project. An early prototype may be developed, as a proof of concept or simply as a showcase, and initially documented using the UMM.

- Elaboration: where the requirements are analyzed in detail, further refined and expanded, and an architectural prototype developed. This prototype serves as a baseline for the overall system.

- Construction: where software development and testing are performed.

- Transition: where further testing and deployment of software occurs.

The view of such software engineering projects is a series of sequential steps, or workflows, moving from technology-independent business process modeling to technology-dependent deployment. A UMM workflow is a logical grouping in a software development process.

The inception and elaboration phases of the UMM concentrate on workflow prerequisites for understanding the business needs and producing business scenarios, business objects and business collaborations. These are as follows [UMM 2003]:

1. The *business modeling workflow* elicits and organizes business processes and information in e-Business applications. This includes the creation of packages to categorize key concepts and business models.

2. The *requirements workflow* uses business models as input to understand the requirements of the resulting e-Business solution. This workflow results in the creation of detailed requirements in the form of UMM use case diagrams.
3. The *analysis workflow* further elaborates the requirement workflow use cases by detailing the activities that occur and collaborations between partners. This workflow produces initial UMM class diagrams.
4. The *design workflow* precisely defines the dynamics of the collaboration, along with the structure of data exchanged between business partners.

Each workflow produces a set of modeling artifacts which, taken together, provide a description of the business case at various levels of detail and from various perspectives. The term artifact is a typical UML/UMM term that refers to any result produced in the software development project. This result may include models, documentation, prototypes, test reports, etc. A subset of the artifacts, known as the deliverables, includes those artifacts that must be formally accepted or are contractually agreed between the project team and the customer or user organization.

The construction and transition phases concentrate on workflow activities that are standard for software development projects and not specific to e-Business integration. These workflows are taken directly from the RUP without any special addition or modification by the UMM, and include [UMM 2003]:

1. The *implementation workflow* that covers software development of the various components in the overall system and covers programming, unit testing and integration;
2. The *test workflow* that covers activities needed to verify the correct interaction and integration of the various components and subsystems, and the correct implementation of all requirements;
3. The *deployment workflow* that addresses operational rollout of the functional production system delivered in a software development project;
4. The *configuration and change management workflow* that covers actions to manage the activities dealt with by other workflows: planning, staffing, and monitoring as well as risk management;
5. The *environment workflow* that sets up and maintains the infrastructure needed to carry out an e-Business development project, including technical services and configuration and management of security services.

The UN/CEFACT Modeling Methodology requires the use of a lexicon. This lexicon contains information and process definitions including relationships and cross-references as expressed in business terminology and organized by industry domain. This knowledge is captured from business experts across multiple domains and evolves over time. The lexicon functionally is a bridge between the specific business or industry language and the UML models through the application of the UN/CEFACT UMM. In addition to the lexicon, models can reuse artifacts from a library of business information objects and processes.

The UN/CEFACT UMM begins with business modeling and produces the Business Domain View (BDV), which is the top view of the UMM metamodel, in the form of a model architecture expressed as UML packages and initial business use cases with descriptions. UMM prescribes a specific way to perform business process and information modeling for electronic business using the Unified Modeling Language. A business use case typically is expressed as a first-cut business activity diagram.

The UMM metamodel underlies the business modeling, requirements and analysis workflows that we described earlier and specifies all of the items that must be produced from the analysis and describes their

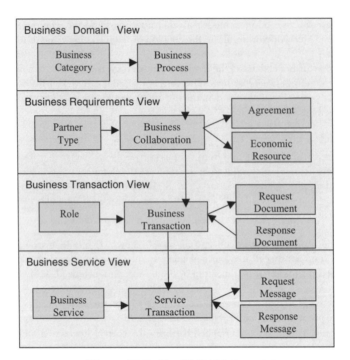

■ **Figure 12.8:** The UMM Metamodel

relationships. The UMM metamodel is a description of business semantics that allows trading partners to capture the details for a specific business scenario (a business process) using a consistent modeling methodology (see Figure 12.8). A business process specification describes in detail how trading partners take on shared roles, relationships and responsibilities to facilitate interaction with other trading partners. The interaction between roles takes place as a choreographed set of business transactions. Each business transaction is expressed as an exchange of electronic business documents. The sequence of the exchange is determined by the Business Process, and by messaging and security considerations. Business documents are composed from reusable business information objects, expressed in an appropriate format (XML, EDI, etc.). At a lower level, business processes can be composed of reusable common business processes, and business information objects can be composed of reusable core components. Common business processes and business information objects reside in a UMM Business Library.

The UMM metamodel supports a set of business process viewpoints that provide a set of semantics (vocabulary) for each viewpoint and form the basis for specification of the semantics and artifacts that are required to facilitate business process and information integration and interoperability. The UMM metamodel structures modeling activities so that each business process and information model can be viewed from a number of perspectives. Each view is briefly described as follows [UMM 2003]:

• The Business Domain View (BDV): The Business Domain View partitions a business domain into business areas, process areas, and business processes. This view establishes the business context of the process, which is a precursor to evaluating the likelihood of finding reusable, previously defined, process descriptions or terminology in the UMM libraries. The BDV defines an overall 'frame of reference' for the business processes being identified. As such it is used to consistently define the business process area boundaries and achieve business process interoperability with future trading partners also following the same business reference model for their operating practices. The BDV also defines basic terms accepted by the given industry segment: for example, the Supply-Chain Operations Reference (SCOR) model – discussed in the next section – which defines a frame of reference for supply chains, or the Telemanagement Forum (TMForum), which enhances the Telecom Operations Map.

- The Business Requirements View (BRV): The Business Requirements View is a view of a business process model that captures the use case scenarios, inputs, outputs, constraints and system boundaries for commercial transactions and their interrelationships. This view defines the choreography of business transactions: the economic resources, economic events and agents involved in a process. The BRV concerns itself with how the business domain expert sees and describes the process to be modeled.

- The Business Transaction View (BTV): The Business Transaction View is a view of a business process model that captures the semantics of business information entities and their flow of exchange between roles as they perform business activities. This view is an elaboration on the business requirements view by the business analyst and is how the business analyst sees the process to be modeled.

- The Business Service View (BSV): The Business Service View is the view of an explicit specification of business process interactions according to the type of transaction, role, security and timing parameters and their message (information) exchange as interactions necessary to execute and validate a business process. The set of interactions is derived from the BTV according to the system requirements. In essence, the BSV captures the syntax and semantics of business messages and their exchange between business services.

These perspectives support an incremental model construction methodology and provide levels of specification granularity that are suitable for communicating the model to business practitioners, business application integrators and network application solution providers.

UMM specifies all information that needs to be captured during the analysis of an e-Business process. It defines the modeling methodology and resulting artifacts for use when analyzing and defining a business process. UMM uses business process and business information analysis worksheets as simple business process aids to capture business process and business information requirements The worksheets and corresponding usage methodology are derived from the UMM. The worksheets can be extended for specific vertical industry needs. The worksheets help collect and organize the information needed to produce the minimum UMM models for a particular work area corresponding to the first three UMM views, i.e. Business Domain View, Business Requirements View and Business Transaction View. Procedures within each of these work areas describe how to populate the worksheets [UMM 2003]. For the fourth UMM view, the Business Service View models are not defined in the UMM User Guide as a work area, as these can be determined as a result of completing the procedures outlined in each of the preceding work areas. Each UMM work area is composed of a set of procedures which build on each other to define the minimum required UMM models for these three views. These procedures are based on use of the worksheets that are used to create MM models. A high-level overview of these worksheets and models can be found in Figure 12.9.

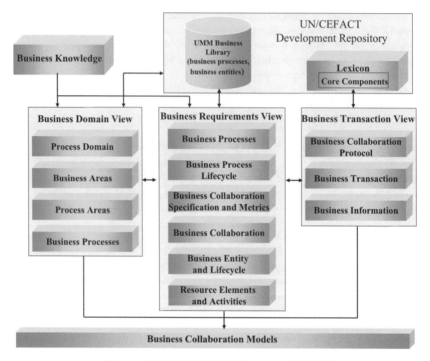

■ **Figure 12.9:** UMM Worksheets and Models

Building a UMM-compliant business model is a top-down modeling activity, which starts off with a clear understanding of the specific domain of business activities within which the entire model exists. It de-emphasizes the use of business documents and transactions to model this view as that approach may capture only one part of the required model. Instead, emphasis is placed on the definition of business entities, their state management, and state lifecycle identification to produce a model that encompasses all instances and can evolve as new business requirements emerge. Bottom-up modeling can also be used as a starting point to fill in parts of the worksheets through use of existing business documents and transactions. It can help identify some model elements. However, the top-down approach must ultimately be applied in order to produce evolvable and maintainable models that support reuse and manage loosely coupled business processes between trading partners on the Internet.

Using the UMM methodology and the UMM metamodel, the user may thus create a complete business process and information model conforming to the UMM metamodel. This model is syntax independent and contains more information than what is required for configuring e-Business collaboration models such as the electronic-business XML (see Chapter 20), EDI, or web services (see Chapter 19). For example, as we are going to see in Chapter 20, the electronic-business XML (ebXML) Business Process Specification Schema draws out modeling elements from several of the UMM views and forms a semantic subset of the UMM metamodel. This subset is provided to support the direct specification of the nominal set of elements necessary to configure a runtime system in order to execute a set of ebXML business transactions. Since the ebXML Business Process Specification Schema (see Section 20.5.2) is a semantic subset of the UMM metamodel, the user may then extract from the Business Process and Information Model in an automated fashion the required set of elements and relationships, and transform them into an ebXML Business Process Specification conforming to the ebXML Business Process Specification Schema.

12.5 The Supply-Chain Operations Reference (SCOR) model

Most of the first generation business process methodologies, such as Business Process Reengineering, the IDEF0 – a standard for functional modeling (`www.idef.com/idef0.html`), – the DMAIC (Define-Measure-Analyze-Improve-Control) methodology (`www.isixsigma.com/me/dmaic/`), and the various methodologies of consulting companies, e.g. Catalysis, and those of the various vendors, e.g. ARIS, approach business process redesign in the same general way. They all rely on analyzing each new business process as if it were unique. One begins by defining the scope of the process to be analyzed, and then proceeds to decompose the process, identifying its major subprocesses, and then the subprocesses of those, identifying their major activities, and so on down to whatever level of granularity the designer chooses. Once the process is laid out in detail, the analysis team usually considers how to change it.

A second-generation approach to business process redesign began to emerge a few years ago. This approach was proposed by the Supply Chain Council (`www.supply-chain.org`) who combined the expertise of supply-chain professionals across a broad cross-section of industries to develop best-in-class business practices and design a specific methodology tailored to the analysis of supply-chain processes. Second-generation software is usually tailored for specific industries or niche markets. The SCC named this second generation methodology the Supply-Chain Operations Reference (SCOR) Framework. SCOR is a business process methodology built by, and for, supply-chain analysis and design.

SCOR is a cross-industry, standardized, supply-chain reference model that enables companies to analyze and improve their supply-chain operations by helping them to communicate supply-chain information across the enterprise and measure performance objectively. SCOR also assists enterprises with identifying supply-chain performance gaps and improvement objectives and influences the development of future supply-chain management software. SCOR's consistent common language enhances communication between supply-chain trading partners and enables quick assimilation of unfamiliar business processes. SCOR provides standard definitions of measures and procedures for calculating the metrics. SCOR metrics stimulate development of indicators that are applicable to the enterprise and balance customization of indicators against compliance with metrics defined by standards.

SCOR also facilitates business process reengineering, benchmarking, and best practice analysis, indicating which technology can guide performance improvement and adoption of best practices. Business process reengineering concepts capture the 'as is' state of the process and derive the desired 'to be' future state. Benchmarking concepts quantify the operational performance of similar companies and establish internal targets based on 'best in class' results. Best practice analysis characterizes the management practices and software solutions that result in 'best in class' performance. Thus SCOR combines all these three concepts into a cross-functional framework. SCOR as a process reference model contains [Kasi 2005]:

- standard descriptions of management practices

- a framework of relationships among the standard processes

- standard metrics to measure process performance

- management practices that produce best-in-class performance

- standard alignment to features and functionality

The SCOR model has been developed to define all business activities associated with the supply chain. It spans: all customer interactions (order entry through paid invoice), all physical material transactions (supplier's supplier to customer's customer, including equipment, supplies, spare parts, bulk product, software, etc.) and all market interactions (from the understanding of aggregate demand to the fulfillment of each order). SCOR does not attempt to describe every business process or activity. Specifically, the SCOR model does not address: sales and marketing (demand generation), product development, research and development, and several elements of post-delivery customer support.

The SCC defined the common supply-chain management processes, matched these processes against 'best practice' examples, and benchmarked performance data as well as optimal software applications. Best supply-chain practices were assembled in a set of models that can be utilized to redesign business processes, determine associated system and infrastructure requirements, and address those issues identified as critical in modern supply-chain operations. Such typical supply-chain project objectives may include the following:

- Creating an enterprise that can swiftly respond to market changes. Configuring process categories and extending the definitions for process elements to an implementation level across the organizations involved in the supply of goods and/or services may implement inter-organization supply-chain strategies.

- Leveraging supply-chain standards for more effective materials-planning forecasts and capacity management. This entails retaining critical strengths while implementing new standardized, cost-effective procurement processes and lowering levels of safety stock inventory.

- Implementing best-in-class improvements by benchmarking supply-chain processes from other organizations. Deliver proven, competitive process improvements through a direct comparison of supply-chain processes using a standardized set of metrics and process element definitions.

- Rethinking *plan*, *source*, *make*, *deliver*, and *return* strategies in light of e-Business capabilities. This entails adapting new technologies and improving the flow of information among the network partners to reduce cost and create collaborative systems that improve planning and demand forecasting.

These objectives resulted in a tool for measuring both supply performance and the effectiveness of supply-chain reengineering, as well as testing and planning for future process improvements.

The SCOR Framework model depicts the supply-chain from a strategic perspective. It profiles the enterprise-wide business scope, establishes the process boundaries, and portrays the interrelationship of activities within the SCOR structure. This end-to-end business process model includes the primary activities by which business partners provide exceptional service to their customers, and it serves as a navigational tool and starting point to access all lower-level workflow models.

The SCOR model consists of five basic processes: Plan, Source, Make, Deliver and Return [Harmon 2003b]. In addition to these basic processes, there are three process types or categories: Enable, Planning and Execute. The SCOR modeling approach starts with the assumption that any supply-chain process can be represented as a combination of the five basic processes: Plan, Source, Make, Deliver and Return. The Plan process balances demand and supply to best meet the sourcing, manufacturing and delivery requirements. The Source process procures goods and services to meet planned or actual demand. The Make process transforms product to a finished state to meet planned or actual demand. The Deliver process provides finished goods and services to meet planned or actual demand, typically including order management, transportation management and distribution management. The Return process is associated with returning or receiving any returned products.

At the core, the SCOR model comprises four levels of processes that guide supply-chain members on the road to integrative process improvement [Harmon 2003b]. These are shown in Figure 12.10. Level 1 describes supply-chain processes at the most general level. It consists of four key supply-chain process types: Plan,

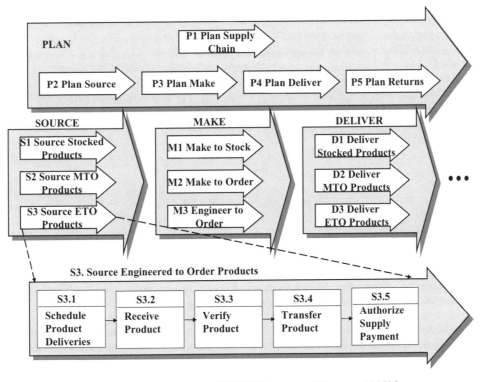

■ **Figure 12.10:** Levels of SCOR Processes [Harmon 2003b]

Source, Make, and Deliver; and assumes that all supply chains are composed out of these four basic processes. In other words, complex supply chains are made up of multiple combinations of these basic processes.

Level 2 defines 26 core supply-chain process categories that were established by the SCC with which supply-chain partners can jointly present their ideal or actual operational structure. Actually, Level 2 provides for variations in the Level 1 processes. These are not in fact subprocesses, but variations in the way the processes can be implemented. Each of the Level 1 processes currently has three variations. In analyzing a process, an analyst first decides that there is a sourcing process (Level 1 process), and then decides which of three (Level 2) variations of sourcing process it is. For example, in the case of Level 1 Source process, the Level 2 variations are S1: Source Stocked Products, S2: Source Made to Order Products, or S3: Source Engineered to Order Product. Figure 12.10 shows all of the four basic SCOR Level 1 processes with current Level 2 variations inside their respective Level 1 process. Each Level 2 process is further defined by a set of subprocesses or activities that define the basic sequence of steps involved in implementing the process. In fact, in SCOR, the Level 3 processes are subprocesses of the Level 1 processes, and are the same, no matter the variation. Figure 12.10 also shows the Level 3 activities that are included in one Level 2 process S3, the Source Engineered to Order Products. Level 3 provides partners with information useful in planning and setting goals for supply-chain improvement. Processes in the first three levels of the SCOR framework serve as the foundation for the development of Level 4 processes. Level 4 processes focus on implementation of supply-chain process improvement efforts and are company-specific practices designed to achieve and maintain competitive advantage in the industry. Level 4 processes are beyond the scope of the SCOR framework.

SCOR provides a well-organized, hierarchically structured vocabulary as well as a notation system for defining the major processes that make up supply chains. In addition, the SCC has also defined a set of measures that one can use to evaluate processes at each level of the process hierarchy. The SCOR model, instead of dictating strategy, defines a measure at a high level. The SCOR model calculates the measures based on precise formulae for each measure defined by a standard definition. The SCOR methodology defines a dictionary of all the definitions of terms and measures to standardize across all domains. The metrics are calculated at each level of the model. The metrics cater to various goals different companies might have. Thus the choice of measures and metrics depends on the company's strategy and focus and it is upto the company to choose the metrics they desire.

The SCOR methodology is divided in six broad phases. These are summarized in what follows:

- *Define the Supply-Chain Process*: This first phase commences after the need for an improved supply chain has been determined. During the first phase a team of analysts undertakes the actual analysis of existing processes. This effort includes decisions about the number and scope of the supply-chain processes to be examined. For example, a complex assembly, like an automobile, might source hundreds of parts or subassemblies from hundreds of different suppliers, who might, in turn, do the same. Analysts characterize processes and create analyses of high-level business processes.

- *Determine the Performance of the Existing Supply Chain*: Once the team of analysts has scoped the existing supply-chain process, it can use historical data to define how the existing supply chain is performing. In addition, the performance of a supply chain can be compared with benchmarks to determine how its processes measure up against similar processes in similar industries. The preexistence of standardized performance measures and benchmark data means that a process analysis team can arrive at an overall evaluation of a supply-chain process fairly quickly. Similarly, since the measures are standardized, a company can quickly compare several S1 processes to see which is more efficient. Once Level 1 processes are examined, and in some cases Level 2, a process development team is in a position to decide if the supply chain should be changed. In effect, it is now ready to review the organization's existing approach to its supply chain and, if necessary, define a new supply-chain strategy, and set some targets, priorities and a budget for any redesign effort [Harmon 2003b].

- *Establish Supply-Chain Strategy, Goals and Priorities*: Once the team of analysts has determined the performance of an existing supply chain, the team is in a position to consider if the supply-chain strategy is reasonable and how it might be improved. One can consider alternative targets for improvement and determine how they might improve the enterprise's performance. Similarly, one can identify which changes would yield the highest return and prioritize any improvement efforts.

- *Redesign the Supply Chain as Needed*: SCOR provides a number of tools to assist in redesigning a supply chain. It provides tools for identifying problems and gaps and suggests the best practices used by enterprises within superior supply chains.

- *Enable the Redesign and Implement*: Once the design is complete, the redesign must be implemented using software and human performance-improvement techniques. Then the new supply chain must be implemented and data must be gathered to determine if the new targets are met.

The major benefit of SCOR is that it gives inter-organizational supply-chain partners a common basis for integration by providing them with a tangible framework to interact and work with. The use of a framework-based business process methodology such as the SCOR model is only possible in cases where a high-level analysis of the processes to be analyzed already exists, and where measures of process success have already been standardized. Obviously, it will help if the standardization is done by a large, neutral standards group, like the Supply Chain Council, since that will assure that the processes and measures are really well thought out and that individual practitioners will more readily accept this common framework [Harmon 2003b].

12.6 Business process modeling notation

From the preceding discussion it is easy to understand that business process modeling would be simplified if notation that is readily understandable by all business users were introduced. This includes the business analysts who create the initial drafts of the processes to the technical developers responsible for implementing the technology that will perform those processes and, finally, business people who will manage and monitor those processes. A major improvement would be if the business process modeling activity led to the execution of the modeled business processes in some standard business process execution language. In this way a standardized bridge could be created for the gap between the business process design and process implementation. These are precisely the primary goals of the Business Process Modeling Notation (BPMN) effort.

Business Process Modeling Notation is an attempt at a standards-based business process modeling language that can unambiguously define business logic and information requirements to the extent that the resultant models are executable [White 2004, Owen 2004]. The net result is that business logic and information requirements are maintained in a model that is consistent with and reflects the actual EIS supporting business activities. This graphical model does need to be completely captured by a rigid and cryptic computer language that is destined to become obsolete one day. BPMN holds out the promise of giving end users management and direct control over their business processes and the information systems supporting them. In this way BPMN addresses the legacy systems' problem that organizations face today by having the primary repository of their intellectual capital invested in older generation systems (see Chapter 16). BPMN is also supported with an internal model that will enable the generation of executable Business Process Execution Language processes. This business process language is representative of a new family of process definition languages intended for expressing abstract and executable processes that address all aspects of enterprise business processes, including in particular those areas important for Web-based services (see Section 19.8).

BPMN has a rich set of semantics that provide a tool for capturing the complexity of an information-rich business process model. BPMN contains notations and semantics for capturing workflows or sequences of activities, decision points and prerequisites, information transformation and flows, collaborations among multiple entities and actors.

BPMN specifies a single business process diagram, called the *Business Process Diagram* (BPD). This diagram is easy to use and understand, offers the expressiveness to model complex business processes, and can be naturally mapped to business execution languages. A business process diagram is defined as a series of activities connected by sequence flow, where the direction of the sequence flow arrowheads determines the order of the sequence. The BPD is made up of a series of graphical elements that include flow objects, connecting objects, swimlanes and artifacts [White 2004].

Flow objects comprise events, activities and gateways. As usual an event signifies the occurrence of an important incident that happens during the course of a business process. An event in BPMN is represented by a circle. Events affect the flow of the process and usually have a cause (trigger) or an impact (result). There are three types of events, based on when they affect the flow: start, intermediate, and end events.

An activity is a generic term for work that a business process performs and is represented by a rounded-corner rectangle. An activity can be atomic or nonatomic (compound). BPMN includes three types of activities: processes, subprocesses, and tasks. Processes represent typical business process activities. Processes can be nested and thus spawn children which are referred to as subprocesses. Finally, tasks are the lowest-level processes, which cannot be further decomposed.

A gateway is used to determine traditional decisions, as well as the forking, merging, and joining of paths and is represented by the familiar diamond shape.

Flow objects in BPMN are connected together in a diagram to create the basic skeletal structure of a business process. There are three types of connecting objects that provide this function: sequence flows, message flows and associations.

A sequence flow is used to indicate the sequence in which activities will be performed in a business process and is represented by a solid line with a solid arrowhead. A message flow is used to show the flow of messages between two separate process participants (business entities or business roles) that send and receive them and is represented by a dashed line with an open arrowhead.

An association is used to associate data, text, and other artifacts with flow objects and is represented by a dotted line with a line arrowhead. Associations are used to show the inputs and outputs of activities.

Flow objects and connectors can be used to specify BPMN process models at a high-level of abstraction for documentation and communication purposes as shown in Figure 12.11. Additional details can be added to the core elements and shown through internal markers to create process models at a higher level of precision, as shown in Figure 12.12. Such models could be subject to detailed analysis or managed by a specific Business Process Management System. As we shall explain in Chapter 18, a Business Process Management System offers the ability to transform the distinct disciplines of workflow, Enterprise Application Integration, and e-Business from a complex high-end solution practiced by a few highly skilled practitioners into an open solution accessible to all kinds of developers, producing new types of loosely coupled applications. The purpose of a Business Process Management System is to orchestrate participants (applications, people, partners) into executable, end-to-end processes and close the gap between business strategy and business process execution.

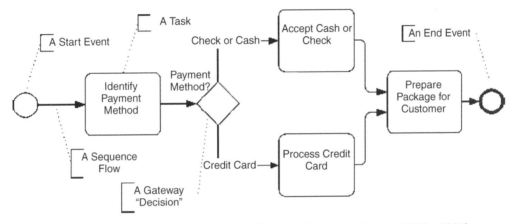

■ **Figure 12.11:** A BPMN Example of a High-level Business Process [White 2004]

In BPMN, swimlanes are a mechanism to organize activities into separate visual categories in order to illustrate different functional capabilities or responsibilities. BPMN supports swimlanes with two main constructs: pools and lanes. A pool represents a participant in a process. Figure 12.13 shows two pools (buyer and seller) and two lanes (order processing and inventory) for a hypothetical order-processing application. A pool also acts as a graphical container for partitioning a set of activities from other pools, usually in the context of e-Business applications. A lane is a subpartition within a pool, for instance the order processing and inventory lanes within the seller pool, which extends the entire length of the pool, either vertically or horizontally. Lanes are used to organize and categorize activities.

BPMN was designed to give business modelers and modeling tools the possibility to extend the basic notation in order to add context appropriate to a specific e-Business modeling situation, such as a vertical industry or market. To achieve this effect, artifacts can be added to a diagram, as appropriate for the context of the

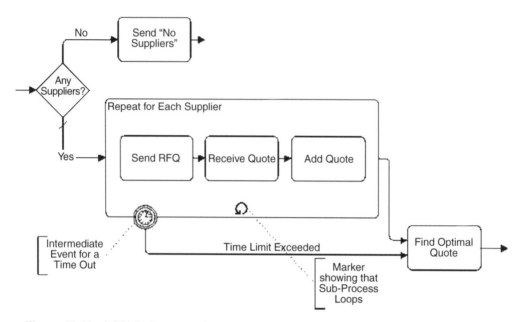

■ **Figure 12.12:** A BPMN Example of a Business Process at High Level of Precision [White 2004]

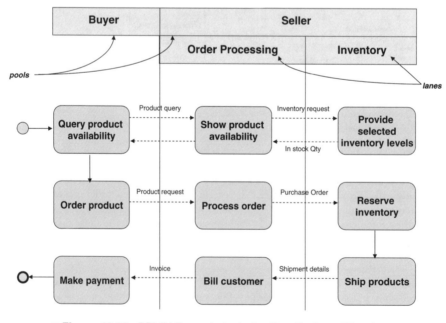

■ **Figure 12.13:** BPMN Example Including Two Pools and Two Lanes

business processes being modeled. The current version of the BPMN specification predefines only three types of BPD artifacts, which are: data objects, groups and annotations.

Data objects are a mechanism to show how data is required or produced by activities. They are connected to activities through associations. The grouping mechanism of BPMN can be used for documentation or analysis purposes, but does not affect the sequence flow. Finally, annotations are a mechanism for a business modeler to provide a textual annotation that can be affixed to any model element.

BPMN represents a vast improvement over the various flavors of process modeling languages that preceded it, as most were designed primarily as communicative tools for human analysis, and are much more ambiguous. Many of the modeling languages developed from industrial engineering are as rich and structured as BPMN, but their focus is on workflows supporting material assembly and transformation. They lack mathematical rigor and are less useful as tools for modeling collaboration and information flow. In contrast to these modeling languages, BPMN is based on the Business Process Modeling Language (BPML) developed by the Business Process Management Initiative (`www.bpmi.org`). BPML is a comprehensive process modeling language that is based on mathematical proof, capable of capturing detailed business activities, business rules, information flows and collaborations at an unambiguous level.

One notable weakness of BPMN is that it does not directly support some of the standard requirements of industrial engineering, such as material flows and assembly/transformations. Additionally, while it can capture process performance data upon execution, it does not provide the ability to directly articulate and capture process performance measures as a notation in the model [Nelson 2004].

Thus while BPMN can be used to represent the process context for information flow between roles in inter- and intra-enterprise transactions, it cannot be used to directly support the standard industrial engineering material flow requirements in the Intel case study presented at the outset of this chapter. It can however, unlike UML 2.0, analyze performance data and identify conformance with performance metrics that measure process performance in the supply chain.

12.7 Comparing BPMN with UML

Although on the surface it seems that BPMN and UML share the same concerns, they have very different approaches to business process modeling [Owen 2004]. UML is a language that helps developers specify, visualize and document models of software systems. It is very much targeted at a technical audience including system architects and software engineers. It takes an object-oriented approach to the modeling of applications and has been developed as a means to streamline the software development process, from architecture design to application implementation. As we already explained in Section 12.3, UML defines a number of diagrams that fall into one of three categories that describe static application structure, dynamic behavior and management and organization of software solutions. Of these three categories, it is only the dynamic behavior diagrams that are often used for modeling business processes, such as the activity diagram and the use case diagram. BPMN is related to UML in the sense that it also defines a graphical notation for business processes that is similar to UML behavior diagrams. BPMN is targeted at both the business process developer and business analyst level and offers a process-centric approach that is more natural and intuitive for them to use. With BPMN, emphasis is on modeling control and message flows of processes, which are modeled first in an e-Business application. In contrast to UML, an object model for the process is defined implicitly rather than explicitly. BPMN also offers business analysts the option of explicitly modeling business objects that may be exposed through business services in their process flows.

UML is an assemblage of diagrams – which are the collective best practices of its founding practitioners – that have not been specifically designed to work with each other. As a result, developers can only model part of their applications with UML; the detailed implementation level is not covered adequately. In contrast, BPMN defines a single type of diagram that has multiple views derived from the same underlying process execution metamodel, which furthermore has a strong mathematical foundation. The natural result of this is that implementation in a business process execution language merely becomes another logical step of the business modeling process.

Finally, unlike BPMN, UML does not define any execution metamodel for the business processes that are modeled with it. Instead, any execution metamodel must be defined using the Model Driven Architecture (see next section) MDA. Figure 12.16 is a typical example of this and indicates that the process of creating executable business process specification in BPEL from UML diagrams is quite a complicated affair. In contrast to this, BPMN is based on BPML's process execution metamodel and can directly produce fully executable BPEL processes.

12.8 The Model Driven Architecture (MDA)

Today enterprises find themselves unable to standardize on a single platform that they can use for the development of enterprise application integration or e-Business applications. Some enterprises find themselves with a number of middleware platforms because their different departments have different requirements, others because mergers or acquisitions created a mix of such platforms. Even the enterprises that rely on a single middleware choice find that they need to use other technologies to interoperate with other enterprises and e-Business markets. These deliberations have triggered an important paradigm shift in the area of information system construction, namely from object and component technology to model technology. The object technology revolution has allowed the replacement of the more than twenty-years-old step-wise procedural decomposition paradigm by the more fashionable object composition paradigm. Surprisingly this evolution seems itself to be triggering today another even more radical change, towards model transformation.

To address these concerns the Object Management Group's *Model Driven Architecture* (MDA) separates the fundamental logic behind a specification from the specifics of the particular middleware that implements it. This allows rapid development and delivery of new interoperability specifications that use new deployment technologies but are based on proven, tested business models. The MDA is motivated by integration and interoperability concerns at the enterprise scale and beyond. MDA is part of a broad effort across the computer industry to raise the level of abstraction in how we develop systems. Through the abstraction process, developers hide all but the relevant data in the system's code – thereby reducing its complexity and increasing development productivity. MDA utilizes models and a generalized idea of architecture standards to address integration of enterprise systems in the face of evolving heterogeneous technology and business domains. MDA addresses integration and interoperability spanning the complete life cycle of a system from modeling and design to construction, assembly, deployment, integration and evolution using open standards. MDA encompasses both the modeling and development spaces and unifies business modeling and implementation into a synergistic environment by codifying and standardizing the steps that take a model through development into implementation.

MDA addresses the challenges of today's highly networked, constantly changing systems environment, providing an architecture that assures the following:

- Portability, increasing application reuse and reducing the cost and complexity of application development and management, now and into the future.

- Cross-platform Interoperability, using rigorous methods to guarantee that standards based on multiple implementation technologies all implement identical business functions.

- Platform Independence, greatly reducing the time, cost and complexity associated with retargeting applications for different platforms – including those yet to be introduced.

- Domain Specificity, through domain-specific models that enable rapid implementation of new, industry-specific applications over diverse platforms.

- Productivity, by allowing developers, designers and system administrators to use languages and conc-epts they are comfortable with, while allowing seamless communication and integration across the teams.

Figure 12.14, which is excerpted from OMG's MDA documentation pages (http://doc.omg.org/mda), shows a high-level representation of how the various pieces fit together in the MDA. At its core is a technology-independent definition of the distributed enterprise computing infrastructure. MDA is built in UML. As already explained, UML allows an application model to be constructed, viewed, developed, and manipulated in a standard way at analysis and design time. This allows the design to be evaluated and critiqued when changes are easiest and least expensive to make, before it is coded. MDA includes the concepts that we recognized as common to the various architectures in the enterprise application integration or e-Business market, representing component-based systems such as Enterprise JavaBeans (see Chapter 14), and loosely coupled messaging-based systems including Web services (see Chapter 19).

The MDA builds upon and leverages the value of OMG's modeling technologies, all based on UML. These include:

- XML Metadata Interchange (XMI): XMI is a standard interchange mechanism used between various tools, repositories and middleware. XMI is a mapping mechanism, which expresses UML models in XML schemas, providing an XML serialization mechanism. In this way it allows XML documents to be moved around an enterprise as we progress from analysis to model to application.

- The Meta-Object Facility (MOF); MOF provides the standard modeling and interchange constructs that are used in the MDA. These constructs are a subset of the UML modeling constructs. This common foundation provides the basis for model/metadata interchange and interoperability, and is the mechanism through which models are analyzed in XMI. MOF also defines programmatic interfaces for manipulating

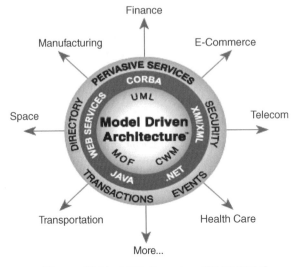

■ Figure 12.14: MDA Overview [OMG 2004]

models and their instances spanning the application lifecycle. These are defined in IDL (see Section 14.8.1) and are being extended to Java.

- The Common Warehouse Metamodel (CWM): This is an established data warehouse industry standard. It covers the full life cycle of designing, building and managing data warehouse applications and supports management of the life cycle.

The annular ring closest to the core of Figure 12.14, shows some of the middleware environments that are current targets for the MDA: CORBA; Java (including Enterprise JavaBeans); C#/.NET; XML and web services. The outermost and largest ring, dominating the diagram, depicts the various vertical markets or domains whose facilities will make up the bulk of the MDA. These facilities are defined as *Platform-Independent Models* (or PIMs) and will be implemented in multiple target platforms. They extend MDA interoperability from the infrastructure level into the applications themselves by standardizing key functions such as product data management and CAD/CAM interoperability for manufacturing; patient identification and medical record access for healthcare; and financial foundations for e-Business.

MDA development starts with the construction of a Platform-Independent Model in this technology-independent UML environment. PIM exhibits a specified degree of platform independence to be suitable for use with a different number of platforms of similar type. A very common technique used for platform independence is to target a system model for a technology-neutral virtual machine. A virtual machine is a set of parts and services, such as communications, scheduling, naming and so on, which are defined independently of any specific platform and which are realized in platform-specific ways for different platforms.

The PIM is platform independent with respect to the class of platforms on the virtual machine that has been implemented. MDA spans a spectrum comprising business models at the top and technology-specific models at the bottom, (see Figure 12.15). Business domain experts work at the top in modeling space. At this level, UML-based tools provide support and the UML language's structure and narrower profiles, i.e. tailored subsets, provide guidance. The UML model is leveraged to support applications throughout their entire lifecycle, extending beyond the design and coding stages through deployment and into maintenance and, ultimately, evolution. The product of the first development step, the PIM, represents the business functionality that this MDA application will execute, in isolation to technological factors.

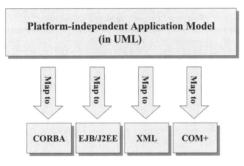

■ **Figure 12.15:** Deriving Platform-specific Artifacts from Platform-independent Models

While we are moving down toward the bottom level, the business domain recedes and technology takes over. In a perfectly efficient world, the MDA might take over directly from the business model at the top to the implementation. As, however, the discontinuities are too great, so the MDA introduces an intermediate step. The artifact produced in this step is termed the *Platform-Specific Model*, or PSM. The PSM is a platform model that provides a set of concepts, representing the different kinds of parts that make up a platform and the services provided by that platform. This platform model also specifies the connections and use of the parts of the platform, and the connections of an application to the platform. The PSM is produced primarily by MDA-enabled tools following OMG standardized mappings and provides the means for developers to annotate the platform model with their preferences about how they wish particular steps to be designed or executed. The completed PSM contains the same information set as a coded application, but in the form of a UML model instead of a specific programming language.

Automating the route set down by the OMG standard, the MDA-based tools produce applications that faithfully meet the functional and non-functional (scalability, security and so on) requirements built into platform models by domain experts and IT architects. Models become the prime development artifact in this environment, not only defining and recording business requirements, but also serving as the basis for development, maintenance and evolution.

MDA focuses on improving the software engineering methods with which business process solutions are implemented by separating the business or application logic from the underlying platform technology and representing this logic with precise semantic models. For instance the MDA could be used to automatically transform a PIM (specified by a UML 2.0 activity diagram) that captures the operational requirements of a business process into an executable PSM – namely, a program in the Business Process Execution Language

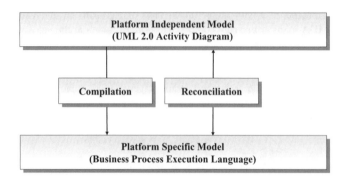

■ **Figure 12.16:** Model-driven Generation of Programs in BPEL using the PIM/PSM Approach

for Web Services (see Chapter 19) that satisfies the operational requirements captured in the PIM [Koehler 2005]. This procedure is shown in Figure 12.16.

As we shall see in Chapter 19, the Business Process Execution Language for Web Services or BPEL4WS has recently emerged as the standard to define and manage business process activities and business interaction protocols comprising collaborating web services. This XML-based flow language defines how business processes interact. Enterprises can describe complex processes that include multiple organizations – such as order processing, lead management, and claims handling – and execute the same business processes in systems from other vendors.

In Figure 12.16 compilation is a one-way process producing code from a model, where the code and the model may remain linked or evolve independently of each other. In contrast to compilation, model reconciliation is used in Figure 12.16 to link models together, such as PIM and PSM, so that they remain synchronized even if those models change, thus requiring bidirectional transformations.

12.9 Chapter summary

The world of e-Business represents a serious opportunity to rethink traditional application software modeling and development processes. Business process models in e-Business define how business processes are described prior to being implemented. The specification for a business process definition enables an enterprise to express its business processes so that they are understandable by other enterprises. Virtually all enterprises are using process modeling techniques before making actual investments in e-Business application or system implementations.

The principal goal of business process models is to specify business processes that allow business partners to collaborate. Business models provide a means of expressing business processes in terms of business activities and collaborative behavior. Business modeling involves designing processes at both the enterprise level and across entire supply chains to take advantage of Internet connectivity. Business modeling is frequently used for analyzing process interrelations, and the impact of making strategic-level changes regarding collaborative processes in the supply chain. Detailed business process models allow analysts to visualize, analyze and improve processes, so that e-Business workflow implementations are tested before design and implementation. Business collaboration activities can be specified by a business process analyst as use cases, requirements and business object flow graphs that define the choreography of business processes.

Business models come under two main flavors: descriptive (or non-normative) and normative. Descriptive models are models where the real world is simply 'described'. Normative models force modelers to select from a prespecified set of constructs and essentially map the perceived system into this prespecified set.

There are several normative models that can be used in the context of e-Business to capture the structure and behavior of complex applications. These include the Unified Modeling Language and standard business methodologies, such as the UN/CEFACT Modeling Methodology, the Supply-Chain Operations Reference model and the Business Process Modeling Notation to model e-Business processes and supply-chain applications. We summarize their main characteristics and functions below, starting with the Unified Modeling Language.

UML defines a standard language and graphical notation for creating models of business and technical systems. UML employs class diagrams to show the static structure of the system being modeled and activity diagrams to model the procedural flow of actions that are part of a larger activity. In projects in which use cases are present, activity diagrams can model a specific use case at a more detailed level. A use case illustrates a unit of functionality provided by the system. Finally, sequence diagrams show a detailed flow for a specific use case or even just part of a specific use case. They show the calls between the different objects in their sequence and can show, at a detailed level, different calls to different objects. UML has recently undergone a major revision advancing from version 1.4 to version 2.0. The goal of this revision was to increase the precision and expressiveness of UML so that it can be effectively used to model large, complex architectures and business processes, and business process interactions.

The Rational Unified Process, or RUP, is a configurable software development process platform that delivers proven best practices and a configurable architecture that enables software developers to select and deploy only the process components needed for each stage of a large-scale software development project. Proven best practices for the RUP are based on the Capability Maturity Model. The Rational Unified Process is designed and documented using the Unified Modeling Language. An underlying object model, the Unified Software Process Model, provides a coherent backbone to the process.

The United Nations Centre for Trade Facilitation and Electronic Business (UN/CEFACT) Modeling Methodology is a methodology for business process and information modeling. UMM is an incremental business process and information model construction methodology that provides levels of specification granularity that are suitable for communicating the model to business practitioners, business application integrators and network application solution providers. UMM prescribes a specific way to perform business process and information modeling for electronic business while the UMM metamodel is a description of business semantics that allows trading partners to capture the details for a specific business scenario (a business process) using a consistent modeling methodology.

SCOR is a cross-industry, standardized supply-chain reference model that enables companies to analyze and improve their supply-chain operations by helping them to communicate supply-chain information across the enterprise and measure performance objectively. SCOR also assists enterprises with identifying supply-chain performance gaps and improvement objectives and influences the development of future supply-chain management software. To achieve this SCOR provides standard definitions of measures and a procedure for calculating the metrics.

A major improvement would be if the business process modeling activity could close the gap between the business process design and process implementation. The Business Process Modeling Notation effort achieves precisely this important goal. BPMN is an attempt at a standards-based business process modeling language that can unambiguously define business logic and information requirements to the extent that the resultant models are executable. BPMN defines a single type of diagram that has multiple views derived from the same underlying process execution metamodel, which furthermore has a strong mathematical foundation. The natural result of this is that implementation in a business process execution language merely becomes another logical step of the business modeling process.

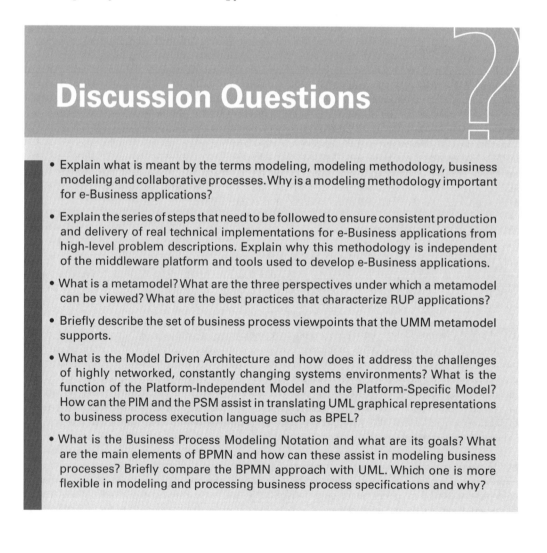

Discussion Questions

- Explain what is meant by the terms modeling, modeling methodology, business modeling and collaborative processes. Why is a modeling methodology important for e-Business applications?

- Explain the series of steps that need to be followed to ensure consistent production and delivery of real technical implementations for e-Business applications from high-level problem descriptions. Explain why this methodology is independent of the middleware platform and tools used to develop e-Business applications.

- What is a metamodel? What are the three perspectives under which a metamodel can be viewed? What are the best practices that characterize RUP applications?

- Briefly describe the set of business process viewpoints that the UMM metamodel supports.

- What is the Model Driven Architecture and how does it address the challenges of highly networked, constantly changing systems environments? What is the function of the Platform-Independent Model and the Platform-Specific Model? How can the PIM and the PSM assist in translating UML graphical representations to business process execution language such as BPEL?

- What is the Business Process Modeling Notation and what are its goals? What are the main elements of BPMN and how can these assist in modeling business processes? Briefly compare the BPMN approach with UML. Which one is more flexible in modeling and processing business process specifications and why?

Assignments

i. Consider the simplified supply-chain management application described in Figures 12.2, 12.3 and 12.4. These figures present a high-level definition of this SCM in the form of a set of UML use cases, activity diagrams, and sequence diagrams. The application being modeled is that of a retailer offering consumer electronic goods to consumers. To fulfill orders the Retailer has to manage stock levels in warehouses. When an item in stock falls below a certain threshold, the retailer must restock the item from the relevant manufacturer's inventory. In order to fulfill a retailer's request, a manufacturer may have to execute a production run to build the finished goods. Use BPMN notation to model this example. Extend the BPMN model to indicate how a manufacturer can order the component parts from its suppliers. The complete BPMN specification can be found at: www.bpmn.org/.

ii. Figure 19.8 uses a UML activity graph of a simple a BPEL process for handling purchase orders. In this scenario, upon receiving the purchase order from a customer, the process initiates three tasks in parallel: calculating the final price for the order, selecting a shipper, and scheduling the production and shipment for the order. The four partners shown in this figure correspond to the sender of the order (customer), the provider of price (invoiceProvider), shipment (shippingProvider), and manufacturing scheduling services (schedulingProvider). Use BPMN to model this particular scenario.

Chapter 13

Security and Reliability for e-Business

e- Business is distributed – often across multiple time zones, geographic, national and corporate boundaries. In addition, enterprises are expected to be always online and available, providing complex applications that deliver information and value to their customers and partners, and provide corporate and customer data. Considering the Web's worldwide reach, these and still more concerns are relentless. As enterprises undertake e-Business integration initiatives and increasingly conduct transactions electronically, they must place additional reliance on electronic means for protecting business-critical information, transactions and communications.

Although e-Business significantly enhances enterprise productivity, it will never achieve its full potential in the absence of adequate trust and security mechanisms. Identifying security and privacy policies, procedures and ongoing active management is essential for e-Business success. In addition to security, quality of service is the key to unlocking the vast potential of e-Business by ensuring the enterprise infrastructure delivers the scalability, security, transaction, and content-based requirements of business services delivered across the Internet.

This chapter presents important issues regarding security, privacy, trustworthiness and quality of service for e-Business. First we discuss quality of service requirements for e-Business and introduce the topics of trust and e-Business risks. Subsequently, we explain that most existing browser-based security mechanisms, generally adequate for low-value business-to-consumer transactions, do not provide the enhanced security or flexibility required for protecting high-value commercial transactions and the sensitive data exchanges that they include. We then describe security principles and mechanisms that can be successfully applied in the context of e-Business.

Case Study

Securing financial services[1]

Wipro Technologies Ltd (`www.wipro.com`) is an IT provider of integrated business, technology and process solutions on a global delivery platform. Wipro's customer was a leading international financial services company with more than 13 million customers and some 20 000 employees worldwide. Its Insurance Operations provide a range of financial products and services including annuities, corporate and individual pensions, with profit bonds and investment products to more than seven million customers.

The financial services company was undergoing a business process reengineering in transforming its customer services and therefore wanted a scalable application security framework that would be capable of integrating with other enterprise applications. The financial company wanted to define a security framework for single sign-on, authentication, effective access control and audit mechanisms. It also wanted to provide a comprehensive security framework for the call center applications that were being developed. The key challenges were to provide a security framework that would plug in easily to the strategic applications that were being planned; to define a secure administration model to manage user profiles seamlessly in extranet and intranet directories; to provide an application security framework that was compliant with the needs of the organization; and finally, to define a solution architecture that would extend to future applications that would be available to independent financial advisers and e-Business portals.

Wipro conducted interviews with the customer's management and users to study the security needs of the business and identify issues existing in the security infrastructure. It analyzed the business applications to be integrated with a single sign-on mechanism and identified the level of authentication and access to be assigned to the users. After gathering customer requirements, Wipro undertook a consulting exercise and came up with a prototype of integrating security via the middleware framework. On successful proof of concept, the customer gave Wipro the responsibility of designing and implementing the security model with the middleware enablement framework.

Wipro proposed and implemented a comprehensive security framework that secured access to applications/components through a middleware enablement framework that provided Single Sign-On to users accessing Web-based J2EE applications

[1] This case study was summarized from: www.wipro.com/itservices/ebusiness/esscasestudy2.htm.

through the middleware enablement framework. The middleware enablement framework provided a common generic authorization model (Role-based Access Control, Fine-grained Access Control) for users to utilize the core business components of the middleware framework and a single point Administration that simplifies system and user management via an enterprise directory. The framework also provided a common audit mechanism to audit user activity/transactions of applications initiating transactions from the framework, and a secure messaging mechanism that would ensure data confidentiality and integrity of messages to back-end systems.

13.1 Reliability and quality considerations

Today a large number of enterprises are becoming e-Businesses enabled. e-Business applications that support remote work forces, wireless access, corporate partnership programs, and CRM systems, among many others, are doing more than ever to increase efficiency and improve relationships with partners and customers. While technology is revolutionizing the way enterprises conduct business, it is also affecting the ways that commercial information and organizations are accessed over networks, introducing new risks along with compliance and legal issues that need to be considered and addressed. This is true not only for individual operations but also for the entire supply chain. Unfortunately, increasing the availability of corporate information also significantly increases security risks. Protecting corporate information assets has taken on a whole new meaning with the rise of communication over the public network. In e-Business environments, traditional network borders – between remote users, branch offices, corporate headquarters and third-party companies, and between intranets, extranets and the Internet – are disappearing. Companies are turning to Virtual Private Networks (VPNs) on the Internet as the transport backbone to establish secure links with business partners, regional offices and remote users, to significantly decrease the cost of communications whilst maintaining and enhancing the level of security.

Fundamentally, e-Business is about creating new services and streamlining business processes by leveraging the company's computing infrastructure and Internet connectivity. The key to unlocking the vast potential of e-Business is highly available, high-performance computing services delivered across the Internet. Enterprise information systems play such a critical role in this endeavor that special measures have to be taken to protect them and to ensure their accurate and reliable functioning. This has been the case ever since computers were introduced into regular business practice. Now that critical business systems are becoming increasingly dependent on large networks, which link enterprise information systems in different locations belonging to different, independent enterprises, everyone's vulnerability to technical malfunctions, unintended faulty actions and human malevolence grows. Schoder and Yin [Schoder 2000b] have suggested that a lack of security, plus the legal issues involved and the fact that one is doing business with suppliers with whom one has no business history, are the main barriers to an enterprise moving its transactions online. The results of bad security are very obvious for an enterprise. They can result in disrupted and damaged corporate networks, damage to reputation, increased costs and ultimately loss of customers and market share.

The security of an enterprise's information systems has become a major management responsibility – security being the sum total of a enterprise's policies, organizational procedures and technical measures, which are used to safeguard the proper functioning of its enterprise information systems. Traditional enterprise security has focused almost entirely on keeping intruders out by using tools such as firewalls and content filters. This approach, however, does not fit the security demands of the emerging world of e-Business.

e-Business environments impose their own requirements. Verification of identities, non-repudiation of agreements and a swarm of other issues often come into play. Alongside such concerns, enterprises solidifying their positions on the e-Business front must protect themselves against a growing number of complex risks. Some of the risks that consistently plague e-Business interactions include the items that are mentioned below:

- Application-level vulnerabilities that allow exploits to pass through firewalls and intrusion detection systems undetected.

- Inadequate security controls for authenticating third parties.

- Unencrypted data residing on web servers and databases without proper authentication/data protection.

As a result, enterprises must adopt complicated controls where delegated authority, non-repudiation and audit trails, as well as stronger authentication, credential verification and access controls, are key elements. e-Business security constitutes a trusted electronic means of communicating with often a large number of trading partners, customers and suppliers over insecure networks such as the Internet. This involves the complex interaction of multiple computer environments, web interfaces, communication protocols, system infrastructures, and policies and procedures that must be considered when implementing secure e-Business integration initiatives.

Secure relationships are the building blocks of all business processes and interactions. To offer the highest standards of service and convenience, companies need to provide their customers with secure Web access to the back-office systems, enabling status assessment, purchases and much more. Also, the business partners may require access to systems in a distributed network environment. All this combined means that companies end up sharing portions of internal systems, applications and knowledge bases with business partners.

e-Business security requires specific technical, organizational and legal measures that must be an integral part of the control environment (a system of internal controls) set up for the enterprise as a whole. Such internal control systems include the separation of duties, clearly defined authority and responsibility, authorization systems, adequate documents and records and physical control over assets and records. These means are traditionally considered as part of internal control and auditing (for which the reader is referred to literature specializing in this field [Weber 1988]).

In addition to security, the key to unlocking the vast potential of e-Business is highly available, high-performance computing services delivered across the Internet. Thus, *quality of service* (QoS) becomes a critical instrument to ensure the enterprise infrastructure and deliver the scalability, security, transaction, and content-based requirements of the business. In devising a QoS plan, an enterprise must deal with issues such as: measuring the business impact of the infrastructure; prioritization of services based on corporate objectives; leveraging internal versus external resources; ensuring the reliability and availability of data; deploying applications and services rapidly and reliably; and measuring the effectiveness of QoS efforts.

The following sections will focus on the role that QoS plays for e-Business and the specific organizational and technical requirements needed for creating a reliable environment for e-Business communication using the Internet.

13.2 Quality requirements

Traditionally, QoS has been measured by the degree to which applications, systems, networks, and all other elements of the IT infrastructure support availability of services at a required level of performance under all access and load conditions [IDC 2000]. Although traditional business metrics apply to QoS, the characteristics of e-Business environments put specific and intense demands on organizations, which it must address. These include expectations regarding performance and reliability and time-to-market demands. Expectations regarding performance and reliability have been raised to very high levels, making it imperative to support e-Business solutions with scalable and dependable infrastructures that can adapt to virtually real-time changes in demand and activity. In addition, the time-to-market of new or enhanced e-Business solutions needs to increasingly become shorter as it is a by-product of the growing competitive nature of e-Business and the high expectations of participating parties.

The major requirements for supporting QoS in e-Business are summarized below and are mainly based on similar concerns raised in [Mani 2002]:

- *Availability*: availability is the absence of service downtime. Availability represents the probability that a service is available. Larger values represent that the service is always ready to use while smaller values indicate unpredictability of whether the service will be available at a particular time. Also associated with availability is time-to-repair (TTR). TTR represents the time it takes to repair a service that has failed. Ideally smaller values of TTR are desirable.

- *Accessibility*: accessibility represents the degree to which a client request is served. It may be expressed as a probability measure denoting the success rate or chance of a successful service instantiation at a point in time. A high degree of accessibility means that a service is available for a large number of clients and that clients can use the service relatively easily.

- *Conformance to standards*: describes the compliance of an e-Business application with standards. Strict adherence to correct versions of standards by service providers is necessary for proper invocation of e-Business applications by service requesters. In addition, service providers must stick to the standards outlined in the service-level agreements (SLAs).

- *Integrity*: describes the degree to which an e-Business application performs its tasks according to its description as well as conformance with its service-level agreement. A higher degree of integrity means that the functionality of a service is closer to its description or SLA.

- *Performance*: performance is measured in terms of two factors: throughput and latency. Throughput represents the number of application requests served in a given time period. Latency represents the length of time between sending a request and receiving the response. Higher throughput and lower latency values represent good performance of an e-Business application. When measuring the transaction/request volumes handled by an e-Business application it is important to consider whether these come in a steady flow or burst around particular events like the open or close of the business day or seasonal rushes.

- *Reliability*: reliability represents the ability of a service to function correctly and consistently and provide the same service quality despite system or network failures. The reliability of an e-Business application is usually expressed in terms of number of transactional failures per month or year.

- *Scalability*: scalability refers to the ability to consistently serve the requests despite variations in the volume of requests. High accessibility of an e-Business application can be achieved by building highly scalable systems.

- *Security*: security involves aspects such as authentication, authorization, message integrity and confidentiality (see Section 13.5). Security has added importance because e-Business application invocation occurs over the Internet. The amount of security that a particular e-Business application requires is described in its accompanying SLA, and service providers must maintain this level of security.

- *Transactionality*: there are several cases where an e-Business application requires transactional behavior and context propagation. A classical example is an application where goods can only be delivered if payment has been made. The fact that a particular activity requires transactional behavior is described in its accompanying SLA, and service providers must maintain this property.

The implementation issues relevant to delivering on QoS obligations include a multitiered e-Business architecture for facilitating integration with legacy applications and a variety of access devices (see Chapter 6); and a middle-tier caching of data, Web page content, and other information that can help effect significant reductions in network traffic. In addition, it requires providing an effective load-balancing strategy that can avoid performance and availability issues as network activities vary over time. Choosing the right technologies along these lines can have a significant impact on QoS success [IDC 2000].

Improvements in computing and network infrastructure and support, coupled with increasing internal performance expectations, have pushed enterprises to more stringently tie financial benefit to the QoS delivered. Detailed strategies for ensuring QoS can be found in [IDC 2000; Hurwitz 2001]. In the following we summarize the necessary measures of the strategy that must employed to guarantee that effective QoS is delivered:

- *Measuring the business impact of the computing infrastructure*. An enterprise must have sufficient management information to intelligently allocate resources to resolve problems. It must allocate resources to infrastructure problems that affect the most critical e-Business services, continuously measuring the business impact of the infrastructure to improve service availability and performance, which is a competitive advantage for e-Businesses. This item requires:
  - *Understanding application requirements and measuring their business impact*. The specific types of e-Business infrastructure management required will depend in great measure on the type of applications and

services being provided. Network performance, middle-tier caching capabilities, and other relevant parameters that affect QoS delivery must, therefore, be matched to the requirements of specific e-Business applications and services. When the nature and business impact of an application is understood, decisions can be made that optimize technology expenditures to solve the most critical problems. For instance, the simple case of a server failure that slows or prevents services to a customer who provides a large percentage of corporate revenues will justify greater effort and quicker response.

To measure the business impact of an enterprise's computing infrastructure requires tools that can identify how many users are experiencing problems, where the problems are occurring geographically, and exactly which services are being affected. In addition, it requires tools that link from the performance customers are seeing to the behavior of the infrastructure delivering the service [Hurwitz 2001a].

- *Ensuring the availability and reliability of data.* Information availability and reliability are critical for online transactions and service delivery; and are means to achieve this goal. Information value increases dramatically as more companies streamline business processes using e-Business services. Such increased information availability improves business process efficiency and acts as insurance against downtime. This protects enterprises from lost productivity, revenue, and opportunity costs.

- *Security and privacy management.* E-Business activities increasingly involve transactions and exchanges that must be trusted and secure. This becomes a more difficult management challenge as the numbers of individuals, organizations, marketplaces, and so forth, grow. Securing data and transactions is necessary to protect an enterprise from the risks of online business activities. The first step is performing a comprehensive risk assessment and security audit to understand not only the 'front-line' security threats, but also the 'back-end' vulnerabilities [Hurwitz 2001a]. Security requires carefully managing of the computing infrastructure as well as security devices, according to corporate security policies, on an on-going basis. To do this, companies require a scalable management system that manages [Hurwitz 2001a]:

  o authentication and access control systems like public key infrastructures (see Section 13.5.1)
  o configuration of all security resources such as firewalls, remote access servers and so on, for compliance with security policies
  o monitoring of all computing resources, such as enterprise information systems, network devices and applications, for changes in configurations that increase security risks

- Deploying e-Business applications and services in a rapid and reliable manner to improve the enterprise's time-to-market. Time-to-market for e-Business services is a critical factor in achieving success. This refers to the speed of decision making, partnering, market emergence, and the impact of commercial events. To compete effectively, enterprises need to bring well-managed online services to market quickly. For this purpose, tools are required that allow enterprises to quickly deploy new e-Business applications and services, as well as customize and expand performance management capabilities for those applications and services. Such tools must deliver [Hurwitz 2001a]:

  o software deployment capabilities that automatically identify and solve distribution and configuration problems
  o software modules that automatically manage software reliability after deployment
  o software management systems that rapidly expand to cover new software technologies

A Service-Level Agreement is an important and widely used instrument in the maintenance of service provision relationships that ensures a guaranteed level of performance is delivered. Where contracts are clearly defined and closely monitored in order to guarantee adherence of all involved parties to the terms agreed upon, then participants are protected by the SLA. An SLA is basically a performance guarantee typically backed up by charge-back and other mechanisms designed to compensate service clients and to force enterprises to fulfill contractual commitments. Both service providers and clients alike need to utilize SLAs in order to work well together.

A service level agreement is a contract between a service provider and a client that specifies, usually in measurable terms, what services the service provider will furnish. It defines mutual understandings and expectations of a service between the service provider and service consumers. The service guarantees are about what transactions need to be executed and how well they should be executed. An SLA may have the following components: purpose – describing the reasons behind the creation of the SLA; parties – describes the parties involved in the SLA and their respective roles (provider and consumer); validity period – defines the period of time that the SLA will cover. This is delimited by start time and end time of the term. An SLA also has a scope that defines the services covered in the agreement, restrictions that define the necessary steps to be taken in order for the requested service levels to be provided, and service-level objectives, which are the levels of service that both the users and the service providers agree on, and usually include a set of service-level indicators, like availability, performance and reliability. Finally, an SLA also specifies penalties in case the service provider underperforms and is unable to meet the objectives in the SLA.

To better understand requirements when entering into an e-Business application SLA, one needs to address several important concerns. These include: the levels of availability that are needed for an application; whether the business can tolerate application downtime and how much; whether there is adequate redundancy built in so that services can be offered in the event of a system or network failure; the transaction volumes expected of e-Business applications and services; whether underlying systems have been designed and tested to meet these peak load requirements and, finally, how important are request/response times.

SLAs are, in conjunction with security policies, reviews of security procedures, staff qualifications and so on, one of the most effective means of dealing with QoS. One important function that an SLA should address is the QoS at the source. This refers to the level of service that a particular service provides [Mani 2002]. QoS is defined by important functional and nonfunctional service quality attributes, such as service metering and cost, performance metrics (e.g. response time), security attributes, (transactional) integrity, reliability, scalability, and availability. Service clients (end-user organizations that use some service) and service aggregators (organizations that consolidate multiple services into a new, single service offering) utilize service descriptions to achieve their objectives. QoS must be aligned with organizational objectives, and it is important to understand to what degree each service supports those objectives [IDC 2000]. The level of management support required for each service must also be ascertained. Determinations made are fundamental, and they feed into subsequent decisions. Without this determination, low-impact services that do not require high levels of QoS support could be an unnecessary drain on resources.

Effective service-level management, i.e. the service objectives and performance targets that are reflected in service management policies and practices of an organization, depends on applying proper metrics. These metrics should assess performance management in terms of how well business priorities and objectives are being met. For successful e-Business, one of these metrics needs to address the agility of the implementation. Agility, in the case of architectures for e-Business, reflects not only the ability to foresee necessary changes to meet performance and scale issues but also a level of adaptability to conditions, the details of which are partially or completely unknown at the time the architecture is designed and built [IDC 2000].

Effective e-Business infrastructure management requires that particular attention be paid to reliability and scalability as these affect the performance and availability of e-Business applications and services. Therefore, reliability and scalability are two important factors to consider when selecting an e-Business infrastructure that contributes to overall QoS. Inherent in this choice is an evaluation of current and future capacity, measured in an application-relevant way, e.g. transactions per unit time, average size of content-based download, and so on. Emphasis must be placed on the ability of an enterprise to scale the overall infrastructure in response to changing conditions in terms of transactions, numbers of users, and other considerations [IDC 2000]. In this context, scalability reflects the ability of the infrastructure to handle effectively such dynamic load requirements.

To handle reliability and scalability requirements, enterprises must assess the current state and future capabilities of their e-Business infrastructure. The overall business plan and the levels of business activity with customers, partners and all relevant parties, and how these change over time, are important issues for this kind of assessment. Consequently, capacity planning must not only address present requirements but also leverage business planning assets to forecast and plan for future infrastructural demands and developments [IDC 2000]. Capacity planning may be defined [Menascé 2000] as the process of predicting when future load levels will saturate the system and determining the most cost-effective means of delaying system saturation as much as possible.

13.3 Trust

Market transactions (including those in hierarchical arrangements between business partners with long-term relations) are affected by a variety of uncertainties and risks. The element of trust and the possibility of opportunistic behavior have therefore received considerable attention in recent business literature [Fukuyama 1995]. Opportunistic behavior has been described [Williamson 1979] as "self-interest-seeking with guile". This issue points to the ever-present risk of one's business partners premeditatedly violating the deals made. It is found in all kinds of business, independent of the channel used, although the shape it takes is different for every business channel and every line of business.

Trust on the other hand is the belief – or the willingness to believe – that one can rely on the fairness, goodness, strength and ability of one's partners, who may be sellers, buyers or any other enterprise or individual with an interest in the transaction at hand. It is an expectation, arising within a community, of regular, honest, and cooperative behavior based on commonly shared norms. Trust therefore applies to all elements of the transaction: buyers expect the delivery of the right products, of the right quality and at the right time, while sellers expect payment as agreed. As Fukuyama [Fukuyama 1995] argues: "People who do not trust one another will end up cooperating only under a system of formal rules and regulations, which have to be negotiated, agreed to, litigated and enforced, sometimes by coercive means". Such a legal and procedural apparatus serves as a substitute for trust, but it entails making transaction costs. Absence of trust thus implies that higher costs will be incurred.

Recently it's has been suggested that there are three kinds of trust: *person-based*, that is, based on the characteristics of a person; *enterprise-based* or tied to the enterprise as an entity; and *institution-based*, which means it is founded on formal mechanisms such as the laws and codes in a particular society. Frequently, a fourth kind of trust is mentioned as well: that *in technology*. This involves the expectation that the technology will function as it should (that is, do what it must do and not do what it must not do) and that any mistakes caused by it will be corrected or compensated for. The correction and compensation element in this description immediately shows that trust in technology, too, is really trust in the people who use it (or the organization which uses it or the rules and regulations under which it is used). We need not, therefore, take a closer look at trust in technology. In global markets, in which the only contact buyers and sellers have with one another may be established through databases and communication networks, it is enterprise-based and institution-based trust which clearly must receive special attention.

To be trusted, a company that embarks on an e-Business initiative needs to protect the information it publishes as well as information it gathers from visitors to its site and from transactions it conducts with its partners. Therefore, a privacy policy should be in place. Each business page or document published on the Web should provide a notice linking to that privacy policy and allowing 'opt-in' and/or 'opt-out' options. Documents published on the Web need expiration dates and a process to remove the documents. Furthermore, consent must be obtained from authors of any published material, and if copying or reuse is prevented, then that should be made clear. If data is collected, then customer notification is absolutely necessary regarding the policies of use, retention and collection of that data. All these issues contribute to building trust relationships between companies.

Since one can never be entirely sure that one's business partners can be trusted, the question arises of how much risk it is acceptable to take. Both individuals and enterprises can seek risks, for example when they expect greater benefits. They may also try to avoid risks or steer a middle course, choosing a route that neither increases nor decreases the risks they run. Generally, the risk one is willing to accept will be determined economically, by the nature of the transactions and the business value involved. Less value and small potential damages usually mean higher risks are acceptable. Another factor is the existence or absence of a previous business relation. It is these previous relations that the European Commission, for instance, has used to made a distinction between traditional e-Business and Internet-based e-Business [EC 1997]. Traditional e-Business generally involves a limited number of participants, usually in one kind of industry, who all know and trust each other. They use closed and secure private IT networks called value-added networks. Essentially, such a market functions like a club. Internet e-Business on the other hand uses an open network, the Internet, and it is a global affair with a theoretically unlimited number of participants, only some of whom you may know. Since the network is open, it is unprotected. Thus, security and authentication (proof of identity) are needed.

Participants who share a history of established business relations are able, in the case of differences of opinion, to rely on the business procedures they know from the physical world. For instance, once enterprises do business together for some time, a certain belief in the continuity of their partners grows and this results in a kind of enterprise-based trust. Such long-term relations enable the enterprises quickly to solve any differences that might arise. Trust that has been built doing physical business can be carried over into the virtual world, for example in the shape of a certain amount of confidence in one's partners' websites. Enterprises without such a history cannot rely on such trust, which renders them dependent on the procedures currently used on the Internet. This frequently slows down the speed with which transactions may be concluded.

One of the most important goals is to align security and privacy policies with business objectives [IBM 2001]. Businesses thus need to address questions, including: What business information and IT resources need to be protected and from whom? What is the cost of a security breach weighed against the cost of protection? What is the likelihood of a breach, and what is the right amount of security and privacy as e-Businesses evolve from simply publishing on a Website to using the Web for full integration of business processes across the enterprise? Identifying and translating the answers to these questions into security and privacy policies, procedures and ongoing active management is essential at each state of e-Business evolution.

13.4 e-Business risks

The emergence of e-Business has introduced new kinds of risks. These are all consequences of the fact that e-Business is done without any direct personal contact. All contact runs through computers, data communication networks and Websites. Contact is frequently established with persons and organizations of which one does not even know in which country they operate, let alone their address or any other specifics. Person-based trust and even institution-based trust are then absent. Another risk is that the business done depends totally on the IT infrastructure's performance – if the infrastructure fails, then all business ceases.

Doing business has gone through many changes. At first, a simple handshake was enough to confirm a transaction. This meant that both parties must always be physically present, but once accepted as the way business was done, it provided maximum security. In fact, in some industries in some parts of the world, business is still conducted in this manner – think of the gold and jewelry trade. But once the procedures involved increase in number and complexity, such methods become impracticable. Modern transactions require all kinds of safety checks and information, for which standard forms are generally used (waybills, insurance policies, invoices). Effectively, the physical flow of goods is accompanied every step of the way by a parallel flow of information. The transaction can thus become a very complex process. Shipping a container with chemical products from Germany to the United States, for example, may involve over 40 different parties and more than 100 different types of documents [Bons 1997]. This shows that it is no longer necessary to meet physically in order to do business reliably.

If there is some doubt with regard to the reliability of a prospective trade partner (that is, if there is a lack of trust), certain measures can be taken. Special agencies, like Dun and Bradstreet, can be hired to investigate enterprises' creditworthiness. If additional financial security is desired, the prospective partner may be asked for a bank guarantee. This means that the bank of the partner whose reliability is in doubt guarantees to pay the money due if the partner cannot pay it himself. Thus, the other partner acquires at least some financial security. Naturally, the bank involved will only give such a guarantee on certain conditions, which usually include a counter guarantee to pay the bank back its money, backed up by some form of collateral. Obviously, taking such measures to shore up confidence in one's reliability as a business partner increases the costs of the transaction.

Trade in virtual environments involves essentially the same questions of trust and reliability as does business in the physical world. But because there is no physical contact, there are specific, additional questions that need to be addressed:

- Can you be sure of the identity of one's prospective partners? – Is the customer the one he claims to be? Is the supplier of goods and services the one he claims to be?

- Can you be sure that business-related data has not been intercepted and tampered with while it was transmitted over the Internet? Has the order been tampered with? Has the payment arrived unchanged?

- Is it possible to deny that a certain transaction has been conducted? Can a customer simply deny ordering? Will it be possible to fight the legality of an order because the person placing it lacked the proper authority for it?

- Is your privacy guaranteed? Can anyone else gain access to the data transferred?

As these questions indicate, conducting business on the Internet does not only involve reliability questions with respect to prospective partners. Even if these are perfectly trustworthy, other individuals or organizations, not involved in the transaction, may interfere. The fraud risks involved in conducting business on the Internet are numerous. The most typical ones can be classified into four categories [Felten 1996; Froomkin 1996]:

- Data may be intercepted and read or even changed. This is called a *man in the middle attack*: a third party intrudes into the data flow between trade partners, reading and changing their messages before relaying them on, and thus manipulating their communication. Sometimes this can be done without the real partners even noticing.

- Intentionally misrepresenting one's identity in order to commit fraud is called *broad spoofing*. Spoofing entails using false e-mail addresses or domain names. In 1998 one of the major West European banks fell victim to a spoofing ploy. Customers logging into their charge accounts believed they were dealing with their bank, while all the time they were diverted to a fake website that could not be distinguished from the real thing.

- *Hacking* is probably the best known of these risks. This involves the unauthorized access to one's network by another network's user.

- Finally, competitors or other malevolent parties may crash the computer system involved: a *denial of service attack*. The result is that the Website becomes inaccessible to customers and much potential revenue is lost.

Today companies that conduct their business over the Internet and other insecure communication networks face increasing risk from network security breaches. Large organizations are attacked on a regular basis through ever new and creative means. The 2004 Computer Crime and Security survey conducted by the Computer Security Institute (CSI) and the FBI revealed that 100% of surveyed companies experienced attacks. Measuring the likelihood of successful attack is very difficult. The CSI/FBI survey on Computer Crime and Security reported that 53% of survey respondents were successfully breached with a cost of damage in excess of $500 000 per incident. The actual percentage could be much higher due to the reluctance of many companies to reveal security information. In fact, 48% of respondents did not report breaches in general, fearing leakage of information. Therefore, securing networks becomes a primary target for large organizations. This requires identifying and fixing vulnerabilities in advance.

There are several factors contributing to escalating security risks for company networks attached to the Internet. Some of the reasons include the following:

- Networks increasingly have multiple entry points – for example, VPNs and wireless access points used by remote employees. This exposes networks to threats from unknown software and unprotected connections.

- Automated tools have made it easier to identify and exploit network exposures, swelling the rate of attacks on networks attached to the Internet.

- Viruses, worms and trojans have evolved into sophisticated, self-propagating attacks, resistant to detection, and boost damage through a multiplier effect: they keep on 'giving' long after the initial incident.

- The lifecycle for network attacks is shorter and as a consequence companies have less time to identify and correct vulnerabilities before they are exploited by hackers and worms.

- Networks and applications have grown more complex and difficult to manage, even as qualified security professionals are scarce and IT budgets have come under pressure.

The security risks for companies that conduct their business over the Internet are significantly reduced if they implement an integrated enterprise-wide security architecture. An integrated enterprise-wide security architecture facilitates the exchange of confidential, mission-critical information securely and in a timely fashion, and can be administered centrally, using a single technology-independent policy-based approach for specifying security requirements and one security policy enterprise-wide. A comprehensive systematic security policy needs to be established and technologies can then be applied in the context of the overall policy. An effective information security policy must include the following six objectives: privacy and confidentiality; integrity; availability; legitimate use (identification, authentication, and authorization); auditing or traceability; and nonrepudiation. If these objectives could be achieved, it would alleviate most of the information security concerns. However, before an enterprise security architecture can be built, the security problem must be understood and articulated from a common frame of reference, including an understanding of how threats exist, how to express requirements to counter them, and how they can be mitigated using security features, mechanisms and products.

In the following we shall examine technologies and elements of an enterprise security infrastructure that provides the building blocks for an enterprise-wide security solution.

13.5 e-Business security

Security is emerging as the essential element that must be woven into the fabric of a corporate network, bringing together critical resources such as the infrastructure, systems, applications and users. In the physical world enterprises rely on conventional security measures to protect and safeguard confidential corporate information. Traditional enterprise security has focused almost entirely on keeping intruders out by using tools such as firewalls and content filters. Firewalls act as a secure interface between a private, trusted enterprise network and external untrusted networks (see section 13.6.2). Firewalls use content filters to permit/deny packet flow on the basis of the origin and destination of the packet's addresses and ports. The firewall can be used to control access to and from the enterprise network. This includes access to resources such as application services and specific hosts. When properly configured to implement a judicious security policy, firewalls can protect an enterprise network from intrusion and compromise.

e-Business is forcing enterprises to move away from private communication networks to open public networks such as the Internet, where enterprises open their private network applications and information assets to customers, suppliers and business partners. This means letting customers and business partners into the private enterprise network, essentially through the firewall, but in a selective and controlled manner, so that they access only applications permitted to them. Hence, enterprises must rely on sophisticated electronic means for protecting business critical information, transactions and communication with a large number of trading partners, customers, and suppliers, over insecure networks such as the Internet. e-Business security involves the complex interaction of multiple computer environments, communication protocols, Web interfaces, policies and procedures that must all be considered when implementing a coherent, consistent approach to e-Business security.

Until recently, enterprises have controlled and managed access to resources by building authorization and authentication into each e-Business application. This piecemeal approach is not only time-consuming but also error-prone, and expensive to build and maintain. Eventually, this technique becomes unsustainable as an enterprise's e-Business portfolio grows, and as online interactions between enterprises become more complex. What is required is a comprehensive e-Business security solution that is easily managed and satisfies a demanding set of user and developer security requirements, and provides capabilities such as performance, speed of deployment and scalability, as well as the flexibility to accommodate evolving technologies such as wireless devices and Web services.

e-Business security marks a departure from traditional security as it poses new security requirements in connection with access (authentication, authorization), confidentiality, nonrepudiation and integrity of information [Yang 2000].

13.5.1 Application security requirements

To address the security issues facing organizations as they adopt e-Business technology, it is essential to apply the principles of *application security*. In order to establish some clarity in the security discussion, the British Standards Institution has provided a definition [BSI 1999] of information security that is now widely accepted [Froomkin 1996; Gartner 1998; Menascé 2000]. According to this definition application security contains five basic requirements, expressed in terms of the messages exchanged between parties [Pilz 2003]. Such messages include any kind of communication between the sender (party who wishes to access an application) and the recipient (the application itself). The five requirements for application-level security can be summarized as follows:

- *Authentication*: This is a combination of identification (claiming an identity) and verification (proving that the identity is as claimed). Authenticity refers to a state in which there can be no dispute about the identity of the communicating partners. It is the most important of the conditions to be met because none of the other aspects can be safeguarded without a reliable authentication mechanism [Ford 1997]. Authentication verifies that the identity of entities is provided by the use of public key certificates and digital signature envelopes. Authentication in the e-Business environment is performed very well by public key cryptographic systems incorporated into a Public Key Infrastructure (PKI), which we will describe later in this section. The primary goal of authentication in a PKI is to support the remote and unambiguous authentication between entities unknown to each other, using public key certificates and trust hierarchies.

- *Authorization*: This ensures that the information sent is accessible only to those who are properly authorized. No third parties must be able to read the information while it is being transferred or stored. Authorization verifies that the identity has the necessary permissions to obtain the requested resource or act on something before providing access to it. Normally, authorization is preceded by authentication.

- *Message integrity*: This involves safeguarding the accuracy and completeness of the information and its processing methods. Integrity ensures that data cannot be corrupted or modified, and transactions cannot be altered. Message (data) integrity comprises two requirements: first, the data received must be the same as the data sent. In other words, data integrity systems must be able to guarantee that a message did not change in transit, either by mistake or on purpose. The second requirement for message integrity is that at any time in the future, it is possible to prove whether different copies of the same document are in fact identical.

- *Confidentiality*: Confidentiality means that an unauthorized person cannot view or interfere with a communication between two parties. It refers to the ability to ensure that messages and data are available only to those who are authorized to view them. Confidentiality is sometimes confused with privacy, which refers to the ability to control the use of personal information.

- *Operational defence*: The system must be able to detect and guard against attacks by illegitimate messages, including XML Denial of Service (XDoS) and XML viruses, and must be operationally scalable with existing personnel and infrastructure.

In addition to the above five requirements, two more requirements must be added for secure e-Business applications, these are: auditability and nonrepudiation.

- *Auditability* means that operations on content must be transparent and capable of being proven. That is, the information system and the information contained in it may readily be audited to check whether they conform to the standards specified, even when there are interruptions.

- *Nonrepudiation* means that two or more parties cannot deny that they have talked to each other. In other words, neither the sender nor the receiver of the information can deny sending or receiving it, respectively.

Finally, one additional issue that is mentioned frequently is *certification*. This issue concerns the legal capacity of the party involved as well as a check on who is given access. For example: is the person contacting you authorized to conclude a legally binding contract for their enterprise, and for what maximum amount of money?

Companies that collaborate in e-Business settings view suppliers, partners and customers (value networks) as extensions of their own business. In fact, core business processes are very tightly coupled with these value networks and are supported by applications run across enterprise boundaries. As explained earlier in this book, these applications may be run in a company's customer, partner or supplier enterprise. This means that functions such as product manufacturing, for example, are then linked with supplier component manufacturing, fulfillment, transportation and logistics. However, pieces of administration, authorization and authentication residing in different companies make it difficult to implement security features across enterprise borders. Organizations should thus harmonize differences in security policies so that they can clearly identify privacy information and maintain equivalent safeguards.

13.5.2 Security mechanisms for e-Business

When considering the application-level security requirements that we addressed in the previous section, it is important to understand that the fundamental need for mechanisms and technologies is that any kind of communication between the sender and the recipient is safe and secure.

In the case of authentication and authorization, all user attempts to access an e-Business application or service are handled by a security infrastructure technology, which authenticates the user (or external application) and grants the appropriate access to the requested resource or system. Many authentication methods exist, ranging from simple usernames and passwords to stronger methods such as tokens and digital certificates. In the following we shall first concentrate on the use of digital certificates as a means of authentication for e-Business applications.

Digital certificates are exchanged during the set up of communication links to verify that the trading partner on the other end of the wire is the intended recipient of a message transmission and to prove the sender's identity. A digital certificate binds an entity's identification to its public key and is issued by a certification authority, which we will describe later in this section. *Digital certificates* are files that contain information that identifies the user or organization that owns the certificate, the time period for which the certificate is valid, the organization that issued the certificate, and a digital signature that verifies the issuing organization's identity.

Digital signatures guarantee that the enterprise/person represented in the digital certificate sent the message. A *digital signature* is a block of data created by applying a cryptographic signing algorithm to some data using the signer's private key. Digital signatures may be used to authenticate the source of a message and to assure message recipients that no one has tampered with a message since the time it was sent by the signer. Digital signatures are attached to the message body to identify the sender. The receiver verifies the digital signature by decrypting it with the sender's public key to retrieve the message. In this way authentication mechanisms ensure that only the intended parties can exchange sensitive information.

Once the supplied digital certificate or other credentials have authenticated a user's identity, the user's access privileges must be determined. Authorization is meant to limit the actions or operations that authenticated parties are able to perform in a networked environment. The classical solution for restricting employee and trading partner access to sensitive information is by means of access control lists (ACLs) on a resource such as a Web page and then evaluating the kind of access requested to determine if the requester has permission to access the resource. None, read-only, add, edit, or full control access rights can be assigned.

Message integrity ensures that information that is being transmitted has not been altered. Secure transactions are the typical mechanism that guarantees that a message has not been modified while in transit. This is commonly known as communication integrity and is often accomplished through hashing algorithms and digitally signed digest codes.

Secure transactions should also guarantee confidentiality. Confidentiality refers to the use of encryption for scrambling the information sent over the Internet and stored on servers so that eavesdroppers cannot access the data. This is also known as 'quality privacy', but most specialists reserve this word for the 'protection of personal information' (confidential or not) from aggregation and improper use.

Nonrepudiation is of critical importance for carrying out transactions over the Internet. It consists of cryptographic receipts that are created so that the author of a message cannot falsely deny sending a message. These tasks fall well within the premises of contract formation and enforcement. Tracking digitally signed messages using a tracking data repository provides an audit trail for guaranteeing nonrepudiation. The receiver saves the digital signature together with the message in the repository for later reference in case a dispute arises.

Application integrated security requires that individual corporate business applications include functionality for achieving secure communications between a client and application server. SSL (*Secure Sockets Layer*), used primarily with web browsers, is the security protocol most commonly used in this approach. Traditionally, the SSL along with the de facto Transport Layer Security (TLS) and Internet Protocol Security (IPSec) are some of the common ways of securing e-Business content. SSL/TLS offers several security features including server and client authentication, data integrity and data confidentiality. SSL/TLS enables point-to-point (server-to-server) secure sessions. More specifically, SSL uses encryption and authentication techniques to ensure communication between a client and a server remain private and to allow the client to identify the server and vice versa. SSL is the mechanism supported by most Web browsers and Web servers. As SSL does not support certificate validation, certificate extensions are currently provided to facilitate certificate validation. Additionally, SSL extensions also provide such features as monitoring, logging and access control authorization, which are traditionally not supported by conventional SSL technology. IPSec is another network layer standard for transport security that may become important for e-Business applications. Like SSL/TLS, IPSec also provides secure sessions with host authentication, data integrity and data confidentiality. However, these are point-to-point technologies. They create a secure tunnel through which data can pass [Mysore 2003]. For instance, SSL is a good solution for server-to-server security but it cannot adequately address the scenario where a message is routed via more than one server. In this case the recipient has to request credentials of the sender and the scalability of the system is compromised. The session-based authentication mechanisms used by SSL have no standard way to transfer credentials to service providers via messages. e-Business applications require much more granularity. They need to maintain secure context and control it according to their security policies.

It is widely accepted that Public Key Infrastructure (PKI) is one of the main technologies for supporting the security requirements of e-Business applications. *Public Key Infrastructure* is a technology that provides the necessary foundation to implement e-Business security. PKI is a system of digital certificates and certification authorities that verify and authenticate the validity of parties involved in Internet transactions. This is illustrated in Figure 13.1. PKI capabilities help create and manage asymmetric cryptographic keys or public/private keys required by e-Business applications. A PKI is a foundation upon which other applications and network security components are built. The specific security functions for which a PKI can provide a foundation are confidentiality, integrity, nonrepudiation and authentication. The following major PKI components provide the necessary capabilities to establish, maintain, and protect trusted relationships [Schlosser 1999]:

- A certification authority that creates and signs digital certificates, maintains certificate revocation lists, makes certificates and revocation lists available, and provides an interface so that administrators can manage certificates.

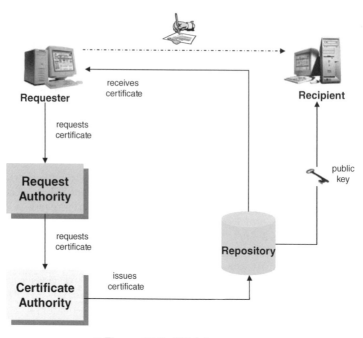

Figure 13.1: PKI Infrastructure

- The registration authority that evaluates the credentials and relevant evidence that an organization requesting a certificate is indeed the organization who they claim to be.

- PKIX, the X.509 standard that defines the contents of public key certificates and a set of proposed IETF standards that are intended to provide interoperability between digital certificates produced by different vendors.

Appropriate extensions to the PKI infrastructure add the ability to ensure the confidentiality of exchanges of digitally signing and encrypting messages as they are sent, and decrypting and authenticating messages when they are received.

PKI is not simply an authentication technology. When there is a risk of fraud, a risk of legal ramifications if a transaction is altered or disclosed, or when the confirmed identity of an individual or business entity is essential, PKI becomes crucial. For this reason, organizations that engage in e-Business, e-government, finance, healthcare, and manufacturing are well positioned to consider implementing PKI.

Other critical functions and benefits that PKI provides include:

- Confidentiality, which protects sensitive information

- Integrity, whereby transactions are guaranteed not to be altered

- Nonrepudiation, which provides evidence that transactions have occurred

- Integration, the ability to integrate with all company functions: marketing, sales, finance, etc., rather than through a piecemeal integration process.

The PKI should offer comprehensive functionality, integrate easily with internal and external applications, scale to large numbers of users, operate flawlessly 24x7, and ensure security. In addition, it should allow enterprises to easily create communities of trust with partners, customers, and suppliers.

13.6 Realizing a secure e-Business infrastructure

Addressing trust issues, avoiding risks, and achieving the security requirements, which we discussed in the previous section, coalesce into three basic quality requirements that the IT infrastructure for e-Business must meet. These are:

1. infrastructure availability;
2. network level security;
3. secure communications.

Anchoring these requirements into the business processes of enterprises, which intend to trade via the Internet, involves considerable development efforts and a specialized infrastructure. Many small and medium-sized enterprises will have difficulty finding the resources to do so. This gives an opportunity to new facilitating intermediaries, trusted third parties (TTPs), to act as go-betweens to guarantee secure e-Business. In the following we will take a close look at the preceding three quality requirements and discuss the role of trusted third parties.

13.6.1 Infrastructure availability

If there is to be e-Business, there must be an IT infrastructure. *IT infrastructure* may be defined as the totality of the resources available for long-term, continuous, common use. The term 'available' means that those resources have the capacity required and can be used whenever required. The availability requirement identifies the functionalities of the infrastructure's hardware and software components and specifies the corresponding service-level requirements [Menascé 2000].

After the network connections, the most important elements of the infrastructure are servers and databases. Servers regulate incoming and outgoing data flows, and at least one Web server is needed to communicate with the Internet. In addition, one or more application servers may be used to handle the application operations between browser-based customers and an enterprise's back-office databases. Subsequently, enterprise information systems servers will be added. These may include existing enterprise information systems such as stock administration systems, possibly developed on the basis of legacy data stored in mainframes, or may be completely new enterprise information systems. Often a client database is set up also, to store financial information regarding purchasing customers, prices, and methods of payment specific to a particular transaction. Many different kinds of databases may be used, for different types of information. Killela [Killela 1998] distinguishes between three basic types:

- Read-only databases, facilitating individual queries (such as the Google or Alta Vista search engines).

- Databases with which to carry out transaction processes such as online credit card verification and providing access to one's bank account; databases of this type are becoming increasingly important for e-Business.

- Databases facilitating complex queries to establish links between large amounts of data; these 'data mining' databases, which are frequently used for marketing purposes, are so complex they are generally not suited for e-Business applications.

IT availability usually means that the infrastructure is available when it is needed. However, different organizations may have different needs with respect to IT infrastructure availability. Some may, for instance, wish to make their infrastructure available for eight hours on every working day, or offer it for continuous periods of seven days and 24 hours per day. Obviously, continuous availability will require extra investments in order to allow for maintenance and making backups. Another question to address is what failure rates are acceptable. Any enterprise requiring seven days and 24 hours availability in combination with a really small chance of failure will have to take some very specific infrastructural measures. One such measure is setting up a redundant system with which data is frequently exchanged. Even for redundant systems there are many different possibilities, from simple systems with hardware maintenance contracts to the so-called 'full swappable redundant systems' or 'hot stand-bys', which allow complete internal or external data diversion. In the latter situation a complete hardware system is set up alongside the hardware in actual use, and it is kept online so that if the original system fails it can restore its functions straightaway. Clearly, the choice of backup system is made on the basis of the failure rate that is acceptable considering the consequences of the system failing.

Availability also means that the capacity to be used is large enough. Here, capacity planning considerations that were discussed in Section 13.2 must be taken into account. What capacity is adequate depends on the service-level agreements for performance measures like response time and availability, as well as on the technologies used and the cost constraints involved. Apart from the Web servers and databases that must be utilized, having a large enough capacity implies having a system with sufficient bandwidth, for it is the bandwidth that determines how many visitors can use the application at any one time. Small bandwidths and large numbers of visitors combine to give long waiting times. Finally, another aspect that must be taken into account is the connection of the system to other systems, especially back-office systems used for stock administration, logistics and finances. If these connections are less than perfect, the application's speed will be slowed down significantly. This means that the amount of data included in the databases used, the intended use of the database, its target performance and many related aspects must be carefully balanced against each other.

13.6.2 Network level security

Companies face increasing risk from network security breaches as networks have grown more complex and difficult to manage and increasingly have multiple entry points – for example, Virtual Private Networks (see later in this section) and wireless access points. This exposes networks to threats from unknown software and unprotected connections.

Network level security incorporates embedded encryption functionality within network devices or operating systems utilizing Internet Protocol Security (IPSec), see Section 13.5.1. Network level solutions are usually designed to terminate the secure connections at the corporate firewall. Enterprises employing network level security solutions rely on two main technologies to protect their networks: firewalls and vulnerability assessment.

Firewalls

Networks must be kept safe from typical e-Business threats, such as spoofing and 'man in the middle' attacks. In order to prevent such trouble arising, the system's network connections and e-Business applications must be managed well. Firewalls play an important role here. A *firewall* (also called a secure internet gateway) supports communication-based security to screen out undesired communications. Firewalls are built between an organization's internal network and the Internet backbone and serve as security beachheads that define the network perimeter where an enterprise meets the Internet.

Firewalls identify incoming traffic by name, IP address, application etc. This information is checked against the rules that have been programmed into the system. Thus any unauthorized communication between the internal and the external network is prevented. In order for a firewall to be effective it must be an integral part of an overall security policy, covering broader corporate policies and user responsibilities; as a stand-alone measure it will have limited effect. Clear organizational structures and procedures are needed to create and maintain effective firewalls. The rules regarding the identification of who and what is accepted or rejected must be made explicit and they have to be maintained. Firewalls are typically configured to filter traffic based on the basis of a deny, unless specifically permitted, policy [Minoli 1998]. Functions typically provide by a firewall include the following [Ford 1997]:

- Limiting the set of applications for which traffic can enter the internal network from the Internet, and limiting the internal addresses to which traffic for different applications can go.

- Authenticating the sources of incoming traffic.

- Limiting the ability of internal enterprise networks and systems to establish connections to the Internet, on the basis of the application used and other relevant information.

- Acting as a security gateway and encrypting and/or integrity checking all traffic over the Internet backbone to or from some other security gateway. Such a continuation is known as a Virtual Private Network. VPNs allow organizations to use their corporate networks and the Internet as a wide area network to achieve secure connectivity with their branches, suppliers, customers and remote users.

Because firewalls determine what traffic is allowed to pass into an enterprise from the Internet, they are the essential first line of defence against hackers. A firewall that is a perfect brick wall admits no outside traffic and ensures perfect security for an enterprise. It is hardly practical, however, because it isolates the company from its customers and partners. Rather, the firewall must selectively admit traffic based on the guidelines a com.5pany defines. This opens the door for potential intruders. What's more, whenever the company modifies its firewall policies – for example, to permit new services or devices to access the Internet, or to update policy – it might inadvertently create new security vulnerabilities.

Figure 13.2 shows a typical enterprise network after deploying a firewall. The enterprise network is likely to include several types of subnetworks. This includes a *demilitarized zone* (DMZ) which is the local area network attached to the unprotected interface of the firewall that communicates with the Internet. This is an area

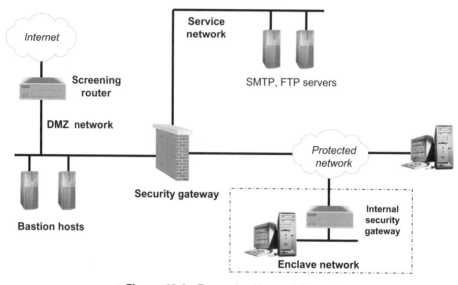

Figure 13.2: Enterprise Network Firewall

where enterprises typically host assets such as web servers. The demilitarized zone is open to the Internet and has less security than an internal portion of the network would. Between the demilitarized zone and the internal corporate network there is a firewall mechanism protecting internal EIS from unauthorized users who might try to gain access to any internal network resources. The firewall usually directs the traffic coming from the Web server directly to internal resources, such as data servers, and prevents any other resources from being accessed by traffic coming from the website server. The enterprise network is shown also to include a service network, which is an internal subnetwork protected by the firewall, which is used to offer services over the Internet such as a FTP access. As Figure 13.2 shows, the main mission of the firewall is to protect an internal trusted network. Finally, Figure 13.2 shows that an enterprise network may include an enclave network. This is another form of internal network protected from the rest of the internal network to mitigate internal threats to sensitive data.

Intrusion detection systems and vulnerability assessment

One possible technology for network protection is Intrusion Detection Systems (IDS). *Intrusion detection systems* monitor and analyze system and network events to find and warn network administrators of unauthorized attempts to access system resources. IDS support network administrators in two ways: They alert them promptly so that planned responses can be invoked, and help them determine whether an unusual traffic pattern is an attack or a random event caused by non-malicious actions. IDS can detect when malicious users are employing an enterprise's site to launch attacks against another site. With IDS, an organization discovers hacking attempts or actual break-ins by analyzing its networks or hosts for inappropriate data or other anomalous activity.

Intrusion detection systems can be designed for network-based and host-based systems:

• Network-based IDS: these are attached to the network and detect attacks by analyzing the content of network packets as they pass across the network. An unusually high number of TCP, UDP, or ICMP packets sent to a single destination can easily be detected. IDS are configured to determine if these packets should be considered attacks or normal traffic.

- Host-based IDS: operate by monitoring hosts for suspicious activity. Host-based IDS can analyze the network packets received on the network interface, as well as the log files written by the operating system or by applications running on the computer. Typically, host-based IDS can detect attacks against web servers by analyzing logs in real time.

IDS solutions raise alerts that an attack may be taking place. However, this is inadequate for e-Business applications. What is needed is a more proactive approach that determines susceptibility to attacks before networks are compromised. This is provided by vulnerability assessment.

Vulnerability assessment is a methodical approach to identifying and prioritizing vulnerabilities, enabling enterprises to non-intrusively test their networks from the hacker's perspective and automatically do the following [Qualys 2003]:

- identify vulnerabilities and network misconfigurations

- identify rogue devices, including wireless and VPN access points

- detect and prioritize vulnerability exposures

- provide remedies for known vulnerabilities

- validate firewall and IDS configurations.

Vulnerability assessment has traditionally been conducted with techniques such as penetration testing by expert consultants. Companies that perform vulnerability assessment typically scan new systems when they are attached to the network, after software is installed or reconfigured, and at regular intervals thereafter. When a vulnerability is detected, the company corrects it and then performs another scan to confirm that the vulnerability is gone. Vulnerability assessment works hand in hand with antivirus, firewall, and IDS systems. The vulnerability assessment identifies potential vulnerabilities before they can be exploited, and the intrusion detection system notifies the company when anomalous activity has occurred. With on-demand security audits and vulnerability management, organizations can detect and eliminate vulnerabilities frequently and at a reasonable cost, closing their networks' windows of exposure. Vulnerability assessment and IDS work synergistically. Vulnerability assessment enables an enterprise to identify and close obvious holes so that the intrusion detection system produces a manageable volume of alerts. Vulnerability assessment also works in conjunction with firewalls to continuously and seamlessly monitor for vulnerabilities that may have inadvertently been introduced by firewall policy changes.

The process of vulnerability management incorporates a combination of processes and technologies that include asset discovery, vulnerability assessment, analysis of audit results, and the management of corrective actions/remediation.

13.6.3 Secure communications

Owing to the fact that e-Business transactions must flow over the public Internet, and therefore involve a large number of routers and servers through which the transaction packets flow, security experts believe that the greatest threats occur at the level of Internet communications. This situation is very different from a private network where dedicated communication lines are established between communicating parties. Several sources such as [Gartner 1998; Mougayar 1998] have identified message security as one of the most important conditions for reliable e-Business. A number of technologies are available to protect the security of Internet communications, the most basic of which is message encryption.

Cryptography is essential for the secure exchange of information across intranets, extranets and the Internet. *Cryptography* is the science of protecting data by mathematically transforming it into an unreadable format and as such it is an important technique with which to address requirements regarding message security. Cryptography enables the user to encrypt and decrypt messages, allowing only authorized persons to read them. Both processes require a key to transform the original text (called plaintext) into a coded message (ciphertext) and back. *Encryption* is a process where the plaintext is placed into a codified algorithm and an encryption key used to transform the plaintext into ciphertext. The *encryption key* is used in the algorithmic formula to scramble the information in question in such a way that it could not easily be descrambled without knowledge of the secret encryption key. Decryption on the other hand is the reversing of encryption with the ciphertext as input and the plaintext as output. The function involves both an algorithm and a decryption key.

The security functions enabled by cryptography address three dimensions of the application-level security requirements we covered in Section 13.5. These are: authentication, confidentiality and message integrity. Cryptography also addresses nonrepudiation.

There are currently three cryptographic techniques that are used to protect the security of Internet communications. These are as follows:

- *symmetric encryption* or secret key cryptography, in which sender and receiver use the same key

- *asymmetric encryption* or public key cryptography, which requires two different keys, one of which is public and the other private; sender and receiver each have their own pair of keys

- *hybrid encryption*, which combines aspects of both symmetric and asymmetric encryption

In both symmetric and asymmetric cryptography, maintaining the secrecy of the encrypting key is of paramount importance. To ensure secrecy, a key management system must be established, including key generation, key distribution, and key installation procedures. Evaluating the key management system is a critical aspect of assessing a cryptosystem's reliability [Weber 1988].

Symmetric encryption

Symmetric key encryption, also called shared key encryption or secret key cryptography, uses a single key that both the sender and recipient possess, see Figure 13.3. This key, used for both encryption and decryption, is called a secret key (also referred to as a symmetric key). Symmetric key encryption is an efficient method for encrypting large amounts of data. Many algorithms exist for symmetric key encryption, but all have the

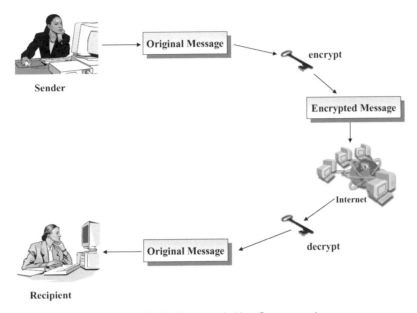

Sender

Recipient

■ **Figure 13.3:** Symmetric Key Cryptography

same purpose – the reversible transformation of plaintext into ciphertext. Ciphertext is scrambled using an encryption key and is meaningless to anyone who does not have the decryption key. Deciphering is accomplished by retracing the key's algorithms in reverse order. Because symmetric key cryptography uses the same key for both encryption and decryption, the security of this process depends on no unauthorized person obtaining the symmetric key.

Parties wishing to communicate using symmetric key cryptography must securely exchange the key before they can exchange any encrypted data. The primary yardstick for the strength of a symmetric algorithm is its key size. Modern symmetric encryption uses a sequence of 40, 56 or 128 bits (that is, 5, 7 or 16 bytes) as a key, which applies mathematical procedures to the plaintext to generate the ciphertext. The longer the key sequence, the harder it is to break the code. With a good cryptographic algorithm and an adequate key size, it is computationally unfeasible for someone to reverse the transformation process and derive the plaintext data from the ciphertext in a practical amount of time.

Three examples of symmetric key encryption algorithms are Data Encryption Standard (DES) Federal Information Processing Standard (FIPS) 46-3, Advanced Encryption Standard (AES) FIPS 197, and International Data Encryption Algorithm (IDEA).

The advantage of symmetric encryption is that it is easily and quickly implemented. If the key is to be used only a few times, it works very effectively because there are only a limited number of previous messages with which to compare a new ciphertext. The disadvantage is that every pair or group of users needs its own key – otherwise everyone can read along – which results in a large number of keys. Of the security requirements, symmetric encryption ensures confidentiality only: nobody but the sender and the receiver can read the message.

Asymmetric encryption

In order to overcome the disadvantages of symmetric encryption, a different cryptographic system, which involves the use of different keys, has been devised. This type of encryption is called asymmetric encryption or public key cryptography.

In contrast to symmetric encryption, the primary characteristic of asymmetric encryption (public key cryptography) is the fact that instead of one key, both the sender and the receiver need two keys, one of which is public and the other private. These two keys share a specific property in that when one of these keys is used to perform encryption, only the other key is able to decrypt the data. All keys are mathematically related to one another, so that data encrypted with one key can be decrypted using the other. This allows applications that are not possible with symmetric key encryption.

The public key can be passed openly between the parties or published in a public repository, but the related private key remains private. Whichever key is used to encrypt requires the other key to decrypt. For instance, data encrypted with the private key can only be decrypted using the public key. Figure 13.4 shows that the sender encrypts their message using the receiver's public key. Therefore, only the receiver can read the original message using its private key. In this way, both parties can communicate without having to exchange private keys. Thus, both confidentiality and the receiver's authenticity are guaranteed (not the sender's authenticity, since anybody can use the receiver's public key). The other security requirements are not met by this system. In Figure 13.4 a sender has the receiver's public key and uses it to encrypt a message, but only

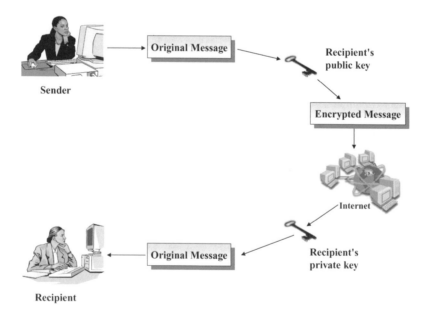

■ **Figure 13.4:** Asymmetric Key Cryptography

the receiver has the related private key used to decrypt the message. Presumably it is impossible to compute a private key on the basis of a public key, but there is as yet no proof for this assumption [Salomaa 1996]. The keys are reversible in the sense that either one can be used to encrypt a message, which can then be decrypted using the other.

The following three public key algorithms are the most commonly used:

- The Rivest-Shamir-Adleman (RSA) cryptographic algorithms are the most widely used public key algorithms today, especially for data sent over the Internet. The algorithm is named after its three inventors, Ron Rivest, Adi Shamir and Leonard Adleman. The security of the RSA algorithm is based on the difficulty (in terms of computer processing power and time) of factoring large numbers [RSA 2003]. The key is generated from two large (about 256 bits) prime numbers multiplied together. The product of these two primes is transmitted along with the public key, but the two prime numbers are kept secret and used for the generation of the private key. If anyone had a method of factoring this very large product they would have enough information to generate the private key. RSA is unique among the commonly used public key algorithms in that it is capable of both digital signature and key exchange operations. Key sizes for RSA usually range from 512 to 1024 bits or larger.

- Diffie-Hellman (DH), the first public key algorithm invented, is named after its inventors Whitfield Diffie and Martin Hellman. It derives its security from the difficulty of calculating discrete logarithms in a finite field. The DH cryptosystem is not really an encryption algorithm, since all it really accomplishes is the exchange of a shared secret key over an unsecured transmission system. But it is still considered a public key system because there is a very large (about 512 bits) prime number and a 'magic number' (a number less than the prime number) that is on some public server that is accessible to anyone. To simplify the algorithm, this magic number is then raised to the power of a random number and sent to the other party over the unsecured transmission system. The other party would do the same thing. From this information both can compute the same number. They can then use this number for a secret key to encrypt some data using a secret key encryption algorithm such as the Data Encryption Standard (DES). The security of DH is based on the fact that no one can calculate the secret random number even though they know the initial magic number and the magic number raised to that secret power.

- The Digital Signature Algorithm (DSA) has been invented by the United States National Security Agency (NSA), and has been incorporated by the US National Institute of Standards and Technology (NIST) into their Federal Information Processing Standard (FIPS) for digital signatures. DSA, like Diffie-Hellman, derives its security from the difficulty of calculating discrete logarithms [Kaufman 1995]. The DSA is a public key cryptosystem used only to calculate digital signatures (and not for data encryption). It uses keys very similar to DH, but it also includes a computed value (which turns out to be one half of the DH exchange) as well as the prime number and the 'magic number' described for DH. All three of these values constitute the public key. In addition, there is a per-message public key that is sent with every signed message. The DSA is optimized for speed of generating a signature, anticipating its use on low-power microprocessors such as those on smart cards or other tokens.

Hybrid encryption

One of the major differences between symmetric and asymmetric encryption is the system's performance. Symmetric systems are faster, which is an advantage when large amounts of data must be sent. In order to combine this advantage with those of asymmetric encryption, a hybrid of both systems is often used. The message is encrypted using a symmetric key, which is then itself encrypted using an asymmetric key and sent along with the message. A digital signature can be processed in the same way. As already explained, the use of a digital signature allows the confirmation of a message's authenticity and integrity, and its incontrovertibility as well.

Hybrid encryption in combination with a digital signature meets the requirements of authentication, confidentiality, integrity and incontrovertibility. No one but the receiver can decrypt the symmetric key and nobody but the sender can encrypt the message digest, hence authentication and incontrovertibility. And nobody can have read the message (if the key is strong enough, that is; then there is confidentiality) and by comparing the two message digests the receiver knows if anything in the message has been changed (integrity).

Implementation of secure communications

To operate business-critical applications over the Internet, enterprises need high-level, certificate-based security provided by PKI. PKI protects applications that demand the highest level of security, enabling online banking and trading, e-Business applications, web services-based business process automation, digital form signing, and enterprise instant messaging. In addition, it protects firewalls, virtual private networks (VPNs), directories, and enterprise applications. Secure communications are implemented using a number of authentication and encryption technologies based on PKI. These include:

- The Secure Socket Layer (SSL) protocol (see Section 13.5): This protocol is used primarily in conjunction with web browsers and uses encryption and authentication techniques to ensure that communications between a client and application server remain private and allow the client to identify the server and vice versa.

- Virtual Private Network: SSL is not the only mechanism available for creating secure communications between systems. The goal of a VPN is to have a set of network sites that can communicate securely with each other, using the Internet backbone to satisfy basic communications needs, with confidence that the private network traffic is not vulnerable to external attack. VPN differs from SSL in that it creates a secure channel between two TCP/IP hosts over which multiple TCP/IP connections can be established.

13.6.4 Digital certification and trusted third parties

In Section 13.5 we explained how the public key infrastructure is used to describe the policies, standards, and software that regulate or manipulate certificates and public and private keys. In practice, PKI refers to a system of digital certificates, certification authorities (CAs), and other registration authorities that verify and authenticate the validity of each party involved in an electronic transaction.

A public key certificate is used for authentication and secures exchange of information on the Internet, extranets and intranets. The issuer and signer of the certificate is known as a certification authority. The entity being issued the certificate is the subject of the certificate. A public key certificate is a digitally signed statement that binds the value of a public key to the identity of the subject (person, device or service) that holds the corresponding private key. By signing the certificate, the CA attests that the private key associated with the public key in the certificate is in the possession of the subject named in the certificate. Certificates can be issued for a variety of functions, including web user authentication, Web server authentication, secure e-mail using Secure/Multipurpose Internet Mail Extensions (S/MIME), IP Security, Secure Sockets Layer/Transaction Layer Security (SSL/TLS), and code signing.

Certificates provide a mechanism for establishing a relationship between a public key and the entity that owns the corresponding private key. The use of public keys allows the encryption and decryption of data and messages. However, there needs to be a guarantee that a certain public key really belongs to a certain identity. In the case of a 'man in the middle' attack it is possible that the intruder could intercept the public key. He can subsequently read, change and forward the messages and data, manipulating the communication between trading parties without either of them realizing it. One potential solution is having the key registered by an intermediary who is trusted by both parties. This intermediary guarantees that the key belongs to the person identified, and announces this by signing and publishing the file containing the key owner's personal specifics and public key. This digital certificate is then sent along with the encrypted message. The intermediary's signature ensures the authenticity, integrity and incontrovertibility of the certificate as well as the accuracy of the public key. In order to prevent a massive spread of certificates, the Internet Engineering Taskforce (IETF) is developing standards for them.

Such an intermediary authority is called a trusted third party (TTP). A *trusted third party* is an independent and impartial organization that offers trust services for the purpose of realizing electronic data communication [Froomkin 1996]. Entrust, Globalsign.com and Baltimore are examples of such enterprises. The first step in their verification process is checking the applicant's identity. If everything is in order, the applicant's personal specifics and public key are laid down in a certificate using the TTP's private key. Thus, the physical identity and its digital representation are connected; the TTP guarantees trust in the connection. Subsequently, the digital certificate is published in a public directory. After publication, the TTP manages the keys when they are used, blocked and renewed. Every TTP publishes a certification practice statement (CPS), a document in which the rules and procedures are described which the TTP uses to publish certificates. This guarantees a certain level of security and trust.

As an example, the PKI is set up by trusted TTPs. These consist of at least one certification authority, one or more registration authorities and the users for whose benefit the certificates are issued. The PKI's heart is the participants' trust in the certification and registration authorities involved, which allows the participants to place their faith in the certificates they use to sign (or verify) and encrypt (or decrypt) messages. The trustworthiness of the registration authorities' work is of crucial importance to the reliability of the certificates issued. In general, TTPs can play several different roles:

- *Certification Authority* – As already explained, a certification authority is an entity trusted to issue certificates to an individual, a computer or any other requesting entity. The role of a CA, within the infrastructure of trust based on asymmetric cryptography, is that of a guarantor of the identity of each user to all others. Froomkin [Froomkin 1996] defines certification authorities as "a body, either public or private, that seeks to fill the need for trusted third party services in electronic business by issuing digital certificates that attest to some fact about the subject of the certificate". A CA accepts a certificate request, verifies the requester's information according to the policy of the CA, and then uses its private key to apply its digital signature to the certificate. The CA then issues the certificate to the subject of the certificate for use as a security credential within a PKI.

- *Registration Authority* – Eurotrust [Nagle 1998] provides the following definition of registration authorities: "An entity that is responsible for identification and authentication of certificate applicants. It is not a certification authority and does not sign or issue certificates." Registration authorities, then, are authorities, which identify and register applications for certificates as well as the blocking of certificates. The applicant's identity is established and all information about them that is needed is collected. The registration authority checks whether the applicant meets all conditions and, if so, approves the application. Then the certification authority can issue a certificate on the basis of this information.

- *Directory* – The certificates are published in a public list called a directory, which allows everyone who wishes to send someone an encrypted message to use the receiver's public key that is given in the certificate. Directories are often managed by TTPs who serve as certification authorities, but managing a directory always remains a distinct responsibility.

13.6.5 Trust services overview

As already explained in Chapter 7, XML has become the preferred infrastructure for e-Business applications. e-Business transactions require trust and security, making it mission-critical to devise common XML mechanisms for authenticating merchants, buyers and suppliers to each other, and for digitally signing and encrypting XML documents like contracts and payment transactions. XML is widely used to describe Internet documents and provide inter-application functionality; therefore developer adoption of XML security methods is desirable.

XML Trust Services is a suite of open XML specifications for application developers, developed in partnership with industry to make it easier than ever to integrate a broad range of trust services into e-Business applications. The main technologies for ensuring trust during Internet transactions are as follows [VeriSign 2003]:

- *XML Signature*: Defines an XML schema for cryptographically authenticating data. The authenticated data may consist of a complete XML document, individual elements in an XML document, or an external data object referenced by an XML document.

- *XML Encryption*: Defines an XML schema for encrypting data. The encrypted data may consist of a complete XML document, individual elements in an XML document, or an external data object referenced by an XML document.

- *XML Key Management Specification* (XKMS): Defines trusted web services for managing cryptographic keys, including public keys. XKMS contains two subparts:
  - XML Key Information Service Specification (X-KISS): Supports services used by a party relying on a cryptographic key (location, and validation)
  - XML Key Registration Service Specification (X-KRSS): Supports services used by the holder of a cryptographic key (registration, revocation, reissue, and key recovery)

- *Security Assertions Markup Language* (SAML): A framework for specifying and sharing 'trust assertions' in XML. A trust assertion can be any data used to determine authorization, such as credentials, credit ratings, approved roles, and so on.

- *XML Access Control Markup Language* (XACML): An extension of SAML that allows access control policies to be specified.

XML signature and encryption

Two recent security initiatives designed to both account for and take advantage of the special nature of XML data are XML Signature and XML Encryption. XML Signature is a joint effort between the World Wide Web Consortium (W3C) and Internet Engineering Task Force (IETF), and XML Encryption is solely a W3C effort. Before we present these two initiatives we shall describe how digital signatures work.

Digital signatures use asymmetric encryption techniques whereby two different keys are generally used, one for creating a digital signature or transforming data into a seemingly unintelligible form, and another key for verifying a digital signature or returning the message to its original form (see Section 13.6.3). The keys of an asymmetric cryptosystem for digital signatures are termed the private key, which is known only to the signer and used to create the digital signature, and the public key, which is ordinarily more widely known and is used to verify the digital signature. A recipient must have the corresponding public key in order to verify that a digital signature is the signer's. If many people need to verify the signer's digital signature, the public key must be distributed to all of them, e.g. by publication in an online repository or directory where they can easily obtain it. Although many people will know the public key of a given signer and use it to verify that signer's signature, they cannot discover that signer's private key and use it to forge digital signatures.

Use of digital signatures comprises two processes, one performed by the signer and the other by the receiver of the digital signature:

- *Digital signature creation* is the process of computing a code derived from and unique to both the signed message and a given private key.

- *Digital signature verification* is the process of checking the digital signature by reference to the original message and a public key, and thereby determining whether the digital signature was created for that same message using the private key that corresponds to the referenced public key.

A more fundamental process, termed a hashing algorithm, is used in both creating and verifying a digital signature. A hashing algorithm creates a message digest of the message. This is a code usually much smaller than the message but nevertheless unique to it. If the message changes, the hash result of the message will invariably be different. Hashing algorithms enable the software for creating digital signatures to operate on smaller and predictable amounts of data, while still providing a strong evidentiary correlation to the original message content.

Figure 13.5 depicts the digital signature creation process. This figure shows that to sign a document or any other item of information, the signer first delimits precisely what is to be signed. The delimited information to be signed is termed the 'message'. Subsequently, a hashing algorithm in the signer's software computes a message digest, a code unique to the message. The signer's software then transforms (encrypts) the message digest into a digital signature by reference to the signer's private key. The resulting digital signature is thus unique to both the message and the private key used to create it. Typically, a digital signature is attached to its message and stored or transmitted with its message. However, it may also be sent or stored as a separate data element, so long as it maintains a reliable association with its message. Since a digital signature is unique to its message, it is useless if wholly dissociated from its message.

Figure 13.6 depicts the verification of a digital signature. As illustrated in Figure 13.6, this is accomplished by computing a message digest of the original message by means of the same hashing algorithm used in

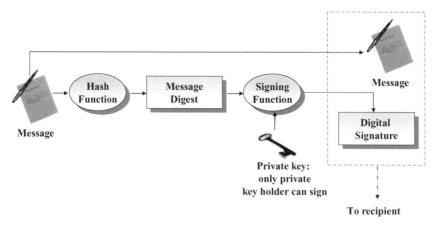

■ **Figure 13.5:** Creation of a Digital Signature

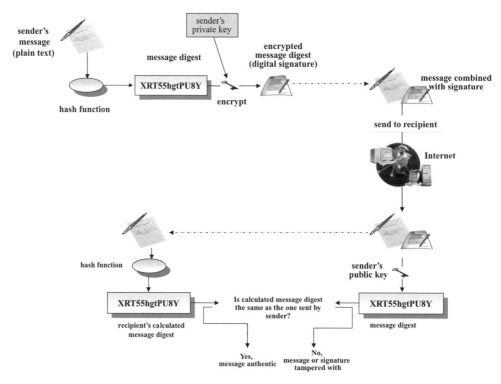

■ **Figure 13.6:** Verification of a Digital Signature

creating the digital signature. The message digest is encrypted by the sender's private key. Subsequently, the message along with the message digest is sent to the recipient. The recipient uses the public key to decrypt the digital signature and check whether the digital signature was created using the corresponding private key. The recipient then uses the same hashing algorithm (which is agreed upon before hand) to calculate its own message digest of the sender's plaintext message. Subsequently, the recipient checks whether the newly computed message digest matches the message digest derived from the digital signature. If the signer's private key was used and the message digests are identical, then the digital signature as well as the original message is verified. Verification thus provides two kinds of indications. Firstly that the digital signature was created using the signer's private key, because only the signer's public key will verify a digital signature created with the signer's private key. Secondly that the message was not altered after it was signed, because the message digest computed in verification matches the hash result from the digital signature, which was computed when the message was digitally signed.

For signature verification to be meaningful, the verifier must have confidence that the public key does actually belong to the sender (otherwise an impostor could claim to be the sender, presenting his own public key in place of the real one). A certificate, issued by a Certification Authority, is an assertion of the validity of the binding between the certificate's subject and their public key such that other users can be confident that the public key does indeed correspond to the subject who claims it as their own.

Various asymmetric cryptosystems create and verify digital signatures using different mathematical formulas and procedures, but all share this overall operational pattern.

Digital signatures deliver critical authentication, tamperproofing and nonrepudiation services for legally enforceable transactions, so they can be easily adopted in the e-Business arena. However, it is doubtful that many e-Business trading communities will rush to implement digital signatures without a flexible, general-purpose standards framework for applying and validating signatures on electronic documents. Fortunately, the standards community is progressing well in defining such a framework: XML Digital Signatures (XML-DSig).

XML signatures are digital signatures designed for use in XML e-Business transactions. The XML-DSig standard defines a schema and series of XML elements for capturing the details of a digital signature operation applied to arbitrary (but often XML) data. The XML-DSig standard is application independent and supports the signing of any content type, XML or non-XML, as long as that content can be addressed across the Internet, extranet or intranet via uniform resource identifiers (URI). A URI attribute of the XML-DSig reference tag points to the location of the signed data. XML-DSig defines procedures for binding cryptographic signatures to one or more URI-addressable local or network resources and for validating those signatures. XML-DSig also specifies an XML syntax for defining signature blocks that can be embedded in all content types. XML signatures provide message and signer authentication, data integrity, and support for nonrepudiation to the data that they sign.

A fundamental feature of XML Signature is the ability to sign only specific portions of the XML tree rather than an entire document. This will be relevant when a single XML document may have a long history in which different portion of a document are authored at different times by different parties, each signing only those portions relevant to itself. This flexibility is also critical in situations where it is important to ensure the integrity of certain portions of an XML document, while leaving open the possibility for other portions of the document to change. Consider, for example, a signed XML form delivered to a customer for completion.

If the signature were over the full XML form, any change by the user to the default form values would invalidate the original signature.

The signed data might be more than one type of resource, e.g. an XML document, independent elements in an XML do.cument, or external data referenced by an XPointer. The XML signature itself will generally indicate the location of the original signed object. Three types of signatures exist [Plouin 2002]:

- Enveloping, where the signature envelops the entire content to be signed via an internal URI. An enveloping signature means that the signed data is in the signature element.

- Enveloped, where the signature is instead inserted (contained) within the document that it is signing via an internal URI. An enveloped signature is part of the signed data.

- Detached, where the signature references a document that is separate from the XML document and where the signature exists via a reference to an external URI. A detached signature means that the signed data is not in the signature element – it is elsewhere in the XML document or in some remote location.

The root element Signature in an XML Signature specification contains among other things a SignedInfo element that provides information that describes how to obtain the message digest, a SignatureValue element containing the value of the message digest encrypted with the private key and a KeyInfo element, which indicates the key to be used to validate the signature. The KeyInfo element may contain keys, names, certificates and other public key management information, such as in-band key distribution or key agreement data.

Signature validation requires that the data object that was signed be accessible. To validate the signature, the recipient decodes the message digest contained in the XML Signature element SignatureValue using the signatory's public key. The recipient then compares it with the message digest obtained by following the instructions in SignedInfo.

An XML document, like any other, can be encrypted in its entirety and sent securely to one or more recipients. This is a common function of SSL or TLS, for example, but what is much more interesting is how to handle situations where different parts of the same document need different treatment. XML Encryption supports encryption of all or part of an XML document.

Because XML encryption is not locked into any specific encryption scheme, it requires that additional information be provided on encrypted content and key information. This is the function of the EncryptedData element and EncryptedKey element. The core element in the XML encryption syntax is the EncryptedData element which, with the EncryptedKey element, is used to transport encryption keys from the originator to a known recipient. Data to be encrypted can be arbitrary data, an XML document, an XML element, an XML element content or a reference to a resource outside an XML document. The result of encrypting data is an XML encryption element that contains or references the cipher data. When an element or element content is encrypted, the EncryptedData element replaces the element or content in the encrypted version of the XML document. When it is arbitrary data that is being encrypted, the EncryptedData element may become the root of a new XML document or it may become a child element. When an entire XML document is encrypted, then the EncryptedData element may become the root of a new document. The EncryptedKey element provides information about the keys involved in the encryption.

The steps for XML encryption include:

- selecting the XML document to be encrypted (in whole or in parts)

- converting the XML to be encrypted to a canonical form, if necessary

- encrypting the resulting canonical form using public key encryption

- sending the encrypted XML to the intended recipient

The process of converting an XML document to canonical form is known as canonicalization.

XML canonicalization is the use of an algorithm to generate the canonical form of an XML document to ensure security in cases where XML is subject to surface representation changes or to processing that discards some information that is not essential to the data represented in the XML, e.g. entities or namespaces with prefixes. XML canonicalization addresses the fact that when XML is read and processed using standard XML parsing and processing techniques, some surface representation information may be lost or modified.

XML Key Management Specification (XKMS)

The *XML Key Management Specification* (XKMS) is used to simplify the integration of PKI and management of digital certificates with XML applications. As well as responding to problems of authentication and verification of electronic signatures, XKMS also allows certificates to be managed, registered or revoked. The potential benefits of combining XML with PKI include the fact that there is no need to delay PKI deployment pending client support, as the XML Key Management Specification moves the complexity of PKI and trust processing to server-side components instead.

Developers can take advantage of XKMS to integrate authentication, digital signature, and encryption services, such as certificate processing and revocation status checking, into applications without the constraints and complications associated with proprietary PKI software toolkits. Figure 13.7 shows how XML Signature and Encryption are related to XKMS. With XKMS, trust functions reside in servers accessible via easily programmed XML transactions. Developers can allow applications to delegate all or part of the processing of XML digital signatures and encrypted elements to a TTP such as VeriSign, shielding the application from the complexity of the underlying PKI [VeriSign 2002].

There are two major subparts of the XML Key Management Specification: these are the XML Key Information Service Specification (X-KISS) and the XML Key Registration Service Specification (X-KRSS). We shall give a brief overview of X-KISS and X-KRSS below.

XML Key Information Service Specification (X-KISS): The XML Key Information Service Specification defines protocols to support the processing, by a relying party, of Key Information associated with a XML digital signature, XML encrypted data, or other public key usage in an XML-aware application. Functions supported include locating required public keys given identifier information, and binding of such keys to identifier information.

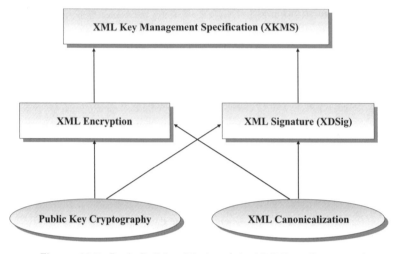

■ **Figure 13.7:** Basic Building Blocks of the XML Trust Framework

Applications that work in conjunction with X-KISS receive messages signed in compliance with the XML Signature specifications. The XML Digital Signature specification defines a few simple types, but applications are often left to define their own key identification and exchange semantics within this element type through the XML namespace facility. The specification indicates that a signatory may provide optional Key Information elements used to authenticate the signature. For instance, a signatory may attach their public key to a message. There are two verification stages for the signature [Plouin 2002]:

• Local verification that is carried out directly by the receiving application. During this stage the document is checked to see whether it has been correctly signed and not been tampered with during transit. This phase comprises decoding the signature with the signatory's public key and then comparing it with the footprint obtained locally.

• Contacting the XKMS service and requesting information on the public key transmitted. During this second stage the identity of the signatory is made known and it is checked whether the key has been revoked (in case it was stolen) and is valid (period of validity has not expired).

The X-KISS protocol is used to perform the checks required in the second stage by means of two services [Plouin 2002]:

• The locate service, which is used to find out the attached information from the data contained in the XML Signature specification Key Information element.

• The validate service that makes sure that a key is valid.

XML Key Registration Service Specification (X-KRSS): The XML Key Registration Service Specification defines protocols to support the registration of a key pair by a key pair holder, with the intent that the key pair subsequently be usable in conjunction with the XKMS. Each of these protocols describes protocol exchanges that consist of a simple request and response exchange with a Trust Service.

The goal of the X-KRSS Specification is to respond to the need for a complete XML client-focused key life cycle management protocol. X-KRSS supports the entire certificate life cycle by means of the following services:

- Key Registration, where an XML application key pair holder registers its public key with a trusted infrastructure by means of a registration server. The public key is sent to the registration server using a digitally signed request in KRSS that may optionally include name and attribute information, authentication information and proof of possession of a private key.

- Key Revocation, which is handled by a protocol similar to the one used in key registration.

- Key Recovery, where the use of file system encryption – as well as broader XML client encryption applications – mandates some form of key recovery provision. In X-KRSS, this function is not supported by standardized protocols but rather is built in.

Security Assertions Markup Language

The Security Assertions Markup Language is a vendor-neutral, XML-based framework for exchanging security-related information, called 'assertions', between business partners over the Internet. SAML enables disparate security services systems to interoperate. It resides within a system's security mechanisms to enable exchange of identity and entitlement with other services. SAML addresses the need to have a unified framework that is able to convey security information for users who interact with one provider so they can seamlessly interact with one another. Users (or applications) should be able to sign on at one website and have their security credentials transferred automatically to partner sites. This would enable users to authenticate once to access applications such as airline, hotel and car rental reservations systems, through websites maintained by associated business partners.

SAML defines mechanisms for user identification, authentication and authorization. SAML does not address privacy policies, however. Rather, partner sites are responsible for developing mutual requirements for user authentication and data protection. It, however, defines the structure of the documents that transport security information among services. SAML implementations provide an interoperable XML-based security solution, whereby user information and corresponding authorization information can be exchanged by collaborating applications or services. The SAML specification establishes assertion and protocol schemas for the structure of the documents that transport security. By defining how identity and access information is exchanged, SAML becomes the common language through which organizations can communicate without modifying their own internal security architectures. For instance, rather than having each e-Business application use a different authentication scheme, they can 'converse' in SAML.

SAML enables single sign-on and end-to-end security for e-Business applications and web services. Because the SAML standard is designed for the exchange of secure sign-on information between a user, or 'relying party', and multiple issuing parties, it allows issuing parties to use their own chosen methods of authentication, for example PKI, hash, or password.

The main components of SAML include the following:

- *Assertions*: SAML defines three kinds of assertions, which are declarations of one or more facts about a user (human or computer). Authentication assertions require that the user prove their identity. Attribute assertions contain specific details about the user, such as their credit line or citizenship. Authorization assertions state whether a client is allowed or denied a request (for example, whether they are authorized to buy a certain product), and the scope of the client's privileges. Authorization assertions permit or deny access to specific resources, such as files, devices, web pages, databases and so on.

- All types of assertions include a common set of elements: the subject, which denotes who the assertion is identifying, the conditions, which denotes conditions under which the assertion is valid and an authentication statement, which denotes advice on how the assertion was made. Each assertion also includes information about the type of request made.

- *Request/response protocol*: This defines the way that SAML requests and receives assertions between trading partners.

- *Bindings*: This element details exactly how SAML requests should map into transport protocols such as the Simple Object Access Protocol (SOAP) for message exchanges over HTTP, see Chapter 19.

- *Profiles*: These dictate how SAML assertions can be embedded or transported between communicating systems.

While SAML makes assertions about credentials, it does not actually authenticate or authorize users. This is achieved by an authentication server in conjunction with the Lightweight Directory Access Protocol directory. SAML links back to the actual authentication and makes its assertion based on the results of that event.

XML Access Control Markup Language

In the previous section we explained that SAML defines how identity and access information is exchanged and lets organizations convey security information to one another without having to change their own internal security architectures. However, SAML can only communicate information. How to use that information is the responsibility of the XML Access Control Markup Language (XACML), an extension of SAML that allows access control policies to be specified. This language, which uses the same definitions of subjects and actions as SAML, offers a vocabulary for expressing the rules needed to define an organization's security policies and make authorization decisions.

XACML has two basic components:

- An access-control policy language that lets developers specify the rules about who can do what and when.

- A request/response language that presents requests for access and describes the answers to those queries.

The access-control policy language is used to describe general access-control requirements, and has standard extension points for defining new functions, data types, combining logic, etc. The request/response language lets users form a query to ask whether or not a given action should be allowed, and interpret the result. The response always includes an answer about whether the request should be allowed using one of four values: Permit, Deny, Indeterminate (an error occurred or some required value was missing, so a decision cannot be made) or Not Applicable (the request can not be answered by this service).

XACML provides for fine-grained control of activities (such as read, write, copy, delete) based on several criteria, including the following:

- Attributes of the user requesting access. Attributes are named values of known types that may include an issuer identifier or an issue date and time, e.g. "Only division managers and above can view this document". A user's name, their security clearance, the file they want to access, and the time of day are all attribute values.

- The protocol over which the request is made, e.g. "This data can be viewed only if it is accessed over secure HTTP".

- The authentication mechanism used.

13.7 Chapter summary

Enterprises solidifying their positions on the e-Business front must protect themselves against a growing number of complex risks. In addition to security, verification of identities, nonrepudiation of agreements and a swarm of other related issues often come into play.

The key to unlocking the vast potential of e-Business is highly available, high-performance computing services delivered across the Internet. Thus, quality of service becomes a critical instrument to ensure the enterprise infrastructure delivers the scalability, security, transaction, and content-based requirements of the business. The major requirements for supporting QoS in e-Business span such concerns as availability, accessibility, conformance, integrity, performance, reliability, scalability, security and transactionality. Several necessary measures of a strategy must be employed to guarantee that effective QoS is delivered. These include understanding application requirements and measuring their business impact, ensuring the availability and reliability of data, security and privacy management, as well as deploying e-Business applications and services in a rapid and reliable manner to improve the enterprise's time-to-market. An important and widely used instrument in the maintenance of service provision relationships that ensures that a guaranteed level of performance is delivered is the Service Level Agreement.

The fraud risks involved in conducting business on the Internet are numerous. Most can be classified into four categories: man in the middle attack, spoofing, hacking and denial of service attack. e-Business is forcing enterprises to move away from private communication networks to open public networks such as the Internet where enterprises open their private network applications and information assets to customers, suppliers and business partners. e-Business security marks a departure from traditional security as it poses new security requirements in connection with access (authentication, authorization), confidentiality, nonrepudiation and integrity of information. To address the security issues facing organizations as they adopt e-Business technology, it is essential to apply the principles of application security. The five requirements for application-level security include authentication, authorization, message integrity, confidentiality, operational defence, auditability and nonrepudiation.

It is widely accepted that Public Key Infrastructure is one of the main technologies for supporting the security requirements of e-Business applications. PKI is a technology that provides the necessary foundation to implement e-Business security. A PKI is a foundation upon which other applications and network security components are built. The specific security functions for which a PKI can provide a foundation are confidentiality, integrity, nonrepudiation, and authentication. Digital certificates and digital signatures are other important security mechanisms for e-Business. Digital certificates are exchanged during the set up of communication links to verify that the trading partner on the other end of the wire is the intended recipient of a message transmission and to prove the sender's identity. Digital signatures guarantee that the enterprise/person represented in the digital certificate sent the message.

To address trust issues, and avoid risks in achieving the security requirements, the IT infrastructure for e-Business must meet three basic quality requirements: infrastructure availability, network level security, and secure communications.

The IT infrastructure availability requirement identifies the functionalities of the infrastructure's hardware and software components and specifies the corresponding service-level requirements.

Network level security incorporates embedded encryption functionality within network devices or operating systems utilizing Internet Protocol Security. Enterprises employing network level security solutions rely on two main technologies to protect their networks: firewalls and vulnerability assessment. Firewalls are built between an organization's internal network and the Internet backbone and serve as security beachheads that define the network perimeter where an enterprise meets the Internet. Vulnerability assessment is a methodical approach to identifying and prioritizing vulnerabilities, enabling enterprises to non-intrusively test their networks from the 'hacker's perspective' and identify vulnerabilities, rogue devices, detect and prioritize vulnerability exposures, provide remedies for known vulnerabilities and validate firewall and intrusion detection systems.

A number of technologies are available to protect the security of Internet communications, the most basic of which is message encryption. There are currently three cryptographic techniques that are used to protect the security of Internet communications. These are: symmetric encryption or secret key cryptography; asymmetric encryption of public key cryptography; and hybrid encryption, which combines aspects of both.

PKI refers to a system of digital certificates, certification authorities, and other registration authorities that verify and authenticate the validity of each party involved in an electronic transaction. Certificates provide a mechanism for establishing a relationship between a public key and the entity that owns the corresponding private key. The use of public keys allows the encryption and decryption of data and messages.

e-Business transactions require trust and security, making it mission-critical to devise common XML mechanisms for authenticating merchants, buyers, and suppliers to each other, and for digitally signing and encrypting XML documents like contracts and payment transactions. XML Trust Services is a suite of open XML specifications for application developers, developed in partnership with industry to make it easier than ever to integrate a broad range of trust services into e-Business applications. The main technologies for ensuring trust during Internet transactions include XML signature and encryption, XML Key Management Specification, Security Assertions Markup Language, and XML Access Control Markup Language.

Discussion Questions

- Explain why quality of service becomes a critical instrument to ensure the enterprise infrastructure and list some of its major requirements. What are the necessary measures that must be employed to guarantee that effective QoS is delivered?

- Explain what application security is and describe the five requirements for application-level security.

- What are the three basic quality requirements which the IT infrastructure for e-Business must meet?

- What are the main components of infrastructure availability? Why is infrastructure availability important for e-Business applications?

- What are the major components of network-level security?

- What are XML trust services? How do they contribute towards the realization of a secure e-Business infrastructure?

Assignments

i. An IT director, working on e-Business issues and related banking matters, realized that PKI could potentially facilitate business and build trust with retail customers. Passwords and ids were currently being used, but not viewed as a long-term security solution for authentication. The IT director decided to form a small group to do a pilot program that would work with retail online banking applications. It was decided that PKI should be used primarily in business to e-Business processes ranging from currency trading applications, to domestic check-clearing applications. Describe the phases and key deliverables for the PKI implementation.

ii. A small auto-parts manufacturing company wishes to deliver its products to several large automobile companies. This company set out to implement an e-Business solution to improve the order and delivery process between its own company and its remote business partners (contractors). In the first instance, the company decided to implement XML signature and encryption for security purposes. Design a solution for this company on Figures 13.5 and 13.6. Use UML use case, activity and sequence diagrams to model the user interactions with the security system at a high level of abstraction.

Chapter 14

Approaches to Middleware

I
n Chapter 6 we presented EDI and workflow systems as examples of collaborative technologies. Whereas EDI and workflow systems support electronic business by automating existing processes and enabling electronic document exchange between separate organizations, a number of other systems approach electronic business by trying to create a single virtual organization. These systems use middleware, a layer of integration code and functionality that allows multiple diverse and distributed systems to be used as though they were a single system. Using these middleware tools, business applications can be built that transparently access the multiple back-end systems.

This chapter introduces middleware approaches for e-Business. It first introduces the concept of messaging, Remote Procedure Calls and Remote Method Invocation and then concentrates on Message-Oriented Middleware. Subsequently, it concentrates on data-access middleware and transaction-oriented middleware. Finally, it introduces distributed objects and distributed-object middleware platforms, such as CORBA and DCOM, and newer generation frameworks that support loosely coupled applications such as .NET and J2EE.

14.1 **What is middleware?**

Middleware is connectivity software that is designed to help manage the complexity and heterogeneity inherent in distributed systems. It builds a bridge between different systems by enabling communication and transfer of data. It is often used in a client/server environment. Middleware can be applied to manage disparate applications both within one single organization and between various independent organizations. Within one single organization middleware will support the collaboration between existing (legacy) applications. When different organizations have to work together, e.g. in the context of an electronic marketplace or of a dynamic networked organization, middleware may create an interface between the different company systems. Middleware may be customized software or purchased as a standard package (called enterprise application integration software). Middleware is often used to connect a Web server to applications or data stored on another computer. The Web server presents information to browser programs available on (client) machines.

More precisely, middleware could be defined as a layer of enabling software services that allow application elements to interoperate across network links, despite differences in underlying communications protocols, system architectures, operating systems, databases, and other application services. Middleware lives above the operating system but below the application program level and provides a common programming abstraction across a distributed system. Middleware services provide a more functional set of Application Programming Interfaces (APIs) than the operating system and network services to allow an application to do the following:

- Locate applications transparently across the network, thereby providing interaction with another or service.

- Shield software developers from low-level, tedious and error-prone platform details, such as socket-level network programming.

- Provide a consistent set of higher-level network-oriented abstractions that are much closer to application requirements in order to simplify the development of distributed systems.

- Leverage previous developments and reuse them rather than rebuild them for each usage.

- Provide a wide array of services such as reliability, availability, authentication and security that are necessary for applications to operate effectively in a distributed environment.

- Scale up in capacity without losing function.

Modern middleware products mask heterogeneity of networks and hardware, operating systems and programming languages. They also permit heterogeneity at the application level by allowing the various elements of the distributed application to be written in any suitable language. Finally, programming support offered by the middleware platform can provide transparency with respect to distribution in one or more of the following dimensions: location, concurrency, replication and failure. This means that applications can interoperate irrespective of whether they are located in diverse geographical locations, whether operations execute concurrently, or whether data is replicated in multiple locations. Finally, middleware component systems and applications will always find themselves in a consistent state despite the possibility of middleware or local system failures.

Currently, there are different types of middleware that provide a different variety of features addressing different integration needs. Middleware encompasses a variety of different types of products with different capabilities that can be divided into five broad segments:

1. Remote Procedure Calls (RPCs);
2. Message-oriented middleware;
3. Data-access middleware;
4. Transaction-oriented middleware;
5. Object Request Brokers (ORBs).

Before we discuss these types of middleware we shall first examine the modes of messaging that these types of middleware support.

14.2 Messaging

Whilst there are different types of middleware, they all can support one, or sometimes two, basic modes of communication. These modes are: synchronous or time dependent; and asynchronous or time independent.

The simplest form of communication is the *synchronous mode of communication*, which employs request/reply communication whereby the sender sends a request and receives a reply from the message recipient. In the synchronous mode, communication is synchronized between two communicating application systems, which must both be up and running. Both the sending and the receiving application must be ready to communicate with each other at all times. A sending application initiates a request (sends a message) to a receiving application. The sending application then blocks its processing until it receives a response from the receiving application. The receiving application continues its processing after it receives the response. Applications that employ the synchronous mode of communication are called *request/response applications*. Synchronous communication is exemplified by remote procedure calls. Figure 14.1 shows this form of synchronous request/response mode of communication.

Synchronous calls imply that the calling process is halted while the called process is executing a function. Even in a Remote Procedure Call scenario (see next section), where the called application executes in a different process, the caller blocks until the called application returns control (and the results) to the caller. As a result the type of middleware that supports synchronous applications is usually referred to as blocking middleware. Synchronous middleware is thus tightly coupled to applications. In turn, the applications themselves are reliant on the middleware platform to process one or more function calls at a remotely hosted application. Because of this, any problems with middleware – such as network or remote server crashes – hinder the application from processing.

When using the *asynchronous mode of communication*, systems and applications communicate by exchanging messages. Programs communicate by sending packets of data called *messages* to each other. The concept of a message is a well-defined, data-driven text format – containing the business message and a network routing header – that can be sent between two or more applications. *Messaging* is a technology that enables high-speed, asynchronous, program-to-program communication with reliable delivery.

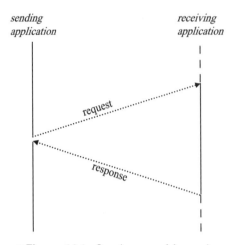

■ **Figure 14.1:** Synchronous Messaging

A message typically comprises three basic elements: a *header*, its *properties* and a *message payload* or *body* [Chappell 2004]. The message header is used by both the messaging system and the application developer to provide information about characteristics such as the destination of a message, the message type, the message expiration time and so forth. The properties of a message contain a set of application-defined name/value pairs. These properties are essentially parts of the message body that get promoted to a special section of the message so that filtering can be applied to the message by clients or specialized routers [Chappell 2004]. The message body carries the actual 'payload' of the message. The format of the message payload can vary across messaging implementations. Most common formats are plain text, a raw stream of bytes for holding any type of binary data, or a special XML message type that allows the message payload to be accessed using any number of common XML parsing technologies.

The message can be interpreted simply as data, as the description of a command to be invoked on the receiver, or as the description of an event that occurred in the sender. The business data usually contains information about a business transaction, such as a sales ordering, payment processing, or shipping and tracking.

When using asynchronous messaging, the caller uses a *send and forget* approach that allows it to continue to execute after it sends the message. With asynchronous communication, an application sends (requester or sender) a request to another while it continues its own processing activities. The sending application does not have to wait for the receiving application to complete and for its reply to come back. Instead it can continue processing other requests. Both application systems do not have to be active at the same time for processing to occur.

The primary advantage of the asynchronous communication model is that, unlike the synchronous mode of communication, the middleware infrastructure does not block the application processing. Since the middleware is decoupled from the application, the application can continue processing at all times without having to wait for – or having to know the status of – any other communicating application.

Asynchronous messaging is usually implemented by some queuing mechanism. Two types of message queue exist, these are *store and forward* and *publish–subscribe*.

Store and forward: Messages are placed on a message queue by the sending application and retrieved by the receiving application as needed. The message queue is independent of both the sender and receiver applications. The message queue acts as a buffer between the communicating applications. In this form of communication, two applications can be senders and receivers relative to the message queue (see Figure 14.2). Asynchronous communication allows work to be performed whenever applications are ready.

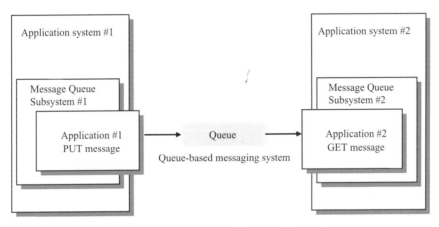

■ Figure 14.2: Store and Forward Messaging

The store and forward queuing mechanism is typical of a many-to-one messaging paradigm where multiple applications can send messages to a single application. The same application can be sender, receiver, or both sender and receiver.

Publish–subscribe: With this type of asynchronous communication, the application that produces information publishes it and all other applications that need this type of information, subscribe to it. Messages containing the new information are placed in a queue for each subscriber by the publishing application (see Figure 14.3). Each application in this scheme may have a dual role: it may act as a publisher or subscriber of different types of information.

The publish–subscribe mechanism is typical of a many-to-many messaging paradigm when multiple applications want to receive the same message or when a group of applications want to notify each other.

Publish–subscribe messaging works as follows. Suppose that a publisher application publishes messages on a specific topic, such as real-time stock quotes on a specific stock symbol. Multiple subscribing applications can subscribe to this topic and receive the messages published by the publishing application. The publish–subscribe facility takes the responsibility of delivering the published messages to the subscribing applications based on the subscribed topic.

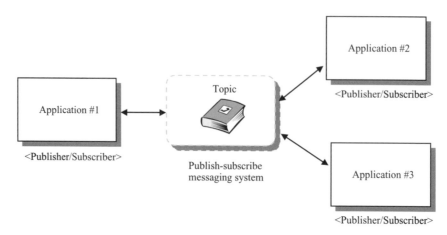

■ **Figure 14.3:** Publish and Subscribe Messaging

Asynchronous communication has a number of implications [Hohpe 2003]:

1. We no longer have a single thread of execution. Multiple threads enable applications to run concurrently, which can greatly improve performance and help ensure that some applications are making progress even while other applications may be waiting for external results.
2. Results (if any) arrive via a callback. This enables the caller to perform other tasks and be notified when the result is available, which can improve performance. However, the caller has to be able to process the result even while it is in the middle of other tasks, and it has to be able to use the result to remember the context in which the call was made.
3. Asynchronous applications can execute in any order. Again, this enables one application to make progress even while another cannot. But it also means that the calling application must be able to run independently in any order, and the caller must be able to determine which result came from which client application and combine the results together. So asynchronous communication has several advantages but requires rethinking how a calling application uses its client applications.

In general, asynchronous communication is often the preferred solution for e-Business, especially when applications want to push data between internal EIS or between the systems of their partners. In those cases the reply from clients may not be important, or if it is, its contents are not. For example, when pushing a group of new product prices out to the EIS of retail partners, the publisher of those messages is not expecting an answer. It simply wants to make sure that the partners have received the information.

14.3 Remote Procedure Calls (RPCs)

The RPC (*Remote Procedure Call*) is a basic mechanism for inter-program communication. In effect, RPC is the middleware mechanism used to invoke a procedure that is located on a remote system, and the results are returned. With this type of middleware, the application elements communicate with each other synchronously, meaning they use a request/wait-for-reply model of communication. The RPC mechanism is the simplest way to implement client/server applications because it keeps the details of network communications out of the application code.

Figure 14.4 shows the relationship between application code and the RPC mechanism during a remote procedure call. In client application code, an RPC looks like a local procedure call, because it is actually a call to a client stub. A *stub* is a surrogate code that supports remote procedure calls. The client stub behaves like a local procedure to the client, but instead of executing the call, it marshals the procedure identifier and the arguments into a request message, which it sends via its communication module to the server. The client stub communicates with the server stub using the RPC runtime library, which is a set of procedures that support all RPC applications. A server stub is like a *skeleton* method in that it unmarshals the arguments in the request message, calls the corresponding service procedure and marshals the return results for the reply message. The server stub communicates its output to the client stub, again by using the RPC runtime library. Finally, the client stub returns to the client application code.

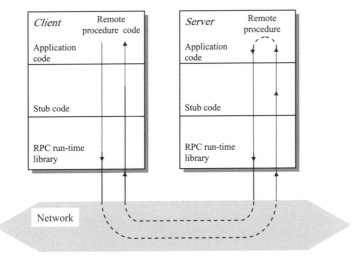

■ **Figure 14.4:** RPC Communication

RPCs work well for smaller, simple applications where communication is primarily point-to-point (rather than one system to many). RPCs do not scale well to large, mission-critical applications, as they leave many crucial details to the programmer, including:

1. handling network and system failures;
2. handling multiple connections;
3. buffering and flow of control;
4. synchronization between processes.

An additional problem with RPCs is that they do not have the means to provide persistence to objects since only single independent calls can be made to functions. This problem is partly overcome by distributed object systems that are written on top of RPCs, adding real object states, but this is done at a cost of efficiency and performance.

Owing to their synchronous nature, RPCs are not a good choice to use as the building blocks for enterprise-wide applications where high performance and high reliability are needed. Under synchronous solutions, applications are integrated by connecting APIs together on a point-to-point basis. If we do this for every application scenario it implies a lot of integration points between applications. The RPC standards have not evolved in any significant way during the past few years, primarily because of the emergence of object request brokers, which will be described later in this chapter.

14.4 Remote Method Invocation (RMI)

Traditional RPC systems are language-neutral, and therefore cannot provide functionality that is not available on all possible target platforms. The Java *Remote Method Invocation* (RMI) provides a simple and direct model for distributed computation with Java objects on the basis of the RPC mechanism.

RMI applications often comprise two separate programs: a server and a client. A typical server application creates some remote objects, makes references to them accessible, and waits for clients to invoke methods on these remote objects. A typical client application gets a remote reference to one or more remote objects on the server and then invokes methods on them. RMI provides the mechanism by which the server and the client communicate and pass information back and forth.

The client communicates with the RMI system through a stub. The server communicates with the RMI system through a skeleton. The stub and the skeleton both act as proxies for the actual remote object that is being processed. In effect the stub/skeleton implements local objects at the client and server that communicate with the remaining layers of the RMI system. The stub/skeleton layer resides on top of the remote reference layer and transport layer, allowing the RMI system to handle the interface (see Figure 14.5). The *reference layer* is connected with the protocol that is to be used for invoking remote methods. For instance, this layer can support a unicast protocol, which results in a single object being sent messages, or a multicast protocol, whereby a number of objects are sent messages. The *transport layer* is concerned with transporting the data that is associated with sending a message to a remote object. This layer supports a number of transport mechanisms, with TCP/IP being the most typical.

The stub and skeleton provide the interface to application programs. The stub classes are client-side images of the remote object classes. The skeleton classes are server-side instances of those remote (to the client) methods. The application developer communicates with any remote objects by sending messages to these local objects, which are commonly known as *proxy* objects. An application using RMI first makes contact with a remote object by finding it in the RMI *registry*. This is illustrated in Figure 14.5. The registry is a Java application that runs on the server and maintains active (object) references to remote objects. It helps the client and remote objects to locate each other. When a client first makes a call to the remote object, it will perform a lookup in the remote registry. Then the registry sends it back to

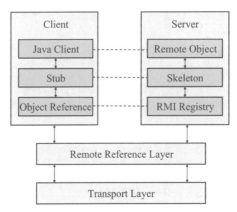

■ **Figure 14.5:** The Java Remote Method Invocation (RMI)

the stub that the client will use from this point onward to connect to the remote object. The client uses this stub to manipulate the remote object, which appears to be another local object to the client. Stubs implement the same interfaces as the remote classes and forward the invoked methods on their instances to the corresponding remote instances. When the remote method is executed, the arguments are runtime encoded and sent over the network to the server. Skeletons intercept the remote method request from the client and then call the actual method on an implementation instance. The server decodes the arguments, invokes the method, encodes the result, and sends the result back. The skeletons capture the returned results and send them back to the client's stub. The client then decodes the received result as if it were the return value of the stub.

The primary advantages of RMI for application integration are as follows:

• Transportable behavior: RMI can transport class implementations (behavior) from client to server and server to client [RMI 2000]. This feature can be useful in business applications. Consider for example the case where employee expense reports need to be checked against current business policies. When an expense report is generated, the client can fetch an object that implements that interface from the server. When company policies change, the server will return a different implementation of that interface that uses the new policies. The constraints will therefore be checked on the client side without installing any new software on the user's system. This provides maximum flexibility as it requires that only one new Java class is written and installed on the server.

• Connection to existing/legacy systems: RMI interacts with existing systems via Java's native method interface JNI. Using RMI and JNI a client can be written in Java and invoke an existing server implementation. When RMI/JNI is used to connect to existing server implementations, parts of the server implementation can be re-written (wrapped) in Java. Similarly, RMI can interface with existing relational databases using Java Database Connectivity (JDBC) without modifying existing non-Java code that communicates with the databases [Sun 2000].

• Portability: RMI is portable to any Java Virtual Machine, therefore guaranteeing maximum portability.

14.5 Message-Oriented Middleware (MOM)

Message-Oriented Middleware (MOM) is the infrastructure that is responsible for relaying data from one application to another by putting it in a message format, akin to the way e-mail works. MOM is a newer technology than RPC that permits time-independent responses as it operates in an asynchronous manner. It also permits applications to be designed in different ways. Thus, it can have serious implications for the overall enterprise integration architecture.

MOM is interposed between the client and the server part of client/server architecture and handles asynchronous calls between clients and servers (see Figure 14.6). MOM also provides an API that abstracts the complexity of the network implementation from the developer. To support this asynchronous model, MOM products typically use message queues to store calls temporarily and allow clients and servers to run at different times. Messages in the queue can consist of formatted data, requests for action or both.

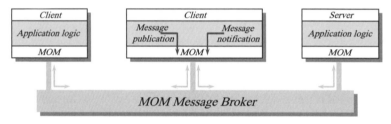

■ **Figure 14.6:** Message-Oriented Middleware

As we already explained earlier in this chapter, asynchronous messaging (or simply messaging) is a method of communication between software components or applications. A messaging system is a peer-to-peer facility: a messaging client can send messages to, and receive messages from, any other client. Each client connects to a messaging agent that provides facilities for creating, sending, receiving, and reading messages. Messaging enables a distributed communication style that is *loosely coupled*. A component sends a message to a destination, and the recipient can retrieve the message from the destination. However, the sender and the receiver do not have to be available at the same time in order to communicate. In fact, the sender does not need to know anything about the receiver; nor does the receiver need to know anything about the sender. The sender and the receiver need to know only which message format and which destination to use. In this respect, messaging differs from *tightly coupled* technologies, such as Remote Method Invocation, which require an application to know a remote application's methods.

Messaging is most attractive in contexts where heterogeneous applications need to automatically or periodically pass data to each other, or when the nature of the integration is event driven. Commonly used services e.g. an account balance service, can be active all the time, processing requests as they arrive. Periodic services can execute on a periodic basis to process requests. Consider for example trading houses, which buy and sell equities and instruments for their clients. At the end of each trading activity, books need to be reconciled to determine the existing inventory. Thus, order management can also be facilitated by a messaging infrastructure.

Typically, business operations running in e-Business applications comprise a number of invocations of different components, often in an event-driven or asynchronous fashion that reflects the underlying needs of business process. For such environments the synchronous approach espoused by RCP and RMI is rather prohibitive as it incurs delays, tight coupling of components and synchronization problems. Asynchronous messaging is often the preferred option.

The asynchronous nature of MOM makes it most appropriate for *event-driven applications* that characterize e-Business. With this approach, when an event occurs, the client application hands off to the messaging middleware application the responsibility of notifying a server that some action needs to be taken. Messages containing requests for action can trigger other messages to be fired. Normally when an event occurs, a notification is required. The natural form of communication here is to publish events to which various listeners (clients) subscribe. For example, consider financial service applications that need to react quickly to stock market fluctuations. A poorly engineered approach to this problem would be to have all client applications active and continually querying the server applications for new data. This solution would lead to performance problems as a tremendous amount of network traffic would be generated. Moreover, this solution is neither scalable nor reliable. The best solution to this problem would be to notify client applications in an event-driven style and push security prices as soon as they change.

MOM products, in general, cover more than just passing information; they usually include services for translating data, security, broadcasting data to multiple programs, error recovery, locating resources on the network, cost routing, prioritization of messages and requests, and extensive debugging facilities. MOM messaging systems also help divide long-running tasks into multiple transactions for greater efficiency. As opposed to RPC and ORB products, MOM does not assume that a reliable transport layer exists. MOM tries to handle all problems that may surface when the transport layer is unreliable.

In general, MOM has demonstrated an ability to deliver the benefits of asynchronous messaging for applications and process-to-process interoperability, distributed transaction processing (such as banking, brokerage, airline reservations), distributed enterprise workflow (such as process manufacturing, insurance claims processing), real-time automation (such utility and process control), and systems management (such as distributed backup, software distribution), among others.

Modern MOM technologies typically possess the following features:

- Message multicast supporting event-driven processing, i.e. the publish–subscribe model.

- Reliability and serialization of messages thus guaranteeing message delivery in the appropriate order.

- Subject-based (textual) names and attributes to abstract from the physical names and addresses that are interpreted and implemented by the network.

- Support for multiple communications protocols such as store and forward, request/reply, and publish–subscribe.

- Support for transactional boundaries. MOM implementations should provide a model for grouping together multiple operations as a single transaction that is locally scoped to an individual sender or receiver. In an MOM environment, applications hand off their messages to the messaging environment using local transactions. The topic of transaction processing is treated further in Section 14.7.1.

There are some features that make MOM particularly attractive when integrating applications. These include – but are not limited to – the following:

- *Prioritization of requests*: In many cases some services need higher priority than others. Consider for example an airline reservations application where there is a business policy that a canceled seat needs to be rebooked as soon as possible and is therefore of higher priority than a new reservation.

- *Load balancing*: The asynchronous nature of MOM provides more flexibility for scalability and load balancing. For example, if an application system is busy then messages could be forwarded to a parallel process in an alternate location – if there exists one.

- *Persistent messaging*: this brings reliability and ensures that messages are guaranteed to be delivered at most once to their subscribers. The combination of persistent messaging with durable subscriptions allows the implementation of integration architectures over unreliable communications media, such as the Internet.

One of the disadvantages of message queues used in MOM is that they can suffer from overloading because of temporary storage leading to an overworked network. It is possible for a client application to keep transferring data messages to a server that is not able to accept them in a timely fashion. A nice feature of many MOM implementations, however, is that they can switch between synchronous and asynchronous communication mode. Although MOM is in principle an asynchronous peer-to-peer protocol, some implementations can handle synchronous message passing too. Compare this to the less flexible RPC protocol with synchronous communication. In RPC, incoming client requests are blocked when servers are down or busy.

14.5.1 Integration brokers

Before leaving the subject of MOM, it would be useful to complement it with a short description of integration brokers. It is best to do this in this section since integration brokers are usually layered on top of some MOM implementation (see Figure 14.6) and therefore the general principles of MOM also apply to integration brokers. Initially integration brokers were called message brokers but this name often led to a mischaracterization and confusion between message brokers and message-oriented middleware. More recently, message brokers have been renamed to integration brokers, which is a more descriptive name for the features they provide.

An *integration broker* is an application-to-application middleware service that is capable of one-to-many, many-to-one and many-to-many message distribution. An integration broker is a software hub that records and manages the contracts between publishers and subscribers of messages. When a business event takes place, the application will publish the message(s) corresponding to that event. The broker reviews its lists of subscriptions and activates delivery to each subscriber for this type of message. Subscribers receive only the data to which they subscribe. A message published by one application can be subscribed to by multiple consumer applications. Similarly, a subscribing application can receive messages from multiple publishing applications.

An integration broker is usually built on a queue manager and routes messages to applications. The integration broker allows multiple applications to implement a published service with the broker providing application integration. In addition to these functions, integration brokers account for any differences at the structural level of applications. Integration brokers take care of structural mismatches by keeping track of message schemas and changing the content of messages accordingly to the semantics of a specific application. These unique capabilities of integration brokers enable them to broker not only between applications but also between types of middleware.

Integration brokers consist of components that provide the following functions:

- message transformation

- business rules processing

- routing services

- directory services

- adapter services

- repository services

- events and alerts

These functions will be explained in some detail in Chapter 17 where we examine integration brokers as part of business integration architectures. We summarize them briefly in this section for reasons of completeness.

The integration broker transforms application-specific messages into commonly understood messages, e.g. between different XML schemas using eXtensible Stylesheet Language Transformations (see Section 7.4.2). To achieve a transformation the integration broker uses transformation rules defined by an application developer by means of a graphical mapping tool. The message transformation functionality 'understands' the format of all messages transmitted between applications. This is possible since the integration broker holds a repository of schemas of interchanged messages. Using this knowledge, the broker can translate between schemas by restructuring the data of these messages. In this way, receiving applications can make sense of received messages.

The business-rules processing functionality is usually implemented as a rules-processing engine within the broker. Often there is a need for a message created in one system to be used in more than one other application, and the broker can follow business rules (see Section 12.4) to decide where the message should be sent. The integration broker allows the application of business rules to messages, so that new application logic can reside within the integration broker. The flow of messages is often bound to business rules that can be expressed in traditional logic (e.g. if, then, else, or). These rules can be constructed with a rules editor provided with the integration broker using scripting-like languages. This moves integration logic out of the applications codifying the business logic, including the sequencing of events and data flow, ensuring the integrity of the business transaction.

The routing functionality takes care of the flow control of messages. It identifies the origin of the message and routes it to the appropriate target application. This functionality uses the message transformation functionality since messages usually have to be translated for a receiving application to understand their content. The rules engine may also be involved to determine under which conditions the message can be sent to the recipient.

The directory services functionality is needed since integration brokers function in a distributed environment and need a way to locate and use network resources. Applications using the integration broker are able to find other applications or hardware on the network.

Many integration brokers use *adapters* as layers between the broker and large enterprises' EIS to convert the data formats and application semantics from the source application to the target application. As business events occur, the adapter publishes the event and related data via the MOM interface and instantiates the integration process controlling the flow of the integration.

Adapters map the differences between two distinct interfaces: the integration broker interface and the native interface of the source or target application. Adapters hide the complexities of that interface from the end user or even the developer using the integration broker. For instance, an integration-broker vendor may have adapters for several different source and target applications (such as packaged ERP applications, like PeopleSoft and SAP), or adapters for certain types of databases (such as Oracle, Sybase, or DB2), or even adapters for specific brands of middleware.

Key features of application adapters include the following [Roch 2002]:

- A development environment and software development kit (SDK) to build customized adapters.

- Configurable adapters for common EIS applications.

- An ergonomic GUI to assist with configuring adapters.

- Support for specific metadata that describes the interfaces and messages particular to applications as well as a metadata repository to store the configuration metadata.

The widespread adoption of standards, such as J2EE and XML, has laid the foundation for a standardized approach to the development of adapters. Perhaps the most significant of these standards for application integration is the *J2EE Connector Architecture* (CA) [Sharma 2002]. The J2EE Connector Architecture defines a standardized approach for the development of adapters connecting the J2EE platform to heterogeneous EISs. EISs can range from legacy applications, such as CICS, to ERP, transaction processing, and database systems. The adoption of standards such as J2EE CA enables organizations to develop adapters that work on any J2EE-compliant application server. This ability to transform messages as they are distributed provides relief for applications by isolating them from the message formats that every other connected application uses.

There are two types of adapters in the world of integration brokers: thin adapters and thick adapters. The most popular integration brokers today offer *thin adapters* that simply bind one API to another. The most typical thin adapters are simple API wrappers, or binders, delivered as a set of libraries, that map the interface of the source or target system to a common interface supported by the integration broker. Thin adapters have the advantage of simplicity in implementation but also have a number of disadvantages.

They can impact performance without improving functionality as they offer nothing more than trading one application interface for another. As most common APIs that are being mapped are almost always proprietary, considerable programming efforts are required. These problems are solved by *thick adapters*, which provide advanced functionality interposed between the integration broker infrastructure and the source or target applications. Thick adapters provide a layer of abstraction that handles the difference between all the applications requiring integration. Hence, there is only a limited need for programming. They are capable of accomplishing this task because they provide a layer of sophisticated software that hides the complexities of the source and target application interfaces from the integration broker user. In many cases, the user can connect many systems through this abstraction layer and through the graphical user interface, without ever having to resort to hand coding. Integration brokers that use the thick adapter scenario employ repositories.

Repository services are implemented by using a database holding extensive information on target and source applications. The database keeps track of input/output to the applications, its data elements, interrelationships between applications and all the metadata from the other subsystems of the broker like the rules-processing component. In short, the repository houses information on rules, logic, objects and metadata. Metadata is one of the key elements of any integration solution as it used to describe the structure of information held in the disparate systems and processes. This may range from the structure of a relational database schema to the description of a process that sets up a new customer account. When repositories are used in conjunction with thick adapters, they enable the integration broker to understand the source and target applications and interact with them by relying on metadata about the source and target applications.

Messages passing through the integration broker may trigger events or alerts based on specified conditions. Such conditions may be used for tracking business processes that move outside given parameters, and then create a new message, run a special purpose application, or send an alert, in response. We shall revisit integration brokers in the context of enterprise application integration in Chapter 17.

14.5.2 The Java Message Service

Until recently, MOM products required use of their own proprietary programmatic interfaces. This meant that all applications needed to be recorded to adapt to a middleware package. Thus, in-house applications that were designed for use with one middleware product could not be used with another middleware product. Several times during the last decade, middleware vendors attempted to standardize programming interfaces to MOM packages, but with little success. This changed in 1999 when Java launched the *Java Message Service* (JMS), a framework that specified a set of programming interfaces by which Java programs could access MOM software.

JMS is a vendor-agnostic API for enterprise messaging that can be used with many different MOM vendors. The JMS acts as wrapper around different messaging products, allowing developers to focus on actual application development and integration, rather than on the particulars of each other's APIs. Application developers use the same API to access many different systems. JMS is not a messaging system itself. It is an abstraction of the interfaces and classes needed by messaging clients when communicating with different messaging systems. JMS does not only provide a Java API for connectivity to MOM systems, it also supports messaging as a first-class Java distributed computing paradigm on an equal footing with RPC [Monson-Haefel 2001].

JMS-based communication is a potential solution in any distributed computing scenario that needs to pass data either synchronously or asynchronously between application elements. A common application for JMS involves interfacing Enterprise JavaBeans (see Section 14.8.2) with legacy applications and sending legacy-related data between the two.

JMS provides the two principal models of MOM messaging: point-to-point queuing and publish-and-subscribe.

The JMS messaging point-to-point model allows JMS clients to send and receive messages both asynchronously and synchronously via queues. A given queue may have multiple receivers, but only one receiver may accept each message. This guarantees that, for example, if a packaging order is sent to multiple warehouses, a single warehouse receives the message and processes the order.

In the JMS publish-and-subscribe messaging model, publishers send messages to a named topic, and subscribers receive all the messages sent to this topic. There may be multiple message listeners subscribed to each topic and an application can be both sender and receiver. The JMS subsystem delivers a copy of the message to each of the topic's subscribers. JMS clients can optionally establish durable subscriptions that allow subscribers to disconnect and later reconnect and collect the messages that were published while they were disconnected.

In addition to this basic messaging functionality, JMS works with other Java technologies, such as the Java Transactions API to provide features like distributed transaction support.

Finally, a few words about the differences between JMS and RMI. JMS and RMI are different objects in Java's enterprise suite. In RMI, the object is physically resident in one place and applications invoke methods on this object via its stub. The remote object is always passed by reference. In contrast to this, JMS messages are passed by value and provide synchronous and asynchronous communication between MOM-based applications.

14.6 Data-access middleware

Enterprise data is typically widely distributed and stored on multiple locations using multiple formats, application-specific design, and a wide variety of semantics. Moreover, the data formats and semantics adhere to application-specific standards, as usually no enterprise-wide standards would have been in place when the original applications and corresponding databases were developed. Data-access middleware addresses most of these problems and can be seen as the type of middleware that facilitates communications with a database, whether from an application or between databases [Linthicum 2001a].

Data-access middleware comes in three flavors: Command Line Interfaces (CLIs), native database middleware and database gateways [Linthicum 2001a].

Command Line Interface is a common API that can manage access to different types of relational databases via a well-defined common interface. The CLI provides a single interface to applications for constructing CLI messages, sending them to CLI-compliant databases and receiving response messages. It provides a useful set of methods for callback registration, database connection pooling, setting up communication mechanisms and protocol options, and others. CLIs also translate common interface calls into any number of relational-database dialects. They also translate and aggregate the responses into a common response that is understandable to the application making the call to the target databases.

A typical example of a CLI is the *Java Database Connectivity* (JDBC) API, which is the standard approach for Java application programs to access multiple databases. The JDBC API gives application developers the ability to make their Java applications independent of the database vendor. Developers can code a JDBC application that accesses a database using standard SQL statements. If the underlying database differs from one vendor's product to another, the JDBC application works without any changes in its code, provided that the code uses standard statements and does not include any proprietary extensions from the first vendor.

Native database middleware accesses a particular database using only native mechanisms rather than a single multi-database API. Native database middleware has an advantage over CLI applications in its ability to provide high-performance database access along with the ability to access features native to a specific database. Its primary disadvantage is its inability to provide access to more than one type of database.

Database gateways, also known as SQL gateways, provide access to data that reside on different types of platforms; typically, data that were once locked inside larger systems such as mainframes and legacy databases. They integrate several databases for access from a single application interface. These gateways are suitable for ad hoc SQL queries only, with little or no support for remote stored procedures and procedure calls [Umar 1997]. To provide access to legacy databases such as IMS and older-generation data-access mechanisms (flat files, ISAM, VSAM, and so on), some database gateways provide converters, e.g. SQL to IMS converters, which change SQL calls to legacy and older-generation data-access calls. This data translation is usually accomplished at the target database server machine through data translators.

Database gateways translate SQL calls into a standard format known as the Format and Protocol (FAP), which is the common connection between the client and the server. FAP is also the common link between different platforms and databases. The gateway translates the API call directly to FAP, it relays the request to the target database and then translates it into that database's native language.

14.7 Transaction-oriented middleware

Transaction processing systems are widely used by enterprises to support mission-critical applications. These applications need to store and update data reliably, provide concurrent access to data by large numbers of users, and maintain data integrity despite failures of individual system components. Most large-scale business applications in the domains of finance, insurance claim processing, banking and so on, rely on transaction processing for delivering their business functionality. Given the complexity of contemporary business requirements, transaction processing is one of the most complex and important segments of business-level distributed applications to build, deploy and maintain.

A transaction is a series of operations performed as a single unit of work that either completely succeeds, or fails with all partially completed work being undone. An *atomic transaction* is a computation consisting of a collection of operations which take place indivisibly in the presence of both failures and concurrent computations. That is, either all of the operations prevail or none of them prevail, and other programs executing concurrently cannot modify or observe intermediate states of the computation. A transaction ends when one of two things happens: the transaction is committed by the application, or the transaction is rolled back by an application or system failure, or when a commit operation fails (for example, because of inadequate resources or data consistency violations). If the transaction successfully commits, changes associated with that transaction will be written to persistent storage and made visible to new transactions. If the transaction is rolled back, all changes made by that transaction will be discarded; it will be as if the transaction never happened at all.

To maintain consistency across resources within a transaction boundary, a transaction must exhibit ACID properties, which are Atomicity, Consistency, Isolation, and Durability:

- Atomicity means that either all of the transaction's operations are applied to the application state, or none of them are applied; the transaction is an indivisible unit of work. If the transaction cannot complete successfully, it will rollback to the state before the beginning of the transaction.

- Consistency means that the transaction must correctly transition data from one consistent state to another, preserving the data's semantic and referential integrity.

- Isolation requires that several concurrent transactions must produce the same results in the data as those same transactions executed sequentially, in some (unspecified) order. Isolation guarantees that the execution of concurrent transactions is controlled and coordinated since they are accessing a shared database and may potentially interfere with one another. Concurrent transactions are executed in a manner that gives the illusion that each transaction is executing in isolation while in reality it may work concurrently with other transactions on the same database items. Isolation is generally implemented using a locking mechanism.

- Durability means that committed updates are made permanent. Failures that occur after a commit cause no loss of data. Durability also implies that data for all committed transactions can be recovered after a system or media failure.

Atomic transactions are useful for activities that manipulate data, transform data from one or more sources to one or more targets, or coordinate multiple transaction participants. The all-or-nothing guarantee ensures that all data changes and messages exchanged in the context of the transaction retain their consistency, regardless of how many steps are required in order to complete the transaction.

Transaction-oriented middleware encompasses two kinds of middleware products: transaction-processing monitors and application servers. These coordinate information movement and method sharing between many different resources.

14.7.1 Transaction-processing (TP) monitors

Transaction-processing (TP) monitor technology provides the distributed client/server environment with the capacity to efficiently and reliably develop, execute and manage transaction applications. TP monitors enable the building of online transaction processing by coordinating and monitoring the efforts of separate applications. TP monitors reside between front-end applications and back-end applications and databases to manage operations on transactional data. TP monitors manage processes and orchestrate applications by breaking complex applications into a set of transactions. The transaction is the mechanism that binds the client to one or more servers. It is the fundamental unit of recovery, consistency, and concurrency in a client/server system. From the perspective of application integration, transactions are more than just business events. They have become an application's design philosophy that guarantees consistency and robustness in distributed systems.

A transaction monitor is needed for transactions requiring guaranteed completion of multiple discreet functions on multiple application systems. Under the control of a TP monitor, a transaction can be managed from its point of origin – typically on a client – across one or more servers and back to the originating client. When a transaction ends, all parties involved agree that it either succeeded or failed. Transaction models define when a transaction starts, when it ends, and what the appropriate units of recovery are in case of failure. TP monitor designs allow APIs to support elements such as heterogeneous client libraries, databases and resource mangers, and peer-level application systems.

TP monitors were invented to run applications that serve large numbers of clients. By interjecting themselves between clients and servers, TP monitors can manage transactions, route them across systems, load-balance their execution, and restart them after failures. The router subsystem of a TP monitor brokers the client request to one or more server processes. Each server in turn executes the request and responds. Typically, the server manages a file system, database, or other mission-critical resources, shared among several clients. A TP monitor can manage transactional resources on a single server or across multiple servers, and it can cooperate with other TP monitors in federated arrangements.

Transaction processing can adversely affect application performance because the processing of a transaction is synchronous, from the point of view of the transaction's requester. The requester must wait until all the processing of the transaction has completed before it can proceed with further computations. Moreover, during the processing of a transaction all the resources used by it are locked until the transaction completes. No other application can use these resources during the execution of a transaction.

Another problem is that TP monitors are much more intrusive than MOM. That means that they demand more modification of the applications themselves in order take advantage of the TP monitor's specific services.

Examples of TP monitors include CICS from IBM, Tuxedo from BEA Systems, and MTS from Microsoft.

14.7.2 Application servers

Until recently applications were classified either as front-office or back-office applications. Front-office applications target the consumer or end user, while back-office applications provide the infrastructure necessary for running the back-end business processes of an enterprise such as inventory, accounting, general ledger, billing and so on. Front-office applications include applications that focus mainly on sales and customer management automation as well as marketing automation. Back-office applications include applications that concentrate on vital information about customers, products, and financial transactions typically provided by ERP systems. As much of the information required by front-office applications – such as customer account details, inventory status and new product information – is contained in back-office applications, traditional middleware and enterprise integration technology focused until now on integrating back-office and front-office applications. Rather than being targeted to the front-office or back-office applications, most middleware applications are now integrated for both the front and back ends and are in addition web-enabled. These days traditional middleware, which focuses on integrating data and applications within the boundaries of an enterprise, is rapidly being transformed into Web-enabled middleware.

Application servers offer an integrated development environment that allows enterprises to connect and manage front-office and back-office applications and combine them with Web-enabled functionality. Application servers provide a robust and scalable platform for application deployment by taking care of much of the system-level plumbing by handling resources such as operating-system processes, memory management, database connections and network sessions. Application servers expose these integrated resources through a single user interface, typically a Web browser. For example, application servers can easily externalize information contained in databases or ERP applications. As a result developers can gain all the application development capabilities they require, including support for programming languages (typically Java) and an integrated development environment.

An application-server architecture is normally based on a three-tier model, which is a popular alternative to two-tier client/server applications. The three-tier applications are partitioned logically into three executable tiers of code: the user interface, the business rules and the data-access software (see Figure 6.4). In an application server requests run on the user interface (front tier), the business application logic and rules run on the middle tier and the data accesses that service them run on the server (back tier). Often the business-rules tier (or business-processing layer) is deployed on the same platform as the data-access tier, or on the same platform(s) as the user interface. In this way application servers can achieve higher performance efficiency by providing more flexibility by separating business application logic from either the presentation or data-access code.

A typical application server offers security, state management, transactional and database connectivity. The connection from the business logic (application server layer) to the data layer is usually accomplished utilizing a standard protocol that supports transactional coordination. This implies that application components deployed on the application server utilize synchronous resource adapters to connect to and provide transactional access to EIS in the data layer. This synchronous messaging allows access to business information that needs to be real time, like pricing, shipping charges, tax calculation and inventory availability. This allows critical and sensitive business data to remain on the back-end applications at the data layer rather than be duplicated and synchronized on the web server.

Adapters implement the support communication with the EIS and provide access to EIS data functions. The most common standard for this is an XA connection although it is also possible for application-server and database-server providers to supply more proprietary connection protocols. An XA-compliant resource adheres to the XA interface which is part of the X/Open DTP (Distributed Transaction Processing) specification that is used to describe the interface between a global transaction manager and a local resource manager under the guidance of the two-phase commit protocol. If the application server does not provide transactional coordination capabilities, then the system will depend on the database servers in the data layer for transaction coordination or on another application server that offers this capability. To keep data consistency simple (non-transactional) there must be only one data access connection for the application server. Advanced application servers also offer load balancing, failure recovery and security features as well as interactive debugging and the facility to reuse tried and tested components. This latter facility reduces development time, leading thus to rapid prototyping of applications, an essential feature for modern enterprises where development requirements change rapidly owing to market pressure.

To maximize the advantages of Web-driven application integration, enterprises are turning to the Java programming language and the Java Enterprise Edition (J2EE) platform. J2EE is a reference (standard) architectural model for building robust component-based applications based on application-server technology centered around the Java programming language [Sharma 2001b]. The J2EE application server consists of several major components: a suite of Java specifications such as Enterprise JavaBeans (covered in Section 14.8.2), Servlets, JavaServer Pages (both covered in Chapter 6), a reference implementation, compatibility tests, and the J2EE Blueprints – an integrated set of documentation and examples that illustrate best practices for developing and deploying J2EE technology-compatible solutions. Each component is designed to address longstanding design and performance issues unique to enterprise web-applications development. The J2EE specification also describes how the server-side components interact with each other, the applications server, the resource APIs like Java Database Connectivity (JDBC) and Java Message Service (JMS), both of which we presented in this chapter.

J2EE has historically been used to build websites and applications around EJB. EJB application servers typically provide access to Java components, applets, and EJB clients. In some cases, application servers also support request-brokering interfaces such as the CORBA Internet Inter-ORB Protocol (IIOP), allowing them to communicate with any CORBA client. Recently, it has been extended to include support for XML and web services. There is a natural complementarity and synergy between XML and the Java programming language. They were both designed for web applications, both are internationalized (because they support Unicode), and both are designed for portability. XML is to data what the Java programming language is to application services.

Application servers are a popular technology for enterprise and e-Business application integration and will be examined in the context of middleware technologies for enterprise application integration that are described in Chapter 17.

14.8 Distributed-object middleware

One alternative for providing inter-application communication is to employ distributed-object middleware. Distributed objects are a development of RPCs that provide an additional layer of interoperability that abstracts the procedure call from the underlying platform and language. Distributed-object middleware shields developers from many tedious and error-prone aspects of programming distributed applications. It helps address these challenges by defining high-level programming abstraction in the form of a distributed-object interface that provides location transparency to client and server components, shielding application developers from low-level network programming details like parameter marshaling and unmarshaling, error handling and so on.

Distributed objects can be classified as middleware as they facilitate inter-application communication. They also provide the mechanisms for distributed application development and data sharing. This section covers a specific breed of distributed-object technology known as Object Request Brokers (ORBs) that can be used as middleware to manage application integration. This technology is used for developing tightly coupled applications on the basis of distributed objects and software components, which we examine in Chapter 15.

14.8.1 Object Request Brokers (ORBs)

An object request broker (ORB) is a distributed-object middleware technology that manages communication and data exchange between objects. ORBs promote interoperability of distributed-object systems because they enable users to build systems by piecing together objects – from different vendors- that communicate with each other via the ORB [Wade 1994]. The implementation details of the ORB are generally not important to developers building distributed systems. The developers are only concerned with the object interface details. This form of information hiding enhances system maintainability since the object communication details are hidden from the developers and isolated in the ORB [Cobb 1995].

An Object Request Broker provides clients and servers of distributed objects with the means to make and receive requests of each other. ORB support in a network of clients and servers on different computers means that a client program (which may itself be an object) can request services from a server program or object without having to understand where the server is in a distributed network or what the interface to the server program looks like. They are a key part of a broader architectural standard for building services and providing inter-application interoperability. ORBs mediate between applications and network services such as security, authentication, performance monitoring and so on. ORBs can also provide object services, such as a naming service that lets clients look up objects by name, or security services that provide for secure inter-object communication. To make requests or return replies between the ORBs, applications use the General Inter-ORB Protocol (GIOP) and, for the Internet, its Internet Inter-ORB Protocol (IIOP). IIOP maps GIOP requests and replies to the Internet's Transmission Control Protocol (TCP) layer in each computer.

ORBS perform the same functions as RPCs, MOMs and distributed transaction-processing monitors that were discussed earlier. Initially, ORBS provided synchronous messaging and operated just like RPCs in a point-to-point manner. More recently, event services were layered on top of ORBS to support asynchronous message servicing. However, ORBs do not provide a consistent set of services that fully replace the functionality of these middleware approaches. Furthermore, ORBs from different vendors are not interoperable. Moreover, the features of communication models of synchronous/asynchronous messaging and transaction-management services provided by different vendors of ORBs vary significantly. At present there are two different standards for ORBS: the Common Object Request Broker Architecture (CORBA) backed by the Object Management Group (OMG), a consortium of over 700 companies; and the Distributed Common Object Model (DCOM) backed by Microsoft.

The Common Object Request Broker Architecture (CORBA)

The strength of CORBA lies primarily in its ability to subsume other forms of existing client/server middleware [Orfali 1997]. Objects are the unifying metaphor to incorporate existing applications while still providing a broad foundation for component-based development. CORBA is a self-describing system in which the specifications of services are separated from the implementation. It was designed to let distributed components discover each other and interoperate on the bus as its basic functionality. But with this it also specifies a broad array of bus-related services and facilities.

CORBA consists of a number of components, depicted in Figure 14.7. The ORB (Object Request Broker) is the core facility that provides clients and servers of distributed objects with the means to make and receive requests of each other. CORBA has an object manager on both the client and server side of a distributed object. Thus, both the client and the server CORBA objects use a separate ORB to talk to each other. This

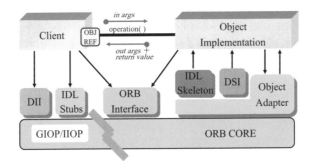

■ **Figure 14.7:** The Common Object Request Broker Architecture (CORBA)

lets any agent in a CORBA system act as both a client and a server of remote objects. ORBs communicate by using IIOP (Internet Inter-ORB Protocol) as a standard protocol making CORBA a platform-independent architecture. ORBs provide interoperability infrastructure interposed between applications allowing distributed objects to communicate, independent of the specific platforms and techniques used to implement the addressed objects.

We can understand best how CORBA operates by examining the sequence of actions involved when a client application invokes a method in a remote object.

In order to invoke a remote object, the client must first obtain its object reference, usually from a name server. When a CORBA object is created it is assigned a unique immutable object reference. A client can get a reference to a remote object by creating an ORB that is connected to the remote server hosting the object, and then asking the ORB to find the object on the remote server. The ORB initialization process will typically include arguments that let the client specify which remote host and port to talk to for remote object transactions [Mowbray 1997; Farley 1998]. The client then binds to this object reference and, as a result, is given access to a stub through which it can invoke the remote object associated with this reference. A stub is a mechanism that effectively creates and issues requests on behalf of a client and allows the client application to view the stubs as proxies for remote objects. Stubs map (or marshal) the arguments and return values of method calls into and out of communication buffers, which are specified in terms of the Generic Inter-ORB Protocol (GIOP). GIOP specifies transfer syntax and a standard set of message formats for ORB interoperation. These are relayed across the network by the IIOP. When the client invokes a method on a remote object, the server ORB receives the request and calls the method on the object implementation through its skeleton interface. The server implementation is interfaced to the underlying ORB much in the same as clients are interfaced to ORB stubs. That is, skeletons are responsible for unmarshaling requests, passing the resulting arguments to the target object implementation and marshaling any results into GIOP reply messages.

Before a client can make requests to an object, it must know the types of operations supported by that object. An object's interface specifies the operations and types that the object supports and thus defines the requests that can be made on the object. Interfaces for objects are defined in CORBA's Interface Definition Language (IDL). IDL is a declarative language that is a platform- and implementation-independent means to define what kinds of operations an object is capable of performing.

Developers can use a variety of programming languages to build networked objects and have to specify their public interface in IDL. IDL has its own set of data types so each programming language has to provide a mapping to IDL types and object definitions. CORBA implementations come with an IDL compiler that takes as input the written classes and their IDL interfaces and delivers as output client stubs and server skeletons. The stubs translate method calls to ORB calls using IIOP and send them to the server ORB that translates the call to a skeleton call, which provides a mapping to a call to the target object.

Once an IDL interface for a distributed object has been written, it can be translated into a client stub and a server skeleton. IDL translators exist for C, C++, Smalltalk, Ada, Java, and other common languages. The stub and skeleton do not have to be compiled into the same programming language. For example, the client could be a Java applet and use a stub in the form of a Java class definition. The server could implement the same object interface in C++ using an object skeleton defined as a C++ class definition. At the server side, implementation instances are registered with the ORB so that their presence can be advertised.

CORBA offers two ways to specify object interfaces: an IDL for static interface definitions, and a Dynamic Invocation Interface (DII), which lets clients access interfaces as first-class objects from an Interface Repository. The above description is a typical example of static IDL definitions, whereby applications have their stubs and skeletons prelinked with their implementation code. Using the DII, a client can invoke requests on any object without having compile-time knowledge of the object's interfaces. This is useful for applications such as browsers and databases for which it would be impossible to link all possible stub and skeleton classes statically [Campbell 1999].

CORBA specifies a range of architectural entities that surround the core ORB. These include: Object Services, Common Facilities and Domain Interfaces.

Object Services are general purpose services that are either fundamental for developing useful CORBA-based applications composed of distributed objects, or that provide an application domain-independent basis for application interoperability [OMA 1997]. These include services for naming, persistence, life cycle, dynamic linking, externalization, event handling, security, transaction management and concurrency control, to name a few. These services are used when locating objects (naming), creating and destructing objects (life cycle), triggering objects to act (events), saving the state of objects (persistence) and so on.

Common Facilities provide a wide range of horizontal facilities that are oriented towards end-user applications. Examples are printing facilities, database facilities, and e-mail facilities.

Domain Interfaces are domain-specific interfaces designed to accommodate objects from vertical industries. These target application domains such as finance, healthcare, manufacturing, telecommunications, e-Commerce, and transportation.

Distributed Component Object Model (DCOM)

The Distributed Component Object Model (DCOM) is Microsoft's proprietary distributed-object technology. DCOM builds on the earlier Component Object Model (COM) architecture that provides a framework for application interoperation within a Windows environment.

COM defines how components and their clients interact. A client that needs to communicate with a (server) component in another process cannot call the component directly, but has to use some form of inter-process communication mechanism provided by the operating system. COM provides this communication transparently by intercepting calls from the client and forwarding them to the component in another process. When client and component reside on different machines, DCOM simply replaces the local inter-process communication with a network protocol. Neither the client nor the component observe any differences irrespective of whether the processes run on the same or different machines.

For a client to get an actual instance of a server object to run, it needs to know that server's class. This information is accessed from the COM library, also called the registry. The client calls the system library by using a function, specifying the desired server class. Subsequently, the client is able to invoke the server object's services by its methods.

Figure 14.8 shows the overall DCOM architecture: The COM run-time provides object-oriented services to clients and components and uses RPC and the security provider to generate standard network packets that conform to the DCOM wire-protocol standard.

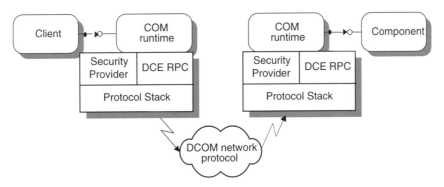

■ **Figure 14.8:** The Distributed Component Object Model

Developers can write their own interfaces with COM's proprietary IDL. To match CORBA's dynamic method-calling capabilities, COM additionally lets developers use ODL (Object Description Language) to register the interfaces in a Type Library so clients can discover dynamically which interfaces a server object supports and what parameters they require. Since the COM specification is at the binary level it allows DCOM server components to be written in diverse languages like C++, Java, Visual Basic and even COBOL.

DCOM is the distributed version of COM and as such is an alternative to CORBA. For example, they both define an IDL and both provide platform and language neutrality and support services such as persistence and security. DCOM is based on an ORPC (Object Remote Procedure Call) layer to support remote objects. The interactions between client and server objects are similar to those in CORBA. Special stubs are generated to exchange remote calls; in COM client stubs are called proxies and server stubs are called simply stubs.

14.8.2 The Enterprise JavaBeans component model

Enterprise JavaBeans (EJB) is a server component model for the development and deployment of enterprise-level Java applications based on a distributed-object architecture [Johnson 1998]. As we shall see in Chapter 15 a component model defines an environment to support reusable application components. Components are predeveloped pieces of application code that can be assembled into working application systems. The EJB architecture supports developers to create reusable components designed to operate on an application server on the middle tier. The EJB specification and APIs provide a vendor-independent programming interface for application servers. The EJB components have the advantage of being able to run in a standard environment that is independent of both the operating system and middleware infrastructure.

The core of the EJB system comprises EJB components, also known as enterprise beans, which provide persistence, business processing, and distributed-processing capabilities for enterprise applications. An EJB component is a Java class, written by an EJB developer, that implements business logic. All other classes in the EJB system either support client access or provide services such as persistence, security, transaction management and so on, to EJB component classes.

Before we introduce the different types of beans that exist, it is useful to explain what session and sessionless processes are. A *session* is a logical connection created by the communications service between two communicating processes. Sessions are typically multiplexed over the underlying network transport mechanism to avoid exhausting network resources. Using a session, name-to-address resolution occurs only once, at session initiation. Sessions are useful when sending many, or very large messages within a short time period to the same process. A communications service may also provide *sessionless communication* where a message is sent without first establishing permission. In this case, name-to-address resolution occurs with each message transmitted, and the receiving process may or may not be able to process the messages being sent. Sessionless transmissions are often useful when fewer messages are being sent during a short time period to the same process, or when messages are broadcasted or multicasted. Some communication services can be invoked repeatedly without having to maintain context or state, while other services may require their context to be preserved from one invocation to the next. The former communication services are called *stateless*, while the latter are called *stateful*.

EJB components come in three types: session, entity and message beans. *Session beans* model processes and act as server-side extensions of their clients, i.e. they manage a client's session state. Session beans are enterprise beans that are suitable for processing or workflow [Alur 2001]. They come in two flavors: *stateful* and *stateless*. A stateful session bean retains the client state between method invocations. Stateless session beans are used when there is no need to store a state between method invocations and there is need to achieve higher performance than that offered by stateful beans. Session beans are used to model business processes that may or may not have session state. Session beans might be used to model business concepts such as a securities broker, loan calculation, currency conversion and so on. Session bean instances pertain to a single user session and are not shared between users. *Entity beans* model persistent business objects and are used when a business component needs to access persistent data that need to be shared among multiple users. Entity beans are usually used for modeling business concepts, e.g. customers, accounts, bills, etc., that have persistent data and may be accessed by multiple clients concurrently. *Message-driven beans* are the newest bean type and are used to model stateless JMS [Monson-Haefel 2001]. A message-driven bean has a pool of instances at run time, each of which is a message listener. These bean instances can concurrently consume hundreds of messages delivered to the message-driven bean. This makes the message-driven bean scalable.

Like session beans, message-driven beans model business processes by coordinating the interaction of other beans and resources according to the messages received and their payloads.

EJB components execute within an *EJB container*, which in turn executes with an *EJB server*. Any server that can host an EJB container and provide it with the necessary services can be an EJB server. The EJB container provides services such as transaction and resource management, versioning, scalability, mobility, persistence and security to the EJB components it contains [Johnson 1998; Anderson 2002]. Since the EJB container handles all these functions, the EJB component developer can concentrate on business rules, and rely for database manipulation and other systems programming details on the container.

Client programs execute methods on remote EJBs by means of an *EJB object*. The EJB object implements the remote interface of the EJB component on the server. The remote interface represents the 'business' methods of the EJB component. The remote interface does the actual, useful work of an EJB object, such as creating an order form. EJB objects and EJB components both implement the same interface (the EJB component's remote interface), however, their mission is quite different. An *EJB component* runs on the server in an EJB container and implements the business logic. The EJB object runs on the client and remotely executes the EJB component's methods.

To create a server-side bean, a client program contacts a server and requests that the server create an Enterprise JavaBean. The server responds by creating the server-side object (the EJB component instance), and returning a proxy object (the EJB object) whose interface is the same as the EJB component's and whose implementation performs remote method invocations on the client's behalf. The client then uses the EJB object as if it were a local object. Figure 14.9 gives a pictorial representation of this arrangement.

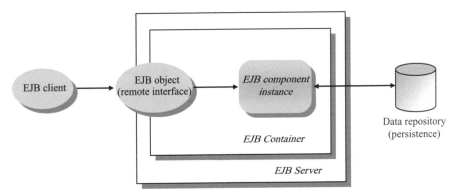

■ **Figure 14.9:** The EJB component Model

The EJB object is created by the container and code-generation tools associated with the container, while the EJB component is created by the EJB developer. To the client, an EJB object looks just like an object from the application domain – an order form, for example. However, the EJB object is just a stand-in for the actual EJB, running on the server inside an EJB container. When the client calls a method on an EJB object, the EJB object method communicates with the remote EJB container, requesting that the same method be called, on the appropriate (remote) EJB, with the same arguments, on the client's behalf [Johnson 1998].

The EJB technology specification requires application servers to provide a host of services that the EJB components may depend upon. Because the services are specified using Java technology interfaces, the bean implementation is not tied to any application-server vendor's implementation of those services. The specification also enables the application-server vendors to provide a robust, scalable, secure and transactional environment to host the EJB components.

14.9 Newer generation frameworks

Newer generation platforms are Web development infrastructures that support the development of loosely coupled applications. The vision is that future applications will be built not only by integration of local services, but integration of services across the Internet (see Chapter 19). For the moment it suffices to say that web services are software modules built using XML for data exchange to help distributed applications, services, and a variety of devices, such as mobile or handheld devices, interoperate. Sharing data through XML allows them to be independent of each other while simultaneously giving them the ability to loosely link themselves into a collaborating group that performs a particular task.

In the following we shall examine the .NET framework and the J2EE platform, which are the two most prominent technologies for developing loosely coupled web-based applications or applications based on web-services technologies that are distributed across the Internet. J2EE and .NET are evolutions of existing application-server technology used to build loosely coupled enterprise applications.

14.9.1 .NET

The Microsoft .NET (http://msdn.microsoft.com/netframework) effort provides an Internet operating system, bridging applications from the traditional desktop to the Internet. Microsoft has recognized that ubiquitous network connectivity has not been fully exploited. The vision is that future applications will be built not only by integration of local services, but integration of services across the Internet. Microsoft sees this effort as a way to decrease time-to-market, to achieve higher developer productivity, and to improve quality. Microsoft is focusing on language independence, as opposed to platform independence. This is a similar approach to that taken by the Common Object Request Broker Architecture. .NET ignores object-model issues, instead focusing on messaging.

Microsoft .NET is a product suite that enables organizations to build smart, enterprise-class web applications. More specifically, .NET technology provides the ability to quickly build, deploy, manage, and use connected, security-enhanced solutions with web services. .NET targets code reuse, code specialization, resource management, support for multiple languages, security, deployment and administration. Microsoft is focusing on language independence, as opposed to platform independence. This is a similar approach to that taken by CORBA that we examined earlier in this chapter. .NET is built on top of XML and ignores object model issues instead focusing on messaging. Microsoft .NET's reliance on XML removes barriers to data sharing and software integration. While designing the .NET platform, Microsoft also improved some features of the current Windows platform on which it is based.

.NET includes several software components that are used to support the development of .NET-connected applications and services. The most notable components are shown in Figure 14.10, which provides an overview of the .NET product suite, and are summarized below.

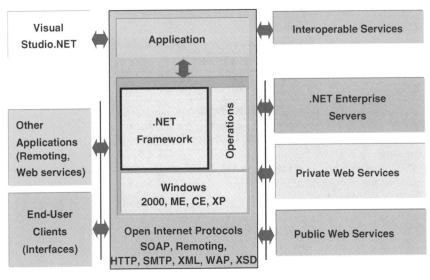

■ **Figure 14.10:** Overview of .NET

One of the main components of the .NET platform is .NET Framework development tools. These include a set of languages such as C# and VB.NET, the .NET version of Visual Basic, to build XML web services; a set of development tools including VisualStudio.NET for the development of web services and Web-based applications; and a comprehensive set of class libraries for building Windows, web services and Web-based applications. VisualStudio.NET is designed to support the rapid development of web services through the integrated development environment that supports multiple languages, cross-language debugging, and XML editing facilities. The .NET development tools rely on a Common Language Runtime (CLR) to execute objects built within this framework.

The server infrastructure for .NET, which includes Windows and the .NET enterprise servers, is a suite of infrastructure applications for building, deploying, and operating XML web services. Key technologies include support for XML, scale out, and business process orchestration across applications and services. These servers include: application center to enable scale-out solutions; BizTalk Server to create and manage XML-based business process orchestration across applications and services; host integration server for accessing data and applications on mainframes; mobile information server to enable use of applications by mobile devices like cell phones; and SQL server to store and retrieve structured XML data.

Figure 14.10 illustrates that the .NET product suite sits on a Windows environment. This can be one of a variety of Windows platforms, including Windows XP, Windows 2000, Windows ME and Windows CE. .NET also provides hooks for device software to facilitate the inclusion of a variety of smart devices. Smart devices include PCs, laptops, workstations, smart phones, handheld computers, tablet PCs, and other devices whose aim is to operate in the .NET universe. A smart device uses a user's .NET identity, profile, and data to enable tailoring of notifications, is responsive to bandwidth constraints and provides support for both online and offline use of applications. In addition, a smart device understands what services are available and discovers and announces other devices, servers, and the Internet and knows how to provide services to them.

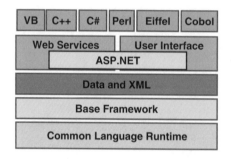

Figure 14.11: .NET Framework

At the core of .NET is the .NET framework (see Figure 14.11), which is a development and runtime environment for implementing business applications on the Windows infrastructure. .NET is not inextricably tied to the Windows operating system and is touted as platform independent. The goal of the Microsoft .NET Framework is to make it easy to build web applications and web services. Microsoft .NET offers language independence and language interoperability. This is one of the most fundamental aspects of the .NET platform. A single .NET component can be written, for example, partially in VB.NET and C#. The source code is first translated into common Intermediate Language or IL. This IL code is language-neutral, and is analogous to Java's platform-neutral byte codes that can be ported across platforms. The IL code is then interpreted and translated into a native executable, which is achieved by the Common Language Runtime (CLR) engine that lies at the heart of the .NET platform. The CLR is analogous to the Java Runtime Environment (JRE).

The Common Language Runtime is an attempt to bring the service paradigm to Dynamic Link Libraries (DLLs). The concept is to define language-independent interfaces to DLLs that include the object code, interface definitions, and a description of the interface. The key element to notice here again is the concept of a contract. The CLR is Microsoft's intermediary between .NET developers' source code and the underlying hardware, and all .NET code ultimately runs within the CLR. The CLR is built on top of operating-system services and manages the needs of running code written in any modern programming language. It supplies many services that help simplify code development and application deployment while also improving application reliability. Code that targets the CLR is called managed code. Managed code simply means that there is a defined contract of cooperation between natively executing code and the runtime itself. Responsibility for tasks like creating objects, making method calls, and so on is delegated to the runtime, which enables the runtime to provide additional services to the executing code. The CLR provides many advanced features not available in earlier versions of Windows, such as automatic garbage collection, exception handling, cross-language inheritance, debugging, simple deployment and versioning, and integrated security services.

The .NET framework also includes a set of class libraries that developers can use from any programming language. Above that sit various application programming models that provide higher-level components and services targeted specifically at developing websites and web services.

14.9.2 J2EE

The Java 2 Platform, Enterprise Edition (J2EE) provides a component-based approach to the design, development, assembly, and deployment of enterprise applications. The J2EE platform offers a multitiered distributed-application model – the tiers are the various information systems such as client, Web and business tiers – reusable components, a unified security model, flexible transaction control, and Web services' support through integrated data interchange on XML-based open standards and protocols. J2EE provides the infrastructure to build various application servers. For example, BEA's WebLogic Web services that are hosted by WebLogic Server, are implemented using standard J2EE components (such as EJB and JMS), and are packaged as standard J2EE enterprise applications. J2EE component-based solutions are platform independent and are not tied to the products and application-programming interfaces of any particular vendor [Armstrong 2004]. Vendors and customers are able to choose the products and components that best meet their business and technological requirements.

As illustrated in Figure 14.12, the J2EE application model divides enterprise applications into three fundamental parts: components, containers and connectors.

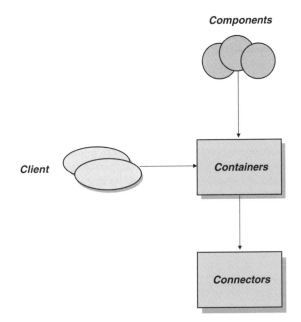

■ **Figure 14.12:** J2EE Components, Containers and Connectors

Components provide the essential parts for application developers to develop enterprise applications. A J2EE component is a self-contained functional software unit that is assembled into a J2EE application with its related classes and files and communicates with other components. Developers develop components as reusable modules that can be shared among multiple enterprise applications.

Containers are standardized runtime environments that provide application components with specific J2EE system-level services, such as life-cycle management, security, deployment, and runtime services. Containers are the interface between a component and the low-level platform-specific functionality that supports the components. As Figure 14.12 illustrates, containers intercede between clients and components, providing services to both.

Connectors sit beneath the J2EE platform defining a portable service API that provides access to database, transaction, naming, directory and messaging services, and legacy applications. The J2EE platform also provides technologies that enable communication between clients and servers and between collaborating objects hosted by different servers.

J2EE components

The J2EE platform uses a distributed multitiered application model for enterprise applications. The tiers are the various information systems, such as client, web, business and database, which interact with each other. Multitiered J2EE applications are divided into the tiers described in the following list.

- Client-tier components are end-user-oriented applications that run on the client machine.

- Web-tier components extend the traditional HTTP Web-server applications through Java Servlets and JavaServer Pages and run on the J2EE server.

- Business-tier components provide the business logic and run on the J2EE server.

- Enterprise information system (EIS)-tier software contains back-end database components and runs on the EIS server.

Figure 14.13 shows two multitiered J2EE applications divided into the tiers described in the above list. Although a J2EE application can consist of the three or four tiers shown in Figure 14.13, J2EE multitiered applications are generally considered to be three-tiered applications because they are distributed over three locations [Armstrong 2004]: client machines, the J2EE server machine, and the database or legacy machines at the back end. Three-tiered applications that run in this way extend the standard two-tiered client and server model by placing a multithreaded application server between the client application and back-end storage.

J2EE applications are made up of components. A J2EE component is a self-contained functional software unit that is assembled into a J2EE application with its related classes and files, and communicates with other components. Using J2EE, application logic is divided into components according to function, and the various application components that make up a J2EE application are installed on different machines depending on the tier in the multitiered J2EE environment to which the application component belongs. The J2EE application parts shown in Figure 14.13 are presented in J2EE components.

Three-tiered applications define corresponding J2EE components: client-tier, Web-tier and business-tier components.

Client-tier components: A J2EE client can be a Web client or an application client. These are components that run on the client machine.

A Web client consists of two parts: dynamic Web pages containing various types of markup language, such as HTML and XML, which are generated by Web components running in the web tier; and a

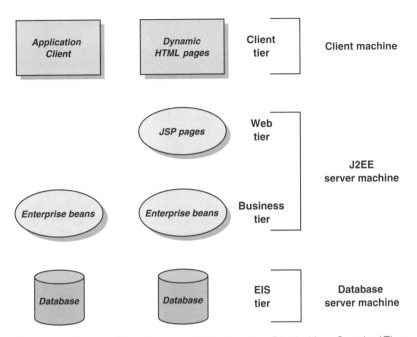

Figure 14.13: Two Multitiered J2EE Applications Divided into Standard Tiers

Web browser, which renders the pages received from the server. A Web client is sometimes called a thin client. Thin clients usually do not query databases, execute complex business rules, or connect to legacy applications. When a thin client is used, such heavyweight operations are off-loaded to enterprise beans executing on the J2EE server, where they can leverage the security, speed, services, and reliability of J2EE server-side technologies.

An application client runs on a client machine and provides a way for users to handle tasks that require a richer user interface than can be provided by a markup language. It typically has a graphical user interface created but a command-line interface is also possible. Application clients interact directly with EJB running in the business tier. However, if application requirements warrant it, a J2EE application client can open an HTTP connection to establish communication with a servlet running on the web tier.

Web-tier components: J2EE Web components are either servlets (see Section 6.3.2) or pages created using JSP technology (JSP pages) that run on the server.

Web components enable a cleaner and more modular application design because they provide a way to separate application programming from Web-page design. Static HTML pages and applets are bundled with Web components during application assembly but are not considered Web components by the J2EE specification. Server-side utility classes can also be bundled with Web components and, like HTML pages, are not considered Web components.

The Web tier, like the client tier, might include a JavaBeans component to manage the user input and send that input to enterprise beans running in the business tier for processing.

Business-tier components: The business tier handles business code, which is logic that solves or meets the needs of a particular business domain such as banking, retail, or finance, by enterprise beans (see Section 14.8.2) running on the server. In the business tier, enterprise beans are used as building blocks to implement modules of business logic on the J2EE server. Enterprise beans often interact with databases found at the EIS-tier.

Figure 14.14 illustrates how an enterprise bean receives data from client programs, processes it, and sends it to the enterprise information system tier for storage. An enterprise bean also retrieves data from storage, processes it, and sends it back to the client program. A J2EE application component might also need access to enterprise information systems for database connectivity.

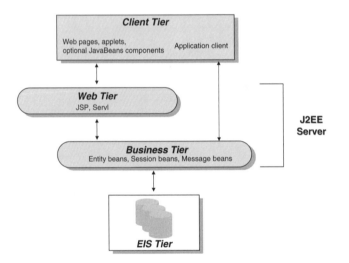

■ **Figure 14.14:** J2EE Client-tier, Web-tier and Business-tier Components

Enterprise Information System Tier: The enterprise information system tier handles EIS software. As we explained in Section 6.6, EIS include enterprise resource planning, customer-relation management systems, mainframe transaction processing, database systems, and other legacy information systems. For example, J2EE application components might need access to enterprise information systems for database connectivity.

J2EE containers

The component-based and platform-independent J2EE architecture facilitates writing J2EE applications because business logic is organized into reusable components. In addition, the J2EE server provides for every component type (EJB, web, JSP, servlet, applet, and application client) corresponding to component-specific services in the form of a container. Developers do not have to develop these services themselves and are thus free to concentrate on solving the business problem at hand.

Containers are standardized runtime environments that provide application components with specific J2EE system-level services, such as life-cycle management, security, deployment, and runtime services. Containers intercede between clients and components, providing services to both. Containers let developers customize components to use the resources available in the environment in which they are deployed.

Before a component can be executed, it must be assembled into a J2EE application and deployed into its container. The assembly process involves specifying container settings for each component in the J2EE application and for the application itself. Figure 14.15 illustrates how a container manages the execution of

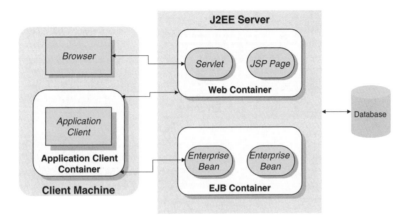

■ **Figure 14.15:** J2EE Containers

the component installed in it. For example, this figure shows that application client components are installed in an application container and that these both run on a client machine. JSP pages and servlet components are installed in a web container. Web-tier components and their corresponding web container run on the J2EE server. Finally, enterprise-bean components are installed in an EJB container. Both enterprise-bean components and their EJB containers run on the EJB server.

Container settings customize the underlying support provided by the J2EE server, including services such as security checks, transaction management, Java Naming and Directory Interface lookups, and remote connectivity (see next section). Application behavior is specified at assembly or deployment time with deployment descriptors. Deployment descriptors are text files that specify component behavior in terms of well-defined XML tags. Containers provide all application components with the J2EE platform APIs.

Because the J2EE architecture provides configurable services, application components within the same J2EE application can behave differently based on where they are deployed. For example, an enterprise bean can have security settings that allow it a certain level of access to database data in one production environment and another level of database access in another production environment.

J2EE APIs

J2EE builds on the existing technologies in the Java 2 Platform, Standard Edition (J2SE). J2SE includes the base Java support and various libraries with support for applets and applications. A J2EE-compliant application implements both the J2EE and J2SE APIs. Figure 14.16 illustrates the availability of the J2EE

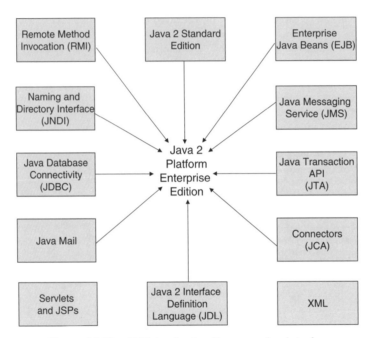

■ **Figure 14.16:** J2EE Application Programming Interfaces

platform APIs in each J2EE container type. The J2EE APIs offer a unified application model across tiers with enterprise beans and a simplified request and response mechanism with JSP and servlets [Armstrong 2004]. The following sections give a brief summary of some of the technologies required by the J2EE platform and the J2SE enterprise APIs that would be used in J2EE applications.

Java Authentication and Authorization Service (JAAS): The Java Authentication and Authorization Service (JAAS) provides a way for a J2EE application to authenticate and authorize a specific user or group of users to run it. JAAS is a Java programming language version of the standard Pluggable Authentication Module (PAM) framework, which extends the Java 2 Platform security architecture to support user-based authorization. The PM library is a generalized API for authentication-related services that allows a system administrator to add new authentication methods by installing new PAM modules and to modify authentication policies by editing configuration files.

Java API for XML Processing: The Java API for XML Processing (JAXP) supports the processing of XML documents using Document Object Model (DOM), Simple API for XML (SAX), and Extensible Stylesheet Language Transformations (XSLT). JAXP enables applications to parse and transform XML documents independent of a particular XML processing implementation. JAXP lets developers use any XML-compliant parser or XSL processor from within their application, and supports the W3C schema. JAXP also provides namespace support, which lets developers work with schemas that might otherwise have naming conflicts.

Java Database Connectivity (JDBC): The JDBC API lets developers invoke SQL commands from Java programming-language methods. Developers use the JDBC API in an enterprise bean when they need to override the default container-managed persistence, or have a session bean access the database. With container-managed persistence, database access operations are handled by the container, and the enterprise-bean implementation contains no JDBC code or SQL commands. The JDBC API can be used from a servlet or a JSP page to access the database directly without going through an enterprise bean. The JDBC API has two parts: an application-level interface used by the application components to access a database, and a service-provider interface to attach a JDBC driver to the J2EE platform.

Java Naming and Directory Interface (JNDI): The Java Naming and Directory Interface (JNDI) provides naming and directory functionality. It provides applications with methods for performing standard directory operations, such as associating attributes with objects and searching for objects using their attributes. Using JNDI, a J2EE application can store and retrieve any type of named Java object. J2EE naming services provide application clients, enterprise beans, and web components with access to a JNDI naming environment. A naming environment allows a component to be customized without the need to access or change the source code of a component. Because JNDI is independent of any specific implementation, applications can use it to access multiple naming and directory services. This allows J2EE applications to coexist with legacy applications and systems.

The Java Transaction API (JTA): The Java Transaction API (JTA) provides a standard interface for demarcating transactions in a manner that is independent of the transaction-manager implementation. The J2EE architecture provides a default autocommit to handle transaction commits and rollbacks. An autocommit means that any other applications that are viewing data will see the updated data after each database read or write operation. However, if an application performs two separate database access operations that depend on each other, the JTA API can be used to demarcate where the entire transaction, including both operations, begins, rolls back, and commits.

A JTA transaction is controlled by the J2EE transaction manager that can span updates to multiple databases from different vendors. The J2EE transaction manager does not support nested transactions.

The Java Message Service (JMS): The Java Message Service API that we have already examined in Section 14.5.2 is a messaging standard that supports sophisticated messaging applications and strives to maximize the portability of JMS applications across JMS providers in the same messaging domain. The JMS API enables communication that is not only loosely coupled but also reliable and asynchronous. To achieve reliable messaging the JMS API can ensure that a message is delivered once and only once. Lower levels of reliability are available for applications that can afford to miss messages or to receive duplicate messages.

J2EE Connector Architecture (JCA): J2EE Connector Architecture has been specifically designed to address the hardships of integrating applications. JCA provides a standardized method for integrating disparate applications in J2EE application architectures. It provides support for resource adaptation, which maps the J2EE security, transaction, and communication pooling to the corresponding EIS technology. JCA defines a set of functionalities that application-server vendors can use to connect to back-end EIS, such as ERP, CRM and legacy systems and applications. Using JCA to access enterprise information systems is akin to using JDBC to access a database. J2EE-tools' vendors and system integrators use the J2EE Connector API (JCA) to create resource adapters that support access to legacy systems that can be plugged into any J2EE product. A resource adapter (see Section 14.5.1) is a software component that lets J2EE application components access and interact with the underlying resource manager of an EIS. Because a resource adapter is specific for a resource manager, there is typically a different resource adapter for each type of database or EIS.

The JCA architecture defines a set of contracts that a resource adapter must support to plug into a J2EE product; for example, transactions, security, and resource management. The resource adapter mediates communication between the J2EE server and the EIS via contracts. The application contract defines the API through which a J2EE component such as an enterprise bean accesses the EIS. This API is the only view that the component has of the EIS. The system contracts link the resource adapter to important services that are managed by the J2EE server. The resource adapter itself and its system contracts are transparent to the J2EE component.

14.10 Chapter summary

Middleware is connectivity software that is designed to help manage the complexity and heterogeneity inherent in distributed systems. It builds a bridge between different systems by enabling communication and transfer of data. It is often used in a client/server environment. Middleware can be applied to manage disparate applications both within a single organization and between various independent organizations. Middleware encompasses a variety of different types of products with different capabilities that can be divided into five broad segments: Remote Procedure Calls, Message-oriented middleware, Data-access middleware, Transaction-oriented middleware, and Object Request Brokers.

Whilst there are different types of middleware, they all can support one, or sometimes two, basic modes of communication. These modes are: synchronous or time dependent; and asynchronous or time independent. The simplest form of communication is the synchronous mode of communication, which employs request/reply communication whereby the sender sends a request and receives a reply from the message recipient. Synchronous middleware is tightly coupled to applications. When using the asynchronous mode of communication, systems and applications communicate by exchanging messages, which are packets of data. The concept of a message is a well-defined, data-driven text format – containing the business message and a network routing header – that can be sent between two or more applications. Asynchronous messaging is usually implemented by some queuing mechanism. Two types of message queues exist: store and forward and publish–subscribe. Asynchronous middleware is decoupled from the application, hence the application can continue processing at all times without having to wait for – or having to know the status of – any other communicating application.

Remote Procedure Call is a basic mechanism for inter-program communication. RPC is the middleware mechanism used to invoke a procedure that is located on a remote system, and the results are returned. With this type of middleware the application elements communicate with each other synchronously. Traditional RPC systems are language-neutral, and therefore cannot provide functionality that is not available on all possible target platforms. The Java Remote Method Invocation provides a simple and direct model for distributed computation with Java objects on the basis of the RPC mechanism.

Message-Oriented Middleware is the infrastructure that is responsible for relaying data from one application to another by putting it in a message format. MOM is interposed between the client and the server part of client/server architecture and handles asynchronous calls between clients and servers. An integration broker is an application-to-application middleware service that is capable of one-to-many, many-to-one and many-to-many message distribution and is layered on top of the middleware infrastructure. An integration broker is a software hub that records and manages the contracts between publishers and subscribers of messages.

Data-access middleware addresses the problem of widely distributed data which is stored on multiple locations using multiple formats, application-specific design, and a wide variety of semantics. Data-access middleware can be seen as the type of middleware that facilitates communications with a database, whether from the side of an application or between databases.

Transaction-oriented middleware encompasses two kinds of middleware products: transaction-processing monitors and application servers. These coordinate information movement and method sharing between many different resources. Transaction-processing monitor technology provides the distributed client/server environment with the capacity to efficiently and reliably develop, execute and manage transaction applications. Application servers offer an integrated development environment that allows enterprises to connect and manage front-office and back-office applications and combine them with web-enabled functionality. Application servers expose these integrated resources through a single user interface, typically a web browser.

One alternative for providing inter-application communication is to employ distributed-object middleware. Distributed objects are a development of RPCs that provide an additional layer of interoperability that abstracts the procedure call from the underlying platform and language. Distributed-object computing middleware defines a high-level programming abstraction in the form of a distributed-object interface that provides location transparency to clients and server components, shielding application developers from low-level network programming details like parameter marshaling and unmarshaling, error handling and so on.

Discussion Questions

- What is middleware and what are its main services?
- Compare and contrast the synchronous and asynchronous types of communication. Clearly state their advantages and disadvantages.

- List the primary advantages of the RMI approach for application integration.

- What is Message-Oriented Middleware, what are its main features and what types of application can it be used for?

- What is the purpose of transaction-processing monitors? Are they being used for synchronous or asynchronous applications? Justify your answer. What are the main drawbacks?

- Briefly describe the two types of distributed-object middleware and describe the relationships between them.

Assignments

i. A client computer needs to access remote objects on a server. As already explained in this chapter each invocation of a remote object requires that operation parameters are collected and marshaled into a byte stream. A connection also needs to be established and the request parameters need to be sent to the target remote object. These tasks need to be performed for each object by the client. Use remote procedure call technology to explain how this approach works. Assume that the client application uses a proxy class for accessing a remote object. The proxy class is supplied with a unique object reference for the remote object, the operation name it invokes on the remote object, and its arguments. Assume that the proxy class can be deployed in two ways. First there may be a single proxy object to handle all object invocations in the server application. In this case multiple requests to the proxy object need to be synchronized. Alternatively, a proxy object can be created every time a client request for a remote object is issued.

ii. Extend the previous approach to handle the following scenario. Assume that we have a message sent with *non-persistent* delivery mode and a durable subscriber/receiver. In this situation, the message producer sends or publishes a message to the destination. An acknowledgement for the message is sent back to the producer. The messaging server realizes that there are durable subscribers that have not received the message and stores the message in its internal store. A provider failure occurs – either the server's internal buffer overflowed, or the client crashed, etc. Since the delivery mode for the message was *non-persistent*, even though there are durable consumers, the message is lost. Again, explain what information should be kept in the queue and if the use of buffers is necessary.

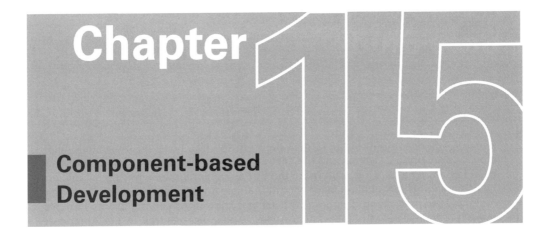

Chapter 15

Component-based Development

Enterprise Application Integration and e-Business integration solutions are geared toward applications that are built as extensions of third-party frameworks by gluing together existing applications or parts thereof. Component technology facilitates this endeavor by allowing a complex system to be built as a combination of smaller cohesive components. The aim with software components is to allow off-the-shelf modules to be quickly assembled into applications with functionality that does not need to be expensively reimplemented for each new system. Software components are used in e-Business as they can be used to shorten an application's development cycle and therefore lower development costs of e-Business applications.

In this chapter we concentrate on one of the technologies that enable the conduct of e-Business: components and explain how components can be used to improve the software development process by assembling new software from prebuilt software components rather than developing them from scratch. This chapter provides an overview of component technology and its characteristics and explains how it fits within an e-Business application development process. The chapter describes architectural approaches, business and modeling requirements, economic models and organizational guidelines all of which are required to facilitate the introduction of component technology in the domain of e-Business.

Case Study

Component business model for Bank of America's Card Services[1]

Bank of America is one of the largest banks in the US, boasting more than 4200 locations covering 21 states and the District of Columbia. Bank of America is also a leader in online banking, with more than three million people, paying 6.4 million bills valued at US$1.9 billion, each month online. The company's Global Corporate and Investment Banking group has offices in 30 countries serving clients in more than 150 countries, with associates in major business centres in the Americas, Europe and Asia. Bank of America is the number one debit card issuer and number four credit card issuer in the United States, uniquely positioning the company to innovate and create efficiencies in electronic payments.

Within Bank of America's Card Services and e-Commerce division, rapid growth resulted in several fragmented strategies and a complex and disconnected IT infrastructure. These needed to be consolidated and simplified in order to streamline the business area and provide better and faster response to customer demand. Their senior management directive was to create a new architecture to help the company get new products to market quicker and with less money, while supporting and extending customers' relationships with the bank. The scope of the IT strategy and architecture realignment project needed to include all consumer card segments, ATM cards and services, and e-Commerce.

Bank of America's staff together with IBM Business Consulting Services built a component business model of its card services business, providing a tight linkage between business and technology objectives (see `www-306.ibm.com/software/ success/cssdb.nsf/cs/GJON-67VNYK?OpenDocument&Site=gicss67fss`). The component business model mapped the bank's technology to its business objectives, identified priorities for transformation and helped create the new supporting IT architecture.

As a result of the component business model implementation Bank of America's Card Services division identified US$40 million of simplification and cost-savings projects over two years. Bank of America's Card Services and e-Commerce division

---

[1] This case study has been summarized from
  `www-306.ibm.com/software/success/cssdb.nsf/cs/GJON-67VNYK? OpenDocument&Site=gicss67fss.`

used the component-based business model methodology to identify opportunities to eliminate redundancies, consolidate systems/applications and rationalize duplicate processes. Along with a business-aligned technology investment strategy, Card Services now has a number of highly leveraged business and technology investment opportunities designed to give disproportionate returns and capable of being self-funding. Card Services also has a multigenerational plan to manage parallel developments, while ensuring regular, integrated delivery of benefits to fund the ongoing migration.

15.1 What are components?

As we explained in Chapters 1, 3 and 4, the business environment has become more dynamic and unpredictable than it ever has been. Business models are consequently shifting to Internet-supported dynamic networked organizations, with possibly changing partners and relations. Besides the increased environmental dynamics, businesses in most industries have to cope with fierce competition. The only way to survive under these circumstances is to react fast to changes (when prediction becomes difficult) and to meet customer demands while outperforming competitors. This represents a challenge for businesses to establish flexible organizational structures, business processes and ways of working and to react adequately with the right decisions and actions to changing market conditions. It is, however, also a challenge for information systems and their developers. An organization just cannot afford to be slowed down by its information technology.

To meet the challenges imposed by this business agenda, interoperable applications have to be developed quickly at competitive cost levels. Traditional (structured) software development methodologies are too slow for such an environment; they are based on a much more static view of the world. Moreover because of their 'proprietary' approach they offer too few opportunities for cross-enterprise interoperability, often even for intra-enterprise interoperability. Agile companies need software parts that can be quickly modified, replaced, reconfigured, combined with others, removed and added. Systems, composed of those software parts must be scalable to support a varying number of users, who are utilizing a variety of platforms.

Until very recently the object-oriented approach was the preferred solution for developing large-scale and complex software applications. The real advantage of the object-oriented approach is that it designs a solution around a model of the problem domain and this can lead to better traceability, better documentation, and more enhanceable systems. Because the problem domain is only likely to change subtly, extensive change of the solution is unlikely too. However, although this technology itself has a sound basis, there were impracticalities in its implementations owing to a bad choice of abstractions that created more problems than they solved. The correct abstractions proved incredibly hard to find on large, complex designs because of the scope that they must cover. Often one complex object model must suffice for the whole system and this leads to brittle and not easily upgradeable solutions. The use of object-oriented technology is not sufficient to address the stringent requirements in software delivery times, development costs and software quality. More importantly for e-Business, it is not geared toward applications that are built as extensions of third-party frameworks or by gluing together existing applications or parts thereof. This is where component technology steps in; components allow a complex system to be built as a combination of smaller cohesive components.

Component based development offers an approach that is assumed to support systems that need to function effectively in a dynamic environment. Since components are potentially reusable, component-based development could reduce the costs of building systems, because organizations could reuse components that have already been used for other applications. In short, components provide an efficient way to integrate diverse software systems. Component technology is an evolution of object-oriented technology that can serve to integrate business functions on the basis of a homogeneous software infrastructure. Rather than creating or buying monolithic in-house end-to-end solutions, components are assembled from smaller modules built either in-house or purchased by a third party. Knitting those pieces together within the confines of a common architecture allows business systems to interoperate while isolating each piece from implementation changes in other pieces.

A *component* is an independent, encapsulated part of a system. Each component is simple enough to be designed well, and built to implement a well-defined set of responsibilities as regards its clients but, just as importantly, has well-defined limits to its functionality. Components are autonomous units of software that may provide a useful service or a set of services to a client, and have meaning in isolation to other components with which they interoperate. Because components are autonomous units of functionality, they provide natural demarcation of development work. A component developer is responsible for making sure that the component fulfills its contract with client programs. Universal interfaces on components mean they can be 'plugged' into other components, development and test tools effortlessly. This removes several issues of other types of software development, e.g. structured or object oriented.

To summarize the above discussion, a component can be defined as a coherent package of software implementation that exhibits the following characteristics:

- It is an encapsulation of business logic (or technical functionality) that performs a set of related functions and that presents a well-defined published interface for the functions (or services) it provides and expects from others. In particular:

  ○ It exhibits all the appealing characteristics of objects such as encapsulation, cohesion, polymorphic behavior, well-defined responsibilities, and well-defined interface.

- It is self-describing. The interface to a component provides enough metadata to make it possible for its clients to know how to use it.

- Although a component can in principle exist in isolation from other components, it is subject to composition from third parties. However, it may be possible to customize some of the component properties, without modifying the components themselves. More specifically:

  ○ A component conforms to a *component model* (see Section 15.4.1) that specifies the rules that must be observed by the component. These rules improve component composability by ensuring alignment of functionality and compatibility of component interfaces with other such components.

Components are not defined by their structure but by the functions they provide. Unlike objects they do not provide structural interfaces, rather they provide functions (or services). The component allows access to data and behavior it encapsulates, i.e. its functionality, only through the interface it provides, see Figure 15.1. A component may contain a variety of structural or object-oriented forms or procedural code in its internals, but these are not what it exposes to the outside world as part of its contract. In other words, its implementation is completely independent from its interfaces. For instance, a purchase-order management component would be used to establish purchase orders, providing services for creating, maintaining and confirming purchase orders. If this interface is, for example, implemented with objects, the object that is used to represent a construct as an order is not exposed as part of the interface. A direct consequence of this freedom from implementation is that a component allows you to replace its implementation without impacting its users.

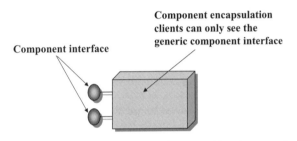

Figure 15.1: Component Interfaces and Implementation

It is possible to think of a component as a mini-application that may be run, tested and used in its own right. It is this separation of components from other components that is the authority behind the rapid building and deployment of component-based systems.

The essence of a component is that it can be built and then continuously improved upon by an expert or organization. By buying a component, a developer can add functionality to an application without sacrificing quality. Indeed, quality should improve, as the component will typically go through several development iterations and reflect feedback from a large number of users.

A component may be developed, tested and deployed in complete isolation to other components within a system; even if it seems unlikely that the component will ever be deployed in isolation, this should still be possible. This is an important criterion for testing and quality. Independent and autonomous components that may be run in isolation dramatically increase the quality of a system because defects can be spotted and corrected early in a component's implementation by testing the components separately from each other without waiting for other parts of the system to be ready.

Component-based applications can be developed using interchangeable parts to assemble components. For one component to replace another, the replacement component need not work in the same way internally. Nevertheless, the replacement component must provide compatibility of interfaces and at least the services that the external environment (container) expects of the original component. Moreover, the replacement component must expect no more services than are provided by what the environment provides to the original component. The supporting runtime environment and support infrastructure in which components are deployed is generally known as its container environment. The *container environment* that surrounds components provides management and control services for components and can be considered as a miniature operating system that contains the following component support facilities:

- create runtime instances of components

- allow components to discover other components

- allow components to communicate with other components

- provide additional common services such as location independence, persistence, transaction management, recovery, security, and monitoring

With a component-based system it is no longer necessary, or even correct, to think of the whole system as one entity, but rather as a loose association of functional entities that may combine in foreseen and sometimes unforeseen ways to conduct useful work. Thus, separation of concerns, encapsulation, and composability are the major issues that concern components and component-based development.

With component-based development, software parts are designed according to predefined specifications, so they can be assembled together to create entire applications. The need to 'retool' new components or the system to which they are being added is essentially eliminated. During component-based development, developers use both internally developed components and open-market components to provide as much functionality as they can for their application. It is notable that these artifacts can have a varying degree of granularity that scales from entire applications down to the smallest functional parts. The developers subsequently write any additional components needed for their application and the 'glue code' that hooks all the components together. Figure 15.2 illustrates how a simple order-processing application can be developed using prefabricated components.

Designers typically store the components they have created in a *component repository*, so that other developers or users can employ the functionality that they have created. This obviously helps lead to software reuse which can bring down the costs of development. For example, if a developer creates a component to access a purchase order in the component repository, then no other developer should have to code that functionality again. Instead, they can find that purchase-order component in their repository, and use it directly in their applications or customize it to satisfy their specific needs.

15.1.1 Component characteristics

A component is made up of three essential parts: the interface, the implementation, and the deployment [McInnis 2000]. The *component interface* informs the client of a component what functions the component is capable of performing. Component clients are not in a position to understand how to use a component if no interface specification is provided. The *component implementation* is the code that makes the component function. For example, a component might possess one implementation that relies on a C++ program, and another that relies on a Java application. Finally, the *component deployment* specifies the particular environment under which the component operates. It is important to note the distinction between implementation

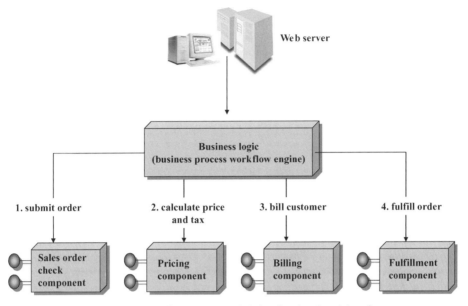

■ Figure 15.2: A Simple Order-processing Application Involving Components

and deployment descriptions. The same implementation can be deployed in different ways. For example, it is possible to create an implementation using C++ and a relational database, and then use the same implementation to create a COM+ deployment or a CORBA deployment.

In addition to these parts, a component must possess certain properties: it must be *encapsulated*, *descriptive*, *replaceable*, and *extensible*. These four properties are essential to the construction of a component, and must be respected by component developers, if a component is to be used in conjunction with other components to assemble a flexible software application [McInnis 2000]:

- *Component encapsulation and implementation independence*: Encapsulation is the process of hiding the implementation or code that drives a component. The component client accesses the component through its interface, which informs the client how the component behaves. A component interface describes only what the component offers, regardless of its implementation. The implementation provides a blueprint of how the component achieves its stated objectives and functionality. There is a strong separation between the external contract provided for the use of a component and its internal implementation of that contract. The implementation may change; however, the contract should not. Therefore, the major advantage of encapsulation lies in a component's ability to accommodate changes in its implementation without affecting its clients since the interface remains undisturbed by component implementers.

- *Component description*: Because a component is encapsulated it can only be accessed via well-defined interfaces, therefore it must furnish information (metadata) about itself to allow potential clients to understand it. Thi s metadata should describe a component's essential parts and characteristics, including its interface(s), implementation(s), and deployment.

- *Component replaceability*: Since a component is encapsulated, implementation details can be changed without affecting the component's client, provided that there is no change in the component interface. Because the interface is fully specified, the consumer does not need to worry about implementation details. These properties make it possible to interchange one component with another as long as the replacement component offers the same set of interfaces and functionality as the original. It is then desirable for the internals of a component to be able to be late-bound, thus providing deployment time and runtime substitutability.

- *Component extensibility*: The extensibility property of a component implies that it is possible to enhance or extend its range of services without affecting its clients. There are two approaches to extensibility – adding interfaces and delegating responsibility:

  1. *Adding Interfaces*: A component developer with access to a component's implementation can extend services by changing the implementation code. The original interfaces of a component may not be altered in order to avoid interfering with other clients' access to this component. To add new services, a new interface must be developed and added to facilitate access to these services.
  2. *Delegating Responsibility*: A component client does not have access to the implementation code. Consequently, the addition of any new services to a component-based system has to be handed over to a new component that is created to offer these new services. *Delegation* is implemented in some specialized programming languages, such as Self [Ungar 1987], and is in essence nothing more than forwarding a message from one object to another one and is used to mimic inheritance. Delegation supports late and dynamic composition [Liebermann 1986], [Ungar 1987]. Composing applications from components based on the principle of delegation results in more flexible software artifacts, but in much more complex solutions if these are not implemented in the appropriate way [Hoelze 1995].

There are two main types of components, *white-box* components and *black-box* components. White-box components are components that are source code and are readable, and directly changeable by the developers that use them. Black-box components are typically in compiled or binary form. They are discrete components that cannot be changed directly. All the developer knows about them is the documentation that describes their functionality, and their published interfaces. These interfaces may include properties, such as attributes that can be viewed, and methods, which allow the component to perform a stated function. They also may include events that are triggered when it is necessary for the component to notify the developer that a specific action has occurred. The benefits of using black-box components outweigh those of white-box components. A developer cannot directly modify black-box components. Instead, they extend their functionality by creating 'wrapper' components to wrap and extend the existing components. This keeps the original functionality intact so that upgrades, bug fixes, and so on, made by the original developer can be implemented.

15.2 Interfaces and contracts

One important characteristic of a component is the explicit separation of its interface from its implementation. This separation is much stronger than that suggested by languages that support separate compilation of interfaces and implementations, such as for example, C++ header files or Ada package specifications [Bachmann 2000].

In languages and systems that support software components, an interface may be implemented by many distinct components and a component may implement many distinct interfaces. A concrete realization of this idea can be found in Microsoft's Component Object Model [Bachmann 2000]. In COM, interface specifications are assigned a globally unique identifier (GUID) at the time they are created. Every time that this interface is revised it is assigned a new GUID. COM components are binary implementations that are bound to the interfaces they implement via these interface GUIDs. Similarly, clients are linked to components via interface GUIDs. Consequently, there is a clean separation of interface and component, with clients and component alike bound directly to interfaces and only indirectly to each other. In a similar manner the Java programming language also distinguishes interface specification from class specification by introducing an interface type. In both COM and Java the idea is that clients depend upon interfaces and never upon implementations, and that components can implement any arbitrary number of interfaces.

The ability to combine components into component assemblies and to develop a market of components depends fundamentally on the notion of component interface. Interface abstraction provides a mechanism to control the dependencies that arise between modules in a program or system. An application programming interface is a specification, in a programming language, of those properties of a module that clients of that module can depend upon. Conversely, clients should not depend upon properties that are not specified by the interface.

A component's interface defines the component's *contract* with the application code that invokes it. The interface defines the *component signature*, i.e. the names, types and order of arguments to the service and the manner in which results are returned from the service. The interface masks the implementation details from any clients of the component. In this way clients of the component are dealing only with the methods that the component exposes. A component's implementation is the core functionality that the component provides and can be implemented in a variety of ways. An important feature of components is their physical packaging into executables. An executable may contain several components, while it also possible that a component is contained in several different executables. Figure 15.3 illustrates the various parts of a component and their interrelationships.

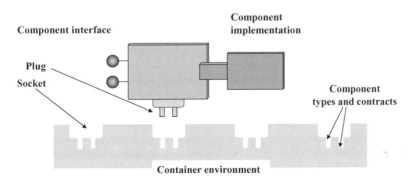

■ **Figure 15.3:** A Component and its Parts

When a client invokes a method specified in a component interface, the called method dispatches the parameter information to the current version of the implementation class method. This explicit separation enables the implementation of the component to be changed, without affecting its called interface or that of its client. By enforcing this criterion, we can achieve the following advantages:

- The responsibilities of each component are well defined and presented through a stable interface. Developers must very carefully consider the placement of functionality, as it is not desirable to simply add another method or functionality, in general, onto the interface.

- Components are combined with each other with minimum effort, since there is no special programming effort required for one component to communicate and interact with a compatible component.

- Each component may be deployed as an independently managed unit and may be replaced with as little impact on client components as possible.

- Each component may be deployed using a specific middleware platform, e.g. CORBA or COM, with minimum effort. To take the CORBA example, a component definition can be easily created in IDL and then the various stubs and skeletons can also be generated. This can be done once for all components rather than once for each component.

Conventional interface specifications, written in object-oriented programming languages such as Smalltalk, C++, Modula-3, and Java, can conveniently express functional properties [Bachmann 2000]. *Functional properties* include the services a module provides and the signature of these services. Conventional APIs are not well equipped to express nonfunctional properties. *Nonfunctional properties* include items like performance, accuracy, availability, latency, security, and so on. These are, however, of importance to components. In many cases components in a component assembly may come to depend upon any of these properties, as a result reducing the probability that one component can be substituted for another.

Several attempts have been made to extend interfaces to make them more expressive of nonfunctional properties. These extensions are motivated by the desire to ensure that interface specifications are sufficiently complete to ensure correct integration. To understand the nonfunctional properties of components, it is useful to differentiate between various kinds of nonfunctional properties. One of the most interesting approaches is that reported by Beugnard *et al.* where the authors define four kinds of property: *syntactic, behavioral, synchronization,* and *quality of service* [Beugnard 1999]. Syntactic properties correspond to functional properties as described in the previous section. The latter three properties are nonfunctional, and the means of expressing them are briefly discussed.

Behavioral specifications define the outcome of operations [Beugnard 1999] and can be written into the program code using pre- and post-conditions and other forms of assertions. This is common practice with programming languages such as Eiffel [Meyer 1992b, 1997]. However, this technique is not available in the more commonly used languages such as Java. Behavioral specification of components deals only with sequential aspects. This is clearly inefficient in a component world, as systems and applications are increasingly distributed and synchronization between the components must be explicitly specified. However, specifying synchronization of components is more of a research challenge and is still not a very well-understood mechanism. Finally, quality of service includes quality attributes such as performance, where it may be possible to specify the complexity of a component, maximum response delay, average response, and precision as well as global characteristics of a component such as its portability, adaptability and so on [Bachmann 2000]. This covers guarantees of availability, mean time between failures, mean time to repair, throughput, capacity, latency, and data safety for persistent state. Quality of service mechanisms are very much an open research topic.

Interfaces specify a one-way flow of dependencies from components that implement services to the clients that use these services. Component interaction involves a number of (usually) tacit agreements between a client and a component. In general, a component client may implement certain services and depends upon the component to provide its services in a specific way. At the same time the supplier component depends upon the client to access and use these services in the appropriate manner. For example, a client depends upon the component to provide a service, and perhaps depends upon a number of nonfunctional component properties as well. In return, the component may depend upon the client to provide data arguments within certain bounds or to have properly initialized the component service. This caller/callee codependence is of major importance to component-based software because of the concept of component pluggability (substitutability). Component interactions that define the context in which substitution occurs can be significantly more complex than in traditional systems.

To address the above requirements, the concept of *interface contract* has become prominent in component-based literature to express the codependence between the services offered by a (supplier) component to associated (client) component(s). A contractually specified interface makes these codependencies explicit [Bachmann 2000]. The idea of interface contract is closely linked to the programming language Eifel [Meyer 1992b, 1997]. Eiffel was designed on the philosophy that classes should resemble abstract data types (ADTs) in order to ensure safe execution of systems.

Contracts are used to concisely specify the obligations and rights of both the supplier and the client during their lifecycles. Contracts are between two or more parties to highlight the nature of supplier/client codependence. This is particularly necessary in component-based systems where multiple components coordinate to implement a single logical interaction.

The specification of contractual conformance serves as a basis for the entire design of an enterprise system based on components, and can be enforced at runtime. Component codependencies can be specified in an interface through the use of an assertion language, most commonly the use of pre- and post-conditions. The contract consists of assertions that are employed in programs using the components and expresses the nature and characteristics of certain component properties during execution by using pre- and post-conditions. Assertions are used in formal languages to express the correctness conditions. Partial correctness can then be proven by using a correctness formulae: $\{Pre\}$ A $\{Post\}$ that needs to be interpreted as follows: excution of statement A can be initiated in a state where condition *Pre* is true, and will end in a state where condition *Post* holds [Meyer 1992a]. The object-oriented programming language Eiffel employs the `require` and `ensure` keywords to represent the pre- and post-conditions.

15.3 Business components and entities

Business components are reusable components that enable rapid application development by providing large independent parts that when assembled together can be used to create a business application. A business component encapsulates both conceptual and physical (software) artifacts, provides clear business semantics, and offers them as third-party products to prospective customers using an explicit interface specification, comprising a limited set of plugs. Components do not store any state in themselves and thus can be relatively easily assembled into a (sub)system by parameterizing their plugs to other components.

Business components come in two flavors: coarse-grained and fine-grained components. *Coarse-grained components* provide large independent parts that can be assembled together to create an entire application. An example of a coarse-grained component that can be used to support an operations and logistics application, which encompasses inventory management, material requirements planning, production planning and shipping, is a product management component. This component can be used to represent services such as product defintion, stock updates, unit conversions to inventory in stock, and product availability calculations. *Fine-grained components* are normally used to provide smaller interrelated parts that can be used to directly support coarse-grained business components. For example, for the operations and logistics application, a typical fine-grained component would be a component that represents an order. As fine-grained components are typical business entities in an application domain, we henceforth reserve the term business component to denote coarse-grained components only.

In the following we briefly describe business entities followed by business components and their characteristics.

15.3.1 Business entities

Business entities are basic component constructs that one or more business components require for their successful operation. A business entity contains information about the entity it represents and the behavior associated with it. For example, the product business entity can describe any specific product within an operations and logistics application together with behavior associated with this specifc product such as lot management.

Busines entities are typically used to establish strong connections to other business entities within their own business domain but they can also be used to connect entities across different business domains. For example, business entities supporting applications within the enterprise resource-planning domain such as order management (providing business tasks such as sales orders and purchase orders) and warehouse management (providing warehouse logistics tasks such as stock movement between warehouses) are closely related to each other. These components exhibit tight coupling between the business entities they represent. In our example, this means that the product business entity is tightly coupled either directly or indirectly to a corresponding warehouse component. Changing the warehouse business entity may have an impact on the product business entity.

Business entities are used to create business components or applications and are built with the expectation that they will need to be extended to fulfill their requirements of their particular usage. Business entities are usually implemented as Enterprise JavaBeans so they are developed using some object-oriented development process that takes into account business application requirements. As it is expected that business entities will be highly reused, they do not completely fulfill all business requirements from end to end; rather they support only the core common piece of these business requirements.

Business entities have a long learning curve due to their numerous connections and dependencies with other such components within the same domain. Business entities are in addition used in many different solutions within the same domain.

15.3.2 Business components

Business components are coarse-grained components that provide business process-level fragments (functionality) of an enterprise application. In many cases, business components are built using business entities. In those cases, business entities are provided as a set of components that work together to solve specific problems. For example, a product management component can be built using the business entities product, warehouse and other related business entities.

Business entities provide reusable, highly customizable content that can be adapted for the particular needs of a business component. This is especialy beneficial when families of related components are being created, since the business entities need not be re-implemented for each variation. As an example consider a general ledger application. The general ledger components provide the structure and default behavior related to managing the accounts on the general ledger for a company or hierarchy of companies. Examples of business tasks that are supported include journaling (creation, validation, processing and posting of general ledger journals) and closing (closing the books for a general ledger accounting period or year). The core of most general ledgers is the same, therefore we can create a set of standard business entity components that can be used to implement this core functionality. These business entity components may include: accounts assets, liabilities, income, and expenses. Such business entity components can be reused to create customizable general ledger applications. In this way a set of general ledger business entity components can be used to build general ledgers for many different countries. However, a single business component would be provided for a particular country. Whenever business entity components are used by a business component they are encapsulated. This means that they are not exposed to the clients of their surrounding business component(s). Figure 15.4 shows the interrelationship between business entity components and business components.

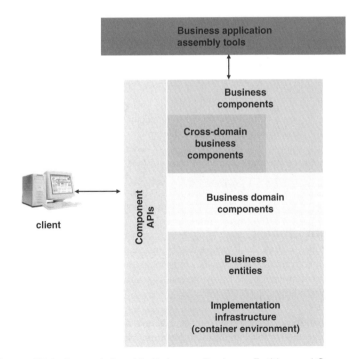

■ **Figure 15.4:** Interrelationship Between Business Entities and Components

The set of functions provided by a business component as well as the services it requires are completely specified by its contract. Each function can be supported by using the services of the component implementation infrastructure. These services may provide session management, security, authentication, event publication and subscription mechanisms, i.e. events that the business component publishes and events to which the component subscribes, transactional services and so on. The component implementation infrastructure also provides management facilities to guarantee dynamic plug-and-play capabilities as well as to manage late binding and loading of new business components. A number of business application assembly tools can be provided to help with the assembly of business applications from business components (see Figure 15.4). These tools allow implementers to couple the outputs of one component to the inputs of another component or as inputs to the presentation layer.

Busines components can be implementated in a number of ways and operate in the context of a component execution environment such as EJB. Busines components can be implemented completely from scratch, from reusable fragments that include both business entities and components, by delegation to an existing (legacy) system and by some combination of the above. For example, a component can be created out of a legacy system that provides budgeting features such as storing different sets of budget figures to project future needs, and comparing projections and automatically creating budgets using prior-year information. For further information on this topic refer to Chapter 16.

In contrast to business entities, business components have a shorter learning curve and provide particular solutions within the domain they are employed.

15.4 Component models and compositions

Two or more components can communicate only if they rely on a common mechanism for finding each other and for exchanging meaningful messages. Therefore, for component-based systems to work properly it is necessary that they rely on a component model that specifies the conventions imposed on developers of component applications comprising compositions. Compliance with a component model is one of the properties that distinguish components from other types of assembled software. In the following we shall concentrate on component models and component compositions and present their basic requirements and characteristics.

15.4.1 Component models

A component model defines the basic architecture of a component, specifying interface definitions, message passing and data transfer conventions by which the component interacts with its container environment and other components. The component model provides guidelines to create and implement components that can work together to form a larger application.

The essence of component-based design is relating several independent components and combining them together as parts of a large and complex application. A component model specifies how components can be plugged together with different interaction schemes connecting them.

A component model is usually expressed in terms of ports and connectors. *Component ports* are the exposed interfaces of a component that define the endpoints of communication between components in terms of plugs and sockets. A *socket* is a well-defined and well-known interface to an external environment into which a plug interface should fit. A socket indicates the set of interfaces that the environment makes available to a component, while the term *plug* indicates the combination of services that the component provides to satisfy the interfaces provided (see Figure 15.3). A plug can be coupled with any socket of a compatible type using a suitable *connector* construct.

There are currently several component models that have gained commercial support. These include: CORBA, DCOM and JavaBeans (refer to Chapter 14 on middleware for more information on any of these three component models). In each case, the component model specifies a means for components under this particular reference model to publish their interfaces, send messages and pass data. Although we have already examined these component models in Chapter 14, we shall examine them again briefly in the context of component-based development.

The CORBA model defined by the Object Management Group as already explained is a language and platform-independent specification that has numerous bindings and implementations on most common platforms.

The DCOM model provides adapters to other component models. It is, however, largely confined to the Windows platform (although there are implementations in other environments by companies such as Hewlett-Packard).

With the introduction of technologies such as Enterprise JavaBeans, server-side enterprise software applications may now be created as a collection of Java components, or enterprise beans. These EJB technology-based applications may now be deployed on any EJB technology-compliant application server, such as Sun-Netscape Alliance iPlanet, IBM WebSphere, BEA Weblogic or IONA iPortal Application Server.

Enterprise JavaBeans technology is now being widely adopted, and so there is a new target market for component authors, who can focus on creating portable and reusable components, rather than spending time on building complex, proprietary middleware services that lock in users.

Whichever of the above three component models is selected would require a dedicated platform and infrastructure. An alternative solution is to connect components using XML. The most likely scenario is that there will still be a variety of component models suited to different platforms or environments, which would communicate using XML. A component can then implement a single interface that accepts XML messages upon whose format the component is then dependent [Hopkins 2000]. This solution is suitable primarily for low-frequency, high-semantic content exchanges, such as, for instance, passing purchase order information, patient records or requests for quotations.

15.4.2 Component compositions

Components are built around the concepts of interfaces, composition and delegation. Most component models today actually make minimal use of implementation inheritance in favor of interface inheritance and composition. This is partly to resolve the implementation pain of a major component advantage: they are language independent. This may get resolved as the component models continue to evolve, with more and more sophisticated abstract middleware mechanisms in place.

Although there is no universal agreement as to what elements should be included in a component model, Bachmann *et al.* [Bachmann 2000] analyze the requirements of component compositions and propose several composition conventions that we summarize in the following.

When analyzing the nature of compositions the designer has to make certain that they are dealing with uniform compositions, meaning compositions in which components can interact only if they share consistent assumptions about what interfaces each of them provides and what each of them requires from the other. Additional requirements are that a composition should possess the appropriate quality. Bachman *et al.* [Bachmann 2000] suggest that if the types of components in a system and their patterns of interaction are standardized, then we can ensure that a system composed of third-party components possesses the desired quality characteristics. A final requirement is that components can be deployed from the development environment into a composition environment and applications that are composed from components can be deployed from the composition environment into the customer environment.

The above requirements motivate the use of composition conventions that include the following constructs [Bachmann 2000]:

- *Component types*: Each component must be defined in terms of a type. A component's type is completely defined in terms of the interfaces it implements. Moreover, a component is polymorphic with respect to the interfaces it implements. It can play the role of any of the interfaces it implements at different times. Polymorphic components offer additional flexibility for component compositions. With composition compositions we rely on this very notion of substitutability of interfaces and the ability to select appropriate interface providers at either deployment or runtime.

- *Interaction schemes*: Components specify how components are located, which communication protocols are used and how qualities of service such as security and transactions are achieved.

- *Resource binding*: The process of composing components is a matter of describing which resources are available to a component and of binding a component to one or more of these resources. A resource is a service provided by some other component or component framework.

Components are composed so that can interact with other components. When assembling a larger component or application out of existing components, the application developer must do the following [D'Souza 1999]:

- select which components to compose

- connect the socket interfaces of one component to the appropriate plug interfaces of other components to plug them together

- develop some connecting code (via a connector module) using scripting or adapters between components

Requirements of component compositions as well as composition conventions motivate the need for component frameworks and design patterns, which we cover in the following section.

15.5 Component frameworks and patterns

Components are considered as self-contained and not tightly coupled to other components. To achieve a loose form of collaboration, components are usually designed to be deployed within a component framework. A *component framework* is prefabricated software that provides a partial solution to a set of related problems that application developers can use to extend or customize for a particular type of solutions [Gamma 1995; Lewis 1995; D'Souza 1999]. A framework is developed to bootstrap implementations of products based on a common architectural style. A framework comprises a set of cooperating classes, some of which may be abstract, that make up a reusable design for a specific type of software application. With frameworks, application developers do not have to start from scratch every time that they need to develop an application. Recall from the previous section that a component model describes which resources are available to components, and how and when components are bound to these resources. Conversely, a framework perceives components as resources that need to be managed.

Frameworks are reusable parameterized semifinished systems, that capture recurring (business) patterns and processes within or between domains, which need to be customized to reflect desirable business characteristics.

15.5.1 Characteristics and types of frameworks

A framework predefines the main data and control flow infrastructure of an application. The implementation of a framework is usually incomplete (it provides only a generic functionality) and can be extended or customized by application developers to deliver a specific functionality and solution. A framework is the glue that binds individual components into applications that can be deployed with ease. The framework itself is usually designed as a set of reusable components creating an aesthetic simplicity. The aim is then that components can be quickly put together to form new applications. For example, an enterprise can use a mixture of 'purchased' and in-house developed components as discrete parts of a complete workflow solution implementing some typical business process.

Frameworks are enabled by the key properties of object-orientation, dynamic binding and inheritance [Gamma 1995], which are mixed with the notion of abstract classes. Dynamic binding implements polymorphism by allowing for runtime checking of the method that is to be called. The method actually executed is determined on the basis of both a message name as well as the dynamic type of the receiver. These properties greatly simplify the extension and adaption of frameworks to match enterprise-specific business logic and policies.

A framework is built from a collection of components, providing support for not only the reuse of code, but also the reuse of the design of the software system [D'Souza 1999]. Consequently, a framework captures both the design and programming expertise required to solve a particular class of problems. Frameworks are characterized by the problem domains they address. The problem domain that a framework addresses can embrace application, domain or support functions:

- *Application frameworks* encapsulate expertise that is applicable to a wide variety of programs. Application frameworks encompass a horizontal slice of functionality that is applied across client domains. The most typical application framework is a commercial graphical user interface (GUI) application framework that supports all kinds of standard functionality required for all GUI applications.

- *Domain frameworks* encapsulate expertise and functionality in a particular vertical domain, such as the automotitive industry, accounting, industrial manufacturing, securities trading framework and so on.

- *Support frameworks* provide system-level functionality such as distributed file access, interprocess communication facilities, and support for security and access rights and so on. Application developers typically use support frameworks directly or they can customise them, e.g. when developing advanced event notification or publish – subscribe functionality.

A *business framework* is a typical domain framework that must conform to a particular vertical domain e.g. automotive, financial, travel, and so forth, and comprises a design and code skeleton of cooperating enterprise components that aims to implement domain-specific entities and business processes based on some default business logic. Business frameworks, like any other framework, are built around the concepts of abstract interfaces, polymorphic composition, and delegation in such a way that designers rely on the substitutability of interfaces and the ability to select appropriate functions either at deployment or runtime. Some examples of business frameworks include business financials (accounts payable/receivable, and general ledger), order management (sales orders, purchase orders, purchase/sales contracts and quotations), and warehouse management (logistics and control functions). For instance, a typical order management framework would cover many of the basic supply-chain functions, with separate component suites for quote and order entry, transportation and distribution, financial interactions and custom configurations. Components for quote and order entry may provide processes including requests for quotes, prices and availability, purchase order management, and queries on order status. Transportation components may provide services such as ship notices, delivery management, claims, and changes. Finally, the financial components may provide invoicing, remittance, product return and reconcilation functions.

Building applications from frameworks can be approached in several ways. The simplest of these is to use the components of the framework without changing them. A second approach is to extend the framework by creating and adding new business components at the top of the framework. A third possibility is to modify the framework by provding additional interfaces to those defined for a component, or by replacing the business logic offered by component interface.

Like components, frameworks come in two types: black or white-box frameworks [Earles 2000]. With *white-box frameworks* clients will either have access to the source code or use inheritance to derive new variations of the framework's abstract interfaces. Use of a white framework necessitates intimate knowledge of the framework implementation. Additionally, white-box frameworks are extremely difficult to version, and therefore such frameworks are often used as a starting point for an implementation – with future versions having no tie to past versions. White-box frameworks rely on inheritance or static embedding to allow code reuse, in addition to the ability to override generic functionality with a more specific one. This introduces tight coupling between the interfaces and components involved in an inheritance relationship. In contrast to white-box frameworks, *black-box frameworks* only provide a description of the external properties and dynamics of framework. Accordingly, black-box reuse of framework functionality is established only on the basis of the interface definitions provided by the framework. Black-box reuse is simpler than white-box reuse, but less flexible. In practice, a mixture of both white and black-box reuse, called gray-box reuse, seems to be more appropriate. Gray-box reuse is based on the philosophy that only a controlled part of the implementation needs to be understood by the developer.

Although frameworks provide several attractive features such as modularity, extensibility and reusability, they also face some serious problems. Some of the problems that frameworks face include [Earles 2000]:

slow performance, increased complexity, a modeling/implementation gap as well as problematic integration with legacy enterprise assets. These are addressed briefly below.

The use of frameworks can lead to decreased performance. This issue is directly related to the complexity of frameworks. Complexity can be reduced by applying the princple of separation of concerns and developing a layered architecture. Although this architecture results in reduced complexity, the improved conceptual clarity is counterbalanced with a slower performance.

A thorough understanding of the workings of frameworks is critical for developers. This understanding can be gained by studying framework documentation, which can be offered as a textual description, UML models or patterns. One serious problem is that the models present some abstraction of the implementation, frequently introducing a gap between modeling an implementation. Integration with legacy systems or other frameworks is problematic, the reason being that frameworks are specified for extension, not for integration. This poses severe problems when embedding frameworks in an existing application environment.

15.5.2 Business patterns

Business frameworks are inherently very complex as they typically comprise several hundreds of enterprise components that collaborate with each other using different business scenarios. The essence of designing a framework is to allow future iterations of applications to be developed with ease. In order to achieve this, the framework must embody flexibility, extensibility and ease of configuration. These properties are provided by *patterns* that form the backbone of flexible framework architectures, encapsulating the areas of variability inside components. Patterns are established for generalized solutions that address problems that are common to different business situations [Eriksson 2000]. A pattern describes a particular design problem that is frequently encountered in specific contexts, and presents a proven, generalized approach to solving it [Buschmann 1996]. Patterns provide value because they capture business knowledge.

Patterns can be found in all the phases of business application development, from business modeling to the actual coding and testing stages. Patterns found in business applications are known as *business patterns*; high-level system patterns that are found in system design are referred to as *architectural patterns*; and patterns closer to programming solutions are called *design patterns* [Eriksson 2000]. We shall first introduce design patterns and subsequently explain how they are related to business patterns.

Business application developers usually employ component-based software development techniques in a specific horizontal or vertical market to reduce their time-to-market and meet the increasing demand for sophisticated business software. The purpose of design patterns within such enterprise applications is to capture successful software designs, very much in a similar manner to what blueprints achieve, and reuse them in ever-new contexts. Thus, design patterns capture the intent behind a design by identifying components, how components interact, and how responsibilities are distributed among them. They constitute a base of experience for constructing reusable software, as they act as building blocks from which more complex designs can be built. Multiple patterns fit together to form an application. Loosely speaking we may state that patterns comprise microarchitectural elements of frameworks that provide a recurring solution to a common software problem.

Patterns for e-Business are a group of proven, reusable assets that drive the design, development, and deployment processes. An application designer first chooses one of a number of business patterns that most closely matches the interaction between participants in the desired e-Business solution. An individual business pattern offers the choice of several application topologies. The different application topologies associated with a business pattern account for differing customer requirements and lead to a particular configuration that focuses principally on the relationship of the application logic and associated data but does not mandate where middleware runs or where data might be stored.

Typical business patterns address problems within a business domain, such as how to model and structure business services that rely on orders, invoices, bills, products, inventory and so on. As an example business pattern, consider such business processes as order processing, order fulfillment or procurement that exist within an order management business framework. Some of the steps involved in order processing include capturing the items and quantities desired, applying promotional or other pricing terms, obtaining shipping and billing addresses, determining required delivery timing, computing shipping, handling, taxes and total costs, completing the transaction and issuing the customer with an order number and updating the inventory or ERP system. Component suites can then be used to implement the steps in the order-processing business process. This order-processing business pattern could constitute part of the order-management business pattern that we described in the preceding subsection.

15.6 Business component architecture

Components can be of widely varying purpose. As we have already indicated in the preceding sections in this chapter, developers may be confronted with at least two types of components:

1. *System-level components*: these are components that act directly upon other components in order to manage their lifecycle or other resources, for example to start, suspend, resume, or terminate component execution. For example, the EJB specification defines framework servers and containers to support the EJB component model (see also Section 14.7.2). Servers are responsible for providing persistence, transaction and security services, while containers are responsible for managing the component life cycle.
2. *Business components*: these provide, as we already explained, a set of meaningful services focused on a particular business concept. Business components may also be combined into reusable groups forming patterns and frameworks.

It is useful to standardize the way that the different kinds of components interact with each other. To achieve this, the most common approach is to define a layered architecture for business components. The basic principle of a layered architecture is that in each layer the components play a similar client role with respect to components in the layer below, and a server role with respect to the components in the layer above.

Recall that the four-tier architecture of client, presentation, processing and data that we introduced in Section 6.3.2 has become accepted as a way to distribute the functionality of Web-based applications. The business component architecture requires that the processing tier in conventional four-tier architecture be divided into two units with separate functions. Figure 15.5 illustrates this particular arrangement.

As shown in Figure 15.5, the classical processing tier is subdivided into two parts: the business process (or workflow) tier and the business component tier. The business process tier contains process components that

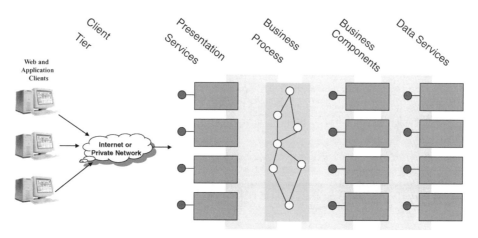

Figure 15.5: Five-tier Component Architecture

are concerned with managing the execution of a particular business process. Business process components call upon the services of business components that implement the business rules, manipulate data, provide information and are reused in different applications. The process components in the business process layer manage business components and sequence the workflow between them. The managing and sequencing activities are delivered in the form of components that contain processes specific to a particular application. The business process tier is enabled for multiple clients in the presentation tier. Presentation components are more likely to be specific to the client technology used. The business component tier can be built on top of component model APIs like J2EE APIs, such as JMS (see Section 14.5.2). The J2EE APIs provide basic distributed-object services. Additional extensions that are commonly required by the business component tier can be written in Java, and can be targeted to EJB server platforms that support the J2EE APIs. These extensions implement mechanisms such as component composition, substitutability, modular encapsulation, independent deployability, component contractual safety and so forth. Business components are provided in a way that is completely independent of the implementation. This means that beyond a thin layer to allow the business components to participate in this five-tier architecture, any technology can be used to implement them. In fact, different component models (COM, CORBA or EJB) can be used at each layer.

Data-tier components should be capable of providing alternative interfaces for different component models. For instance, a data service could use SQL statements to access a relational database and then present the results through COM, CORBA or EJB interfaces.

The connections between business components and data-tier components are supported by system-level components. System-level components provide a variety of services including location, transaction management, security, and event notification. Location services are used by components to locate the services that they require. Examples of standards for location services include the Java Naming and Directory Interface and CORBA's naming and trading service. Transaction management services can be implemented using the Java Transaction API (see Section 14.5.2). As we already explained in Chapter 14, a JTA transaction is coordinated by the J2EE platform. JTA allows applications to access the application server's transaction management services in a way that is independent from any specific implementation. A principal benefit of a JTA transaction is that it enables the combining of multiple components and EISs accesses into a single atomic transaction with little programming effort. JMS works in tandem with JTA to provide features like distributed transaction support for business components.

The fact that requests in the five-tier architecture (depicted in Figure 15.5) are made only in a single direction helps reduce dependencies between components. Moreover, since components are accessed via published interfaces, the implementation of a component on any tier can be exchanged with minimum impact on the components on either side of it.

15.7 Business component-based design and development

Component-based development is a software development approach where all aspects and phases of the development life cycle, including analysis, design, construction testing and deployment, as well as the supporting technical infrastructure are based on the concept of components [Herzum 2000]. In particular, the business component approach extends component-based development by defining a conceptual framework for large-scale e-Business systems development and integration. It is a set of technologies, processes, guidelines and techniques about how business systems should be conceived, analyzed, architected, designed, developed and evolved. Obviously this approach focuses on its core concept, the business component concept.

In this section we investigate existing applications for potential component functionality, consider component reusability and finally discuss the importance of business knowledge and how it applies to component development.

15.7.1 Designing components

When designing components, emphasis should be given to both functional and nonfunctional requirements of components. The various component concepts and model artifacts that are used during component design can be represented using UML, very much in the spirit of what we presented in Chapter 12. For this purpose, UML can be extended by means of using stereotypes to represent new kinds of modeling elements. These resemble, of course, built-in UML types. However, it is not the purpose of this book to illustrate how UML can be used to express component designs. Instead, we shall concentrate on issues relating to component design and development. Interested readers can refer to the book by Cheesman and Daniels [Cheesman 2001] that is an excellent source for demonstrating how UML can be used to specify components.

In the following, we shall examine design guidelines that can be used for functional and nonfunctional component design.

Functional component design guidelines

Functional component design encompasses the following steps:

- identifying candidate components

- managing component granularity

- designing for reuse

- designing for component composability

Identifying candidate components: Understanding how an enterprise component works and how component functionality differs, or can get adjusted between applications, is an important milestone when identifying suitable component candidates.

When designing an application, developers must first analyze application functionality and develop a logical model of what an enterprise does in terms of business components and the services the business requires from these business components (what are the shipping and billing addresses, what is the required delivery time, what is the delivery schedule and so on). The developer may implement these concepts as a blend of business entities and components.

The key factor is being able to recognize functionality that is essentially self-sufficient for the purposes of a business component. A business component should be specified with an application or the user of the service in mind where component realization may be provided by a software package, e.g. an ERP package, a special purpose-built component, commercial off-the-shelf applications (COTS), or a legacy application. It is important when designing a component to identify the functionality that should be included in a specific component and the functionality that is best incorporated into another component. Good candidates for business components are those business concepts that represent commonly required functionality for EAI or e-Business such as sales order management, credit checking and inventory management. Components of this type are designed to provide comprehensive support to very specific services in sharply focused, narrower information and process domains, and can be integrated with existing back-office and custom storefront applications.

A component should allow a developer to integrate a precise solution as opposed to one that provides features over and above a basic requirement. Defining component scope helps ensure that a component does not become monolithic and mimic an entire application. Unbundling functionality into separate components will prevent the component from becoming overly complex and difficult to maintain. For example, designing an enterprise component that handles online purchasing would require the removal of packaging and shipping information and costs to different components. In this example the three functions are mutually exclusive and should be implemented separately. The functionality included in these components is not only discrete and identifiable but it is also loosely coupled to other parts of the application. Tightly coupled functionality is one of mitigating factors against flexibility and extendibility and is thus very difficult to componentize. Developers usually look at the functions encapsulated in their own and other applications to assess the commercial viability of componentizing particular functions. Relationships between the components are increasingly implemented in the form of messages between the components.

Managing component granularity: The granularity of components should be the prime concern of the developer responsible for providing component implementations. An enterprise component can be of various gran-ularity levels. The smallest level of granularity is normally a component implemented by a component model such as EJB, CORBA or COM. Larger granularities are compositions of smaller-grained components and possibly other artifacts, where the composition taken as a whole conforms to the enterprise component definition.

Identifying the appropriate level of granularity for a component is a difficult undertaking as granularity is very much application-context dependent. In general, there are several heuristics that can be used to identify the right level of granularity for enterprise components. These include clearly identifiable business concepts, highly usable and reusable concepts, concepts that have a high degree of cohesion and low degree of coupling and must be functionally cohesive [Herzum 2000]. Many vertical sectors, e.g. automotive, travel industry and so on, have already started standardizing business entities and processes by choosing their own levels of granularity. It is important that the developer who implements the service still thinks about granularity so they can change parts of the implementation with the minimum of disruption to other components, applications and services.

Designing for component reusability: When designing components it is important to be able to design them for reuse so that they can perform a given function wherever this function is required within an enterprise. To design for component reuse one must make components more generic, abstracting away from differences in requirements between one situation and another, and attempting to use the generic component in multiple contexts where it is applicable. Designing a solution that is reusable requires keeping it as simple as possible. There are intuitive techniques that facilitate reuse that are related to design issues such as identification and granularity of components. These include [McInnis 1999]:

- looking for common behavior that exists in more than one place in the system

- trying to generalize behavior so that it is reusable

- planning to build facade interfaces that will make use of generalized components

When designing a component-based application, it is possible to extract common behavior and provide it by means of a generic interface so that multiple clients can use it directly. It is important, however, when designing enterprise components that business logic is kept common and consistent across the enterprise so that generalization is not required. Nevertheless there are cases where fine-tuning, specialization or variation of business logic functionality is required. Consider for instance, discounting practices that differ depending on the type of customer being handled. In those cases it is customary to produce a generalized solution with customization points to allow for variations. These solutions are normally developed on the basis of façade interfaces. A *façade interface* is a type of interface that passes control to other interfaces and provides many of its services by consuming the services of another interface [McInnis 1999]. Figure 15.6 illustrates a sales-order component that provides billing services by calling the services of a billing component.

When designing generic interfaces it will be necessary to build façade interfaces since in many cases application-level clients will require specialized functions or variant component versions based on generic components. To understand the usefulness of the façade interface, consider the common requirement to establish a business-wide service to support a unified view of an organization to the outside world. This requires resolving the issues created by perhaps many different existing business systems operating disparate applications, which manage customers and accounts in different, uncoordinated ways. Components offering customer relationship services can be implemented by wrapping and complementing existing legacy applications. These components provide narrowly focused services that present a façade to existing applications. In essence they provide access to the same service, bypassing preexisting business systems and logic, and can thus be reused by both existing and future applications. This approach is superior to acquiring a new CRM package as it enables a custom solution with reduced construction time and costs. The same

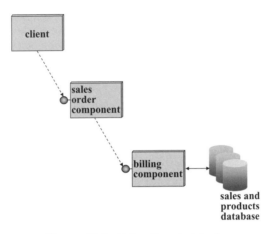

■ Figure 15.6: Using Façade Interfaces

approach can be adopted for a wide range of purposes precisely because the component interfaces to the services they provide are rigorously defined.

When designing interfaces for an application, a designer can create an application that has multiple interfaces with associations between them. The designer can create all of these interfaces during the design of an application, or they may know of already existing interfaces that can be incorporated into the application design. In general, interfaces can be designed to use other interfaces at deployment time or at runtime. The choice of which type of interface to use will affect the design of the application interfaces.

If interfaces are associated with each other at deployment time, it means that component implementations in the specified application must fully support the interfaces as they are designed. If an interface utilizes the services of another at runtime, the clients of the latter interface cannot be certain that it is actually being used to realize the entire interface implementation. Although this latter interface may fulfill its contractual obligations with respect to its client, it may rely on external component providers to perform its services. Each of these external providers may provide only partial implementations based on which interface is constructed.

Designing for component composability: In order to design useful and reliable services we need to apply sound service design principles that guarantee that components are self-contained, modular and support component composability. The design principles that underlie component reusability revolve around two well-known software design guidelines: coupling and cohesion.

It is important that grouping of activities in business processes is as independent as possible from other such groupings in other processes. One way of measuring service design quality is *coupling*, or the degree of interdependence between two business processes. The objective is to minimize coupling, that is to make (self-contained) business processes as independent as possible by not having any knowledge of or relying on any other business processes. Low coupling between business processes indicates a well-partitioned system that avoids the problems of service redundancy and duplication.

Coupling can be achieved by reducing the number of connections between services in a business process, eliminating unnecessary relationships between them, and by reducing the number of necessary relationships, if possible. Decoupled business processes are easier to achieve.

Cohesion is the degree of the strength of functional relatedness of operations within a service. Designers should create strong, highly cohesive business processes, business processes whose services and service operations are strongly and genuinely related to one another. There are two broad guidelines by which to increase component cohesion: *functional cohesion* and *logical cohesion*. A functionally cohesive component contains services that all contribute to the execution of one and only one problem-related task, e.g. customer billing. At the same time, the operations in the services that the component provides must also be highly related to one another. A logically cohesive component is one whose activities all contribute to tasks of the same general category, e.g. logistics and distribution, which include business processes such as warehousing, distribution and management inventory.

High cohesion increases the clarity and ease of comprehension of the design; simplifies maintenance and future enhancements; achieves service granularity at a reasonable level; and often supports low coupling. Highly related functionality supports increased reuse potential as a highly cohesive component can be used for specific purposes.

Nonfunctional component design

A component design methodology would be incomplete if we did not take into account other important nonfunctional design criteria such as a payment model, component policies, and quality of component. In general, nonfunctional component characteristics describe the broader context of a component, e.g. what business function the component accomplishes, how it fits into a broader business process as well as characteristics of the hosting environment such as whether the component provider ensures security and privacy, what kind of auditing, security and privacy policy is enforced by the component provider, what levels of component quality are available and so on. As these issues are very specific to component design, only some of them are examined briefly in this book. More information about nonfunctional issues can be found in several other popular publications in software component literature such as [Allen 2001aa; Whitehead 2002; Cheesman 2001]. Unfortunately, all of these books cover nonfunctional component design issues in a rather dispersed manner and none of them systematically taxonomizes them.

In the following we summarize the most typical elements of nonfunctional component design. We do not explicitly mention quality of service requirements for components as these are identical to the requirements for supporting QoS in e-Business that we discussed in some detail in Section 13.2.

Component provisioning strategies: An important nonfunctional characteristic worth considering is the commercial viability of a component. Market demand determines whether a component is commercially viable or should be used only within its own organization. As components become acceptable from industry, organizations realize that there are several intricate issues pertaining to the deployment aspects of revenue-generating components. Component provisioning is a complex mixture of technical and business aspects for supporting component client activities and involves choices for component realization, component enrollment, auditing, metering, billing and managing operations that control the behavior of a component during its use [Allen 2001a].

Component realization strategies: The separation of specification from implementation allows components to be realized in different ways. It becomes important then to plan effectively when deciding how to realize or provision components, consider the diversity of realization alternatives and make the right choice.

Component realization relies on gap analysis techniques [Allen 2001a]. *Gap analysis* is a technique that decides the component realization strategy by incrementally adding more implementation details to an abstract component interface. During this process a component realization architecture can be used to express how the component interface is connected to and assembled from the interfaces of the components from which it is composed.

A gap analysis strategy may be developed in stages and results in a recommendation to do development work, reuse or purchase components. For example, there may exist software components that provide a good match. These may include component implementations previously developed by the enterprise and externally supplied component realizations available on a subscription or pay-per-use basis. Component realizations may be a blend of component and non-component implementations.

In addition to component reuse, component realization strategy involves choosing from an increasing diversity of different options for components, which may be mixed in various combinations including the following:

- Purchasing/leasing/paying-per-use for components. This option is covered in some detail in the following section on component metering and billing.

- Outsourcing component design and implementation. Once a component is specified, the design of its interfaces or sets of interfaces and the coding of its actual implementation may be outsourced.

- Using wrappers and/or adapters. Non-component implementations for components may include database functionality or legacy software in the form of adapters or wrappers. Wrappers reuse legacy code by converting the legacy functionality and encapsulating it inside components, see Section 15.7.2 and Chapter 16 for more details on wrapping of legacy code. Adapters use legacy code in combination with newly developed component code. This newly developed component may contain new business logic and rules that supplement the converted legacy functionality.

Component development strategies can lead to identifying opportunities to eliminate redundancies, consolidating systems/applications and rationalizing duplicate processes such as in the case of the Bank of America's Card Services and e-Commerce division that we introduced at the beginning of this chapter.

Component billing strategies: Increasingly, business models for commercial component provisioning will become a matter of concern to component providers. From the perspective of the component provider a complex trading component is a commercializable software commodity. For example, a component provider may decide to offer simple components (with no quality of component guarantee) for free, while it would charge a nominal fee for use of its complex (added-value) components. Obviously, with complex enterprise components the quality of the component plays a very important role and the component is offered for a price. For complex enterprise components, the component provider may have different charging alternatives. These may include the following [Allen 2001a]:

1. Payment on a per use basis. With this alternative a client is charged some nominal fee each time they invoke the component. Small organizations that use components on an infrequent basis would probably opt for the pay-per-use model.
2. Payment on a subscription basis. With this alternative a client is charged a set amount of money for a given period of time. This charging model is more appealing to large enterprises that make more frequent use of components.
3. Payment on a leasing basis. This alternative is similar to subscription; however, it is geared towards components that may provide high value for a shorter period of time.
4. Lifetime components. These components are offered for a set amount of money for their entire lifetime. This may apply for a period of a few weeks to a few months or even years.
5. Free components. An advantage of this model is that components could be offered to requesters for free for a period of time and then they can be moved into some payment plan.

A component design methodology should take into account several important aspects relating to the accounting process for component provisioning. This process requires that component providers come up with viable business cases that address factors such as component metering, rating and billing:

- *Component metering model*: Use of a component by a client must be metered if the component provider requires usage-based billing. Then the component provider needs to audit the component as it is used and bill for it. This could typically be done on a periodic basis and requires that a metering and accounting model for the use of the component be established. The model could allow the establishment of a component contract for each new subscriber, tracking, and billing for using the subscribed hosted components.

- *Component rating/billing model*: Software organizations that are used to the traditional up-front license/ongoing maintenance pricing structure for software should come up with annuity-based pricing models for the components they provide. The pricing (rating) model could determine subscriber rates based on subscription and usage events. For example, the pricing model could calculate charges for components based on the quality and precision of the component and on individual metering events based on a component-rating scheme. The billing model associates rating details with the correct customer account. It provides adequate information to allow the retrieval and payment of billing details by the client and the correct disbursement of payments to the component provider's suppliers.

Component policy management models: As a wide range of components is provided across a network, it is only natural that components would benefit from the use of policy management models, which could determine the configuration of a network of *differentiated components* according to business rules, QoS or application-level policies. There are many reasons why businesses might want to give different levels of component to different customers or why they might need different levels of priority for different business transaction models involving components. Therefore, it is not surprising that such criteria constitute important elements of a component design methodology and are considered equally important to technical policies such as security or authentication.

Consider for example a component that displays the company's share price. Under normal circumstances, the component displays share prices with a 20-minutes delay to inhibit the use of this component for trading purposes. However, a few select customers (or employees) could be allowed to know the current share price together with perhaps other important financial information such as, for example, analysts ratings and financial reports. Component providers can mix different levels of component precision, granularity, timeliness and scope. Another possibility is to differentiate components based on technical service-quality details such as response time, performance bandwidth used, security and authentication models, transactionality and reliability (for more details about QoS requirements, see Section 13.2). If a component is designed to cover a wide spectrum of component levels according to some set of policies then it is likely that this component would achieve much higher levels of use [Veryard 2000].

15.7.2 Developing components

During development, software components are generated on the basis of functional and nonfunctional requirements identified during the design process. There are several fundamental challenges in developing software applications that component technology is evolving to solve. The core challenges of developing software applications that use a component-based development approach can be generalized as follows:

- building customizable components

- controlling component change

- wrapping legacy applications

These challenges are briefly examined in the following.

The fact that components should not be modified does not imply that they should not be customized externally. A component can be designed to provide, in addition to the interfaces for its primary services, additional interfaces for plug-ins that customize the behaviors of its primary services. Components can be designed for customization at the time that they are assembled into an application. To assist the application developer with customization, components should provide enough metadata for use by the assembly environment to inquire about their capabilities.

In general, a reusable component is built to offer generalized services that can be used on an 'as-is' basis in several cases, while in other cases a variant or specialization of the services provided by the component is needed. To customize a component for a specific use, a developer may decide to use façade interfaces and delegate requests to the reusable component where appropriate. Normally, as we already explained in Section 15.7.1, these façade interfaces implement customization interfaces by providing controlled customization of a component, e.g. by handling additional code sections. Customized requests could be handled either locally without invoking the corresponding service in the reusable component, by possibly employing additional logic prior or after the invocation, or simply delegated to the reusable component [Whitehead 2002]. Another possibility is to employ parameterization techniques whereby alternate code sections may be included or excluded from the component implementation based on options selected by the application developer.

When components are designed for reuse, *change management* becomes a critical factor. The key requirement in managing change is keeping change localized – minimizing its scope and impact so that changes do not end up being propagated through the complete solution. This is because these parts of the solution have a dependency. Minimizing dependencies between the elements in a solution is the key to managing change.

As components are defined with immutable interfaces, when a change is made it should be handled by defining a new interface, such as a façade interface. Subsequently, the upgraded component can be included in an application without any changes having to be made. Another obvious point when changing a component is that the nature of the service needs to remain constant. There is no need to subvert an existing service to make it capable of carrying out some new upgraded function [Whitehead 2002]. Instead, a new interface providing this service should be added.

Components are ideal choice for wrapping legacy assets. The premise behind wrapping is that it fully replaces the legacy software from the point of view of its client. When components are used to assist with wrapping, legacy assets are encapsulated inside components. Legacy transformation and wrapping is a topic that is of paramount importance to e-Business applications; thus we have devoted an entire chapter to it in this book. In Chapter 16, which covers legacy systems' transformation for e-Business, we discuss among other things component wrapping in some detail.

15.7.3 Certifying components

Enough information should be provided in order to determine whether a component is useful within the context for which it is being evaluated. An item of importance is whether one can trust the component's quality. Component certification involves two separate actions [Bachmann 2000]:

1. Establishing that a component possesses particular properties, most often in *conformance* with some specification against which the component or framework is certified.
2. It is foreseeable that an independent trusted group within an organization or even a third party might certify that components are fit for their stated purpose and attest to the truth of this conformance.

The first of these actions has consequences on the engineering discipline, in that application developers can work with 'known quantities'. The second of these actions has consequences on the development of consumer trust. Both of the above actions are necessary for component certification.

To establish that a component or framework possesses some desired property we need to use knowledge to predict properties that an assembled application may attain. Certification depends on *compositional reasoning* [Bachmann 2000]. Compositional reasoning identifies which properties of components and frameworks are material for predicting or achieving some end-system properties, such as performance, safety, scalability and so on, and how to predict the 'values' of end-system properties from component and framework properties. These contractual specifications must be expressive enough to capture all of the properties imposed by frameworks that will lead to end-system quality attributes, and measurement techniques must be in place to determine, to a desired level of confidence, the degree to which a component exhibits these properties. Such component properties are specified contractually in a component model. The effectiveness of a certification regime improves as our ability to undertake compositional reasoning improves.

15.8 Advantages and limitations of component-based development

There are several advantages to building e-Business applications from components, including faster application development, reduced development and maintenance costs, higher productivity, as well as leveraging vertical domain expertise.

Components yield several advantages, and perhaps their main benefit lies in faster application development. The most significant way in which creating software applications with components can serve to reduce development costs is through reuse. Instead of having to design, develop and test code, developers can acquire prebuilt components that have been written by experts. Often, many system functions can be achieved by reusing existing components instead of designing entirely new ones. For example, BEA's EJB technology-based e-Commerce components can help an organization save an estimated 80% on development time by offering ready-made components commercially. This obviates the need for company developers to write all of the different pieces of an application themselves. The development team can then concentrate their efforts on adding features that will differentiate their solution for competitive advantage.

In addition to reducing costs, reusing existing components increases productivity since application development teams don't have to begin building new applications from scratch. Relying on components also makes it possible to facilitate parallel development. Because they possess well-defined boundaries, and can be built on their own, it is possible for multiple teams to develop different components at the same time.

Building with components also reduces maintenance costs. Since components are encapsulated, it is possible to make changes to their implementation without affecting all the systems that rely on them.

The economic benefits of component-based development are that the use of standard components within a standard process can result in the development of standard project estimates, schedules and costs [Due 2000]. Return on investment can be measured with precise technical metrics, one of which is function-point analysis. This measures how quickly functionality can be placed into an application, for example, as function points to dollars spent, or function points to person-hours of development. The consequences of reusable estimates and schedules are these [Due 2000]:

1. Management can realistically plan and control component-based development projects. There exist component standards, component blueprints and development techniques that can be used as a basis to manage large development projects and compare them with other such projects, teams and organizations.
2. Quality assurance and EDP audit personnel can measure the effectiveness, and efficiency of a particular project against historical standards for each task and each work product.
3. Project managers can concentrate on risk minimization and contingency planning for those tasks on a critical component-based development path that have the largest variances from the historical standards identified in step 2.

Components constitute a solution for Enterprise Application Integration, which we shall examine in Chapter 17. EAI solutions address integration within an enterprise and are typically designed as a *tight bound implementation* of – or *tightly coupled integration* approach to – connecting systems that rely on a homogeneous distributed infrastructure. Component technologies such as CORBA, EJB, and COM solve many integration problems. Unfortunately, barriers prevent them from scaling to the Web. Each technology erroneously assumes that it is ubiquitous (i.e. each requires the same technology for both caller and receiver) and thus results in a tightly coupled integration model. Industry support for each component standard (where there is a standard) is fragmented. Applications based on these technologies require them to be written using that particular technology, often from a particular vendor. Integrating different component models is difficult owing to differences in object models, communication mechanisms and protocols, type systems and differences in exception handling, especially runtime vs. application exceptions. For example, calling EJB services from CORBA requires reverse-mapping EJB into CORBA IDL with the resulting IDL specifications being quite cumbersome and messy. Moreover, components do not possess the scalable communication protocols required for Web-based applications and they do not offer firewall traversal capabilities in the form of protocols that are not blocked by firewalls with a standard configuration. These requirements hinder widespread acceptance of component-based applications on the Web.

In summary, component systems are best suited to building systems with well-defined architectural considerations that are very much oriented towards the intranet and the enterprise architectures of a single enterprise. This can be attested to by our case study where the Bank of America's Card Services and e-Commerce division built a component business model of their card services that provided a tight linkage between internal business and technology objectives. The component business model mapped the Bank's technology to its business objectives, identified priorities for transformation and helped create the new supporting IT architecture. It is difficult for component technology to create the technical agreement and coordination needed to build distributed systems that span enterprises.

In Chapter 19 we shall examine an approach that addresses the requirements for developing Web-based e-Business applications and surmounts the problems introduced by tightly coupled technologies such as component-based systems. This technology is known as Web services, which are a *loose bound implementation* of connecting systems to provide a standard framework for distributed Internet applications to communicate and interoperate with each other. Web services are best suited for implementing shared business tasks between enterprises. The component and Web-service technologies are largely complementary. Components provide the underlying infrastructure for the systems that run inside a single enterprise, while Web services provide the connectivity between collaborating systems in independent enterprises. A Web service provides a common façade for cross-enterprise-specific systems, making it easier to create the service-level agreement needed for business-to-business integration.

15.9 Chapter summary

A component is an independent, encapsulated part of a system that can be designed and built to implement a well-defined set of responsibilities as regards its clients. Components are autonomous units of software that may provide a useful service or a set of services to a client, and have meaning in isolation to other components with which they interoperate. Because components are autonomous units of functionality they provide natural demarcations of development work.

A component is made up of three essential parts: the interface, the implementation, and the deployment. The interface informs the client of a component about what functions the component is capable of performing. The component implementation is the code that makes the component function. For example, a component might possess one implementation that relies on a C++ program, and another that relies on a Java application. Finally, the deployment specifies the particular environment in which the component operates. It is important to note the distinction between implementation and deployment descriptions. The same implementation can be deployed in different ways.

Component-based applications can be developed using interchangeable parts to assemble components. It is this separation of components from other components that is the authority behind the rapid building and deployment of component-based systems. A component conforms to a component model that specifies the rules that must be observed by the component. These rules improve component composability by ensuring alignment of functionality and compatibility of component interfaces with other such components.

Business components are reusable components that enable rapid application development by providing large independent parts that when assembled together can be used to create a business application. To achieve a loose form of collaboration, components are usually designed to be deployed within a component framework. A framework is prefabricated software that provides a partial solution to a set of related problems that application developers can use to extend or customize for a particular type of solution. A business framework is a typical domain framework that must conform to a particular vertical domain, e.g. automotive, financial, travel, and so forth, and comprises a design and code skeleton of cooperating enterprise components that aim to implement domain-specific entities and business processes based on some default business logic. Finally, patterns for e-Business are a group of proven, reusable assets that drive the design, development and deployment processes. An application designer first chooses one of a number of business patterns that most closely matches the interaction between participants in the desired e-Business solution.

As with other middleware approaches to e-Business, it is useful to standardize the way that the different kinds of components interact with each other. To achieve this, the most common approach is to define a layered architecture for business components. The classical processing tier in the component architecture is subdivided into two parts: the business process (or workflow) tier and the business component tier. The business process tier contains process components that are concerned with managing the execution of a particular business process. Business process components call upon the services of business components that implement the business rules, manipulate data, provide information and are reused in different applications. The process components in the business process layer manage business components and sequence the workflow between them.

Component-based applications rely on component-based development methodology which is a software development approach where all aspects and phases of the development life cycle, including analysis, design, construction testing and deployment, as well as the supporting technical infrastructure, are based on the concept of components. This methodology defines a conceptual framework for large-scale e-Business systems development and integration. It is a set of technologies, processes, guidelines and techniques about how business systems should be conceived, analyzed, architected, designed, developed and evolved.

Discussion Questions

- Why is an object-oriented approach not the preferred solution for developing large-scale and complex software for Enterprise Application Integration or e-Business integration applications?

- Explain what a component is and discuss its main characteristics. Explain whether components provide structural interfaces like objects.

- Explain what is meant by white-box and black-box components. What are the benefits of using black-box components?

- What is a framework, what are its main characteristics and types? What is a business framework? What are black and white frameworks? Discuss the major advantages and major drawbacks of business frameworks. Give a detailed example of a typical business framework.

- What is a business pattern and what are its main characteristics and types? How does a business pattern relate to a business framework?

- What is component-based development? Discuss in some detail the design guidelines that are used for functional and nonfunctional component design.

Assignments

i. Design an order management framework using business components. Define typical business patterns within this framework including order processing, order fulfillment, inventory management, and materials procurement.

ii. Design policy models and policy guidelines for the components that you developed in assignment 1. Make sure that the policies and the QoS characteristics of individual components within the component assemblies in the order management framework do not conflict with each other. Use as guidelines the QoS requirements for e-Business that we covered in Section 13.2.

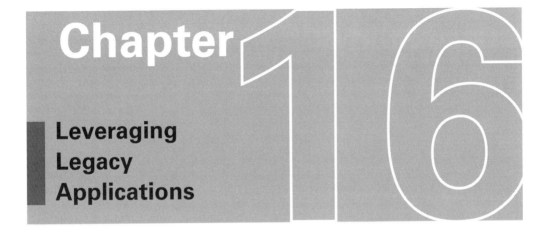

Chapter 16

Leveraging Legacy Applications

Established enterprises that are trying to get into the e-Business arena are being hindered by their legacy information assets, which are systems that have been in use for a long time and that continue to be used to avoid the high cost of replacing them. The value of business logic in the legacy systems combined with the huge investments companies have already made in the development of their existing systems, are a powerful incentive to leverage these systems into modern business initiatives rather than replace them or recreate them with modern technologies. The ever-expanding universe of the new generation of enterprise applications requires retaining the business process knowledge embedded in the legacy systems while at the same time enabling those systems to work with Web-enabled applications and connecting them into coherent large-scale e-Business solutions.

This chapter focuses on legacy systems and provides insights into establishing a legacy infrastructure, and overviews strategies and deployment options for managing, modernizing and integrating legacy applications with modern technologies so that they can function without hindrance in the environment surrounding e-Business applications.

Case Study

National City Corporation extends the life of existing assets using enterprise application modernization technology[1]

National City Corporation (NCC) is the 13th-largest bank holding company in the USA with $89 billion in total assets. Like most financial services firms, NCC relies on its core applications to run its business. In fact, those applications shape much of the firm's interactions with customers and partners. NCC is no stranger to the realities of technology change. NCC decided to upgrade its Corporate Automation System (CAS) application to a Web-based environment, with greater flexibility, lower costs, and reduced maintenance issues became a significant priority.

NCC considered a number of options for the CAS application, including eliminating it altogether, replacing it with a packaged application, upgrading to the latest version of its existing proprietary environment, or moving the system to a more modern architecture. The company decided that eliminating or replacing the CAS system was impractical: the company would in effect be throwing out several years' worth of intellectual assets and starting from scratch. NCC concluded that the most efficient, cost-effective way to harness the value of its existing assets and renovate its current application. To do so, they chose to work with Relativity Technologies and their enterprise application modernization technology (www.relativity.com).

Relativity Technologies' Modernization Workbench is a software solution that drives down the cost and accelerates the modernization, management, and maintenance of business-critical enterprise applications. Relativity's Modernization Workbench product uses sophisticated algorithms to isolate and manage your essential business rules, giving an organization greater control over how its application portfolio reflects its business' needs. The solution contains highly customizable modules that address the specific needs of organizations in each stage of enterprise application modernization.

The solution enabled complex code to be partitioned and selected on the functions that required application migration, thus providing a Web-based front-end to access NCC's systems without disrupting their main functionality.

By using enterprise application modernization to rearchitect their applications and code, NCC simplified the overall maintenance of their system, reduced costs

[1] This case study was summarized from: www.relativity.com/pages/fssuccess.asp.

> while boosting organizational flexibility. The application modernization solution enabled NCC to maintain the crucial functionality it depended on while allowing it to take advantage of new technologies and reduce costs – with no disruption to their normal business activities. Internal estimates put the return on investment as being 200 to 300%.

16.1 Enterprise information systems and legacy enterprise assets

Essentially e-Business involves a more or less radical change in business models, as has been discussed in previous chapters, which results in a number of legacy problems. The e-Business enabled company focuses on core competencies, which leads to outsourcing and possibly insourcing of activities or of entire business processes. New business models are customer-centric, which initiates an internal change from a traditional functional organization to a process oriented organization. New business models are networked, which necessitates building relationships with suppliers, customers and other business partners. These models smoothen their operations and use modern information systems to link to their business partners, for example, by establishing relations through electronic market places.

Each of these changes has major implications for the information systems in place. Out- and insourcing trigger a more or less fundamental change in a company's activities and lead to a change in information needs and consequently in information systems. Support of entire business processes, like product development, distribution, handling customer orders, instead of functions, like sales, production, procurement, require systems that cross the boundaries of traditional functions. In the traditional landscape of island automation, systems typically focus on one or two functions, with no interface between them. e-Business requires an unhindered flow of information from a company's customers to its suppliers and vice versa. For supply chain integration, traditional islands of automation need to be abolished. Integration is difficult to achieve within the boundaries of one enterprise, it is even more difficult when it involves integration with systems of suppliers and customers, the so-called extended supply chain. Besides business changes, changes in IT infrastructure also affect the existing applications. Replacing mainframe based computer systems by client server networks typically involves a complex effort to install new application software, which replaces the existing software.

Legacy Enterprise Information Systems are critical assets of any modern enterprise as they provide access to mission critical business information and functionality and thus control the majority of an organization's business processes.

Established enterprises are finding that the shortcomings of their mission critical legacy systems are preventing them from expanding their corporate IT systems beyond the boundaries of the traditional enterprise. Typical shortcomings of mission critical legacy systems include among other things: the impediment that they present to corporate growth, inability to deal with competitive threats, slow response to growing customer demands, and the lack of integration with trading partners' systems. The ever-expanding universe of enterprise applications requires connecting dissimilar (legacy) systems with newer generation applications.

Although there is strong corporate desire to replace legacy systems with modern technologies, the desire to replace these legacy systems is offset by real world constraints, such as massive long-term accumulated investments in the legacy systems and a significant loss of knowledge about the inner workings of these systems. The value of business logic in the legacy systems combined with the huge investments companies have already made in the development of their existing systems, are a powerful incentive to leverage these systems into modern business initiatives rather than replace them or recreate them with modern technologies. Consider, for instance, our case study where the NCC decided to upgrade its Corporate Automation System and against reimplementing it from scratch.

Although legacy information assets support conventional business operations, it is extremely complicated and expensive to implement new business logic that incorporates the core business processes entrenched in legacy EIS. Replacing or redesigning them is not only costly, but may also lead to a loss of customized business logic that has been programmed over the years into those systems. A question that comes up, and which is discussed in this chapter, is how can existing legacy applications be re-engineered in such a way that they can be adjusted to the new requirements of an e-Business environment making sure that loss of embedded business logic and a costly transition to new systems is prevented.

For over thirty years, enterprises have been developing and enhancing mainframe based EIS applications. Most large enterprises still rely on legacy applications and databases that serve critical business needs. According to Ulrich [Ulrich 2002] *legacy applications systems* (or simply legacy systems) are defined as "any production-enabled software, regardless of the platform it runs on, language is written in, or length of time it has been in production". Legacy applications are technically obsolete mission critical elements of an organization's infrastructure – as they form the core of larger enterprises' business processes – but are too frail to modify and too important to discard.

Legacy enterprise assets may be aging software systems that were constructed to run on various obsolescent hardware types, programmed in obsolete languages, and may suffer from the fragilities and brittleness that results from prolonged maintenance. These legacy systems support core business tasks such as taking and processing orders, initiating production and delivery, generating invoices, crediting payments, distribution, inventory management, and related revenue-generating cost-saving and accounting tasks. In general, legacy systems manage the people and processes required to support an enterprise's core functions. A key part of the value of legacy systems is that they incorporate business process expertise that reflects how the business operates, i.e., how both employees and customers expect the business to operate. This business process knowledge ensures consistency and reliability.

The majority of legacy systems are domain-specific: they support the needs of individual functional business domains, not those of the entire enterprise. As a result, these systems have a limited focus – that of the domain they target – and are unable, to grow or to integrate with modern technologies as the focus of the enterprise changes. The high cost of replacement of legacy systems, coupled with the urgency with which enterprises must make new systems fully operational, means that they have to leverage the value tied up in their existing EIS applications, rather than discarding them and creating new applications. Theoretically, this will make it easier in the future to update and improve applications progressively over time without having to rewrite them entirely. In addition to moving to new programming languages and support environments, enterprises redistribute the locations of applications and data.

Legacy systems have been developed over many years at a substantial cost and typically contain redundant code that supported business processes that are no longer relevant in the modern world. Typical examples of legacy systems are: CICS and Cobol programs and applications, flat files (such as ISAM and VSAM), older generation databases and data sources. A typical legacy system comprises a very large number of individual programs that work together in a hard-wired series of business process flows. Geography, database incompatibilities, and corporate mergers can fragment them. But still there is a requirement to maximize enterprise assets by protecting, managing, integrating, and modernizing legacy EIS.

In general, legacy systems continue to run on the platforms for which they were developed. Typically, new development environments are responsible for continuing to support legacy systems and data. Consequently, older generation applications must be continuously updated and modernized to reflect evolving business requirements and practices. However, repeated modifications have cumulative effects on the complexity of EIS, and the rapid evolution of technology renders existing technologies obsolete. The challenge is to keep the legacy systems operational, while converting them to newer, more efficient applications, which use modern technology and programmer skills.

16.2 Strategies for modernizing legacy systems

A large organization is likely to have a number of applications located on heterogeneous platforms with the core applications residing on a proprietary mainframe. Often the legacy code is of such an age that integration with more modern systems and applications is almost impossible. Therefore, in order to participate in e-Business, as well as to make internal systems more efficient, the legacy systems need to be moved into a more open environment so that they can be integrated more easily with other systems across the extended enterprise.

When considering mission-critical legacy systems it is useful to distinguish between two conceptual parts of an application:

- Its *environmental part* that manages the application's underlying operating environment such as its hardware and communications infrastructure, operating systems and databases.

- Its *business part* that deals with its perceived business functionality. The business part contains the application's business rules and business process flows. It is the business process flows that tie the application's business rules into unified processing units.

It is handy to examine these two parts separately when dealing with legacy application system modernization.

The environmental part of a legacy system is concerned primarily with system migration techniques. Legacy system migration involves starting with a legacy EIS and ending with a comparable target EIS [Brodie

1995]. The essence of legacy system migration is to move an existing, operational system to a new platform, retaining the functionality of the legacy system while causing as little disruption to the existing operational and business environment as possible. There are two strategies for migrating legacy EIS [Brodie 1995]:

- The cold turkey strategy which involves redeveloping a legacy system from scratch using modern architecture, tools and databases running on a new hardware platform. This strategy is a huge and risky undertaking.

- The chicken little strategy which aims to provide support for mission-critical legacy systems by incrementally selecting and migrating parts of the legacy EIS and by allowing the legacy and target system to interoperate during migration. In this way the legacy EIS and the target EIS form a composite EIS, which collectively provides the required mission-critical functions. Interoperability is provided by a gateway, which is a software module interposed between the operational software components to mediate between them.

Environmental modernization of legacy systems has received considerable attention over the past few years and we refer the interested reader to Brodie and Stonebraker [Brodie 1995] who provide an excellent account of how to achieve EIS migration.

In this book we divert our attention to the modernization of legacy systems whose aim is to provide the business capabilities and functionality for new applications, such as e-Business. When dealing with the modernization of legacy systems that provide business level support, it is imperative that application developers understand the functionality of the business part of the legacy system. This is no easy task as there is very often little or no surviving documentation. Even in cases where the development work was originally documented, chances are that the systems have been amended in the intervening years to address new business requirements in such a way that trying to reverse engineer the documentation to find where the business logic resides is a task not to be undertaken lightly.

In order to cost-justify legacy application reuse, some strategy for assessing the value of both legacy and new applications must devised. This strategy is useful in assessing build, lease and reuse options along with variations of these options. Evaluating legacy assets can be done in several different ways by taking into account, for instance, the legacy application's contribution to the business and valuing legacy software based on its replacement cost [Ulrich 2002]. Techniques for evaluating application development can be found in [Ulrich 2002].

Deciding whether to modernize a legacy system and which method to use depends on the degree of the system's uniqueness to the enterprise and on its "health", i.e., the quality and flexibility of its code. Best candidates for modernization are low-quality strategic legacy applications often found in industry sectors such as banking, insurance and brokerage. The best strategy for such cases is to preserve the business part of these applications by organizing them into new workflows. Other candidates for modernization are high-quality legacy systems with standard functionality [Erlikh 2001]. These applications are most likely candidates for integration with modern enterprise solutions and e-Business applications. In most cases these legacy systems should be modernized by extending their use to a Web environment. Such applications can continue functioning in their present platforms but can be easily accessed through well-defined APIs from Web-based applications.

There are a number of ways in which legacy modernization can be achieved. Here, we distinguish between two broad categories of approach to legacy system modernization:

- *Non-invasive* approaches require that the existing application flow remain intact.

- *Invasive* approaches intrude upon the functional legacy code and require that the legacy system be modified.

Each of these approaches has advantages and disadvantages, which we shall cover below. Regardless of the approach taken, the decision should proceed primarily not only from the technology point of view but also from business driven criteria such as cost, benefit and risk.

Before introducing non-invasive versus invasive approaches to legacy system integration and assessing their relative merits, it is useful to recall that most conventional business systems have three tiers that are present regardless of the operating platform or host. These are: the presentation tier, the processing (or business logic) tier and the data tier, see Section 6.2. Most legacy host applications do not provide a clear separation of these three tiers. These are typically inextricably tied together, thus making it complex, time-consuming and even impossible to separate and distribute the tiers for integration purposes.

16.3 Non-invasive approaches

Non-invasive approaches enable existing business functions to be accessed through a new presentation interface, typically created through screen scraping, APIs, wrapping, or middleware access. Because these approaches use existing interfaces to legacy systems and legacy systems are tied so closely to the original program functionality and flow, non-invasive approaches tend to be very limited in the amount of flexibility they can provide. While a complicated presentation tier (front end) to legacy systems can be created to handle the mapping of client requests to legacy functions, such approaches can result in extremely high maintenance overheads when the legacy system changes. In many cases legacy systems that are modernized by non-invasive approaches are almost impossible to maintain.

16.3.1 Refacing

Refacing is the process of replacing a standard terminal emulation (dialogue) screen, e.g., VT100/220, with a user-friendly graphical interface. This approach enables a given host application to blend in seamlessly with GUI desktop environments. This approach is relatively inexpensive and can be achieved in a short time. However, it suffers from a very serious drawback: the end result is only marginally different from the original legacy system. Although, the presentation layer is enhanced the business logic still remains unchanged.

16.3.2 Repurposing

Repurposing entails capturing, encapsulating and exposing screen-based EIS without modifying the legacy host application. Like refacing, repurposing is a non-intrusive approach that results in an application that blends in with GUI desktop environments [Ryan 2000]. Instead of replacing standard emulation screens with a user friendlier GUI as is done in refacing, this approach redesigns the dialogue by employing different

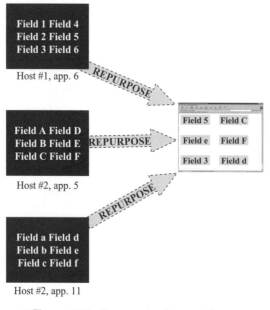

Figure 16.1: Repuposing Legacy Systems

screen sequences, data capture mechanisms and presentation logic (see Figure 16.1). While refacing an application merely replaces terminal emulation screens on a one-to-one basis with a GUI, repurposing exploits the fact that the business logic of a legacy application is to a large extent exposed by the sequence of terminal emulation screen evoked by user actions. Repurposing serves to capture and encapsulate this business logic by combining multiple screens into a more useable form.

Repurposing not only integrates data from different host applications into a single presentation, it also may involve building new business logic for various purposes such as, for instance, updating data sources, performing calculations, triggering events, and automating tasks in general. It is more time consuming and costly than refacing but ultimately yields better results, especially when the business logic and the flow of work are not suitable for new users.

Repurposing results in applications that can be substantially different from the legacy systems involved. Despite the fact that repurposing is considered to be a non-intrusive approach, developers are frequently required to alter the workflow of involved applications to better suit the business processes in the enterprise, streamlining these processes and increasing productivity [Ryan 2000].

16.3.3 Presentation tier modernization techniques
One of the most successful methods for modernizing the presentation layer of legacy systems is a technique known as *screen scraping* that can be used for both refacing and repurposing [Carr 1998].

With screen scraping, a client-based emulator or server-based application sends and receives data streams intended for a mainframe terminal and interprets them as graphical presentations in line with modern desktop applications (see Figure 16.2). The application retrieves from those data streams the data the end-user needs to access or wishes to modify on the host.

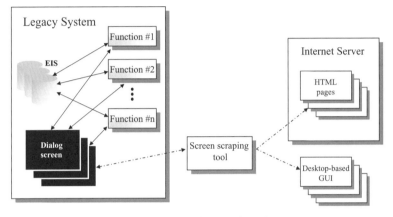

■ **Figure 16.2:** Screen Scraping

Screen scraping avoids making any changes to the legacy system while making it easier to use. It can, however, enable fairly extensive modifications to the sequence of information presented to the user by combining several screens into a single graphical representation. This gives the effect of modifying the application while in reality business logic remains intact. Usually, a screen-based application provides the correct business logic for accessing the data. For example, if a user needs to create a new customer record, they can be certain that the host application will update and notify all programs and databases that are affected by such a change. There is no need to discern the internal host database structure and application logic in order to ensure that the new application will perform all the required steps.

Screen scraping allows the legacy system to be accessed from different platforms (including the Internet and World Wide Web, as shown in Figure 16.2). From the perspective of the legacy system, the new GUI is indistinguishable from an end user entering text in a dialogue screen. From the user's perspective, screen scraping is successful as the new system gives the feel of a modern user friendly GUI. However, from the perspective of the enterprise, screen scraping is only a cosmetic mapping of dialogue screen to windows and the new system is as inflexible and difficult to maintain as the legacy system.

Screen scraping products range widely in their degree of sophistication, scalability and robustness. In the older two-tier applications, the client application that provides the new user interface can communicate directly with legacy back-end systems. More recent products provide programming intensive APIs generated from legacy interfaces. In this way, developers can issue API calls from their preferred development environment.

16.4 Invasive approaches

Invasive approaches in which the legacy system is actually modified are inherently far more powerful and flexible than non-invasive approaches. Business functions and logic can, for example, be separated from workflow and implemented as components that provide specific business services. The usual drawback to this approach is that it can be difficult to analyze and modify legacy systems by hand, and there is potential for introducing errors into production systems. New tools that automate such transformations make invasive techniques much more attractive and enable such tools to complement EAI approaches.

16.4.1 Maintenance

Legacy maintenance is an incremental and iterative process during which small discrete changes are made to the overall system [Weiderman 1997a]. These changes are often corrections to bugs or small functional enhancements and do not involve major structural or functional changes. We may define software maintenance as a fine-grained, short-term activity focused on localized changes. A typical example of localized software maintenance was the Year 2000 (Y2K) problem. This was because dates were most often handled idiosyncratically throughout the system rather than by one single procedure that is called in many places. Software will always have these low-level maintenance requirements, and some of these changes can add value rather than merely maintaining the value of the software.

With software maintenance, the structure of the system remains relatively constant and the changes produce few economic and strategic benefits. There is a tendency to respond to one software requirement at a time. Legacy system maintenance has a number of limitations [Comella-Dorda 2000]:

1. Competitive advantages derived from adopting new technologies are seriously hampered. For example, Web-centric computing or graphical user interfaces are typically not considered as part of maintenance operations.
2. The compound impact of many small changes can be devastating due to the erosion of the legacy
   - system's conceptual integrity. EIS tend to expand with time and maintaining them to adapt to changing business needs becomes almost impossible.
3. Finding required expertise in obsolete technologies becomes increasingly difficult and expensive.

Only through structural change can the software provide leverage for further development efforts. Thus the requirement is to try to increase the asset value of software by making it capable of accepting substantive structural changes [Weiderman 1997a].

16.4.2 Replacement

Legacy replacement is the appropriate strategy when legacy systems can no longer be maintained cost-effectively or for cases where the legacy systems cannot cope with business needs and for which modernization efforts and costs are prohibitive. Replacement is normally used for systems that are undocumented, outdated or non-extensible. Replacement allows the implementation of parts of the application to be replaced without affecting other parts. The key to success when replacing a legacy application is to refine its business logic and processes to match the requirements of the new application and to ensure that it integrates well with the existing application environment.

Replacement usually amounts to building a new application (to replace the legacy) from scratch and is a very cost intensive and laborious task. However, in some cases it is also possible to replace a legacy application with off-the-shelf software packages. As a general rule we should typically try to replace a low-quality legacy application that offers a generic industry solutions with off-the-shelf ERP packages. Prime candidates for ERP replacement are such applications as accounting, payroll and human resources (HR) applications.

Building applications from scratch involves high risks that must be evaluated before choosing this strategy. This type of replacement has these requirements:

- the enterprise's goals, objectives and customer needs are carefully reassessed

- legacy assets are carefully evaluated analyzing all possible cost tradeoffs and

- planning, design, extensive testing and evaluation of the new application are undertaken.

Building or purchasing new applications always requires the ability to leverage information regarding existing applications. If this is not realized then fundamental problems relating to software quality may ensue.

When considering replacement as a technical strategy, one should focus on the degree of business process automation and on how closely this legacy application is coupled with other applications. The less a business process is automated and the looser its coupling with other processes and applications, the lower the risks of the legacy replacement strategy. If, for example, a business process is supplemented with manual activities then the risks of the replacement strategy failing decrease.

The greater the flexibility of the business process the greater the chances of success of the replacement strategy. The flexibility of a business process is measured in terms of structure of the process itself and the degree of its coupling with other processes. Inflexible processes are those that are highly tuned, very efficient, involve very large capital investments and have problematic labor relation agreements [Estes 2001]. For example, if we consider business processes in the automobile manufacturing sector, then these are highly inflexible since there is very little likelihood that they are going to change. Changing the way that an automobile manufacturer is building or producing its cars is an extremely expensive and lengthy undertaking. By contrast, a consulting company that offers customized services can be flexible in its business processes, providing a unique (customizable) service to each client.

16.4.3 Re-engineering and transformation

The approaches to legacy system modernization are changing rapidly along with the changing technology and business requirements. These two factors are pushing the evolution of legacy systems in several ways. The two invasive approaches to software evolution that we described in the previous section appear to be on the decline [Weiderman 1997a]. Firstly, it is rarely possible, because of huge investments in legacy systems that have evolved over many years, to completely replace those applications and start from scratch. Therefore the so-called "big bang" approach to legacy system integration is not often feasible. Secondly, it is increasingly less attractive to continue maintaining functional legacy systems at the lowest level of abstraction, expecting them to evolve into maintainable assets. Therefore, the fine-grained maintenance approach is also undesirable because it neither adds value to the asset nor provides for future leverage. This leaves re-engineering and transformation as the most appropriate approach to legacy system integration.

Legacy re-engineering and transformation uses legacy systems and data in the broad context of the business and its information architecture. The primary focus of legacy re-engineering and transformation are businesses, business processes, the enterprise information architecture and how a legacy system can contribute to implementing the architecture without propagating the weaknesses of past designs and development methods.

Re-engineering encompasses a variety of tasks related to understanding and modifying software applications. In particular legacy system re-engineering is a technique that combines reimplementation of parts of the legacy system and the addition of new capabilities. Re-engineering is defined as "the examination of a subject system to reconstitute it in a new form and the subsequent implementation of the new form" [Chikofsky 1990].

Re-engineering involves the transformation of business functions and data into different structures, with modern languages, e.g., Java, and a different surrounding environment. It poses its own technical challenges such as transforming the legacy system implementation language, extracting objects, reallocating functions and providing the equivalence of functionality [Sneed 1995]. Consider, for instance, the NCC case study, where complex code was partitioned, based on its functionality and upgraded with modern technology.

Re-engineering embraces the concept of legacy system modernization by seeking to implement a new environment that builds on past investments and seeks to preserve past investments by reusing legacy artifacts. Software modules undergo restructuring, conversion, testing and post-documentation. The ultimate aim of a proper re-engineering strategy is to hide (encapsulate) legacy systems and applications behind well-defined interfaces that more closely relate to the business environment and processes and allow changing or replacing implementations without affecting other systems and applications.

The legacy system re-engineering process involves the disciplined evolution of an existing legacy system to a new "improved" environment by reusing as much of it (implementation, design, specification, requirements) as possible. The resulting system may or may not run on a different platform. There are many factors that would suggest such a move, such as, for instance, the discontinuation of the old platform. In its most fundamental form the process of re-engineering includes three basic tenets. These are:

• understanding of the existing application, resulting in one or more logical descriptions of the application

• restructuring or transformation of those logical descriptions into new, improved logical descriptions and

• development of the new application based on these new logical descriptions.

The application resulting from the modernization must meet several business requirements. However, as the legacy system already partially satisfies these requirements, it is essential for the success of the modernization that the functionality of the legacy system and how it interacts with its domain be understood. Understanding of a legacy system's structure and operations is critical to transforming it intelligently to a new architecture. A poor understanding of the legacy system will lead to an incorrect specification of requirements for the target system and ultimately a failed migration project. Application understanding is a prerequisite for system re-engineering and is based on program understanding techniques. Application understanding is critical to the ability to evolve unproductive legacy assets into reusable enterprise assets. This process involves identifying and analyzing the execution paths, data flows and business processes within the applications. On the downside this approach is time consuming and costly. A typical legacy system has often millions of lines of code distributed over hundreds or even thousands of individual programs.

Once legacy system analysis is achieved, enterprises can determine whether the business rules are obsolete and need changing or whether they can be changed. As a result, the ensuing code segmentation and integration with new e-Business applications can be initiated in an organized manner. Application understanding is based on program understanding techniques. *Program understanding* is the process of acquiring knowledge about a software artifact through analysis, abstraction, and generalization [Tilley 1996, 1997].

Legacy transformation is focused on deriving a detailed grasp of an enterprise's legacy environment by extracting key logical information that describes the existing legacy system. The information extracted is typically extremely detailed and establishes the data model, process model, business logic, interface model, and usage model for the application. This information is then used as a basis for either developing or deploying a new application. Sophisticated tools in this space automate much of the reverse engineering process to obtain an understanding of the legacy system and automate some of the aspects of forward engineering new software components [Erlikh 2001]. *Forward engineering* is defined as "the traditional process of moving from high-level abstractions and logical, implementation-independent designs to the physical implementation of a system" [Chikofsky 1990].

Re-engineering involves more extensive changes than maintenance, but conserves a significant portion of the existing system. Changes often include system transformation or restructuring, important functional enhancements or the incorporation of new software attributes [Comella-Dorda 2000; Seacord 2001]. *Restructuring* can be defined as the process of transforming one form of representation to another at the same relative level of abstraction provided that the resulting representation preserves the semantics and external behavior of the original representation.

In retrospect, re-engineering is used when a legacy system requires more pervasive changes than those achieved during maintenance. Its aims are to increase the strategic and economic value of the legacy software that needs to be preserved by making it easier to integrate with modern and other modernized legacy software and to make it more of an asset than a liability (see Figure 16.3). Figure 16.3 shows that calls which were direct only to the presentation tier can now be divided into appropriate calls to the presentation business logic and data tiers without modifying application semantics.

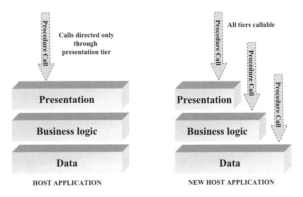

Figure 16.3: Application Restructuring

Types of legacy system re-engineering

We may distinguish between two approaches for program understanding depending on whether an understanding of the internals of a legacy system is required or just understanding the external interfaces of the application modules is required. The former technique is referred to as *white-box re-engineering*, the latter, *black-box re-engineering* [Weiderman 1997a]. Each of these techniques encompasses a form of *reverse engineering* that can lead to substantive structural change being performed on different modules within an application.

Reverse engineering is defined as "the process of analyzing a subject system to identify the system's components and their interrelationships, and create representations of the system in another form or at a higher level of abstraction" [Chikofsky 1990]. White-box re-engineering encompasses a form of reverse engineering that emphasizes deep understanding of individual modules and internal restructuring activities. Black-box re-engineering encompasses a form of reverse engineering that emphasizes an understanding of module interfaces and wrapping techniques.

In deciding which of the two transformation paths to follow, several activities must be undertaken. These include assessing the health of the application specifically as it relates to encapsulation, modularity, coupling, and cohesion; assessing personnel skills and capabilities of the technology accessible within the business unit; assessing costs, time-frame and risks of the various courses of action; modeling of the application domain, architectural principles, and system components; and selecting decision analysis tools [Weiderman 1997a].

In [Weiderman 1997b] the authors assert that the nature of program understanding should refocus its emphasis from a bottom up understanding of the internals of software modules (white-box approach) to a top-down understanding (black-box) of the interfaces between software modules as white-box re-engineering is the more technically challenging of the two activities and requires the legacy system to be in a healthier state.

In the following we draw the distinction between these two forms of program understanding and focus on the activities necessary for white- and black-box re-engineering.

White-box re-engineering: White-box re-engineering concentrates on reverse engineering techniques to gain an understanding of the internal structure and operations of an application. It aims at recovering lost structure and documentation and involves extracting information from the code using appropriate reverse-engineering and extraction mechanisms to create abstractions that help in the understanding of the underlying application structure. Usually, legacy code can be difficult to understand as it may have been created using ad hoc methods and unstructured programming and maintained with no updates to its documentation. Moreover, there may be little or no conceptual integrity of its architecture and design.

Automated analysis and understanding of legacy programs and code is a risky and laborious task with no guarantee of accurate results [Estes 2001]. Thus, it is not surprising that software and systems engineers spend inordinate amounts of time trying to reproduce the system's high-level architecture from low-level source code.

Once the legacy code is analyzed and understood, white-box re-engineering normally includes some form of restructuring. Restructuring can come in two forms: *application* (or system) *restructuring* and *code restructuring*.

Legacy restructuring and transformation is focused on deriving a detailed understanding of an organization's legacy environment by extracting key logical information that describes the existing system. One of the appealing properties of restructuring is the reuse of legacy assets. Reusing legacy assets is appealing for many of the same reasons that component-based development is appealing: reuse of existing application logic and the ability to assemble applications out of pre-tested components with well-known quality. However, one of the major problems of this approach is the need to be able to partition (decompose) monolithic legacy applications into collections of self-contained, encapsulated components with restructured but well-defined business functional boundaries. The process of creating a component involves being able to extract discrete logic from the legacy environment with the desired level of granularity. This logic is then wrapped so that it effectively becomes a component with a well-defined interface. Automatic extraction of business rules is not possible in all circumstances; for instance, some business rules may not be expressed in the source code, but may instead exist in the data.

After the application is restructured, white-box re-engineering often includes some code restructuring. Chikofsky *et al.* [Chikofsky 1990] define code restructuring as the process of transforming one program representation form into another at the same level of abstraction while preserving the functionality and semantics of the original form. This type of transformation is normally used to enhance some quality aspect of the application such as performance or maintainability. Here componentization can be used again as a means to deliver effective code restructuring solutions.

The activities that are specific to white-box transformation include the following items [Weiderman 1997a]:

- Using conceptual modeling techniques to create domain-specific models of the application.

- Using appropriate extraction mechanisms to analyze and understand source program code.

- Creating abstractions that facilitate program understanding and permit navigation, analysis, and presentation of the resultant data structures.

Black-box re-engineering: What transpires from the preceding discussion is that it is more sensible and economical to re-engineer legacy systems by treating their constituent components as black boxes and by reinterfacing them, than it is to fully understand what is inside these boxes. Hence, legacy system understanding should de-emphasize the fine-grained, bottom-up, exhaustive, computationally intensive techniques used in the white-box re-engineering approach in favor of coarse-grained, top-down, targeted analysis. Back-box re-engineering involves studying the inputs and outputs of legacy systems within an operating context in order to gain an understanding of the system interfaces. Black-box re-engineering is often based on legacy wrapping techniques that we shall examine in Section 16.5.1.

In general, the black-box approach is preferred to white-box re-engineering because the technology for interfacing and integrating is developing much faster than the technology for program analysis and understanding. Thus with black-box re-engineering approach, instead of changing software only at the level of instructions in a higher level programming language, change is made at its architectural level. The system architecture and high-level understanding of the structure of the legacy system must be the focus of a system understanding effort.

A more detailed treatment of white-box and black-box re-engineering can be found in [Weiderman 1997a, 1997b]. The authors of these articles have developed an approach for legacy system re-engineering that has been employed in production-quality tools and used to transform legacy systems. The steps that are particular to legacy system black-box re-engineering can be briefly summarized as follows:

1. Understand the legacy application at a high level of abstraction using software engineering techniques, paying particular attention to interfaces and abstractions. Find components of the legacy application that can be potentially wrapped, assess them and build on them.
2. Consider wrapping technologies for encapsulating sub-applications and creating components that form the basis for product line systems. Apply those technologies in accordance with the framework identified in the previous item.
3. Consider using the Web for expanding the scope of the legacy system and as a development tool.
4. Develop an incremental implementation strategy towards the desired re-engineering targets. Having a goal and a strategy simplifies the problems associated with transitioning the new application into operational use (by decomposing into manageable and predictable pieces) and allows for mid-course corrections based on actual field experience and customer/user feedback.

Benefits of the re-engineering approach are derived from the ability of this strategy to leverage past IT infrastructural investments, at both a structural as well as at a semantic level, thereby ensuring its optimized reuse or basis for promoting evolution in the IT infrastructure. High levels of flexibility and utility therefore characterize this strategy. This is because the legacy transformation strategy is the only invasive approach that provides a logical basis for understanding the semantics of the existing IT environment. Both re-engineering approaches are not only adept at supporting evolution of the legacy system environment within the context of past IT investments; they are also equally accomplished in supporting evolution of the business environment.

Hybrid techniques

In many situations a combination of different approaches is required. With such a hybrid legacy system modernization technique, parts of the legacy system can be effectively maintained, others can be transformed by white-box techniques, others can be transformed by black-box techniques, while others can be replaced. The hybrid approach strives to address each part of the whole system in the most appropriate manner possible. When considering a hybrid approach, a careful analysis of the legacy system is necessary on several fronts. Several factors need to be carefully considered and evaluated, such as, for instance, what is the internal health of the application, how well it is satisfying application needs, what fragments of the whole system require the most treatment, what are the most cost-effective technologies that can be used, and so on.

Planning the legacy system re-engineering

Legacy system re-engineering is a very expensive procedure that carries a definite risk of failure. Hence, it is not surprising that the overriding business concern is whether re-engineering is worth the effort or whether legacy systems should be replaced with new ones. Justifying re-engineering of legacy systems is more difficult than justifying an ordinary application development as, in many cases, re-engineering may be viewed as a last resort. Consequently, before any decision is taken, an intensive study should be undertaken to quantify the risks and benefits, and fully justify the development of the legacy system involved [Slee 1997]. The projected target environment needs to be considered carefully in terms of the legacy system functionality and legacy environment to identify expected benefits in both the long and short term. The costs involved in the actual migration should be weighed against these benefits to provide a significant cost benefit analysis and an estimation of the possibility of failure. Sneed [Sneed 1995] identifies five major steps to the legacy system re-engineering planning process:

1. *Project justification*: Justifying a re-engineering process requires that the quality of the existing software also needs to be analyzed using measurement programs and tools. The maintenance of the exiting software is assessed using adequate metrics to determine the application's reliability and maintainability. Finally, the business value of the application needs to be assessed using business value analysis techniques that take into account the market value of the legacy system, contribution to profit, and the significance of information the application provides.
2. *Portfolio analysis*: Portfolio analysis requires that the applications that are candidates for re-engineering be prioritized according to their technical quality and business value. Business objectives are derived from business strategies and processes, while technical assets are mapped against these objectives and evaluated using a comprehensive set of metrics [Slee 1997]. If an application has low business and technical quality it can be retired. If it has low business value and but high technical quality it should be carefully reassessed. If the application has business value and low technical quality it must be redeveloped. Finally, if an application has high business and technical quality it must be modernized.
3. *Cost estimation*: Cost estimation is a function that involves identifying and weighing all the software components to be re-engineered to estimate the cost of the re-engineering project. For example, the size of code is counted, as well as the executable statements, the data elements, the database accesses, while code complexity and quality is estimated.
4. *Cost-benefit analysis*: In this step, the cost of re-engineering is compared with the expected maintenance cost savings and value increases.
5. *Contracting*: The goal of this step is to achieve a maximum level of application re-engineering distribution in order to avoid bottlenecks.

Legacy system re-engineering methodology

One of the major problems during the process of re-engineering of legacy systems is identifying critical factors, risks and alternatives and in general developing a strategy that can be used to guide all the stages of the process of re-engineering legacy systems. The objective is to identify choices, illuminate benefits and risks, and provide insight into the implications of selecting a particular option. In the following, we present the elements of legacy system re-engineering methodology that is based on findings reported in [Surer 1996] and identify several fundamental tasks for performing legacy system re-engineering. These tasks are performed in sequence and include the following:

1. Analysis and understanding of the goals and resources of the enterprise with respect to the legacy re-engineering project. This task concentrates on such issues as the enterprise's strategic goals and objectives, the operational context of the enterprise, enterprise customer needs, as well as current legacy systems with respect to their current and future operational environment. This item contains elements of the project justification step described in the previous section.
2. Determining whether the cost and benefit of re-engineering are favorable for an application and a candidate set of services that can replace some functionality within the application. This task encompasses the portfolio analysis and cost estimation steps of the legacy system planning strategy covered in the previous section.

3. Identification of the execution environment in which the re-engineered application will be deployed. This task involves describing the impact of the differences between this deployment environment and the execution environment of the original application and of tools needed to re-engineer the legacy system.

4. Baselining the legacy system. This task involves obtaining, building, installing, configuring, testing and running the legacy code in the re-engineered environment. Performing this step may necessitate fixing parts of the application that depend on aspects of the legacy environment that are not consistent with the re-engineering and deployment environment.

5. Obtaining new services. This task involves identifying and installing new services, which can be invoked via an object interface by the legacy system. These services could be newly developed, purchased from a third party, or be a component encapsulation of some existing functionality, i.e., a wrapped service.

6. Analyzing the legacy code. Once the legacy system and services are installed in the re-engineered environment, the code in the legacy system that implements the functionality to be replaced needs to be identified. Once this happens we next need to determine how to modify that code to use the new services in the previous step. This task makes extensive use of reverse engineering tools to provide high-level architectural descriptions, detailed dependency lists, source code organization and naming conventions, and the calls to the duplicate code.

7. Re-modularizing the legacy system code. The legacy system code may be partitioned into modules that do not reflect the functional decomposition of the application. Therefore, the code may need to be re-modularized to isolate functions that correspond to the new services. In this way the replacement of duplicated code is simplified and it is easier for the application to use new services developed in the future.

8. Connecting the re-modularized application to the new services. Once an application contains the appropriate modules described above it can be connected to the new services using some form of mediation to adapt to small mismatches and resolve code dependencies.

9. Integration testing of the re-engineered application. Objective of this task is to demonstrate that the migrated application meets the goals of the migration when running in the target environment with the new (modernized) services.

10. Documenting the migrated application. The final task concentrates on appropriately documenting th e migrated application and concerns itself with the description of the object definitions, service calls, and re-engineered code of the modernized application.

This methodology concentrates on maintaining flexibility throughout a re-engineering project's duration in order to minimize the risk and cost of unanticipated problems.

A few years ago, Bergey and colleagues at the Carnegie Mellon Software Engineering Institute [Bergey 1999, 2001] proposed a conceptual approach, called the *Options Analysis for Reengineering* (OAR) method, for analyzing re-engineering options to enable better software re-engineering decision making. This method provides a coherent technique for making technical, organizational, mission and programmatic choices in practical re-engineering decision making that can complement the legacy system re-engineering methodology we just described. The OAR method is a systematic, architecture-centric approach for identifying and mining reusable software components within large, complex software systems that addresses the following questions:

- How does one efficiently and cost-effectively rehabilitate legacy software?

- Which legacy components are worth extracting for reuse in a new software product line or with a new architecture?

- What types of changes need to be made to the components?

- What are the risks and costs involved in identifying and reusing legacy components?

In summary, OAR enables users to screen candidate software components; identify the best candidates for reuse; analyze, isolate and aggregate candidate components; and estimate the level of difficulty, cost, and effort required to mine and rehabilitate the software components selected. Using OAR results, a re-engineering team can focus its efforts on those high-value components that meet the technical and programmatic needs of the software product line or the new single system architecture.

16.5 Legacy modernization techniques

It is clear from the preceding discussion that it is not possible to properly integrate legacy systems into e-Business frameworks without invasive modifications to these systems. These modifications need to reshape legacy systems to provide a natural fit with Web-enabled application requirements.

Modernization of legacy systems introduces many challenges due to the size, complexity, and frailty of the legacy code. Size and complexity issues often dictate that these systems are incrementally modernized, and new functionality is incrementally deployed before the modernization effort is concluded. This in turn requires that legacy fragments operate side by side with modernized components in a business system.

In this section we discuss approaches for modernizing legacy systems, including consideration of the advantages and disadvantages of each approach.

16.5.1 Legacy componentization

Exposing legacy business services for use by e-Business systems raises integration issues. Legacy systems are largely self-contained and any integration required with other systems is usually accomplished at the data level (e.g., database extracts). This approach usually leads to the duplication not only of data between systems but also of the logic required maintaining that data.

The component-based nature of modern architectures has simplified the task of integrating modern systems, and the critical issue for organizations is how to integrate modern and legacy architectures as rapidly as possible. Componentization alleviates this problem by allowing access to one set of logic responsible for accessing and maintaining the data in the supplying (callable) system and facilitating entry of data in a single place. Componentization also streamlines the integration process by reducing the number of integratable pieces required to construct an application while retaining the appealing properties of object-orientation, such as reuse and specialization.

The philosophy behind component architectures is one of *isolation*: isolate one process from the inner workings of another process. To achieve this, components communicate via well-defined and published interfaces. The processes internal to a component are encapsulated, or hidden, from the calling process. These interfaces, once published and consumed, are immutable. The implementation of these types of interfaces to components facilitates the rapid development of highly integrated systems. However, when developing modern e-Business applications, the requirement to access reusable processes in legacy or packaged systems poses some interesting challenges.

The principle of componentization can be exploited for legacy systems. More specifically, legacy componentization involves surrounding the legacy system with a layer of component software that hides the unwanted complexity of the old generation system and reveals a modern interface to give it a new and improved functionality. The componentized legacy system acts as a server that performs the functions required by external clients, while shielding them from the legacy service implementation details. This means providing external clients with appropriate component interfaces to legacy systems, such that from the outside they look like any other component.

Legacy componentization allows complex legacy systems to be partitioned into a collection of functional components that can subsequently be deployed on different platforms of choice, e.g., on the client platform – including the existing legacy platform. Moreover, legacy componentization allows componentized legacy systems to be more naturally integrated in the overall enterprise architecture.

Legacy systems were, for the most part, not implemented in a fashion that lends itself to componentization. Presentation logic is often intertwined with business logic, which in turn is intertwined with data access logic. Legacy applications as already explained need to be analyzed and have business logic separated from presentation and data access logic only where reusable processes have been identified. This transformation makes these processes callable by other processes. It should be noted that componentization of reusable legacy processes and applications does not imply or require the massive conversion of an entire system.

In order to achieve relatively simple and highly integrated systems required for e-Business applications, *component wrappers* (or simply wrappers) need to be employed to encapsulate legacy and/or package functionality. A component wrapper is a component that provides service implemented by legacy software. A wrapper can be used to hide existing system dependencies, and provide legacy functionality for new component-based solutions in much shorter time than it would take to build a replacement from scratch and recreate those dependencies. In its ideal form, wrapping is a black-box re-engineering task whereby only the legacy interface is analyzed and the legacy system code and software module internals are ignored.

The purpose of wrappers is to insulate calling processes from all changes to the called systems. Consequently, component wrappers are responsible for accessing legacy and/or package functionality and present a consistent interface to the calling processes. For example, if a legacy system were to be replaced by a standard COTS package, the only instruments requiring changing would be the internal workings of the wrappers of the existing application, as opposed to all calling components. See Figure 16.4 for a schematic representation of this.

A component wrapper can provide a standard interface on one side, while on the other it interfaces with existing application code in a way that is particular to the existing application code [Whitehead 2002]. The wrapper with the existing application code it uses, forms a virtual component that is accessed via a standard component interface by any other component (see Figure 16.4). The component wrapper provides part of the functionality of the resulting component and part of it is provided by the legacy system that is wrapped.

In a nutshell, component wrappers perform specific business functions, have clearly defined APIs and can appear as "standard" components for clients and can be accessed by using modern industry

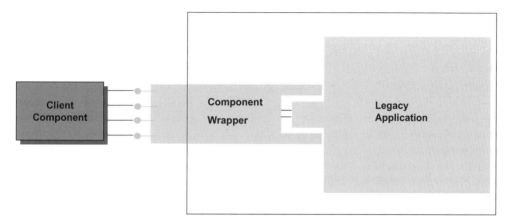

■ **Figure 16.4:** Component Wrappers: Connecting Client Components to Legacy Applications

protocols. Components wrappers are normally deployed in modern, distributed environments, such as J2EE or .NET.

When a legacy business process is wrapped, its realization comprises code to access an adapter that invokes the legacy system. The adapter may be built-in or may possibly be vendor supplied separate code. An adapter, unlike a wrapper, does not contain presentation or business logic functions [Whitehead 2002]. It is rather a software module interposed between two components in order to convert between their different technical representations and perceptions of their interfaces. Recall from Section 14.5.1 that an adapter is a piece of software that translates between the service invocation issued by a client and the service invocation expected by a server component. The role of the adapter is to insulate both the client and legacy system from any incompatibilities between them. An adapter interface may contain interface conversion facilities and protocol conversion, e.g., connecting CORBA to COM+ applications. In broad terms, the adapter must satisfy the external requirements of the program element and provide a mapping function between legacy and componentized functionality.

Normally, wrappers are employed perform the following functions [Whitehead 2002]:

- to wrap non-componentized legacy code

- to wrap an existing component so that its functionality can be extended

- to provide part of a component's functionality on a different platform, e.g., on the client platform – in which case the wrapper acts as proxy

There are several advantages to the componentization approach for wrapping legacy systems:

- It insulates new component-based software from legacy code and from the effects of changes to it.

- It reuses code in a component-based environment.

- Its migration to component-based technology, while preserving investments in existing legacy codes and applications. With relatively limited effort, the advantages of component-based systems are supported. We can, for example, build new components that use wrapper components in unanticipated ways, greatly improving system flexibility.

- After wrapping the functionality of the legacy system, we can reimplement wrapper components one at a time, without having to go through a "big-bang" replacement of the entire legacy system. This is possible because the system and the clients would not notice any disruption as the reimplemented component maintains the same interfaces provided by the wrapper. In time, it is possible to replace a legacy system completely.

A wrapper can be used to hide (encapsulate) existing system dependencies and provide legacy functionality for modern component-based solutions in a much shorter time and in a more effective manner than building a replacement from scratch. The wrapper component usually provides standard interfaces, such as for example EJB or COM+.

16.5.2 Requirements for componentization

The componentization of legacy applications is an activity that depends on the execution of several preliminary stages that involve sound software engineering principles. A number of activities should be performed before proceeding to the details of a wrapping implementation policy. The most important activities include:

1. assessment of legacy applications for componentization;
2. identification of specific component candidates;
3. selection of levels of abstraction for componentization;
4. code slicing;
5. modernizing business logic and
6. creating component wrapper APIs.

These are examined in some detail in the following subsection.

Assessing legacy systems for component wrapping

The ability to create components from a legacy environment is highly contingent upon how well-structured the source code is. Code that lacks structure (too few sub-routines or too many go-to statements) can be exceedingly difficult to componentize. In many cases component wrapping is not practical and it often requires understanding of the internals of software modules using white-box engineering techniques [Comella-Dorda 2000]. Thus, although wrapping is often tempting, it needs careful analysis if pitfalls are to be avoided.

There are several legacy system wrapping evaluation techniques that can be used to assess whether a legacy system can be wrapped, whether it is actually worth it, and how much work is involved. Justification for wrapping depends on a wide variety of factors, including quality of the legacy system, complexity or fragility of code, cost savings, and so on. In the following we summarize the most important considerations:

1. *Legacy application correctness*: In wrapping a legacy application we are making the assumption that the application fills the needs of the business. As the analysis of the business needs progresses it may be found

that the legacy application is so dated in regards to the enterprise needs that attempting to wrap it as part of a new solution is impractical. A system that does not properly model the business needs tends to complicate the design of other components that must compensate for its design flaws.

2. *Revenue increase/cost savings*: An important consideration when introducing components is to determine the costs for reimplementing parts of, or even entire, legacy systems directly versus the costs of wrapping parts of, or even entire, applications with components. The costs, savings and benefits of delivering each approach should be determined. In general, the costs for wrapping applications with business components from an existing design tends to be much lower than the cost of traditional application development. However, the learning curve and initial costs must be considered when making this decision. In addition, the economic benefit of expediting the crossover to a more efficient environment should be considered. This return on investment (ROI) approach appears to be fairly straightforward but can involve numerous variables that are difficult to discern.

3. *Component affinity*: Traditional monolithic applications tend to implement and control sets of business components. The business components that are tied together will probably need to be reimplemented at the same time. Identification of the dependent and independent business components is thus required and is achieved by examining the legacy systems.

4. *Performance*: wrapping a legacy system with component functionality will incur performance penalties. The degree of those penalties can only be determined on a case by case basis that considers environmental factors, application factors, use factors and the tools used to wrap the application.

5. *Targeting high-impact areas*: In all likelihood, all non-componentized legacy systems will eventually be reimplemented directly with components. But this transition must be gradual. Targeting the high-impact and/or costly legacy systems, or parts thereof, first, can smooth a transition.

Identification of candidate components and levels of abstraction

A typical legacy system is composed of a large number of independent programs. These programs work together in a hard-wired net of business process flows. In order to refine the legacy system into components it is important to segregate these programs into clearly identified collections that perform in-kind business functions. The top-down process of legacy system componentization begins by establishing logical subject areas of business functionality, which should be performed by a subject-matter analyst. Each of the identified business areas serves as a foundation for components. Each business area should be examined for size and complexity by using industry accepted measurement statistics. If desired, large-sized business areas can be refined progressively until each business area is composed of a manageable number of programs and contains clearly defined target business functionality [Erlikh 2001].

Once the initial set of business areas is defined, every program within the legacy system is analyzed and examined on a macro level and is allocated into one specific subject business area. An attempt is made to fit each program into a single business area. If a particular program does not provide a clean fit into a single business area is restructured to produce a better fit. Alternatively, the program can be replicated into several business areas under a different name.

Selection of levels of abstraction for componentization

Once candidates for wrapping have been identified, the appropriate level of abstraction for components must be determined. The granularity of components should normally be defined at the level of subsystems where the scope of a component is expanded to include a number of data stores, along with a number of programs, as opposed to techniques that advocate decomposing subsystems and programs into multiple functions for separate wrapping. When it comes to wrapping and legacy componentization one should concentrate on identifying coarse-grained components. Reusing a larger component saves more effort, and thus larger components have greater value. Smaller components are more likely to be frequently reused, but their reuse saves less effort. This implies that fine-grained components are less cost-effective. Very large components also suffer some limitations. They are inflexible in the face of change, with changes taking longer to achieve.

Choices of appropriate levels of wrapping are likely to be driven largely by the ease of decomposition of legacy software and the time and cost constraints at any given stage of a legacy modernization.

Code slicing

The purpose of evolving monolithic code and integrating it with new environments is to create reusable component-based code. One of the biggest problems during this process is that code that was designed to process data sequentially, does not necessarily adapt easily to the object paradigm. In order for legacy code to maintain all of its functionality once it has been decomposed, the rules for partitioning have to be strictly enforced on the basis of complex algorithms.

Code slicing, also known as code splitting, involves the moving of select data and process logic definitions from one source module into a new source module [De Lucia 2001]. A given module may result in two or more source modules that could be implemented as subroutines or as standalone programs in a subsequent job step. The resulting modules perform the same functions as the original. Specific objectives of code slicing include:

• reducing the size of cumbersome, monolithic source modules;

• eliminating code that no longer has a business function or use;

• improving system clarity where overly complex source modules are involved and

• realigning code along more suitable functional boundaries.

Program slicing is a decomposition technique that determines the statements in a program that are relevant for a particular computation. A *program slice* is an executable subset of program statements, which preserves the original behavior of the program with respect to a subset of variables at a given program point [Weiser 1984].

From a formal point of view the definition of a slice is based on the concept of a slicing criterion. According to Weiser [Weiser 1984], a slicing criterion is a pair $<p, V>$, where p is a program point and V is a subset of program variables. A program slice on the slicing criterion $<p, V>$ is a subset of program statements that preserves the behavior of the original program at the program point p with respect to the program variables in V, i.e., the values of the variables in V at program point p are the same in both the original program and the slice.

In Weiser's approach, computing consecutive sets of indirectly relevant statements processes slices according to data flow and control flow dependencies. This type of slicing is commonly known as *static slicing* since only static information is used for computing slices.

In contrast to static slicing, *dynamic slicing* identifies the statements that affect a particular computation while also considering the information about a particular execution of the program. Usually, dynamic slices are determined considering *execution histories*, which are records of the statements executed during a run of the program. As during the execution of a program, a statement can be executed more than once, the slicing criterion for identifying a dynamic slice is extended so that it also points to a particular occurrence of the statement under analysis [Binkley 1996]. Hence, a dynamic slicing criterion specifies the input, the variable of interest, and distinguishes between different occurrences of a statement in the execution history.

In general, there are two main strategies for dealing with code slicing that are applied to the two different types of slicing:

- A data flow approach, where a program is modeled as a *control flow graph* (CFG), computes the data flow information (the set of relevant variables for each program statement/node in the CFG) and then extracts the slice.

- A graph reachability approach, where a program representation is based on *program dependence graphs* (PDG). PDG is a program representation technique where nodes represent statements and predicates, while edges carry information about control and data dependencies. The slicing algorithm is performed on the PDG and then the slice from the PDG is translated into the corresponding program slice.

Although constructing the PDG is more complicated than building a CFG for the same program, the slicing approach is based on PDG and is much more efficient. The entrance criteria for code slicing include:

- determination of business objectives driving the slicing approach;

- completion of the process flow analysis task of the technical assessment;

- application staging for code slicing candidates;

- completion of the code flow analysis and removal of dead code;

- functional hierarchy analysis based on requirement to achieve some degree of functional realignment/coupling between ensuing components.

Legacy system componentization is conducted on the basis of code slicing tools that support operations on legacy programs, including backward slicing, forward slicing, and chopping techniques that can help the program analyst gain an understanding of what legacy code does and how it works. A code slicing tool typically consists of a package for building and manipulating control flow graphs and program dependence graphs.

From the program analyst's perspective, the code slicing tool's main capabilities must include the ability to perform:

- forward and backward slicing with respect to a given set of program components

- chopping of a program with respect to given sets of source and target components and

- illustrating control and/or flow dependences between program components.

Typical code slicing tools support *static analysis*, *code restructuring* and *code remodularization* tasks. These tools are used to represent information as required by the code slicing task.

The static analysis task must be able to graphically analyze code to produce information on how interrelated portions of code are. The analysis is used to identify favorable split points at which to create reusable code.

The restructuring task identifies and removes dead code from the restructured output; many of the restructuring tools can be used in conjunction with brief manual code changes to split programs.

The main goal of a code remodularization task is to perform code slicing to carve out segmented functions of a program and to turn them into new called modules. The slicing tool must be able to perform automated slicing based on multiple situation-dependent criteria.

The final stage of process transformation is the actual creation of the component wrappers that have been defined after partitioning. If these components are targeted to specific middleware, the middleware wrappers are automatically generated to complete the process.

As part of the transformation process, a special class of components that exist in every system needs to be identified. These components perform common system utility functions such as error reporting, transaction logging, and date-calculation routines, and usually work at a lower level of abstraction than business components. To avoid processing redundancy and to ensure consistency in system behavior, these components need to be standardized into a system-wide reusable utility library.

Business logic modernization techniques

Legacy systems typify the accumulated knowledge of the business processes of an enterprise. These business processes implement the business rules that run the enterprise. Moving into future generation technologies without a full understanding of this knowledge base is risky at best and may prove to have potentially disastrous consequences for the smooth functioning of the enterprise.

Recall that business rules are core business policies that capture the nature of an enterprise's business model and are buried in a legacy application. For instance, for a healthcare application, business rules may include policies on how new claim validation, referral requirements, or special procedure approval are implemented. Because these rules are fundamental to a business model they are technology independent.

Business rules exist within legacy applications in many different guises. In older generation procedural code, business rules may be difficult to identify due to their close association with presentation logic and/ or data management activities. Structured code generally reflects more easily identifiable business rules. The extraction of business rules from legacy code is generally termed *business rule recovery*. The accuracy with which this task is performed is key to application modernization whether this means re-engineering, replacement, or enhancement.

During the legacy modernization process, core business logic must be identified and mapped out to show the interrelationships of the code performing the application's business function (see, for instance, the NCC case study). The solution is to extract the business rules from an application program by building a map of the relationship of the code necessary to perform the business function of the application. This may happen using similar techniques to code slicing whereby program-affinity analysis is performed to produce call maps and process flow diagrams. Call maps, PDGs and process flow diagrams tie the application's business rules into unified process units and contain program-to-program call/link relationships. These maps and diagrams make it possible to visually identify connected clusters of programs, which are good indicators of related business activity. In this way legacy programs can be arranged into clearly defined collections that perform similar business functions, which means establishing logical subject areas.

Once core business logic is identified and mapped, it can be broken up into standalone components deployable on client/server and Web-based environments for use in e-Business applications. This process creates collections of programs that perform a specific business function.

Organizations may find it more convenient to break up the conversion process into two steps:

1. translation of existing code, data migration, and associated testing and
2. addition of new functionality.

Before making any changes to program logic and structure, organizations should first test the end-result of the migration process for functional equivalence with the original legacy application.

A variety of *knowledge mining* techniques can be used for best-fit approaches to business rule extraction [Erlikh 2001]. Knowledge mining is the process of determining and understanding what application assets exist within existing applications. An objective of knowledge mining is to identify the business rules that are currently supporting an organization's operations and to use these as input into the planning process for modernization initiatives. This technique identifies, extracts, and translates vital business rules and workflow, selectively moving only relevant parts of a legacy system to the new platform.

Knowledge mining of business rules from existing applications is at the core of fine-grain componentization [Erlikh 2001]. Although business rules are, in effect, not object-oriented by nature they provide a high degree of modularity and encapsulation of a specific business function and can form the basis for reuse. Thus, they provide a solid foundation for fine-grained componentization. Through knowledge mining techniques, legacy applications can be partitioned into collections of self-contained, encapsulated components with well-defined business functional boundaries.

Modern tools such as Relativity's RescueWare [Hurwitz 2002] provide aids to facilitate legacy system analysis, reconditioning, extracting value from legacy applications, and, in general, moving legacy assets closer to the software architectures that underlie new development. Such tools use sophisticated mathematical models, based on advanced graph theory algorithms for automated business rule identification and extraction. Once the business rule and its point of origin are identified, the RescueWare tool extracts the business rule itself automatically. The analytic information is presented in easy-to-comprehend diagrams that the user can visually examine to identify the origin of business rule extraction, i.e., the location in the program where the final result of the business rule computation is available.

An important requirement when selecting a migration tool is that organizations need to consider the quality of the generated code. Tools that map every component in the legacy language to a code equivalent in the target language can be considered as a cost-effective option as they provide major time savings.

Creating component wrapper APIs

After code slicing, business modernization and restructuring techniques are applied to a legacy system, a series of component wrappers are generated. At this point the boundaries of the newly established component wrappers are well defined but the modernized legacy system as a whole is still tightly coupled with components hard-wired to each other via program-to-program calls. The e-Business approach to large-scale system coupling is to remove from the individual component wrappers any direct knowledge of any other such components. This can be accomplished by breaking up program-to-program connectivity and replacing it with component APIs that are coupled with one of the emerging EAI techniques such as publish-and-subscribe, or business-process automation integration, see Chapter 17 for more details on EAI techniques.

Identification of component APIs is conducted on the premise that every mission-critical program is composed of three distinct layers:

- Business Rules

- Process Flows

- Environmental Support

As already explained several times in this book, business rules embody the fundamental business practices and policies of the enterprise. They provide the business foundation of the underlying system. They are a very stable and technology independent aspect of such systems.

Process flows tie the system's business rules into unified processing units. The flows are subject to greater change than the underlying business rules. In the case of Enterprise Application Integration, such process flows can be further factored outside the application code into an EAI engine.

Lastly, a significant portion of any system is dedicated to managing the physical aspects of the underlying operating environment. These tasks include screen interface, storage, and interprocess communications management. Environmental support is vital for the smooth functioning of component wrappers and modern components; however, it is considered a secondary activity to componentization.

16.6 Chapter summary

Established enterprises are finding that the shortcomings of their mission critical legacy systems are preventing them from expanding their corporate IT systems beyond the boundaries of the traditional enterprise. The ever-expanding universe of enterprise applications requires connecting dissimilar (legacy) systems with newer generation applications. Although legacy information assets support conventional business operations, it is extremely complicated and expensive to implement new business logic that incorporates the core business processes entrenched in legacy EIS. The desired solution is thus legacy system modernization.

There are two broad categories of approaches to legacy system modernization: non-invasive and invasive. Non-invasive approaches require that the existing application flow remain intact. Invasive approaches intrude upon the functional legacy code and require that the legacy system be modified. Regardless of the approach taken, the decision should proceed not only from a technology point of view but also from business driven criteria such as cost, benefit and risk.

Non-invasive approaches include refacing, repurposing and presentation-tier modernization techniques that enable existing business functions to be accessed through a new presentation interface, typically created through screen scraping, APIs, wrapping, or middleware access. Because these approaches use existing interfaces to legacy systems and legacy systems are tied so closely to the original program functionality and flow, non-invasive approaches tend to be very limited in the amount of flexibility they can provide.

Invasive approaches include maintenance, replacement, and re-engineering and transformation. Using these techniques the legacy system is actually modified. Thus they are inherently far more powerful and flexible than non-invasive approaches. Business functions and logic can, for example, be separated from workflow and implemented as components that provide specific business services. The usual drawback to this approach is that it can be difficult to analyze and modify legacy systems by hand, and there is potential for introducing errors into production systems. However, new tools that automate such transformations make invasive techniques much more attractive and enable such tools to complement EAI approaches.

Modernization of legacy systems introduces many challenges due to the size, complexity, and frailty of the legacy code and requires that legacy fragments operate side by side with modernized components in a business system. Such activities are supported by legacy componentization, a technique that allows complex legacy systems to be partitioned into a collection of functional components that can subsequently be deployed on different platforms of choice. In addition, legacy componentization allows componentized legacy systems to be more naturally integrated into the overall enterprise architecture.

Discussion Questions

- Legacy systems are preventing enterprises from expanding their corporate information systems beyond the boundaries of the traditional enterprise. Explain the shortcomings of legacy systems and why they need to be leveraged and not replaced.

- Re-engineering is a methodology to deal with legacy systems integration. Why is re-engineering the most appropriate approach to legacy systems integration? What are the main problems when dealing with the re-engineering methodology?

- What are the two major types of legacy system re-engineering and how do they differ? Why is the black-box transformation approach preferred to the white-box transformation approach? What activities are specific to white-box transformation and what are specific to black-box transformation?

- What is the philosophy behind legacy system componentization and what problem does componentization solve?

- Describe the major legacy system wrapping evaluation techniques that can be used to assess whether a legacy system can be wrapped. Explain whether each technique is actually significant and how much work is involved in performing it.

- How is business rule recovery and knowledge mining related to componentization activities?

Assignments

i. Suppose that a company wishes to replace several screen-based enterprise information systems with browser-based user interfaces. Explain how this company can use Web-enablement solutions and screen scraping and wrapping techniques to extend access to its applications with Web-enabled interfaces. Describe in some detail the steps that this company needs to undertake in order to modernize its EIS interfaces.

ii. A software development manager in a company has been given the task of performing an assessment of the legacy systems and suggesting whether they should be maintained or re-engineered. Describe how this software development manager might set up a program to analyze the maintenance vs. re-engineering process and discover appropriate metrics for her company.

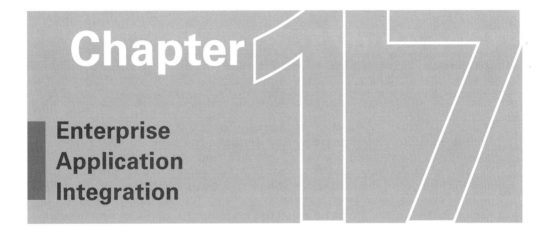

Chapter 17

Enterprise Application Integration

A pplications within an enterprise have been developed to provide various service functions for the organization. These may include functions such as customer tracking or account management systems, or they may be more inwardly focused employee management systems. To be competitive, an organization's core business applications – such as Enterprise Resource Planning, Supply Chain Management, and legacy systems – must be seamlessly integrated with Customer Relationship Management and Web-based applications to enable connectivity to suppliers, partners, and customers. For instance, if a customer's address or account status changes in the ERP system, it should be updated automatically in the CRM system, and vice versa, to keep these systems synchronized.

The main objective of modern enterprises is to respond effectively and quickly to competitive challenges and streamline business processes by integrating the various packaged and home-grown applications found spread throughout the enterprise. This challenge is addressed by *Enterprise Application Integration*. EAI is an integral part of the assembly process that facilitates integrating multiple applications at the enterprise level that were independently developed, may use incompatible technology and remain independently managed.

In Chapters 6 and 14 we presented e-Business technologies and middleware approaches that can be used in the context of EAI. These include event-triggered actions, data transformation, and messaging-based integration, and transaction-awareness. In this chapter we shall explain how these can be used in the context of singular or collaborating enterprises to support business integration activities.

Case Study

End-to-end supply management solution for Audi Hungaria[1]

With a workforce of 4800 and an installed capacity of 6600 engines in four engine families and 250 vehicles per day, Audi Hungaria has been Hungary's biggest investor and exporter and one of its highest-earning enterprises for years. Audi Hungaria quickly grew beyond its process and IT structures. To be prepared for the future challenges of the market, the company decided to integrate its corporate processes and to switch to on-demand functionality. The company decided that it wanted to develop an integrated enterprise infrastructure with standard software from SAP and other IT manufacturers.

An international team consisting of Audi Hungaria and IBM Business Consulting Services staff embarked on modernizing Audi Hungaria's structures with state of the art processes and infrastructure. Within two years, the experts implemented SAP R/3, SAP for Automotive, SAP Business Information Warehouse (BW), SAP Netweaver, Seeburger EDI and WebEDI interfaces, an optical archiving system and a comprehensive radio-frequency infrastructure and integrated them in the corporate IT. The plant's processes were extensively restyled in parallel.

Program planning is realized by means of SAP R/3 and takes place from the product group level right down to the type level. Over 350 variants of the four engine families produced by Audi Hungaria are manufactured. The planning process ends with the MRP net requirement calculation for external procurement of the engine and vehicle parts. SAP NetWeaver is a comprehensive integration and application platform that unifies and aligns people, information, sources and business processes across technologies and organizations and allows them to achieve enterprise application integration. It provides independence from existing databases and operating systems, full support for platform-independent Web services and business applications, and an open, standards-based development environment.

The enterprise application infrastructure targeted end-to-end supply chain management activities. Standard activities such as customer forecast delivery schedule, detailed forecast delivery schedule, programme planning, MRP requirement calculation, forecast delivery schedule, notification, goods receipt,

---

[1] This case study was summarized from: www-1.ibm.com/industries/automotive/us/en/content/ gcl_xmlid/21681/nav_id/casestudies.

invoice verification, warehouse management, production supply, packaging, warehousing, shipping and invoicing are all now possible in real-time because the new system integrates all processes across companies. Contact with customers and suppliers is realized via an EDI and WebEDI solution that is standardized throughout the company. In addition, smaller-scale partners are informed about forecast delivery schedules via an e-Business supplier platform providing notification of goods receipt in the same way. Therefore, suppliers are also completely integrated in Audi Hungaria's procurement processes.

Due to the seamless business process and application integration techniques and links with its partners, the company is able to resist and withstand fluctuations in the market. This is making it possible for of Audi Hungaria to concentrate on its core business and to shape prices variably, thus optimizing total cost of ownership.

17.1 The application integration imperative

In today's competitive global economy it is fundamental that businesses react quickly and efficiently to shifts in market trends. Responsiveness to market forces has become a necessity in ensuring the viability of the enterprise. This means that organizations do not have the luxury of being able simply to replace systems to meet integration requirements. Mergers, acquisitions, decentralization and other business decisions are forcing enterprises to modify and expand their application portfolios. Enterprises frequently find themselves having to reorganize their internal structure, and adopt new technologies and computing platforms as they strive for competitive advantages or when they try to merge with other enterprises. Increased acquisitions and mergers activity results in a need to integrate business processes of corporations in different geographical locations. In every instance, integration of applications and databases across these business units becomes an obvious by-product of the mergers and acquisitions. Integration across enterprise applications, ERP systems and databases can create significant opportunities for enterprises to provide a single unified face to the customer and stimulate collaboration and efficient end-to-end processes. In addition, the outsourcing of parts of the business process to specialist organizations continues, but now, because of the real-time information needs, it requires the information systems of the service provider to be integrated as well.

Enterprises need to be cautious in how they respond to the challenge of application integration. Unplanned, ad hoc integration will only exacerbate the problem. Unfortunately, the common practise until recently was for enterprises to create stovepipe applications – stand-alone, non-integrated systems – based on the distributed client/server model, serving the needs of specialized departments and divisions. For the past two or so decades, the idea of autonomy superseded the need for corporate consistency and application unity. It also became too hard, too costly and too risky for enterprises to write new, custom applications for the majority of their computing needs, so commercial off the shelf (COTS) systems, e.g., ERP packages, and applications were purchased.

This architecture fitted well the classical bureaucratic organization, with its grouping of activities and responsibilities by function, like sales, manufacturing and procurement. People are allocated to departments based on the type of work they do. For large organizations, like multinationals, a higher level grouping will combine activities into (strategic) business units based on similarity of products or region; in this type of grouping functional departments are being multiplied (e.g., each business unit may have a sales department). This type of organization functions well in relatively stable and predictable environments, as these types of environment do not require a high degree of cross-functional coordination. This organizational form benefits to a maximum from specialization; coordination is assumed to be easy to achieve with the common hierarchy and standard operating procedures being the main coordination mechanisms. As a consequence information systems, in this type of organization, are primarily designed to support functional departments.

The results of this evolution were multi-functional businesses that were effectively being run in silos, where "islands of automation" and mission-critical data were "locked" within disparate and ad hoc legacy systems. In fact, today most medium and large enterprises have a number of organizational and technological silos that have arisen as a result of functional specialization and evolution over time. Application systems within such enterprises generally ran as autonomous independent automated stovepipes exchanging data through batch file transfer, if they exchanged data at all. Often there are boundaries of product lines, business units, channels and geographies that create rigid walls that diminish an organization's ability to share information and create obstacles in providing value to the customers.

Figure 17.1 illustrates how a stovepipe architecture is comprised of independent applications, belonging to diverse departments disconnected from each other, and implemented as monolithic or client/server applications. This architecture comprises two elements, islands of data and islands of automation.

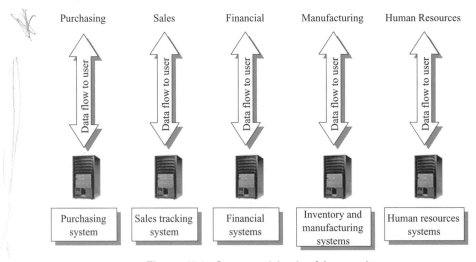

■ **Figure 17.1:** Corporate Islands of Automation

Islands of data: have the following three main consequences:

1. Each island of data has its own meaning of business objects, such as customers, invoices, shipments and sales.
2. There is data replication between the islands, creating data consistency and integrity problems.
3. None of the islands contain complete information about business objects, making it necessary to integrate data from multiple islands to create a unified enterprise-wide view of business objects.

Islands of automation: have the following three main consequences:

1. Each island automates only a limited and select set of activities.
2. There is duplication between processes contained in different islands of automation, which require synchronization and coordination between them.
3. Multiple islands need to cooperate to create enterprise-wide processes.

The islands of data and automation resulted in replication of data and application code within an organization, which required considerable effort for synchronization and data consistency by introducing transformation and updating rules scattered between multiple applications. Some of these applications were the result of specific developments while others were packaged solutions, such as ERP and CRM solutions. The resulting enterprise information systems, e.g., enterprise application programs, ERP applications, database and legacy applications, were thus heterogeneous with company takeovers, mergers and reorganizations being factors adding to this trend. In response, many enterprises adopted a strategy of Web-enabling each stovepipe independently. This approach achieves the short-term objective of making these systems available over the Web, but the resulting Web presence is fractured and difficult for customers to navigate. More importantly, this approach makes it extremely difficult to combine the functionality of various stovepipes and create new value-added services. For example, an enterprise might separately Web-enable its order entry system and its inventory system. Although this allows customers to check on product availability and order products, it does not enable them to check availability as part of the order entry process, let alone suggest alternative products as substitutes for out-of-stock items.

17.1.1 Target applications

Customer demands and competitive pressures are driving more and more companies to integrate not only their internal applications and processes but also to extend this integration to the suppliers, partners and customers that populate their business community. This overwhelming need to share data more efficiently internally, with members of the supply chain, and even across industry and national boundaries is driving companies to consider integration of applications.

To appreciate the application integration initiatives requires understanding the target applications to be integrated. The prime target for application integration is Enterprise Information Systems (see Section 6.5). Without EIS integration, information is confined to individual disparate systems. For example, a sales order is entered into a sales EIS, passed on to the account department, re-entered there in another system, and a credit check may be required that involves the credit control department. Each manual step introduces the potential for error in handling the information and significant delays as office workers normally rely on slow communication media such telephone and fax. Moreover, exceptions in the processing of the sales order, such as exceeding a credit limit require multiple steps to coordinate across all involved departments. This need for synchronization and interoperation between heterogeneous stovepipe applications caused the first attempts to interconnect the disparate islands and their underlying EIS. Integration of information systems may be defined as bringing together information systems that were previously isolated from one another.

As explained earlier in this book, today's business environment has become very dynamic and unpredictable. The traditional stovepipe organizational structures proved to be too slow and unresponsive to meet these changing demands. Actually in these organizations, the lack of coordinative ability, which is an essential characteristic of the functional structure, proved to be the major impediment. As a result, in many corporations the individual activities were being executed according to high standards; however, the overall process, of which an activity is a part, was slow, expensive and ineffective. This situation threatened the competitive position of many firms and necessitated a fundamental change in organization design: the "machine bureaucracies" had to transform to "organic" structures or "adhocracies". Companies moved from vertical to horizontal structures or, in other words, from function-based to process-based structures. This transition cannot be realized without an accompanying change in the information systems architecture. The new challenge for information systems is that besides supporting individual activities, in this environment they have to support connectivity and shareability of information.

In this environment the ability to leverage information within and outside the enterprise, where data must be exchanged between applications that are owned by different organizations, is essential for businesses to be competitive. Initiatives such as customer relationship management, supply chain management and knowledge management depend upon the integration of information from diverse data sources. What companies need is the ability to quickly build new systems that work with existing systems, integrate different applications, and upgrade applications to take advantage of new technologies like the Web. It is important to "reuse" applications and their data with no, or minimal, modification, whether they be legacy applications, newly developed applications or vendor packages. However, as enterprises rely mostly on purchased packages, achieving consistent data formats and semantics across all the different applications has become virtually impossible. For years, modern organizations have turned to packaged applications to automate many internal processes. As a result a large number of enterprises rely on different packaged software for their key business functions, such as ERP, SCM, CRM and vertical products. While these applications may deliver on their promise to speed operations and boost productivity, they are not necessarily designed to integrate with other function-specific applications. Enterprise computing has become inescapably a patchwork of disparate applications that are built at different times by different internal and external development groups, each operating without knowledge of the others' choices of tools and designs. An incredible wealth of information remains segregated among these different applications and their supporting databases. This makes it difficult for organizations to respond rapidly to change and, accordingly, remain competitive. Thus, a major requirement is that back-end functionality offered by core business applications such as ERP, be integrated with front-end functionality and supply chain management functionality to gain efficiencies throughout the supply chain. Other packaged software products and legacy business applications need to be integrated as seamlessly with each other and with CRM tools and also application servers that provide access to Web-based applications and services, which supply outward-facing connectivity to suppliers, partners and customers.

An additional component driving the need for architectures to support application integration is industry specific niche software applications. COTS applications, such as trouble ticket management and trading and risk management for energy marketing and trading companies, require not only complex integrations but also require complex workflows. Many of these niche COTS applications do not have the commercial market size to justify entry by larger ERP vendors. Therefore, it will be necessary for businesses to develop an integration strategy to address COTS applications [Roch 2002].

Few, if any, of the existing applications have been designed or built with future integration requirements in mind. Only recently have some package vendors begun to deliver interfaces to their applications to facilitate integration, and some operating system and middleware solutions become more interoperable. Even so, they often still require the adoption of an architecture which is at odds with the major applications and parts that an organization needs to integrate. It is the lack of common business and technical architectures that makes integration complex. It is not simply the differences in data formats or interfaces that matters, but the lack of common definition of the business concepts that underlies the different sources to be integrated. Hence, the pressure is to create an environment in which there is a controlled sharing of business data and processes. Because of these reasons, many organizations have realized that they can no longer standardize on a common set of software and integration tools. Instead, they need business software and integration tools to support *common integration standards*, so that the customers can integrate their own business applications as well as integrate up and down their supply chain. This calls for an integration strategy so that enterprises can increase their agility in responding to customer, market and other strategic requirements.

Such issues will be examined throughout this chapter.

17.2 Operational and financial drivers

In Chapter 10 we discussed Venkatraman's model, which shows that higher levels of IT-induced business transformation (e.g., moving from local exploitation to internal integration) result in higher potential benefit levels. As a result, the business motivation for an information systems integration initiative is basically the improved business performance. Benefits that come from an integration effort are tangible and intangible. The most important reported tangible benefits of systems integration are the reduction of costs, in particular, inventory costs and personnel costs, productivity improvement, and improved cycle time. With regard to intangible benefits, improved availability of information throughout the organization, improved processes and responsiveness are considered to be key. These benefits occur in a stable business setting; they become even stronger in a dynamic setting. Organizations are constantly driven to change, to keep up with today's business environment. New business unit formation and the removal of existing business units cause IT to re-work existing integration or to build new integration to both legacy applications and purchased products. In addition these requirements many organizations are acquiring new business units or selling other business units. These pose new challenges for integration as there is a strong likelihood that merging companies will differ in numerous ways such as diverse EIS infrastructure, business processes and organizational cultures.

The focus on the supply chain, rather then on the individual firm, requires the enterprise to integrate firmly with suppliers and customers at the process level, not just the data level. This integration must be accomplished quickly and cost-effectively for organizations to compete effectively. These applications may take the form of e-Business in order management, billing, payments, transportation, and customer service.

Several enterprises have tried to address the integration challenge by standardizing on a single provider. However, according to the Open Applications Group Integration Specification (OAGIS) (`www.openapplications.org`), this approach presents several limitations:

- The inability of any one software provider to cover the entire range of applications that a modern organization requires.

- Internal drivers requiring support for fast reorganizations and integration with legacy applications or internally developed applications.

- External drivers requiring integration with business partners such as customers, suppliers, and transportation providers.

Expanding software choices have created a marketplace with at least four categories of software that many organizations must integrate such as ERP, SCM, CRM and specific vertical software for the organization. While these choices have created a wealth of options, they have also created the requirement for organizations to purchase software from several sources and integrate it with all business software it touches, including legacy applications.

Unfortunately, without a common approach, and without the cooperation of the technology vendors, this approach falls short of its promise. The primary reason for this shortfall is that this issue has too many dimensions for any one organization to solve. To respond to marketplace demands for cross-vendor industry capability, a number of the largest ERP vendors (including SAP, Oracle, PeopleSoft and J.D. Edwards) have moved rapidly to ensure that their offerings can be implemented as components. An outcome of this fact has been the vendors' efforts to create standards for inter-product communication and cooperation. Thus the major ERP suppliers founded the Open Application Group (OAGi) (`www.openapplications.org`) to develop interoperability specifications and standards for open application development at the business process level.

The costs of integration are not well documented. Many IT organizations do not keep specific records of the cost of integration. However, some estimates put the amount spent on application integration at approximately 100 billion dollars annually in the USA alone. This cost is not limited to installing new applications. The larger expense in time and money comes from the huge task of maintaining the APIs once they have been built and deployed.

17.3 What is Enterprise Application Integration?

One of the key enabling technologies that has emerged to help organizations achieve internal integration is Enterprise Application Integration. EAI seeks to eliminate islands of data and automation caused by disparate software development activities and to integrate custom and package applications (including legacy) to drive operational efficiency within an organization. EAI is not a technology per se, but a collection of tools, techniques and technology that enable applications to interoperate effectively. EAI may involve applications running on the same computer, on disparate computers within the same data center or on computers distributed across an enterprise network. EAI-based connectivity is the precursor to developing an integrated e-Business infrastructure and the automated support needed to fulfill e-Business transactions.

EAI is a strategy that does not specify products, tools or technology for its inception. It is an on-going process, utilizing new technology within the technical infrastructure to allow applications to mirror the ideal workflow of the business. EAI can be defined as the requirement to integrate the operational behavior, or business rules, of disparate systems, as well as the data that underlies them, into new business processes. EAI is non-intrusive: the applications being integrated do not change, or the changes are slight and insignificant.

The ultimate goal of EAI is to encapsulate the enterprise in a single virtual application of heterogeneous and autonomous parts working together in a cohesive system. At the core of EAI is the approach to the solution. Too many integration projects, in particular ERP systems, have come from a "bottom-up" perspective, where integrating the data was the objective, leading to processes having to fit around the data. EAI, on the other hand, demands that integration is driven by the business need, and thus uses technology as a means to an end.

Traditional EAI software provides the infrastructure to rapidly connect and interface information and systems between an organization's internal applications. The major characteristics of EAI are follows:

- EAI provides the infrastructure to *reuse, rapidly connect, interface* and *unify* information and business processes between an organization's internal applications into a cohesive corporate framework within the enterprise.

- EAI represents both the products and the process of integrating new and legacy applications (including packaged applications) with data files and databases.

- The purpose of EAI is to integrate custom and package applications and map data between applications to drive operational efficiency within the corporation. Typically, this means extending the major customer-interactions – such as registration and order management, invoicing and payment – and management of customer transactions, for example, accommodating requests from the Web for products and services and integrating the vast amounts of customer information. EAI includes both front-end and back-end processes – such as inventory, order management, and customer service – required for complete fulfillment of customer requests.

- EAI seeks to enable enterprises to react with consistency and speed through access to business information in real-time.

- EAI is non-intrusive: the applications being integrated do not change, or the changes are slight and insignificant.

From an e-Business perspective the most pressing requirements for application integration are twofold: *internal* or *intra-enterprise integration* and *external* or *inter-enterprise integration.* Internal enterprise integration is the classical form of EAI that we presented above. External integration is usually known as *e-Business integration* and refers to the technologies that extend a corporation's internal process and data and connect them with business processes, transactions and data of external enterprises; see Figure 17.2. We shall present the subject of e-Business integration in Chapter 18.

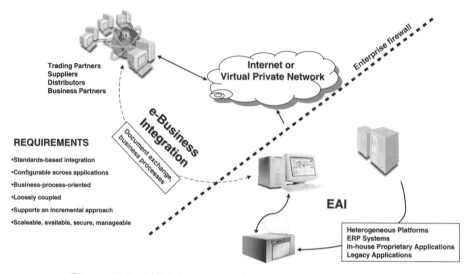

Figure 17.2: A High-Level View of EAI and e-Business Integration

One of the important characteristics of EAI is that it strives not only to integrate data within an enterprise but also business processes. Until very recently, enterprises used to deploy enterprise resource planning systems and software to add automation to business processes. ERP systems significantly improve internal organization efficiencies by integrating manufacturing, distribution, and financial data and workflows. However, they fall short as the Internet redefines the end points of business processes. New initiatives such as advanced planning, CRM, and e-Procurement provide chances for increased efficiency and collaboration by extending the reach of the enterprise beyond its barriers. As a result, many enterprises are acquiring a growing list of pre-packaged, point solutions designed to fulfill specific e-Business needs. However, to achieve the desired benefits, these systems must be integrated with enterprise back-end systems. This need for interoperation among the growing number of enterprise applications has given rise to EAI solutions. EAI products provide internal messaging mechanisms and infrastructure necessary for connecting applications together so that they can share information.

17.4 Typical topologies for enterprise application integration

Application to application integration is important because enterprises are under pressure to streamline business processes by customers, suppliers and trading partners. These individuals are demanding a consistent set of interfaces across all points of access, including corporate and division Web sites.

For two or more applications to effectively collaborate, they must communicate using a pre-negotiated protocol. Instead of modifying the original applications to conform to the protocol, integration techniques can be used to bridge heterogeneous contents and formats and transform incoming messages to a scheme that the destination system can understand and utilize.

On the technical front, significant changes are also contributing to the rise of EAI. As already explained in Section 17.1.1, ERP systems have been added as core elements to the enterprise-computing infrastructure and CRM systems were installed to meet business demands. Application servers are maturing as tools for developing and deploying distributed Web- and non-Web-based applications and services. Legacy application services and data are becoming components (see Chapters 15 and 16), liberated from the confines of legacy.

The history of application integration is linked to MOM and message brokering technologies, which remain a core EAI technology. Massage brokering technology minimizes the impact on both the source and target systems, thus reducing the cost of EAI and maximizing flexibility. Typical product suites in the EAI segment include:

- a message (integration) broker (i.e., a set of services for transformation and routing)

- various development tools for specifying the transformation and routing rules

- tools for building adapters into applications

- off-the-shelf adapters

- monitoring, administration, and security facilities, and

- message-oriented middleware, business process management facilities and portal services.

The different approaches to application integration are based on a different set of assumptions and observations about the nature of topologies used in conjunction with application integration, and each has its own strengths and limitations.

This section introduces the three most commonly encountered topologies in which application integration plays a major part and discusses their relationship with the middleware infrastructure we introduced in Chapter 14. Other topologies are also possible but are generally hybrids of these.

17.4.1 Point-to-point topology

For many years, IT departments have been trying to integrate disparate systems by building point-to-point bridges between them; see Figure 17.3. *Point-to-point integration* means applications are linked through hand-coded, custom-built connectivity systems and data is interchanged directly between any two systems. The approach is generally to "build an interface" for each connection. The interfaces are usually unique and the number of them keeps growing. Each one is designed and coded for a unique use. The sending system interface needs to convert its internal data format to a format acceptable for the interface of the receiving system. Examples would be direct TCP/IP socket interfaces between systems, flat file export/import, direct read/write to target database schemas. For example, a point-to-point implementation may be designed to access data from the flat files of a mainframe system and data by an order fulfillment application used by an enterprise's merchandise distribution system. However, this tactical approach has limitations. With each new connection, point-to-point solutions become unyielding, unmanageable, and unproductive. To realize the benefits of e-Business integration, enterprises need a more efficient way to link their systems together and extend them to the Web.

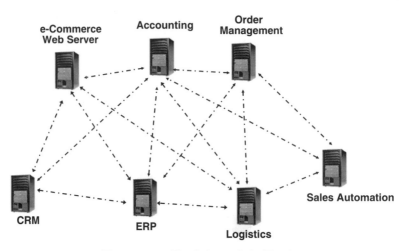

■ Figure 17.3: The Point-to-Point Topology

Point-to-point integration is a model for unbounded growth of interfaces. To look at this mathematically, the number of possible integration points between systems (assuming two-way integration for each system connection) is given by $n \times (n-1)$, where n is the number of systems to be integrated. For example, for integrating 2 systems, the minimum number of connections between them is 2. For 10 systems, the minimum number of connections is 90, for 20 software systems, the number grows to 380!

To understand the financial implications of this model consider that each interface usually requires some amount of time to build and then some amount of time and effort to maintain. This effort involves large amounts of work with no end in sight and it can drain organizational resources simply to maintain it. For instance, if maintaining one interface takes 5% of a person's time, which is roughly one day a month, the effort required to maintain the interfaces for 10 software components, where 90 is the number of connections needed, is the equivalent of 4.5 full time persons – just to maintain interfaces.

Traditional integration approaches concentrated on building non-invasive point-to-point solutions that required two interfaces per application integration point. Examples in inter-organizational settings are the traditional EDI connections between suppliers and buying firms, which have been especially efficient in stable supply situations with high volume transactions as found, for instance, in the automotive industry. Similar examples exist within large multinational firms where business units deliver goods and services to each other. Originally this was controllable since enterprises only required a select few systems to be integrated. Point-to-point integration is typically a tactical approach to address an isolated business need, and is not suitable for cost-effective reuse across other business areas. With the large number of legacy systems to be integrated within an enterprise, this practice does not scale well and incurs high costs through continuous maintenance and support. Point-to-point integration has several drawbacks:

- It is not scalable, is very complex as the number of integration points increases and can quickly become unmanageable.

- It is hard to manage and maintain as it introduces a tighter form of coupling (transport protocols, document formats) that makes it harder to change either of the two systems involved in an interchange without impacting other systems.

- It is inherently a static form of integration as it does not allow for rapid changes (e.g., swapping in of a new application) often required when integrating business applications both internally and externally.

- Moreover, it is expensive as it is not reusable. Each time there is a change in requirements or a new data source needs to be added, additional custom coding is required.

Point-to-point solutions tend to grow on the back of technology such as EDI. It should be noted that point-to-point solutions may also be used in the realm of e-Business. There they are generally used to connect an organization with a small number of key suppliers or even customers. The level of integration is typically very close, for instance, directly connecting a company's ERP solution with that of another, allowing the direct placing of orders and close inventory control. In order to achieve this, both organizations need to have rationalized their internal integration problems otherwise the solution will fail. Point-to-point solutions tend to provide for high traffic, dedicated requirements, supporting a small network (within an organization or between organizations that trade widely and frequently with one another) and a very tightly coupled integration pattern.

In summary, a patchwork of point-to-point links is a weak foundation for strategic a multi-source data integration system. It frequently requires maintenance and upgrading and significant investments, and delivers limited business value.

17.4.2 Publish–subscribe (shared bus) topology

A better approach to the point-to-point integration strategy is to provide an integration backbone capability by means of a publish–subscribe topology, which enables fast assembly and disassembly of business software components. A *publish–subscribe topology* uses an integration "backbone" that allows any application to be installed and integrated with the rest of the business by amending its connector to the integration hub that manages all its interactions. This topology allows integration to be accomplished by following the rules of making information available via publishing (broadcasting) mechanisms. Many asynchronous message-oriented middleware products are based on this architecture.

All publish–subscribe technologies (see Section 14.2) use subject or topic names as the loosely coupled link between publishers and subscriber systems. Publishers produce messages on a particular subject or topic name and subscribers receive those messages by registering interest in the subject name either explicitly or through some broader subscription scheme using wildcards. Publish–subscribe allows subscribing applications to select messages that these applications receive by topic (as specified by the publishing application) or by content (by specifying filters). Which applications receive the messages they send is not important for publishing applications. Any messages addressed to a topic are delivered to all the topic's subscribers. Every subscriber receives a copy of each message. Information is automatically *pushed* to subscribing applications without them having to *pull* or request it. Publish–subscribe topologies publish messages directly to the bus or network (see Figure 17.4). These types of topologies are known as *shared bus-based* solutions.

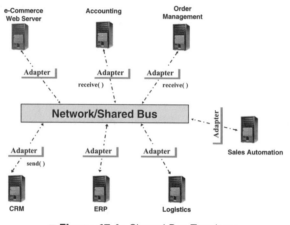

■ **Figure 17.4:** Shared Bus Topology

In a shared bus architecture, there is no centralized message server to coordinate the distribution of messages. Instead, each application client contains the functionality typically found in a message server, such as security and transaction support. All application clients are connected to a common message bus, typically the network layer of the IP multicast protocol. This multicast network layer routes messages among each of the application clients; however the clients themselves must perform all checks and balances to ensure that the message is delivered securely and reliably.

As the shared bus messaging model calls for a "many to one" integration model instead of a "many to many" integration model, the mathematical formula is simplified to a flat growth rate of 2n. The shared bus messaging topology uses the same principle as used in TCP/IP routing, where TCP/IP clients know a router or gateway that then routes all traffic onwards. If we now assume the same costs for maintaining an interface as we did in the point to point model above, then for n = 10 components, we need 20 connections. The effort required to maintain the interfaces for 20 software components could be as low as 1 full time equivalent person.

In the publish–subscribe messaging model the producer sending the message is not dependent on the consumers (subscribers) receiving the message. Optionally, clients that use the publish–subscribe model can establish durable subscriptions that allow publishers to disconnect and later reconnect to the bus and collect messages that were published while they were disconnected. Consider the following example. Every time a buyer in the purchasing department of a manufacturing firm places an order, notification is required of the accounting department, the receiving department, the central warehouse, the invoice control department, and the manufacturing department. As large firms may place more than 1000 buying orders per month, efficiency and speed in this process is mandatory. When an order is placed, e.g., through a supplier's Website, the buyer's purchasing information system will be updated; next the respective information systems of the departments mentioned above (the accounting IS, the receiving IS, etc) will be notified automatically. When an application needs to use publish–subscribe messaging, it must also hook into a messaging system that provides these mechanisms. The application uses an API exposed by the messaging system to access the messaging services. The messaging system uses a messaging adapter to implement the messaging API.

Thus, the publish–subscribe topology has the ability to transform messages of different types to enable applications that were not designed to work together to do so. Most EAI applications that rely on the publish–subscribe enterprise messaging model use the Java Message Service [Monson-Haefel 2001].

Modern publish–subscribe EAI messaging tools are based on the multicast model. With this model messages are published by being sent once in such a way that they are received simultaneously by all subscribers of the message. A multicast publish–subscribe application typically specifies the multicast address (a unique logical identifier) along with a topic name. The bus uses routers and switches that work in concert to track subscribers and route messages. Since this is being done within the network (bus) layer, multicast publish–subscribe can yield performance improvements and efficiencies when disseminating messages to large numbers of subscribers. These qualities are a major driver for adopting multicast publish–subscribe.

One of the distinct features of publish–subscribe EAI messaging is that it frees a source application from the need to understand anything about the target application. The source application simply sends the information it publishes to the network, which is responsible for routing it further. This requires that the network interprets and transforms the information being sent. The network then redistributes this information to any interested applications. For instance, if a financial application wants to make all accounts receivable information available to other applications that subscribe to it, it informs the network. The network then makes this information available to any application that subscribes to it. This feature of the publish–subscribe EAI topology can become a major liability. Typical EAI scenarios, such as general ledger, order fulfillment or invoice application interfaces, involve a limited number of consumers (typically one) with distinct message formats [Timberlake 2002]. Publish–subscribe by its own very nature implies that the publisher's message format, i.e., message structure, tag names, etc., is acceptable to all subscribers. For the majority of legacy or packaged applications, this characteristic is likely to be inappropriate [Timberlake 2002].

A more appropriate approach for EAI is a unicast-based message transport, such as message queuing organized into a hub and spoke model. This approach delivers messages efficiently to a limited number of consumers typically found in EAI scenarios.

17.4.3 Hub and spoke topology

The *hub and spoke topology* uses a central node that manages all interactions between applications. The central node prevents an application from having to integrate multiple times with several other applications, and simply carries out one integration process on the central node. The central node then handles communication with other applications. The most popular hub and spoke EAI solution for the inter-enterprise arena is integration brokering.

Recall from Section 14.5.1 that an integration broker resides between multiple source and target applications and enables them to work together by performing all translation, transformation and routing necessary for these applications to interoperate. Integration brokers direct traffic by identifying the source of the request and directing the necessary response based on predefined business rules and protocols. They achieve this by placing a processing layer between the disparate applications and platforms, accounting for the differences in application semantics, data formats, and operating systems within the integration broker. Integration brokers perform necessary content and format transformation to translate the incoming message into a scheme that the destination system(s) can understand and utilize. Integration broker software is underpinned by MOM software; see Figure 17.5.

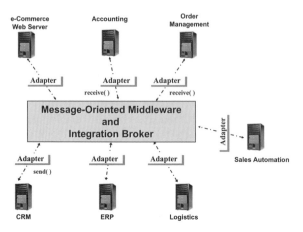

■ **Figure 17.5:** The Hub and Spoke Topology

This architecture is a vast improvement over point-to-point hand-coded interfaces, and it greatly simplifies the design, implementation and management of an integration solution. Changes are made at the hub, minimizing the impact of change and decreasing the time required to implement the new solution. The key disadvantage for integration brokering is that the hub may quickly become a bottleneck. In addition, while the EAI solution preserves business logic held in applications including legacy, some business logic is ultimately distributed into the integration broker itself. As usage grows, unpredictable workloads driven through existing mainframe on-line transaction processing environments such as CICS can considerably impact overall performance of the integration broker. In addition, geographically distributed enterprises face many difficulties implementing the single hub architecture. As integration infrastructures become larger and more geographically distributed, hub and spoke architectures could limit the scalability and flexibility of the solution. As integration solutions grow, so will the number of messages that need to get translated, transformed and routed.

Compared to the hub and spoke model, the shared bus model is more scalable, and can offer better performance, but implementation of the shared bus model is, in general, more complex. In addition, the shared bus model can be hard to administer as the environment grows. Both models support looser forms of integration.

The hub and spoke approach can also be used for e-Business marketplace solutions (see Chapter 8) by providing simple integration capabilities for a predictable and manageable cost. This opens opportunities for integrating to a wider audience, incorporating smaller players as well as infrequent business transactions. This is a key benefit of the e-Market approach where there is little incentive in investing in dedicated links if organizations only trade sparsely.

17.4.4 Conclusion

The choice of the EAI topology depends on its fit within the organization and on the scale and type of integration solution required. A number of vendors supply more than one of the approaches mentioned above. In a large-scale integration project where scalability is highly likely to be an issue, a form of distributed computing architecture should be seriously considered. This includes message-oriented middleware, distributed objects and object- and component-oriented middleware (e.g., ORBs), and remote data access middleware. Also, tools are emerging to address various types of EAI, including application integration, data integration, and process automation.

An EAI infrastructure may well become the mixture of different architectures, including hub and spoke, shared bus and distributed operations.

17.5 Types of application integration: passive vs. active

There are two ways in which application integration can occur: a passive and an active approach. In the passive approach existing applications and systems are integrated and communicate with each other without end-user interaction. In contrast, with the active approach end-users can interact with business processes and transactions to change the process flow and reroute transfers, if necessary.

With the *passive application integration* approach, processing is largely driven by the existing applications themselves and thus no end-user input is required. Integration is limited to entities that can pass or receive data in a message. The applications produce a message triggers the sequence of actions that follow. This type of EAI is supported by traditional MOM and message-oriented products such as integration brokers. Passive EAI approaches rely on an asynchronous application architecture, where the synchronization points are not naturally supported. These messaging technologies are suited towards delivering high volumes of data, without the need for responses from receiving applications. When an application requires synchronization, passive EAI approaches require explicit representation of the response in the form of an event. This makes the business process highly complex and cluttered.

According to the passive approach any external application that needs to be integrated has to be event-enabled to be able to interoperate with other existing applications. To mitigate this problem, most EAI vendors supply default adapters or connectors to common third party applications [May 2001], see Section 14.5.1. However, these adapters usually need to be tailored to cater for specific applications. This requires extensive programming and maintenance efforts.

The *active application integration* approach is based on Business Process Management and workflow technologies, which provide facilities for creating, manipulating, tracking and managing business processes. BPM technology is discussed further in Section 17.6.4. With the active approach, end-users interact with the BPM workflow to drive the execution of businesses processes and transactions and business processes are composed of a frequently changing combination of human and automated tasks using an end-to-end business process model. The active approach offers a combination of synchronous and asynchronous delivery. Tasks within the process model can be fast (using synchronous connectivity between applications) or slow (using asynchronous connectivity), but must cooperate to deliver the improved efficiency required. As such the business processes can be viewed, modeled and managed in an end-to-end manner against the requirements of constant change.

The active EAI approach is supported by newer generation application servers and constitutes the preferred solution when integrating e-Business applications.

17.6 Layers of EAI integration

EAI enables the collaboration between disparate systems across the divisions of an enterprise. Until very recently the majority of EAI efforts have concentrated on integrating existing data and application assets. Today, EAI requirements are encompassing not only integration of existing organization assets but the full spectrum of communications, business processes and transactions occurring electronically. It is thus convenient to perceive EAI as a conceptual multi-layered framework addressing integration issues at several hierarchical levels including:

1. transportation layer
2. data integration layer
3. application programming interface integration layer and
4. business process integration layer.

Each of these layers addresses a different and increasingly complex level of integration as we move up the integration stack; see Figure 17.6. Here, we can distinguish between the two fundamental paradigms for data. In particular, lower layers in the integration stack provide the basic infrastructure upon which higher layers build to guarantee the right level of integration. It is important to stress that these layers include the necessary ingredients that can be used for the EAI topologies that we examined in Section 17.4. It must be noted that since the business process integration layer is traditionally associated with e-Business integration initiatives, it will be revisited in Chapter 18 that deals with e-Business integration.

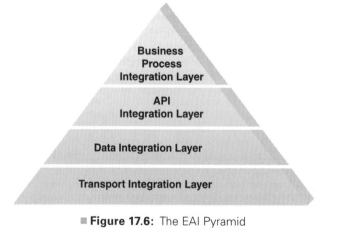

■ **Figure 17.6:** The EAI Pyramid

17.6.1 Transportation layer

The *transportation layer* handles connectivity to an application and transports data to it from other applications. Applications can be either external or internal to an enterprise. The transportation layer provides message encryption and network connectivity. In particular, this foundation layer involves the communications protocols and standards-based technologies employed to interconnect heterogeneous hardware platforms, operating systems and applications. Integration may take place at the protocol level where two or more systems exchange data through a common protocol for communication or through the use of more sophisticated concepts such as message queues. It typically includes TCP/IP (Transmission Control Protocol/Internet Protocol), which is the global standard for communications and is used to route data within and beyond enterprise walls. When communicating across enterprises the common means of transport occurs through the use of HTTP (Hypertext Transfer Protocol) that operates over TCP/IP connections. The goal of HTTP is to facilitate communications between Web-enabled systems by providing rules of conversation, including requests and responses. It comprises a set of messages that are used in e-Business to penetrate company firewalls, which are usually configured to accept HTTP and FTP service requests.

The transport integration layer also includes the messaging middleware that provides an interface between applications, allowing them to send data back and forth between systems. Here we can distinguish between the two fundamental paradigms for data transfer: synchronous vs. asynchronous (previously described in Section 14.2).

The synchronous communication mode, as explained earlier in this book, requires that data be transferred in a request/reply manner by establishing and maintaining a communication channel between the sending and receiving systems. Synchronous messaging mechanisms are exemplified by distributed technologies such as the Java Remote Method Invocation. Consider the following example. A customer is placing an order through the website of a company. Before the order is accepted by the Web-based application, first a check of the current debtor status (provided by the accounting information system) of the customer is checked (to ascertain that the company is willing to accept the order), next the inventory status (the inventory information system) is checked (to ascertain that the company is able to deliver). Only if the two checks are positive will the Web-based order application send a message to the customer that his order has been accepted.

The asynchronous communications paradigm allows the sender to be loosely coupled to the receiver as messages can be stored in a message queue and can then be forwarded to the receiving system when it becomes available to process the message. Messaging technologies such as IBM MQseries, Microsoft MSMQ and Tibco Rendevous provide reliable asynchronous communications.

17.6.2 Data integration layer

The transition from the supply chain to the value chain has increased the value of the data assets that are owned by an organization. This transition has been facilitated by the implementation of applications that utilize their own data sources and data models. A value chain requires open access precisely to these data sources and the data integration layer traditionally handles this.

The *data-integration layer* goes beyond simply transporting messages between two end points. This layer refers to the ability to exchange relevant business data from the applications available and integrate it with other such related data items despite differences in data formats, structures and intended meaning of business terms under possibly diverse company standards. A data integration solution deals with moving data between multiple databases and solves the problem of sharing data across multiple applications created by implementing numerous proprietary back-end systems. What makes data-level EAI appealing is the fact that accessing databases can be accomplished without any changes to the application code.

The guiding philosophy behind integration at the data level is that the real currency of the enterprise lies in its data and that the best path to this data is usually not through the original application but rather through the database level; see Figure 17.7. Consider as an example a financial analyst at a large multi-national company that needs to obtain cumulative roll-up of net income, net sales and total assets for a given fiscal year for this company. This request involves interacting with several database systems that not only may have structural differences – which may require data cleansing and transformation to a common format for access – but also may not conform to the same standards, e.g., may have country dependent (different) names for the company, different scale factors and different currencies. This requires translating application messages to a common data format and communication protocol. It is also necessary to convert message content to and from the specific data structures used internally by each application.

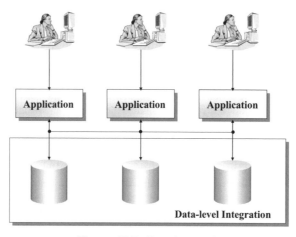

■ **Figure 17.7:** Data Integration

Each application has its own data structures, based on the information that it stores and uses internally. For example, suppose you need to move information from an "employee" application to a "mailing list" application. The employee application may contain records that consist of fields like employee number, name, address, city, state, country, salary, etc. The mailing list records might have a simpler structure – name and address information only. Even where corresponding fields exist – such fields that store the city name – they could have different internal names and different internal characteristics in each application.

It is not simply the differences in data formats or interfaces that matters, but the lack of common definition of the business concepts that underlies the different sources to be integrated. Hence, there is pressure is to create an environment in which there is a controlled sharing of business data by resolving differences in data formats and structures as well as reconciling semantic differences. This problem, known as the semantic integration problem, is a serious obstacle to successful data integration and will be treated in some depth in Section 18.7.

For the above reasons it is common for this type of solution to create an enterprise-wide meta-data repository that describes the structure and the usage of data throughout the organization. It will also define mappings, and where necessary, transformations, which are required to move data between applications.

Data-level integration is used when the applications do not provide any APIs or client interfaces, and developers understand how business operations affect an application's data schema. Data-level integration can be push- or pull-based [JavaWorld 2002]. With push-based data-level integration, one application makes SQL calls through database links or stored procedures on another application's database relations. Push-based data-level integration thus pushes data into another application's database. In contrast, pull-based data-level integration uses triggers and polling. Triggers capture changes to data and write the identifying information to interface meta-data tables. Adapters can then poll these interface meta-data tables and retrieve the pertinent data. Pull-based data-level integration is used when an application requires simple notification of updates that occur within another application's data.

Translation is the responsibility of the integration broker (hub) or application server and adapters. These translate the codes used, the data structures, and the format of the fields, and may reorder and remove fields and even add needed data. However, it must be noted that conventional data integration tools provide very little, if any, support for semantic data integration.

We can distinguish four major mechanisms of data-level integration solutions that are worth examining [Linthicum 2001a]. These are staged integration, data replication, data federations and data integration servers.

Staged integration

With this approach source data is exported into an intermediate format for eventual transformation and importing into the new target application's data structures (schemas). This approach isolates the two applications from each other while enabling the sharing of data.

The primary limitations of this approach are: data latency, data inconsistency and cost overhead. Data latency is the result of the staged nature of the transformations. In most cases, transformations exhibit batch characteristics, i.e., they are scheduled to occur at predefined intervals, for instance, hourly, daily, weekly, etc. The very nature of this latency affects data integrity since changes in the source data are not immediately reflected in the target data and vice versa. As new applications use out of date information inconsistencies and errors occur.

Data replication

Data replication is an attempt to rectify the drawbacks of the staged nature of data integration. Data replication is a synchronous process whereby triggering mechanisms, i.e., event-based data integration, are employed to automatically transform and copy data from the source application to the target application on the basis of business rules. For example, rules can be set up that every time a new order has been taken by the Web interface of a given enterprise, the order is automatically recorded by the back-end customer order system and an invoice is automatically generated and sent to the customer. This environment implies distinct schema definitions for the EIS involved, where changes to one database system trigger updates in another. Because the schema definitions and layouts of data in the source and target do not exactly match, a meta-data mapping between the two systems is needed to define a synchronization profile. Meta-data is used in this context to include not only descriptions of enterprise data and their structures but also business rules and logic that apply to that data.

Most relational database vendors and system tool vendors provide data replication products. Replication can be straightforward if both database systems use technologies provided by the same database vendor. However, data replication is quite complex with a multi-vendor solution.

Data federation

The function of a *data federation* is to create a virtual integration model so that applications can access schemas and data from different data sources using the same interface. This results in a federated database that envelops an enterprise's legacy data with integrated distributed relational front-end servers, providing a single integration portal accessing all enterprise data. A federated database system bypasses older applications that originally controlled access to legacy data. Developers can use this virtual database as a single point of accessing data from applications in the enterprise through the single database interface. The result is similar to having a single unified database for all the applications.

With a federated approach to data integration, data remains intact within data sources ensuring that it is current for real-time access and query from the applications that need it. Federated database operations follow the client/server (or push) architecture model. Major drawbacks of this approach concern performance and cost considerations as well as the need to create the logic for integrating the applications with the databases.

Data integration servers

The function of a *data integration server*, also known as a data server or data portal, is to provide data access (retrieval and modification), transformation (reformatting and repackaging) and movement (posting, forwarding, replication and so on). Data integration servers add push capabilities to the normal client/server model. These can occur through scheduled or triggered mechanisms that enable data replication and synchronization between systems originating from different vendors. Data integration servers do not require centralized hubs as in the case of a federated database, an architectural freedom that allows them to act as portals and/or hubs based on application requirements.

Data integration servers are ideal for bringing data from disparate systems, e.g., islands of information, together for new application platforms such as the Internet. They achieve this by adhering to common standards in accessing enterprise data, while preserving it in its original form and by bypassing proprietary access modes.

Integration servers must be evaluated based on speed, scalability and scope of coverage. In addition, they do not offer any data cleansing capabilities. Fortunately, they allow easy integration with data cleansing tools so that access, reporting and cleansing of heterogeneous data can be performed.

To facilitate integration of data across different systems, data integration servers are adopting XML as the standard format for data exchange. EAI tools translate relational data into XML and vice versa. Once data is translated into XML, XML documents containing this data can subsequently be transformed into specific XML business protocols such as Electronic Business XML (ebXML) or RosettaNet. Such transformed XML data is also integrated with business processes by using XSL stylesheets.

EAI is designed to bridge the gap between applications via a message infrastructure; as such it is primarily designed for process integration and not data integration. Hence its capabilities for data integration are limited. Despite the fact that complex business transactions often require information that is distributed across multiple sources, EAI systems do not provide the means for aggregating and processing data under these conditions. Typical EAI solutions only provide access to one data source at a time.

17.6.3 Application programming interface integration layer

The data integration level concentrates on the coordinated sharing and seamless integration of enterprise data while the *application programming interface integration layer* concentrates on the sharing of business logic between applications. The basic premise of the API integration layer is the integration of two systems and the passing of information between them. It differs from the data integration level as the interface is created with the application rather than its underlying database. This implies that access is not only provided at the data level but also the business logic and rules that are built into the application can be used as part of the integration link to maintain the integrity and consistency of the information that flows between applications. In addition to accessing application data it is also possible to access an application's methods. Application Programming Interfaces are used for this purpose.

APIs are hooks that can be used to connect to an application to invoke its business logic and retrieve its underlying data. API integration allows enterprises to integrate through the sharing of common business logic exposed using pre-defined programming interfaces; see Figure 17.8. As many modern applications are constructed with distributed component technology externalizing interfaces as a point of access, this layer is also known as the message or component integration layer.

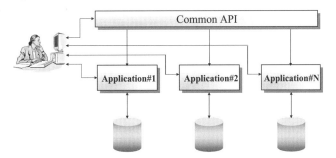

■ **Figure 17.8:** API Integration Layer

Applications normally provide a callable interface in the form of an API. For example, major COTS vendors also provide APIs to allow integration with their underlying applications. This API does not necessarily have to make use of component technologies, such as CORBA or DCOM, though they provide wider levels of interoperability than most proprietary interface standards. These are examples of APIs:

- Component interfaces such as CORBA, DCOM, or JavaBeans.

- Transaction processing interfaces such as IBM's CICS or BEA's Tuxedo.

- Packaged application interfaces such as SAP's Business API (BAPI), which, themselves, can be made available in the form of a component interface such as COM.

Sharing of business logic between applications is an important aspect of EAI as it promotes reusability of business logic throughout an enterprise and ensures application consistency. Applications normally contain important business logic that needs to be shared between applications in order to provide efficient EAI solutions [Yee 2001]. To understand this, consider the following example. Consider an enterprise that wishes to upgrade its CRM to conduct periodic credit risk analysis on its customers. Assume that the same functionality is already part of a sales automation system that allows for the same risk analysis to be conducted on prospective customers. Instead of developing that facility within the CRM it would be beneficial if this functionality were to be reused directly from the sales management system. This is precisely the type of integration provided by the API-level.

API-level integration is synchronous in nature and requires that interacting applications be available and running. It is an inherently point-to-point integration mesh, which may result in tightly coupled systems and reduced reusability. API-level integration traditionally requires that integrated applications support RPC or distributed component technology.

API-level integration can only be enabled if both communicating systems use the same type of technology such as distributed components (see Chapter 15) as a means of encapsulating business logic. Most of the efforts on API integration have concentrated on developing industry standard frameworks for application and component interoperability that allow the development of aggregating (front) applications that invoke the APIs (or functional methods) of other applications. OMG's CORBA, Microsoft's DCOM, and Sun's Enterprise JavaBeans (EJB) framework are examples of industry standard frameworks. Like data replication, APIs work well when both communicating systems are using the same framework. Cross-platform integration is a far more difficult proposition.

As the interface exposed by the source application rarely matches the interface of the target application, some form of transformation must take place. Instead of using point-to-point transformations, the data could be abstracted to an intermediate format, such as XML, so that the transformation is created only once for each application. The benefits of XML for such purposes includes that it provides a flexible interface that is independent for both the application itself and the middleware and enables a common platform approach to middleware. In general, XML is well suited to the loose style of integration that is required for applications that require extending business processes outside the enterprise. One potential disadvantage of XML is that the volume of data that needs to be moved between applications is increased. This could prove to be a stumbling block for applications where the use of high bandwidth is a problem.

The major disadvantages of API-level integration stem from the tight application coupling in front-end components (applications). Often, changes in an integrated application API break the front application components and the applications that rely on them.

17.6.4 Business process integration layer

Data and API integration are the traditional tenets of EAI and occur at the information level by exchanging data and defining information flows between diverse systems. These information flows are defined at the physical level and do not take into account abstract business concepts such as business processes (refer to Chapter 4 for the features of business processes and to Chapter 12 for business process modeling techniques) and shared business agreements (see Chapter 20) that are critical for e-Business application integration. Businesses need to take a holistic view of business processes. The larger view of integrating processes brings elements that are necessary for part of an integration strategy as these contain transactions.

The *business process integration* layer provides the core infrastructure that permits business processes to cross enterprise boundaries, link and interact with counterpart processes operated by the enterprise's suppliers and trading partners. For instance, consider the end-to-end supply chain management activities of Audi Hungaria in our case study and how it interconnects its systems with its partners. Organizations that integrate processes across departmental boundaries and deepen the understanding of processes within vertical applications will reap the benefits of an overall integration strategy.

Traditionally EAI technology does not include process technology; however, the evolution of EAI technology coupled with competitive pressures and the need to connect enterprises across the Internet has recently shifted attention to process oriented business architectures. These fall naturally into the realm of e-Business integration.

Business process integration is at the center of attention when developing e-Business solutions and may present the broadest range of variations in integration practices ranging from simple application-to-application data exchange links to very complex arrangements involving transaction integrity support for business processes, workflow routing for processes residing in different systems and enterprises, and so on.

Business processes are the defining elements of a particular organization in that they control and describe precisely how business is conducted both internally and externally. This can relate to how customers place orders, how goods are requisitioned from partners and suppliers, and how employees update internal systems. Thus it is not surprising that enterprises have come to realize that they need to create end-to-end business processes for internal and cross-enterprise integration in order to bring ultimate value to their customers. It is indeed the entire value chain, not a single enterprise that delivers the products or services and makes enterprises competitive and successful. Value-chain management is now clearly recognized as the next frontier for gaining new productivity and competitive advantage. Consequently, internal and cross-enterprise integration initiatives must be managed and deployed in a systematic and coherent fashion.

Business process integration

Business process integration (BPI) can be described as the ability to define a commonly acceptable business process model that specifies the sequence, hierarchy, events, execution logic and information movement between systems residing in the same enterprise (viz. EAI) and systems residing in multiple interconnected enterprises (viz. e-Business integration). BPI is an integration solution that provides enterprises with end-to-end visibility and control over the contributing parts of a multi-step information request or transaction, which include people, customers, partners, applications, and databases [Hurwitz 2001b]. For instance, this might include all the steps in an order management, inventory management or fulfillment process, while e-Business processes can include service provisioning, supply chain management, and multi-step purchasing transactions.

The primary problem with business process integration is not that of the translation of data formats and routing, but rather that of the business process embedded in one application being bridged into the process of another. The business processes linked together are not defined as information but rather are described in terms of activities or workflows.

Figure 17.9 illustrates a typical business process integration scenario involving an order fulfillment process. This typical business process is shown spanning multiple functional areas within an enterprise. This figure

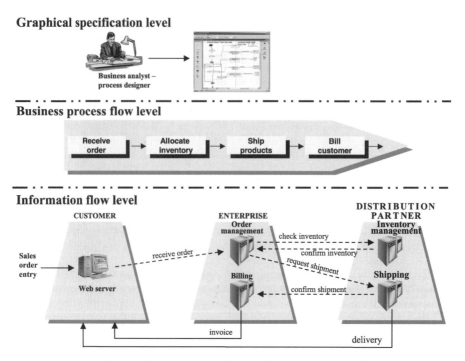

Figure 17.9: Business Process Integration Scenario

also illustrates that business process developers can – with the assistance of business process modeling and automation tools – specify cross-application and cross-enterprise business processes. Process modeling and automation tools use graphical tools to define business process models and business rules that specify the flow of processes and information between the applications that constitute the overall business process (see Chapter 12). Activities in the order fulfillment process include receiving the sales order, allocating inventory, shipping products, billing, and making sure that the payment is received. Some of these processes may execute for long periods of time, while others may execute in milliseconds. The technologies that support the order fulfillment BPI might range from typical order entry and payment systems to ERP systems such as SAP to modern component-based systems running on IBM WebSphere or Microsoft application servers. The Internet adds another dimension of complexity to this example as the enterprise dealing with the order fulfillment may have outsourced the shipping function to a trading partner such as UPS or FedEx. Inside the firewall the business processes must span heterogeneous stovepipe applications such as the ones shown in Figure 17.1, which were originally conceived as standalone systems. Outside the firewall, the business processes must interact with systems operated by customers, suppliers and trading partners. Even if the systems are outsourced, the enterprise needs to stay tightly linked to them to function cohesively [MetaServer 2001].

BPI solutions allow enterprises to take advantage of systems that are already in place by automating and managing the business processes that span these systems. With BPI, enterprises can preserve major investments in legacy systems and avoid the expense of having to write new code to replicate existing functionality. BPI requires considerable changes in the overall enterprise architecture and application structures that include [Lubinsky 2001b]:

1. dividing applications into distinct parts for front and back-office tasks. Front-office applications access the functionality of the back-office systems, which include ERP systems that let users manage purchasing, inventory, materials resource planning, and financial reporting. Front-office applications such as CRM systems allow effective integration of Web-based customer service and back-office applications supporting their functionality, and
2. defining business processes that implement the overall enterprise functionality. Back-office applications are not exposed directly in these processes, they are rather wrapped in the sub-processes that interact with them as part of their execution.

The process integration approach ultimately leads to a *loosely-coupled architecture* whereby back-office applications do not communicate directly with front-office applications, they rather communicate with each other through processes and thus they do not need to have specific knowledge of one another.

A critical element beyond pure automation remains human intervention with both operational and, importantly, strategic implications. The shift in BPI is now toward the human level, either through PDA or e-mail notification, or a graphical representation through a portal. This allows alerts to business processes that have gone out of boundaries, based on key performance indicators and indices used to set their tolerances. Thus in addition to extending critical business processes outside the enterprise firewall, modern BPI tools provide the ability to intercede at the human management level to adjust or refine or optimize business processes. In this way enterprises can respond quickly and effectively to changing business conditions without time-consuming and expensive programming activities.

Business process management
The extension of BPI with management aspects is commonly referred to as *Business Process Management* (BPM). BPM emphasizes the management aspect of automating processes to achieve maximum ongoing flexibility with minimum development cost and time.

BPM is a commitment to expressing, understanding, representing and managing a business (or the portion of business to which it is applied) in terms of a collection of business processes that are responsive to a business environment of internal or external events [McGoveran 2004]. BPM entails a *strategic business position* statement that is in line with the corporate or enterprise e-Business strategy level we examined in Section 2.6. The definition also entails an *operational position* statement. The term management of business processes includes process analysis, process definition and redefinition, resource allocation, scheduling, measurement of process quality and efficiency, and process optimization. Process optimization includes collection and analysis of both real-time measures (monitoring) and strategic measures (performance management), and their correlation as the basis for process improvement and innovation.

A BPM solution is a graphical productivity tool for modeling, integrating, monitoring, and optimizing process flows of all sizes, crossing any application, company boundary, or human interaction; see Figure 17.9. BPM is driven primarily by the common desire to integrate supply chains, as well as internal enterprise functions, without the need for even more custom software development. This means that the tools must be suitable for business analysts, requiring less (or no) software development. They must reduce maintenance requirements because internally and externally integrated environments routinely require additions and changes to business processes. Currently, the vendors most active in BPM include IBM with WebSphere, HP with HP Process Manager, BEA with WebLogic, and Vitria with BusinessWare. Microsoft BizTalk is also a good example of a BPM integration product, but its use is limited to Microsoft Windows and .NET servers.

BPM codifies value-driven processes and institutionalizes their execution within the enterprise [Roch 2002]. This implies that BPM tools can help analyze, define and enforce process standardization. BPM provides a modeling tool to visually construct, analyze and execute cross-functional business processes. Design and modeling of business processes is accomplished at the graphical specification level shown in Figure 17.9.

BPM products must implement the entire business process as much as possible within the product, using minimum custom code. This requires that BPM products have separate runtime engines, require validation, testing and monitoring tools and create new applications. Consequently, the five tenets of BPM are modeling, integration, monitoring, measuring and optimization (shown in Figure 17.10). These are defined and briefly described in what follows:

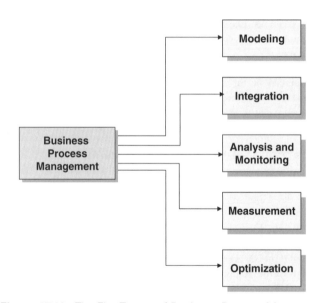

■ **Figure 17.10:** The Five Tenets of Business Process Management

1. *Modeling.* This item includes tools for graphically defining or building a business process representation that accounts for all needed process assets, multiple steps within a process, process branching and event routing, parallel process execution sequences, business rules, exception handling, and error handling. Modern business process modeling tools include business process analysis functionality of capturing, designing, and modifying business processes and their properties, resource requirements, such as definition

and selective enforcement of process standards, and facilitate the expression process views at different levels of abstraction depending on authorization, functional responsibility and the level of detail desired. Process modeling is totally separated from process execution. Therefore, enterprises do not need to rely on programmers to define business processes. A business analyst can use a graphical process design tool, as shown in Figure 17.9 to define processes. Modeling is both wide and deep in that multiple participants can be included in end-to-end processes, at any level of nesting and detail, from organizational unit participants down to individual EIS and component systems. Once the design and modeling exercise is accomplished, the execution occurs inside a BPM execution engine, which offers facilities for sequencing of tasks and integration of tasks with outside applications.

2. *Integration.* Connecting the process elements so that they can seamlessly exchange information to achieve business goals. For applications this means using APIs and messaging. For people this means creating a workspace on the desktop or wireless device for fulfilling their part of the process.

3. *Analysis and Monitoring.* This involves providing graphical administrative tools that illustrate processes that are in progress and that are completed, and integrate business metrics and key performance indicators with process descriptions. It provides a wide-angle view of the time and resources consumed by enterprise-wide processes. Analytical tools guide business process improvement and deployment. Graphical reports can also be produced to check the status of all running and finished processes. These tools include facilities to query the state of live business processes and to intervene to resolve exceptions if required. For example, they can check for processes awaiting further inputs in order to complete execution, such as a process waiting for new inventory to come in. This process can then be observed and appropriately monitored.

4. *Measurement.* Managing processes first requires aggregating process data in business-oriented metrics such as key performance indicators and balanced scorecards. If the process is "out of bounds" or service level agreements are not being met, the next step is to optimize it by reconfiguring resources or modifying business rules – dynamically and "on the fly". The ability to capture the definition of familiar business metrics and relate them to computational measurements is an essential part of BPM [McGoveran 2004]. Business metrics definitions have an impact on which raw computations are made. However, the distinction between business metrics and raw computational measurements is essential. For example, expected time-to-completion of a business transaction is of immense interest to the business analysts and management, whereas mean queue times, mean activity service times and most probable path to completion are too technical and too detailed.

5. *Optimization.* Optimization means process improvement, which should be an ongoing activity. This item involves optimizing process flows of all sizes, crossing any application or company boundary and connects process design and process maintenance. For example, it automatically detects bottlenecks, deadlocks and other inconsistencies in processes across the whole extended enterprise and acts on or changes processes in real-time to minimize inefficiencies.

These five tenets of BPM should not be considered as separate from each other. They work in concert and represent a cohesive set of actions that deliver BPM solutions.

BPM is more than process automation, or workflow. It adds conceptual innovations and technology from EAI and e-Business integration (see Chapter 18) and reimplements it on an e-Business infrastructure based on Web and XML standards. BPM software thus really means the combination of workflow, EAI, and e-Business components in an integrated modeling and execution environment based on Web technology standards. BPM within the context of EAI and e-Business integration provides the flexibility necessary to automate cross-functional processes. Consider a typical e-Business scenario involving the linking of purchasing and sales applications. While such applications may provide workflow features, these features work only within their local environment. Automating cross-functional activities enables corporations to manage processes by exception based on real-time events driven from the integrated environment [Roch 2002]. Process execution then becomes automated, requiring human intervention only in situations where exceptions occur or manual tasks and approvals are required.

17.7 Workflow, EAI, and BPM technologies: A comparison

In general, business processes can range from being straightforward and fully automated to complex and intricate processes that require human input and intervention. This is where workflow technology needs to be embedded into the integration solution. The rules that govern when, which and how users need to interact with the business process, need to be clearly identified and incorporated in the workflow solution.

Workflow technology models and automates "long-running" processes lasting days or even months. Flows include both automated tasks and human interaction, with interactive tasks distributed to users based on organizational roles (see Section 6.4.2). Workflow technology tends to relegate integration functions, such as synchronizing data between disparate packaged and legacy applications, to custom code within its activities – and thus outside the scope of the process model [Silver 2003]. Moreover, it uses a tightly coupled integration style that employs low-level APIs and that has confined workflow to local, homogeneous system environments, such as the department or division. Therefore, traditional workflow implementations are closely tied to the enterprise in which they are deployed, and cannot be reliably extended outside organizational borders to customers, suppliers and other partners. As a consequence, one of the major limitations of workflow management systems is integration: they are not good at connecting cross-enterprise systems together. Modern workflow technology tries to address this deficiency by extending this functionality to cross-enterprise integration.

Traditional EAI solutions have predominantly relied on a tightly coupled integration style based on synchronous communications, such as remote procedure calls and infrastructures such as DCOM or CORBA. Newer generation EAI introduces a more flexible, loosely coupled style of integration via messaging. Messaging allows integration of applications with dissimilar platforms and APIs, and tolerates interruptions in the communications link or unavailability of the application. EAI also involves a process flow of sorts – usually a simple, short data flow between applications – but for the most part, has not tried to automate long-running end-to-end processes involving many steps, nor include interactive activities in which a person (rather than an automated program) does some work and makes a decision [Silver 2003].

On the surface modern workflow and BPM technologies seem to be the same as they try to target the same problem, i.e., integration of applications across organizational boundaries. However, they have subtle differences. Their differentiation lies deep in their architecture and applicability.

BPM provides an enterprise infrastructure that may cross enterprise boundaries and which manages and automates processes that have both human and system related tasks. The distinction between BPM and workflow is mainly based on the management aspect of Business Process Management systems. BPM tools place considerable emphasis on management and business functions. This fact accentuates the business applicability of BPM, instead of a technological solution, which is the case with workflow systems. BPM solutions, just like workflow solutions, define and enact processes. However, managing processes from a business perspective is the key part of BPM, therefore, tools that do not support the business management aspect are not considered BPM tools.

BPM technology covers the same space as EAI and workflow, but its focus is on the business user, and it provides more sophisticated management and analysis capabilities. In fact, BPM can be considered as the convergence of workflow, EAI, and unstructured or ad-hoc processes. With a BPM tool the business user is able to manage all the process of a certain type, for example, claim processes, and should be able to study them from historical or current data, produce costs or other business measurements, and produce on the basis of these measurements business charts or reports. In addition, the business user should also be able to analyze and compare the data or business measurements based on the different types of claims.

17.8 When to use synchronous or asynchronous communication

Recall from Chapter 14, where we examine the role of middleware, that synchronous communication involves one entity, usually a client, in the message passing process sending a message, and a second entity, usually a server, receiving the message, carrying out some processing and then sending some response to the client. The client blocks (waits) while the server is carrying out the processing and cannot proceed with any other work. If the server fails then the client will be left waiting for a response locking up the system until the server comes up or a time out mechanism is exercised.

With asynchronous communication the client makes a request and proceeds to other processing tasks, not waiting for a response. When the server is ready with the response it notifies the client, which then accepts. For example, the server could be executing some processor-intensive task for another service it provides, before it returns the response to the client. With the asynchronous form of communication there is no close coordination between message passing entities. One way of handling this mode of communication would be to place the messages on some intermediate queue. For example, one application server may receive many requests from EAI application clients, which it queues for another application server to handle. The first application server does not wait for a response but when one is received from the second application server, the first relays it to the appropriate client.

The increased breadth of applications in e-Business settings requires connecting to business systems that are not managed locally and are therefore unpredictable. When application servers are upgraded, network problems or remote server breakdowns occur, due to the tightly coupled nature of applications. They can bring down other remote applications and associated business processes if a synchronous communication solution such as remote procedure calls is adopted. In addition to this, middleware solutions based on synchronous messaging require broad bandwidth, as many calls should be made across the network to execute a synchronous function call. Thus they do not scale well. For these reasons it is clear that the asynchronous mode of communication is the better option when integrating both modern EAI and e-Business applications. This communication paradigm offers advantages over the more traditional synchronous function calls of distributed object computing technologies such as Java RMI, CORBA and DCOM, unless the systems being integrated have identical availability characteristics. Some of these advantages include highly decoupled system relationships, recoverable messages, and technology independence [Bond 2002]. An obvious question that arises is whether we need synchronous communication at all.

There is a fundamental difference between these two modes of communication and this is in connection with guaranteed response times, as well as with technical requirements such as transactional integrity during data updates, which require synchronous communication. In applications that require information without requiring updates there is no real difference between using synchronous or asynchronous communication. Because of the fact that an enterprise cannot rely solely on asynchronous messaging as an integration strategy, many EAI vendors provide synchronous request/reply functionality as an extension of their MOM products. Although with such products the interaction appears to be synchronous to the initiating application, the underlying messaging transport remains asynchronous.

Asynchronous communication between application servers (business systems belonging to separate enterprises) imposes a design burden on application developers as they have to take into account the impact of time synchronization between applications that require concurrent updates. However, the benefits outweigh this drawback as business systems can always operate independently if required. This independence is mandatory in e-Business integration where the requirement is to integrate business applications that originate from different enterprises by providing a non-invasive fit into the existing application server architectures.

To summarize this section, *timing* (synchronization) is an important element of the application integration infrastructure. Timing deals with the exchange of information between applications. Events in one application typically trigger the need to send or request information from another. However, this could take place synchronously, perhaps requiring two-phase commit, or asynchronously via message queues. Events may have to be handled immediately for real-time action or queued for overnight replication. The integration infrastructure may monitor events in applications, or in the information that exchanges them, and initiate other dependent actions. The following are various models of how the interaction between the applications should take place [Wilkes 1999]:

- Request and Reply: An application requests information from another and blocks (waits) for the reply to arrive.

- Conversational (or Synchronous): Information is passed between two sources in a series of related exchanges. A reply must be received before processing continues.

- Publish and Subscribe: An information source publishes events that other anonymous information sources can subscribe to.

- Asynchronous: A reply to a message is not required before processing continues.

The timing ingredient of the application integration infrastructure therefore provides services for the following:

- Scheduling, i.e., the precise timing of information exchange.

- Events, i.e., the events that need to be monitored and the applications that are affected by them or need to be informed about them.

- Interaction Model – are synchronous and asynchronous activities supported and are publish and subscribe techniques required?

17.9 Elements of the application integration architecture

To summarize the points that we have raised so far and associate the material in this chapter with material that we introduced in Chapter 14, where we presented middleware structures, we introduce a high-level view of EAI. Figure 17.11 shows the elements involved in this kind of logical EAI architecture. The EAI architecture includes a suite of products including MOM, an integration broker, EIS adapters, business process management and business activity monitoring tools.

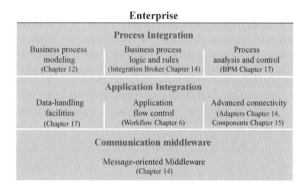

■ **Figure 17.11:** Elements of EAI Architecture

Message Oriented Middleware is the basic layer in the EAI architecture and is important to EAI because it ensures asynchronous and reliable delivery of messages between applications, providing the means for the integration broker and the target applications to communicate in a distributed manner. MOM also provides an API that abstracts the complexity of the network implementation from the developer. The API is used to create a message, give it a payload (its application data), assign it routing information, and then send the message to the MOM which delivers it asynchronously to one or more intended recipients. The same API is used to receive messages produced by other applications. The message should be self-describing in that it should contain the entire necessary context required to allow the recipients to carry out their work independently. While a MOM vendor implements its own networking protocols, routing and administration facilities, the basic semantics of the developer API provided by different MOMs are the same. This makes it possible for vendor-agnostic APIs such as JMS to be used with many different MOM platforms [Monson-Haefel 2001].

Although MOM does not traditionally incorporate distributed transaction processing, with some approaches, e.g., BEA's MessageQ, a developer can write business transactions using workflow as the mechanism of process execution. These mechanisms incorporate distributed transaction control of legacy programs as well as service calls. Hence, a call could be made to, for example, an ERP process as part of a workflow process that incorporated update of databases. Failure of the ERP process would result in the update being aborted.

Integration brokers are responsible for brokering messages exchanged between two or more applications, providing the ability to transform, store, and route messages and also to apply business rules and respond to events. Integration brokers are essentially run-time products that are built on top of other communication middleware such as, for instance, RPC and MOM. They focus on the message and process flow, with little human interaction. Integration brokers use messaging systems to move information between systems and as such they may include process and workflow management, which introduce the capability to manage state and long-running transactions. Most integration brokers support some sort of asynchronous transport layer, either proprietary or open. Some integration brokers offer the ability to select any number of messaging systems, even to mix and match messaging systems to meet the requirements of the problem domain.

Integration brokers may utilize several abstraction layers around the types of applications to be integrated. For example, there may be an abstraction for common middleware services (such as distributed objects, message-oriented middleware, and transactional middleware). There may also be an abstraction layer for packaged applications; another layer addresses the integration of relational and non-relational databases. The complexities of the interfaces that each entity (middleware, packaged applications, and databases) employs are hidden from the end user.

The integration broker deploys communications middleware and associated protocols of various types as applicable to the particular application target. Adapters are invoked to complete the access to the target applications. The adapters may reside in the integration broker or in the target application environment. Adapters link an application in one environment with one in another taking advantage of the application's API. They provide the integration broker with both data and process access to disparate applications within an enterprise. As business events occur, the adapter publishes the event and related data in real time via the MOM interface. The integration broker then receives the message via the MOM interface and instantiates the integration process controlling the transactional logic and flow of the integration.

Business process management, as explained in some detail in a previous section, is a set of services and tools that provide for explicit management of cross-functional business processes, e.g., process modeling, analysis, definition, execution, monitoring and administration, including support for both human and application level interaction. BPM tools are emerging now from many sources including integration brokers, application servers, Web integration servers and so on. BPM contains tools to analyze and model processes, using a graphical process designer targeted for business analysts who decompose old and compose new business flows. The run-time environment can monitor task execution time and exceptions, providing empirical data to base further process decomposition and optimization. BPM executes automated tasks via process definitions within the integration broker and human tasks via a defined workflow. BMP systems monitor and synchronize the execution of automated and human tasks.

Business activity monitoring provides real-time access to critical business performance indicators to improve the speed and effectiveness of business operations. Business activity monitoring is the convergence of operational business intelligence and real-time application integration targeting business goals. Business activity monitoring includes event and alert management, dashboards and other graphical administrative tools. Unlike traditional real-time monitoring, business activity monitoring draws its information from multiple application systems and other internal and external sources. This enables a broader and richer view of business activities. Business activity monitoring targets the enterprise strategy level (see Sections 2.5 and 2.6) by facilitating the enablement of new business strategies, reduced operating costs, improved process performance and other areas important to enterprise and e-Business strategy. The ultimate beneficiary of a successful EAI solution is the entire organization. Users in both technical and business units will benefit from having access to an accurate, consolidated view of the enterprise.

To interconnect an enterprise with the outside world application servers are used (see Section 14.7.2). An application server is a natural point for application integration as it provides a platform for development, deployment and management of Web-based, transactional, secure, distributed and scalable enterprise applications. Application servers are the platform of choice for applications that are developed using a multi-tier architecture.

Application servers can be used in tandem with integration brokers through a cooperative interface (see next section). In this way the integration broker functions as an application integration backbone while the application server hosts custom business logic in the middle tier. In this mode the integration broker functions as a service provider to the application server by providing data access, transformations and content-based routing.

17.10 Implementing business process-level EAI

Traditionally, ERP and CRM vendors provide an API to their software and leave the integration work to customers, who might write custom code, hire a systems integrator or invest in integration middleware to make the necessary application connections. Working with APIs often requires manual coding, and they do not provide for a scalable integration method. A manual interface through a proprietary API provides a means for one application to make requests of another application and pull in data. But when an application pulls in data through an API and duplicates that data in its own repository, there are two instances of the data that need to be kept in sync to maintain its quality. Conversely, when applications share the same resources, data does not have to be duplicated in application-specific repositories, and information and processes can be tied together. This is achieved by means of appropriately integrating business processes.

The first step in effective business process integration is to integrate disparate business applications internally and optimize operations within the enterprise before linking processes with trading partners. Only when enterprise business applications and processes are aligned with Web applications can an enterprise truly consider itself to have a competitive e-Business strategy. The evolution of middleware technologies has culminated in two, well-established key types of middleware products commonly used for implementing business process integration: integration brokers and application servers [Dolgicer 2004].

Today, application servers and integration brokers still represent a significant polarization. They do not share a common technology base, and one is built around standards, while the other has mostly grown from proprietary implementations, although this is changing rapidly, too.

17.10.1 Integration broker-based process-level integration

To integrate disparate business applications one must concentrate on the characteristics and functions of integration brokers. An integration broker, built primarily on messaging middleware, provides an end-to-end integration platform addressing the critical business components required to completely automate business processes across the extended enterprise, which may also include trading partners. It provides wide-ranging, pre-built application adapters, and bi-directional connectivity to multiple applications, including packaged and mainframe applications. For instance, the SAP NetWeaver in our case study is a comprehensive integration and application platform that unifies and aligns information sources and business processes across technologies and organizations and allows them to achieve enterprise application integration. It achieves this by providing independence from existing databases and operating systems, and an open, standards-based development environment.

Integration brokers are able to share information with a multitude of systems by using an asynchronous, event-driven mechanism, thus constituting an ideal support framework for asynchronous business processes. This type of middleware is responsible for brokering messages exchanged between multiple applications, providing the ability to transform, store, and route messages, and also the ability to apply business rules and respond to events.

Initially, integration brokers originated as hub and spoke systems, where the integration broker-based BPI is implemented at a central integration hub, see Section 17.4.3, and the applications needed to be integrated, i.e., every existing EIS in this architecture, being connected only to the integration broker and not to each other. These are some typical integration broker products:

- Adapter technology to establish connectivity to legacy and packaged applications.

- Some form of asynchronous, MOM infrastructure to propagate events and data.

- A business rules engine to govern message routing and transformation.

Figure 17.12 presents a high-level view of the typical architecture for implementing integration broker-based process-level EAI. This figure illustrates that the integration broker is the system centerpiece. The integration broker facilitates information movement between two or more resources (source and target applications) and accounts for differences in application semantics and heterogeneous platforms. The various existing (or component) EIS, such as inventory management, order management billing systems, transaction processing monitors, legacy systems and so on, in this configuration are connected to the integration broker by means of adapters; see Figure 17.12. The purpose of the adapters is to provide a reliable insulation layer between application APIs and the messaging infrastructure. These adapters enable non-invasive application integration in a loosely coupled configuration.

An integration broker extracts data from the source node at the right time, transforms the data, converts the schema, and routes the data to the target node. Here, the node can be an application, a program, or a person – as defined in the business process workflow. Communication between applications and an integration broker occurs mostly in the form of messages. An integration broker also provides a repository for archiving, searching, and retrieving these messages. An integration broker does not replace traditional middleware such as MOM, RPC, or distributed TP monitors. It is rather built on top of existing middleware technology, most often on messaging middleware.

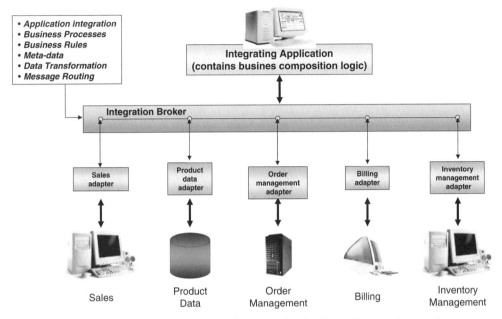

■ **Figure 17.12:** Integration Broker Topology for Business Process Integration

Most brokers provide the ability to support a suite of APIs and allow applications to communicate with each other and guarantee delivery of transactions. Both the integration broker and the EAI services are expecting the message in the standard internal format used by the integration broker. Hence, thick adapters are usually used to provide the mapping between the integrated EIS and applications and the integration broker native interfaces. The adapter is normally responsible for transforming component EIS schema and data content and putting it into the internal format expected by the integration broker. As there are no standards for message formats, this translation will be dependent on the middleware product used. If, for example, MQSeries is used, the message will be translated by the adapter into an MQSeries message format; if the middleware is BEA MessageQ, the message will be in BEA MessageQ format, and so on.

The integration broker infrastructure is responsible for accomplishing the following tasks (see Figure 17.12):

- Support for different types of messaging: The integration broker supports store and forward, store and retrieve and event-driven messaging. Some of the applications that communicate with each other may not able to initiate the session, while others may. The broker must be able to emulate the interface with which the legacy application expects to communicate and deal with any inconsistencies.

- Message routing: The broker must be able to send and receive messages and status information. All the messaging in the BPI occurs between applications and EIS and the integration broker. Once the integration broker receives a message from an EIS it routes it to appropriate component EIS. Message routing includes:

o Managing the delivery of the messages over communication connections including protocol conversion, flow of control, and guaranteed delivery.
o Multi-point message decomposition/re-composition to enable one to many and many to one routing.

- Status information is an important element of the integration broker. Consider, for instance, a legacy application that sends shipping instructions out to geographically dispersed warehouses. A local process at the warehouse will load the information into the recipient application. If it fails, the application needs to send a status update back to the broker, which is trapped and recorded and in the audit system of the broker. In this way the broker "realizes" that the operation has not completed successfully. However, without this type of information developers need develop complex programmatic solutions to manage and coordinate multiple systems.

- Data transformation: The integration broker contains data and message transformation facilities. For process integration transformation is between different API or message formats, whereas for data integration it is transformations between different data repository schema and semantic definitions. Data transformation facilities enable transforming between data elements having different structural representations and formats. Message transformation is the process of dynamically converting the message format, content and vocabulary of messages. Most modern integration brokers provide graphical user interface-based data transformation tools to assist with transformations.

- Meta-data support: Most advanced integration brokers use some form of meta-data to facilitate data-transformation. Typical meta-data that assist data transformations include schema-based data type descriptions, such as descriptions of relations, attributes, data element relationships, primary/foreign key constraints, and other EIS-centric meta-data. It also includes business rules and business process related meta-data. Meta-data is discussed further in Chapter 18 in the context of semantic interoperability.

- Business rules implementation: Business rules are important parts of business process definitions, as they govern the flow of business processes. These rules dictate not only the decision to send a given message to an application, but also the format of that message. The routed message may be an XML document and the decision to send it may be based on the content of another XML document. The integration broker is responsible for applying the enterprise business rules to the interacting business processes. Most integration brokers provide built-in graphical interfaces for defining simple business rules. More complex business rules can be implemented as Java classes.

- Ability to allow transaction recovery in a consistent format: In addition to event-triggered actions, data transformation, and messaging-based integration, EAI introduced another critical element generally missing from conventional workflow technology: transaction-awareness. EAI software can aggregate multiple process activities as a single unit of work, or business transaction, with rollback recovery and compensating activities explicitly defined in the model and executed automatically at runtime. Data can change structure during its journey and have several identification codes to track it in different formats. For instance, several transactions could originally be contained in a single application. In such cases the application would be split into the individual transactions, each transaction would be mapped to a different format and the new transactions would pass to the recipient application. A broker must be able to track transactions and their associated data based on their original formats and allow users to track transactions by date, time, sending/receiving application, and so on.

• Business process support: The integration broker is responsible for supporting business processes. Again, most modern integration brokers provide built-in graphical interfaces for representing business processes.

The integration broker architecture presents several advantages in the task of reducing the application integration effort by providing pre-built functionality common to many integration scenarios. The value proposition rests on reuse (in terms of middleware infrastructure and the application integration logic) across multiple applications and initiatives. Modern integration brokers incorporate integration functionality such as transformation facilities, process integration, business process management and trading partner management functionality, packaged adapters, and user-driven applications through front-end capabilities such as Java Server Pages. Integration brokers also present some disadvantages, including most notably:

1. Inability to automatically define implementation-level data-flows between distributed application instances: Almost all integrations require data to be routed in some order between different applications running on distinct machines in a heterogeneous network. Such integrations are surprisingly hard to set up within existing process driven integration broker suites, since such suites provide no in-built GUI tools to automatically configure the flow of data between physically executing application processes. Instead all actual data flows have to be manually configured, typically using JMS, MQSeries or other messaging middleware, increasing the time and complexity of the implementation.
2. Inability to easily define "ad-hoc" workflows and distributed applications across multiple component-models and platforms deployed within an organization: All current integration broker suites are limited in their support for multiple component-models and platforms, being heavily biased towards development using particular component models such as EJB, J2EE (for most vendors) and .NET for Microsoft-based solutions. As such, current brokers are unable to easily compose distributed integrations across multiple component models already deployed within an enterprise. This complicates cross-platform integration efforts enormously.
3. Inability to easily configure different adapters and applications participating in an integration: Most integration brokers do not provide adequate support to configure the adapters and applications running at the network end-points that actually participate in the integration workflow. Traditional integration broker suites do not allow the pre-existing GUI of each adapter to be called from within the integration framework to ease configuration. Instead, they require the configuration of each adapter or application to be manually updated within a centralized repository. This problem can result in significant implementation complexity.

The integration broker architecture also presents some limitations in connection with the support of end-to-end business processes. The most notable disadvantages are that end-to-end transactions are not supported due to the asynchronous messaging nature of this architecture. The solution is to use compensating transactions in the form of additional business processes. Integration brokers present low-level APIs to users as there are no standard ways to define standard interfaces to business operations such as funds withdrawal, funds transfer, credit check and so on. The lack of standard APIs for integration brokers makes end-to-end security difficult to implement. However, it is expected that XML and the emerging security suite standards around it, such as the Security Assertion Markup Language and XML Access Control Markup Language will provide some reasonable solution in the future. Refer to Section 13.6.5 for more details on these two emerging security standards.

Leading commercial integration broker solutions have evolved into comprehensive (and complex) product suites. Typical products include IBM MQSeries Integrator; Extricity; BEA eLink; WebMethods B2B Enterprise; Mercator Enterprise Broker, WebBroker, CommerceBroker; NEON eBusiness Integration Servers; SeeBeyond eBusiness Integration Suite; Tibco ActiveEnterprise, ActivePortal and ActiveExchange; Vitria BusinessWare; CrossWorlds Software; and Microsoft BizTalk Server. Today, many integration vendors have built out their adapter offerings and most provide a universal layer that supports proprietary MOM; Simple Object Access Protocol (SOAP), see Chapter 19, for message transfers; and, other forms of file transfer.

17.10.2 Application server-based process-level integration

Application servers enable the separation of application (or business) logic from interface processing, and also coordinate many resource connections. Application servers offer critical features such as secure transactional execution environment, load balancing, application-level clustering across multiple servers, failover management should one of these servers break down, and other elements of application serving infrastructure. Application servers provide application connectivity and thus access to data and functions associated with EIS applications, such as ERP, CRM and legacy applications. While application servers are focused on supporting new application development, they do not natively support integration.

Application servers typically provide Web connectivity for extending existing solutions and bring transaction processing mechanisms to the Web. In essence, an application server is simply a collection of services that support the development, run-time execution, and management of business logic for Web-enabled applications. The application server middleware enables the functions of handling transactions and extending back-end business data and applications to the Web. Application servers retrieve information from many existing enterprise systems and expose them through a single interface, typically a Web browser. This makes application servers ideal for portal-based EAI development. Unlike integration brokers, they do not integrate back-end systems directly.

Application server developers have all the necessary facilities for application development including programming language support and an integrated development environment. Further, Web application developers do not have to deal with heterogeneity. Information sources can be switched without affecting the application too much and clients can be changed at will without opening any client code. This is a perfect illustration of the concept of loose coupling.

Because application servers were created for Web-based transactions and application development and because of their ability to provide component-based integration to back-end applications, they are useful as support framework for integrating business processes.

Figure 17.13 presents a high-level view of the typical architecture for implementing application server-based process-level EAI. As this figure illustrates, the application server is the system centerpiece for a wholesale application that brings together ERP capabilities with sophisticated customer interfaces to open up new models of sales and distribution. The component wrappers in this figure achieve point-integration of component systems, e.g., ERP, CRM and distributor databases, as they introduce each of them to the application server. Execution in this type of architecture occurs among component wrappers within the application server. These component wrappers wrap back-end resources such as databases, ERP, transaction mainframe systems and legacy systems so that they can express data and messages in the

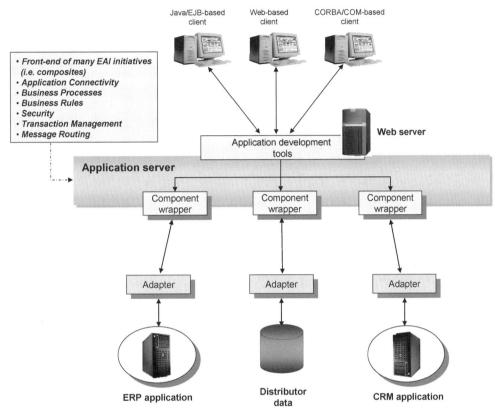

- *Front-end of many EAI initiatives (i.e. composites)*
- *Application Connectivity*
- *Business Processes*
- *Business Rules*
- *Security*
- *Transaction Management*
- *Message Routing*

■ **Figure 17.13:** Application Server Topology for Business Integration

standard internal format expected by the application server. The application server is oblivious to the fact that these components are only the external facade of existing EIS that do the real processing activities [Lubinsky 2001a].

The adapter/component wrapper pairs in the architecture illustrated in Figure 17.13 are responsible for providing a layer of abstraction between the application server and the component EIS. This layer allows for EIS component communications, as if the component EIS were executed within the application server environment itself. Traditional application servers constitute an ideal support framework for synchronous business processes. However, newer generation application servers also offer asynchronous communication.

The application server is responsible for accomplishing the following tasks:

- Message routing: All the messaging occurs between the enterprise information systems and the application server. The application server is responsible for involving the appropriate components at the appropriate time. Message routing includes additional requirements such as "intelligent" routing capabilities, which are defined in terms of content-based or rules-based routing capabilities.

- Data transformation: The application server provides transformation facilities for transforming between data elements and messages having different structural representations and formats. From the perspective of EIS components, wrapped EIS components appear as objects within the application server.

- Meta-data support: Meta-data services contain meta-data to facilitate data-transformations, such as typical EIS related meta-data as well as business rules and business process related meta-data.

- Business process and business rules support: The overall business processes must be coded within the application server. The application server is also responsible for applying the company business rules to the interacting business processes.

- Transaction support: This service enables multiple application operations to be coordinated to provide atomic and deterministic end results. This service employs a two-phase commit protocol that ensures that ACID (atomicity, consistency, isolation, durability) properties are preserved. Transactional services provide a commit and rollback facility that works with XA-compliant resources to ensure that either all the updates are made permanent or they are rolled back.

- Component support: This service provides support for developing component-based applications. It provides componentized access to EIS in order to seamlessly communicate among themselves through published programmatic interfaces supported by middleware platforms such as CORBA, COM and EJB.

Web application server platforms already provide database connectivity, transaction management, EAI-style connectors, message queuing, and are gradually evolving into business process execution engines. This architecture presents several advantages. It facilitates reliability, scalability, and availability, while at the same time automating application development tasks. The application server relieves application developers from the need to develop complex low-level middleware services and lets them concentrate more on coding business rules, creating and reusing business processes. The application server provides a central control facility for this throughout the enterprise. End-to-end transactions can be implemented with this approach if EIS support transactions. Finally, this approach allows transforming EIS components to objects for the application server.

Application servers also present several disadvantages. They are not strong in providing back-end integration or application-to-application integration. For instance, they do not provide data transformation between different data structures and semantics, rules-based and syntax validation and intelligent routing of data. Nor do they provide the fundamentals of true business process management, which includes functionality such as: long-lived transaction support, time-based exception handling, real-time monitoring and analysis of running processes, and dynamic management and change of the process. The main disadvantages of the application broker approach originate from the fact that all processing occurs synchronously (if asynchronous communication is not supported). This leads to a strong degree of coupling between component EIS. Moreover, long-lived processes can starve application server resources. There is often a mismatch between the life cycle of business processes and the components hosted by the application server [Lubinsky 2001a]. If asynchronous communication is supported between application servers (business systems belonging to separate enterprises), applications that require concurrent updates need to be synchronized.

Currently, application servers are available from a host of vendors such as BEA, Borland, HP, IBM, Oracle, Sun, and others. The criteria for selecting an application server may be varied, but key elements should include adherence to the J2EE specification and ability to support technologies such as Java Message Service, Java Database Connectivity and Secure Socket Layer.

In general terms an application server is an application development environment including a run-time engine on which applications can be deployed and run. Unfortunately, the term "application server" is no longer just associated with its original purpose of providing a comprehensive environment for application development and deployment. Recently, application servers have started to embrace application integration challenges [Dolgicer 2004]. They exploit their strength as a standards-based, central hub for new business components to also function as an integration hub. The integration capabilities have evolved from proprietary connectors (adapters) that facilitated point-integration of legacy systems and packaged applications to new technologies based on J2EE standards. These include support for JMS, the Java 2 Connector Architecture, and Web services.

17.11 Summary of application integration infrastructure functions

Table 17.1 summarizes the most typical characteristics and functions of application servers, integration brokers and object request brokers that are used for the purpose of application integration. From this table we can deduce that application servers are the most flexible infrastructure that can be considered as the infrastructure that targets e-Business application integration; see also Chapter 18. The modern version of the application server provides the essential functionality required for integration applications

	Comunication mode	Web presence	EAI-type	Coupling	Business processes	API	Transport	Transaction	Translation	Timing	Integration rules
Application server	synch/ asynch	Yes	Active	Loose	Yes	Yes	Yes	Yes	Yes	Yes	Yes
Integration broker	asynch	No	Passive	Loose	No	Yes	Yes	Yes	Yes	Yes	Yes
Object reques broker	synch	No	Passive	Tight	No	Yes	Yes	Yes	Yes	Yes	Yes

■ **Table 17.1:** Summary of Application Server, Integration Broker and ORB Functions

across the Internet, such as, for example, synchronous and asynchronous communications, active application integration, a loose form of coupling between cross-enterprise applications, support for business processes, standard APIs, translation, transaction and timing facilities. Integration brokers, on the other hand, have several appealing properties that make them an ideal choice for inter-enterprise application integration.

So far we have left unexplained the last column in Table 17.1. This column deals with the rules that determine application integration. Complex integration rules occur when multiple applications need to be integrated, or when there are multiple steps in the integration process. Integration takes place within the context of a business process, and relies on ready-modeled or custom-made solutions to drive it. Integration rules determine the characteristics of the integration and can be applied in several obvious situations, e.g., how data is transformed, or which application messages are sent to, and so on. However, there may be more complex business (integration) rules that require the content of information to be checked. For example, in EAI applications, the type of customer, e.g., customers with preferential status, may determine which customer information sources need to be updated. Therefore, for more complex integration tasks, services are needed in the application integration infrastructure that address the following aspects [Wilkes 1999]:

1. Multiplexing – determining whether one-to-many and many-to-many interactions between applications are required and how they are managed.
2. Business rules – can business rules that determine integration be expressed, and how? Where are they coded?
3. Workflow – are there end-to-end business processes that must be executed to effect the integration? Is the integration a business process in its own right? Does the integration require multiple steps, with different sources being integrated, to complete?

When the integration rules are complex, the integration tasks require application development. Typically all application integration solutions, such as the ones examined in Table 17.1 provide the necessary application development tools and environment for this purpose.

17.12 Chapter summary

To be competitive, an organization's core business applications – such as Enterprise Resource Planning, Supply Chain Management, and legacy systems – must be seamlessly integrated with Customer Relationship Management and Web-based applications to enable connectivity to suppliers, partners, and customers. This challenge is addressed by Enterprise Application Integration.

EAI is defined as the requirement to integrate the operational behavior, or business rules, of disparate systems as well as the data that underlies them into new business processes. EAI provides the infrastructure to reuse, rapidly connect, interface and unify information and business processes between an organization's internal applications into a cohesive corporate framework within the enterprise. It represents both the products as well as the process of integrating new and legacy applications (including packaged applications) with data files and databases. EAI is an integral part of the assembly process that facilitates integrating multiple applications at the enterprise level that were independently developed, may use incompatible technology and remain independently managed.

The most commonly encountered topologies in which application integration plays a major part are point-to-point, publish–subscribe, and hub and spoke topologies. Each of them has a series of advantages and disadvantages with the most serious disadvantages being associated with point-to-point solutions.

EAI is a conceptual multi-layered framework addressing integration issues at several hierarchical levels including the transportation layer, the data integration layer, the application programming interface integration layer and the business process integration layer. The transportation layer handles connectivity to an application and transports data to it from other applications. Applications can be either external or internal to an enterprise. The data integration level concentrates on the coordinated sharing and seamless integration of enterprise data while the application programming interface integration layer concentrates on the sharing of business logic between applications. The business process integration layer provides the core infrastructure that permits business processes to cross enterprise boundaries and link and interact with counterpart processes operated by the enterprise's suppliers and trading partners.

Business process integration is the primary aim when developing EAI and e-Business solutions and may present the broadest range of variations in integration practices ranging from simple application-to-application data exchange links to very complex arrangements involving transaction integrity support for business processes, or workflow routing for processes residing in different systems and enterprises.

The term Business Process Integration can be described as the ability to define a commonly acceptable business process model that specifies the sequence, hierarchy, events, execution logic and information movement between systems residing in the same enterprise and systems residing in multiple interconnected enterprises. The term management of business processes extends BPI techniques by including process analysis, process definition and redefinition, resource allocation, scheduling, measurement of process quality and efficiency, and process optimization.

Synchronization is an important element of the application integration infrastructure as it deals with when information should be exchanged between applications. This determines whether applications should be integrated in a synchronous or asynchronous manner.

Process-level EAI is implemented by means of standard infrastructure including integration brokers and application servers.

Integration brokers are responsible for brokering messages exchanged between two or more applications, providing the ability to transform, store, and route messages and also for applying business rules and responding to events. Application servers are used to interconnect an enterprise with the outside world. An application server is a natural point for application integration as it provides a platform for development, deployment and management of Web-based, transactional, secure, distributed and scalable enterprise applications. Application servers can be used in tandem with integration brokers through a cooperative interface. In this way the integration broker functions as an application integration backbone while the application server hosts custom business logic in the middle tier of a multi-tiered EAI architecture.

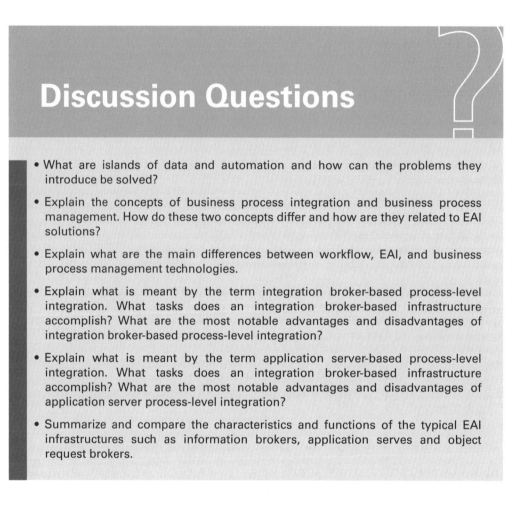

Discussion Questions

- What are islands of data and automation and how can the problems they introduce be solved?

- Explain the concepts of business process integration and business process management. How do these two concepts differ and how are they related to EAI solutions?

- Explain what are the main differences between workflow, EAI, and business process management technologies.

- Explain what is meant by the term integration broker-based process-level integration. What tasks does an integration broker-based infrastructure accomplish? What are the most notable advantages and disadvantages of integration broker-based process-level integration?

- Explain what is meant by the term application server-based process-level integration. What tasks does an integration broker-based infrastructure accomplish? What are the most notable advantages and disadvantages of application server process-level integration?

- Summarize and compare the characteristics and functions of the typical EAI infrastructures such as information brokers, application serves and object request brokers.

Assignments

i. A typical operation and business support environment embraces various disparate systems, from a customer servicing system to the provisioning, billing and mediation systems. In addition, this niche of operation and business support environment consists of numerous third-party systems in order to complete the communication backbone of the enterprise. These systems vary technically and functionally and need to be connected using a single or multiple integration methodology/products. For instance, the CRM System needs to communicate with various other systems such as billing, order management and provisioning to facilitate the order processing. Use an integration broker/application server (integration broker with application server stack) topology to interconnect all these diverse systems together. Explain how this company can communicate with external partners to conduct its business.

ii. Design a business integration platform that can deploy a Business Activity Monitoring solution that provides an organization with a way to monitor and alert enable transactional or operational systems such as ERP, supply chain management, customer relationship management, or any relational data store. Designed for use by business and technical users alike, the business integration system should notify and alert decision-makers, just in time, to issues with customer relationships, supply chain activity, sales and financial performance, or any other business event. The business integration system should enable the real-time, event-driven sharing of information between disparate heterogeneous systems and across departmental boundaries and help managers make smart decisions to shape the direction of their business. It should also enable the enterprise to inform employees with interactive notification of time-critical events as they occur. This enables the recipients to take action to resolve issues which arise. Typical alerts include customer shipment notifications, inventory out of stock notifications, inventory safety level reached, order behind schedule alert, order cancellations, purchase receipts due, purchase order requiring approval, strategic customer on credit-hold, receipt of payment from customer on credit-hold, and so on. The end-result recipient alerts (which can be by way of SMTP e-mail, HTML Web Pages, XML, and SMS for cell phones or pagers) are all configured from a single screen interface. Assume that the data sources in this organization can be relational databases, data warehouses and also the data files of legacy applications. The architecture should combine application integration, business process automation, business activity monitoring, event-notification middleware and legacy integration modules.

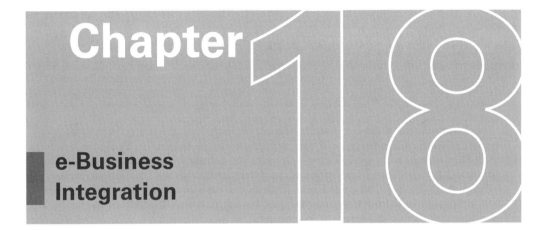

Chapter 18

e-Business Integration

Enterprises strive to integrate, automate, and streamline core internal and external business processes to improve their performance in the e-Business environment. By their very nature, supply chains require that each participant integrate their information services with the others, as they all become part of an extended network. To achieve end-to-end process integration requires integration with back-end systems and business processes. These business processes drive a company's e-Business interactions with their customers, partners, distributors, and suppliers; they can also streamline the company's internal business. The requirement is to effectively combine the enterprise's best practices with a means of automating the time- and cost-intensive business tasks involved in the entire information supply chain. In this way enterprises can form partnerships with others to provide a totally integrated experience for their customers.

This chapter provides a detailed introduction to e-Business integration concepts and techniques. It first presents the key characteristics and types of automated business processes and then an overview of e-Business and the standards used for e-Business integration. Different e-Business topologies are introduced and the use of workflow technology for e-Business integration solutions is explained. Business integration patterns that are the result of strategic e-Business decisions are described and the concept of semantic interoperability is introduced. In addition, we explain the desired level of integration (tight vs. loose) between local and remote applications on the basis of the types of relationship between trading partners. Finally, e-Business integration requirements are revisited and e-Business integration is compared with EAI solutions described in Chapter 17.

Case Study

Deutsche Bank's Global Integration Platform[1]

The Deutsche Bank Group, headquartered in Frankfurt, Germany, is one of the world's largest financial institutions with total assets exceeding EUR 758 billion (US $866 billion) and over 77 000 employees. The company has approximately 2300 branches in more than 76 countries serving the needs of over 13 million customers. Through its Global Corporates and Institutions division, the company provides an integrated investment and commercial banking service to many of the world's leading companies and financial institutions.

The company's back-end IT applications handle all of the processes associated with buying and selling securities from each of its business divisions. Company traders worldwide manually enter transaction information into separate order management applications and investment banking systems. To streamline its operations and reduce order entry errors, Deutsche Bank wanted an e-Business platform to integrate each independent order management application, enabling the communication of transaction data in real time and providing shared access to the company's trading information worldwide. As Deutsche Bank expanded its back-end application architecture and merged several of its existing legacy applications, the company wanted a flexible e-Business platform that could handle the addition of applications and support a globally distributed system. The company wanted a platform that could support constant usage and could perform under strenuous network traffic. To further optimize its operations, Deutsche Bank needed to standardize the hardware and software used in each of its locations that perform similar mission-critical activities.

After evaluating several solutions, Deutsche Bank selected Vitria's BusinessWare platform (www.vitria.com) which handles high volumes of data transactions, for its publish and subscribe messaging technology and secure and reliable data communications infrastructure. The company created an application management service named dBus, using BusinessWare, Visual Basic and Java to integrate systems that were previously independent and facilitate securities trading worldwide. When Deutsche Bank traders, in any location, place buy or sell orders for stocks, bonds and other securities through dBus, the trading information is disseminated throughout the company's back-office systems. dBus users access

[1] This case study was summarized from www.vitria.com.

the system to gain an integrated view of securities trading activity worldwide. The bank, after being successful with rolling out the platform for a select number of 17 business divisions worldwide, expects to expand the dBus application to Deutsche Bank's over 50 business divisions worldwide and anticipate publishing hundreds of thousands of records daily.

Deutsche Bank has integrated its various independent back-end order and transaction management applications and legacy systems without having to code point-to-point interfaces. By making the dBus platform a standard enterprise-wide medium the company has facilitated application integration throughout the entire company and was able to extend its technology throughout the enterprise without increasing overhead. The company has also experienced a reduction in implementation time when adding new systems to its IT infrastructure.

18.1 Business processes and e-Business integration

e-Business integration grows on the back of successful internal EAI solutions and provides the capability to link together disparate processes between interacting business entities. Business processes drive a company's e-Business interactions with their customers, partners, distributors, and suppliers. Moreover, business processes can also streamline the company's internal business. Among the target business processes for e-Business integration and automation are design and specification, manufacturing and testing, procurement, sales fulfillment, customer service, and planning. e-Business integration manages the end-to-end processes of the entire value chain, creating a seamless and efficient environment. In this way enterprises can form partnerships with others to provide a totally integrated experience for their customers.

An example of a totally integrated solution can be an automotive industry network among manufacturers, dealers, retail system providers in the automotive distribution value chain, and banks to provide customers with a one-stop-shopping experience. This network may include online car research and selection, pricing the vehicle, possible construction of a tailor-made vehicle, choosing the payment scheme and agreement on the delivery date. These types of partnerships allow enterprises to align their services with the most important priorities of their customers, e.g., variety, quality, competitive pricing and fast delivery and require a high degree of integration, along with the flexibility to quickly enable new partnerships in an automated fashion.

Business processes are fundamental elements of EAI or e-Business integration. The ability to manage business processes is the key to integrating applications, systems and people into a single integrated solution. Business processes consolidate enterprise-wide tasks, actions, decisions, and events into a continuous flow that keeps business activities moving forward. Business processes can be as brief as a single transaction, or they can be long-running activities, spanning days or even weeks.

In the context of integration, a business process refers to any multi-step activity that manipulates data or business logic from multiple systems. Business processes are long running and very dynamic, responding to demands from customers and to changing market conditions. For example, a single instance of an order-to-cash process may run for months; it is the pipeline that links booked orders to the collection of revenue and is often so full of blockages, alternatives and escape clauses that many booked sales cannot be easily translated directly into cash received.

Business processes are usually large and complex, involving the flow of materials, information and business commitments. They are widely distributed and customized across boundaries within and between organizations, often spanning multiple applications with very different technological infrastructure.

Business processes can be internal to a business, coordinating simple interactions between different departments, or they can be public processes that orchestrate collaboration between trading partners. We may thus distinguish between two kinds of processes within an enterprise.

> *Private business processes*: these are processes internal to an enterprise. They are not exposed outside the enterprise, and customers or trading partners do not interact with them directly. Private processes are usually integrated with back-end business systems. A private process might handle the interaction between an enterprise and its customers, but the interaction takes place through a Web site. For example, placing an order on a Web site might trigger a private business process that performs the following tasks: inventory check; credit card validation; transmission of a confirmation; order building and order shipment. The design, definition and management of private processes are specific to a particular enterprise.

> *Public business processes*: these enable the interaction with trading partners in a collaborative, e-Business arrangement by choreographing the exchange of business messages between them. These inter-enterprise processes have unique requirements that exceed those of private processes. Public business processes are typically integrated with *private* business processes. For example, a private process can execute an internal business activity, such as retrieving information from a database, and then it can return the result to a public process, which, in turn, forwards the result to a trading partner. The design and management of these processes is subject to the agreement of the trading partners. They are part of a formal contract that defines the content and semantics of the messages exchanged by the partners, and they may be standardized across an industry or industry segment.

In addition, we may also distinguish between two primary types of business processes for integration purposes [Lubinsky 2001b]:

- *Synchronous business processes*: Synchronous processes have strict timing and transactional requirements. They usually occur in real time and must deliver either a result within the duration of the request or an error. A typical example of synchronous processes is ticket reservations.

- *Asynchronous business processes*: Asynchronous processes have less rigid timing requirements when compared with synchronous processes. These are started as part of an execution request, where the requester is not blocked and can continue with its processing activities rather than wait for them to finish. A typical example of asynchronous business processes is order fulfillment.

Business processes are sometimes designed to be started and stopped by users (people), or to include tasks that must be performed by people. These tasks frequently include making discretionary decisions, handling exceptions, or troubleshooting problems [BEA 2002]. Business processes can be started in a variety of ways, depending on their design [BEA 2002]. More specifically they can be:

1. called by another application or workflow system;
2. invoked manually by people using a business process-based application;
3. timed to start automatically at a predefined time interval or
4. triggered by the receipt of an event notification, e.g., an incoming order, in the form of an XML message; this XML message may originate from another application, another workflow system, or a trading partner.

18.2 Business process redesign

Making key business processes available over the Internet may involve relatively straightforward extension of existing processes out to the Internet or may involve complex re-engineering efforts to make the business processes Web-enabled.

Typically, the logistic flow of a business process follows a trajectory across different (functional) departments. As a result the execution of business processes is often hampered by many inefficiencies, like:

1. the workflow being managed per department, and independently per department;
2. departments checking each other's work;
3. the workflow being supported by different information systems, and
4. nobody really being responsible for the entire workflow.

Redesign of business processes based on a critical analysis of the workflow and taking the enabling possibilities of modern IT into account has been seen as seen as a way to significantly improve an organization's operational performance. BPR (business process redesign) may be defined as "the critical analysis and radical redesign of business processes to achieve breakthrough improvements in performance measures" [Teng 1994], such as cost, quality and speed. Essential in this definition is the word radical, as opposed to incremental improvements. The aim is to achieve significant improvement in operational results (e.g., tenfold improvements) through direct actions aimed at a fundamental redesign of the process, taking a "clean slate" approach.

A company wide approach to BPR may encompass the following steps [Davenport 1993]:

1. Develop a business vision and process objectives. BPR for a specific company is driven by key performance measures that are critical for the company's competitive position. The BPR vision gives direction to how BPR should be targeted, e.g., at cost reduction, time reduction, and quality improvement, or learning and empowerment.
2. Identify the processes to be redesigned. A distinction can be made between a high impact approach and an exhaustive approach. The former focuses on the most important processes or on those that conflict most with the business vision. The latter involves identification of all processes and prioritizing them in order of urgency.

3. Understand and measure the current processes to provide a bottom line for future improvements.
4. Identify the IT levers in order to understand how IT should impact the process design.
5. Design and build a prototype of the new process. Typically process design will evolve after a number of iterations.

The redesign of the business process itself could follow the following steps:

1. Organize around results and outcomes, not around tasks and so combine several jobs into one.
2. Make those who process information, use the information: workers make decisions.
3. Information-processing work should be subsumed into the real work that produces the information, so that steps are performed in a natural order.
4. Treat geographically dispersed resources as if they were centralized.
5. Put decision points where the work is performed, and incorporate checks and controls into the process (as such exogenous controls are reduced).
6. Capture information once and at the source (work is performed where it makes most sense).
7. Do not forget that processes have multiple versions.
8. Appoint case managers who provide a single point of contact.

Notwithstanding the promises, 70% of BPR projects have been reported to fail. The reasons for this high failure rate are similar to those for any radical organizational change: lack of management commitment, unrealistic scopes and expectations, and badly handled resistance to change. In particular, an overemphasis on tactical aspects and neglect of the strategic considerations are perceived as a major obstacle to success [King 1998]. Also, the effectiveness of a company-wide, top-down approach as described above is questioned. Instead, there are signs that bottom-up approaches may be more successful. Business re-engineering proves to be successful starting with a small experiment in an inconspicuous part of the organization [Caron 1994]. This approach offers the organization the opportunity to learn from successes and failures, and to transfer this knowledge to larger projects in more complex parts of the organization. In this way an organizational memory of what succeeds and fails is built up [Caron 1994], which in the end can make business redesign work effectively. It general it is not the concept of BPR, which is considered as the reason for failure, rather then the way it is implemented [Teng 1994].

18.3 e-Processes

As already explained earlier in this book, managing and optimizing business processes using IT is a competitive necessity for every company. In particular, workflow systems have helped to automate, streamline and also redesign existing processes.

Also the Internet is exerting its influence. The Internet helps to design new processes and to redesign existing ones [Nah 2004]. The term *e-Business process management* is being used to indicate the (re-) design and management of business processes facilitated by the Internet. e-Business process management encompasses the design and management of collaborative processes supported by the Internet. Such collaborative processes may involve interaction with customers, suppliers and trading partners, so e-Business management faces a number of new challenges [Nah 2004]. An e-Business process combines activities from at least two independent organizations, which requires an integration of different organizational practices, cultures etc. Internet-enabled self-services offer new opportunities and challenges in process design. Examples are customer self-services where customers become the drivers of an entire business process and supplier self-services as a part of supply chain management systems.

Compared to traditional business processes e-Business process management presents new challenges. A few examples may serve as an illustration [Nah 2004]:

1. An e-Business process spans more than one organization. Processes are being made available to customers, suppliers and other trading partners. Consequently differences between legally and economically independent firms have to be bridged. Differences in company objectives, priorities, ways of working, in culture etc., and probably in IT platforms have to be overcome before a joint design of a process can be established. This is difficult and takes time! Companies have invested in their existing business, including procedures, information systems, standards etc. Abandoning or adapting them to the needs of the external business partner is costly. Crossing company borders with a process also requires transmitting data to another organization and may face legal limitations. For example, in the case of sharing patient data between different care providers and an insurance company, privacy issues will have to be dealt with.
2. The Internet also offers opportunities for new alternatives in process design. For example, supplier self-services, where suppliers become the drivers of a business process (in particular ordering and replenishment), form an indispensable part of modern supply chain management.
3. The Internet can significantly reduce transaction costs, and so contributes to outsourcing entire business processes.

Finally, e-process (or simply e-Business process) management may imply a rather fundamental shift in organizational practice. Traditional organizations were built around processes. The execution of processes was bound by the "physical" boundaries of the firm. The work was done physically within the firm. Moreover, for decades organizations and their processes did not change very much. Today, with modern IT, processes are run by people that do not necessarily reside within the "physical" boundaries of their organization. Actually the work, and the tools needed to do the work, can be moved to the people, on their laptops, PDAs etc. Moreover, under the pressure of market dynamics, value chains are being bundled and unbundled, and processes are no longer contained within the same organizational borders. They must cross not only the departmental borders imposed by the company's organizational structure, but also the boundaries of different companies.

Despite the potential promises of e-Process management, there is too high a level of optimism associated with this topic [Davenport 2004]. Setting up efficient and effective processes in a single organization and making those available to external business partners, are two different things, he argues. As key factors that slow down the process of adoption he mentions the fact that business partners have to agree on meanings (semantics), on how to set up interorganizational business processes, and on how to embed process flows into their existing systems. So it will take time, and it will be more like an evolution than a revolution.

18.4 Overview of e-Business integration

e-Business is about coordinating the flow of information and processes among enterprises and their underlying EIS. The aim of e-Business integration is to facilitate supply, distribution and customer information exchange, coordination and collaboration between multiple trading partners. e-Business integration typically combines automated services from multiple providers, such as partners for the supply chain, to support extended transaction management and, more importantly, information exchange, coordination and collaboration across the extended value chain [Davydov 2001].

An e-Business transaction may involve many enterprises with varying interests in the transaction such as the products or services, payment arrangements or monitoring and control. Every business transaction generates multiple business processes such as credit checks, automated billing, purchase orders, stock updates and shipping on the back-end systems of the enterprises involved. The challenge is how to integrate operational systems and enterprise data with the Web applications, to enable customers, partners and suppliers to transact directly with an enterprise's corporate systems such as inventory, accounting and purchasing. One thing that all the enterprises involved in an e-Business transaction have in common is the need for information for their decisions, their actions and for the synchronization of these actions. While the physical transport and handling of goods constitute a flow made up of a straightforward series of activities, the corresponding information flow shows a more varied and complex pattern. The purpose of the information flow, which combines the flow of data and the invocation of functionality among disparate (and possibly heterogeneous) systems across enterprises, is to provide and manage smooth and efficient flows of goods and payments. To this end, the information in each step has to be accurate and reliable. It has to meet the needs of each receiver and be presented in an appropriate form and in a timely manner. Consider for instance the case where containers are introduced in transport. Handling and transport of goods becomes faster and this, in turn, calls for faster processing and communication of related information. The documents exchange between the enterprises involved in the e-Business transaction have to reflect that containers are the handling units, in addition to describing the goods in them. The containerized transport systems attract high-value goods, and this puts even more emphasis on the information being accurate, timely and reliable. Any inaccuracies and errors in the information flow may have immediate consequences for the receiver organization's ability to proceed with its part of the transaction.

The following ten main characteristics of the loosely coupled e-Business application integration model summarize the previous discussion. These are also graphically depicted in Figure 18.1:

1. The e-Business integration model interlinks seamlessly the operational behavior, or business rules, disparate systems as well as the data that underlies them into new business processes spanning organizations.
2. e-Business integration reaches beyond the enterprise to provide the automated support needed to fulfill e-Business transactions between corporate entities. In fact, the e-Business model advances the idea of an e-Market composed of discrete transactions from various corporate entities. The e-Business integration model assumes support for long running complex transactions and event sharing without excessive latency.
3. e-Business integration is an application-to-application concept, always functioning in near real time, and typically at the back-end with limited end-user influence.
4. e-Business integration uses of the notion of reuse in addition to distribution of business processes and data between several linked enterprises.
5. The e-Business integration model assumes that scalability and fast response time are requirements and not just goals.
6. e-Business integration must employ advanced security standards to ensure that information moving between enterprises is not visible to others on the public networks.

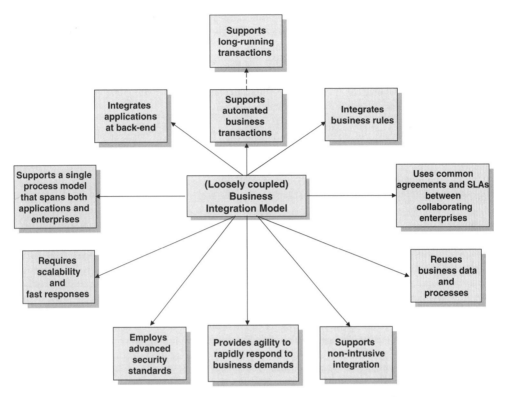

Figure 18.1: Characteristics of e-Business Integration Model

7. e-Business integration uses the notion of common agreements between trading organizations, and supports those agreements as information is exchanged between them.
8. The e-Business integration model provides agility to rapidly respond to competitive business demands using process modeling and automation.
9. e-Business integration assumes that source and target systems cannot be altered to support inter-enterprise application integration, so the points of integration must be non-intrusive.
10. e-Business integration takes into account the differences between integrating applications within and between enterprises, and supports a single process model that spans both.

18.4.1 Choosing the type of integration

Companies are at a wide variety of stages in implementing e-Business initiatives, from simple connection to a trading exchange for procurement, to creating electronic communities – a group of companies forming tighter trading relationships for mutual business advantage – to sophisticated trading networks where e-Business relationships are formed as loosely and as dynamically as required. With the evolution of e-Business models such as virtual organizations, extended value chains, electronic marketplaces, public and private exchanges, trading hubs and so on, new opportunities arise to make e-Business partnerships for key business functions. All these require some form of integration on the technical level.

One of the most important requirements for e-Business integration is the level of independence between application implementation and a remote application server interface or processing. In other words, how likely it is that changes to the e-Business application will lead to changes to the server interface or changes to the integration processing environment. The degree of invasiveness can affect the remote server application processing and even require changes to the partner application. The further across the e-Business integration topology a change ripples, the more complicated and expensive this change will be. The degree of invasiveness is often described in terms of coupling.

Coupling can be defined as the degree of interdependence between two business processes. With tight coupling the calling system requires detailed knowledge of the technology, e.g., components, of the called system and precise definition of the call structure and the arguments in it. In contrast to this, *loose coupling* implies call structure and technology independence. With loosely coupled systems an application does not need to know the intimate details of how to deal with the interfaces of another application. Each participant in a loosely coupled multi-step process flow is a standalone unit of work that need be concerned only with ensuring that it can send a message to another application. The same terms are also used frequently to describe the type of connection to a system (or component), with tightly-coupled meaning synchronous request/response connection, the integration approach offered by component platforms (see Chapters 15 and 17), and loosely-coupled meaning asynchronous store and forward connection.

When integrating e-Business applications, the objective is to minimize coupling, that is, to make (self-contained) business processes as independent as possible by not having any knowledge of, or relying on, any business processes originating in other organizations. This loose coupling of applications has several advantages but also some disadvantages. With a loosely coupled integration between a source and a target application, the source application can continue processing client requests without blocking on target application server performance or communication problems. This improves fault tolerance and scalability. However, the price to pay is that application developers may find it difficult to program an asynchronous messaging system as these systems do not support the propagation of transaction and security contexts. A classical example of loose coupling is event-driven applications and the service-oriented approach espoused by Web-services, which we shall examine in Chapter 19.

As opposed to loose coupling, which is often used for linking applications to one another, tight coupling is frequently used within an application. This means that the same messaging (homogeneous) technology is required within, for example, the same component model, and the semantics and structure of the message have to be agreed by the message sender and recipients before hand.

The goal of EAI middleware is to create a single unified view of a virtual organization. Consequently, classic middleware systems (including components) typically involve tight coupling between the systems and processes at the various organizations. By closely coupling the organizations, classic middleware systems are able to provide rich functionality, but require expensive initial deployments and carefully coordinated ongoing deployment management. These systems are thus most appropriate for use in a single distributed organization or across long-term and closely coordinated business partnerships. For instance, EDI solutions result in tight coupling between the transaction systems used by the participants.

Component systems and architectures (see Chapter 15), such as CORBA and Enterprise JavaBeans, provide middleware for integrating application components written in different languages. CORBA, RMI and COM were all designed for tightly coupled applications. They are based on an RPC (synchronous) model and assume a great deal of similarity between the calling and called systems. For the purpose of interaction, an application component needs to know only the interfaces to other components written in a suitable middleware integration language (for example, the Interface Definition Language or IDL in CORBA, Java, or platforms such as Windows). Such tightly coupled architectures make it difficult for arbitrary systems to interoperate. In such environments, typically, the applications are executed as short ACID (atomicity, consistency, isolation, durability) transactions. The underlying middleware provides necessary runtime services, for instance, naming, transaction, and resource allocation. For the automation of the e-Business interactions, no common, shared, underlying middleware can be assumed for distributed applications spanning organizational boundaries and using a public network, such as the Internet. Setting up such a common software infrastructure requires tight coupling of the business partners' software platforms.

Even if such a homogeneous software connection could be established, ACID and/or complex extended transaction models would not be appropriate for e-Business interactions. Implementation of such protocols necessitates tight coupling of operational states across business applications, which is highly undesirable. The application components in one organization may lock the resources in other enterprises for an extended period of time, resulting in a loss of autonomy. Moreover, rollback and/or compensation of application steps is no longer under the control of a single enterprise. Some of these issues will become clearer once we have discussed the characteristics and functionality of Web services and Web-service transactions in Section 19.9.

For the above reasons component architectures are normally used to support internal applications rather than to support communication between applications or with the external world. In general, tight coupling between applications limits an enterprise's ability to react to changing business requirements.

18.4.2 The role of standards

Business interactions center on cross-enterprise application integration, collaborative business process and workflow technologies. Many of the early EAI solutions fall short of expectations when dealing with cross-enterprise solutions. Enterprises may decide to adopt proprietary messaging technologies to integrate their applications internally. This may mean that trading partners need to adopt multiple infrastructures, as it is unreasonable to expect that all trading partners would commit to identical messaging solutions.

Open standards have driven the e-Business revolution. Networking protocols such as TCP/IP and HTTP, have enabled universal communication via the Internet and the World Wide Web. In addition, programming standards based on Java have enabled the portability of applications and the reuse of application components. Java represents a good programming language choice for EAI because of its portability, it runs on most operating systems, and boasts good support from EAI tool vendors. However, XML-based standards are receiving increased attention as they enable the exchange and sharing of data across multiple systems connected by the Internet.

XML has emerged as the messaging standard to address many of these cross-enterprise application issues; see Chapter 7. XML is a perfect vehicle to describe messages and for publishing data definitions and meta-data for wrapping diverse message formats. Because of its extensible nature and the self-describing meta-data within documents, XML can support a flexible and dynamic e-Business environment for application interoperability. It can provide the e-Business communication standard for both shared data and data definitions. It also provides flexible graphical tools to edit and view business objects, as well as transform and share business objects and data. XML provides an excellent data transformation facility for standardizing message transformation between trading partners. XML messages can be easily extended outside the enterprise and existing XML standards have predefined message data for several business patterns. There are at least three ways in which XML can be used in e-Business applications:

1. *Extending EDI functionality*. EDI has traditionally been associated with a set of standards that have been created for data interchange between enterprises (see also Section 7.6). These are currently binary standards, but there are initiatives to enable the use of XML in EDI. In this way the limitations of EDI that lie in the cost of integration and deployment to smaller business partners can be surmounted. With XML, there is no reason for some of the costly EDI requirements such as the use of Value Added Networks; instead, trading partners can exchange structured data across the Internet using XML. However, the current EDI standards are optimized for large volumes whereas XML over the Internet is not optimized to the same extent. Therefore, XML is not a total replacement for the EDI standards but is rather complimentary. For example, trading partners can exchange not only old structures of EDI data, but also business process templates and business rules. The XML/EDI group (www.xmledi-group.org) is currently looking at this fusion of XML/EDI to extend the advantages of Web-based EDI to small and medium enterprises.
2. *Interoperating with Java technologies*. Whereas Java is used as a means to making applications platform independent, which is an advantage when deploying distributed Web applications, XML provides a way of representing data in an application independent way. Thus, XML and Java are ideally suited as complementary technologies that can have major impacts on e-Business. Both are very flexible in that they can be extended to suit virtually any EAI or e-Business environment by integrating and interoperating easily with external systems. Increasingly, developers are taking advantage of the flexibility of XML to communicate more than just business data, such as describing workflows, process state information, and collaborative business processes.
3. *Defining industry-wide standards*. The lack of standards is one of the biggest obstacles to XML's viability and acceptance. Different industries are currently using different transaction information and formats, e.g., orders, to mean the same thing. Recently, standard-setting bodies and vertical industries have started working together to define their documents, transaction sets and collaborations, security handling and exception definitions to facilitate the conduct of e-Business. These activities are discussed later in this chapter and in Chapter 20, where we introduce business standards and protocols.

18.4.3 Initial comparison between EAI and e-Business integration

Although EAI and e-Business integration share many of the same approaches and technologies, they do have unique characteristics. EAI typically deals with the integration of applications, business processes and data sources within an enterprise to solve a local problem. EAI lacks the pure business-to-business integration features, such as the use of XML, support for business standards, EDI and the need for sophisticated security mechanisms. In contrast, e-Business integration is the integration of systems between organizations to support any business requirement, such as sharing information with trading partners to support a supply chain or collaborating on a product design [Linthicum 2001b]. While e-Business integration software provides many of the features EAI solutions lack, it does not provide deep, non-intrusive integration with internal enterprise applications that need to participate within a trading community.

e-Business integration extends EAI by enabling integration of data, processes and transactions across organizational boundaries. The technologies enabling e-Business integration include partner management, process management, support for e-Business standards, including XML and EDI, and e-Business security (non-repudiation, encryption, support for multiple firewall configurations). e-Business is also based on business protocol and standard support for managing the format, semantics and function of any business process, as well as business conversation dialogues between trading partners regardless of industry.

Initially, EAI and e-Business integration were considered as separate domains. EAI focused on synchronizing data and functionality from disparate systems within an enterprise's firewall, including those spread across separate business units and locations. e-Business integration also addressed the problem of integrating multi-vendor IT infrastructures, however, its primary emphasis was in exchanging data and invoking functionality between different organizations across the Internet. Despite the fact that EAI and e-Business integration address different business needs, the technology used and the approaches applied to both types of solutions are similar. For example, they both may employ middleware solutions, such as integration brokers, so that data is transformed and routed from application to application, and similar approaches to systems integration. It is thus not surprising that most experts agree that these two domains will soon merge. In fact, EAI products have gradually shifted emphasis from conventional middleware products to e-Business enabling platforms. As we will see later in this chapter, application servers, integration brokers, and assorted integration engines now occupy the leading role in the center of a multi-tier enterprise topology that aims not only to integrate data and business processes within the confines of a single enterprise but also aims to integrate them with business processes, transactions and data from multiple enterprises. Logic obviously suggests that internal information systems must be integrated before they can be externalized to foreign systems residing with trading partners. As can be seen from Figure 17.2, EAI is morphing with e-Business to simply form a continuum extending from inter-enterprise to intra-enterprise application integration. Hence, we can view EAI and e-Business as clearly integrated concepts that leverage much from each other.

18.5 Topologies for e-Business integration

Classical core EAI technologies such as integration brokers and MOM are incapable of addressing the characteristics and requirements of e-Business integration summarized in the previous section.

Application servers address most of the drawbacks of integration brokers and MOM technologies and can be considered as the main development platforms targeting e-Business integration. An application server is the natural point for e-Business integration because it provides a platform for development, deployment and management of Web-based business applications. Application servers are the platform of choice for applications that are developed using a multi-tier architecture. Application servers provide a flexible platform for integrating business applications, as they can be interconnected using either synchronous or asynchronous communication methods.

The application server-based topology has been presented earlier in this book when we addressed three-tier architectures and middleware in Chapters 6 and 14 and studied further in the context of EAI solutions in Section 17.10.2. Recall that as explained in Chapter 6 (see Figure 6.6), the application server implements the processing-tier in a multi-tier architecture and thus acts as an intermediary between browser-based front-ends, and back-end data bases and legacy systems.

Application servers primarily provide the infrastructure support for executing distributed applications together with technology integration capabilities. The application server provides both the development tools and run-time platform for developing applications on the Web. Application servers provide the infrastructure for developers to write business logic that turns disparate and geographically distributed applications into integrated applications. Although the main function of an application server has been to host business logic, these days they also include integration brokering capabilities (see Section 17.10.2). The integration brokering functionality is required for the purposes of integrating business processes that span enterprises.

The ability to interconnect application servers is a key requirement for integrating e-Business applications. An important requirement, as in the case of the multi-tier application architecture, is that business logic reside in the application server. When we try to integrate e-Business applications this needs to be achieved at the business-process level. In an e-Business topology, such as the one depicted in Figure 18.2, sharing business logic between applications is an important factor when attempting to integrate applications that originate from different enterprises. This moves integration logic out of the applications codifying the business logic including the sequencing of events and data flow ensuring the integrity of the business transaction.

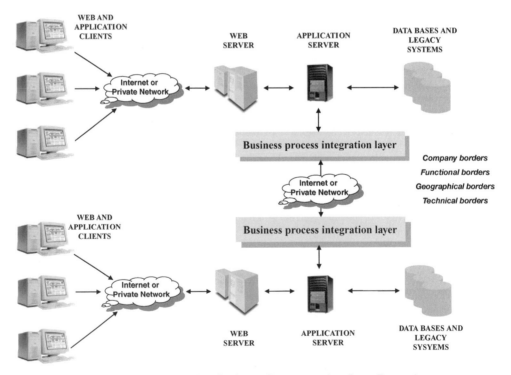

■ Figure 18.2: Integrating Business Processes that Span Enterprises

Application servers coordinate the sequence of complex integration steps with support for checkpoints and transaction boundaries.

In general, the following criteria indicate an application server solution [Wilkes 1999]:

- The prime need is to deliver a Web-based business processes, with reasonable development of new functionality.

- The focus is technology integration and legacy systems.

- Sources of integration are already well structured and have clear interfaces.

- New components that run on the Web server are being developed.

- A hub and spoke mechanism is being provided.

- Run-time management of applications is being provided.

As the business logic that defines and drives business processes for specific applications resides in the application server layer, it is only natural that when we are discussing integration of business processes, we are really talking about interconnecting application servers. Figure 18.2 illustrates how an application server can be used for integration with existing applications and heterogeneous enterprise information systems. The application server can extend the enterprise processes and interlink them with counterpart processes in external organizations by supporting secure transactions and XML data exchanges through the Internet. External data exchanges drive internal processes through the application server.

Figure 18.2 illustrates that business-process integration introduces an additional independent coordination layer that provides a non-invasive fit into the existing application server architectures. Rather than being primarily focused on integrating physical entities such as data or business components, the business process integration layer involves the integration of logical entities represented as business process elements. The application server thus encapsulates the process logic of application integration in its business process integration layer. This moves integration logic out of the applications codifying the logic, including the sequencing of events and data flow, and ensuring transaction integrity. Application servers coordinate the sequence of complex integration steps with the support for checkpoints and transaction boundaries. As business rules change, the business process definition can be changed within the application server development environment, thereby reducing application maintenance and providing flexibility.

The e-Business topology in Figure 18.2 assumes that integration broker functionality is built upon an application server stack. An important point to note about this type of e-Business topology is that integration brokers including those that are built upon an application server, require that the entire integration broker/ application server stack be installed everywhere that the integration broker functionality is necessary. This is clearly shown in Figure 18.2.

In many situations where high volumes of interaction are required, such as, for instance, the situation described in the Deutsche Bank case study, integration brokering capabilities need to be distributed across a more loosely coupled integration environment involving the use of federated enterprise buses. Recall from our case study that the Deutsche Bank e-Business integration platform needs to access back-end applications on a continual basis and needs to perform under strenuous network traffic.

The *Enterprise Service Bus* (ESB) is an open standards-based message bus usually based on publish–subscribe and event-notification mechanisms that is designed to enable the implementation, deployment, and management of e-Business integration solutions with a focus on assembling, deploying, and managing distributed service-oriented architectures. The ESB provides the distributed processing, standards-based integration, and enterprise-class backbone required by the extended enterprise; see Figure 18.3.

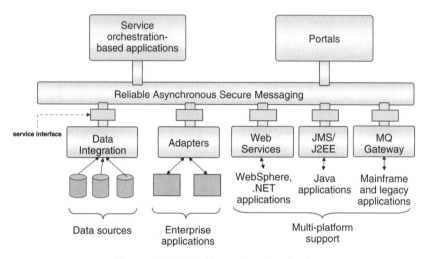

■ Figure 18.3: The Enterprise Service Bus

The ESB offers a whole range of functions designed to provide a manageable a standards-based IT backbone that extends Messaging Oriented Middleware functionality throughout the entire business value chain, connecting heterogeneous components and systems [Chappell 2004]. In addition to "backbone" style communications, the ESB also offers integration with the broad spectrum of components likely to be encountered through the use of various "standard" binding approaches such as Web services, J2EE Connector Architecture, JMS, COM, and other common mechanisms. The ESB is designed to provide interoperability between larger grained applications and other components via standards-based adapters and interfaces. The bus functions as both transport and transformation facilitator to allow distribution of these services over disparate systems and computing environments.

Conceptually, the ESB has evolved from the store-and-forward mechanism found in middleware products and now is a combination of EAI, Web services, XSLT, and orchestration technologies. To achieve its operational objectives the ESB draws from traditional EAI broker functionality in that it provides integration services such as connectivity and routing of messages based on business rules, data transformation, and adapters to applications [Chappell 2004]. These capabilities are spread out across the bus in a highly distributed fashion and hosted in separately deployable service containers. This is crucial difference from traditional integration brokers, which are usually highly centralized and monolithic in nature.

18.6 Workflow, BPM, EAI and e-Business

Recently, we are witnessing that enterprises have a renewed interest in workflow technologies to automate the rules for connecting and sequencing activities for joint business initiatives. In fact, workflow technologies are considered as essential in building cross-enterprise integrated value chains, (see Section 10.5).

Before BPM, traditional workflow systems were departmental, forms (or documents) driven, and did very little analysis. Traditionally, a workflow usually referred to the automation of such front-end processes as document management that build and manage processes from the flow of documents, e.g., orders or bills, irrespective of whether these are interacting with EIS or humans. While this reflects many processes common in business, it is too restrictive for being able to support a broad range of business processes, some of which can be represented in the form of documents.

When we look at modern BPM technology it is easy to understand that it is more than process automation, or workflow. BPM adds conceptual innovations and technology from EAI and e-Business integration and re-implements all of it on the new e-Business infrastructure based on Web and XML standards. BPM software thus really means the combination of workflow, EAI, and e-Business components in an integrated modeling and execution environment based on Web technology standards.

Workflow is an enabling technology that can be used throughout the enterprise, and beyond the enterprise, to support various business functions. Modern workflow systems that offer BPM functionality do not distinguish between internal (EAI) and external (e-Business) processes within the process modeling and design environment, but provide the means of including all participants within end-to-end process that span multiple enterprise applications and enterprise boundaries. These processes typically separate process control flow and data flow. All data flow uses neutral XML formats, based on XML schema where these are available. They also include a process level security complementing network security firewalls. In this way they allow public–private access policies between different organizations to be enforced through a process interface design [BEA 2002]. These designs can adhere to industry standards when required.

When combined with the workflow capabilities of BPM, business processes can be tailored to specific events or customer/supplier classes optimizing supply chain execution. For example, it is possible for an automated processes to determine that a customer support call is from a high-value customer and to execute an expedited process with more human checkpoints. BPM can therefore address the escalating demands for improved customer service [Roch 2002].

When numerous workflow engines need to operate in concert to achieve e-Business functionality, synchronization of processes and related process control information across workflow engines (belonging to the same or different organizations) is necessary. Consider, for instance, an application which requires a consistent view of a certain customer's credit position. This application needs information from a sales application regarding orders in flight, from an accounting application for outstanding invoices and from a credit control application for credit history. It is essential to synchronize the processing of the multiple systems involved, as a single customer may have many orders in various stages of processing at any given time. Only in this way can a true picture of that customer's credit situation be given.

Process synchronization requires that one workflow engine makes requests of another workflow's engine to effect the selection, instantiation, and enactment of known business process definitions by that other engine. The requesting workflow engine is also able to pass context data (workflow relevant or application data) and receive back status information and the results of the enactment of the process definition. Business applications interface with a workflow enactment service via WAPIs (Workflow APIs) and interchange formats. The support of these interfaces in workflow management products allows the implementation of front-end applications that need to access workflow management engine functions (workflow enactment services). The WAPI enables interoperability between business applications and components of workflow management systems (see Figure 18.4 which shows how workflow technology is used to link processes within and between organizations). Interchange formats provide support for the automated interchange of workflow information between different workflow management products.

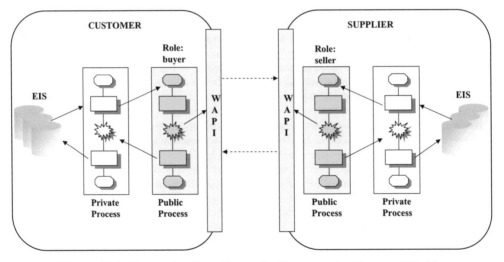

■ **Figure 18.4:** Connecting Cross-Enterprise Processes by Means of Workflows

There is a list of three criteria that must be satisfied by advanced process-based workflow tools that enable integration and synchronization of business processes, which we describe below. These come in addition to the BPM functionality described in Section 17.6.4:

- *Integration with external workflows, components and applications* Business processes never act in isolation so it is important that they can integrate with workflows and applications. It is therefore essential that enterprise workflow tools integrate with other such tools and applications by opening up their operations in the form of WAPIs. The workflow tools in an e-Business architecture coordinate existing systems, which may be components, such as CORBA or EJB, or middleware (MOM for message sending or RMI type of RPCs). These may also include legacy systems and packaged enterprise applications in the form of components.

- *Provision of transaction management capabilities* Business processes span everything from short-lived real-time transactional systems to long-lived extended collaborations. This creates demanding requirements for transactional integrity, resilience and scalability. A process-based workflow system must be able to support advanced transaction management facilities, including distributed coordinated transactions, open-nested transactions, recovery and compensation. Compensation involves undoing a completed process by means of compensating transactions, in case it cannot be rolled back because a required resource is external, or non-transactional, or connected via asynchronous messaging.

- *Management of a standard exchange vocabulary* When business processes belonging to diverse organizations collaborate it is vital that they adhere to a standardized business vocabulary. Defining a proprietary format with one's partners should be avoided as it does not allow further collaborations. There are a number of initiatives that aim to standardize XML vocabularies so as to prevent too-tight coupling between collaborating e-Business organizations.

Two examples of advanced workflow tools that provide process-based functionality are BEA's WebLogic Process Integrator and IBM's WebSphere MQWorflow and Crossworlds.

BEA's WebLogic Process Integrator provides a workflow management system that automates business processes within and between enterprises and runs on BEA's WebLogic server. The WebLogic Process Integrator provides workflow design functions, data administration functions such as modeling business processes and system users and creating calendars that control the execution of workflows, and workflow monitoring functions such as displaying the status of running workflows and modifying activities associated with running workflows. BEA's WebLogic server is a J2EE-compliant tiered architecture that facilitates the separation of presentation, business logic and data. It provides the underlying core functionality necessary for the development and deployment of business-driven applications including support for advanced transactions.

IBM's WebSphere MQWorflow provides the infrastructure to automate and manage complex business processes and help ensure business process integrity. Business processes can be modeled in a tool easy for business mangers and analysts to use. Once a business process is captured in this tool, it can be simulated and optimized based on cost and capacity factors. The process can then be deployed by the WebSphere MQWorflow run-time engine and actually executed. IBM's Crossworlds provides the process automation facilities required to execute and streamline business processes. It also manages industry templates and business objects, such as customer or order information, across various systems and applications and automates the synchronization of information both inside and outside an enterprise's firewall.

18.7 Integration challenges: the semantic interoperability problem

The issues that arise when attempting to integrate disparate systems within and across organizations continue to plague not only large enterprise alliances, but also most businesses across all industries. Today there exist several EAI products and technical solutions that deal with the challenges relating to actual physical connectivity and communication of the systems involved in a given exchange by sharing APIs and messages or using tightly coupled workflows. However, what is lacking from most available technology solutions that would improve the odds for integration success is the ability to exchange meaningful, context-driven data, messages and business processes between autonomous systems. The challenges of enabling each system to appropriately understand the information that is being shared relates to the logical aspect of using and sharing data and business processes based on their intended meaning. This is part of a broader problem known as the *semantic interoperability problem*. The semantic interoperability problem for EAI and e-Business needs to be examined and solved both at the data and the process-level. Semantic interoperability is part of the interoperability challenge for networked organizations, which we discussed briefly in Chapter 10. As semantic interoperability is broader than the technology, syntax and practice levels, and encompasses elements of them, it deserves to be discussed further.

18.7.1 Semantic issues at the data level

To understand the semantic interoperability problem at the data level, consider airline reservation systems that belong to a given alliance. The logical concerns of data-level EAI involve understanding what the data in one airline reservation system actually means in that system, and how it relates to data found in each and every one of the other alliance partners' passenger systems. Addressing these semantic concerns involves discovering how information is used differently by each of the members in the alliance, and how that information maps to the normative alliance view.

A data-level integration technique must focus on a complete picture that delivers more than data, objects or messages. It needs to focus on conveying meaning to create fluency. Meaning, in a practical sense, is about meta-data, business rules and user supplied application context to facilitate robust information transformation between disparate systems and applications.

Most EAI software tools and solutions focus on the transportation of data and messages between heterogeneous systems. EAI tools perform the basic syntactic transformation tasks required for the applications to interoperate. These include, for instance, string transformations, conversion routines, mathematical operations, and filtering. However, as already explained in Section 17.6.2, these tools cannot facilitate the transformation of an entire schema domain representation to another partially compatible schema domain representation. The prime tenet of a true data integration approach is to maximize the exchange of meaning in terms a target system can understand. This means that EAI and e-Business support tools need to be able to preserve the semantics of applications while transforming the context.

Solutions

Currently, most semantic interoperability issues are handled by the following means:

- a common vocabulary of terms that each party must adhere to when communicating to a group of trading partners, and/or

- custom-coded, point-to-point bridges that translate one particular vocabulary to the group's vocabulary or to that of a trading partner.

There are two core elements that need to support any semantic-based interoperability solution. These are meta-data and ontology:

1. *Meta-data* is data describing the data in a database, such as schema data, business domain data, company related data and so on. Typical meta-data include schema-based data type descriptions, descriptions of data relationships, relations, attributes, primary/foreign key constraints, and other database-centric meta-data. The descriptive information meta-data supplies allows users and systems to locate, evaluate, access and manage online resources. To fully enable efficient communication and interoperation between systems, you need appropriate meta-data extensions such as, for example, including human-defined context and business rules. However, the use of meta-data alone is not a complete solution. Meta-data has to be connected to an ontology.

2. *An ontology* is a set of vocabulary definitions that express a community's consensus knowledge about a domain. This body of knowledge is meant to be stable over time and can be used to solve multiple problems [Gruber 1993]. Formal ontology definitions include a name of a particular concept, a set of relations to other concepts and a natural language description that serves strictly as documentation. In e-Business, an ontology can serve as the reference model of entities and interactions in some particular domain of application and knowledge. The ontology provides meaning to data because it puts raw structured or unstructured data in the form of a structured conceptual specification.

Typical semantic interoperability solutions at the data level exhibit the following three key characteristics [Pollock 2002]:

1. *Semantic inter-mediation*: Semantic interoperability solutions use a common ontology as a mediation layer in order to abstract data terms, vocabularies and information into a shareable distributed model. This is analogous to creating a model-driven enterprise which uses core information models as a means to refract enterprise data in whatever form is required.

2. *Semantic mapping*: Mapping to an ontology preserves the native semantics of the data and eliminates the need for custom developed code. In semantic interoperability solutions, mapping accounts for much more than simple many-to-many data formatting rules or data syntax arbitrations. It is about how the semantics are captured, aligned, and structured in relation to the data itself, thereby creating useful information out of semantically poor data repositories.

3. *Context sensitivity*: The meaning of any data item is bound to a specific context. Consequently, any semantic interoperability solution must accommodate the fact that the same data item may mean different things from different semantic viewpoints. Typically, the business rules, context definitions, and environmental meta-data are captured and stored in meta-data repositories so that they can be used during the semantic mapping process.

18.7.2 Semantic issues at the business process level

In addition to the semantic interoperability problems on the data level, there exist additional semantic problems when attempting to integrate business processes that span organizations. Recall that at the process-level enterprises need a solution that can cohesively weave together business processes wherever they reside in or across the extended enterprise. The lack of agreement about how business processes are defined and managed can lead to serious problems including serious process re-engineering, corresponding implementation efforts and organizational changes. These efforts are more about redesigning business processes than about making them easy to change and combine with those of customers, suppliers and business partners. Although interoperability within a supply chain is an important goal, interoperability *between* supply chains is equally important; see Section 10.5. An enterprise rarely interacts only within a single supply chain, but rather must connect with several supply chains as product offerings and business dictate.

The lack of effective solutions regarding custom coding, vocabulary and business-process standards has led to limited success among serious e-Business projects. We can encounter three types of semantic problems with business process-level e-Business:

1. business terminology fluctuations (which are identical to the semantic problems that we examined for data-level EAI);
2. lack of commonly acceptable and understood processes; and
3. lack of commonly accepted business protocols.

We will briefly discuss the latter two in the following as we have already discussed business terminology fluctuations in the preceding subsection.

The objective for process-level integration is to provide a method for defining, automating and managing cross-application and cross-enterprise business processes. Before engaging in such a course of action, it is imperative that collaborating enterprises understand each other's business processes.

In many cases in vertical industries we can identify a *standard* shared set of business processes that have common accepted meaning. We can additionally identify *industry neutral business processes* that are generic in nature. The generic nature of these business processes enables one to reuse them with specific context and business rules within different vertical industries. On some occasions these shared business processes may require slight modifications to fulfill the requirements that are unique to the business process within a specific context. The context that drives the process may modify the way the business information used. The contexts essentially guide how the base set of business information must be adapted for use in the narrower (specialised) context. Consider for example an e-Procurement business process used in the European Union vs. an e-Procurement business process used in the US or some other part of the world. In such situations it is important that trading partners not only identify such standard and common processes but also various components of a common business process specification (reference model) that can be reused to create new business processes, e.g., the components for procurement, payment and shipping for a particular industry. Such core components are defined using identity items that are common across all businesses. Reuse of core components will typically occur at the business process, business collaboration, business transaction, and business document model components. This enables users to define data that is meaningful to their businesses while also maintaining interoperability with other business applications.

Business processes should be able to capture the information and exchange requirements, identifying the timing, sequence and purpose of each business collaboration and information exchange. This is the aim of a business protocol, which is associated with business processes and governs the exchange of business information and messages between trading partners across differing EIS, middleware platforms and organizations. The business protocol should also be able to specify collaboration or contractual agreements that exist between two or more trading partners (see Chapter 20).

Solutions

The lack of agreement on the terminology, grammar and dialogue that constitute e-Business processes demonstrates the need for standards. As a consequence, several business process standards and business protocols have been developed recently. In addition to these, industry-specific (vertical) e-Markets that offer e-Business solutions have also been developed.

Business Standards and Protocols: Business standards and protocols typically manage the structure for defining form, fit and function of any product or service, regardless of the industry. In addition, they specify the structure and format and semantics of the business content of a message as well as the message exchange choreography (also referred to as business conversation dialogue) between trading partners. They use specialized business and technical dictionaries to provide commonly used domain-specific terminology and accepted values. To develop meaningful business standards and protocols, vendors have begun to work together, facilitated by standards bodies, and in unison with business experts to define global XML standards like ebXML (ebXML.org), RosettaNet (www.rosettanet.org), cXML (cxml.org) and others which will enable a new generation of BPM products specifically for process-centric e-Business.

Enterprises are exploring open XML-based standards that help remove the formidable barriers associated with developing a common business process language and process methodology for Internet-based collaboration, communication and commerce. Without any form of standardization the flexibility of XML will become the biggest single obstacle to implementation within the e-Business domain. Flexibility must be managed in a manner which will enable re-usability and facilitate harmonization. Without this each non-standard XML dialect will not openly and cost effectively communicate beyond the boundaries of its own implementation domain. The benefits of XML will then only be realized by users who are dominant within their value chains.

For reasons of completeness we will give a brief introduction to some of the XML-based standards. Details about these standards can be found in Chapter 20, which is entirely devoted business protocols and standards.

ebXML (Electronic Business extensible Markup Language) is a collection of specifications that was initiated by a consortium of businesses, vendors, and governments and is sponsored by UN/CEFACT (United Nations Centre for Trade Facilitation and Electronic Business) and Structured Information Standards, a nonprofit organization dedicated to the creation of international interoperability specifications based on open, public standards. The vision of ebXML is to create a single global electronic marketplace where enterprises of any size and in any geographical location can meet and conduct business with each other through the exchange of XML-based messages. To facilitate this, ebXML provides an infrastructure for data communication interoperability, a semantic framework for commercial interoperability, and a mechanism that allows enterprises to find each other, establish a relationship, and conduct business. In other words it provides the facilities for enterprises to discover each other and the products and services they have to offer, to determine which business processes and documents are necessary to obtain those products and services, and to determine how the exchange of information will take place and then agree on contractual terms and conditions. Once all of this is accomplished, enterprises can then exchange information and products/services according to these agreements.

RosettaNet is an independent, nonprofit consortium of major IT, electronic component and semiconductor manufacturing companies dedicated to the collaborative development and rapid deployment of industry wide, open e-Business process standards. These standards form a common e-Business language, aligning processes between supply chain partners on global high-technology trading network. To support its mission RosettaNet provides specifications for the RosettaNet Implementation Framework (RNIF), the RosettaNet Partner Interface Processes (PIPs), and business and technical dictionaries.

PIPs define business processes between trading partners. PIPs fit into seven groups of core business processes that represent the backbone of the trading network. Each group is broken down into segments –

cross-enterprise processes involving more than one type of trading partner. PIPs are specialized system-to-system XML-based dialogues. Each PIP specification includes a business document with the vocabulary, and a business process with the choreography of the message dialogue. Typical PIPs include order management, inventory management, marketing information management, service and support and manufacturing. The RNIF acts as the grammar and provides common exchange protocols while PIPs form the dialogue. The RNIF together with the dictionary, which provides a common set of properties for business transactions and products, form the basis for the implementation of RosettaNet PIPs.

cXML (Commerce XML) began as a collaborative effort among IT companies looking to reduce the costs of online business. cXML is a new set of document type definitions (DTD) for the XML specification. cXML works as a meta-language that defines necessary information about a product. cXML defines a request/response process for the exchange of transaction information. cXML is used to standardize the exchange of catalogue content and to define request/response processes for secure electronic transactions over the Internet. These business processes include purchase orders, change orders, acknowledgments, status updates, ship notifications and payment transactions. The main types of cXML documents are catalogues, punchouts, and purchase orders.

Industry-specific e-Markets: Today, trading exchanges are forming at a rapid pace and as a result several industry-specific partnerships have been announced for just about every major manufacturing sector of the economy. Many industry standards groups are working on domain-specific XML standards including, the Automotive Industry Action Group, the Open Travel Alliance, the Association for Retail Technology Standards, Health Care and Medical Equipment, and the ACORD standards group for the insurance industry. Due to the relatively low barriers to entry, significant cost savings that come from reduced transaction costs and reduced processing costs, the automation of supply chains and increased productivity, such online marketplaces attract smaller companies that establish partnerships with them.

Most e-Markets provide common business process definitions (promoting industry-based standards through XML formats and defined APIs) and a standard terminology to combat semantic interoperability problems. This results in a universal foundation for conducting global electronic business, ensuring the integrity of fast, clean business transactions, guaranteeing common semantics and data integrity across the Internet, backed with the industry representation.

Three recent interesting developments in industry-wide collaboration and industry-based standards come from the automotive industry, retail grocery industry and the travel industry, respectively. These are indicative of the efforts that are currently happening in other industry domains.

STAR (Standards for Technology in Automotive Retail) is a nonprofit, auto industry-wide auto industry group to create standards for the data elements and transmission format for communication among manufacturers, dealers and retail system providers in the automotive distribution value chain. The aim of the STAR alliance is to define the standard XML message for dealer-to-original equipment manufacturer business transactions such as parts order, sales lead, and credit application, define a standard IT infrastructure based on ebXML to support these messages between dealers and original equipment manufacturers and standardize the IT infrastructure at dealerships. Recently, STAR and OAGi (Open Applications Group) have jointly approved seven XML standards for automotive dealer-to-manufacturer transactions. The published standards cover parts order, parts pick list, parts return, repair-order, sales lead, vehicle service history and warranty reconciliation. OAGi (www.openapplications.org) is a nonprofit consortium focused on building reusable, interoperable XML messages and schemas for various business transactions. All the new standards are based on OAGi's XML message methodology.

The goal of the Uniform Code Council's (UCC) retail grocery industry, known as UCCnet (`www.uccnet.org`), is to create a trading community designed to interconnect trading partners with electronic markets and provide enhanced services for its subscribers. UCCnet provides access to industry standards through the adoption of XML technologies and business process models defined by the current trading community. UCCnet shares XML, schemas, process models, and functional and technical specifications with all compliant exchanges and solution providers, standardizing the functionality across a wide range of solutions. It also facilitates data-driven collaboration among trading partners by providing common data definitions, standard formats for data communication and a data synchronization that ensures that supply chain information and business processes are correct and updated with the EIS of trading partners.

The OpenTravel Alliance (OTA) (`www.opentravel.org`) has specified a set of standard business processes and standard terminology for searching for availability and booking a reservation in the airline, hotel and car rental industry, as well as the purchase of travel insurance in conjunction with these services. OTA specifications use XML for structured data messages to be exchanged over the Internet or other means of transport. This specification relies upon the work of other standards developer organizations, specifically, the ebXML initiative, and the work of the World Wide Web Consortium. OTA specifications also reference standards developed by the International Organization of Standards (ISO), and the International Air Transport Association (IATA), that are used by the travel industry to provide standardized message structures and data for its members.

18.8 Business integration patterns and their implications

It is important to understand that business process integration may result in several business integration patterns whose aim is to manage and support business automation and integration across distributed enterprises. Thus before embarking on an e-Business integration solution the nature of the relevant business integration pattern must first be determined. In the following we shall introduce three primary business (organizational) patterns and briefly discuss their implications and impacts on the structure of an enterprise as well as their advantages and disadvantages. These business integration patterns are applied after strategic decisions regarding the application architecture and e-Business infrastructure (see Figure 2.4) have been made at the enterprise level. The business process integration patterns include [Jarman 2002]:

1. Integrated enterprise
2. Brokered enterprise
3. Federated enterprise.

Selecting the most appropriate business process pattern for an organization depends on the business needs, structure and business priorities of an enterprise.

18.8.1 Integrated enterprise business pattern

The integrated business pattern is about ensuring that end-to-end business processes are managed and monitored in a complete fashion across and within all business units. Business processes are viewed across the entire enterprise, where activities span organizational units and are carried out by separate business sections that have a responsibility for them. There is a common view and accountability for business process across the enterprise and any process improvement or process re-engineering is managed across the entire enterprise [Jarman 2002].

This business pattern is driven by management recognition that process management should cross enterprise business unit boundaries to maximize process improvement benefits and that the entire enterprise must take responsibility for providing and maintaining a BPI infrastructure. This business integration pattern assumes that workflow and integration processes may cross organizational units, and are managed by a group within the enterprise. This group is also responsible for setting policies on toolset selection and on message standards. The integrated enterprise business pattern is most suitable for small enterprises or larger enterprises where a common standard integration toolset is imposed.

The integrated business pattern is supported by EAI integration brokering and workflow infrastructure. Integration brokering provides message routing and distributed processing infrastructure, while workflow technology provides support for process-driven automation middleware. In particular the integrated enterprise business pattern can make use of an Enterprise Service Bus.

The Enterprise Service Bus is an open standards-based message bus designed to enable the implementation, deployment, and management of Service Oriented Architecture solutions (see Section 19.5) with a focus on assembling, deploying, and managing distributed service-oriented architectures. The ESB provides the distributed processing, standards-based integration, and enterprise-class backbone required by the extended enterprise. There are two key ideas behind this approach: loose coupling of the systems taking part in the integration and breaking up the integration logic into distinct easily manageable pieces. The ESB is designed to provide interoperability between larger grained applications and other components via standards-based adapters and interfaces. The bus functions as both transport and transformation facilitator to allow distribution of these services over disparate systems and computing environments. To achieve its operational objectives the ESB draws from traditional EAI broker functionality in that it provides integration services such as connectivity and routing of messages based on business rules, data transformation, and adapters to applications [Chappell 2004].

Figure 18.5 shows a large enterprise employing the integrated enterprise business pattern. In this figure, end-to-end business process flows are depicted as dotted arcs between departmental units. In the example, an end-to-end business process is shown in this figure, and the activities carried out in the various departments can be treated as organizational activities rather than business unit activities. The role of the various business units is simply to identify the responsibility to carry out activities and, as such, business unit boundaries have no impact on the business process flow. This figure shows that an external partner is responsible for carrying out the logistics and distribution processes such as warehousing, distribution and management inventory. The logistical workflow, which is seamlessly integrated into the end-to-end business processes of the large enterprise depicted in Figure 18.5, is dependent on the exchange and processing of consignment notes, goods advice, invoices and other business documents.

A major advantage of the integrated enterprise BPI scheme is that it provides enterprise-wide process management so that business processes can be easily tracked and monitored. Enterprise-wide improvement of business processes are easier identified and applied, while reuse of process activities and functionality can be easily identified and managed. Disadvantages of this approach are that it requires implementing business

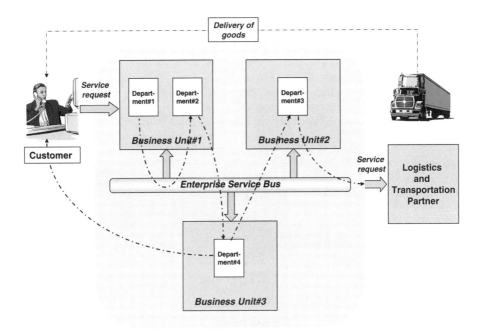

■ **Figure 18.5:** The Integrated Enterprise Pattern

process management across the entire organization and that the ESB can be a point of contention for fairly large enterprises.

18.8.2 Brokered enterprise business pattern

The brokered enterprise business process pattern is about ensuring that processes are managed and monitored across all business units by means of a broker business unit to provide both infrastructure and business process management [Jarman 2002]. This is a distributed business enterprise scheme, where business units are fairly autonomous but use the business broker to manage communication and interoperation. Each individual business unit may manage any business process improvement or re-engineering; however, business processes can be viewed across the entire organization.

The brokered enterprise BPI scheme is driven by management recognition that business process monitoring should cross business unit boundaries to maximize the benefits of business process tracking, while still maintaining the autonomy of individual business units. With the brokered enterprise business process pattern, the broker business unit takes responsibility for providing and maintaining a business process infrastructure and determines the standards for any service interfaces individual business units provide. The broker business unit acts as a broker for all service requests between business units and can provide some level of end-to-end business process monitoring; see Figure 18.6. The individual process units still own the processes provided, but must maintain standards for both messages and inter-business unit processing and must register the services they provide and the processes supporting them with the broker unit registry.

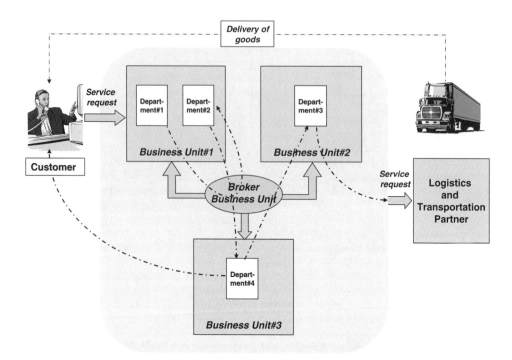

■ Figure 18.6: The Brokered Enterprise Business Pattern

With this scheme all requests are handled by the broker unit, so a service client is not aware of which organizational unit provides the business process handling the service. The brokered enterprise pattern is applicable to organizations where the individual organization units want to maintain their autonomy but benefit from the advantages of a hub-style service management and a common messaging infrastructure.

The brokered business pattern, just like the integrated business pattern, is supported by EAI integration brokering and workflow infrastructure. An advantage of the brokered enterprise BPI pattern is that the number of relationships that need to be managed and coordinated between business units is drastically reduced. Each business unit is autonomous and publicizes its processes and services through a central unit that can manage and support end-to-end business processes. The main disadvantage of this pattern is that when business processes are viewed externally they provide a fragmented image of the enterprise. This is due to the fact that each business unit is responsible for monitoring the progress of its segment of the enterprise's business processes, including those handling a customer service related request. In addition, enterprise-wide business improvement is harder to identify and implement.

18.8.3 Federated enterprise

In circumstances where the organizational or geographically dispersed units need to act independently from one another, the infrastructure may become more physically distributed while retaining at least logically the central control over configuration. The federated enterprise pattern is about keeping the business units autonomous with common message standards provided for cooperating business units [Jarman 2002]. This business pattern is similar to "pure" e-Business integration, where business units must cooperate with each other to support end-to-end business processes. Any process improvement or re-engineering occurs within individual business units.

This pattern is driven by the expectation that individual business units are completely autonomous and are expected to cooperate when there is a need for it. As there is no overall business management and monitoring, business processes are not viewed end-to-end and each unit is responsible for providing and maintaining standard interfaces so that it can cooperate with other such units. Common standards for messaging and for describing the services provided are introduced with each business unit managing its own service repository. The federated enterprise pattern is applicable to organizations where the individual organization units want to maintain their autonomy but benefit from the advantages of cooperating with other business units in the organization and the use of a common messaging infrastructure and cooperation standards.

The federated business pattern, just like the integrated and brokered business patterns, could be supported by EAI integration brokering and workflow infrastructure. However, it is more typically supported by e-Business infrastructure and e-Business process management support facilities. The e-Business infrastructure provides messaging and distributed processing support over the Internet (e-Business) or a private internal network with appropriate encryption and security facilities. The e-Business process management infrastructure focuses on providing support for monitoring and managing business processes across enterprise boundaries. The federated enterprise business process integration pattern leverages e-Business standards to provide effective e-Business processes and services. Applicable architectural styles here include the Service Oriented Architecture (see Chapter 19), and standards include the Web Services Description Language, Universal Description Discovery and Integration framework and the Electronic Business extensible Markup Language (ebXML), covered in Chapters 19 and 20, respectively.

The federated enterprise BPI pattern is shown in Figure 18.7, which illustrates a distributed ESB allowing different enterprises units or enterprises, such as manufacturers, suppliers and customers, to plug together their integration domains into a larger federated integration network. This topology allows for local message traffic, integration components and adapters to be locally installed, configured, secured and managed, while allowing for a single integrated transaction and security model. In this figure a federated ESB solution is used to form a virtual network of business units and possibly trading partners across industries and services able to take advantage of the wider range of options and partnering models.

An advantage of the federated enterprise BPI pattern is that each business unit is truly autonomous and free to publicize its own processes and services. It additionally provides hooks for e-Business integration and for managing e-Business style processes. A main disadvantage of this scheme is that each business unit promotes its own process and services and provides little support and accountability for process management and enterprise-wide process improvement identification and implementation. Another disadvantage of this scheme is, like the brokered enterprise BPI pattern, that when business processes are viewed externally they provide a fragmented image of the enterprise. Again, the reason is that each business unit is responsible for monitoring the progress of its segment of the enterprise's business processes, including those handling customer service related requests.

18.9 e-Business integration requirements revisited

As e-Business integration has multiple dimensions to it, enterprises need to address more than one type of integration problem. This leads to a large number of issues that have to be faced when introducing e-Business

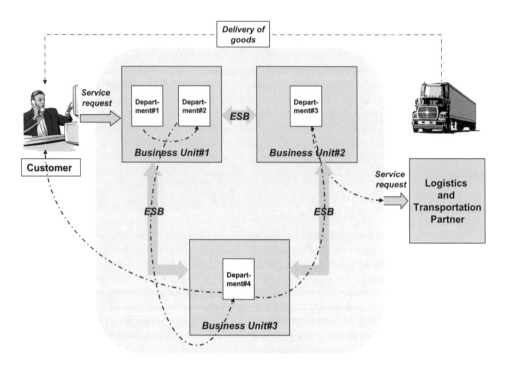

■ **Figure 18.7:** The Federated Enterprise Business Integration Model

solutions to the enterprise level. Apart from e-Business strategy and business governance issues that we introduced in Chapters 2 and 5, technical issues are concerned with security, privacy, autonomy, heterogeneity in software and platforms managing internal and external communications, and, more importantly, managing complexity of process interactions. In the following we will summarize and discuss these technical issues again so that the reader can understand and appreciate the nature of e-Business integration and its requirements. We will place more emphasis on the issues that have either not been discussed so far or received only cursory treatment in this chapter but have been covered in other parts of this book.

1. *Application connectivity that links various internal applications to share and leverage information and processes*: This element describes the ability of internal applications and systems to communicate and interoperate at both the data and the process level. This is essentially the EAI techniques and infrastructure that we described throughout the previous chapter.
2. *Information integration that leverages information across and beyond the enterprise*: This element describes the ability of systems to leverage information within and outside the enterprise.
3. *Process/information coordination*: Leveraging information is only the first step in e-Business integration. Business process integration provides current information, helps synchronize key business information and the ensuing decision making processes and, in general, makes an enterprise's IT infrastructure more agile and event-driven by enabling communications and making it easier to adapt business processes in response to business changes.

4. *Leveraging legacy systems*: EAI and e-Business endeavor to constantly increase the value of IT investments as a whole. Thus a major objective is not only to continue to extract value from legacy systems by simply building wrappers around them, but to increase that value through their approach to integration. Consequently, proper component interfaces should be developed to integrate with already existing systems and hide the internals of their implementations. In this way legacy systems can be leveraged and effectively integrated with the core modern systems that run an enterprise.
5. *Support for advanced security infrastructure*: Beyond conventional techniques for secure access, e-Business also requires techniques such as digital signatures on transactions and digital certificates (to handle authentication) with different levels of validation, mutual authentication and policy-based security management – offering higher degrees of protection against unauthorized access without burdening authorized users. A communication infrastructure for e-Business should support security standards such as Secure Sockets Layer, a Public Key Infrastructure, and Virtual Private Networking. It also requires toolkits that provide a set of APIs for incorporating specific security needs into e-Business applications.

Successful enterprises rely on an infrastructure that meets the following three e-Business infrastructure design criteria [Overtveldt 2001]:

1. *Flexibility*: for rapidly evolving e-Business models through the addition of new application functionality and the integration of systems, processes and applications with customers, business partners and suppliers. This type of connectivity can only be achieved through the use of open standards using Internet standards such as TCP/IP and HTTP, SSL and PKI for secure communications and so on.
2. *Scalability*: for accommodating unpredictable fluctuations in customer demands and user workload. This is especially true for enterprises that interface directly with end customers. In this case the number of customers and generated workload can be very hard to predict.
3. *Reliability/availability*: to help ensure continuous operation and availability of e-Business applications to end users.

18.10 Wrapping up: the real differences between e-Business and EAI

Despite the similarities between e-Business integration and internal enterprise integration as advocated by EAI, there are some meaningful differences, although most of these are becoming less significant over time. These are briefly discussed in the following.

1. *e-Business interactions are likely to run over the Internet*: Many e-Business interactions still use VANs or direct private network links rather than the Internet. However, the increased use of secure infrastructure such as PKI and VPNs enables organizations to use their corporate networks to achieve Internet connectivity with their branches, suppliers, customers and remote users. In addition, a growing number of intra-enterprise connections also use the public Internet, e.g., to connect mobile users, retail outlets, small offices and home offices.
2. *e-Business transfers are more likely to use XML than are intra-enterprise transfers*: XML has several things going for it when used as a common format for data representation in Internet enabled e-Business. It is entirely represented as text and can be processed without change regardless of the receiving platform. XML

includes provisions to support different character sets and languages. Finally, XML is the primary format used with such protocols as HTTP and SMTP so it does not need any special handling when used with most widely employed protocols of the Internet. Hence, e-Business transfers are more likely to leverage XML data formats today than are intra-enterprise transfers. However, the intra-enterprise adoption of XML has already begun and is certain to grow dramatically during the next several years.

3. *e-Business transactions involve additional security measures*: Traditional intra-enterprise transmissions are unencrypted because they rely on the supposed safety of the private enterprise network and its firewalls. However, encryption is becoming more common both for internal and external traffic as security demands increase. It is not uncommon today for firewalls to be placed at points within an enterprise network not just for external network links.

4. *Non-repudiation is only applicable to e-Business transactions*: Non-repudiation protocols are aimed at preventing parties in a business communication from falsely denying having taken part in that communication. This is rarely an issue for EAI transactions.

5. *e-Business interactions are driven by business protocols and standards*: The core objective of business standards is to build a collection of standards that allow organizations (including small and medium-sized businesses) to participate in e-Business exchanges across the Internet. This is rarely an issue for EAI transactions.

6. *Business process management differs between intra-enterprise and e-Business applications*: Business process management in an e-Business context tends to consist of relatively short duration business conversations between only two end-point enterprises. Consider the public process aspect of RosettaNet PIPs or the business transactions of the ebXML Business Process Specification Schema (refer to Chapter 20 for further details). These types of processes usually have shorter duration and are simpler than the business processes that occur within the enterprise. Internal business processes tend to involve more applications, more steps, more complex conditional logic and are also frequently of longer duration. Because of these differences, it is sometimes useful to apply a different type of BPM tool to internal integration than to e-Business integration. One complication is that most EAI tools have not built in the rich human side of BPM (business process monitoring, optimization and management) and have concentrated mainly on automating processes. The main reason is that EAI tools were designed initially as MOM products and have been retrofitted from delivering messages to process-oriented management. However, some of today's better BPM tools are so broad that they can, for many applications, satisfy both sets of requirements without requiring the enterprise to acquire a second tool.

18.11 Chapter summary

To achieve end-to-end process integration requires integration with back-end systems and business processes that span organizations. These business processes drive a company's e-Business interactions with its customers, partners, distributors, and suppliers; they can also streamline the company's internal business. This is the primary purpose of the e-Business integration initiative.

Making key business processes available over the Internet may involve relatively straightforward extension of existing processes out to the Internet or may involve complex business process re-engineering efforts to make the business processes Web-enabled. The term e-Business process management is being used to indicate the (re-) design and management of business processes facilitated by the Internet. e-Business process management encompasses the design and management of collaborative processes that are supported by the Internet.

Companies could implement e-Business initiatives in different ways ranging from simple connections to electronic communities and to sophisticated trading networks where e-Business relationships are formed as loosely and as dynamically as required. For such implementations the type of coupling between organizational processes should be determined. There are two types of coupling that have enormous implications for the kind of technology chosen to implement an e-Business solution. These are tight and loose coupling. With tight coupling the calling system requires detailed knowledge of the technology of the called system and precise definition of the call structure and the arguments in it. Tightly coupled solutions are normally based on component technology such as CORBA and DCOM. In contrast to this approach, loose coupling implies call structure and technology independence. Loosely coupled solutions are normally implemented using asynchronous middleware such as message passing or publish–subscribe and Web services technologies. Typical loosely coupled solutions are driven by open standards based on XML.

Integration of e-Business applications needs to be achieved at the business-process level. This leads to multi-tiered topologies where the business process integration layer involves the integration of logical entities represented as business process elements. In such topologies the application server can encapsulate the process logic of application integration in its business process integration layer.

One of the most important technical challenges of e-Business integration is enabling each system to appropriately understand the information that is being shared with other similar systems. This relates to the logical aspect of using and sharing data and business processes based on their intended meaning and is part of a broader problem known as semantic interoperability. The semantic interoperability problem for EAI and e-Business needs to be examined and solved both at the data and the process-level. The two core elements that need to support any semantic-based interoperability solution are meta-data and ontology. As a result of the lack of agreement on the terminology, grammar and dialogue that constitute e-Business processes, several generic and industry-specific business process standards and business protocols have been introduced recently. The goal of these business standards and protocols is to manage the structure for defining form, fit and function of any product or service. In addition, they specify the structure, format and semantics of the business content of a message as well as the message exchange choreography (also referred to as business conversation dialogue) between trading partners.

Before embarking on an e-Business integration solution it is important to understand and determine the business integration pattern that will drive the e-Business integration platform. Selecting the most appropriate business process pattern for an organization depends on the business needs, structure and business priorities of an enterprise. There are three patterns that are typical of e-Business solutions. These are the integrated business pattern, the brokered enterprise business process pattern, and the federated enterprise pattern. The integrated business pattern is about ensuring that end-to-end business processes are managed and monitored in a complete fashion across and within all business units. The brokered enterprise business process pattern is about ensuring that processes are managed and monitored across all business units by means of a broker business unit to provide both infrastructure and business process management. Finally, the federated enterprise pattern is about keeping the business units autonomous with common message standards provided for cooperating business units. This business pattern is similar to "pure" e-Business integration, where business units must cooperate with each other to support end-to-end business processes.

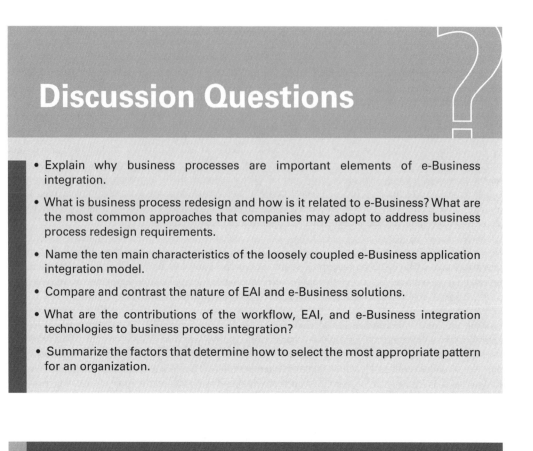

Discussion Questions

- Explain why business processes are important elements of e-Business integration.

- What is business process redesign and how is it related to e-Business? What are the most common approaches that companies may adopt to address business process redesign requirements.

- Name the ten main characteristics of the loosely coupled e-Business application integration model.

- Compare and contrast the nature of EAI and e-Business solutions.

- What are the contributions of the workflow, EAI, and e-Business integration technologies to business process integration?

- Summarize the factors that determine how to select the most appropriate pattern for an organization.

Assignments

i. Consider the Deutsche Bank integration platform that we described as part of our case study. The main objectives of the Deutsche Bank integration platform involve four interrelated aspects:

- Facilitating communication between independent order management applications in real-time,
- integrating globally distributed application systems,
- consolidating IT infrastructure management to one location, and
- implementing an e-Business platform to handle high volumes of transactions.

Design a publish–subscribe solution based on a federated enterprise bus to explain how these objectives can be achieved.

ii. Consider the example of a manufacturing company that would like to streamline its manufacturing and fulfillment processes across multiple factories and warehouses, as well as partners' facilities. The company has realized that it is more profitable to outsource the manufacturing of low-margin parts that are not in inventory when orders are placed. Depending on the available-to-promise inventory levels, the company will either fulfill the order from one of its warehouses or place the order directly with one of its established partners for outsourced manufacturing. To effectively manage such a process the enterprise decided to:

- gather service level metrics from distributed services (inventory, manufacturing, warehouse, and so on);
- monitor processes it does not control (for example, response times for a UPS shipping service);
- make real-time decisions based on historical data, defined goals and business objectives (use historical performance numbers to select from a list of tax calculation services);
- rapidly locate problems within a process and determine their impact;
- preemptively address issues before there are compliance failures (for example, if the response time of the cost rollup service is degrading, automatically route the step to a backup service).

Develop an end-to-end business process integration architecture for this order fulfillment process that covers multiple inter- and intra-company business processes. Describe the process flows in this architecture.

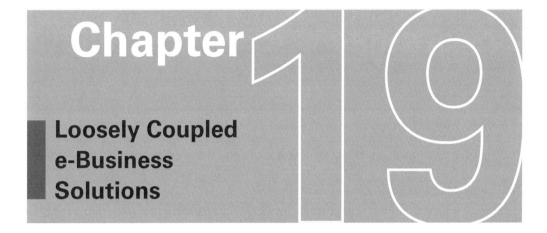

Chapter 19

Loosely Coupled e-Business Solutions

Web services are an emerging technology that avoids the problems of using distributed component technologies (see Chapter 15) over the Internet to enable communication between heterogeneous business systems and applications. As we have explained already in earlier chapters, heavyweight, symmetrical object models such as CORBA and DCOM have proved extremely complex to implement. Furthermore, the protocols they use are often incompatible with existing architectures and, in particular, conflict with standard security enforcement rules implemented in firewalls. Web services have emerged as a solution to overcome the limitations of heavyweight or proprietary architectures and the incompatibilities they create as they are centered round the use of open and complementary standards and assist with both EAI and e-Business implementations.

Web services technologies allow applications to describe and implement different ways to communicate with each other on the basis of loose coupling. Loosely coupled systems can communicate with each other and interact in ways that maintain flexibility by minimizing inter-system dependencies, which are appealing properties for achieving end-to-end process integration.

This chapter introduces the concept of software as a service and describes Web services and their typical characteristics. It then introduces the service-oriented architecture, which results in packaged software applications used either as internal or external services and explains how current Web services standards contribute to this architecture. Finally, the chapter explains how business processes can be created out of orchestrated services, discusses Web service transactions and security concerns and concludes by explaining how Web services can help implement EAI solutions.

Case Study

Virgin Mobile Integration Framework[1]

Virgin Mobile USA is a joint venture between Virgin Group and Sprint that has set the pace as the fastest growing wireless carrier in the USA while redefining the entire prepaid category. Virgin Mobile is the first mobile virtual network operator in the USA and the first wireless service to solely target the youth market.

As a mobile virtual network operator, Virgin Mobile faces the unique challenge of owning the entire customer relationship, including call management, without owning the mobile network. This requires extensive application and systems integration between Virgin Mobile's IT infrastructure and the legacy systems that powered the Sprint PCS network. Virgin Mobile also faces intense time-to-market pressure and in order to maintain a competitive advantage, the company is forced to roll out new features continually.

To address these imposing challenges, and implement a world-class mobile service with telecommunications-grade reliability and scalability, the company decided to develop an e-Business integration solution that also had to manage its own IT home grown infrastructure. Virgin Mobile based its integration infrastructure on BEA's WebLogic Platform (www.bea.com), which supports all of its integration requirements, innovative messaging services as well as interactive e-Commerce and customer service portal. Virgin Mobile is utilizing a service-oriented architecture (SOA) implemented on BEA WebLogic Platform 8.1 to integrate and manage all aspects of its operation. The flexible SOA enables the company to reuse software for delivering services across multiple channels. Those channels include handsets that support the wireless application protocol (WAP) and short message service (SMS), interactive voice response (IVR), the At Your Service call center, and the Web.

The BEA infrastructure links together a customer relationship management system from Siebel Systems, a pre-paid billing solution from Telcordia Technologies, and value-added services from a variety of content providers. In addition, Virgin Mobile built 26 application interfaces on the BEA platform for such core business functions as point-of-sale order entry, product fulfillment, and mobile service provisioning. Most of these interfaces were built as Web services, enabling synchronous and asynchronous real-time communication.

[1] This case study was summarized from www.bea.com/contents/news_events/white_papers/BEA_VirginMobile_cs.pdf.

The scope of the integration work was a major driver behind the company's decision to use an SOA and Web services. Because Web services are based on open standards, Virgin Mobile is able to create and expose the services much faster than would have been possible using traditional "one-off" development and integration techniques. And the reuse of services eliminates wasteful, redundant development projects. Virgin Mobile also leveraged the flexibility of BEA's end-to-end platform as it implemented a security system that includes SSL encryption ranging from 128 to 768 bit, multiple firewalls, and rules-based access to applications based on password authentication.

Virgin Mobile succeeded in meeting its aggressive go-to-market timeline. The highly personalized wireless service was rolled out after sevens months of work and is able to handle over two million Web service transactions per day. In addition to providing an integration framework for Virgin Mobile vendors, the BEA platform facilitates integration with content partners that provide access to music news, games and customized ring tones.

19.1 Introduction

In Chapter 18 we explained that e-Business integration is about coordinating the flow of information among enterprises and their business support and information systems. Building integration bridges that span independent organizations and their systems is challenging as it requires linking the elements of business together into a cohesive whole despite different computing platforms, operating systems, database technologies and applications.

Today, most of the implementations of the business-to-business transactions are little more than automated versions and extensions of traditional corporate business processes. The business-to-business connections are usually created virtually point-to-point with human direction at every stage of the process and result in tightly coupled systems. After the laborious implementation a human agent has to discover for each business-to-business transaction potential matches between two businesses, negotiate a contract, decide on the exchange mechanisms and program the flows of information between any two collaborating organizations. EAI solutions can make this task easier, but even these solutions are brittle and require dedicated infrastructure. Although, EAI solutions have been designed to effectively integrate systems within an enterprise, they typically cannot provide the open and scalable integration critical for e-Business applications. These traditional forms of business-to-business communication have not been able to adequately address the challenges of integrating multiple customers, suppliers and other strategic partners. Consequently, they must be augmented by new technologies that allow organizations to communicate more efficiently using the Internet. Web services refers to the set of technologies that are designed to solve this problem.

Web services constitute a distributed computer infrastructure made up of many different modules trying to communicate over the network to form virtually a single logical system. Web services are modular, self-describing, self-contained applications that are accessible over the Internet [Papazoglou 2003a]. A *Web service* is a collection of business functions or capabilities that can be published to a network using standard protocols for use by other services or applications. A Web service is a service available via a network such as the Internet that completes tasks, solves problems or conducts transactions. Each Web service is a building block that enables the sharing of software functionality with other applications residing outside the Web service's native environment. A function deployed as a Web service uses common XML-based protocols to communicate with other Web services and systems that can receive XML-based data. Web services are the answer to the problems of rigid implementations of predefined relationships and isolated services scattered across the Internet.

Web services can vary in function from simple requests (for example, currency conversion, credit checking and authorization, inventory status checking, or a weather report) to complex business applications that access and combine information from multiple sources, such as an insurance brokering system, a travel planner, an insurance liability computation or a package tracking system. Enterprises can use a single Web service to accomplish a specific business task, such as billing or inventory control or they may compose several Web services together to create a distributed e-Business application such as customized ordering, customer support, procurement, and logistical support. As an example, we may consider how Web services could be used for aspects of supply chain integration; see Chapter 10. A supply chain management application, for instance, could utilize Web service components to automatically publish and execute orders, query and consolidate shipping capacity, and aggregate and schedule production needs among various participants in an enterprise's value chain. This becomes a purely automatic function, ensuring that inventory for production is always at sufficient levels. Obviously, manual interaction and approval can be inserted, where necessary.

When Web services are used as part of a purchase order application, tracking and adjusting purchase orders due to unexpected events such as the buyer initiating a purchase order change or cancellation involves a lot of coordination work. This calls for the use of reactive services. For instance, if a single event in the purchase order needs to change or is cancelled, the entire process can unravel instantly. Employing a collection of Web services that work together to adjust purchase orders for such situations creates an automated solution to this problem. In the case of a purchase order cancellation the purchase service can automatically reserve a suitable replacement product and notify the billing and inventory services of the changes. When all of these Web services interactions have been completed and the new adjusted schedule is available, the purchase order Web service notifies the customer sending her an updated invoice.

In another example, an insurance company may decide to offer an on-line quoting Web service to its customers. Rather than developing the entire application from scratch, this enterprise looks to supplement its home grown applications with modules that perform industry standard functions. Therefore, it may seamlessly link up with the Web service of another enterprise that specializes in insurance liability computations. The insurance liability Web service may present a quote form to the customer to collect customer information based on the type of the desired insurance. Subsequently, the Web service would present the customer with a quote including a premium estimate. If the customer selected to buy that particular insurance policy, the system will take the customer's payment information and run it through a payment system offered by yet another company (service provider) Web service. This payment Web service will ultimately return billing information to the customer and to the originating company.

Services such as these can be deployed independently or orchestrated as part of overall processes by the EAI server or a more advanced Business Process Management server. Web services are leveraged when appropriate in these processes, creating a virtual library of loosely coupled yet tightly integrated services that tie together various supply chain functions [Hernocki 2003]. They enable developers to construct Web-based applications using any platform and programming language that is required. Once a Web service is deployed, other applications and Web services can discover and invoke that service. The eventual goal of Web services technology is to enable distributed applications that can be dynamically assembled according to changing business needs, and customized based on device and user access. The idea of creating and exposing a service that can be easily consumed by other applications in possibly remote organizations without expensive integration costs is compelling.

Figure 19.1 illustrates a supply planning application for an extended value chain comprising collaborating business processes (implemented by Web services) such as demand tracing, distribution planning, inventory replenishment and logistics [Hoque 2000]. Supply planning incorporates information from immediate suppliers all the way to the collection of raw materials and its purpose is to identify where to manufacture or acquire products and evaluates production, storage and transportation constraints to maximize profits. Supply planning involves multi-supplier and multi-site sourcing techniques, supply allocation to multiple plants and distribution centers, and seamless integration with the enterprise procurement management applications. In Figure 19.1 the distributed supply planning application is shown to combine inventory, replenishment, demand planning and logistics Web services to fulfil its mission.

Extended value chain applications, such as the one depicted in Figure 19.1 must be able to react to changing market and supply conditions by ensuring that supplier models are flexible enough to integrate

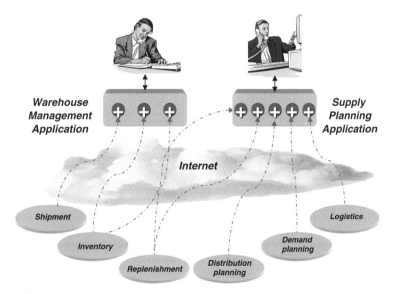

■ **Figure 19.1:** Using Web Services to Develop Distributed Applications

and disintegrate new and different business partners without installing and uninstalling complex software applications.

Web services can provide an answer to the barriers to intra-enterprise communication (required by EAI applications) and cross-enterprise communication (required by e-Business applications). To achieve this, Web services provide an essential infrastructure for using pre-existing business functionality in an enterprise, making it accessible on all platforms, responding to new business needs without breaking the pre-existing functionality, and seamlessly integrating new development with existing and future IT infrastructure. In this way, enterprises can build a bridge between their internal systems and the systems of their existing and prospective trading partners and can mix and match Web services to perform transactions with minimal programming efforts. Web services become even more important as the range of computing devices (such as handheld computers, cellular telephones, or appliances) and software platforms (e.g., UNIX or Windows) becomes more diverse. Because Web services provide a uniform and ubiquitous information distributor for all of these devices and platforms, they are the next logical step for Web-based computing.

19.2 The concept of software as a service

Web services are very different from Web pages that also provide access to applications across the Internet and across organizational boundaries. Web pages are targeted at human users, whereas Web services are developed for access by other applications. Web services are about machine-to-machine communication, whereas Web pages are about human-to-machine communication. As terminology is often used very loosely it is easy to confuse someone by describing a "service" as a Web service when it is in fact not. Consequently, it is useful to examine first the concept of software as-a-service on which Web services technology relies and then compare Web services with Web pages and Web-server functionality.

The concept of software-as-a-service is revolutionary and appeared first with the ASP (Applications Service Provider) software model. *Application Service Providers* are companies that package software and infrastructure elements together with business and professional services to create a complete solution that they present to the end customer as a service on a subscription basis. The ASP industry Consortium [ASP 2000] defined that application service providers are service organizations that deploy, host, manage, and enhance software applications for customers at a centrally managed facility, offering application availability, performance and security. End-uses access these applications remotely using the Internet or leased lines. Applications are delivered over networks on a subscription or rental basis. In essence, ASPs were a way for companies to outsource some or even all aspects of their information technology needs.

The basic idea behind an ASP is to "rent" applications to subscribers. The whole application is developed in terms of the user interface, workflow, business and data components that are all bound together to provide a working solution. An ASP hosts the entire application and the customer has little opportunity to customize it beyond set up tables, or perhaps the final appearance of the user interface (such as, for example, adding company logos). Access to the application for the customer is provided simply via browsing, and manually initiated purchases and transactions occur by downloading reports.

Although the ASP model introduced the concept of software-as-a-service first, it suffered from several inherent limitations such as the inability to develop highly interactive applications, inability to provide complete customizable applications and inability to integrate applications [Goepfert 2002]. This resulted in monolithic architectures and highly fragile, customer-specific, non-reusable integration of applications based on tight coupling principles.

The Web services paradigm allows the software-as-a-service concept to expand to include the delivery of complex business processes and transactions as a service, while permitting applications be constructed on the fly and services to be reused everywhere and by anybody.

We may distinguish four key differences between Web services and the Web-based applications used in an e-Business environment [Aldrich 2002]:

1. Web services act as resources to other applications that can request and initiate those Web services, with or without human intervention. This means that Web services can call on other Web services to outsource parts of a complex transaction to those other Web services. This provides a high degree of flexibility and adaptability not available in today's Web-based applications.
2. Web services are modular, self-aware and self-describing applications. A Web service knows what functions it can perform and what inputs it requires to produce its outputs and can describe this to potential users and to other Web services. A Web service can also describe its non-functional properties: for instance the cost of invoking the service, the geographical areas the Web service covers, security measures involved in using the Web service, contact information and more.
3. Web services are more visible and manageable than Web-based applications. The state of a Web service can be monitored and managed at any time by using external application management and workflow systems. Despite the fact that a Web service may not run on an in-house (local) system or may be written in an unfamiliar programming language it still can be used by local applications, which may detect its state (active or available) and manage the status of its outcome.
4. Web services may be brokered or auctioned. If several Web services perform the same task, then several applications may place bids for the opportunity to use the requested service. A broker can base its choice on the attributes of the "competing" Web services (cost, speed, degree of security).

19.3 What Web services are

Web services form the building blocks for creating distributed applications that can be published to and accessed over the Internet and corporate intranets. They consist of a set of open Internet standards that allow developers to implement distributed applications – using different tools provided by many different vendors – to create corporate applications that join together software modules from systems in diverse organizational departments or from different enterprises. But more importantly, Web services can also be combined/programmed by distributed applications, behind the scenes and even on the fly, to perform virtually any kind of (business-related) task or transaction, see Figure 19.1. These applications usually already exist within an enterprise or may be developed from scratch using a Web services toolkit.

A Web services toolkit exposes the useful business service in an Internet-accessible format. For instance, an IBM Web services development environment or Microsoft Visual Studio .NET toolkit may be used to expose the inventory level query application (being originally coded in, say, C or Visual Basic) as a Web service that can be accessed over the Internet by any other module as part of a distributed application. Consequently, the modularity and flexibility of Web services make them ideal for e-Business application integration. For example, an inventory Web service referenced above can be accessed together with other related Web services by a business partner's warehouse management application or can be part of a new distributed application that is developed from scratch and implements an extended value chain supply planning solution; see Figure 19.1.

Web services can be viewed from two perspectives. An application that provides, and possibly publishes, Web services functionality that can be invoked in a standard format is called a *provider* (the host) of Web services. Distributed applications that call/invoke external Web services are known as *clients* or *requesters* (the users) of this Web service.

One important aspect of Web services is that they distinguish between an interface and implementation part. The interface part defines the functionality visible to the external world and how it is accessed. The implementation realizes the interface and the implementation details are hidden from the users of the Web service; see Figure 19.2. Different service providers using any programming language of their choice may implement the same interface. One Web services implementation might provide the direct functionality itself, while another service implementation might use a combination of other Web services to provide the same functionality. This leads to a hierarchical service dependency process whereby a certain service provider may rely on the services of other service providers to supply a client with the required Web services functionality. The term Web service used in this book refers to both the Web service interface (the description of functionality provided by the Web service) and the Web service implementation (the software component realizing the functionality).

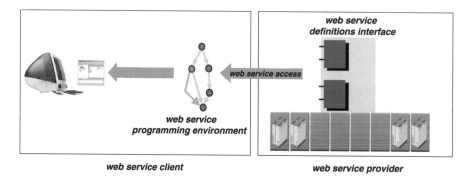

web service client   **web service provider**

■ **Figure 19.2:** Web Services Clients and Providers

The Web service implementation strategy involves choosing from an increasing diversity of different options for services, which may be mixed in various combinations including [Papazoglou 2002]: in-house service design and implementation, purchasing/leasing/paying for services, outsourcing service design and implementation using wrappers and/or adapters (see Section 16.5.1). Non-component implementations for services may include database functionality or legacy software accessed by means of adapters or wrappers.

Web services can discover and communicate with other Web services and trigger them to fulfill or outsource part of a higher-level transaction by using a common vocabulary (business terminology) and a published directory of their capabilities according to a reference architecture called the Service Oriented Architecture; see Section 19.5. A Web service can be a specific service, such as an online car rental service; a business process, such as the automated purchasing of office supplies; an application, such as a language translator program; or an IT resource, such as access to a particular database.

At this stage a more complete definition of a Web service can be given. A Web service is a platform-independent, loosely coupled, self-contained programmable Web-enabled application that can be described, published, discovered, orchestrated and programmed using XML artifacts for the purpose of developing distributed interoperable applications. Web services possess the ability to engage other services in a common computation in order to:

- complete a task,

- conduct a business transaction, or

- solve a complex problem, and

- expose their features programmatically over the Internet (or intra-net) using standard Internet languages and protocols like XML.

They can be implemented via a self-describing interface based on open Internet standards. Now, let us examine this definition more closely and deconstruct its meaning.

Web services are loosely coupled software modules. Web services interact with one another dynamically and use standard Internet technologies, making it possible to build bridges between systems that otherwise would require extensive development efforts. Traditional application design depends upon a tight interconnection of all subsidiary elements. The complexity of these connections requires that developers thoroughly understand and have control over both ends of the connection; moreover, once established, it is exceedingly difficult to extract one element and replace it with another. Loosely coupled systems, on the other hand, require a much simpler level of coordination and allow for more flexible reconfiguration. As opposed to tight coupling principles that require agreement and shared context between communicating systems as well as sensitivity to change, loose coupling allows systems to connect and interact more freely (possibly across the Internet). Loose coupling also implies that a change in the implementation of the Web services functionality does not require a subsequent change in the client program that invokes it or in the conditions and cost of using the service.

Web services semantically encapsulate discrete functionality. A Web service is a self-contained software module that performs a single task. The module describes its own interface characteristics, i.e., the operations available, the parameters, data-typing and the access protocols, in a way that other software modules can determine what it does, how to invoke its functionality, and what result to expect in return. In this regard, Web services are contracted software modules as they provide publicly available descriptions of the interface characteristics used to access the service so that potential clients can bind to it. The service client uses a Web service's interface description to bind to the service provider and invoke its services.

Web services can be accessed programmatically. A Web service provides programmable access – this allows the embedding of Web services into remotely located applications. This enables information to be queried and updated in real time, thus, improving efficiency, responsiveness and accuracy – ultimately leading to the provision of high added value to the Web service clients.

Web services can be dynamically found and included in applications. Web services can be assembled, even on the fly, to serve a particular function, solve a specific problem, or deliver a particular solution to a customer. By employing a Web service architecture, dynamic, loosely coupled applications can be created based on different Web services accessible by a variety of devices such as personal computers, workstations, laptops, WAP-enabled cellular phones, PDAs, and even household appliances fitted with computer chips.

Web services are distributed over the Internet. Web services make use of existing, ubiquitous transport Internet protocols like HTTP. By relying on the same, well-understood transport mechanism as Web content, Web services leverage existing infrastructure and can comply with current corporate firewall policies.

Web services are described in terms of a description language that provides functional as well as non-functional characteristics. Functional characteristics include operational characteristics that define the overall behavior of the service while non-functional characteristics include service availability, reliability, security, authorization, authentication, performance characteristics, e.g., speed or accuracy, timeliness information and payment schemes on a "Finance it", "Lease it", "Pay for it" or "Pay per use" basis.

In e-Business applications that provide seamless connectivity between business processes and applications external to an enterprise and the enterprise's back office applications – such as billing, order processing, accounting, inventory, receivables, and services – for security reasons the firewall, which is essential for the survival of a business site, prevents access to back office systems in order to maintain the integrity of business data stored in business databases and guarantee privacy. The approach with the firewall is that it disallows any kind of binary method invocation, except on pre-designated guarded, i.e., secure, ports. As a result even if all the Web sites come equipped with the same component technology such as, for instance, CORBA, firewalls prevent calls from going through. Web services address the problems of firewall blocking and singular solutions by using the Simple Object Access Protocol (SOAP) as a transport protocol to transport the call from one Web site to the next; see Section 19.7.1. SOAP combines the proven Web technology of the "firewall-friendly" HTTP with the flexibility and extensibility of XML. It facilitates interoperability among a wide range of programs and platforms, making existing applications accessible to a broader range of users. Web services exploit this technology by allowing service providers to provide their clients with secure, personalized access to their back-office information and processes.

19.4 Web services: types and characteristics

We can distinguish between four models of Web services on the basis of the business functionality they provide: informational services, complex trading services, programmatic services and interactive services.

Informational services are services of a relatively simple nature; they either involve simple request/response sequences between interacting services thus providing access to content (content services) or they expose back-end business applications to other applications located outside the firewall (business process services). In the context of e-Business, informational services are normally used for sharing with partners/subsidiaries.

Examples of informational services include access to content such as simple financial information and financial calculations, stock quote information, design information, pricing, calculating quotes, access to product lists and catalogues and so on. They also include services that can provide a seamless aggregation of information across disparate systems and information sources, including back-end systems, giving programmatic access to a business service so that the requester can make the best decisions, such as reserving a rental car, submitting a purchase order or declaring an incident. Finally, they also include services offered by third parties and run the whole range from business-enabling services, such as logistics, payment, fulfillment, and tracking services.

Informational Web services exhibit an important characteristic: they are *stateless*. This means that each time a consumer interacts with a Web service, an action is performed. Web services in their pure form do not keep any memory of what happens to them between requests. After the results of the service invocation have been returned, the action is finished. There is no assumption that subsequent invocations are associated with prior ones. Consequently, all the information required to perform the service is either passed with the request message or can be retrieved from a data repository based on some information provided with the request.

Informational services require support by the three core standards:

• Communication Protocol (SOAP)

• Service description (Web services Description Language or WSDL) and

• Service Publtication and Discovery (Universal Description and Discovery and Integration or UDDI); see Section 19.7.

For businesses to obtain the full benefit of Web services, transactional Web services functionality is required. True business-to-business collaboration requires functionality that relies on numerous document exchanges, multi-party, long running transactions (or "business conversations") that involve sophisticated security techniques, such as non-repudiation and digital signatures, as well as business process management. Business-to-business collaboration usually involves business agreement descriptions, which define roles such as buyer and seller and a purchasing protocol between them. The agreement definition outlines the requirements that each role must fulfill. For example, the seller must have Web services that receive request for quote (RFQ) messages, purchase order (PO) messages and payment messages. The buyer role must have Web services that receive RFQ response messages, invoice messages and account summary messages. This choreography of Web services into business roles is critical for establishing multi-step, service-oriented interactions between business partners and modeling business agreements. This type of functionality is exhibited by *complex Web services*. Complex Web services, just like informational services, require the support of standards such as SOAP, WSDL and UDDI. However, they also require emergent standards for the following:

• business processes and associated XML messages and content

• a registry for publishing and discovering business processes and collaboration protocol profiles

- collaboration partner agreements

- standard business terminology and

- a uniform message transportation layer

Complex services are *stateful* meaning that transient information between operation invocations is kept. Typically, business processes specify stateful interactions involving the exchange of messages between partners, where the state of a business process includes the messages that are exchanged as well as intermediate data used in business logic and in composing messages sent to partners.

Web services can also be categorized according to the way they are programmed in applications. Some Web services exhibit programmatic behavior whereas others exhibit mainly interactive behavior where input has to be supplied by the user. This makes it natural to distinguish between the following two types of Web services:

1. *Programmatic Web services*: Programmatic Web services encapsulate a programmatic business processes and expose the business logic functionality of the applications and components that underlie them. Programmatic business services expose function calls, typically written in programming languages such as Java/EJB, Visual Basic or C#. Applications access these function calls by executing a Web service through a standard WSDL programmatic interface. The exposed programmatic services perform a request/response type of business task and return a concrete result; in this sense they can be viewed as "atomic" operations. The clients of these Web services can assemble them to build new applications. An example typical of programmatic behavior could be an inventory checking function of an inventory management system, which is exposed as a Web service accessible to applications via the Internet. The inventory checking Web service can then be invoked by a create order service that also uses a create purchase order Web service from an order entry system to create orders, if the inventory is available.

2. *Interactive Web services*: these expose the functionality of a Web application's presentation (browser) layer. They expose a multi-step Web application behavior that combines a Web server, an application server and underlying database systems and typically deliver the application directly to a browser. Clients of these Web services can incorporate interactive business processes into their Web applications, presenting integrated (aggregated) applications from external service providers.

Obviously, the programmatic and the interactive can be combined, thus delivering business processes that combine typical business logic functionality with Web browser interactivity.

The complex Web services standards are still evolving and are converging on SOAP, WSDL, UDDI and the Web services Business Process Execution Language (BPEL) currently under standardization at OASIS. Two key emerging business protocols that are widely accepted by industry on which complex Web services can rely are ebXML (electronic-business XML) and RosettaNet; see Chapter 20.

19.5 The service-oriented architecture

To build integration-ready applications the Web service model relies on the service-oriented architecture (SOA). The term *service-oriented architecture* signifies the way that Web services are described and organized so that dynamic, automated discovery and use of network-available services can take place. This architectural approach is particularly applicable when multiple applications running on varied technologies and platforms need to communicate with each other.

SOA is a logical way of designing a software system to provide services to either end-user applications or other services distributed in a network through published and discoverable interfaces. The basic SOA defines an interaction between software agents as an exchange of messages between service requesters (clients) and service providers. Clients are software agents that request the execution of a service. Providers are software agents that provide the service. Agents can be simultaneously both service clients and providers. Providers are responsible for publishing a description of the service(s) they provide. Clients must be able to find the description(s) of the services they require and must be able to bind to them.

The service-oriented architecture builds on today's Web services baseline specifications of SOAP, WSDL, and UDDI. The main building blocks of the Web services architecture are three-fold and they are determined on the basis of three primary roles that can be undertaken by these architectural modules. These are the service provider, the service registry and the service requester.

A logical view of the service-oriented architecture is given in Figure 19.3. This figure illustrates the relationship between the three roles and the three operations mentioned above. First, the Web services provider publishes its Web service(s) with the Web services broker. Next, the Web services requester searches for desired Web services using the registry of the Web services broker. Finally, the Web services requester, using the information obtained from the Web services broker, invokes (binds to) the Web services provided by the Web services provider [Boubez 2000].

Since SOA is based on open standards and is frequently realized using Web services, developing meaningful Web services and business process specification is an important requirement for SOA applications that leverage Web services. Web services design and development has certain similarities to component-based design and development (see Section 15.7) and also quite distinct characteristics due to its business process-centric nature. Readers are referred to [Papazoglou 2006] for a detailed description of the techniques and methodologies used during the Web services development life cycle.

19.5.1 Roles of interaction in the service-oriented architecture

The first important role that can be discerned in the Web services architecture is that of the Web services *provider*. The Web services provider is the organization that owns the Web services and implements the business logic that underlies the service. From an architectural perspective this is the platform that hosts

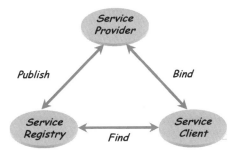

■ **Figure 19.3:** Web Services Roles and Operations

and controls access to the service. The Web services provider is responsible for publishing the Web services it provides in a service registry hosted by a service broker. This involves describing the business, service and technical information of the Web services and registering that information with the Web services registry in the format prescribed by the Web services broker.

The next major role in the Web services architecture is that of the Web services *requester* (or client). From a business perspective this is the enterprise that requires certain functions to be satisfied. From an architectural perspective, this is the application that is looking for, and subsequently invoking, the service. The Web services requester searches the service registry for the desired Web services. This effectively means discovering the Web services description in a registry provided by a Web services broker and using the information in the description to bind to the service.

The last important role that can be distinguished in the Web services architecture is that of the Web services *registry* which is a searchable directory where service descriptions can be published and searched. Service requestors find service descriptions in the registry and obtain binding information for services. This information is sufficient for the service requester to contact, or bind to, the service provider and thus make use of the services it provides.

It is unreasonable to assume that there would be a single global registry containing all of the information required to find and interact with businesses throughout the world. What we will see are local communities of service providers and requesters organized in vertical markets and gathering around portals. These marketplace portals will consist of UDDI registries containing business data for that specific vertical market. This gives rise to the idea of a Web services broker that is the organization (acting as a third trusted party) whose primary activities focus on hosting the registry, publishing and promoting Web services. The service broker can further improve the searching functionality for Web services requesters by adding advertising capabilities to this infrastructure and by supporting facilities for Web services matchmaking between providers and requesters.

19.5.2 Operations in the service-oriented architecture

For an application to take advantage of the Web services interactions between the three roles in the SOA, three primary operations must take place. These are *publication* of the service descriptions, *finding* the service descriptions and *binding* or invocation of the service based on its service description. These three basic operations can occur singly or iteratively.

Publishing a Web service so that other users can find it actually consists of two equally important operations. The first operation is describing the Web service itself; the other is the actual registration of the Web service.

If a service provider wishes to publish its Web services with the registry then the first requirement is to properly describe these Web services in WSDL. Publication includes information on the Web services provider (service information); information about the nature of the Web service (service information); and finally, technical information about the invocation methods of the Web service.

The next step in publishing a Web service is registration. Registration deals with storing the Web services descriptions in the Web services registry provided by the Web services broker. For Web services requesters to be able to find a Web service these need to be published with at least one Web services broker.

In a similar fashion to publishing, finding Web services is also a twofold operation. Finding the desired Web services consists of first discovering the services in the registry of the Web services broker and then selecting the desired Web service(s) from the search results. Discovering Web services involves querying the registry of the Web services broker for Web services matching the needs of a Web services requester. A query consists of search criteria such as type of service, preferred price range, what products are associated with this service, with which categories in company and product taxonomies is this Web service associated (as well as other technical characteristics; see Section 19.7.3) and is executed against the Web service information in the registry entered by the Web services provider.

Selection deals with deciding about which Web services to invoke from the set of Web services the discovery process returned. Two possible methods of selection exist: manual and automatic selection. Manual selection implies that the Web services requester selects the desired Web service directly from the returned set of Web services after manual inspection. The other possibility is automatic selection of the best candidate between potentially matching Web services.

During the binding operation the service requester invokes or initiates an interaction at run-time using the binding details in the service description to locate and contract to the service. The technical information entered in the registry by the Web services provider is used here. Two different possibilities exist for this invocation. The first possibility is direct invocation of the Web service by the Web services requester using the technical information included in the description of the service. The second possibility is mediation by the Web services broker when invoking the Web service. In this case all communication between the Web services requester and the Web services provider goes through the Web services registry of the broker.

19.6 The Web services technology stack

By intent, Web services are not implemented in a monolithic manner, but rather represent a collection of several related technologies. The more generally accepted definition for Web services leans on a stack of specific, complementary standards, see Figure 19.4.

The core layers that define basic Web services communication have been widely accepted and are implemented quite uniformly. Higher-level layers that define strategic aspects of business processes still remain an open problem and it is quite likely that different vendors will propose divergent approaches. The development of open and accepted standards is a key strength of the coalitions that have been building Web services infrastructure.

Core layers
- Although not specifically tied to any specific transport protocol, Web services build on ubiquitous Internet connectivity and infrastructure to ensure nearly universal reach and support. In particular, Web services will take advantage of HTTP, the same connection protocol used by Web servers and browsers.

- *Extensible Markup Language*: XML is a widely accepted format for exchanging data and its corresponding semantics. It is a fundamental building block for nearly every other layer in the Web services stack.

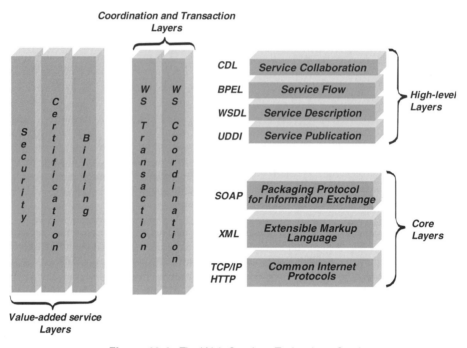

■ **Figure 19.4:** The Web Services Technology Stack

- *Simple Object Access Protocol*: SOAP is a simple XML-based messaging protocol that implements a request/response model for communication between interacting Web services.

Higher-level layers

The key to Web services interoperability is reliance solely on the following standards found in the higher levels of the Web services technology stack.

- *Service Description layer*: Web services are easy to use when a Web services and its client rely on standard ways to specify data and operations, to represent Web services contracts, and to understand the capabilities that a Web service provides. To achieve this, the functionality of Web services is first described by means of a Web services Description Language and subsequently, published in a Universal Description and Discovery and Integration service repository for discovery. WSDL defines the XML grammar for describing services as collections of communicating endpoints capable of exchanging messages. Companies publish WSDL specifications for services they provide and other enterprises can access those services using the description in WSDL.

- *Service Publication layer*: Web services publication is achieved by UDDI, which is a public directory that provides publication of on-line services and facilitates eventual discovery of Web services. It stores and publishes the WSDL specifications of available Web services. Searches can be performed on the basis of company name, specific service, or types of service. This allows enterprises providing or needing Web services to discover each other, define how they interact over the Internet, and share such information in a truly global and standardized manner in order to create value added applications.

- *Service Flow layer*: this describes the execution logic of Web services based applications by defining their control flows (such as conditional, sequential, parallel and exceptional execution) and prescribing the rules for consistently managing their unobservable business data. In this way enterprises can describe complex processes that include multiple organizations – such as order processing, lead management, and claims handling – and execute the same business processes in systems from other vendors. This layer is representative of a family of XML-based process definitions, most representative of which is the Business Process Execution Language for Web services [Andrews 2003]. BPEL is a block-structured workflow-like language that describes business processes that can orchestrate Web services. This XML-based flow language defines how business processes interact.

- *Service Collaboration* layer: this describes cross-enterprise collaborations of Web services participants by defining their common observable behavior, where synchronized information exchanges occur through their shared contact-points, when commonly defined ordering rules are satisfied. This layer is materialized by Web services Choreography Description Language (WS-CDL) [Kavantzas 2004], which specifies the common observable behavior of all participants engaged in business collaboration.

Coordination/transaction layer

Currently there are attempts underway towards defining transactional interaction among Web services. The WS-Coordination [Cabrera 2002a] and WS-Transaction [Cabrera 2002b] initiatives complement BPEL4WS to provide mechanisms for defining specific standard protocols for use by transaction processing systems, workflow systems, or other applications that wish to coordinate multiple Web services. These three specifications work in tandem to address the business workflow issues implicated in connecting and executing a number of Web services that may run on disparate platforms across organizations involved in e-Business scenarios.

Value-added services layer

Additional elements that support complex business interactions must still be implemented before Web services can automate truly critical business processes. These are defined in the value-added services layer; see Figure 19.4. Mechanisms for security and authentication, contract management, quality of service, and more will soon follow, some as standards, others as value-added solutions from independent software vendors.

19.7 Web services standards

For there to be widespread acceptance of Web services there needs to be a set of clear, widely adopted standards. Fortunately, there is wide agreement across the industry on a set of standards to support Web services. The three sets of services that we cover in this section have emerged as the basis for standards in Web services.

19.7.1 SOAP: Simple Object Access Protocol

In the emerging world of Web services, it will be possible for enterprises to leverage mainstream application development tools and Internet application servers to bring about inter-applications communication, which has been historically associated with EDI technology. For this paradigm to become a reality the tools and common conventions required to interconnect proprietary systems running on heterogeneous infrastructures are needed. To address this problem Web services rely on SOAP, an XML-based communication protocol for exchanging information between computers regardless of their operating systems, programming environment, or object model framework. *Simple Object Access Protocol* is defined as lightweight protocol for exchange of structured and typed information between computers and systems in a decentralized and distributed environment such as the Internet or even a LAN [Cauldwell 2001].

The goal of SOAP is to diffuse the barriers of heterogeneity that separate distributed computing platforms. SOAP achieves this by following the same recipe as other successful Web protocols: simplicity, flexibility, firewall friendliness, platform neutrality and XML messaging-based (text-based). SOAP provides a *wire protocol* that specifies how service related messages are structured when exchanged across the Internet. SOAP is a lightweight protocol that allows applications to pass messages and data back and forth between disparate systems in a distributed environment enabling remote method invocation. By lightweight we mean that the SOAP protocol possesses only two fundamental properties. It sends and receives HTTP (or other) transport protocol packets, and processes XML messages.

Although SOAP may use different protocols such as HTTP, FTP or RMI to transport messages and locate the remote system and initiate communications, its natural transport protocol is HTTP. Layering SOAP over HTTP means that a SOAP message is sent as part of an HTTP request or response, which makes it easy to communicate over any network that permits HTTP traffic. SOAP uses the HTTP protocol to *transport* XML-encoded serialized method argument data from system to system. *Serialization* is the process of converting application data to XML. XML is then a serialized representation of the application data. The process of generating application data from XML is called *deserialization*. SOAP's serialization mechanism converts "method calls" to a form suitable for transportation over the network, using special XML tags and semantics. The serialized argument data is used on the remote end to execute the client's method call on that system's, rather than on the client's local system. Because SOAP can reside on HTTP, its request/response method operates in a very similar way to HTTP. When a client makes an HTTP request, the server attempts to service the request and can respond in one of two ways. It can either respond that communication was successful by returning the requested information. Alternatively, it can respond with a fault message notifying the client of the particular reason why the request could not be serviced.

Structure of a SOAP message

The current SOAP specification 1.1 describes how the data types defined in associated XML schemas are serialized over HTTP or other transport protocols. Both the provider and requester of SOAP messages must have access to the same XML schemas in order to exchange information correctly. The schemas are normally posted on the Internet, and may be downloaded by any party in an exchange of messages. A SOAP message contains a payload, the application specific information it delivers. Every SOAP message is essentially an XML document. SOAP messages can be broken down to three basic parts:

- *SOAP envelope*: Conceptually, the SOAP envelope is the overall set of descriptors and container for message data. The SOAP envelope serves to wrap any XML document interchange and provide a mechanism to augment the payload with additional information that is required to route it to its ultimate destination. The SOAP envelope is the single root of every SOAP message and must present for the message to be SOAP compliant. All elements of the SOAP envelope are defined by a W3C XML Schema (XSD).

- *SOAP header*: The header contains processing or control information about a specific message, such as the identification of the requester, the point of origin of the message, information about where the document shall be sent, authentication information, security and encryption information, authentication or transaction control-related information, quality of service, billing or accounting information regarding an application and more technical data as to how the request should be processed. The SOAP header in Listing 19.1 deals with the transactional integrity rules associated with the payment of orders.

- *SOAP body*: The SOAP body defines the content of a request. The body is the area of the SOAP message method call information and its related arguments are encoded. The body must be contained within the envelope, and must follow any headers that might be defined for the message. It is where the response to a method call is placed, and where error information can be stored. The structure of the SOAP body depends on the requested service. The interface requested by the Web service (specified in a WSDL document) determines the structure. If the data elements of the request message as defined to the SOAP body do not conform to an expected structure, e.g., the required element containers, containers ordered in the necessary sequence, and appropriate data types, then the Web service will not be able to process the request. In essence, the design of the SOAP body is similar to the development of a prototype XML transaction and a constraining schema. The SOAP body in Listing 19.1 shows details regarding a hypothetical purchase order.

The SOAP communication model

The Web services communication model describes how to invoke Web services and relies on SOAP. SOAP supports two possible communication styles: *remote procedure call (RPC)* and *document* (or *message driven*).

```
<soap: Envelope xmlns:soap=http://www.w3.org/2001/06/soap-envelope>
    <soap: Header>
        <tx:transaction-id
            xmlns:tx="http://www.transaction.com/transaction"
            env:mustUnderstand='1'>
            512
        </tx:transaction-id>
    </soap: Header>
    <soap: Body>
        <n:purchaseOrder xmlns:n="urn:OrderService">
            <from><person> John Smith </person>
                <dept> Accounting </dept></from>
            <to><person> James F. Phelps </person>
                <dept> Provisions </dept></to>
            <order><quantity>1</quantity>
            <item> Photocopier </item></order>
        </n:purchaseOrder>
    </soap: Body>
</soap: Envelope>
```

■ **Listing 19.1:** A Simplified Hypothetical Purchase Order in SOAP

In a remote procedure call (RPC) style, a Web service appears as a remote object to the client application. The interaction between a client and an RPC-style Web service centers around a service-specific interface. Clients express their request as a method call with a set of arguments, which returns a response containing a return value. RPC style supports automatic serialization/deserialization of messages, permitting developers to express a request as a method call with a set of parameters, which returns a response containing a return value. Because of this type of bilateral communication between the client and Web service, RPC-style Web services require a synchronous tightly coupled model of communication between the client and service provider. RPC-style Web services are normally used when an application exhibits the following characteristics [BEA 2001]:

- The client invoking the Web service needs an immediate response.

- The client and Web service work in a back-and-forth conversational way.

- The Web service is process-oriented rather than data-oriented.

Examples of typical simple information services with an RPC-style include returning the current price for a given stock; providing the current weather conditions in a particular location; or checking the credit rating of a potential trading partner prior to the completion of a business transaction.

Document-style Web services are message driven. When a client invokes a document-style Web service, the client typically sends it an entire document, such as a purchase order, rather than a discrete set of parameters. The Web service is sent an entire document, which it processes. However, it may or may not return a response message. This style is thus *asynchronous* in that the client invoking the Web service can continue with its computation without waiting for a response. The document style does not support automatic serialization/deserialization of messages. Rather it assumes that the contents of the SOAP message are well-formed XML documents, e.g., a purchase order. Document-style Web services promote a looser coupling between the client and service provider, as there is no requirement for a tightly coupled request/response model between the client and the Web service.

Document-style Web services are normally used when in an application the client does not require (or expect) an immediate response, or when the Web service is data-oriented rather than process-oriented. Examples of document-style Web services include processing a purchase order; responding to a request for quote order from a customer; or responding to an order placement by a particular customer. In all cases, the client sends an entire document, such as a purchase order, to the Web service and assumes that the Web service is processing it in some way, but the client does not require an immediate answer.

While it is important to understand the SOAP foundation for services, most Web services developers will not have to deal with this infrastructure directly. Most Web services use optimized SOAP bindings generated from WSDL. In this way SOAP implementations can self-configure exchanges between Web services while masking most of the technical details.

19.7.2 WSDL: Web services description language

WSDL is the service representation language used to describe the details of the complete interfaces exposed by Web services and thus, is the means to accessing a Web service. It is through this service description that the service provider can communicate all the specifications for invoking a particular Web service to the service requester. For instance, neither the service requester nor the provider should be aware of each other's technical infrastructure, programming language or distributed object framework (if any).

WSDL provides a mechanism by which service providers can describe the basic format of Web requests over different protocols (e.g., SOAP) or encoding (e.g., Multipurpose Internet Messaging Extensions or MIME).

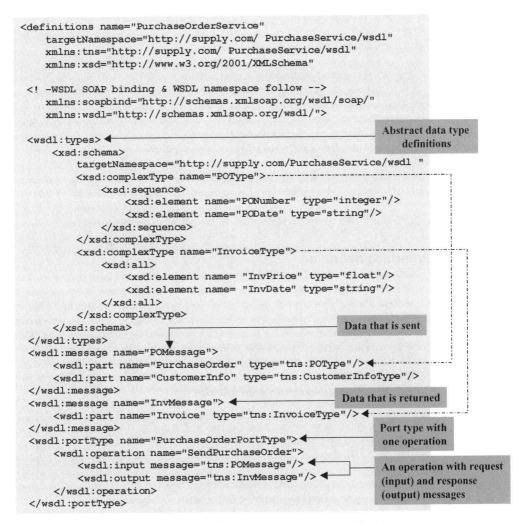

```
<definitions name="PurchaseOrderService"
    targetNamespace="http://supply.com/ PurchaseService/wsdl"
    xmlns:tns="http://supply.com/ PurchaseService/wsdl"
    xmlns:xsd="http://www.w3.org/2001/XMLSchema"

<! -WSDL SOAP binding & WSDL namespace follow -->
    xmlns:soapbind="http://schemas.xmlsoap.org/wsdl/soap/"
    xmlns:wsdl="http://schemas.xmlsoap.org/wsdl/">

<wsdl:types>                                              Abstract data type
    <xsd:schema>                                            definitions
        targetNamespace="http://supply.com/PurchaseService/wsdl "
        <xsd:complexType name="POType">
            <xsd:sequence>
                <xsd:element name="PONumber" type="integer"/>
                <xsd:element name="PODate" type="string"/>
            </xsd:sequence>
        </xsd:complexType>
        <xsd:complexType name="InvoiceType">
            <xsd:all>
                <xsd:element name= "InvPrice" type="float"/>
                <xsd:element name= "InvDate" type="string"/>
            </xsd:all>
        </xsd:complexType>
    </xsd:schema>                                   Data that is sent
</wsdl:types>
<wsdl:message name="POMessage">
    <wsdl:part name="PurchaseOrder" type="tns:POType"/>
    <wsdl:part name="CustomerInfo" type="tns:CustomerInfoType"/>
</wsdl:message>
<wsdl:message name="InvMessage">                Data that is returned
    <wsdl:part name="Invoice" type="tns:InvoiceType"/>
</wsdl:message>
<wsdl:portType name="PurchaseOrderPortType">    Port type with
    <wsdl:operation name="SendPurchaseOrder">     one operation
        <wsdl:input message="tns:POMessage"/>
        <wsdl:output message="tns:InvMessage"/>    An operation with request
    </wsdl:operation>                               (input) and response
</wsdl:portType>                                    (output) messages
```

■ **Figure 19.5:** Simple WSDL Interface Definition

WSDL is an XML based specification schema for describing the public interface of a Web service. This public interface can include operational information relating to a Web service such as all publicly available operations, the XML message protocols supported by the Web service, data type information for messages, binding information about the specific transport protocol to be used, and address information for locating the Web service. WSDL allows the specification of services in terms of XML documents for transmission under SOAP. We can think of Web services as objects that are accessed via SOAP.

A WSDL document describes how to invoke a service and provides information on the data being exchanged, the sequence of messages for an operation, protocol bindings, and the location of the service. WSDL represents a contract between the service requester and the service provider, in much the same way that an interface in an object-oriented programming language, e.g., Java, represents a contract between client code and the actual object itself. The prime difference is that WSDL is platform- and language-independent and is used primarily (but not exclusively) to describe SOAP-enabled services.

The WSDL specification can be conveniently divided into two parts: the service interface definition (abstract interface) and the service implementation (concrete endpoint) [Kreger 2001]. The *service-interface definition* describes the general Web service interface structure. This contains all the operations supported by the service, the operation parameters and abstract data types. The *service implementation part* binds the abstract interface to a concrete network address, to a specific protocol and to concrete data structures. A Web service client may bind to such an implementation and invoke the service in question.

The service interface definition together with the service implementation definition make up a complete WSDL specification of the service. The combination of these two parts contains sufficient information to describe to the service requester how to invoke and interact with the Web service at a provider's site. Using WSDL, a requester can locate a Web service and invoke any of the publicly available operations.

Web service interface definition

The Web services interface definition describes WSDL messages in a platform and language independent manner. It describes exactly what types of message need to be sent and how the various Internet standard messaging protocols and encoding schemes can be employed in order to format the message in a manner compatible with the service provider's specifications. A service interface definition is an abstract service description that can be instantiated and referenced by multiple concrete service implementations. This allows common industry-standard service types to be defined and implemented by multiple service implementers. The service interface contains the WSDL elements that comprise the reusable portion of the service description, these include: the `<portType>`, `<operation>`, `<message>`, `<part>` and `<types>` elements. These are briefly summarized in the following:

- A type attribute in WSDL is comparable to a data type in Java or C++. The WSDL `<type>` element is used to contain XML schemas or external references to XML schemas that describe the data type definitions used within the WSDL document. WSDL uses a few primitive data types that XML Schema Definition defines, such as `int`, `float`, `long`, `short`, `string`, `Boolean` and so on, and allows developers either to use them directly or to build complex data types based on those primitive ones before using them in messages. This is why developers need to define their own namespace when referring to complex data types. Any complex data type that the service uses must be defined in an optional `<types>` section immediately before the `<message>` section.

- Messages are abstract collections of typed information cast upon one or more logical units, used to communicate information between systems. A <message> element corresponds to a single piece of information moving between the invoker and the service. A regular round trip method call is modeled as two messages, one for the request and one for the response.

- A message can consist of one or more <part> elements with each part representing an instance of a particular type (typed parameter). When WSDL describes an object, each part maps to an argument of a method call. If the method returns void, the response is an empty message.

The WSDL <portType> element describes the interface of a Web service. It is simply a logical grouping of operations. The <portType> element is central to a WSDL description; the rest of the elements in the definition are essentially details that the <portType> element depends upon. The <portType> is used to bind the collection of logical operations to an actual transport protocol such as SOAP, thus providing the linkage between the abstract and concrete portions of a WSDL document. A WSDL definition can contain zero or more <portType> definitions. Typically, most WSDL documents contain a single <portType>. This convention separates out different Web services interface definitions into different documents. This granularity allows each business process to have separate binding definitions, providing for reuse, significant implementation flexibility for different security, reliability, transport mechanisms and so on [Cauldwell 2001].

Figure 19.5 shows an excerpt from a WSDL interface definition describing a purchase order service. This service takes a purchase order number, a date and customer details as input and returns an associated invoice. The root element in Figure 19.5 (and every WSDL specification) is the <definitions> element, in which a complete description of the Web service is provided. The <definitions> element consists of attributes, which define the name of the service, the target namespace of the service, and other standard namespace definitions (such as SOAP) used in the service specification. In Figure 19.5 the <definitions> element contains an attribute called targetNamespace, which defines the logical namespace for information about the service, and is usually chosen to be unique to the individual service (a URL set to the name of the original WSDL file). This helps clients differentiate between Web services and prevents name clashes when importing other WSDL files. These namespaces are simply unique strings – they usually do not point to a page on the Web. The xmlns:tns (sometimes referred to as *this* namespace) attribute is set to the value of targetNamespace and is used to qualify (scope) properties of this service defintion. The namespace definitions xmlns:soap and xmlns:xsdl are used for specifying SOAP-specific information as well as data types, respectively. The final statement defines xmlns: as the default namespace for all WSDL elements defined in a WSDL specification such as messages, operations, and portTypes. The wsdl:types definition encapsulates schema definitions of all types using XSD.

The <types> element is a container that contains all abstract data types that define a Web service interface. Part elements may select individual type definitions contained in a <types> element. The chosen type definition is directly attached to <part> element. Figure 19.5 illustrates two complex types that have been defined in its <types> section: POType and InvoiceType. The elements <sequence> and <all> is a standard XSD element. The construct <sequence> requires that the content model follows the element sequence defined, while the construct <all> denotes that all the elements that are declared in the <complexType> statement must appear in an instance document. XSD is also used to create the type namespace, and the alias xsdl is used to reference these two complex types in order to define messages.

The central element externalizing a service interface description is the `<portType>` element. This element contains all named operations supported by a service. The WSDL example in Figure 19.5 defines a Web service that contains a `<portType>` named `PurchaseOrderPortType` that supports a single `<operation>`, which is called `SendPurchaseOrder`. If there are multiple `<portType>` elements in a WSDL document then each `<portType>` element must have a different name. The example assumes that the service is deployed using the SOAP 1.1 protocol as its encoding style, and is bound to HTTP.

Operations in WSDL are the equivalent of method signatures in programming languages as they represent the various methods being exposed by the service. An operation defines a method on a Web service, including the name of the method and the input and output parameters. A typical operation defines the input and output parameters or exceptions (faults) of an operation.

The `<operation>` element `SendPurchaseOrder` in Figure 19.5 is called using the message `POMessage` and will return its results using the message `Invoice Message`. Operations can be used in a Web service in four fundamentals patterns: request/response, solicit/response, one-way and notification. The operation `SendPurchase` is a typical example of a request/response style of operation as it contains an input and an output message.

An operation holds all messages potentially exchanged between a Web services consumer and a Web services provider. If fault messages had been defined, these would also be part of the `<operation>` element. As shown in Figure 19.5 message `POMessage` is linked by name to the input message element of the `SendPurchaseOrder` operation. This message represents the data that is sent from a service requester to a service provider. Similarly, the message `InvMessage` is linked by name to the output message element of the `SendPurchaseOrder` operation. This message encapsulates the data of the return value. The input and output message elements of an operation link the services method, `SendPurchaseOrder` in the case of Figure 19.5, to SOAP messages that will provide the transport for input parameters and output results. The operation patterns are described in Section 19.7.2.

A message consists of `<part>` elements, which are linked to `<types>` elements. While a message represents the overall data type formation of an operation, parts may further structure this formation. In Figure 19.5 the input message called `POMessage` contains two `<part>` elements that refer to the complex types `POType` and `CustomerInfoType`, respectively. `POType` consists of `PONumber` and `PODate` elements. The dotted arrow at the right hand side of the WSL definition in Figure 19.5 links the `POType` definition to the input message. The same applies to the output message `InvMessage` and the `InvoiceType` definition.

WSDL implementation

In the previous section, WSDL operations and messages have been defined in an abstract manner without worrying about the details of implementation. In fact, the purpose of WSDL is to specify a Web service abstractly and then to define how the WSDL developer will reach the implementation of these services. The service implementation part of WSDL contains the elements `<binding>` (although sometimes this element is considered as part of the service definition), `<port>` and `<service>` and describes how a particular service interface is implemented by a given service provider. The service implementation describes where the service is located, or more precisely, to which network address the message must be sent in order to invoke the Web service. A Web service is modeled as a WSDL service element. The Web services implementation elements are summarized below.

- In WSDL a `<binding>` element contains information of how the elements in an abstract service interface (`<portType>` element) are converted into concrete representation in a particular combination of data formats and concrete protocols. The WSDL `<binding>` element defines how a given operation is formatted and bound to a specific protocol.

- A `<port>` defines the location of a service and we can think of it as the URL where the service can be found.

- A `<service>` element contains a collection of (usually one) WSDL `<port>` elements. A `<port>` associates an endpoint, for instance, a network address location or URL, with a WSDL binding element from a service definition. Each `<service>` element is named, and each name must be unique among all services in a WSDL document.

The example in Figure 19.6 is a description of WSDL implementation for the abstract service interface listed in Figure 19.5. The central element of the implementation description is the `<binding>` element. The `<binding>` element specifies how the client and Web service should exchange messages. The client uses this information to access the Web service. This element binds the port type, i.e., the service interface description, to an existing service implementation. It provides information about the protocol and the concrete data formats expected by a service offered from a distinct network address [Zimmermann 2003]. The binding name must be unique among all the `<binding>` elements in a WSDL document.

The structure of the `<binding>` element resembles that of the `<portType>` element. This is no coincidence as the binding must map an abstract port type description to a concrete implementation. The `<type>` attribute identifies which `<portType>` element this binding describes. As illustrated in Figure 19.6 the `<binding>` element POMessageSOAPBinding links the `<portType>` element named PurchaseOrderPortType (refer to Figure 19.5) to the `<port>` element named PurchasePort. This is affected through the binding name POMessageSOAPBinding as can be seen from the dotted arrow in Figure 19.6. Several bindings may represent various implementations of the same `<portType>` element. If a service supports more than one protocol, then the WSDL `<portType>` element should include a `<binding>` for each protocol it supports. For a given `<portType>` element, a `<binding>` element can describe how to invoke operations using a single messaging/transport protocol, e.g., SOAP over HTTP, SOAP over SMTP or a simple HTTP POST operation, or any other valid combination of networking and messaging protocol standards. Currently, the most popular binding technique is to use SOAP over HTTP. It must be noted that a binding does not contain any programming language- or service implementation-specific details. How a service is implemented is an issue completely external to WSDL.

In Figure 19.6 the `<binding>` element is shown to contain a second `<binding>` element (in this case `<soap:binding>`) that specifies the protocol by which clients access the Web service. More specifically, the purpose of the SOAP binding element `<soap:binding>` is to signify that the SOAP protocol format is going to be used as a binding and transport service. This declaration applies to the entire binding. It signifies that all operations of the PurchaseOrderPortType are defined in this binding as SOAP messages. It then becomes the responsibility of SOAP to take the client from the abstract WSDL specification to its implementation. Since SOAP is used for this purpose, SOAP's namespace must also be used.

Figure 19.6 indicates that the transport attribute specifies HTTP as the lower-level transport service that this binding will use. The style attribute defines the type of default operations within this binding, which

```xml
<!-- wsdl:binding states a serialisation protocol for this service -->
<!-- type attribute must match name of portType element in Figure-19.5 -->
<wsdl:binding name="POMessageSOAPBinding"
              type="tns: PurchaseOrderPortType">

<!-- leverage off soap:binding asynchronous style -->
<soap:binding style="document"
      transport="http://schemas.xmlsoap.org/soap/http"/>

<!-- semi-opaque container of network transport details classed by soap:binding above -->
<wsdl:operation name="SendPurchase">

<!-- again bind to SOAP -->
<soap:operation soapAction=" "/>

<!-- furthur specify that the messages in the wsdl:operation " " use SOAP -->
<wsdl:input>
    <soap:body use="encoded"
        encodingStyle="http://schemas.xmlsoap.org/soap/encoding/"
        namespace="http://supply.com/PurchaseOrderService/wsdl"/>
</wsdl:input>
<wsdl:output>
    <soap:body use="encoded"
        encodingStyle="http://schemas.xmlsoap.org/soap/encoding/"
        namespace="http://supply.com/ PurchaseOrderService/wsdl"/>
</wsdl:output>
</wsdl:operation>
</wsdl:binding>
<wsdl:service name="PurchaseOrderService">
<wsdl:port name="PurchasePort" binding="tns: POMessageSOAPBinding">
<!-- give the binding a network endpoint address or URI of service -->
<soap:address location="http://supply.com:8080/PurchaseOrderService/"/>
</wsdl:port>
</wsdl:service>
</definitions>
```

Bind an abstract operation to this implementation &

map the abstract input & output messages to these concrete messages

Service name

Network address of service

■ **Figure 19.6:** WSDL Implementation Description

is "document"; with the other type being "rpc" (see Section 19.7.1). The transport and style attributes are part of the SOAP binding element `<soap:binding>` (not to be confused with the WSL `<binding>` element). The abstract operation SendPurchase together with its input and output messages from the abstract service interface description (see Figure 19.5) is mapped to SOAP messages.

The `<operation>` element contains instructions on how to access the `PurchaseOrderService`. The `<operation>` element provides the actual details for accessing the Web service. Here, the `<soap:operation>` element is used to indicate the binding of a specific operation, e.g., SendPurchase, to a specific SOAP implementation. The SOAPAction attribute in the `<soap:operation>` element is an attribute that a SOAP client will use to make a SOAP request The SOAPAction attribute is a server specific URI used to indicate the intent of request. It can contain a message routing parameter or value that helps the SOAP runtime system dispatch the message to the appropriate service. The value specified in this attribute must also be specified in the SOAPAction attribute in the HTTP header of the SOAP request. The purpose of this is to achieve interoperability between client and service provider applications. The SOAP client will read the SOAP structure from the WSDL file and coordinate with a SOAP server on the other end.

The `<soap:body>` element enables applications to specify the details of the input and output messages and enable the mapping from the abstract WSDL description to the concrete protocol description. In the case of `PurchaseOrderService`, the `<soap:body>` element specifies the SOAP encoding style and the namespace URN associated with the specific service. The `<input>` and `<output>` elements for the `<operation>` SendPurchase specify exactly how the input and output messages of this operation should appear in the SOAP message. Both input and output contain a `<soap:body>` element with the value of its namespace corresponding to the name of the service that is deployed on the SOAP server. Consider, for example, the `<input>` elements for the SendPurchase operation. The entire POMessage message from the `<portType>` declaration for the SendPurchase operation is declared to be abstract. This is indicated by the `use="encoded"` attribute. This means that the XML defining the input message and its parts are in fact abstract, and the real, concrete representation of the data is to be derived by applying the encoding scheme indicated in the `encodingStyle` attribute [Graham 2002]. This implies that the message should appear as part of the `<soap:body>` element and that the SOAP runtime system on the service provider's network should deserialize the data from XML to another format, e.g., Java data types, according the encoding rules defined in the SOAP specification.

The `<port>` element represents the actual network endpoint(s) on which the service communicates. A Web service exchanges messages in a defined format through a `<port>` element. More precisely, the `<port>` element is a single protocol-specific address to an individual binding element. Here, a mandatory location URI must be provided to denote the physical endpoint that requesters must use to connect to the service. The `<soap:binding>` attribute is a SOAP extension to WSDL used to connect the port (URI) with the protocol in the `<binding>` element. The `<soap:address>` attribute is another SOAP extension to WSDL and is used to signify the URI of the service or the network endpoint. A Web service client is expected to bind to a port and interact with the service, provided that it understands and respects the concrete message expected by the service. The same service may be offered with various data formats over multiple ports. A client that wishes to interact with the service can then choose one of these ports.

A `<service>` is modeled as a collection of related ports – where a `<port>` element is a single endpoint defined as a combination of binding and a network address – at which a service is made available.

The <service> element may be the starting point for a client exploring a service description. A single service can contain multiple ports that all use the same <portType>, i.e., there could be multiple service implementations for the same service interface provided by different service providers. Service providers all have different bindings and/or addresses. Port addresses are specified by the <soap:address> element of <port>, as already explained. In the case of multiple ports, these ports are alternatives, so that the client of the service can choose which protocol they want to use to communicate with the service (possibly programmatically by using the namespaces in the bindings), or which address is closest [Cauldwell 2001].

The previous example contains only one Web service, viz. the PurchaseOrderService, thus only the <port> element named PurchasePort (refer to Figure 19.6) is used to reveal the service location. However, the service PurchaseOrderService could, for instance, contain three ports all of which use the PurchaseOrderPortType but are bound to SOAP over HTTP, SOAP over SMTP, and HTTP GET/POST, respectively. This would give the client of the POMessage service a choice of protocols over which to use the service. For instance, a PC-desktop application may use SOAP over HTTP, while a WAP application designed to run on a cellular phone may use HTTP GET/POST, since an XML parser is typically not available in a WAP application. All three services are semantically equivalent in that they all take a purchase order number and date and return its associated invoice. By employing different bindings, the service is more readily accessible on a wider range of platforms [Cauldwell 2001].

WSDL interaction patterns

WSDL interfaces (port types in the WSDL terminology) support four types of operations. These operations represent the most common interaction patterns for Web services. Since each operation defined by WSDL can have an input and/or an output, the four WSDL interaction patterns represent possible combinations of input and output messages [Cauldwell 2001]:

- A *one-way operation* is an operation in which the service endpoint receives a message, but does not send a response. An example of a one-way operation might be an operation representing the submission of an order to a purchasing system. Once the order is sent, no immediate response is expected.

- A *request/response operation* is an operation in which the service endpoint receives a message and returns a message in response. In the request/response message pattern a client requests that some action is taken from the service provider. An example of this is the SendPurchase operation, which receives as input message a containing a purchase order number and date and responds with a message containing its corresponding invoice.

- A *solicit/response operation* is an operation in which the service endpoint sends a message and expects to receive an answering message in response. This is the opposite of the request/response operation since the service endpoint is initiating the operation (soliciting the client), rather than responding to a request. An example of this operation might be a service that sends out order status to a client and receives back a receipt.

- A *notification operation* is an operation in which the service endpoint sends a message and receives no response. This type of messaging is used by services that need to notify clients of events. An example of this could be a service model in which events are reported to the service and where the endpoint periodically reports its status.

19.7.3 UDDI: Universal Description, Discovery, and Integration

One of the main reasons for enterprises engaging in electronic business is to open new markets and find new sources of supply more easily than with conventional means. To achieve this desired state, however, enterprises need a common way of identifying potential trading partners and cataloguing their business functions and characteristics. The solution is the creation of a service registry architecture that presents a standard way for enterprises to build a registry to describe and identify e-Business services, query other service providers and enterprises, and enable those registered enterprises to share business and technical information globally in a distributed manner. To address this challenge, the *Universal Description, Discovery and Integration* specification was created. UDDI is a cross-industry initiative to create a registry standard for Web services description and discovery together with a registry facility that facilitates the publishing and discovery processes. UDDI provides a global, platform-independent, open framework to enable service clients to:

- discover information about enterprises offering Web services,

- find descriptions of the Web services these enterprises provide, and

- find technical information about Web service interfaces and definitions of how the enterprises may interact over the Internet.

UDDI is designed for use by developer tools and applications that use Web services standards such as SOAP/XML and WSDL. UDDI is a group of Web-based registries designed to house information about businesses and Web services they provide in a structured way. One key difference between a UDDI registry and other registries and directories is that UDDI provides a mechanism to categorize businesses and services using taxonomies. For example, service providers can use a taxonomy to indicate that a service implements a specific domain standard, or that it provides services to a specific geographic area [Manes 2003]. Such taxonomies make it easier for consumers to find services that match their specific requirements. Once a Web service has been developed and deployed it is important that it is published in a registry, such as UDDI, so that potential clients and service developers can discover it; see Figure 19.3. Web service discovery is the process of locating and interrogating Web service definitions, which is a preliminary step for accessing a Web service. It is through this discovery process that Web service clients learn that the Web service exists, what its capabilities are, and how to properly interact with it.

The core concept of the UDDI initiative is the UDDI business registration, an XML document used to describe a business entity and its Web services. Conceptually, the information provided in a UDDI business registration consists of three inter-related components: "white pages" including address, contact, and other key points of contact; "yellow pages" classification information according to industrial classifications based on standard industry taxonomies; and "green pages", the technical capabilities and information about services that are exposed by the business including references to specifications for Web services and pointers to various file and URL based discovery mechanisms. Using a UDDI registry, enterprises can discover the existence of potential trading partners and basic information about them (through white pages), find companies in specific industry classifications (through yellow pages), and uncover the kind of Web services offered to interact with the enterprises (through green pages).

UDDI data structures

Although UDDI is often thought of simply as a directory mechanism, it also defines a data structure standard for representing company and service description information. Through UDDI, enterprises can publish and discover information about other businesses and the services they provide. This information can be classified using standard taxonomies so that information can be discovered on the basis of categorization. UDDI contains also information about the technical interfaces of an enterprise's services.

The UDDI specification provides a platform-independent way of describing services, discovering businesses, and integrating business services using the Internet. The UDDI data structures provide a framework for the description of basic business and service information, and architects an extensible mechanism to provide detailed service access information using any standard service description mechanism. The data model used by the UDDI registries is defined in an XML schema. The data UDDI contains is relatively lightweight; as a registry its prime purpose is to provide network addresses to the resources it describes, e.g., schemas, interface definitions, or endpoints, in locations across the network.

The UDDI XML schema defines four core types of information that provide the white/yellow/green page functions. These are: business entities; business services; binding templates; and information about specifications for services (technical or tModels). A service implementation registration represents a service offered by a specific service provider. It specifies information about the business entity e.g., a company, that offers the service (<businessEntity>), describes the services exposed by the business (<businessService>), and captures the binding information (<bindingTemplate>) required to use the service. The <bindingTemplate> captures the service endpoint address, and associates the service with the <tModel>s that represent its technical specifications. Each business service can be accessed in one or more ways. For example, a retailer might expose an order entry service accessible as a SOAP-based Web service, a regular Web form or even a fax number. To convey all the ways a service is exposed each service is bound to one or more <tModels> via a binding template.

The data model hierarchy and the key XML element names that are used to describe and discover information about Web services are shown in Figure 19.7. These are outlined briefly in the following:

- *Business information*: Partners and potential clients of an enterprise's services that need to be able to locate information about the services provided would normally have as starting point a small set of facts about this service provider. They will know, for example, either its business name or perhaps some key identifiers, as well as optional categorization and contact information (white pages). The core XML elements for supporting publishing and discovering information about a business – the UDDI Business Registration – are contained in an element named <businessEntity>. This element serves as the top-level structure and contains information about a particular business unit itself. The XML element <businessEntity> contains information such as the company name and contacts (white page listing). The <businessEntity> construct is a top-level structure that corresponds to "white pages".
- Business service information: The <businessService> structures represent logical service classification about a family of Web services offered by the company. The top-level entity <businessEntity> described above can contain one or more <businessService> elements for each of these service families. The <businessService> structure is a descriptive container that is used to group a series of related Web services related to either a business process or category of services. It is used to reveal service related information such as the name of a Web service aggregate, a description of the Web service or categorization details. Examples of business processes that would include related Web service information include purchasing services, shipping services, and other high-level business processes. <businessService> information sets, such as these, can each be further categorized – allowing Web service descriptions to be segmented along combinations of industry, product and service or geographic

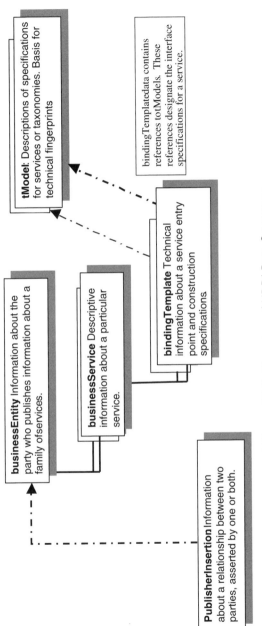

tModel: Descriptions of specifications for services or taxonomies. Basis for technical fingerprints

bindingTemplatedata contains references totModels. These references designate the interface specifications for a service.

bindingTemplate Technical information about a service entry point and construction specifications

businessEntity Information about the party who publishes information about a family ofservices.

businessService Descriptive information about a particular service.

PublisherInsertionInformation about a relationship between two parties, asserted by one or both.

■ **Figure 19.7**: Overview of UDDI Data Structures

category boundaries. The kind of information contained in a `<businessService>` element maps to the "yellow pages" information about a company.

- *Binding information*: The access information required to actually invoke a service is described in the information element named `<bindingTemplate>`. The `<bindingTemplate>` (the structure that models binding information) data structure exposes a service endpoint address required for accessing a service from a technical point of view. Technical descriptions of Web services – the "green pages" data – reside within sub-structures of the `<businessService>` element. Within each `<businessService>` reside one or more technical Web service descriptions. These structures provide support for determining a technical endpoint or optionally support remotely hosted services, as well as a lightweight facility for describing unique characteristics of a given implementation. This information is relevant for application programs and clients that need to connect to and then communicate with and invoke a remote Web service. Each `<businessService>` may potentially contain multiple `<bindingTemplate>` structures, each of which describes a Web service (see Figure 19.7).

- *Specification pointers and technical fingerprints*: It is not always enough simply to know where to contact a particular Web service through its endpoint address revealed by a `<bindingTemplate>` data type. For instance, if we know that a business partner provides a Web service that accepts purchase orders, knowing the URL for that service is not very useful unless technical details such as what format the purchase order should be sent in, what protocols are appropriate, what security is required, and what form of a response will result after sending the purchase order, are also provided. Integrating all parts of two systems that interact via Web services can become quite complex and thus requires information about compatibility of service specifications to make sure that the right Web services are invoked. For this reason, each `<bindingTemplate>` data type contains a special `<tModel>` data structure (short for "Technology Model") which provides information about a Web service interface specification. For instance, in the case of a purchase order, the Web service that accepts the purchase order exhibits a set of well-defined behaviors if the proper document format is sent to the proper address in the right way. A UDDI registration for this service would consist of an entry for the business partner `<businessEntity>`, a logical service entry that describes the purchasing service `<businessService>`, a `<bindingTemplate>` entry that describes the purchase order service by listing its URL, and a reference to a `<tModel>` that is used to provide information about the service's interface and its technical specification. The `<tModel>` contains metadata about a service specification, including its name, publishing organization, and URL pointers to the actual specifications themselves.

The UDDI, just like WSDL, draws a sharp distinction between abstraction and implementation. In fact, the primary role that a `<tModel>` plays is to represent technical information about an abstract interface specification. An example might be a specification that outlines wire protocols, interchange formats and interchange sequencing rules [Ehebuske 2001]. These can be found in the RossettaNet Partner Interface Processes, the Open Applications Group Integration Specification and various Electronic Document Interchange efforts and so on. A corollary of the `<tModel>` structure is the `<bindingTemplate>`, which is the concrete implementation of one or more `<tModel>`s. Inside a binding template, businesses can register the access point for a particular implementation of a `<tModel>`. `<tModel>`s can be published separately from `<bindingTemplate>`s that reference them. For instance, a standards body or industry group might publish the canonical interface for a particular use case or vertical industry sector, and then multiple enterprises could code implementations to this interface. Accordingly, each of those business's implementations would refer to the same `<tModel>`. A set of canonical `<tModel>`s has been defined that standardize commonly used classification mechanisms. The UDDI operator sites have registered a number of canonical <tModels> for NAICS (an industry code taxonomy), UNSPC (a product and service code taxonomy) and ISO 3166 (a geographical region code taxonomy), identification taxonomies like Dun and Bradstreet's D-U-N-S and Thomas Register supplier identification codes.

Due to the fact that both the UDDI and WSDL schema have been architected to delineate clearly between interface and implementation, these two constructs are quite complementary and work together naturally. The WSDL-to-UDDI mapping model is designed to help users find services that implement standard definitions. The WSDL-to-UDDI mapping model describes how WSDL <portType> and <binding> element specifications can become <tModel>s; how the <port>s of WSDL become UDDI <bindingTemplate>s; and how each WSDL service is registered as a <businessService> [Manes 2003]. By decoupling a WSDL specification and registering it in UDDI, we can populate UDDI with standard interfaces that have multiple implementations, providing a landscape of business applications that share interfaces.

UDDI Application Programming Interface

UDDI uses SOAP as its transport layer, so enterprises can interact with UDDI through SOAP-based XML API calls in order to discover technical data about an enterprise's services. In this way enterprises can link up with service providers and invoke and use their services.

The UDDI API is an interface that accepts XML messages wrapped in SOAP envelopes [McKee 2001]. All UDDI interactions use a request/response model, in which each message requesting service from the site generates some kind of response. A developer would not be creating messages in this format – there are toolkits available that shield developers from the task of manipulating XML documents. These toolkits (or the APIs they provide) internally "talk" to the UDDI registry using the XML message formats defined by the UDDI protocol. Developers can build applications in Java, VisualBasic or any other language to access UDDI registries and either publish their services, find services provided by other companies or unpublish their service listings. Currently, UDDI client side libraries/toolkits exist for Java, VisualBasic and Perl [Cauldwell 2001].

The UDDI specifications define two types of exchanges with UDDI registered sites: *enquiries* and *publishing*.

Enquiries enable parties to find businesses, services, or bindings (technical characteristics) meeting certain criteria. The party can then get the corresponding <businessEntity>, <businessService>, or <bindingTemplate> information matching the search criteria. The UDDI enquiry API has two usage patterns: *browse* and *drill down*. A developer would, for instance, use a browse pattern (find() API calls) to get a list of all entries satisfying broad criteria to find the entries, services or technical characteristics and then use the drill down pattern (get() API calls) to get the more specific features. For example, a find_business() call could first be issued to locate all businesses in a specific category, and then a get_BusinessDetail() call could be used to get additional information about a specific business.

The browse pattern uses four methods. These locate specific bindings within a registered business service, locate one or more business entries that match search criteria, locate information about business entity registrations related to the business entity, return a list of business services that match search criteria, and return a list of <tModels>.

The drill-down pattern uses five methods. These return the run-time binding information (`<bindingTemplate>` structure) used for invoking methods against a business service, the complete `<businessEntity>` object for one or more business entities, extra attributes in case the source registry is not an operator node, the complete `<businessService>` object for a given business service, and finally `<tModel>` details.

UDDI sites use *publishing* functions to manage the information provided to requestors. The publishing API essentially allows applications to save and delete the five data structures supported by UDDI and described earlier in this section. These calls are used by service providers and enterprises to publish and un-publish information about themselves in the UDDI registry. These API calls require authenticated access to the registry, unlike the enquiry API [Cauldwell 2001]. UDDI does not specify authentication procedures, but leaves them up to the operator site.

19.8 Web services orchestration

The full potential of Web services as a means of developing e-Business solutions will be achieved only when applications and business processes are able to integrate their complex interactions by using a standard process integration model. When looking at Web services, it is important to differentiate between baseline specifications of SOAP, UDDI and WSDL that provide the infrastructure that supports the publish, find and bind operations in the service-oriented architecture (see Figure 19.3) and higher-level specifications required for e-Business integration. These higher-level specifications provide functionality that supports and leverages Web services and enables specifications for integrating automated business processes found in both EAI and e-Business integration applications.

Models for e-Business interactions typically require specifying sequences of peer-to-peer message exchanges between a collection of Web services, both synchronous and asynchronous, within stateful, long-running interactions involving two or more parties. Such interactions require that business processes are described in terms of a business protocol (or abstract business model) that precisely specifies the mutually visible message exchange behavior of each of the parties involved in the protocol, without revealing their internal implementation. It also requires modeling the actual behavior of participants involved in a business interaction.

Business Process Execution Language for Web services is an XML-based flow language for the formal specification of business processes and business interaction protocols. BPEL extends the Web services interaction model and enables it to support business transactions. BPEL can be used to integrate diverse applications based on Web services such as, for instance, Mobile Virgin's customer relationship management system and pre-paid billing solution (which are described as services in WSDL) and link those with value-added services from a variety of content providers that provide access to music, news, games and customized ring tones.

BPEL provides support for both executable and abstract *business* processes. An executable process models the actual behavior of participants in the overall business process, essentially modeling a private workflow. This can be perceived as a control "meta-process" that is laid on top of Web services controlling their invocations and behavior. The logic and state of the process determine the nature and sequence of the Web service interactions conducted at each business partner, and thus the interaction protocols. Abstract processes are modeled as business protocols in BPEL. Their purpose is to specify the public message exchanges of each of the parties leveraging the protocol. Unlike executable business processes, business protocols are not executable and do not reveal the internal details of a process flow. Abstract business processes link Web service interface definitions with behavioral specifications that can be used to control the business roles and define the behavior that each party is expected to perform within the overall business process.

A BPEL process is a flow-chart-like expression specifying process steps and entry-points into the process that is layered on top of WSDL, with WSDL defining the specific operations allowed and BPEL defining how the operations can be sequenced [Curbera 2003]. The role of BPEL is to define a new Web service by composing a set of existing services through a process-integration type mechanism with control language control. The entry-points correspond to external clients invoking either input-only (request) or input–output (request/response) operations on the interface of the composite service. BPEL provides a mechanism for creating implementation and platform-independent compositions of services woven strictly from the abstract interfaces provided in the WSDL definitions. The definition of a BPEL business process also follows the WSDL convention of strict separation between the abstract service interface and service implementation. In particular, a BPEL process represents parties and interactions between these parties in terms of abstract WSDL interfaces (<portTypes> and <operation>s), while no references are made to the actual services (binding and address information) used by a process instance. Both the interacting process and its counterparts are modeled in the form of WSDL services. Actual implementations of the services themselves may be dynamically bound to the partners of a BPEL composition, without affecting the composition's definition. Business processes specified in BPEL are fully executable portable scripts that can be interpreted by business process engines in BPEL-conformant environments. BPEL processes are exposed as a Web service using WSDL where WSDL describes the public entry and exit points for the process. In addition, WSDL data types are used within a BPEL process to describe the information that passes between requests.

We distinguish four main sections in BPEL: the message flow, the control flow, the data flow, and the process orchestration sections:

- The *message flow section* of BPEL is handled by primitive activities that include invoking an operation on some Web service (<invoke>), waiting for a process operation to be invoked by some external client (<receive>), and generating the response of an input–output operation (<reply>). As a language for composing Web services, BPEL processes interact by making invocations to other services and receiving invocations from clients. The former is done using the <invoke> activity, and the latter using the <receive> and <reply> activities.

- The *control flow section* of BPEL is a hybrid model halfway between block structured and state transition control flow definitions. The control flow part of BPEL includes the ability to define an ordered sequence of activities (<sequence>), to have branching (<switch>), to define a loop (<while>), and to execute one of several alternative paths (<pick>). Its main structured activity is the <flow> statement that allows defining sets of activities (including other flow activities) that are connected via <links>. A flow activity in BPEL may create a set of concurrent activities and enables expressing synchronization dependencies between these activities.

- The state of a business process includes the messages that are exchanged as well as intermediate data used in business logic and in composing messages sent to partners. The *data flow section* of BPEL requires that information be passed between the different activities.

• The process orchestration section of BPEL uses service links to establish peer-to-peer partner relationships. A <partner> could be any service that the process invokes or any service that invokes the process. Each <partner> is mapped to a specific role that it fills within a process. A specific partner may play one role in one business process but completely different role in another process. For example, a process representing a loan servicing system may offer a single Web service, but only parts of it are accessible to the customer applying for the loan, while other parts are accessible to the customer service representative, and the entire service is accessible to the loan underwriters. The approach of using partners to model clients allows the process to indicate that certain clients may only invoke certain operations.

Figure 19.8 uses some of the BPEL constructs we introduced in this section as part of a UML activity graph. In particular, Figure 19.8 presents a UML example of an activity graph of a simple a BPEL process for handling purchase orders. In this scenario upon receiving the purchase order from a customer, the process initiates three tasks in parallel: calculating the final price for the order, selecting a shipper, and scheduling the production and shipment for the order. The four partners shown in this figure correspond to the sender of the order (customer), the providers of price (invoiceProvider), shipment (shippingProvider),

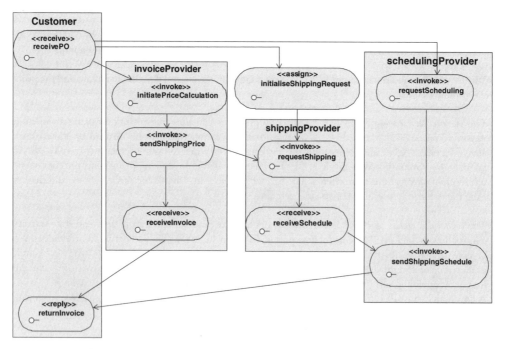

■ **Figure 19.8:** Example of a Purchase Order Process Flows in BPEL

and manufacturing scheduling services (`schedulingProvider`). Activities that involve a message send or receive operation to a partner appear in the corresponding partition. Partitions in the BPEL process diagram correspond to WSDL `<portTypes>`.

The arrows in Figure 19.8 indicate the order in which the process performs the activities. The purchase order process begins by receiving a purchase order request from a customer (`<receive>` message in Figure 19.8). The purchase order process asks for an initial price, shipping information, and production schedule. The `initiatePriceCalculation`, `initialiseShippingRequest` and `requestScheduling` activities begin executing, triggering further activities as they complete. The arrows on the graph indicate control links. An activity starts when all of its preceding activities have completed. Note that the `requestScheduling` activity requires that both the `initialiseShippingRequest` and `sendShippingPrice` activities have taken place before it begins. When price and shipping information are available, the invoice provider calculates final price and sends an invoice to purchase order process. The purchase order process asks a production scheduling provider to determine when each order item will be produced and instructs the scheduling provider to send the production schedule to the customer. Finally, the `returnInvoice` activity returns a response back to the customer. Each activity has a descriptive name and an entry action detailing the work performed by the activity.

BPEL processes are stateful and have instances therefore in BPEL this scenario is implemented as a `PurchaseOrder` process which would have an instance for each actual purchase order being processed. Each instance has its own state which is captured in BPEL variables. In the UML profile, a process is represented as a class with the stereotype `<<Process>>`. The attributes of the class correspond to the state of the process (its variables in BPEL4WS 1.1 terminology). The UML class representing the purchase order process corresponding to the activity graph in Figure 19.8 is shown in Figure 19.9.

Figure 19.10 is a code snippet that shows the process flow for an abbreviated PurchaseOrder process which uses some of the constructs shown in Figure 19.8 and employs WSDL interface definitions for the purchase order service described in Figure 19.5.

The `<variables>` section in Figure 19.10 defines the data variables used by the process, providing their definitions in terms of WSDL message types. Variables allow processes to maintain state data and process history based on messages exchanged.

The `<partners>` section defines the different parties that interact with the business process in the course of processing the order. The partners in this section correspond to the sender of the order (customer), as well as the providers of price (invoiceProvider), shipment (shippingProvider), and manufacturing scheduling services (schedulingProvider). The latter two are not shown in this figure for reasons of brevity. Each partner is characterized by a service link type and a role name. This information identifies the functionality that must be provided by the business process and by the partner for the relationship to succeed, that is, the `<portType>`s that the purchase order process and the partner need to implement.

The structure of the main processing section is defined by the outer `<sequence>` element, which states that the three activities contained inside are performed in order. The customer request is received (`<receive>` element), then processed (inside a `<flow>` section – not shown in this figure – that enables

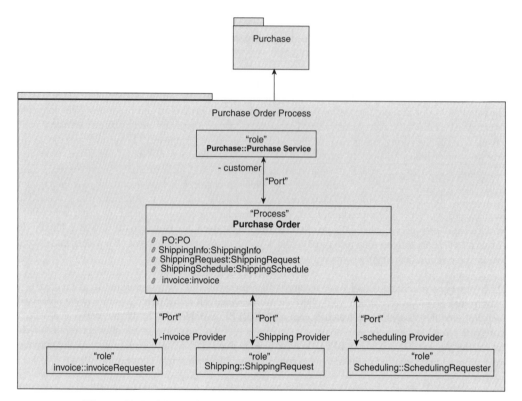

concurrent behavior), and a reply message with the final approval status of the request is sent back to the customer (<reply>). Note that the <receive> and <reply> elements are matched respectively to the <input> and <output> messages of the SendPurchaseOrder operation[2] invoked by the customer, while the activities performed by the process between these elements represent the actions taken in response to the customer request, from the time the request is received to the time the response is sent back (reply).

It is important to notice that BPEL is used for orchestrating Web services. *Orchestration* describes how Web services can interact with each other at the message level, including the business logic and execution order of the interactions from the perspective and under control of a *single* endpoint. Orchestration is different from *choreography* of Web services. Choreography is typically associated with the *globally visible* message exchanges, rules of interaction and agreements that occur between multiple business process endpoints, rather than a specific business process that is executed by a single party [Pelz 2003]. Choreography is more collaborative in nature than orchestration. Choreography tracks the sequence of messages that may involve multiple parties and multiple sources, including customers, suppliers, and partners, where each party involved in the

---

[2] This operation is part of the PurchaseOrder <PortType> defined in section 19.7.2.

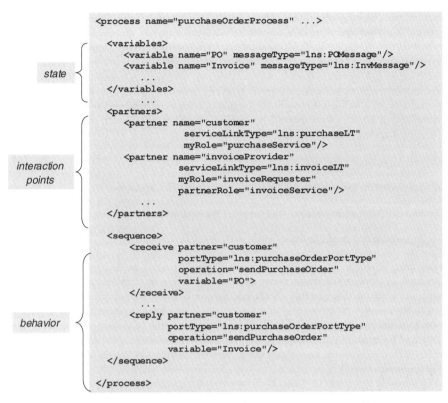

```
<process name="purchaseOrderProcess" ...>

    <variables>
        <variable name="PO" messageType="lns:POMessage"/>
        <variable name="Invoice" messageType="lns:InvMessage"/>
        ...
    </variables>
        ...
    <partners>
        <partner name="customer"
                    serviceLinkType="lns:purchaseLT"
                    myRole="purchaseService"/>
        <partner name="invoiceProvider"
                    serviceLinkType="lns:invoiceLT"
                    myRole="invoiceRequester"
                    partnerRole="invoiceService"/>
        ...
    </partners>

    <sequence>
        <receive partner="customer"
                    portType="lns:purchaseOrderPortType"
                    operation="sendPurchaseOrder"
                    variable="PO">
        </receive>
        ...
        <reply partner="customer"
                    portType="lns:purchaseOrderPortType"
                    operation="sendPurchaseOrder"
                    variable="Invoice"/>
    </sequence>

</process>
```

state — (variables block)

interaction points — (partners block)

behavior — (sequence block)

Figure 19.10: BPEL Process Flow for a `PurchaseOrder` Process

process describes the part they play in the interaction and no party "owns" the conversation. Web services choreographies are specified in terms of the Choreography Description Language (WS-CDL) [Kavantzas 2004], which defines a common view as well as the complementary observable behavior of all participants engaged in business collaboration.

19.9 Web services transactions

One key requirement in making cross-enterprise business process automation happen is the ability to describe the collaboration aspects of the business processes, such as commitments and exchange of monetary resources, in a standard form that can be consumed by tools for business process implementation and monitoring. As already explained in Section 6.4.2, enterprise workflow and business process management systems today support the definition, execution and monitoring of long running processes that coordinate the activities of multiple business applications. However, the loosely coupled, distributed nature of the Web prevents a central workflow authority (or a centralized implementation of middleware technology) from exhaustively and fully coordinating and monitoring the activities of the enterprise applications that expose the Web services participating in message exchanges [Papazoglou 2003b].

Business collaboration requires transactional support in order to guarantee consistent and reliable execution. Database transactions are a well-known technique for guaranteeing consistency in the presence of failures. A classical transaction is a unit of work that either completely succeeds, or fails with all partially completed work being undone. Classical transactions have ACID properties:

- Atomicity: executes completely or not at all.

- Consistency: preserves the internal consistency of an underlying data structure.

- Isolation: runs as if it were running alone with no other transactions running.

- Durability: the transaction's results will not be lost in the event of a failure.

The ACID properties of atomic transactions ensure that even in complex business applications consistency of state is preserved, despite concurrent accesses and failures. This is an extremely useful fault-tolerance technique, especially when multiple, possibly remote, resources are involved. However, traditional transactions depend upon tightly coupled protocols, and thus are often not well suited to more loosely-coupled Web services based applications, although they are likely to be used in some of the constituent technologies. Strict ACIDity and isolation, in particular, is not appropriate to a loosely coupled world of autonomous trading partners, where security and inventory control issues prevent hard locking of local resources that is impractical in the business world.

A Web services environment requires the same coordination behavior provided by a traditional transaction mechanisms to control the operations and outcome of an application. However, it also requires the capability to handle the coordination of processing outcomes or results from multiple services, in a more flexible manner. This requires more relaxed forms of transactions – those that do not strictly have to abide to the ACID properties – such as collaborations, workflow, real-time processing, etc. Additionally, there is a need to group Web services into applications that require some form of correlation, but do not necessarily require transactional behavior. In the loosely coupled environment represented by Web services, long running applications will require support for coordination, recovery and compensation, because machines may fail, processes may be cancelled, or services may be moved or withdrawn.

The concept of a *business transaction* is central to Web services applications as it defines a shared view of messages exchanged between Web services from multiple organizations for the purpose of completing a business process [Papazoglou 2003b]. A business transaction is a consistent change in the state of the business that is driven by a well-defined business function. Business transactions, just like database transactions, either execute to completion (succeed) or fail as a unit. Usually, a business process is composed of several long-running business transactions. A business transaction in its simplest form could represent an order of some goods from some company. The completion of an order results in a consistent change in the state of the affected business: the back-end order database is updated and a document copy of the purchase order is filed. More complex business transactions may involve activities such as payment processing, shipping and tracking, coordinating and managing marketing strategies, determining new product offerings, granting/

extending credit, managing market risk and so on. Such complex business transactions are usually driven by interdependent workflows, which must interlock at points to achieve a mutually desired outcome. This synchronization is one part of a wider business coordination protocol that defines the public, agreed interactions between interacting business parties.

The problem of choreographing Web services is tackled by a trio of standards that have been recently proposed to handle this next step in the evolution of Web services technology.

The standards that support business process orchestration while providing Web services transactional functionality are: Business Process Execution Language for Web services (see Section 19.8), WS-Coordination [Cabrera 2002a] and WS-Transaction [Cabrera 2002b]. WS-Coordination and WS-Transaction complement BPEL4WS to provide mechanisms for defining specific standard protocols for use by transaction processing systems, workflow systems, or other applications that wish to coordinate multiple Web services. These three specifications work in tandem to address the business workflow issues implicated in connecting and executing a number of Web services that may run on disparate platforms across organizations involved in e-Business scenarios.

The *WS-Coordination* specification describes an extensible framework for providing protocols that coordinate the actions of distributed applications. Such coordination protocols are used to support a number of applications, including those that need to reach consistent agreement on the outcome of distributed transactions. WS-Coordination provides developers with a way to manage the operations related to a business activity. A business process may involve a number of Web services working together to provide a common solution. Each service needs to be able to coordinate its activities with those of the other services for the process to succeed. WS-Coordination sequences operations in a process that spans interoperable Web services to reach an agreement on the overall outcome of the business process.

WS-Transaction provides transactional coordination mechanisms for Web services. An important aspect of WS-Transaction that differentiates it from traditional transaction protocols is that it does not assume a synchronous request/response model. This derives from the fact that WS-Transaction is layered upon the WS-Coordination protocol whose own communication patterns are asynchronous. WS-Coordination provides a generic framework for specific coordination protocols, like WS-Transaction, to be plugged in. The WS-Transaction specification leverages WS-Coordination by extending it to define specific protocols for transaction processing.

WS-transaction defines two transaction types: *atomic transaction* and *business activity*. Atomic transactions are suggested for transactions that are short-lived atomic units of work within a trust domain, while business activities are suggested for transactions that are long-lived units of work comprising activities of potentially different trust domains. Atomic transactions compare to the traditional distributed database transaction model (short-lived atomic transactions). The coordination type correspondingly comprises protocols common to atomic transactions, where resource participants register for the two-phase commit protocol. The business activity coordination type supports transactional coordination of potentially long-lived activities. These differ from atomic transactions in that they take a much longer time to complete and do not require resources to be held. The WS-Transaction specification monitors the success of specific, coordinated activities in a business process. WS-Transaction uses the structure that WS-Coordination provides to make sure the participating Web services end the business process with a shared understanding of its outcome. For example, a purchase process contains various activities that have to complete successfully but might run simultaneously (at least to some extend), such as credit check, inventory control, billing and shipment. The combination of WS-Transaction and WS-Coordination makes sure that these tasks succeed or fail as a unit.

More information and examples about Web services transactions can be found in [Papazoglou 2006].

19.10 Web services security and policy considerations

As Web services use the insecure Internet for mission-critical transactions with the possibility of dynamic, short-term relationships, security is a major concern. An additional concern is that Web services applications expose their business processes and internal workflows. This calls for securing them against a wide range of attacks, both internal and external. With Web services, more of the application internals are exposed to the outside world.

Web services can be accessed by sending SOAP messages to service endpoints identified by URIs, requesting specific actions, and receiving SOAP messages. Within this context, the broad objective of securing Web services breaks into providing facilities for securing the integrity and confidentiality of the messages and for ensuring that the service acts only on requests in messages that respect the assertions expressed by policies. Public key infrastructure (see Section 13.5.1) plays an essential role in Web services security, enabling end users and Web services alike to establish trusted digital identities which, in turn, facilitate trusted communications and transactions.

When securing Web services, enterprises should focus on authentication, authorization, confidentiality, and data integrity, as well as threat detection and defense (see Section 13.5). The requirement for securing Web services concentrates on mutually authenticating all trading partners and communicating infrastructure, i.e., users and servers. Authorization is particularly important because of the need for tiered security administration in service-oriented environments. This situation is even more complex when multiple, heterogeneous systems are involved, either within an enterprise or across two or more companies. Every company will likely have its own security policies, in addition to its own authorization technology. Therefore, the ability to provide and administer authorization across multiple systems is an important issue that a Web services specification known as WS-Security is intended to address [Atkinson 2002].

WS-Security specifies an abstraction layer on top of any company's particular application security technology (PKI, Kerberos, etc.) that allows such dissimilar infrastructures to participate in a common trust relationship. WS-Security provides a set of SOAP extensions that can be used to implement message integrity, confidentiality and authentication. It is designed to provide support for multiple security tokens, trust domains, signature formats and encryption technologies. No specific type of security token is required by WS-Security. It is designed to be extensible (e.g. support multiple security token formats). For example, a requester might provide proof of identity and proof that they have a particular business certification. Message integrity is provided by leveraging XML Signature in conjunction with security tokens (which may contain or imply key data) to ensure that messages are transmitted without modifications, (see Section 13.6.5). Similarly, message confidentiality is provided by leveraging XML Encryption in conjunction with security tokens to keep portions of SOAP messages confidential.

While current technologies enable an e-Business to authenticate users and manage user access privileges, it takes considerable effort and cost to extend these capabilities across an enterprise or share them among trading partners. Security Assertions Markup Language (SAML) [SAML 2003] addresses this challenge. SAML is an XML-based framework that enables Web services to readily exchange information relating to authentication and authorization. SAML defines a protocol by which clients can request assertions from SAML authorities and receive responses from them (exchange of security information). This protocol, consisting of XML-based request/response message formats, can be bound to many different underlying communications and transport protocols. The security information is expressed in the form of assertions about subjects. A subject is an entity that has an identity in some security domain. Assertions can convey information about authentication acts performed by subjects, attributes of subjects, and authorization decisions about whether subjects are allowed to access certain resources.

The two specifications WS-Security and SAML, which are closely related, ensure the integrity and confidentiality of XML documents. They differ from existing capabilities in that they provide mechanisms for handling whole or partial documents, making it possible to address varying requirements for access authority, confidentiality and data integrity within one document.

In order to successfully compose Web services, one must fully understand the service's WSDL contract along with any additional Quality of Service capabilities and requirements (see Section 13.2). The QoS for Web services description publishes important functional and non-functional service quality attributes, such as service metering and cost, performance metrics (e.g., response time), security attributes, (transactional) integrity, reliability, scalability, and availability. These Web services capabilities and requirements can be expressed in terms of *policies*. For example, knowing that a service supports a Web services security standard such as WS-Security is not enough information to enable successful composition. The client needs to know if the service actually requires WS-Security, what kind of security tokens it is capable of processing, and which one it prefers.

WS-Policy [WS-Policy 2003] fills this gap by providing building blocks that may be used in conjunction with other Web services and application-specific protocols to accommodate a wide variety of policy exchange models. The Web services Policy Framework provides a general purpose model and corresponding syntax to describe and communicate the policies of a Web service. WS-Policy defines a base set of constructs that can be used and extended by other Web services specifications to describe a broad range of service requirements, preferences, and capabilities. WS-Policy defines a policy to be a collection of one or more policy assertions. A policy assertion represents an individual preference, requirement, capability, or other general characteristic.

19.11 EAI and Web services

Web services and EAI are sometimes misunderstood to be one and the same. Web services are traditionally associated with making cross-enterprise business process automation happen while EAI takes a holistic approach of tightly integrating all internal applications and systems that support a single enterprise's business by using, for instance, distributed component technologies. EAI tends to be more specific to a particular business process, such as connecting a specific order processing application to a specific inventory control application. Moreover, EAI is typically designed as a much tighter bound implementation of connecting systems. As we already emphasized several times Web services are a loosely bound collection of services and they are easy to plug in and out, discover, and bind to dynamically. In fact we may consider Web services are the next logical extension of EAI because the technology standardizes communication, description, and discovery mechanisms. The strengths of EAI still remain: distributed transaction integrity, complex process and workflow automation, business rule automation, and so on.

A few essential differences between traditional EAI solutions and Web services can be summarized as follows [Samtani 2002]:

- Scope and scalability: EAI enables integration of an enterprise's internal applications so different departments and divisions within an enterprise can communicate and share information. This internal application integration happens within the enterprise's firewall. Enterprises can adopt each other's systems and applications for business collaboration, but because the collaboration needs to take place beyond each company's firewall, scalability and application upgrades are difficult to achieve and fairly complicated. Many enterprises leverage their investment in EAI solutions to provide some level of connectivity to customers and partners over the Internet. In many ways Web services can be considered as a natural evolution of the EAI paradigm expanded outside the enterprise whereas EAI strictly deals with the complexities of heterogeneous systems inside an enterprise.

- Proprietary vs. open communication mechanisms: EAI vendors traditionally relied on proprietary technology to map information between various software packages. This means that the integration solution itself becomes proprietary and fairly inaccessible because its internal communication mechanisms are undecipherable. Unlike proprietary EAI solutions, Web services are based on open interoperable standards such as SOAP, HTTP and UDDI and this is one of the most important factors that would lead to the wide adoption of Web services. The fact that they are built on existing and ubiquitous protocols eliminates the need for enterprises to invest in supporting new network protocols [Samtani 2001]. Because Web services functionality can be attached to EAI software packages, thus allowing them to be integrated with other packages (including legacy applications) the need for intrusive third-party EAI adapters and connectors are expected to diminish [Erlikh 2002], [Holland 2002].

- Simplicity and flexibility: Web services are much easier to design, develop maintain and use in comparison to a typical EAI solution that involves distributed object technology such as DCOM or CORBA. Moreover, EAI solutions tend to be rigid, thus difficult to maintain and upgrade. In contrast to this, Web services-based integration is quite flexible as it is based on loose coupling between the application publishing the services and the application consuming the services.

- Granularity and efficiency: EAI solutions such as integration brokers, integrate applications treating them as single entities whereas Web services allow enterprises to break down complex applications into small independent logical units of functionality and build wrappers around them [Samtan 2001]. This makes the integration of applications easier as it is performed at a granular basis. Accordingly, Web services solutions can be considered as a more efficient alternative than traditional EAI solutions.

- Reuse: An EAI solution does not make the reuse of existing functionality and alignment or integration with external business processes any easier. In contrast to this, Web services continue the long ascension of object-oriented design in software development. The service-based model allows developers to reuse the building blocks of code created by others to assemble and extend them in new ways.

- Dynamicity: Web services provide a dynamic approach to integration by offering dynamic interfaces, whereas traditional EAI solutions are pretty static in nature.

It is expected that enterprises will first deploy Web services internally to improve operational efficiencies and gain a unified view of complex business processes. Forrester Research (`www.forrester.com`) projects that enterprises will initially use Web services to provide visibility into delivery and payment status. For example, an enterprise may integrate its Web-based shipping and legacy accounts payable systems in order to track order delivery so that it can bill in real time and more accurately predict cash flow. One of the advantages of starting internally is that it is relatively easy to ensure that chosen technologies and standards are available and compatible. This means that current EAI solutions that predominantly focus on integrating applications will have to be altered significantly. Legacy applications, databases, packaged applications and new in-house applications will all have to expose their functions and business methods as services in a SOA setting using technologies such as SOAP, WSDL and UDDI. Consequently, EAI solutions will have to provide a broad support for service integration rather than application integration.

As a second step it is expected that when Web services are successfully utilized internally, enterprises will likely extend them to customers, partners, and suppliers with which they have already negotiated agreements. Enterprises will migrate existing applications to a Web services platform to automate the processes that implement an ongoing contract or supply chain relationship. During this phase, transaction protocols and security standards will become critical to the success of Web services-enabled applications.

19.12 Chapter summary

Web services technology has been designed to effectively integrate systems within an enterprise and provide the open and scalable integration critical for e-Business applications. Web services technology addresses the traditional forms of business-to-business communication required for integrating multiple customers, suppliers and other strategic partners. A Web service is a collection of business functions or capabilities that can be published to a network using standard protocols for use by other services or applications. It is a service available via a network such as the Internet that completes tasks, solves problems or conducts transactions. A function deployed as a Web service uses common XML-based protocols to communicate with other Web services and systems that can receive XML-based data.

The Web services paradigm is built on the basis of the software-as-a-service concept and further expands it to include the delivery of complex business processes and transactions as a service. We can distinguish between four models of Web services on the basis of the business functionality they provide: informational services, complex trading services, programmatic services and interactive services. Informational services are stateless services of relatively simple nature that either involve simple request/response sequences between interacting services or provide access to content or expose back-end business applications to other applications located outside the firewall. Complex Web services are stateful Web services that specify the choreography of individual Web services into business processes and roles and are thus critical for establishing multi-step, service-oriented interactions between business partners and modeling business agreements. Programmatic Web services encapsulate a programmatic business process and expose the business logic functionality of the applications and components that underlie them. Finally, interactive Web services expose the functionality of a multi-step Web service that has interactive business processes as clients at the Web browser layer.

To build integration-ready applications the Web service model relies on the service-oriented architecture. SOA is a logical way of designing a software system to provide services to either end-user applications or other services distributed in a network through published and discoverable interfaces. SOA discerns three roles in the Web services architecture: service requesters, service providers and service brokers. A service provider publishes its Web service(s) with the Web services broker. The services requester searches for desired Web services using the registry of the Web services broker. The services requester, using the information obtained from the Web services broker, invokes (binds to) the Web services provided by the Web services provider

The service-oriented architecture builds on today's Web services baseline specifications of Simple Object Access Protocol, Web services Description Language, and Universal Description, Discovery and Integration infrastructure. SOAP is an XML-based lightweight protocol that allows applications to pass messages and data back and forth between disparate systems in a distributed environment enabling remote method invocation. The Web Services Description Language is an XML-based service representation language used to describe the details of the complete interfaces exposed by Web services. It is through this service description that the service provider can communicate all the specifications for invoking a particular Web service to the service requester. The WSDL specification is divided into two parts: the service interface definition (abstract interface) and the service implementation (concrete endpoint). UDDI is a cross industry initiative to create a registry standard for Web services description and discovery together with a registry facility that facilitates the publishing and discovery processes. UDDI provides a global, platform-independent, open framework to enable service clients to discover information about enterprises offering Web services, find descriptions of the Web services these enterprises provide, and find technical information about the Web service interfaces.

The baseline specifications of SOAP, UDDI and WSDL provide the infrastructure that supports the publish, find and bind operations in the service-oriented architecture. To be able to integrate applications and business processes and their complex interactions, a standard process integration model developed on the basis of Business Process Execution Language for Web services is necessary. BPEL is an XML-based flow language for the formal specification of business processes and business interaction protocols. It is used for orchestrating Web services in a way that describes how Web services can interact with each other at the message level, including the business logic and execution order of the interactions from the perspective and under control of a single endpoint. Orchestration is different from choreography of Web services. Choreography is typically associated with the globally visible message exchanges, rules of interaction and agreements that occur between multiple business process endpoints.

Business transaction semantics for Web services applications are provided by WS-Transaction and WS-Coordination. WS-Transaction provides transactional coordination mechanisms for Web services and leverages WS-Coordination by extending it to define specific protocols for transaction processing. Finally, when securing Web services, enterprises focus on authentication, authorization, confidentiality, and data integrity, as well as threat detection and defense. Such concerns are addressed by a family of Web services standards that include WS-Security, WS-Policy and WS-Authorization.

Discussion Questions

- What are Web services? What characteristics of Web services can be used for e-Business applications?

- Describe the four major differences between Web services and Web-based applications used in support of e-Business.

- What are stateful and non-stateful Web services? Is statefulness an important characteristic for e-Business applications? Where can it be used?

- Why is it important for Web services to distinguish between interface description and implementation? How does WSDL assist with this undertaking?

- Explain the difference between a Web services orchestration and a Web services choreography language.

- What is the purpose of the Business Process Execution Language for Web services? Is BPEL an orchestration or a choreography language?

Assignments

i. Use WSDL interface definition constructs to extend the simple purchase order depicted in Figure 19.5. The extended purchase order service should be able to link the goods and services ordered by a buyer (order line) to a seller. An order should be represented by a unique order identifier and should include such key operations as creating a new purchase order, sending a purchase order to a vendor, amending a purchase order, withdrawing a purchase order and paying a purchase order. The purchase order process begins with the order initiator creating a new purchase order and ends with the order initiator paying for an outstanding order or with an order being cancelled.

ii. Figure 19.8 presents an example of a UML activity graph of a simple BPEL process for handling purchase orders. Use a similar UML activity graph to represent an integrated solution involving Virgin Mobile's customer relationship management system, pre-paid billing solution and content partner services that provide access to music, news, games and customized ring tones.

Chapter 20

Business Standards and Protocols

Companies across all industries are realizing the fundamental benefits of using the Internet to integrate their supply chains. As e-Business solutions become more global in reach and capacity – and therefore more sophisticated – it becomes increasingly important to provide additional capabilities to ensure global availability, increased trading network capabilities, and improved progression toward e-Business interoperability on the basis of universally accepted standards.

e-Business standardization is about interoperability of business content and message exchange between business systems of different enterprises, as well as the process automation associated with them. Recognizing the need for standardizing these resources, the aim is to provide additional capabilities to baseline XML and service-based solutions in terms of naming and defining data, and harness this with the drive of the emerging communities to build a common understanding of business processes and data to be transferred across existing and future platforms. Such a conceptual framework will remain relatively stable over time as technologies, standards and implementation details evolve. Because of the nature of complexity, it is unrealistic to have any single group or standard body make all the decisions. It requires collaboration of both vertical (within a single industry, e.g., electronics, automotive) and horizontal (across industries) standards bodies and industry leaders to work together to drive e-Business standards definition and convergence. As a result there are currently many initiatives that explore the use of open, XML-based standards for deployment of e-Business efforts.

This chapter introduces the concept of business standards and protocols for e-Business, examines their value and examines some of their salient features. The

**chapter also briefly introduces two such standards for e-Business integration and
discusses their convergence with Web service technologies.**

20.1 Introduction

The past few years have seen an extensive and accelerating amount of work on providing practical
implementations and technical specifications to enable the development of open interoperable e-Business
interactions (see Section 18.7.2). This work is focused around utilizing XML syntax and the Internet as the
underpinning technologies. This helps remove the formidable barriers associated with developing a single
common business language and process methodology for Internet-based collaboration, communication and
commerce.

When examining how the Internet is developing as a platform for electronic business, two major e-Business
trends are worth noting [Wilson 2000]:

• The first trend is the increasing development of *vertical industry portals* on the Internet that are emerging
  as brokers for particular industry sectors. Sectors ranging from financials to chemicals through to global
  freight each have deep portals to act as brokers for their industries. There are developments within many
  of the sectors to provide a central shared catalogue, such as UDDI, so that the goods and services can
  be described in a common way. This combats terminology problems (see Section 18.7.2) minimizes the
  amount of conversion required between different descriptions while providing common product numbers
  for given goods items. The main advantage suggested by deep portals is that they can be organized
  according to the specific requirements of an industry. Conversely, the main disadvantage is that a supplier
  to several industry sectors will have to work with different portals.

• The second trend is the emergence of *electronic marketplaces*. As we already explained in Chapter 8,
  e-Markets (or collaborative business communities) provide among other things a foundation for conducting
  global electronic business, ensuring the integrity of business transactions, an international electronic
  trading environment for buyers and sellers in a community setting, where transactions, payments and
  regulatory requirements can be managed in a secure way. Vertical industry e-Markets initiatives based on
  XML include the automotive, chemical and petroleum, retail, finance, healthcare, telecommunications,
  and insurance industries. An illustrative example, in addition to those mentioned in Section 18.7.2, is the
  Worldwide Retail Exchange (WWRE). The WWRE (www.worldwideretailexchange.org) is
  a retail e-Market that aims to enable participating retailers and manufacturers to simplify, rationalize,
  and automate supply chain processes, thereby eliminating inefficiencies in the supply chain. The WWRE
  enables retailers and manufacturers in the food, general merchandise, textile/home, and drugstore sectors
  to substantially reduce costs across product development, e-Procurement, and supply chain processes.

There are many similarities between e-Markets exchanges and vertical portals, including bringing buyers
and suppliers together to drive down prices, but also one crucial difference. Whereas vertical portals are more
akin to a virtual meeting place for informational purposes, e-Market exchanges provide a more integrated
approach to interoperability solutions built around common business processes [Wilson 2000]. The act of
bringing together groups of companies in marketplace exchanges which have traditionally been considered
as major competitors has galvanized the need to simplify e-Business trading practices. As a result, there

has been a shift towards more cooperative partnerships, providing a streamlined market around common business requirements. The opportunities for supply chain integration are greater in marketplace exchanges, leading to common definition of business processes and further driving down prices as a result.

20.2 Why are business standards and protocols needed?

As a consequence of the activities that center on using the Internet as a platform for electronic business, several industry organizations have been triggered to propose a wide array of business standards both horizontal (universal) and vertical (supply chain- or e-Market-specific) and protocols for creating a common e-Business language.

The use of the Internet as a medium for e-Business has helped encourage the development of XML-based solutions that promise more flexibility. Although EDI allows for not only the capture of common data-interchange formats but also the tackling of the challenge of capturing those formats, i.e., messages, by defining the business processes in which they are used, due to its limitations it is rather impractical to use as the standard for the conduct of e-Business. In Chapter 18 we stated that the limitations of EDI for e-Business lie in its inflexibility and the cost of integration and deployment to smaller business partners. Another important reason is that the EDI transaction sets or messages need to cover a wide range of business scenarios and most industries and individual companies have found them too generic to be practical for day-to-day business use [Kotok 2002]. As a result, industries and even individual enterprises, have written implementation guidelines picking and choosing among the EDI data segments, elements, and codes in the generic standards that apply to them. They have also added specific industry codes for use in industry transactions or messages. This process gives trading partners structured and predictable electronic business messages. However, it also means each vertical industry, and enterprises in the same industry, use EDI differently. EDI provides a common syntax, but the semantics vary as they apply to business processes and as they use specific terminology codified in the industry guidelines.

At the same time, XML showed great promise as means for conducting e-Business but has resulted in a proliferation of industry- or trading partner-specific vocabularies. This has also perpetuated the use of industry-specific and incompatible business semantics. This necessitates the use of a common e-Business standard based on XML. In this way trading partners can understand each other without engaging in the process of human agreement that adds so much to the difficulty of establishing cross-enterprise automated business processes.

Business standards typically manage the structure for defining form, fit and function of any product or service, regardless of the industry. They use specialized business and technical dictionaries to provide commonly used domain-specific terminology and accepted values. In addition, they specify the structure, format and semantics of the business content of a message as well as the message exchange requirements between trading partners. A common e-Business standard should provide the following functionality [Irani 2002]:

- definition of common business processes that characterize business transactions e.g., sending a purchase order

- definition of common data-interchange formats i.e., messages that are exchanged in the context of the above processes/transactions

- definition of a common terminology at the level of data items and messages seeking a way to bridge varying industry terminologies

- definition of a mechanism to describe an enterprise's profile, i.e., the enterprise's capabilities and the business transactions that an enterprise can perform, in such a way that it can be stored in a common repository accessible to all other organizations for querying

- definition of a mechanism that allows enterprises to negotiate on the business conditions before they commence transactions

- definition of a common transport mechanism for exchanging messages between enterprises

- definition of a security and reliability framework

This will not only allow trading partners to integrate with other partners more easily and to conduct business electronically but will also result in increased flexibility since an enterprise will have a larger number of potential trading partners to choose from.

The information and exchange requirements, identifying the timing, sequence and purpose of each business collaboration and information exchange, are captured by a *business protocol*. A business protocol is associated with business processes and governs the exchange of business information and messages between trading partners across differing EIS, middleware platforms and organizations. It specifies the structure and semantics of business messages, how to process the messages, and how to route them to appropriate recipients. It may also specify the characteristics of messages related to persistence and reliability. A business protocol is bound to a business conversation definition and a delivery channel for a trading partner. The business protocol should also be able to specify collaboration or contractual agreements that exist between two trading partners and contain configuration information required for the partners to interoperate. A business protocol is indirectly bound to such a collaboration agreement through its associated conversation definition and associated trading partner delivery channel.

To develop meaningful business standards and protocols, vendors have begun to work together, facilitated by standards bodies, and in unison with business experts to define global (horizontal) and vertical business standards based on XML. *Horizontal business standards*, like ebXML (ebXML.org), are developed in depth for use within any vertical industry. On the other hand, *vertical business standards*, like RosettaNet (www.rosettanet.org) and business protocols such as the RosettaNet Partner Interface Processes (PIPs), enable the development of process-centric e-Business applications. We shall examine both the RosettaNet business standard and the global e-Business standard ebXML in this chapter.

20.3 XML technology stack for e-Business integration

Before discussing typical business protocols and business standards, it is useful to understand how e-Business can be conducted within a single supply chain environment and between diverse (integrated) supply chain environments or e-Markets (see Chapter 8). We base part of the discussion that follows on an adaptation of a white paper by RosettaNet that focuses on standards required to support e-Business based integration [RosettaNet 2001].

20.3.1 Components in support of e-Business within a single supply chain

As explained earlier in this book, technology stacks illustrate how technologies are built on other technologies. The upper layers in a technology stack are built on top of lower-level layers, while the lower-level layers typically support lower-level computer processing and message transport details. Each layer describes a different level of abstraction that builds upon the lower layer.

The four basic components depicted in Figure 20.1 illustrate how e-Business is conducted within the context of a single supply chain. The foundation (or bottom layer) is the Messaging Service. The Messaging Service

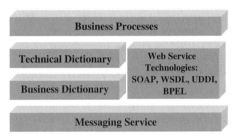

■ **Figure 20.1:** Basic Components in Support of e-Business Within a Single Supply Chain

specifies how the information for an e-Business transaction between trading partners in a single supply chain is physically packaged, transferred and routed securely between trading partners and trading networks. Ideally, trading partners use the same messaging service protocol to share information regardless of supply chain. Once a common messaging service is defined, trading partners must agree upon a common set of Business and Technical Dictionary components and conventions for the content of the business messages being exchanged [RosettaNet 2001]. These are specialized business and technical dictionaries that provide commonly used domain-specific terminology and accepted values, provide business properties for defining products, partners, and are for use in business transactions. The Business Dictionary designates the properties for defining business transactions between trading partners. The Business Dictionary serves as a central repository of the properties for reference and reuse. The Technical Dictionary provides common language for defining high technology products and services. The Technical Dictionary eliminates the need for trading partners to utilize separate dictionaries when trading electronically and is not supply chain-specific, allowing it to be used in a variety of supply chain applications. This dictionary coupled with the Business Dictionary, provides a common vocabulary for conducting e-Business, eliminating confusion in the procurement process due to companies' uniquely defined terminology.

The business and technical content exchanged between trading partners logically forms a complete business process, which in turn, specifies the structure, format and semantics of the business content of a message (also referred to as a payload). It also encompasses the message exchange requirements between trading partners, i.e., the dialogue or message exchange choreography that trading entities must engage in to complete a particular business process or activity. Figure 20.1 shows that the business processes can be orchestrated using for instance Web service technology and specifications in business process execution languages, such as BPEL.

20.3.2 Components in support of e-Business within an e-Market

The rapid adoption of e-Business models is shaping the future of global businesses. An enterprise is no longer limited to its internal systems, but may use systems that span the entire value chain, incorporating trading and distribution partners as well as customers. As a consequence, businesses increasingly integrate their supply chains by redesigning their structures to move from hierarchical organizations – with a focus on management control – to horizontal organizations, which are built around business processes, teamwork and empowerment; refer to Chapters 4 and 10. Thus, by coordinating, collaborating and integrating with other partners, enterprises create an extended virtual enterprise or an e-Market when the aim is an international electronic trading environment for buyers and sellers in a community setting.

As we explained in Chapter 10, supply chain integration can be defined as the process by which multiple enterprises within a shared market segment collaboratively plan, implement and manage the flow of goods, services and information along the value system in a way that increases customer-perceived value and optimizes the efficiency of the chain [Dobbs 1998]. Company value chains are transformed into integrated value systems if they are designed to act as an "extended enterprise", creating and enhancing customer-perceived value by means of cross enterprise collaboration. The same principles apply to companies that collaborate within the context of e-Markets, which is the natural superset of integrated supply chains. Integrated supply chains and e-Markets are expected to have major impact, allowing companies, and ultimately customers, to benefit from reduced inventories, cost savings, improved value added goods and services to customers, and tighter links with business partners. In an e-Market (e-Trading) network an enterprise's business systems can no longer be confined to internal processes, programs and data repositories; rather they must interoperate with other such systems that support links in the supply chain wherever these are. An enterprise must connect with several supply chains or trade with several partners within an e-Market as product offerings and business dictate. To support the highly specialized needs of a given e-Trading network, and at the same time optimize interoperability between supply chains and within trading partners in an e-Trading network, there is a need for using both *horizontal* and *vertical* XML-based components. In developing this model, we need to identify components that are ideally universal, i.e., may be applied uniformly across all e-Trading networks as well as those that are e-Trading network-specific, i.e., must be unique to meet the specialized requirements of a specific e-Trading network.

Figure 20.2 illustrates the technology stack for e-Trading networks. As shown in this figure, the technology stack for e-Trading networks builds upon and extends the technology stack for a single supply chain (see Figure 20.1).

As we explained in the preceding section, the focus of the Common Messaging Services is on defining a communications-protocol-neutral method for exchanging secure and reliable electronic business messages between trading partners or trading networks using various existing communication protocols. It defines specific enveloping constructs supporting reliable, secure delivery of business information. Furthermore, the specification defines a flexible enveloping technique, permitting messages to contain payloads of any format type. This versatility ensures legacy electronic business systems employing traditional syntaxes (i.e., UN/EDIFACT, or ASC X12) can leverage the advantages of the Common Messaging Service infrastructure along with users of emerging technologies.

The Common Messaging Services specification may include descriptions of: (1) the message structure used to package payload data for transport between parties, and (2) the behavior of the message service handler sending and receiving those messages over a data communications protocol. This specification is independent of both the payload and the communications protocol used.

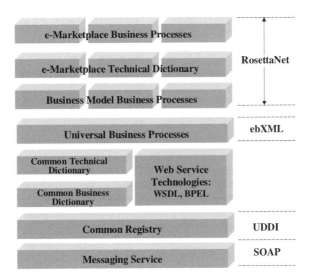

■ **Figure 20.2:** The Technology Stack for e-Trading Networks

The structure of the Simple Object Access Protocol ideally suits the needs of the transport, routing and packaging functions of the Common Messaging Service. The Common Messaging Services could be defined as a set of layered extensions to the base SOAP that provides the message packaging, routing and transport facilities for this infrastructure. It must be noted that security and reliability features are not provided in the SOAP and these need to be addressed separately.

Registries and repositories play a major part in e-Business as they facilitate searching for specifications and trading partners. A *registry* provides a set of services that enable sharing of information and technical fingerprints between trading partners for the purpose of enabling business process integration between these parties. The shared information is then maintained in a *repository* managed by the registry services. A classical example of this is the Web services registry, UDDI, which we introduced in Section 19.7.3.

The technology stack for e-Trading networks should provide distributed registries for listing industry processes, messages, and other business objects required for the conduct of e-Business, rather than storing these elements in either a central repository or in each user's system. Trading Partner Agreements (TPAs)[1] – which spell out the business process with its associated electronic transaction sets to be exchanged, responsibilities of sender and receivers, versions of standards used and exception procedures for handling potential problems – are part of the Common Registry and Repository.

The *Common Business Dictionary* specifies the structure and properties of content fields, elements, constraints, code lists and objects needed to define transactions between trading partners *within business processes*. It describes

---

[1] Trading Partner Agreements are also widely known as Service Level Agreements (see Section 13.2). Given the fact that Electronic Business XML refers to them as TPAs we decided to use this term instead of the familiar term SLA in this chapter for compliance with the ebXML description.

all of the business content, attributes and relationships between elements that exist in business documents. It would, for instance, include product quantity, product identification, global currency code, and monetary amount as business field descriptors for a price and availability request. Each of these descriptors contains, among other things, a data type value (whether it is a string or an integer) and a minimum and maximum value, where at least one choice may be mandatory.

The *Common Technical Dictionary* manages the structure for defining form, fit and function of *any product or service*, regardless of the industry. More specifically, it specifies the structure of the specialized technical dictionary or dictionaries used to obtain common domain-specific terminology, term definitions and accepted values.

Universal Business Processes are industry-neutral business processes that are generic in nature. The generic nature of these business processes enables one to reuse them with specific context and business rules within different vertical industries. Industry-neutral processes contain the minimum amount of specificity required to support core business processes across geographies, business models, supply chains and vertical industries. For example, in almost any industry, it is common for a company to purchase a product or service from a supplier. In that exchange, a purchaser typically asks a supplier for information regarding product price and availability, places an order, and then asks for an acknowledgement of that order. Relatively simple industry-neutral purchasing business processes could be defined that might support the majority of e-Business purchasing transactions across vertical industries, supply chains, regions, and business models. In some occasions these shared business processes may require slight modifications to fulfill the requirements that are unique to the business process within a specific context. The context that drives the process may modify the way the business information used.

For trading partners to complete a transaction on-line, business process standards should specify both the structure and format of the business content of a message as well as the message exchange choreography that trading entities must engage in to complete a business process.

A business model involves an extremely complex combination of multiple business processes. These involve multiple companies, locations, and so on; see Chapter 3. As such, the business model can be viewed as the externalization of the internal business processes. The Business Model (based) Business Processes architectural component specifies business process definitions for a particular business model. For example, the manufacturing processes and informational requirements of a manufacturer of discrete products (computers) may differ significantly from those of a process-based (semiconductor) manufacturer [RosettaNet 2001]. Often, there may be a range of business models used within an e-Trading network or even a supply chain, and it is common to use the same business models across several industries.

The e-Markets Technical Dictionary specifies the structure, form, fit and function of each product and service within an e-Market as well as semantics of the business content of a message and the message exchange choreography (also referred to as business conversation dialogue) between trading partners. The e-Markets Technical Dictionary provides commonly used domain-specific terminology and accepted values. This is particularly important for business processes attempting to automate the update of electronic catalogs and support of end-user product-based parametric searches over the Internet. When describing a modem, for example, the computer industry must agree upon a common set of attributes that can be used consistently by any company that manufactures modems (speed, electrical current, etc.) Whenever a modem manufacturer introduces a new product, it must then describe it in terms of the attributes as prescribed by the e-Market's technical dictionary.

The e-Markets Business Processes component in Figure 20.2 identifies the business process that is unique to a particular e-Trading network. For example, the business process and informational needs in the computer supply chain are quite different than those of insurance, pharmaceuticals, clothing, or book-publishing supply chains. Each vertical industry or supply chain has different ways of designing, forecasting, ordering, manufacturing and distributing their products. Most of these differentiating factors are concrete and non-debatable. For trading partners to complete a transaction online, business process standards should specify both the structure and format of the business content of a message as well as the message exchange choreography.

The three upper layers of the technology stack in Figure 20.2 can be found in the RosettaNet standard while Universal Business Processes are realized by another e-Business integration standard, the Electronic Business XML. We examine these two standards in turn in the remainder of this chapter.

20.4 RosettaNet

The RosettaNet Consortium (`www.rosettanet.org`) is an independent, nonprofit consortium of major information technology, electronic component, and semiconductor manufacturing companies working to create and implement industry-wide, open e-Business process standards designed to standardize the electronic business interfaces used between supply chain partners. RosettaNet has surveyed the XML-related standards space and has developed a conceptual model that that puts individual XML component standards into context and enables the comparison of horizontal and vertical XML standards efforts. The model identifies nine distinct components required to provide a total e-Business process. RosettaNet provides the following architectural elements to scale e-Business transactions:

1. *RosettaNet Implementation Framework (RNIF)*: RosettaNet developed a number of horizontal components in order to provide a robust, complete solution for its supply chains. At the foundational layer of the standard, is the RosettaNet Implementation Framework. The RNIF is a specification that describes how RosettaNet partners exchange information. The RNIF 2.0 includes a transfer protocol independent container that packs together the business payload along with the header components and other elements that must all be exchanged between two endpoints of a RosettaNet e-Business standard interaction. The RNIF core specification provides the packaging, routing, and transport of all PIP messages and business signals that RosettaNet processes use to communicate. The RNIF specification is a guideline for applications that implement RosettaNet Partner Interface Processes. These PIPs are standardized electronic business processes used between trading partners.
2. *Partner Interface Processes (PIPs)*: PIPs are the specifications that define the sequencing, choreography, business documents and elements contained by those documents, necessary to complete an exchange, which fulfill the business requirements of a pre-defined business process. In essence, RosettaNet PIPs define the public processes in which trading partners participate while performing e-Business transactions. RosettaNet PIPs are specialized system-to-system XML-based dialogues that define business processes between trading partners. Each PIP specification includes a business document with the vocabulary, and a business process with the choreography of the message dialogue. Each PIP provides common business models and documents to enable system developers to implement RosettaNet e-Business interfaces. Trading partners participating in PIPs need to implement the public process defined by their role in the

PIP and need to connect their internal systems and their private processes and workflows to the public process. PIPs are designed to fit into seven clusters, representing the core industry business processes of a trading network. PIPs apply to the following core industry processes: Partner, Product and Service Review; Product Information; Order Management; Inventory Management; Marketing Information Management; Service and Support; and Manufacturing. PIPs include: XML documents that specify PIP service, transactions, and messages including dictionary properties, class and sequence diagrams in UML, a validation tool and an implementation guide. Each cluster is broken down into segments which are cross-enterprise processes involving more than one type of trading partner. Within each segment are individual PIPs. RosettaNet specifies the Data Universal Numbering System (DUNS) for global identification of companies and the Global Trade Item Number (GTIN) for global identification of products in its PIPs. As an example of a PIP, consider the PIP "Manage Purchase Order" (PIP 3A4), whose specification is given in Figure 20.3. PIP 3A4 is a key component for a large number of RosettaNet e-Business process standards and serves as a "building block" for a variety of other PIPs. This PIP supports a process for trading partners to issue and acknowledge purchase orders, and cancel and change them based on acknowledgment responses. This PIP encompasses four complementary process segments supporting the entire chain of activities from purchase order creation to tracking-and-tracing, each of which is further decomposed into multiple individual processes. The provider's acknowledgment may also include related information about delivery expectations. When a provider acknowledges that the status of a purchase order product line item is "pending", the provider may later use PIP 3A7, "Notify of Purchase Order Acknowledgment" to notify the buyer when the product line item is either accepted or rejected. The process of issuing a purchase order typically occurs after checking for price and availability and requesting quotes. The process of issuing a purchase order may be followed by changing

```
<ProcessSpecification xmlns=http://www.ebxml.org/BusinessProcess name="PIP3A4RequestPurchaseOrder">
  <BusinessDocument name="Puchase Order Request“            ← Definition of Business Document (P.O.R)
     nameID="Pip3A4PurchaseOrderRequest“ specificationLocation="PurchaseOrderRequest.xsd">
  </BusinessDocument>
  <BusinessDocument name="Puchase Order Confirmation"       ← Definition of Business Document (P.O.C)
     nameID="Pip3A4PurchaseOrderConfirmation“ specificationLocation="PurchaseOrderConfirmation.xsd">
  </BusinessDocument>
  <BusinessTransaction name="Request Purchase Order" nameID="RequestPurchaseOrder_BT">
     <RequestingBusinessActivity name="Purchase Order Request Action" nameID="PurchaseOrderRequestAction“
        isAuthorizationRequired="true" isNonRepudiationRequired="true"
        timeToAcknowledgeReceipt="P0Y0M0DT2H0M0S">
       <DocumentEnvelope businessDocument="Puchase OrderRequest“
          businessDocumentIDRef="Pip3A4PurchaseOrderRequest" />
    </RequestingBusinessActivity>
    <RespondingBusinessActivity name="Purchase Order Confirmation Action“
       nameID="PurchaseOrderConfirmationAction" isAuthorizationRequired="true" isNonRepudiationRequired="true“
       timeToAcknowledgeReceipt="P0Y0M0DT2H0M0S">
       <DocumentEnvelope businessDocument="Purchase Order Confirmation“
          businessDocumentIDRef="Pip3A4PurchaseOrderConfirmation" />
     </RespondingBusinessActivity>
  </BusinessTransaction>
  <BinaryCollaboration name="Request Purchase Order" nameID="RequestPurchaseOrder_BC">
     <InitiatingRole name="Buyer" nameID="BuyerId" />
     <RespondingRole name="Seller" nameID="SellerId" />
     <Start toBusinessState="Request Purchase Order" />
     <BusinessTransactionActivity name="Request Purchase Order" nameID="RequestPurchaseOrder_BTA“
        businessTransaction="Request Purchase Order"businessTransactionIDRef="RequestPurchaseOrder_BT“
        fromAuthorizedRole="Buyer" fromAuthorizedRoleIDRef="BuyerId"
        toAuthorizedRole="Seller" toAuthorizedRoleIDRef="SellerId" timeToPerform="P0Y0M0DT24H0M0S"/>
  </BinaryCollaboration>
</ProcessSpecification>
```

Figure 20.3: Example of a RosettaNet Business Process Manage Purchase Order (PIP 3A4).

the purchase order, canceling the purchase order, querying for purchase order status, and distributing purchase order status.

3. *Dictionaries*: The RosettaNet Business and Technical Dictionaries contain properties for products and services, a common vocabulary for conducting e-Business as well as basic business roles and elements which are required in fields of business documents or schemas which are necessary to support PIP exchanges. The RosettaNet Business Dictionary designates the properties used in basic business activities and the properties for defining business transactions between trading partners. These are Business Data Entities and Fundamental Business Data Entities in PIP Message Guidelines. The RosettaNet Technical Dictionary provides properties for defining products, services, partners, and business transactions. The RNTD eliminates the need for partners to utilize separate dictionaries when implementing multiple PIPs and is not supply chain-specific, allowing it to be used in a variety of supply chain applications.

4. *e-Business Processes*: RosettaNet PIPs create new areas of e-Business process alignment between the IT supply chain partners. This allows companies to take advantage of e-commerce applications and the Internet for scaleable, worldwide e-Business integration.

20.5 Electronic business XML

The ebXML (`www.ebXML.org`) initiative is sponsored by the United Nations Centre for Trade Facilitation and Electronic Business (UN/CEFACT) and the Organization for the Advancement of Structured Information Standards (OASIS). It seeks to enable the exchange of electronic business data on a global scale using XML. The focus of the ebXML initiative is to develop a single global electronic market based on an open public XML-based infrastructure enabling the global use of electronic business information in an interoperable, secure and consistent manner by all parties. A primary objective of ebXML is to lower the barrier of entry to electronic business in order to facilitate trade, particularly with respect to small- and medium-sized enterprises (SMEs) and developing nations.

ebXML consists of a set of XML document type definitions that are common for business-to-business (ANSI X12 EDI) transactions across most industries. Its purpose is to preserve and extend the EDI infrastructure, by leveraging semantics and structure of EDI standards such as X12 and EDIFACT. Some concepts and constructs needed in these "vertical" specifications apply to all business domains and are expressed in a common way across vendors to enable ebXML-based e-Business. These constructs include descriptions of businesses, products and individuals, measurements, date, time, location, currencies, business classification codes and so on. Translation services can be developed to handle the mapping from one company's XML documents onto document formats used by its trading partner and into data formats required by its own legacy systems. A complete business integration solution along the lines of ebXML requires: standardized tags (meta-data) for each industry sector; a means for mapping between different meta-data descriptions; and means for processing XML documents and invoking business applications and services provided by business processes and workflows.

20.5.1 Conducting business via ebXML
Before concentrating on the architecture and technical details of ebXML, it is useful to understand the expectations of implementing a full ebXML business scenario to place everything in context. Enabling this scenario forms the core of the ebXML technical architecture specification.

It is important to realize that the role of ebXML is to provide a framework where trading partners can create consistent, robust and interoperable e-Business services and components seamlessly within an integrated global e-Business market.

Figure 20.4 shows a conceptual model for two trading partners, engaging in a simple business transaction interchange. This model is provided as an illustration of the process and steps that may typically be required using ebXML applications and related components and is adapted from [ebXML 2000]. In Figure 20.4, Company A requests an ebXML specification from an ebXML Registry that contains a set of ebXML specifications in order to determine if it wants to become an ebXML compliant participant (Figure 20.4, step 1). Company A, after reviewing the specification that it receives, decides to build and deploy its own ebXML compliant application (Figure 20.4, steps 2 and 3). For example, if Company A specializes in e-Health applications and wants to sell consumable items to most hospitals, it must have product identifiers that comply with the Health Industry Bar Code specifications. Company A then submits its own implementation details, reference links, and Trading Partner Profile (TPP) as a request to the ebXML Registry (Figure 20.4, step 4). The TPP submitted describes the company's ebXML capabilities and constraints, as well as its supported business scenarios (XML versions of the business processes). Subsequently, the TPP is verified and acknowledged by the ebXML Registry (Figure 20.4, step 5).

Following this, Company B is informed by Company A that it would like to engage in a business transaction using ebXML. Subsequently, the Company B queries the ebXML Registry about Company A and Company A's profile is retrieved (Figure 20.4, steps 6 and 7). Based on the TPP, the application determines that it is able to execute a specific scenario that Company A supports. Before engaging in that the scenario Company B submits a proposed Trading Partner Agreement directly to Company A's ebXML compliant software interface. The TPA outlines the e-Business scenario and specific arrangement(s) it wants to use with

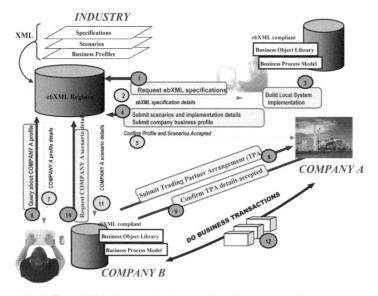

■ **Figure 20.4:** The ebXML Approach; Automating Business-to-Business Interactions

Company A, as well as certain messaging, contingency and security-related requirements (Figure 20.4, step 8). Company A accepts the TPA and acknowledgement is sent directly to Company B (Figure 20.4, step 9). Since the scenario from Company A was not available in the software package that Company B is using, the application requests it and receives it from the ebXML Registry (Figure 20.4, steps 10 and 11). Based on the business processes (contained in the process models) and business messages exchanged Company A and B are now engaging in e-Business transaction utilizing ebXML specifications via their respective software applications (Figure 20.4, step 12).

20.5.2 Architectural model of ebXML

In order to make sense of the technical architecture for ebXML it is important to first understand the conceptual thinking behind the initiative. From the outset the technical architecture team approached the project from the standpoint of business workflow, selecting the objects common to many business processes, such as address, party and location. With the advent of XML it was easier to identify and define these objects with attributes (data) along with the functions that could be performed on those attributes. A cornerstone of the project was allowing these objects to be reused so that ebXML could provide for the means to unify cross-industry exchanges with a single consistent lexicon.

Interoperability in ebXML is achieved by applying business objects across business models that enable representation of business relationships between interacting companies in a shared business process. Business objects and business processes are contained in a business library, which is used in conjunction with a lexicon that contains data and process definitions as expressed in business terminology and organized per industry sector.

The architectural model of ebXML uses two views to describe the relevant aspects of all business interactions. These two views are referred to as the Business Operational View (BOV) and the Functional Service View (FSV) [Webber 2000; ebXML 2000]. These two views originate from early work on OpenEDI by UN/CEFACT and are adopted in the RosettaNet implementation framework and can also be found in the architectural model of ebXML. They address different aspects of e-Business transactions and different human actors are involved with them.

The *Business Operational View* addresses the semantics of business data in business transactions, and associated message exchanges. It is also concerned with business rules for business transactions, including operational conventions agreements and mutual obligations, which are part of business transactions. These specifically apply to the business needs of ebXML trading partners.

The *Functional Service View* addresses the supporting services of the information systems that implement the information exchange. The FSV meets the deployment needs of ebXML. The implementation of the FSV of ebXML has three major phases; implementation, discovery and deployment, and the runtime phase. The implementation phase deals specifically with procedures for creating an application of the ebXML infrastructure. The discovery and deployment phase cover all aspects of the actual discovery of ebXML-related resources and is self-enabled into the ebXML infrastructure. Finally, the run time phase addresses the execution of an ebXML scenario with the actual associated ebXML transactions.

The FSV focuses on functional capabilities, service interfaces and communication protocols including initiating, operating and tracking the progress of ebXML transactions, security, protocols and data or message translation.

When working at the BOV level, appropriate methods and tools are used. The modeling tools used at that level are increasingly based on UML which is used both for modeling software and modeling business collaborations and transactions. The BOV uses tools such as a lexicon (dictionary) that contain data and process definitions including relationships and cross-references as expressed in business terminology and organized by industry domain.

By contrast when working at the FSV level, document format and message encoding are important considerations as are issues such as security, message compression, or application interfaces and data translation layers (for example, from XML to a legacy EDIFACT interface) [Chappell 2001].

The ebXML reference architecture

It is convenient to think of ebXML in terms of its reference architecture, which contains its architectural elements (components) and the systems analysis and development methodology. The latter is referred to as the *process architecture* and has as purpose to provide an analysis and development methodology for the reference architecture.

The ebXML reference architecture is composed of the following five major architectural components illustrated in Figure 20.5. The lower-level layers in this stack support lower-level functionality, e.g., computer processing and message transport details or registry functions, required for the implementation of the higher-level components. The architectural components of the ebXML reference model are as follows:

1. *Messaging Service*: This provides a standard way to exchange business messages between organizations. It provides for means to exchange a payload, which may or may not be an XML business document or traditional and encrypted payloads, over multiple communications services, e.g., SMTP or HTTP, reliably and securely. It also provides means to route a payload to the appropriate internal application once an organization has received it.

■ **Figure 20.5:** ebXML Key Components

2. *Registry and repository*: Integral to the ebXML architecture is the registry component, which is necessary to deliver on the BOV and FSV. The ebXML registry is a document based e-Business registry that also captures descriptive information about each document in the form of metadata. The registry not only holds the ebXML base reference specifications, but also the Business Process and Information meta-models developed by industry groups, SMEs, and other organizations. These models allow for the development of individual business process models and are compliant with the ebXML meta-model and related methodologies. The ebXML meta-model specifications constitute a set of XML structures that can be populated and stored in an ebXML registry and repository system. These XML structures may utilize a classification system, compatible with the registry and repository architecture requirements. In order to store the models they are converted from UML to XML. ebXML registries store these models as instances of XML that are compliant with the ebXML meta-model. Examples of items in the registry might be XML schemas of business documents, definitions of library components for business process modeling, and trading partner agreements. Both the documents and their associated metadata are stored in the repository. Clients can access the content of the ebXML registry through the registry service interface.

3. *Trading Partner Information*: This is known also as the Collaboration Protocol Profile (CPP) and Collaboration Protocol Agreement (CPA). The CPP/CPA defines the capabilities of a trading partner to perform a data interchange and how this data interchange agreement can be formed between two trading partners. The CPP provides the definition (XML schema) of an XML document that specifies the details of how an organization is able to conduct business electronically. It specifies such items as how to locate it, contact it and other information about the organization, the types of network and file transport protocols it uses, network addresses, security implementations, and how it does business (a reference to a Business Process Specification). The CPA specifies the details of how two organizations have agreed to conduct business electronically and is formed by combining the CPPs of the two organizations.

4. *Business Process Specification Schema* (*BPSS*): The BPSS provides the definition (in the form of an XML) of an XML document that describes how documents can be exchange between trading organizations. While the CPP/CPA deals with the technical aspects of how to conduct business electronically, the BPSS deals with the actual business process. It identifies such things as the overall business process, the roles, transactions, identification of the business documents used (the DTDs or XML schemas), document flow, legal aspects, security aspects, business level acknowledgments, and status. A XML BPSS can be used by a software application to configure the business details of conducting business electronically with another organization.

5. *Business Processes*: Business processes define the ways in which trading partners engage each other, to the point of configuring their respective systems to actually do business. This is accomplished in such a way that business practices and interactions are represented both accurately and independently of any specific ways of implementing these transactions. Business process specifications are expressed as XML schemas (or DTDs) or in UML. BPSS and business processes will be revisited below.

6. *Core Components*: ebXML gives particular attention to business objects that appear in multiple domains, and calls the multiple reusable data items that cut across many industries *core components*. A core component captures information about a business concept, and relationships between that concept and other business concepts. A core component is a piece of basic business information that is designed to take into account commonality across industry business processes and can thus be used to facilitate many different processes across different industry sectors. In the most basic sense a core component is syntax/domain-neutral, as it has no business semantics associated with it. Some examples of core components are "date of purchase order", "sales tax", and "total amount". A number of core components can be aggregated to form a building block used to support ebXML business transactions and business processes. In some cases it is possible that aggregates may not be associated with any specific business semantic, and are thus

domain-neutral and highly reusable, while in other cases they may form aggregates, which are required specifically within a particular domain with possibly a high degree of reusability within this domain. The major parts of the core components work are:

- methodology for discovering core components from existing business documents or new business processes, analyzing them for harmonization and reuse, and extending core components into domain components for use in specific industries and situations

- naming conventions that describe the parts of a core component name, based on ISO 11179, and rules for developing the names

- catalogues of core components that may be used "as is" or extended to build definitions of business messages

- catalogue of context drivers containing the types of information describing the contexts in which core components may be extended. These include such things as geographic region, industry, role, and product

The ebXML infrastructure is modular and with few exceptions the infrastructure components may be used somewhat independently. They are therefore only loosely related. The elements of the infrastructure may interact with each other, but in most cases are not required to. For example, the messaging services may be used completely independently, although a message header may contain a reference to a CPA.

The process architecture

The ebXML process architecture is based on UN/CEFACT's Unified Modeling Methodology and its meta-model (see Section 12.4.3) The BPSS specification is strongly influenced by UMM; in fact it represents a subset of the information in the UMM meta-model and thus shares much of its terminology. Ideally, the BPSS should be developed by going through the full UMM process. However, ebXML developed worksheets to enable analysts to document the information necessary for the BPSS without needing to follow the UMM. Worksheets are an alternative to encoding the results of UMM workflows. A worksheet is a template that provides a predefined structure to organize the results of a UMM workflow. In addition, ebXML developed an analysis methodology and several contributions related to it that are summarized in what follows:

- *Business Process Analysis Worksheet and Guidelines*: This item contains a set of worksheets and guidelines for using them. The worksheets are designed to assist an analyst in gathering the data necessary to describe a business process. The information can subsequently be used to create a BPSS XML document describing the business process. The worksheets can be used as a basis for developing business process editors that can guide the user in collecting the information and automatically generate the XML business process specification.

- *Catalogue of Common Business Processes*: This item contains a cross-listing and description of business processes which may be common to several industries.

- *e-Commerce Patterns*: This item contains examples and descriptions of common business patterns. The only one listed to date is for simple contract formation.

The relationships between the business process elements are fairly obvious. The analysis worksheets draw on the catalogue of common business processes and e-commerce patterns to develop a specification document that covers the essential set of data specified by the UMM meta-model [RosettaNet 2001]. The relationships of the core component specifications to each other are similar.

Similar to the modular nature of the technical infrastructure, the parts of the process architecture may also be used independently. It is quite possible to develop XML schemas for business documents in a bottom-up fashion strictly from core and domain components without doing any formal business process analysis. Conversely, it is also quite possible to generate XML document schemas from UML business process models using invented business information objects or objects from a source other than ebXML core components.

Lastly, there is only one strong link between the reference and the process architecture. That link is the BPSS, which is a machine interpretable encoding of a business process. It is compliant with the UMM meta-model (see Section 12.4.3), but does not necessarily need to be developed using the full UMM process. Instead, as noted above, it can be generated from a business process editor that implements the business process analysis worksheets.

Business processes and Business Process Specification Schema

As explained in Section 12.4.3, UMM meta-model is a description of business semantics that allows trading partners to capture the details for a specific business scenario (a business process) using a consistent modeling methodology. A business process describes in detail how trading partners take on shared roles, relationships and responsibilities to facilitate interaction with other trading partners. The interaction between roles takes place as a choreographed set of business transactions. Each business transaction is expressed as an exchange of electronic business documents. The sequence of the exchange is determined by the business process, and by messaging and security considerations. Business documents are composed from reusable business objects. At a lower level, business processes can be composed of reusable common business processes, and business objects can be composed of reusable core components. Common business processes and business objects reside in a UMM Business Library.

The UMM meta-model supports a set of business process viewpoints that provide a set of semantics (vocabulary) for each viewpoint, and forms the basis of specification of the semantics and artifacts that are required to facilitate business process and information integration and interoperability. Using the UMM methodology and the UMM meta-model, the user may thus create a complete business process and information model. This model contains more information than what is required for configuring ebXML compliant software [Dubray 2005]. Also the model is syntax independent and not directly interpretable by ebXML compliant software.

The Business Process Specification Schema [Dubray 2005] is a relatively simple schema that describes public processes and aims to support the specification of business transactions and their choreography into business collaborations. The BPSS provides a view (semantic subset) of the UMM meta-model. This subset is provided to support the direct specification of the nominal set of elements necessary to configure a runtime system in order to execute a set of ebXML business transactions. Using the ebXML Business Process Specification Schema the user may thus create a Business Process Specification that contains only the information required to configure ebXML compliant software. BPSS supports a long-running business transaction model based on proven e-Business transaction patterns used by other standards such as RosettaNet. Business transactions within the BPSS are applied to the semantic business level with a simplistic protocol defined for the interaction between two parties (requesting and responding) and determination of success or failure of the transaction.

The relationship between BPSS, the UMM meta-model, ebXML business transactions and choreographies, and core components is shown in Figure 20.6. Using the UMM methodology, and drawing on content from the UMM Business Library, a user may create a complete business process and information model conforming to the UMM meta-model. Since the BPSS is a semantic subset of the UMM meta-model, the user may then in an automated fashion extract from the business process and information model the required set of elements and relationships, and transform them into business process schema conforming to the ebXML BPSS.

A BPSS is in essence the machine interpretable run-time business process specification needed for an ebXML business service interface. The BPSS is thus referenced by ebXML trading partner Collaboration Protocol

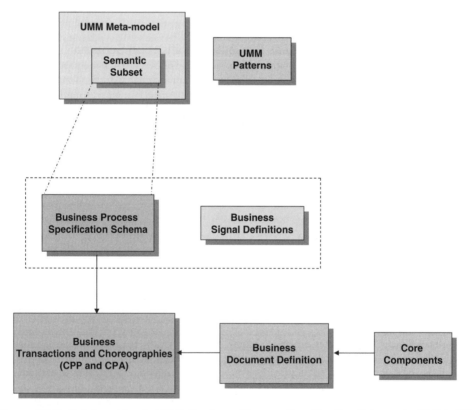

■ **Figure 20.6:** Relationship of ebXML Business Process Specification Schema to UMM, CPP/CPA and Core Components

Profiles and Collaboration Protocol Agreements, as shown in Figure 20.6. Each CPP declares its support for one or more roles within a business process specification. Within these CPP profiles and CPA agreements are then added further technical parameters resulting in a full specification of the run-time software at each trading partner. Business signals in Figure 20.6 are application level documents that "signal" the current state of the business transaction. These business signals have specific business purpose and are separate from lower protocol and transport signals as defined in the ebXML Message Service Specification. The state of a given business transaction activity instance can be explicitly calculated at run-time by evaluating these signals. As such they are instrumental in establishing a business collaboration protocol that insures that the representation of the state of a business collaboration instance for each party is the strictly identical for both parties. For example, an "Acceptance Acknowledgement" signal is generated after an application or service has successfully processed and validated a business document. The BPSS provides both the structure and choreography of business signals, while the Message Service Specification provides a reliable messaging infrastructure for them.

The strength of the ebXML technical architecture is that it provides a framework for electronic business collaboration. The architecture enables businesses to work together to specify business processes, discover each other, negotiate collaboration agreements, and execute business processes. In general terms, an ebXML business process is defined as a sequenced set of business transactions. In ebXML a business transaction is a clearly defined exchange of business messages resulting in a new legal or commercial state between the two partners. The business semantics of each business transaction are defined in terms of the business objects affected, and the commitment(s) formed or agreed. The technical semantics of each commercial transaction are defined in terms of a "handshake" protocol of required message (signal) exchanges.

An ebXML business transaction represents business document flows between requesting and responding partners. This is shown in Figure 20.7. In any ebXML business transaction there always is a requesting business document, and optionally, a responding business document. Each business transaction request or response may require that a receipt acknowledgement be returned to the sender. For contract-forming transactions such as purchase order requests an acceptance acknowledgement may need to be returned to the requester. Time constraints can be applied to the return of responses and acknowledgements. If an ebXML business transaction fails on either side, the other side is notified so that both sides can carry out any actions necessary to process the failure in their internal systems. An ebXML business transaction can be viewed as a type declaration, while business transaction activities (which reference a unique business transaction type) are the usage of this transaction within a particular choreography. As explained earlier, each business transaction can be implemented using one of many available standard UMM patterns, which determine the actual exchange of business documents and business signals between trading partners to achieve the required electronic business transaction.

A BPSS business collaboration is essentially the specification of business transaction activities between the two partners, their associated document flow, and the choreography of these business transaction activities; see Figure 20.7. BPSS describes public processes as collaborations between roles, with each role abstractly representing a trading partner. There are two types of collaborations: binary collaborations and multi-party collaborations. Multi-party collaborations are decomposed to binary collaborations. The business collaboration specifies all the business messages that are exchanged between two trading partners, their content, and their precise sequence and timing. This part of the "agreement" provides a shared understanding of the interaction. The way the contract is implemented is private but the expectations are public. An ebXML collaboration is conducted by two parties, each using a human or an automated

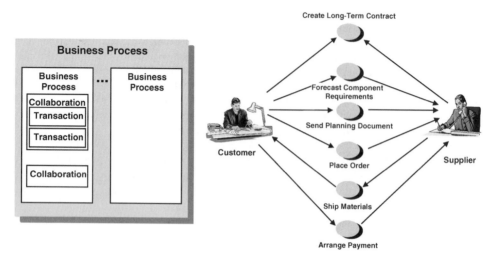

■ **Figure 20.7:** Business Processes and Transactions

business logic system that interprets the documents transmitted and decides how to (or whether to) respond. All collaborations are composed of combinations of atomic transactions, each between two parties. Multi-party arrangements must be decomposed into bilateral transactions. The sequencing rules contained in a collaboration definition are not between messages but between business transaction activities.

The ebXML BPSS is available in two stand-alone representations, a UML version, and an XML version. The XML version is intended to be interpretable by ebXML compliant software. Listing 20.1 is an example specification of an ebXML business transaction with one request and two possible responses, a success and a failure. A document flow is not modeled directly. Rather it is modeled indirectly as a `<DocumentEnvelope>` sent by one role and received by the other. The `<DocumentEnvelope>` is always associated with one `<RequestingBusinessActivity>` and one `<RespondingBus inessActivity>` to model the flow. There is always only one named `<DocumentEnvelope>` for a `<RequestingBusinessActivity>`. The `<DocumentEnvelope>` represents the flow of documents between the activities. Each `<DocumentEnvelope>` carries exactly one primary `<BusinessDocument>`. There may be zero, one, or many mutually exclusive, named `<DocumentEnvelope>`s for a `<RespondingBusinessActivity>`. For example, the response `<DocumentEnvelope>`s for a purchase order transaction might be named `PurchaseOrderAcceptance`, `PurchaseOrderDenial`, and `PartialPurchaseOrder Acceptance`. In the actual execution of the purchase order transaction, however, only one of the defined possible responses will be sent. A `<DocumentEnvelope>` can optionally have one or more attachments, all related to the primary `<BusinessDocument>`. The document and its attachments in essence form one transaction in the payload in the ebXML Message Service message structure. Associated with each document flow can be one or more business signals acknowledging the document flow. These acknowledgment signals are not modeled explicitly but parameters associated with the transaction specify whether the signals are required or not.

```
<BusinessDocument name="Purchase Order" specificationLocation="someplace"/>
<BusinessDocument name="PO Acknowledgement" specificationLocation="someplace"/>
<BusinessDocument name="PO Rejection" specificationLocation="someplace"/
<BusinessDocument name="Delivery Instructions" specificationLocation="someplace"/>

<BusinessTransaction name="Create Order">
   <RequestingBusinessActivity name="..">
      <DocumentEnvelope isPositiveResponse="true",
      BusinessDocument="ebXML1.0/PO Acknowledgement">
        <Attachment
    name="DeliveryNotes"
    mimeType="XML"
    BusinessDocument="ebXML1.0/Delivery Instructions"
    specification=".."
    isConfidential="true"
    isTamperProof="true"
    isAuthenticated="true">
        </Attachment>
      </DocumentEnvelope>
   </RequestingBusinessActivity>
   <RespondingBusinessActivity name="..">
      <DocumentEnvelope
    BusinessDocument="ebXML1.0/POAcceptance"/>
      </DocumentEnvelope>
      <DocumentEnvelope isPositiveResponse="false"
         BusinessDocument="ebXML1.0/PORejection"/>
      </DocumentEnvelope>
   </RespondingBusinessActivity>
</BusinessTransaction>
```

■ **Listing 20.1:** Example of an ebXML Transaction

Listing 20.2 defines a simple Binary Collaboration using the business transaction defined in Listing 20.1. A `<Binary Collaboration>` consists of one or more business activities. A business activity can be either a `<Business Transaction>` activity or a `<Binary Collaboration>` activity. These business activities are always conducted between the two authorized roles of the binary collaboration. For each activity one of two roles is assigned to be the `<InitiatingRole>` and the other to be the `<RespondingRole>`.

Business conversations

In business applications it is expected that trading partners can communicate through conversation sequences. A *conversation sequence* is a long-running sequence of interactions, e.g., documents exchanges, between two or more interacting services [Frolund 2001]. For example, a master purchasing agreement, which permits

```
<BinaryCollaboration name="Product Fulfillment" timeToPerform="P5D">
  <Documentation>
        timeToPerform = Period: 5 days from start of transaction
  </Documentation>
  <InitiatingRole name="buyer"/>
  <RespondingRole name="seller"/>
  <BusinessTransactionActivity name="Create Order"
      businessTransaction="Create Order"
      fromAuthorizedRole="buyer"
       toAuthorizedRole="seller"
       isLegallyBinding="true" />
  <BusinessTransactionActivity name="Notify shipment"
          businessTransaction="Notify of advance shipment"
          fromAuthorizedRole="buyer"
          toAuthorizedRole="seller"/>
</BinaryCollaboration>
```

■ **Listing 20.2:** Example of an ebXML Collaboration

the placing of orders for components by known buying organizations, allows a buyer and a seller to create and subsequently exchange meaningful information about the creation and processing of an order. Such agreements, commonly known as Trading Partner Agreements, stem from business negotiations and are specific to a particular trading community, e.g., a vertical e-Market such as semiconductors, chemicals or the travel industry.

The TPA is an electronic contract that uses XML to stipulate the general terms and conditions, participant roles, e.g., buyers and sellers, communication and security protocols, and a business protocol (such as valid actions and sequencing rules). A TPA thus defines how trading partners will interact at the transport, document exchange, and business protocol levels. Agreements usually result in the specification of shared or canonical data formats and of the messages that carry those formats, and their permitted sequences, all of which are needed for an automated implementation of an agreement. A TPA relates to a conversation between the trading partners. This conversation is a unit of business under the TPA and there may be many conversations running concurrently between the partners. A conversation is represented as a set of related business transactions each of which are represented by an interchange of messages between the partners.

Each party is responsible for maintaining the correlation between messages within a conversation – in effect the conversation state. A party is also responsible for correctly invoking its own business process implementations upon receipt of a request message and generating an appropriate response that is returned to the other party. A conversation is a short- or long-lived series of business messages exchanged between trading partners. A conversation definition typically includes a unique conversation name and version, specifies the roles that the trading partners play in the conversation; it is linked to a specific business protocol (e.g., RosettaNet PIPs) and TPA; and typically references a business process management collaborative workflow template for each role.

Figure 20.8 depicts a hypothetical conversation between two trading parties, which engage in a bidding procedure to settle on mutually acceptable prices. The figure also shows that a successful conversation may lead to the formulation of a contractual agreement between the trading parties.

The Collaboration Protocol Profiles/Collaboration Protocol Agreements specification is the implementation of trading partner agreements in ebXML. An ebXML business collaboration specifies as part of a Collaboration Protocol Agreement an "agreement" between two or more trading business partners [ebXML

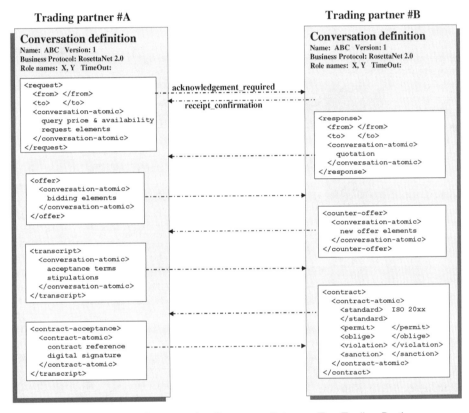

■ **Figure 20.8:** Conversation Sequence Between Two Trading Parties

2002]. The CPA is connected to business process specifications and their related business transactions (both expressed in BPSS). The ebXML working group has adopted the term CPA to mean a machine interpretable version of a TPA. A CPA is created between two trading partners who wish to interoperate. Accordingly, the CPA requires knowledge of each partner's technical capabilities. These capabilities include communication protocols the partners support (HTTP, SMTP, FTP, etc.), messaging service messaging protocols and requirements, security requirements that they place upon the message exchanges, interface requirements, and links to the business processes they support. These technical capabilities are described along with contact information and business classification information in a Collaboration Protocol Profile. Each party has a CPP that is a public description of their capabilities. The CPA is then an intersection of the two parties' CPPs with the results of negotiation variable parameters in the profiles. The CPA includes an agreed common set of technical capabilities together with a definition of what business processes are to be performed between the two parties.

In Figure 20.9, party A and party B use their CPPs to jointly construct a single copy of a CPA by calculating the intersection of the information in their CPPs. The resulting CPA defines how the two parties will behave in performing their business collaboration. Thus, a CPA can contain the following key information [Ibbotson 2001]:

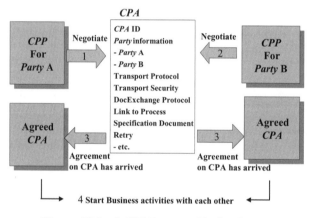

■ **Figure 20.9:** A CPA Between Trading Partners

- Overall Properties. This section contains information relating to the overall CPA, e.g., the duration of the agreement.

- Identification. This section identifies the parties to the agreement. It includes nominated contacts with their addresses together with other party identifiers.

- Communication Properties. This section identifies what communication protocols the parties support. It also includes, where necessary, parameters such as timeouts needed to ensure interoperability between the parties.

- Document Exchange Properties. This section establishes the messaging protocol to be used in exchanging business documents. It includes a description of the set of messages that can be exchanged, their encoding, and any parameters associated with reliable delivery.

- Security Properties. This section includes information needed to ensure a secure interchange of information between the parties. It includes parameters for non-repudiation such as certificates, protocols, hash functions and signature algorithms. It also includes digital certificates and encryption algorithms that can be used for security purposes.

- Roles. This section associates a party with a role defined in the CPP. In general, this description is defined in terms of roles such as "buyer" and "seller". The CPP identifies which role or roles a party is capable of playing in each collaboration protocol referenced by the CPP.

- Business Transactions. This section defines the business transactions or services that the parties agree to interchange. It describes the interfaces between the parties and the business application functions that actually perform the business transactions.

- Comments. This section is a free format section that can be used for additional information such as reference to any legal documents relating to the partner agreement.

Figure 20.10 shows an example of two trading companies involved in a purchase order. One of these companies acts as a buyer while the other acts as a seller. The CPA defines that the two parties have agreed to perform their business collaboration according to RosettaNet PIP 3A4 (which we described earlier in Section 20.4).

Trading partners may also wish to exchange proposed terms without making an assertion of intent to be legally bound. This is analogous to the paper contracting practice of exchanging unsigned drafts or term sheets. Naturally, trading parties may interrogate proposed business processes in a CPP or CPA independently, and then communicate about the suitability and desirability of the specified process. The

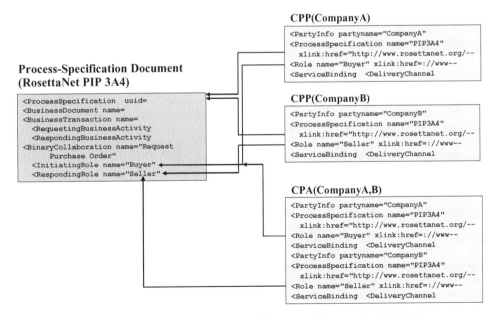

■ **Figure 20.10:** CPP/CPA Example Involving RosettaNet PIP 3A4

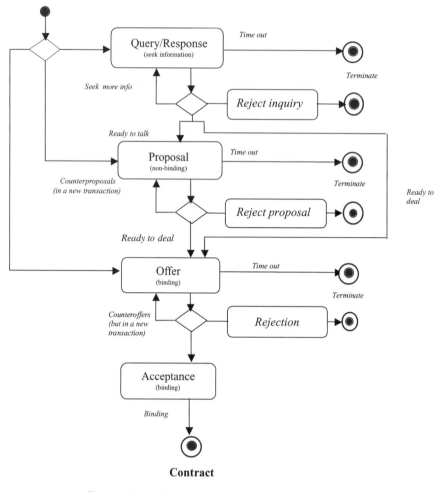

■ **Figure 20.11:** The ebXML Contract Negotiation Process

generalized flow of events resulting from the foregoing approach is illustrated in the activity diagram shown in Figure 20.11.

Figure 20.11 shows how an interaction sequence takes place between two partners seeking to conduct business together. Notice that negotiations are broken down to sets bilateral collaborations, even if they may actually be part of a broader marketplace and associated agreements. The diagram has an annotated set of conventional items encountered during a business negotiation that leads to a formal agreement of terms and conditions. Subsequent to this, the BPSS structure stores those items in a registry and uses them to show how they relate to the business process definitions and messages exchanges. As mentioned earlier in this section, the ebXML registry provides the means to store and retrieve these items and to reuse them between trading partners.

Finally, Figure 20.12 shows how collaboration agreements (CPAs in BPSS), business conversations and trading partner representations are connected with each other. This figure shows that a collaboration agreement is governed by a business protocol that specifies the interactions between partner roles and the sequencing rules that determine the order of requests. The business protocol layer is the interface between the collaboration agreement actions and the business application functionality. When a given collaboration agreement can be reused for different pairs of parties, a template can be specified in terms of role parameters rather than specific party names. Roles are defined by generic terms such as buyer and seller. The document exchange layer defines the properties exchanged by the trading parties [Dan 2001]. Any document formats agreed to by the two parties may be used. The document exchange layer accepts a document from the business protocol layer. It can encrypt, add a digital signature and pass the document

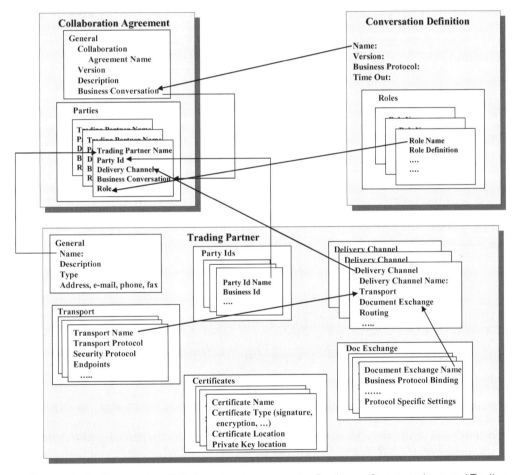

■ **Figure 20.12:** Connecting Collaboration Agreements, Business Conversations and Trading Partners

to the transport layer for transmission to the other party. The transport layer is responsible for message delivery using selected communication and security, e.g., authentication and encryption, protocols. The communication properties define the system-to-system communication used between interacting parties. A delivery channel consists of one transport definition and one document exchange definition. It corresponds to a single communication and document-processing path. The collaboration agreement may include multiple transport and document exchange definitions, which can be grouped into delivery channels with different characteristics.

20.6 Convergence between Rosetta, ebXML and Web services

In the previous sections we have presented two important standards in the world of e-Business, RosettaNet and ebXML because of their wide adoption and industry backing. In this section we will review and compare the compatibility of these standards and will consider them in conjunction with Web services which are the technical infrastructure supporting the conduct of e-Business between enterprises.

RosettaNet is a widely adopted standard that provides message content, choreography and transport specifications and standards development processes that target the high-technology manufacturing industry. Although RosettaNet publishes messaging specifications (such as RNIF2.0) its vision is to develop standards that pertain to the industry processes. This involves creating message content specifications and choreography with a reduced focus on the infrastructure that supports such activities.

ebXML is a set of standards developed to enable enterprises to conduct business over the Internet. Its stated objective is similar to RosettaNet's, although the specific standards developed are different. It produces specifications for messaging, registries, and business processes. Unlike RosettaNet, ebXML is a horizontal standard; it is not targeted at any particular industry. Whereas ebXML focuses on XML and on the technical foundation, and bases its architecture on incorporating current best-of-breed ideas, RosettaNet borrows more architectural ideas from EDI [Chiu 2002]. Currently, RosettaNet and ebXML are complementary in the following ways:

- The ebXML BPSS supports a long-running business transaction model based on robust, proven e-Business transaction patterns used by RosettaNet. ebXML's Business Process Specification Schema provided a suitable fit for this information. The BPSS Schema allows the specification of the collaboration between two or more parties using RosettaNet PIPs. The schema can contain elements for specifying the roles, activities, and other parameters needed to configure PIPs. A normative specification for the use of ebXML BPSS to RosettaNet PIP is being undertaken by the RosettaNet PIP specification program. It will produce BPSS specifications for future PIPs and therefore address the issue of producing machine-readable specifications for PIPs.

- The configuration of system connectivity is an implicit requirement for RosettaNet. This configuration contains information about the identity of their partners, the necessary certificates for security purposes, as well as the network endpoints. The exchange of this information is currently informal, for example, by exchange of emails or of softcopy documents. The use of ebXML's Collaboration Protocol Profile and Collaboration Protocol Agreement can be applied to this scenario. The CPP document defines the message exchange capability of a partner. This information includes details of transport, messaging, security constraints and public process bindings described by the BPSS document.

- There are notable similarities between the RosettaNet property dictionaries and ebXML core components.

- There is a possibility that an entire RosettaNet message may be used as the payload in an ebXML environment. RosettaNet has announced its intention to publish RNIF version 3.0 as an ebXML Message Services-compliant specification [Chappell 2001].

The above factors indicate that convergence between these two initiatives is technically feasible, advantageous and likely at some stage in the future. RosettaNet is likely to continue working adding value in business process standards for the high-technology industry, while ebXML will focus on cross-industry (horizontal) standards.

As Web services constitute the infrastructure for developing complex e-Business applications they can be used as an implementation vehicle for implementing business standards such as ebXML and RosettaNet. There are, however, some issues that need to be explained before we concentrate on this.

Asynchronous and stateful communication between Web services is critical to the development of e-Business applications and the facilitation of next generation business models. BPEL provides Web services with the necessary means to enable e-Business dialogues between peers and create asynchronous stateful interactions.

When considering Web services as an implementation platform for RosettaNet it is fairly easy to model the PIP receipt and messages as WSDL operations by converting DTDs to XML Schema documents [Masud 2003]. RosettaNet message definitions contain the types used in the message and these can be mapped to the types definitions of WSDL, while RosettaNet message definitions, including message names, can be mapped to the message definitions in WSDL. The actions in a RosettaNet PIP are mapped to operations in WSDL.

Choreography from the RosettaNet PIP can be implemented in the choreography of the abstract and executable business process in BPEL. Exception messages from RosettaNet RNIF can be mapped to the exception handling mechanisms of BPEL. The partnerLink construct in BPEL can be used to implement PIP partner roles. The messaging layer from RosettaNet RNIF provides methods for packing and unpacking messages and transporting them in a secure and reliable manner. BPEL and WSDL provide their own methods for encoding, transporting, and securing messages. The workaround is to use best practices from RosettaNet in the Web services paradigm.

BPEL and RosettaNet are ideally suited for use as a powerful combination, with BPEL as a language to define e-Business processes, and RosettaNet to create standardized industry e-Business processes. It is conceivable that RosettaNet can use BPEL as a standard e-Business process definition language to describe its e-Business processes.

As both ebXML and Web services have the same foundational technologies (XML), they have many things in common. Their difference lies in the fact that ebXML provides a complete solution in the e-Business integration domain, while Web services are considered as an e-Business-enabling infrastructure and are broader in scope and include application and e-Business integration as well as traditional Web interactions. ebXML addresses several of the layers in the Web services technology stack (see Figure 19.4). At the core layers, the ebXML messaging specification provides secure, reliable communication on any transport, uses SOAP for packaging, and defines a rich set of meta-data for carrying out e-Business transactions between trading partners [Patil 2003]. At the higher-level layers and in particular the description level, the ebXML Collaboration Protocol describes the trading partner's business services, the concrete binding where the service can be addressed, and so on. BPSS also defines the collaboration aspects between processes and, thereby, how services are orchestrated. The Collaboration Protocol covers the business and service-level agreements. Finally, at the publication and discovery level, the ebXML registry allows publication, sharing and discovery of different business artifacts such as trading-partner information, business process definitions, and business document types. When considering Web services as an implementation platform for ebXML it is fairly easy to use WSDL to describe Collaboration Protocol Profiles. BPEL can also be used to implement BPSS. BPSS can be used to describe the overall business processes and then BPEL can be used to define components in the BPSS. Predefined BPEL components can be included into BPSS diagrams as nodes.

20.7 Chapter summary

e-Business standardization is about interoperability of business content and message exchange between business systems of different enterprises, as well as the process automation associated with them.

The inflexibility and cost of integration and deployment to smaller business partners, and the generic nature of EDI transactions have made conventional EDI undesirable for e-Business interactions. Instead, industries and enterprises have turned to XML, which has shown great promise as means for conducting e-Business, to develop e-Business protocols and standards. To develop meaningful business standards and protocols, vendors have begun to work together, facilitated by standards bodies, and in unison with business experts to define global (horizontal) and industry-specific (vertical) XML standards.

In e-Trading networks, which are targeted by both horizontal and vertical business standards, business systems can no longer be confined to internal processes, applications and data repositories, rather they span networks of enterprises, incorporating systems of trading- and distribution-partners as well as customers. The technology stack for e-Trading networks comprises such architectural elements as messaging services (realized by SOAP), common registry infrastructure (realized by UDDI), common business and technical dictionaries, universal business processes (realized by ebXML), business-model based business processes, e-Market technical dictionaries and business processes. The latter three are realized by RosettaNet.

The RosettaNet Consortium is an independent, nonprofit consortium of major information technology, electronic component, and semiconductor manufacturing companies working to create and implement industry-wide, open e-Business process standards designed to standardize the electronic business interfaces used between supply chain partners. RosettaNet has developed a conceptual model that that puts individual XML component standards into context. The model identifies nine distinct components required to provide a total e-Business process. RosettaNet provides architectural elements to scale e-Business transactions that include the RosettaNet Implementation Framework, Partner Interface Processes, Dictionaries and e-Business Processes. Of particular interest are PIPs which help define the sequencing, choreography, business documents and elements contained by those documents, necessary to complete an exchange, which fulfill the business requirements of a pre-defined business process.

The objective of ebXML is to develop a single global electronic market based on an open public XML-based infrastructure enabling the global use of electronic business information in an interoperable, secure and consistent manner by all parties. A primary target of ebXML is to lower the barrier of entry to electronic business in order to facilitate trade, particularly with respect to SMEs and developing nations. ebXML consists of a set of XML document type definitions that are common for business-to-business (ANSI X12 EDI) transactions across most industries. Its purpose is to preserve and extend the EDI infrastructure, by leveraging semantics and structure of EDI standards such as X12 and EDIFACT.

The ebXML reference architecture is composed of five major architectural components. These include a messaging service, a registry and repository, trading partner protocols, a Business Process Specification Schema, and business processes. Of particular interest is the Business Process Specification Schema, which is a relatively simple schema that describes public processes and aims to support the specification of business transactions and their choreography into business collaborations.

Several factors, such as support for a business processes model and a transaction model, configuration of system connectivity, and use of common business and technical dictionaries, suggest that convergence between the RosettaNet and ebXML initiatives is technically feasible, advantageous and likely at some stage in the future. RosettaNet is likely to continue working adding value in business process standards for the high-technology industry, while ebXML will focus on cross-industry (horizontal) standards.

Discussion Questions

- What are vertical industry portals and how do they relate to e-Markets?
- Why are standards necessary for e-Business? What kind of functionality should a common e-Business standard provide?
- What is the purpose of RosettaNet and what are its major architectural elements?
- Explain how e-Business can be conducted between two trading companies that employ ebXML as a business integration protocol?
- What is a Collaboration Protocol Profile and what is a Collaboration Protocol Agreement? How are they related?
- What are the major differences between RosettaNet and ebXML? How are these two e-Business standards related to Web services?

Assignments

i. As an example of a PIP consider PIP 3A2, which defines the process that a customer performs with a product supplier to receive information about the price and availability of goods that the customer wants to buy and the product supplier wants to sell. A price and availability request may be complex and require business rule analysis to generate a response. To facilitate communications between the buyer and the supplier, the request includes both query lines and incomplete results lines. After processing the query, the supplier completes the results lines, adds additional product information as appropriate, and returns the information to the buyer. Visit the RosettaNet site (`www.rosettanet.org`) to find more about the definition and usage of this PIP and construct a UML activity sequence and use case diagrams for this PIP.

ii. Figure 20.13 depicts an example of a general business model that consists of demand forecast, forecast reply and order placement processes in RosettaNet. Demand information

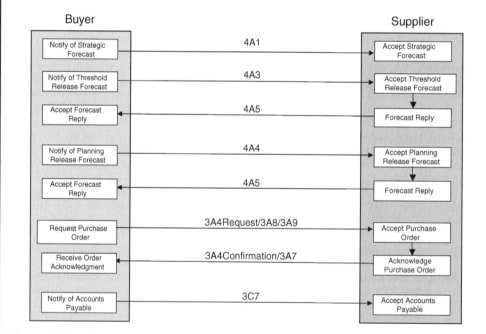

Figure 20.13: Combining Demand Forecast and Order Management Processes (Source [RosettaNet 2004])

is provided using PIP 4A3 or 4A4. Moreover, there is also a case where PIP 4A1 is used as strategic demand information over a long period of time. The combination of PIP 3A4, 3A8, 3A7, and/or 3A9 is used for ordering processes, and PIP 3C7 is used for account payable information. Visit the RosettaNet site (`www.rosettanet.org`) to find more about the usage of demand forecast (PIP 4A3, 4A4) and ordering processes (PIP 3A4, 3A8, 3A7, 3A9) and construct UML activity sequence and use case diagrams on the basis of the diagram in Figure 20.13 and on the descriptions of these processes in the RosettaNet site.

.NET   A Microsoft technology that provides the ability to quickly build, deploy, manage, and use connected, security-enhanced solutions with Web services

Accessibility   The degree to which a client request is served

ACID   The key properties of a database transaction: atomicity, consistency, isolation, durability

Active application integration   End-users drive the execution of businesses processes and transactions

Activity   A logical step in a workflow

Activity diagram   A UML diagram that describes business workflows (similar to a flowchart)

Adapter   A system that maps between interfaces to hide the complexities of an interface from the end user or developer

Ad-hoc workflow   A system that allows users to create and amend processes

Administrative workflow   A predefined workflow with low business value but high repetition, such as the steps required to place an order

Advocate role of change agent   A change agent who focusses on inspiring people to adopt a change

Application framework   A framework that encompasses a slice of functionality that is applied across client domains (e.g. a GUI)

Application server   An integrated development environment that allows enterprises to combine front-office and back-office applications with Web-enabled functionality

Application service provider   A company that packages software and infrastructure with business and professional services to create a subscription service

Architectural pattern   A generalized solution in system design

Asset specificity   The degree to which a transaction is supported by assets that are specific to this transaction alone

Asymmetric encryption   Public key cryptography: sender and receiver each have a pair of public and private keys

Asynchronous business process   A process that does not depend of the timing of other processes

Asynchronous communication   A communication mode in which the sender and receiver do not have to be active at the same time

Atomic transaction   A collection of operations which are trated as a single operation: they must all succeed or all fail

Auction   A method of procurement in which an organization bids against others to buy goods from a supplier

Auditability   A requirement that operations on content are transparent and can be proven

Authentication   a requirement that there is no dispute about the identity of the communicating partners

Authorization   A requirement that information is accessible only to those who need it

Availability   The absence of service downtime

Back-office process   An internal process of an organization, such as distribution, manufacturing, and accounting

Biased market   A market that favors certain buyers or sellers

Black-box framework   A framework for which the developer does not need the implementation details

Black-box re-engineering   A reverse-engineering technique in which the developer need only understand the external interfaces of the application modules

Bounded rationality   A term used to indicate that the capacity of human beings to formulate and solve complex problems is limited

Brokered enterprise   A distributed business enterprise scheme that uses a broker business unit to provide infrastructure and business process management

Business component   A part application that can be used with others to create a business application

Business conversation   The choreography of a message exchange

Business framework   A domain framework that conforms to a particular vertical domain

Business logic   The calculations and validations, workflow and data access required by a business system

Business model   A model that specifies the relationships between participants in a commercial venture, the processes and structure of a organization, or how an organization is seen from the perspective of a marketplace

Business modeling   Abstracting and representing business processes

Business operational view (BOV)   A view from the architectural model of ebXML that addresses the semantics of data in business transactions

Business pattern   a generalized solution for a business application

Business process   One or more related activities that together respond to a business requirement for action and manipulate data or business logic from multiple systems

Business process analysis worksheet and guidelines   An ebXML tool designed to assist an analyst in gathering the data necessary to describe a business process

Business process diagram   A BPMN diagram that shows a series of activities connected by sequence flow

Business Process Execution Language for Web Services (BPEL)   An XML-based flow language for the formal specification of business processes and business interaction protocols

Business process integration   A business process model that specifies the sequence, hierarchy, events, execution logic and information movement between systems residing in interconnected enterprises

Business process management   Purposeful control of processes by automated means to achieve maximum ongoing flexibility with minimum development cost and time

Business process modeling notation (BPMN)   A standards-based business process modeling language that defines business logic and information requirements to the extent that the resultant models are executable

Business process specification schema (BPSS)   A simple ebXML schema that describes public processes

Business registry   A set of documents in ebXML that define base reference specifications and the Business Process and Information meta-models developed by industry groups, SMEs, and other organizations

Business rule   A precise statement that describes, constrains and controls the structure, operations and strategies of an enterprise

Buyer-centric purchasing model   A model in which a buying organization implements software to support its procurement processes and aggregates the catalog data from its contracted suppliers into a single internal catalog for the use of its purchasing officers

Buyer-dominated marketplace   A market that is set up by a large buyer to make it easier to buy from several suppliers

Buyer-managed e-Catalog   A catalog in which a buyer hosts data from a number of suppliers

Buy-grid model   An analysis of the organizational buying process

Buy-side e-Business   An organization that uses e-Business facilities for its buying needs, such as spot purchasing or enterprise-wide procurement needs

Catalog aggregation   A supplier creates an e-Catalog and disseminates it through distribution channels, updating it automatically when necessary

Catalog hub   An industry-specific system that brings together many suppliers

Certification   A requirement that the legal capacity of a party is certified

Certification authority (CA)   An organization that creates and signs digital certificates

Change agent   Someone who plans a change and builds business-wide support for it

Class diagram   A UML diagram that describes the static structure in a business

Client/server architecture   A computational architecture that involves client processes requesting service from server processes (the client performs user interface and simple validation functions and the server performs data processing)

Client-side programming   Associating program code with Web pages that are downloaded into a client and running the code on the client installation

Coarse-grained component   A large component that forms a self-contained application

Code slicing   Moving select data and process logic definitions from one source module into a new source module

Collaboration protocol agreement (CPA)   A document that specifies how two organizations have agreed to conduct business electronically (by combining the CPPs of the two organizations)

Collaboration protocol profile (CPP)   A document that specifies how an organization is able to conduct business electronically

Collaborative network   A long-term collaboration on a strategic level

Collaborative planning, forecasting and replenishment   A process in which manufacturers, distributors, and retailers work together to plan, forecast, and replenish products

Collaborative process   A process that is implicit in the behavior and interaction between multiple business entities described as having different roles

Collaborative product development   A process that integrates an organization's design and test cycles with those of its suppliers to develop products in a short span of time while maintaining quality and reducing cost

Collaborative product development model   A business model that coordinates companies or organizational units involved in developing a product

Collaborative workflow   Processes that have high business value but infrequent execution

Command line interface   An API that manages access to different types of relational databases via a well-defined common interface

Commerce Network-managed e-Catalog   See third-party-managed e-Catalog

Common business dictionary   A document that specifies the structure and properties of content fields, elements, constraints, code lists and objects needed to define transactions between trading partners

Common Gateway Interface (CGI)   a language-independent interface that allows a server to start an external process on behalf of the client

Common Object Request Broker Architecture (CORBA)   An OMG component architecture that enables clients to use services

Common technical dictionary   A document that specifies the structure for defining form, fit and function of any product or service, regardless of the industry

Competitive strategy   A strategy for increasing the structural attractiveness of a firm

Complex type   An XSDL element that defines its content in terms of elements that may consist of further elements and attributes

Complex Web service   A service that keeps transient information between operation invocations

Component deployment   A specification of the environment under which a component operates

Component framework   Prefabricated software that provides a partial solution to a set of related problems

Component implementation   Code that makes a component function

Component interface   A specification of how a component functions

Component model   The basic architecture of a component

Component port   The exposed interfaces of a component

Component signature   The component interface (the names, types and order of its arguments and the manner in which results are returned from it)

Component wrapper   A component that provides service implemented by legacy software

Component-based development   Rapid application development using components

Confidentiality   A requirement that an unauthorized person cannot view or interfere with a communication between two parties

Connectivity management   Coupling a supplier's systems with a company's internal financial and logistic systems

Content management   Managing the data involved in an e-Procurement process

Content service   An infomediary provides product content, such as independent evaluations or directory services

Context-related success factor   A condition under which an electronic market operates that is beyond the control of the market maker

Contract negotiation process   A process in which two partners seek to conduct business with each other

Coordination cost   The cost of all the information processing necessary to coordinate the work of people and machines that perform the primary processes

Corporate-level plan   Objectives that determine the overall direction for the organization

Critical mass   The minimum number of users of a system for it to become self-sustaining

Cross-industry relationship   A relationship between companies in different industries

Cryptography   The science of protecting data by mathematically transforming it into an unreadable format

Customer relationship management (CRM) system   A front-office system that helps an enterprise deal directly with its customers

Cybermediaries business model   A business model based on the idea that multi-organization structures will play an important role in electronic markets

Cybermediary   An Internet-based intermediary

Data federation   An integration model that enables applications to access schemas and data from different data sources using the same interface

Data integration server   A server that provides data access, transformation, and movement; it adds push capabilities to the normal client/server model

Data replication   A synchronous process whereby triggering mechanisms automatically transform and copy data from a source application to a target application

Data tier   A server that holds permanent data associated with applications

Data-access middleware   Middleware that facilitates communication with a database

Decision point   A point in a workflow that determines which branch of the flow a work item may take in the event of alternative paths

Degree of collaboration   The extent of collaboration between functions involved in a particular process

Degree of mediation   The sequential flow of functions involved in a process and how directly they contribute to the outcome

Demilitarized zone   A local area network attached to the unprotected interface of the firewall that communicates with the Internet

Descriptive markup   Markup that categorizes part of a document

Descriptive model   A model that describes the real world in whatever way the modeler wishes

Design pattern   A generalized solution in programming

Digital certificate   A file that identifies the user or organization that owns the certificate

Digital signature   Block of data created by applying a cryptographic signing algorithm to some data using the signer's private key

Disintermediation   Removing the need for middlemen in business

Distributed Component Object Model (DCOM)   An ORB architecture backed by Microsoft

Division-level plan   (also known as a strategic business unit plan) objectives that determine the direction of major areas or groups of related products offered by an organization

Document type definition (DTD)   A special form of document definition in XML that defines a content model and document elements

Domain framework   A framework that encompasses functionality and expertise in a specific client domain

Dyadic supply-chain relationship   A relationship between a company and a direct supplier

Dynamic network   A network in which organizations form temporary alliances to respond to actual market forces

e-Business   The conduct of automated business transactions by means of electronic communications networks

e-Business integration   The capability to link together disparate processes between interacting business entities

e-Business model   A business model that realizes the economic and other objectives of an organization but also aims to leverage the unique qualities of Internet-enabled e-Business processes

e-Business process management   The redesign and management of business processes facilitated by the Internet

e-Business strategy   A strategy that helps an organization identify its e-Business concerns, assess its information needs, and analyze its systems in order to ensure that electronically mediated communication contributes to the corporate strategy

e-Catalog   A catalog that allows buying companies to browse, search, and place orders online

e-Commerce   A forerunner of e-Business that described a focus on buying and selling products and services on the Internet

Economy of scale   A relatively small incremental cost for adding transactions to some maximum

Economy of scope   A relatively small incremental cost for transferring the resources and expertise acquired during the development and operation of one system to other systems

Electronic brokerage   A market in which buyers and suppliers are connected and deals are brokered electronically

Electronic business XML (ebXML)   A UN initiative that strives to create a single global electronic marketplace

Electronic communication   A means of communicating via networked computers

Electronic Data Interchange (EDI)   A method for collaborating companies to transfer structured trading data or documents between applications

Electronic integration   Suppliers and buyers use information technology to create joint, interpenetrating processes

Electronic market hypothesis   A prediction by [Malone 1987] that electronic markets would become the favored mechanisms for coordinating material and information flows among organizations

e-Market   An electronic meeting place for buyers and sellers

e-Marketplace model   A model in which a third party forms a hub that enables buying and selling organizations to trade through a common marketplace

Emergent strategy   A strategy that emerges over time rather than being planned

Encryption   The process of transforming data into an unreadable format

End-to-end business transaction   A succession of automated business processes that provide seamless interoperation and interactive links between the members of an extended demand and supply chain

Enterprise JavaBeans (EJB)   A Java technology that conveys benefits in terms of distribution, transaction processing capabilities, and persistence

Enterprise resource planning (ERP) system   A management information system that integrates and automates many of the business practices associated with the operations or production aspects of a company

Enterprise service bus (ESB)   An open standards-based message bus that enables the implementation, deployment, and management of e-Business integration solutions

e-Procurement   The application of Internet technology to the buying and selling of goods and services

Exchange   An electronic market closely related to a traditional commodity exchange

Extended enterprise   A group of organizations that collaborate

Extensible Stylesheet Language (XSL)   A language that transforms source XML documents into target languages and specifies how data are displayed

Facilitator role of change agent   A change agent who focusses on creating the conditions necessary for change (ideas, well-built IT, organizational conditions)

Federated enterprise   Autonomous business units with common message standards to help them cooperate

Fine-grained component   A small component that supports other components

Firewall   A secure interface between a private, trusted enterprise network and external untrusted networks

Forward engineering   A process of moving from high-level abstractions and logical designs to the physical implementation of a system

Frequency of transactions   Transaction volume

Front-office process   A process that connects an organization to its customers or suppliers

Functional property   A service a module provides and the signature of the service

Functional service view (FSV)   A view from the architectural model of ebXML that addresses the implementation of information exchange

Functional-level planning   (Also known as operating-level planning) Objectives that determine the direction of specific departments of an organization

Gap analysis   A technique that decides a component realization strategy by adding implementation details to an abstract component interface

Geographic transformation   Documents or other carriers of data are transported from one place to another

Governance structure   The organizational form, rules, and institutions that structure a value exchange

Horizontal business standard   A general standard developed for use in any industry

Horizontal e-Market   An e-Market that focusses on products

Hub and spoke topology   An architecture that uses a central node to manage interactions between applications

Industry value chain (or Value system)   A collection of individual business unit value chains that together produce and deliver the goods and services to the final customer

Infomediary   An intermediary who provides information services, usually relating to physical goods and services

Informational service   An infomediary that provides dynamic pricing and notification services; a stateless Web service that involves simple request/response sequences, provides access to content or exposes back-end business applications to applications outside the firewall

Infrastructure service   An infomediary provides facilities for conducting secure transactions via the Internet

Innovative network   A network in which organizations join their research and development activities and share knowledge

Institutional infrastructure   A legal and regulatory framework that makes a market function efficiently

Integrated enterprise   End-to-end business processes managed and monitored across and within all business units

Integration broker   An application-to-application middleware service

Intended strategy   Actions that are the result of a purposeful planning activity

Interactive Web service   A service that exposes the functionality of a Web application's presentation layer

Interest group network   A network that tries to defend its participants' interests and help them gain a stronger position

Interface contract   An explicit statement of codependence between components

Intermediary   An economic agent that buys from suppliers in order to resell to customers, or that helps consumers and suppliers to meet and transact

Intermediation–disintermediation–reintermediation (IDR) cycle   A cycle in which intermediaries appear between business, disappear as communication networks take over their role and then reappear as they provide specialized services

Internal network   A network within a company

Internet EDI link   An inexpensive EDI connection between a supplier and a customer

Internet-enabled business model   A business model that leverages the unique qualities of Internet-enabled e-Business processes

Interoperability   Interorganizational information systems communicating and working with other systems

Interorganizational system (IOS)   A system that connects the systems of different organizations

Intrusion detection system (IDS)   A system that monitors system and network events for unauthorized attempts to access system resources

IS strategy   A set of goals and plans with regard to the use of information systems in an organization

J2EE   Java Enterprise Edition platform

J2EE Connector Architecture   A standardized approach for connecting the J2EE platform to heterogeneous EISs

Java Database Connectivity (JDBC)   a CLI that enables application developers to make their Java applications independent of database vendors

Java message service   A framework that specifies how Java programs can access message-oriented middleware

JavaScript   a browser scripting language

JavaServer Pages (JSP)   A technology that is an extension of the servlet technology created to support authoring of HTML and XML pages

Knowledge management   The identification and analysis of available and required knowledge assets and related processes

Legacy system   Older generation software that provides access to mission critical business data and functionality

Legacy system componentization   Wrapping a legacy system with a layer of component software

Legacy system maintenance   An incremental and iterative process during which small discrete changes are made to the overall system

Legacy system re-engineering   Modernizing a legacy system by transformation into a new form and reinterpretation of parts of it

Legacy system refacing   The process of replacing a standard terminal emulation screen with a GUI

Legacy system repurposing   The process of capturing, encapsulating and exposing a screen-based EIS without modifying the legacy host application

Legacy system transformation   Understanding a legacy system and using the information to develop new software

Linguistic transformation   Data are transformed from one language to another, e.g., translated from Dutch to English

Logical partitioning   Deploying an application as a number of executables split into functional tiers

Logistics   A function responsible for moving materials between locations

Loosely coupled communication   A system in which senders and receivers need to know only which message format and destination to use

Loosely coupled network   A network in which trading partners preserve their independence

Market maker   A company that operates a marketplace

Market transparency   Participants have knowledge about the market around them and their competitors

Marketing model   A model that encompasses both the business model and the strategy of an organization

Market-managed e-Catalog   See third-party-managed e-Catalog

Markup language   A set of conventions used for encoding texts

Mass customization   The delivery of products and services that meet the specific needs of individual customers in mass markets

Matching service   An infomediary matches buyers requirements to products

Message integrity   A requirement that data cannot be corrupted or modified, and transactions cannot be altered

Message-oriented middleware (MOM)   An infrastructure that is responsible for relaying data between applications

Meta-data   Data that describes data

Meta-language   A means of formally describing a language

Middleware   Connectivity software that manages the complexity and heterogeneity inherent in distributed systems

Mission statement   The fundamental purpose of an organization's existence; part of the strategic plan

Model Driven Architecture (MDA)   An OMG system architecture that separates the logic of a specification from its middleware implementation

Modeling language   A notation and standards for modeling business processes and data

Move-to-the-middle hypothesis   A prediction that companies will move to a greater degree of outsourcing and develop long-term partnerships with a small group of suppliers

MRO hub   A provider of a horizontal e-Market that enables systematic sourcing of operating inputs

Multi-tier architecture   A three-tier architecture with processing tier implemented in more than one layer or in a distributed environment

Network   A system of connected computers; a structure of ties among actors in a social system

Network externality   A benefit for individual participants in an e-Market that increases as more businesses join

Network organization   An organization based on a network

Neutral marketplace   A model in which many companies sell products and services to many other companies

Neutral model   A model in which a third party is at the hub, with buying and selling organizations trading with each other through the common marketplace

Non-functional property   A property of a module that relates to the way it performs, rather than its function

Nonrepudiation   A requirement that parties cannot deny that they have talked to each other

Non-transaction-oriented IOSN   An interorganizational system that facilitates communication and other coordinative processes

Normative model   A model that defines how a system is represented, ensuring that the modeler selects predefined constructs

Object request broker (ORB)   An architecture that enables clients to use services using an object-oriented approach

One-to-one marketing   Marketing activities targeted individual customers

Online auction system   A tool that provides simple negotiation mechanisms

Online bidding system   A tool that provides simple negotiation mechanisms

Ontology   A vocabulary that expresses a community's consensus about definitions in a domain

Open buying on Internet (OBI) A common set of business requirements built for e-Business applications

Open trading environment An e-Procurement environment that allows buyers and sellers to establish systems that meet their requirements without imposing them on their trading partners

Operating-level planning (Also known as functional-level planning) Objectives that determine the direction of specific departments of an organization

Operational defence A requirement that a system detect and guard against attacks by illegitimate messages

Operational network A short-term collaboration between companies on an operational and tactical level

Operational plan A way of maximizing the profitability of current operations

Operational-level e-Business relationship A low-level relationship between companies in which they do not share information except that which is required to trade specific items

Operations and logistics The part of the supply chain process that plans, implements and controls the efficient, effective flow and storage of goods, services and related information

Operative network A set of contractual relations covering common agreements on electronic exchanges

Opportunism An attempt to exploit a situation to one's own advantage

Options analysis for reengineering (OAR) A method for analyzing re-engineering options to enable better software re-engineering decisions

Organizational buying behavior The decision-making process by which formal organizations establish the need for purchased products and services, and identify, evaluate, and choose among alternative brands and suppliers

Pareto analysis A small number of important articles represents a major share of the value purchased, while a large number of articles represents only a small part of the value

Passive application integration Applications drive the execution of businesses processes and transactions without user intervention

Personalized markets A market with personalized decision aids

Person-to-system communication Applications that require or facilitate human intervention

Physical partitioning Deploying application executables across a number of platforms

Platform-independent model (PIM) An MDA model that is not related to a specific platform

Platform-specific model (PSM) An MDA model that is related to a specific platform

Point-to-point integration Applications are linked through hand-coded, custom-built connectivity systems and data is interchanged directly between any two systems

Portal A Website that acts as a gateway to information and services

Pragmatic standards Standards for the practices and protocols triggered by specific messages, such as orders and delivery notifications

Prescriptive markup Markup that defines what processing needs to be carried out at a particular point in a document

Presentation tier   A server that is responsible for the graphical user interface (GUI) layer

Price-discovery mechanism   A way of determining the cost of an item

Primary activity   An activity that involves a direct relationship with an organization's customers

Privacy protection service   An infomediary protects the privacy of clients

Private business process   A process internal to an enterprise

Procedural markup   Markup that defines what processing needs to be carried out at a particular point in a document

Process outsourcing model   An e-Business-enabled business model that transfers the responsibility for one or more processes to external suppliers

Process-based workflow   A model that shows actors, sequencing of activities, parallel paths, and logical decision points

Process-centric company   An organization whose managers conceptualize it as a set of business processes

Processing tier   A server that holds the business logic and is responsible for the processing associated with applications

Process-related success factor   A characteristic of the trading processes in a market that is within the control of the market maker

Procurement and order management   A system that uses an integrated electronic ordering process and other online resources to increase efficiencies in their purchasing operations

Production workflow   A system for managing core tasks and optimizing productivity in an enterprise

Program management   The management of a portfolio of projects that need to be controlled as a whole

Program slicing   A decomposition technique that determines the statements in a program that are relevant for a particular computation

Program understanding   The process of acquiring knowledge about a software artifact through analysis, abstraction, and generalization

Programmatic Web service   A service that encapsulates business processes and exposes the business logic of the applications and components that underlie them

Project management   The management of a structured set of activities that deliver a defined capability to an organization on an agreed schedule

Public business process   A process that enables interaction with trading partners

Public key infrastructure (PKI)   A system of digital certificates and certification authorities that verify and authenticate parties involved in Internet transactions

Publish–subscribe   A type of asynchronous communication in which an application publishes information to which other applications subscribe

Pull models   A supply chain management model in which products are built in response to customer orders

Purchasing portfolio model   Kraljic's matrix that defines a company's position in the buying market

Push model   A supply chain management model in which assembly and distribution are based on forecasts

Quality of Service (QoS)   A critical instrument to ensure the enterprise infrastructure and deliver the scalability, security, transaction, and content-based requirements of the business

Rational Unified Process   A configurable software development process platform that delivers best practices and a configurable architecture

Reciprocal relationship   A collaborative relationship between companies

Reference model   A representation of a specific type of organization

Registration authority   An organization that evaluates the credentials of an organization requesting a certificate

Reliability   The ability of a service to function correctly and consistently despite system or network failures

Remote Method Invocation (RMI)   A simple and direct RPC model for distributed computation with Java objects

Remote Procedure Call (RPC)   A middleware mechanism used to invoke a procedure on a remote system and return the results

Request/response application   An application that uses synchronous communication

Requisition management   Managing the process that enables end users to place and transact orders

Resource binding   A description of which resources are available to a component

Resource-based view   A view of an organization as a collection of resources and capabilities; a theory of economic development in which innovation is the source of value creation

Restructuring   The process of transforming one form of representation to another at the same relative level of abstraction while ensuring that the resulting representation preserves the semantics and external behavior of the original

Reverse auction   A method of procurement in which an organization sets a price it is willing to pay and suppliers then bid to fulfill it

RosettaNet Consortium   An independent consortium working to create open standards for electronic business interfaces between supply chain partners

RosettaNet Implementation Framework (RNIF)   A specification that describes how RosettaNet partners exchange information

RosettaNet Partner Interface Processes (PIPS)   Standardized electronic business processes used between trading partners

Scalability   The ability of a service to consistently serve the requests despite variations in the volume of requests

Schema component   Part of an abstract data model

Schema language   A tool for modeling business information

Search engine   Software that enables buyers to search for products

Search service   An infomediary helps buyers in the search process

Secure sockets layer (SSL)   A common Internet security protocol

Security   A vital element of an e-Business system

Security Assertions Markup Language (SAML)   An XML framework for specifying and sharing data used to determine authorization

Seller-centric purchasing model   A model in which buyers use a supplier's system, over the Internet, to browse the supplier's catalog and place orders

Sell-side e-Business   An organization that sells its products via e-Business applications

Semantic inter-mediation   Using a common ontology as a mediation layer

Semantic interoperability   Enabling a system to appropriately understand the information that is being shared

Semantic mapping   Mapping to an ontology to preserve the native semantics of the data and eliminate the need for custom developed code

Semantic standards   Standards for the meanings of terms used in an interorganizational system

Semantic transformation   A change in the contents of data due to assessments, judgements, mathematical operations leading to some form of decision

Sequence diagram   A UML diagram that describes the dynamic interactions between employees and the items they manipulate

Server stub   A method that unmarshals the arguments in a request message, calls the corresponding service procedure and marshals the return results for the reply message

Server-side programming   Storing program code on a Web server and executing it when the client sends a particular request

Service level agreement   A contract between a service provider and a client that specifies what services the service provider will furnish

Service-Oriented Architecture (SOA)   An architecture in which dynamic, automated discovery and use of network-available services can take place

Servlet   A Java component that can be plugged into a Java-enabled Web server to provide server extensions

Simple Object Access Protocol (SOAP)   A transport protocol

Simple type   An XSDL element that defines its content in terms of elements that can only contain data

Skeleton method   *see* server stub

Stable network   A network in which there are long-term, stable relationships between limited numbers of carefully selected suppliers, producers, and distributors

Staged integration   A technique in which data is exported into an intermediate format for eventual transformation and importing into the new target application's schemas

Stateful service   A service that keeps transient information between operation invocations

Stateless service   A service that does not keep transient information between operation invocations

Store and forward   A type of asynchronous communication in which the sending application places messages on a queue from which the receiving application takes them

Strategic alignment   A state of harmony between an organization's strategic objectives and its investment in information technology

Strategic analysis   An analysis of internal and external factors that are important to the organization; part of the strategic plan

Strategic business unit plan   (Also known as a division-level plan) Objectives that determine the direction of major areas or groups of related products offered by an organization

Strategic choice   Evaluation and selection of options that an organization will pursue; part of the strategic plan

Strategic impact of IT   The new business models and strategies enabled by IT

Strategic implementation   The tasks that must be executed in order to realize a plan; part of the strategic plan

Strategic network   Companies operating in different areas cooperate on research and development, production and marketing

Strategic plan   An organization's external positioning in its competitive environment, comprising a mission statement, a strategic analysis, a strategic choice, and a strategy implementation

Strategic planning process   The process of producing a strategic plan

Strategic positioning   An organization doing things differently from its competitors in a way that delivers unique value to its customers

Strategic-level e-Business relationship   A collaborative relationship between companies

Stylesheet   A document that defines formatting instructions

Supplier-dominated marketplace   A market that is set up by a large supplier to make it easier to sell to several customers

Supplier-managed e-Catalog   A catalog in which a supplier hosts data that is delivered over the Internet to the buyers

Supply chain   The chain of suppliers and producers

Supply chain management (SCM) system   A system that allows an enterprise to anticipate demand and deliver the right product to the right place at the right time, at the lowest price to satisfy its customers

Supply chain operations reference (SCOR) framework   A business process methodology built by, and for, supply-chain analysis and design

Support activity   An activity that does not involve a direct relationship with an organization's customers

Support framework   A framework that encompasses system-level functionality

Switching cost   The investment that an electronic market requires from its participants

Symmetric encryption   Secret key cryptography: sender and receiver use the same key

Synchronous business process   A process that depends on the timing of other processes

Synchronous communication   A communication mode in which the sender and the receiver have to be connected at the same time

Syntactic transformation   Data are transformed from one data structure to another or a standard representation of a well-known construct, e.g., invoice descriptions or currency exchange

Syntax standards   Standards for integrating applications based on the structure or 'language' of the messages exchanged

System-to-system communication   Supply chain applications in business-to-business settings that operate with no human intervention

Tactical plan   A way of structuring the resources of an organization

Tactical-level e-Business relationship   A longer-term relationship between companies that involves joint planning

Technical standards   Standards for technology: middleware, network protocols, security protocols, etc.

Technological transformation   Data are transferred from one carrier to another, e.g., from a physical document to some electronic form

Teleworking model   An e-Business-enabled business model that involves large numbers of individuals or groups collaborating with the assistance of networking and communication technologies

Thick adapter   Advanced functionality interposed between the integration broker infrastructure and source or target applications

Thick network   A network of intensive relationships and communication patterns

Thin adapter   An API wrapper that maps the interface of a source or target system to a common interface supported by an integration broker

Thin network   A network of companies that communicate extensively but are not integrated in various ways

Third-party-managed e-Catalog   An aggregated catalog containing the data of many suppliers, which is made available to buying companies on a commercial basis

Three-tier architecture   An application partitioned into three logical tiers: the presentation tier, the processing tier, and the data tier

Tightly coupled communication   A system in which senders and receivers need to know a remote application's methods

Tightly coupled network   A stable network of trading partners with shared planning and control cycles

Trading partner agreement   The ebXML term for a service level agreement

Trading partner information   The Collaboration Protocol Profile and Collaboration Protocol Agreement

Traditional role of change agent   A change agent who focusses on implementing technology changes, without considering the organizational aspects

Transaction cost   The cost of all the information processing necessary to coordinate the work of people and machines that perform the primary processes

Transaction set   The set of electronic documents sent between trading partners

Transactional intermediary   An intermediary who moves, stores and delivers physical goods

Transactionality   The property of ensuring that transactions cannot be partially complete

Transaction-cost economics   A theory that attempts to explain an organization's choice between internalizing and buying goods and services from the market

Transaction-oriented IOS   An interorganizational system that facilitates transactions

Transaction-processing (TP) monitor   Technology that provides the distributed client/server environment with the capacity to efficiently and reliably develop, execute and manage transaction applications

Trust   A vital element of an e-Business relationship

Trusted third party (TTP)   An independent and impartial organization that offers trust services

Two-tier architecture   An application partitioned such that the client performs user interface and simple validation functions and the server performs data processing

Typology of organizations   Mintzberg's classification of organizations by their dependency on the complexity and uncertainty of the environment in which they operate

UN/CEFACT modeling methodology (UMM)   A methodology for business process and information modeling based on the Open EDI Reference Model

Unbiased market   A market that is open to all parties

Unbundling value chain   Outsourcing non-core activities

Unified Modeling Language (UML)   A standard language and graphical notation for creating models of business and technical systems

Unified Software Development Process   A development process that builds on UML and is complementary to it

Uniform Resource Identifier   A string of characters that uniquely identifies a resource on the Internet

Uniform Resource Locator   A URI that uses a traditional addressing scheme

Uniform Resource Name   A URI that uses a newer addressing scheme to address Internet resources in a location-independent manner

Universal business process   A generic, industry-neutral business process

Universal Description, Discovery and Integration (UDDI)   A cross-industry initiative to create a registry standard for Web services description and discovery

Use case diagram   A UML diagram that describes the business context and shows processes in a non-sequential representation

Value chain   A model that describes a series of value-adding activities connecting a company's supply side with its demand side

Value stream   The set of specific actions required to bring a specific product to market

Value web business model An emerging form of fluid and flexible organization that consists of markets, hierarchies, networks, information technology, and new-old business models

Value-added network An EDI system that alleviates network problems by operating on a subscription basis

Value-adding function A way in which an intermediary enhances the business environment

Value-chain analysis Identification of activities and the economic implications of those activities

Value-chain integration model An e-Business-enabled business model that uses Internet technology to improve communication and collaboration between supply chain parties

Vertical business standard A standard that is specific to a process in a vertical industry

Vertical e-Market An e-Market that focusses on a particular industry

Virtual organization model An e-Business-enabled business model that provides for a temporary or permanent collection of geographically dispersed individuals, groups and organizational units who are linked electronically

Vulnerability assessment A methodical approach that enables enterprises to test their networks non-intrusively

Web service implementation A software component that realizes the functionality provided by a Web service

Web service interface A description of functionality provided by a Web service

Web services A distributed computing infrastructure made up of many different functional modules communicating over the Internet to form a single logical system

Web Services Choreography Description Language (WS-CDL) A language that specifies the common observable behavior of all participants engaged in business collaboration

Web Services Description Language (WSDL) The service representation language used to describe the complete interfaces exposed by Web services

Web services registry A register of Web services

Web services requester An enterprise looking for Web services

Well-formed XML document A document that consists of a prologue and a document (root) element

White-box framework A framework of which the developer must know the implementation details

White-box re-engineering A reverse-engineering technique in which the developer need to understand the internals of the application modules

Workflow A sequence of processing steps during which information and physical objects are passed from one processing step to the other

Workflow reference model A model that identifies interfaces which enable applications to interoperate at a variety of levels

Workflow system An automated business process in which documents, information, or tasks are passed from one participant to another

WS-Coordination   An initiative to develop standards for coordinating Web services

WS-Security   A Web services security specification that enables dissimilar infrastructures to participate in a common trust relationship

WS-Transaction   An initiative to develop standards for Web service transactions

XA-compliant   A resource that complies with the XA specification in coordinating two-phase commit transactions

XML access control markup language (XACML)   An extension of SAML that allows access control policies to be specified

XML attribute   A method of putting data into an XML document

XML document   A structured document that enables businesses to exchange information

XML document type   A definition of the elements contained in a document

XML element   A basic building block of an XML document, which is used to describe an entity or an attribute in logical data modeling terms

XML encryption   An XML schema for encrypting data

XML key management specification (X-KISS)   A technology that supports services used by a party relying on a cryptographic key (location and validation)

XML key management specification (XKMS)   A technology that defines trusted services for managing cryptographic keys, including public keys

XML key registration service specification (X-KRSS)   A technology that supports services used by the holder of a cryptographic key (registration, revocation, reissue, and key recovery)

XML namespace   A way to distinguish between elements that use the same local name but are different

XML schema   An XML document that defines the elements and attributes that may be contained in a document that conforms to the schema

XML signature   An XML schema for encrypting data

XML/EDI   A standardized framework in which EDI-based business documents and messages are described using XML syntax

XPath   A sub-language that defines search expressions that locate document elements

XSL transformation (XSLT)   A language for transforming source XML documents into target languages

Yield manager   Someone who creates a spot market for common operating resources with a high degree of price and demand volatility

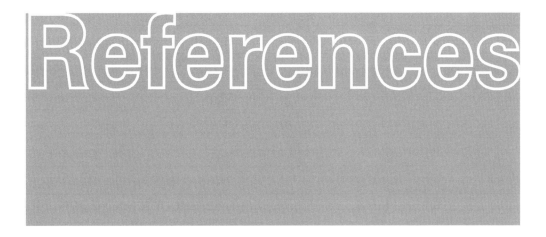

References

[Abell 1980] D. F. Abell. *Defining the Business: The Starting Point of Strategic Planning.* 1980.

[Aberdeen 2001] Aberdeen Group. e-Procurement. *Market Viewpoint* 14(2). March, 2001.

[Adams 2001] J. Adams, S. Koushik, G. Vasudeva, G. Galambos. *Patterns for e-Business.* IBM Press, 2001.

[Alba 1997] J. Alba, J. Lynch, B. Weitz, C. Janiszewski. Interactive home shopping: Consumer, retailer, and manufacturer incentives to participate in electronic market places. *Journal of Marketing* 61(3). 1997.

[Aldrich 1999] D. F. Aldrich. *Mastering the Digital Market Place: Practical strategies for competitiveness in the new economy.* John Wiley & Sons, 1999.

[Aldrich 2002] S. E. Aldrich. Anatomy of web services. Patricia Seybold Group, Inc. 2002. Available at www.psgroup.com.

[Allen 2001a] P. Allen. *Realizing e-Business with Components.* Addison Wesley, 2001.

[Allen 2001b] R. Allen. Workflow: An introduction. *In Workflow Handbook 2001.* Workflow Management Coalition, 2001.

[Alur 2001] Alur D., Crupi J., Malks D. *Core J2EE Patterns.* Prentice Hall, 2001.

[Amit 1993] R. Amit and P. Schoenmaker. Strategic and organizational rent. *Strategic Management Journal* 14. 1993.

[Amit 2001] R. Amit, C. Zott. Value creation in e-Business. *Strategic Management Journal* 22. 2001.

[Anderson 2002] G. Anderson, P. Anderson. *Enterprise Java Beans Component Architecture.* Prentice Hall Inc., 2002.

[Anderson 2003] S. Anderson *et al.* (eds). Supply chain management use case model. April 16, 2003.

[Andrews 2003] T. Andrews *et al.* Business process execution language for web services. Version 1.1, March 2003.

[Ansoff 1968] H. I. Ansoff *Corporate Strategy: An analytic approach to business policy for growth and expansion.* Penguin Books, 1968.

[Ansoff 1984] H. I. Ansoff. *Implanting Strategic Management.* Prentice Hall, London, 1984.

[Ansoff 1987] I. Ansoff. *Corporate Strategy.* Penguin Business, 1987 (revised edition).

[Applegate 2003] L. M. Applegate, R. D. Austin, F. Warren McFarlan. *Corporate Information Strategy and Management*, 6th edition. McGraw-Hill, 2003.

[Armstrong 2004] Amstrong et al. The J2EE 1.4 tutorial. Sun MicroSystems, June 2004. Available at http://java.sun.com/docs/books/j2eetutorial/index.html#second.

[ASP 2000] ASP Industry Consortium. Internet Survey. 2000. Available at `www.aspindustry.org/surveyresults.cfm`.

[Asuncion 1997] R. Asuncion. Potentials of electronic markets in the philippines. *International Journal of Electronic Commerce & Business Media* 7(2). 1997.

[Atkins 1998] M.H. Atkins. The role of appropriability in sustaining competitive advantage: An electronic auction system case study. *Journal of Strategic Information Systems* 7, 1998.

[Atkinson 2002] B. Atkinson et al. Web services security (ws-security). April 2002. Available at `www.ibm.com/developerworks/library/ws-secure/`.

[Bachmann 2000] F. Bachmann *et al*. Technical concepts of component-based software engineering. Technical Report, Carnegie-Mellon Univ., CMU/SEI-2000-TR-008 ESC-TR-2000-007, 2nd Edition, May 2000.

[Bailey 1997] J. P. Bailey, J. Y. Bakos. An exploratory study of the emerging role of electronic intermediaries. *International Journal of Electronic Commerce* 1(3). Spring 1997.

[Baker 1993] W. E. Baker. The network organization in theory and practice. In N. Nohria, R. G. Eccles (eds). *Networks and Organizations*. Harvard Business School Press, Boston, 1993.

[Bakos 1991] J. Y. Bakos. A strategic analysis of electronic marketplaces. *MIS Quarterly* 15(3). 1991.

[Bakos 1998] J. Y. Bakos. Towards friction free markets: The emerging role of electronic marketplaces on the internet. *Communications of the ACM* 41(8). 1998.

[Bakos 1999] J. Y. Bakos, E. Brynjolfsson. Bundling information goods: Pricing, profits and efficiency. *Management Science* 45(12). 1999.

[Barney 1991] J. B. Barney. Firm resources and sustained competitive advantage. *Journal of Management* 17. 1991.

[Barney 1997] J. B. Barney. *Gaining and Sustaining Competitive Advantage*. Addison Wesley, Reading, MA., 1997.

[Barney 2001] J. B. Barney, M. Wright, D. J. Ketchen. The resource-based view of the firm: Ten years after 1991. *Journal of Management* 27, 2001.

[Baron 2000] J. P. Baron, M. J. Shaw, A. D. Bailey jr. Web-based e-Catalogue systems in B2B procurement. *Communications of the ACM* 43(5). May 2000.

[BEA 2001] BEA Systems. BEA weblogic server: Programming weblogic web services. December 2001. Available at `www.bea.com`.

[BEA 2002] BEA Systems. Introducing B2B integration. 2002. Available at . [Beach 1999] P. V. Beach, S. V. Gudmundsson, R. Walczuk. The development of electronic markets in logistics. *International Journal of Logistics Management* 10(2). 1999.

[Bell 2003] D. Bell. *UML Basics: An introduction to the Unified Modeling Language*. Rational Software, June 2003. Available at `www.therationaledge.com/content/jun_03/f_umlintro_db.jsp`.

[Benjamin 1990] R. I. Benjamin, D. W. De Long, M. S. Scott Morton, M.S. Electronic data interchange: How much competitive advantage? *Long Range Planning* 23(1). 1990.

[Benjamin 1995] R. Benjamin, R. Wigand. Electronic markets and virtual value chain on the information superhighway. *Sloan Management Review*, Winter, 1995.

[Benson 1985] R. J. Benson, M. M. Parker. Enterprise-wide information management: An introduction to the concept. IBM LASC Report G320-2768, 1985.

[Bergey 1999] J. Bergey, D. Smith, N. Weiderman, S. N. Woods. Options analysis for reengineering (OAR): Issues and conceptual approach. Technical report CMU/SEI-99-TN-014. Software Engineering Institute, Carnegie Mellon University, 1999. Available at `www.sei.cmu.edu/publications/documents/99.reports/99tr014/99tr014abstract.html`.

[Bergey 2001] J. Bergey, L. O'Brien, D. Smith. OAR: Options analysis for reengineering: Mining components for a product line or new software architecture. International Conference on Software Engineering, 2001 (ICSE, 2001). Toronto, Canada, May 2001.

[Berghel 2000] H. Berghel. Predatory disintermediation. *Communications of the ACM* 43(5). 2000.

[Berners-Lee 1998] T. Berners-Lee, R. Fielding, L. Masinter. RFC 2396: Uniform resource identifiers (URI): Generic syntax. August 1998. Available at `www.ietf.org/rfc/rfc2396.txt`.

[Beugnard 1999] A. Beugnard, J. M. Jezequel, N. Plouzeau, D. Watkins. Making components contract aware. Computer 32(7). July 1999.

[Binbasioglu 2002] M. Binbasioglu, E. Winston. Knowledge-based IS implementation support: An application to the IS change agent role problem. In *Proceedings of the 35th Hawaii International Conference on Systems Sciences*. 2002.

[Binkley 1996] D. W. Binkley, K. B. Gallagher. Program slicing. Advances in Computers. 1996.

[Bock 2003] C. Bock. UML 2 activity and action models. Journal of Object Technology 2(4). July–August 2003.

[Boehm 1996] B. W. Boehm. Anchoring the software process. *IEEE Software*, 13(4). July 1996.

[Boey 1999] P. Boey, M. Grasso, M. Sabatino, I. Sayeed. Architecting e-Business solutions. The Cutter Edge, 2(7). Cutter Consortium, 1999. Available at `www.cutter.com/research/1999/crb990831.html`.

[Bond 2002] D. Bond. When to use synchronous EAI messaging. *EAI Journal*, July 2002.

[Bons 1997] R. W. H. Bons. Designing trustworthy trade procedures for open electronic commerce: A methodology for the automated analysis of inter-organisational controls. PhD thesis. Erasmus University, Rotterdam, 1997.

[Booch 1998] G. Booch, J. Rumbaugh, I. Jacobson. *Unified Modeling Language User Guide*. Addison Wesley, 1998.

[Boubez 2000] T. Boubez. Web services architecture overview: The next stage of evolution for e-Business. IBM DeveloperWorks Web Architecture Library, October 2000.

[Boutell 1996] T. Boutell. *CGI Programming in C and Perl*. Addison Wesley, 1996.

[Brand 1995] N. A. Brand, J. R. P. vd Kolk. *Werkstroomanalyse en ontwerp (workflow analysis and design)*. Kluwer Moret, Ernst & Young Management Consultants, 1995.

[Brodie 1995] M.L. Brodie and M. Stonebraker. Migrating legacy systems: Gateways, interfaces and the incremental approach. Morgan Kaufman, 1995.

[BSI 1999] British Standard Institution (BSI). Information security management – Part 1: Code of practice for information security management. BS7799-1, 1999.

[Buschmann 1996] F. Buschmann *et al. Pattern-Oriented Software Architecture, volume 1: A System of Patterns*. Wiley Publishing, Inc., 1996.

[Buzzel 1995] R. D. Buzzel, G. Ortmeyer. Channel partnerships streamline distribution. Sloan Management Review 36, 1995.

[Cabrera 2002a] F. Cabrera et al. Web services coordination (WS-Coordination). August 2002. Available at `www.ibm.com/developerworks/library/ws-coor/`.

[Cabrera 2002b] F. Cabrera et al. Web services transaction (WS-Transaction). August 2002. Available at `www.ibm.com/developerworks/library/ws-transpec/`.

[Campbell 1999] A. T. Campbel, Coulson, M. E. Kounavis. Managing complexity: Middleware explained. *IEEE IT Pro*, September/October 1999.

[Canzer 2003] B. Canzer. e-Business: Strategic thinking and practice. Houghton Miffin Co., Boston, MA, 2003.

[Caron 1994] . J. R. Caron, S. L. Jarvenpaa, D. B. Stoddard. Business reengineering at CIGNA corporation: Experiences and lessons learned from the first five years. *MIS Quarterly*. September 1994.

[Carr 1998] D. F. Carr. *Web-enabling Legacy Data when resources are Tight*. Internet World, August 1998.

[Castelli 1993] F. Castelli, C. Leporelli. Critical mass of users versus critical mass of services in a multiproduct information service system. *Information Economics and Policy* 5, 1993.

[Cauldwell 2001] P. Cauldwell, et al. (2001). XML web services. Wrox Press Ltd., 2001.

[Cavinato 1992] J. L Cavinato A total cost/value model for supply chain competitiveness. *Journal of Business Logistics*, 13(2). 1992.

[CEC 2004] Commission of the European Communities. Legal barriers in e-Business: The results of an open consultation of enterprises. Commission Staff Working Paper SEC (2004) 498. Brussels, April 2004.

[Chaffey 2002] D. Chaffey. e-Business and e-Commerce management. Financial Times. Prentice Hall, 2002.

[Chandler 1979] A. Chandler, H. Daems. Administrative coordination, allocation and monitoring: A comparative analysis of accounting and organization in the USA and Europe. *Accounting, Organizations and Society*, 4, 1979.

[Chappell 2001] D. A. Chappell *et al. ebXML Foundations*. Wrox Press Ltd., 2001.

[Chappell 2004] D. A. Chappell. *Enterprise Service Bus*. O'Reilley, 2004.

[Cheesman 2001] J. Cheesman, J. Daniels. *UML Components: A Simple Process for Specifying Component-based Software*. Addison Wesley 2001.

[Chen 2001] S. Chen. *Strategic management of e-Business*. John Wiley & Sons, 2001.

[Chieu 2002] E. Chiu. ebXML simplified. J. Wiley, 2003.

[Chikofsky 1990] E. J. Chikofsky, J. H. Cross. Reverse engineering and design recovery: A taxonomy. IEEE Software 7(1). January 1990.

[Chircu 1999a] A. Chircu, R. Kauffman. Strategies for internet middlemen in the intermediation/disintermediation/reintermediation cycle. *Electronic Markets* 9(2). 1999.

[Chircu 1999b] A. Chircu, R. Kauffman. Analyzing firm-level strategy for internet-focused reintermediation. In R. Sprague (ed.). *Proceedings of the 32nd Hawai'i International Conference on Systems Science*, Los Alamitos, CA. IEEE Computer Society Press, 1999.

[Chircu 2000a] A. Chircu, R. Kauffman. The EBay of blank: Digital intermediation in electronic commerce. In S. Barnes (ed.). *E-Commerce and V-Business*. Butterworth Heinemann, London, 2000.

[Chircu 2000b] A. Chircu, R. Kauffman. Reintermediation strategies in business-to-business electronic commerce. *International Journal of Electronic Commerce* 4(4). 2000.

[Choudhury 1998] V. Choudhury, K. S. Hartzel, B. R. Konsynsky, B. R. Uses and consequences of electronic markets: An empirical investigation in the aircraft parts industry. *MIS Quarterly* 22(4). December 1998.

[Christiaanse 1995] E. Christiaanse, J. Huigen. Institutional dimensions in information technology implementation in complex network settings. In *Proceedings of the 3rd European Conference on Information Systems*, 1995.

[Christopher 1998] M. Christopher. *Logistics and Supply Chain Management*. Prentice Hall, 1998.

[Clark 1999] J. Clark. XSL transformations (XSLT). Version 1.0. W3C Recommendation. November 1999. Available at www.w3.org/TR/xslt.

[Clark 1996] T. H. Clark, D. B. Stoddard. Interorganizational business process redesign: Merging technological and process innovation. *Journal of Management Information Systems* 23(2). 1996.

[Clark 2000] T. H. Clark and H. G. Lee. Performance, interdependence and coordination in business-to-business electronic commerce and supply chain management. *Information Technology and Management* 1(1). 2000.

[Clemons 1993] E. Clemons, S. Reddi, M. Row. The impact of information technology on the organization of economic activity: The 'move to the middle' hypothesis. *Journal of Management Information Systems* 10(2). 1993.

[Coase 1973] R.H. Coase. The nature of the firm. *Economica* 4. 1973.

[Cobb 1995] J. Cobb, E. Edward. TP monitors and ORBs: A superior client/server alternative. *Object Magazine* 4(9):57–61, February 1995.

[Comella-Dorda 2000] S. Comella-Dorda, K. Wallnau, R.C. Seacord, J. Robert. A survey of legacy system modernization approaches. Technical Note CMU/SEI-2000-TN-003, Software Engineering Institute, Carnegie Mellon University, April 2000. Available at `www.sei.cmu.edu/publications/pubweb.html`.

[Conner 1994] D. Conner. *Managing at the speed of change*. Villard Books (Random House Inc.). New York, 1994.

[Cort 1999] S. Cort. Industry corner: Industrial distribution: How goods will go to market in the electronic marketplace. *Business Economics*. January 1999.

[Coyle 2002] F.P. Coyle. *XML Web Services, and the Data Revolution*. Addison Wesley, 2002.

[Cruijssen 2004] F. Cruijssen. A survey on european inter-organizational data sharing implementations in transportation. Klict, 2004.

[Curbera 2003] P. Curbera, R. Khalaf, N. Mukhi, S. Tai, S. Weerawarana. Web services, the next step: A framework for robust service composition. In M.P. Papazoglou and D. Georgakopoulos (eds). *Communications of ACM, Special Section on Service-Oriented Computing*. October 2003.

[D'Aveni 1994] R.A. D'Aveni. *Hyper competition: Managing the dynamics of strategic maneuvering*. The Free Press, New York. 1994.

[Dai 2002] Q. Dai, R. J. Kauffman. Business models for internet-based B2B electronic markets. *International Journal of Electronic Commerce* 6(4). Summer 2002.

[Damsgaard 1998] J. Damsgaard. Electronic markets in Hong Kong's air cargo community: Thanks, but no thanks. *International Journal of Electronic Commerce & Business Media* 8(3). 1998.

[Dan 2001] A. Dan *et al*. Business-to-business integration with tpaML and a business-to-business framework. *IBM Systems Journal* 40(1). 2001.

[Daniel 1999] E. Daniel, G. Klimis. The impact of electronic commerce on market structure: An evaluation of the electronic market hypothesis. *European Management Journal* 17(3). 1999.

[Davenport 1993] T. H. Davenport. *Process Innovation: Reengineering work through information technology*. Harvard Business School Press, 1993.

[Davenport 2004] T. H. Davenport. The e-process evolution. *Business Process Management Journal* 10(1). 2004.

[Davidow 1992] W. H Davidow, M.S. Malone. *The Virtual Corporation*. Edward Burlingame Books/Harper Business, NewYork, 1992.

[Davies 1987] S. Davies. *Future Perfect*. Addison Wesley, Reading, 1987.

[Davis 1993] T. Davis. Effective supply chain management. *Sloan Management Review* 34, 1993.

[Davydov 2001] M. M. Davydov. *Corporate Portals and e-Business Integration*. McGraw-Hill, 2001.

[De Lucia 2001] A. De Lucia. Program slicing: Methods and applications. *1st IEEE International Workshop on Source Code Analysis and Manipulation*, Florence, Italy, 2001.

[DeRose 2001] S. DeRose, E. Maler, D. Orchard. XML linking language (XLink) version 1.0. June 2001. Available at `www.w3.org/TR/2001/REC-xlink-20010627`.

[Dobbs 1998] J. H. Dobbs. Competition's new battleground: The integrated value chain. Cambridge Technology Partners, `www.ctp.com`, 1998.

[Dobler 1990] D. W. Dobler, D.N. Burt, L. Lee Jr. *Purchasing and Materials Management*, 5th edition. McGraw-Hill 1990.

[Dolgicer 2004] M. Dolgicer, G. Bayer. Message brokers vs. application servers. *Business Integration Journal*, March 2004.

[Dominique 1998] N.P. Dominique. Exchange costs as determinants of electronic market bearings. *International Journal of Electronic Commerce & Business Media* 8(1). 1998.

[Doorduin 2004] D. Doorduin. Redesign of TFA. Master's thesis. Tilburg University, 2004.

[Douma 1998] S. Douma, H. Schreuder. *Economic Approaches to Organizations*. Prentice Hall, Englewood Cliffs, New Jersey, 1998.

[D'Souza 1999] D. D'Souza, A.C. Wills. Objects, components, and frame-works with UML: The catalysis approach. Addison Wesley, Boston, MA, 1999.

[Dubray 2005] J. J. Dubray, S. St. Amand (eds). ebXML business process specification schema v2.0. Working Draft 054, January 2005. Available at `www.oasis-open.org/ebxmlbp/docs`.

[Due 2000] R.T. Due. The economics of component-based development. Information Systems Management, Winter 2000.

[Earles 2000] J. Earles. Framework evolution. Castek Software Factory Inc., 1999. Available at `www.cdb-hq.com/articles/2000`.

[ebXML 2000] ebXML. ebXML technical architecture specification. OASIS, October 2000.

[ebXML 2002] ebXML Collaboration Protocol Profile and Agreement Technical ommittee. Collaboration-protocol profile and agreement specification version 2.0. September 2002. Available at `www.oasis-open.org/committees/ebxml-cppa/documents/ebCPP-2.0.pdf`.

[EC 1997] European Commission. A european initiative in electronic commerce. COM (97) 157, Communication to the European Parliament, the Council, the Economics and Social Committee and the Committee of the Regions. Available at `www.cordis.lu/esprit/src/ecomcomx.htm`.

[Economides 1991] N. Economides. Compatibility and the creation of shared networks. in M.E. Guerin-Calvert and S.S. Wildman, *Electronic services networks: A business and public policy challenge*. New York, 1991.

[Ehebuske 2001] D. Ehebuske, D. Rogers and C. von Riegen. UDDI version 2.0 – data structure specification. UDDI.org, June 2001.

[Elliot 2002] S. Elliot. Introduction to B2C strategies and models. in S. Elliot (ed.), *Electronic Commerce: B2C Strategies and Models*. Wiley and Sons, 2002.

[Elliot 2002] S. Elliot (ed.). *Electronic Commerce: B2C Strategies and Models*. John Wiley & Sons, 2002.

[Eriksson 2000] H. E. Eriksson, M. Penker. Business modeling with UML. John Wiley & Sons, Inc., 2000.

[Erlikh 2001] L. Elrikh. Leveraging legacy systems in modern architectures. Relativity Technologies, 2001. Available at `www.relativity.com`.

[Erlikh 2002] L. Erlikh. Integrating legacy systems using web services. *EAI Journal*, August 2002.

[Estes 2001] D. Estes. Legacy.Net. *Cutter IT Journal* 14(1). January 2001.

[Evans 1997] P. B. Evans, T. S. Wurster. Strategy and the new economics of information. *Harvard Business Review*, Sept–Oct, 1997.

[Evans 1999] P. Evans, T. Wurster. Blown to bits: How the new economics of information transforms strategy. Harvard Business School Press, Boston, MA, 1999.

[Fairchild 2003] A.M. Fairchild. Possible disintermediation: What role for banks in electronic invoicing (EIPP). In *Proceedings of the 16th Bled Electronic Commerce Conference*, June 9–11, 2003.

[Fairchild 2004a] A. M. Fairchild. Using electronic invoicing to manage cash forecasting and working capital in the financial supply chain. In Proceedings 12th ECIS Conference, June 14–16 2004, Turku.

[Fairchild 2004b] A.M. Fairchild, P.M.A. Ribbers, A. Nooteboom. A success factor model for electronic markets: Defining outcomes based on stakeholder context, and business process. *Business Process Management Journal* 10(1). 2004.

[Farley 1998] J. Farley. *Java Distributed Computing*. O'Reilly, 1998.

[Felten 1996] E.W. Felten et al. Web spoofing: An internet con game. Technical report 540-96, Department of Computer Science, Princeton University, 1996. Available at `www.cs.princeton.edu/sip`.

[Fong 1998] T. Fong, D. Fowler, P.M.C. Swatman. Success and failure factors for implementing effective electronic markets. *International Journal of Electronic Commerce & Business Media* 8(1). 1998.

[Ford 1997] W. Ford, M.S. Baum. *Secure Electronic Commerce: Building the infrastructure for digital signatures and encryption*. Prentice Hall, 1997.

[Forrester 1961] J.W. Forrester. *Industrial Dynamics*. MIT Press, Cambridge, MA, 1961.

[Forrester 2000] Forrester Research. Books unbound. Forrester Report, 2000.

[Freed 1996] N. Freed, N. Borenstein. Multipurpose internet mail extensions (MIME): Media types. November 1996. Available at `www.ietf.org/rfc/rfc2046.txt`.

[Frolund 2001] S. Frolund, K. Govindarajan. Transactional conversations. In *W3C Web Services Workshop*, July 2001. Available at `www.w3.orgt/2001/03/WSWS-popa`.

[Froomkin 1996] A.M.Froomkin. The essential role of TTPs in electronic commerce. 1996. Available at `www.law.miami.edu/~froomkin`.

[Fukuyama 1995] F. Fukuyama. *Trust: The social virtues and the creation of prosperity*. The Free Press, New York, 1995.

[Galliers 2003] R. D. Galliers, D.E. Leidner, (eds). *Strategic Information Management*. Butterworth-Heinemann, 2003.

[Gamma 1995] E. Gamma, R. Helm, R. Johnson, J. Vlissides. *Design patterns: Elements of reusable object-oriented software*. Addison Wesley, 1995.

[Gardner 2002] J. Gardner, Z. Rendon. *XSLT and Xpath*. Prentice Hall , 2002.

[Gartner 1998] Gartner Group. The Future of E-Commerce, Symposium Itxpo98, Cannes.

[Gartner 2001] Gartner Group. B2B internet invoicing & payments: Cash is king. GartnerGroup Report. Stamford, CT, January 2001.

[Gates 1995] W. Gates. *The Road Ahead*. Viking, London, 1995.

[Gates 1999] W. Gates. *Business @ the Speed of Thought: Using a digital nervous system*. Warner Books, New York, 1999.

[Gebauer 1998] J. Gebauer, C. Beam, A. Segev. Impact of the internet on procurement. *Acquisition Review Quarterly*, February 1998. Available at `www.haas.berkeley.edu/cmit/procurement`.

[Gettys 1999] J. Gettys, et al. Hypertext transfer protocol – HTTP/1.1. June 1999. Available at `www.ietf.org/rfc/rfc2616.txt`.

[Ghosh 1998] S. Gosch. Making business sense of the internet. Harvard Business Review, May–June 2000.

[Goepfert 2002] J. Goepfert, M. Whalen. An evolutionary view of software as a service. IDC White paper. 2002. Available at `www.idc.com`.

[Goldfarb 2001] C.F. Goldfarb, P. Prescod. *The XML Handbook*. Prentice Hall, 2001.

[Graham 2002] S. Graham et al. Building *Web Services with Java* SAMS Publishing, 2002.

[Granovetter 1985] M. Granovetter. Economic action and social structure: The problem of embeddedness. *American Journal of Sociology* 91(3). 1985.

[Grover 2001] V. Grover, J. T. C. Teng. E-commerce and the information market. *Communications of the ACM* 44(4). 2001.

[Gruber 1993] T.R.Gruber. Toward principles for the design of ontologies used for knowledge sharing. KSL-93-04. Knowledge Systems Laboratory, Stanford University, 1993.

[GTNews 2003] GTNews. Working capital survey: Electronic invoice presentment & payment. Available at `www.gtnews.com`, 2003.

[Gulati 1995] R. Gulati. Does familiarity breed trust? The implications of repeated ties for contractual choice in alliances. *Academy of Management Journal*, 38(1). 1995.

[Gurbaxani 1991] V. Gurbaxani, S. Whang. The impact of information systems on organizations and markets. *Communications of the ACM* 34(1). 1991.

[Hall 2001] M. Hall. *Servlets and Java Server Pages*. Prentice Hall, 2001.

[Hammer 1990] M. Hammer. Reengineering work: Don't automate, obliterate. Harvard Business Review, July–August 1990.

[Handfield 2002] R. B. Handfield, E.L. Nichols. *Supply Chain Redesign*. Prentice Hall 2002.

[Hannon 2002] D. Hannon. E-procurement strategies: E-procurement adoptions progress slowly and steadily. *Purchasing*, www.purchasing.com, June 20, 2002.

[Harmon 2003a] P. Harmon. Business process architecture and the process-centric company. Business Process Trends 1(3). March 2003.

[Harmon 2003b] P. Harmon. Second generation business process methodologies. *Business Process Trends* 1(5). May 2003.

[Harmon 2003c] P. Harmon. Managing business processes. *Business Process Trends* 1(5). May 2003.

[Hernacki 2003] P. Hernacki, R. Pruett. Solving the supply chain puzzle. *Business Integration Journal*, October 2003.

[Herzum 2000] P. Herzum, O. Sims. *Business Component Factory*. John Wiley & Sons Inc., 2000.

[Hess 1994] C. M. Hess, C.F. Kemerer. Computerized loan origination systems: An industry case study of the electronic market hypothesis. *MIS Quarterly* 18(3). 1994.

[Higginson 1997] J. K. Higginson, A. Alam. Supply chain management techniques in medium-to-small manufacturing firms. *The International Journal of Logistics Management* 8, 1997.

[Hinterhuber 1994] H. H. Hinterhuber, B. M. Levin, B. M. Strategic networks: The organization of the future. *Long Range Planning* 27(3). 1994.

[Hoelze 1995] U. Hoelze. Adaptive optimisation for self: Reconciling high performance with exploratory programming. PhD thesis. Dept. of Computer Science, Stanford Univ., 1995. Available as technical report SMLI TR-95-35, Sun Laboratories, Mountain View, CA., 1995.

[Hoffman 1995] D. Hoffman, T. Novak, P. Chatterjee. Commercial scenarios for the web: Opportunities and challenges. *Journal of Computer-Mediated Communication*, 1(2).

[Hohpe 2003] G. Hohpe, B. Woolf. *Enterprise Integration Patterns*. Addison Wesley, 2003.

[Holland 1995] C.P. Holland. Cooperative supply chain management: The impact of interorganizational information systems. *Journal of Strategic Information Systems* 4(2). 1995.

[Holland 2002] P. Holland. Building web services from existing applications. *EAI Journal*, September 2002.

[Hollinsworth 1995] D. Hollinsworth. The workflow reference model. Technical Report TC00-1003. Workflow Management Coalition, January 1995.

[Hopkins 2000] J. Hopkins. Component primer. *Communications of the ACM* 43(10). October 2000.

[Hoque 2000] F. Hoque. *e-Enterprise*. Cambridge University Press, 2000.

[Hosmer 1995] L.T. Hosmer. Trust: The connection link between organizational theory and philosophical ethics. *Academy of Management Review* 20. 1995.

[Hurwitz 2001a] Hurwitz Group. e-Business infrastructure management. April 2001. Available at www.hurwitz.com.

[Hurwitz 2001b] Hurwitz Group. Ten pillars for world class business process management. 2001.

[Hurwitz 2002] Hurwitz Group. New value for the next generation: Legacy modernization. Hurwitz Group, 2002. Available at www.hurwitz.com.

[Ibbotson 2001] J. Ibbotson. ebXML trading-partners specification. In *XML Europe* 2001. Brussels, May 2001.

[IBM 2001] IBM. Linking security needs to e-Business evolution. July 2001. Available at ibm.com/security.

[IDC 2000] IDC. Quality of service for e-Business. IDC Executive Brief, IDC #23679, December 2000. Available at www.idc.com.

[IEC 2000] International Engineering Consortium. Specification and description language (SDL). Available at www.iec.org/online/tutorials/sdl/.

[Ince 2002] D. Ince. *Developing Distributed and E-Commerce Applications*. Addison Wesley, 2002.

[Inge 1995] R. Inger, A. Braithwaite, M. Christopher. Creating a manufacturing environment that is in harmony with the market: The 'how' of supply chain management. *Production Planning and Control* 6, 1995.

[Intel 2002] Intel. SCOR experience at intel: Methods and tools for supply chain management. Information Technology White Paper, August 2002. Available at `www.intel.com/business/bss/swapps/supply/scor.pdf`.

[Irani 2002] R. Irani. An introduction to ebXML. In P. Fletcher, M. Waterhouse (eds). *Web Services Business Strategies and Architectures*. Expert Press, Birmingham, UK, 2002.

[ISO 1997] International Organization for Standardization. Open EDI reference model. ISO/IEC 14662:1997. ISO 1997.

[IT Governance Institute 2003] IT Governance Institute. Board briefing on IT governance. 2nd Edition. 2003. Available at `www.itgi.org`.

[Jacobs 2002] Ian Jacobs (editor). Architectural principles of the world wide web. Working Draft. W3C, August 2002. Available at `www.w3.org/TR/webarch/`.

[Jacobson 1997] I. Jacobson, M. Griss, and P. Jonsson. *Software Reuse: Architecture, process and organization for business success*. Addison Wesley, 1997.

[Jarillo 1988] J. C. Jarillo. On strategic networks. *Strategic Management Journal*, 9. 1988.

[Jarman 2002] P. Jarman. Business process integration patterns for distributed organizations. *eAI Journal*, January 2002.

[Java servlets] Sun Microsystems. Java servlet technology – documentation. Available at `http://java.sun.com/products/servlet/docs.html`.

[JavaWorld 2002] JavaWorld. Enterprise application integration using J2EE. August 2002. Available at `www.javaworld.com/javaworld/jw-08-2002/jw-0809-eai_p.html`.

[Johnson 1998] M. Johnson. A beginner's guide to enterprise java beans. JavaWorld, Oct. 1998. Available at `www.javaworld.com/javaworld/jw-10-1998/jw-10-beans.html`.

[Johnson 1999] G. Johnson, K. Scholes. *Exploring Corporate Strategy*. Prentice Hall, 1999.

[Johnston 1988] R. Johnston, P.R. Lawrence. Beyond vertical integration: The rise of the value-adding partnerships. *Harvard Business Review* 66(4). July–August, 1998.

[JSP] Sun Microsystems. Java server pages technology – dynamically generated web content. Available at `http://java.sun.com/products/jsp`.

[Kambil 1998a] A. Kambil, A. Ginsberg, M. Bloch. Reinventing value propositions. Working Paper. NYC Center for Research on Information Systems, 1998.

[Kambil 1998b] A. Kambil, E. van Heck. Reengineering the Dutch flower auctions: A framework for analyzing exchange organizations. *Information Systems Research* 9(1). 1998.

[Kanter 1992] R.M. Kanter. Think like the customer: The new global business logic. *Harvard Business Review* 70(4). 1992.

[Kaplan 1999] S. Kaplan, M. Sawhney. B2B E-Commerce hubs: Towards a taxonomy of business models. 1999.

[Kaplan 2000] S. Kaplan,M. Sawhney. E-Hubs: The new B2B marketplaces. Harvard Business Review, May–June, 2000.

[Kasi 2005] V. Kasi. Systemic assessment of SCOR for modeling supply chains. *Proceedings of the 38th Hawaii International Conference on System Sciences*, January 2005.

[Kaufman 1995] C. Kaufman, R. Perlman, M. Speciner. *Network Security, Private Communication in a Public World*. Prentice Hall, 1995.

[Kaufmann 2001] R. Kaufmann, E. Walden. Economics and electronic commerce: Survey and research directions. *International Journal of Electronic Commerce* 5, `http://eric.akindofmagic.com/documents/ecomreview3.pdf`., 2001.

[Kavantzas 2004] N. Kavantzas. Web services choreography description language 1.0. Editor's Draft, April 3 2004. Available at `http://lists.w3.org/Archives/Public/www-archive/2004Apr/att-0004/cdl_v1-editors-apr03-2004-pdf.pdf`.

[Keen 1998] P. W. Keen. *Competing in Time: Using telecommunications for competitive advantage*. Cambridge, MA, 1998.

[Killela 1998] P. Killela. *Web performance tuning*. O'Reilly. October 1998.

[King 1998] W. R King. Process reengineering: The strategic dimensions. *Information Systems Management* 11(2). 1998.

[Klein 1978] B. Klein, R.A. Crawford, A. A. Alchian. Vertical integration, appropriable rents, and the competitive contracting process. *Journal of Law and Economics* 21. 1978.

[Klein 1996] S. Klein. The configuration of inter-organizational relationships. *European Journal of Information Systems* 5, 1996.

[Kobryn 2004] C. Kobryn. UML 3.0 and the future of modeling. *Software and Systems Modeling* 3(1). 2004.

[Koehler 2005] J. Koehler, R. Hauser, S. Sendall, M. Wahler. Declarative techniques for model-driven business process integration. *IBM Systems Journal* 44(1). 2005.

[Kotok 2002] A. Kotok, D. R. R. Webber. *ebXML: The new global standard for doing business over the Internet*. New Riders, 2002.

[Kotok 2002] A. Kotok. New XML e-Business model seeks to break semantic interoperability barriers. November 2002. `www.webservices.org`.

[Kraljic 1983] P. Kraljic. Purchasing must become supply management. *Harvard Business Review*, 1983.

[Kraut 1998] R. E. Kraut, Rice, C. Cool, R. S. Fish. Varieties of social influence: The role of utility and norms in the success of a new communication medium. *Organization Science* 9(4). 1998.

[Kreger 2001] H. Kreger. Web services conceptual infrastructure (WSCA 1.0). IBM Software Group, May 2001. Available at `www.ibm.com/software/solutions/webservices/pdf/WSCA.pdf`.

[Kruchten 2004] P. Kruchten. *The Rational Unified Process: An Introduction*, 3rd edition. Addison Wesley-Longman, Reading, MA, 2004.

[Kubicek 1992] H. Kubicek. The organization gap in large scale EDI systems. in R. J. Streng, C. F. Ekering, E. van Heck, J. F. H. Schultz, *Scientific research on EDI*, Proceedings of the EDIPUUT workshop 1992, the Netherlands, SAMSOM BedrijfsInformatie, Alphen aan den Rijn, 1992.

[Kubler 1999] J. Kubler. Electronic commerce on the web. Informal Paper. United Nations Economic and Social Council, December, 1999.

[Kurose 2003] J. F. Kurose, K. W. Ross. *Computer Networking: A top-down approach featuring the Internet*, 2nd edition. Addison Wesley, 2003.

[Kyte 2001] A. Kyte. Procurement: An overview of electronic catalogue commerce. Research Note. Gartner Group, January 2001.

[Laudon 2003] K. C. Laudon, C. G. Traver. *E-Commerce: Business, Technology, Society*. Addison Wesley, Boston MA, 2003.

[Laudon 2004] K.C. Laudon and J.P. Laudon. *Management Information Systems*, 8th edition. Prentice Hall, 2004.

[Lee 1996] T. H. Lee, T.H. Clark. Market process reengineering through electronic market systems: Opportunities and challenges. *Journal of Management Information Systems* 13(3). Winter 1996–97.

[Lee 1998] H. G. Lee. Do electronic markets lower the price of goods? *Communications of the ACM* 41(1). January 1998.

[Lee 2001] H. L. Lee, S. Whang. Supply chain integration over the internet. *Commercenet*, report 01-01, Cupertino, CA, USA, 2001.

[Lewis 1995] T. G. Lewis. *Object-Oriented Application Frameworks*. Prentice Hall 1995.

[Leymann 2000] F. Leymann, D. Roller. *Production Workflow*. Prentice Hall, Upper Saddle River, New Jersey, 2000.

[Liebermann 1986] H. Liebermann. Using prototypical objects to implement shared behavior in object-oriented systems. *Proceedings of OOPSLA, ACM SIGPLAN Notices* 21(11). 1986.

[Linthicum 2001a] D.S. Linthicum. *B2B Application Integration*. Addison Wesley, 2001.

[Linthicum 2001b] D. Linthicum. B2B application integration. *Software Magazine*. April/May 2001.

[Lubinsky 2001a] B. Lubinsky. Achieving the ultimate EAI implementation. *EAI Journal*. February 2001.

[Lubinsky 2001b] B. Lubinsky, M. Farrel. Enterprise architecture and J2EE. *EAI Journal*. November 2001.

[Lucking 2001] J. Lücking. B2B E-Marketplaces: A new challenge to existing competition law rules? *Conference on Competition Law and the New Economy*, July 2001.

[Maholtra 1998] Y. Maholtra. Business process redesign: An overview. *IEEE Engineering Management Review* 26(3). Fall 1998. Available at `www.brint.com/papers/bpr.htm`.

[Malone 1987] T. W. Malone, J. Yates, R. I. Benjamin. Electronic markets and electronic hierarchies. *Communications of the ACM* 30(6). 1987.

[Manes 2003] A. T. Manes. Registering a web service in UDDI. *Web Services Journal* 3(10). October 2003.

[Mani 2002] A. Mani, A. Nagarajian. Understanding quality of service for web services. IBM Developer Works. January 2002. Available at `www-106.ibm.com/developerworks/library/ws-quality.html`.

[Margretta 2002] J. Margretta. Why business models matter. *Harvard Business Review*, 2002.

[Markus 1996] M. L. Markus, R. I. Benjamin. Change management strategy. *MIS Quarterly* 20(4). December 1996. Also in R.D. Galliers, D. E.Leidner, B. S. H. Baker (eds). *Strategic Information Management: Challenges and strategies in managing information systems*, Butterworth Heinemann, 2001.

[Marshak 2003] D. S. Marshak, P. B. Seybold. An executive's guide to portals. P. Seybold Group, 2003. Available at `www.psgroup.com/vm/portals/`.

[Masud 2003] S. Masud. Rosettanet based web services. *IBM Developer Works*. July 2003.

[May 2001] M. May. The creative destruction of EAI. *EAI Journal*. October 2001.

[McGoveran 2004] D. McGoveran. An introduction to BPM and BPMS. *Business Integration Journal*. April 2004.

[McInnis 1999] K. McInnis. Component-based design and reuse. Castek Software Factory Inc., 1999. Available at `www.cdb-hq.com/articles/1999`.

[McInnis 2000] K. McInnis. Component-based development. Castek Software Factory Inc., 2000. Available at `www.cdb-hq.com/articles/2000`.

[McKee 2001] B. McKee, D. Ehnebuske and D. Rogers. UDDI version 2.0 – API specification. UDDI. org, June 2001.

[Menascé 2000] D.A. Menascé, V.A.F. Almeida. *Scaling for E-Business: Technologies, models, performance, and capacity planning*. Prentice Hall, 2000.

[MetaServer 2001] MetaServer, Inc. The power of business process integration. 2001.

[Meyer 1992a] B. Meyer. Applying 'design by contract'. *IEEE Computer* 25(10). October 1992.

[Meyer 1992b] B. Meyer. *Eiffel: The Language*. Prentice Hall, New York, NY 1992.

[Meyer 1997] B. Meyer. *Object-Oriented Software Construction*, 2nd edition. Prentice Hall International, London, UK, 1997.

[Miles 1986] R. E. Miles, C. C. Snow. Organizations: New concepts for new forms. *California Management Review* 28(3). 1986.

[Miles 1992] R. E. Miles, C. C. Snow. Causes of failure in network organizations. *California Management Review*, Summer 1992.

[Millen 2002] D. R. Millen, M. A. Fontaine, M. J. Miller. Understanding the benefits and costs of communities of practice. *Communications of the ACM* 45, 2002.

[Minoli 1998] D. Minoli, E. Minoli. *Web Commerce Technology Handbook*. McGraw-Hill 1998.

[Mintzberg 1983] H. Mintzberg. *Structure in Fives: Designing effective organizations*. Prentice Hall, 1983.

[Mintzberg 1994] H. Mintzberg. The Rise and Fall of Strategic Planning. Prentice Hall, 1994.

[Monczka 2000] R. M. Monczka, R. B. Handfield, T. B. Scannell, G.L. Ragatz, D. J. Frayer *New Product Development: Strategies for supplier integration*. ASQC/Quality Press, 2000.

[Monson-Haefel 2001] R. Monson-Haefel, D. A.Chappell . *Java Message Service*. O'Reilly, 2001.

[Moore 2000] B. Moore, M. Fielding. *e-Marketplace Pattern*. IBM Redbooks, `ibm.com/redbooks`, Nov. 2000.

[Mougayar 1998] W. Mougayar. *Opening Digital markets: Battle Plans and Business Strategies for Internet E-Commerce*, 2nd edition. McGraw-Hill, 1998.

[Mowbray 1997] T.J. Mowbray, W.A. uh. Inside CORBA: *Distributed Object Standards and Applications*. Addison Wesley Longman, Inc., 1997.

[Mysore 2003] S. Mysore. Securing web services: Concepts, standards, and requirements. Sun Microsytems, October 2003. Available at `sun.com/software`.

[NACHA 2001] NACHA. Business-to-business EIPP: Presentment models, part 1. The Council for electronic billing and payment. National Automated Clearing House Association, 2001.

[Nagle 1998] J. Nagle, S.Grufferty, G. Reinke, P. Sylvester. Report to the commission of the european communities for the eurotrust pki pilot service. *European Commission DG XIII*, 1998.

[Nah 2004] F. H. Nah, M. Rosemann, E. Watson. E-Business process management. Business *Process Management Journal*, 10(1).

[Nartovich 2001] A. Nartovich, T. Abou Aly, V. Mathur, P. Teh. *IBM framework for e-Business: Technology, Solution and Design Overview*. IBM Red Books, September 2001. Available at `ibm.com/redbooks`.

[Negron 2002] P. Negron, R. Alpen. Embedding business management technology: IJET travel intelligence. In L. Fischer (editor). *Workflow Handbook* 2002. Future Strategies Inc., 2002.

[Nelson 2004] M. Nelson. Enterprise architecture modernization using the adaptive enterprise framework. *Business Process Trends*, January, 2004. Available at `www.bptrends.com`.

[Niks 2000] W. Niks, P. Plasmeijer, E. Peelen. E-commerce: Transactiemodel voor het internet. Adfo Specialists Group, Deventer, the Netherlands, 2000.

[Nohria 1992] N. Nohria, R. Eccles. *Networks and Organizations*. Harvard Business School Press, 1992.

[Noorderhaven 1995] N.G. Noorderhaven. *Strategic Decision Making*. Addison Wesley, Oxford, 1995.

[Nooteboom 2001] A. O. Nooteboom. Success factors of electronic markets. Graduation thesis. Tilburg University, 2001.

[Nunes 2000] P. Nunes, D. Wilson, A. Kambil. The all-in-one market. *Harvard Business Review*, May–June 2000.

[OMA 1997] Object Management Group. *Introduction to OMG's specifications*. Available at `www.omg.org/gettingstarted/specintro.htm#OMA`.

[OMG 2004] Object Management Group. Unified modeling language: Superstructure, version 2.0. Document ptc/04-10-02, October 2004. Available at `www.omg.org/cgi-bin/doc?ptc/2004-10-02`.

[Orfali 1997] Orfali R., Harkey D., Edwards J. *Instant CORBA*. John Wiley and Sons Inc., 1997.

[Overtveldt 2001] S. van Overtveldt. Creating an infrastructure for e-Business. *e-Business Report*. IBM Corporation, April 2001.

[Owen 2004] M. Owen, J. Raj. BPMN and business process management: An introduction to the new business process modelling standard. *Business Process Trends*, March 2004. Available at `www.bptrends.com`.

[Papazoglou 2000] M. P. Papazoglou, P. Ribbers, A. Tsalgatidou. Integrated value chains and their implications from a business and technology standpoint. *Decision Support Systems* 29(4). 2000.

[Papazoglou 2002] M. P. Papazoglou, J. Yang. Design methodology for web services and business processes. *Workshop Technologies for Electronic Services*. Hong Kong, September 2002.

[Papazoglou 2003a] M. P. Papazoglou, D. Georgakopulos. Service oriented computing. *Communications of the ACM* 46(10). October 2003.

[Papazoglou 2003b] M. P. Papazoglou. Web services and business transactions. *World Wide Web Journal* 6(1). March 2003.

[Parker 1988] M. M. Parker, R. J. Benson, H. E. Trainor. *Information Economics*. Prentice Hall, 1988.

[Parker 1999] M. M. Parker. Theory and practice of business/IT organizational interdependencies. Ph.D. thesis. Tilburg University, 1999.

[Patil 2003] S. Patil, E. Newcomer. ebXML and web services. *IEEE Internet Computing*. May 2003.

[Paulk 1993] M. Paulk, et al. Capability maturity model for software. version 1.1, technical report SE-93 TR-024. Software Engineering Institute, Pittsburgh, 1993.

[Pelz 2003] C. Pelz. Web services orchestration: A review of emerging technologies, tools, and standards. Technical report, 2003. Available at `http://devresource.hp.com/drc/technical/whitepapers/WSOrch/WSOrchestration.pdf`.

[Pemberton 2000] S. Pemberton et al. XHTML 1.0: The extensible hypertext markup language: A reformulation of HTML-4 in XML 1.0. January 2000. Available at `www.w3.org/TR/xhtml1/`.

[Peppard 1999] Peppard, J. Information management in the global enterprise: An organizing framework. *European Journal of Information Systems* 8, 1999.

[Peppers 1993] D. Peppers, M. Rogers. *The One to One Future*. Currency Doubleday, New York, 1993.

[Peppers 1997] D. Peppers, M. Rogers. *Enterprise One to One: Tools for competing in the interactive age*. Currency Doubleday, New York, 1997.

[Peteraf 1993] M. A. Peteraf. The cornerstones of competitive advantage: A resource-based view. *Strategic Management Journal* 14(3). 1993.

[Pettinga 1998] P. J. Pettinga, G.E. Hilgers. Content management het kloppend hart van een e-Procurement systeem (content management the beating heart of an e-Procurement system). *Tijdschrift voor Inkoop & Logistiek*, October 1998.

[Philips 2000] C. Philips, M. Meeker. The B2B internet report: Collaborative Commerce. Morgan Stanley Dean Witter, 2000.

[Pilz 2003] G. Pliz. A new world of web services security. *Web Services Journal*, March 2003.

[Pine 1993] B. J. Pine. *Mass Customization: The new frontiers in business competition*. Harvard Business School Press, Boston, 1993.

[Platier 1996] E. A. H. Platier. Een logistieke kijk op bedrijfsprocessen, concepten ten behoeve van business process redesign en workflow management (A logistic view on business processes, concepts for BPR and WFM). PhD thesis. Eindhoven University of Technology, 1996.

[Plesmus 2002] C. Plesmus. Introduction to workflow. In *Workflow Handbook 2002*. Workflow Management Coalition, 2002.

[Plouin 2002] G. Plouin, G. Bort. XML trust: Technology and implementation. TecMetrix technical white paper, April 2002. Available at `www.techmetrix.com`.

[Pollock 2002] J. T. Pollock. Integration's dirty little secret: It's a matter of semantics. White Paper. Modulant Inc., February 2002. Available at `www.modulant.com`.

[Porter 1980] M. E. *Porter. Competitive Strategy*. The Free Press, New York , 1980.

[Porter 1985a] M. E. Porter. *Competitive Advantage: Creating and sustaining superior performance*. The Free Press, New York , 1985.

[Porter 1985b] M. E. Porter, V.E. Millar. How information gives you competitive advantage. *Harvard Business Review* 63(4). 1985.

[Porter 1990] M. Porter. *The Competitive Advantage of Nations*. The Free Press, New York , 1990.

[Porter 1997] M.E. Porter. Creating tomorrow's advantages. In R. Gibson (ed.). *Rethinking the Future*. Nicholas Brealey, London, 1997.

[Porter 1999] M. Porter. The net won't transform everything. *Interactive Week*, October 25, `www.zdnet.com./zdnet/stories/news/0,4586,2381095,00.html.`,1999.

[Porter 2001] M.E. Porter. Strategy and the internet. *Harvard Business Review*, March 2001.

[Prahalad 1991] C. K. Prahalad and G. Hamel. The core competence of the corporation. in Montgomery and Porter (eds). *Seeking and Securing Competitive Advantage*. Harvard Business School Press, Boston, 1991.

[Prahalad 1998] C. K. Prahalad. Managing discontinuities: The emerging challenges. *Research Technology Management* 37(3). 1993.

[Qualys 2003] Qualys Inc. On-demand security audits and vulnerability management. November 2003. Available at `www.qualys.com`.

[Quinn 1990] J. B. Quinn, T.L. Doorely and P.C. Paquette. Beyond products: Services based strategy. *Harvard Business Review* 68, 1990.

[Raggett 1999] D. Raggett, A. Le Hors, I. Jacobs. HTML 4.01 Specification. December 1999. Available at `www.w3.org/TR/1999/REC-html401-19991224/`.

[Rayport 1995] J. F. Rayport, J. J. Sviokla. Exploiting the virtual value chain. *Harvard Business Review*, November–December, 1995.

[Reck 1998] M. Reck. The formal and systematic specification of market structures and trading services. *Journal of Management Information Systems* 15(2). 1998.

[Ribbers 2002a] P. M. Ribbers, K-C Schoo. Program management and compexity of ERP implementation. *Engineering Management Journal*, Vol. 14, No. 2, June 2002.

[Ribbers 2002b] P. M. Ribbers, A. M. Fairchild, E. van Heck, J. Kleijnen. Creating alternative electronic trading mechanisms in time-sensitive transaction markets. In J.E.J. Prins *et al.* eds. *Trust in Electronic Commerce: The role of trust from a legal, an organizational and a technical point of view*. Kluwer Law International, The Hague, (2002).

[RMI 2000] Sun Microsystems. Fundamentals of RMI. 2001. Available at `http://developer.java.sun.com/developer/onlineTraining/rmi/RMI.html`.

[Robinson 1967] P. J. Robinson, C.W. Faris, Y. Wind. *Industrial Buying and Creative Marketing*. Allyn & Bacon. Boston, 1967

[Roch 2002] E. Roch. Application integration: Business and technology trends. *EAI Journal*. August 2002.

[RosettaNet 2001] RosettaNet. Standards required to support XML-basesd B2B integration. 2001. Available at `www.xmlglobal.com`.

[RosettaNet 2004] RosettaNet Implementation Guide. Cluster 3: Order management segment a: Quote and order entry PIPs 3A4, 3A7, 3A8, 3A9. April 2004. Available at `www.rosettanet.org/usersguides/`.

[RSA 2003] RSA, Inc. RSA-based cryptographic schemes. 22 June 2003. Available at `www.rsasecurity.com/rsalabs/rsa_algorithm/index.html`.

[RUP 2001] Rational Software Corporation. Rational unified process: Best Practices for software development teams. Technical Paper TP026B, Rev. 11/01. November 2001. Available at `www.therationaledge.com`.

[Ryan 2000] J. Ryan. Extending the enterprise: Managing the transition to e-business with web-to-host software solutions. Applied Technologies Group, The Technology Guide series, `www.techguide.com`, 2000.

[Salomaa 1996] A. Salomaa. *Public Key Cryptography*. Springer-Verlag, 1996.

[SAML 2003] OASIS XML-Based Security Services Technical Committee (SSTC). Security assertions markup language: Overview. OASIS, December 2003. Available at `xml.coverpages.org/saml.html`.

[Samtani 2001] G. Samtani. EAI and web services: Easier enterprise application integration? Web Services Architect, October, 2001.

[Samtani 2002] G. Samtani, D. Sadhwani. Enterprise application integration and web services. in P. Fletcher, M. Waterhouse (eds). *Web Services Business Strategies and Architectures*. Expert Press, Birmingham, UK, 2002.

[Sandelands 1994] E. Sandelands. Building supply chain relationships. *International Journal of Physical Distribution & Logistics Management* 24. 1994.

[Sarkar 1995] M.B. Sarkar, B. Butler, C. Steinfield. Intermediaries and cybermediaries: A continuing role for mediating players in the electronic market place. Available at `www.businessmedia.org/netacademy/publications.nsf/all_pk?1305`, 1995.

[Sarkar 1996] M. B. Sarkar, B. Butler, Ch. Steinfield. Intermediaries and cybermediaries: A continuing role for mediating players in the electronic marketplace. *Journal of Computer Mediated Communication* 1(3). `http://jcmc.huji.ac.il/vol1/issue3/ sarkar.html`, 1996.

[Sarkar 1998] M.B. Sarkar, B. Butler, C. Steinfield. Cybermediaries in the electronic marketspace: Toward theory building. *Journal of Business Research*, 41(3). 1998.

[Schlosser 1999] M. Schlosser. IBM application framework for e-Business: Security. Nov. 1999. Available at `www-4.ibm.com/software/developer/library/security/index.html`.

[Schmelzer 2002] Schmelzer et al. *XML and Web Services*. SAMs Publishing, 2002.

[Schmid 1997] B.F. Schmid. Requirements for electronic markets architecture. International *Journal of Electronic Commerce & Business Media* 7(1). 1997.

[Schmitz 2000] S. Schmitz. The effects of electronic commerce on the strf intermediation. *Journal of Computer-Mediated Communication* 5(3). 2000. Available at `www.ascusc.org/jcmc/vol5/issue3/schmitz.html`.

[Schoder 2000a] D. Schoder. Forecasting the success of telecommunications services in the presence of network effects. *Information Economics and Policy* 12, 2000.

[Schoder 2000b] D. Schoder, P.L. Yin. Building firm trust online. *Communications of the ACM* 43(12):73–9.

[Schoo 1999] K-C Schoo. *Engineering Complex Software Implementation Programmes*. VDE Verlag, Berlin, Offenbach, 1999.

[Schumpeter 1939] J. Schumpeter. *Business Cycles: A theoretical and statistical analysis of the capitalist process*. McGraw-Hill, New York, 1939.

[Seacord 2001] R. C. Seacord, S. Comella-Dorda, G. Lewis, P. Place, D. Plakosh. Legacy system modernization strategies. Technical report, CMU/SEI-2001-TR-025, ESC-TR-2001-025, Software Engineering Institute, Carnegie Mellon University, July 2001. Available at `www.sei.cmu.edu/publications/pubweb.html`.

[Segev 1997] A. Segev, C. Beam. Automated negotiations: A survey of the state of the art. *WirtschaftsInformatik* 39, 1997.

[Selic 1994] B. Selic, G. Gullekson, P.T. Ward. *Real-Time Object-Oriented Modeling*. John Wiley & Sons, 1994.

[Selz 1999] D.Selz. *Value webs: Emerging forms of fluid and flexible organizations*. Sankt Gallen.

[Shapiro 1999] C. Shapiro, H.R. Varian. *Information Rules: A strategic guide to the network economy*. Harvard Business School Press, Boston, MA., 1999.

[Sharma 2001b] R. Sharma, B. Stearns, T. Ng. *J2EE Connector Architecture and Enterprise Application Integration*. Addison Wesley, 2001.

[Sharma 2002] R. Sharma. *J2EE connector architecture*. Available at `http://java.sun.com/j2ee/connector/`.

[Sheombar 1995] H. Sheombar. Understanding logistics coordination. Tutein Nolthenius, S'Hertogenbosch, PhD thesis. Tilburg University, 1995.

[Silver 2003] B. Silver. BPM 2.0: Process without programming. Bruce Silver Associates, September 2003. Available at `www.brsilver.com`.

[Singh 2002] N. Singh. *Electronic Commerce: Economics and Strategy*. Prentice Hall, 2002.

[Skonnard 2002] A. Skonnard, M. Gudgin. *Essential XML Quick Reference*. Addison Wesley, 2002.

[Slee 1997] C. Slee, M. Slovin. Legacy asset management. *Information Systems Management*. Winter 1997.

[Smits 1997] M.T. Smits, K.G. van der Poel, P.M.A. Ribbers. Assessment of information strategies in insurance companies in the Netherlands. *The Journal of Strategic Information Systems*, 6. 1997

[Sneed 1995] H. M. Sneed. Planning the re-engineering of legacy systems. *IEEE Software* 12(1). January 1995.

[Somers 2001] T. M. Somers, K. Nelson. The impact of critical success factors across the satges of enterprise resource planning implementations. *Proceedings of the 34th Hawaii International Conference on Systems Sciences*, IEEE 2001.

[Spulber 1996] D. F. Spulber. Market microstructure and intermediation. *Journal of Economic Perspectives* 10(3). Summer 1996.

[Staff 2002] Staff. e-Procurement adoptions progress slowly and steadily. *Purchasing*, June 20, 2002.

[Statham 2001] S. Statham, P. Knowledge. The emergence and impact of e-Marketplace on SME supply chain efficiencies. Prime Faraday Partnership, May 2001. Available at `www.primetechnologywatch.org.uk/`.

[Strader 1997] T. J. Strader, M. J. Shaw. Characteristics of electronic markets. *Decision Support Systems*, 21(3) 1997.

[Sun 2000] Sun Corporation. RMI. Available at `http://java.sun.com/products/jdk/rmi/examples.html`.

[Surer 1996] S. L. Surer, A. S. Rosenthal, A. L. Schafer, E. R. Hughes, R. S. Hyland. Distributed object mangement integration system: Methodology. MITRE, Centre for Intelligence Systems, Massachusetts, Oct. 1996.

[Sydow 1993] J. Sydow, A. Windeler. Managing corporate networks: A structurationist perspective. In Ebers and Mark (eds). *Proceedings of the Interorganizational networks: Structures and processes workshop*. Paderborn, 192–236.

[Talbott 1995] S. Talbott. *The Future Does Not Compute*. O'Reilly, Sebastopol, CA, 1995.

[Tapscott 1996] D. Tapscott. *The Digital Economy: Promise and peril in the age of networked intelligence*. McGraw-Hill, 1996.

[Teece 1997] D. Teece, G. Pisano, and A. Shuen. Dynamic capabilities and strategic management. *Strategic Management Journal* 18(7). 1997.

[Teng 1994] J. T. Teng, V. Grover, K.D. Fiedler. Business process reengineering: Charting a strategic path for the information age. *California Management Review* 36(3). Spring 1994.

[Teng 1994] J. T. Teng, V. Grover, K. D. Fiedler. Business process reengineering: Charting a strategic path for the information age. *California Management Review* 36(3). Spring 1994.

[Tilley 1996] S. Tilley, S. Paul, D. Smith. Toward a framework for program understanding. in *Proceedings of the 4th Workshop on Program Comprehension*. IEEE Computer Society Press, Berlin, Germany, March 1996.

[Tilley 1997] S. Tilley, D. B. Smith. On using the web as infrastructure for reengineering. In 5th International IEEE Workshop on Program Comprehension (WPC '97). Dearborn, MI, USA, May 1997.

[Timberlake 2002] P. Timberlake. The Pitfalls of using multicast publish/subscribe for EAI. ebizQ, July 2002. Available at `http://messageq.ebizq.net/communications_middleware/timberlake_1.html`

[Timmers 1998] P. Timmers. Business models for electronic markets. *Electronic Markets Focus theme*, 8(2). 1998.

[Timmers 1999] P. Timmers. *Electronic Commerce: Strategies and models for business-to business trading*. John Wiley & Sons, 1999.

[Toppen 1998] R. Toppen, M. Smits, P. Ribbers. Financial securities transactions: A study of logistic process performance improvements. *Journal of Strategic Information Systems*, 7, 1998.

[Toppen 1999a] R. Toppen. Improving the performance of electronic business networks – a research into information technology enabled redesign of market networks and processes in the financial sector. PhD thesis. Tilburg University, 1999.

[Toppen 1999b] R. Toppen, P. Smits, P. Ribbers. Improving process performance through market network redesign: A study of the impact of electronic markets in the financial securities sector. Proceedings of the 32nd Hawaii International Conference on Systems Sciences, 1998.

[Ulrich 2002] W. Ulrich. *Legacy Systems – Transformation Strategies*. Prentice Hall, 2002.

[Umar 1997] A. Umar. *Application (Re)Engineering: Building Web-based Applications and Dealing with Legacies*. Prentice Hall, New Jersey, 1997.

[Umar 1997] A. Umar. *Client/Server Internet Environments*. Prentice Hall, 1997.

[UMM 2003] United Nations center for trade Facilitation and Electronic Business. UN/CEFACT modelling methodology (UMM) user guide. CEFACT/TMG/N093, www.utmg.org, September 2003.

[Ungar 1987] D. Ungar, R. B. Smith. Self: The power of simplicity. Proceedings of OOPSLA, ACM SIGPLAN Notices 22(12). 1987.

[Urwick 1943] L. Urwick. *The Elements of Administration*. Pitman, London, 1943.

[USHER 2001] USHER Project. The current and future barriers to SMe-volution. 2001. Available at www.usherproject.org.uk/support/scenarios/barriers.pdf.

[USHER 2002] USHER Project. e-Business adviser handbook: Section 2.7 – e-Procurement. Version 2, 30 November 2002. Available at www.usherproject.org.uk/support/hb/HBs27v2.pdf.

[Valentine 2002] C. Valentine, L. Dykes, E. Tittel. XML schemas. Sybex, 2002.

[van de Putte 2001] G van de Putte, L. Gavin, P. Sharp. *Business Process Management using MQSeries and Partner Agreement Manager*. IBM Redbooks, May 2001. Available at www.redbooks.ibm.com/abstracts/sg246166.html?Open.

[van den Heuvel 2002] W.J. van den Heuvel. Integrating modern business applications with objectified legacy systems. PhD thesis. Tilburg University, Center, 2002.

[van Heck 1996] E. van Heck, P.M. Ribbers. Economic effects of electronic markets. CentER Discussion paper(9669. Tilburg University, 1996.

[van Heck 1997] E. van Heck, P. Ribbers, E. E. C. van Damme, J. P. C. Kleijnen, . New entrants and the role of information technology: The case of the teleflower auction in the Netherlands. In J. F. Nunamaker & R. H. Sprague (eds). *Proceedings of the Thirtieth Annual Hawaii International Conference on System Sciences (HICSS)*. 3:228–37. IEEE Computer Society Press, Los Alamitos, 1997.

[van Heck 1998] E. van Heck, P. M. Ribbers. Introducing electronic auction systems in the Dutch flower industry: A comparison of two initiatives. *Wirtschaftsinformatik* 40(3). 1998.

[van Heck 2000] E.van Heck, P. M. Ribbers. Experiences with electronic auctions in the Dutch flower industry. In J. C. Westland and T. H. K. Clark, *Global Electronic Commerce: Theory and case studies*. The MIT Press, 2000.

[van Slyke 2003] G. van Slyke, F. Belanger. *e-Business Technologies: Supporting the net-enhanced organization*. John Wiley & Sons, 2003.

[van Stekelenborg 1997] R. van Stekelenborg. *Information Technology for Purchasing*. Eindhoven University of Technology, 1997.

[van Tuijl 2002] M. van Tuijl. E-Commerce and the prospects for intermediaries. SOBU, 2002.

[van Weele 1994] A. Van Weele. *Purchasing Management: Analysis, Planning and Practice*. Chapman & Hall, London, 1994.

[Venkatraman 1991] N. Venkatraman. IT-induced business reconfiguration. In M.S. Scott Morton (ed.), *The Corporation of the 1990s: Information technology and organizational transformation*. Oxford University Press, New York, 1991.

[Venkatraman 1994] N. Venkatraman. IT-enabled business transformation: From automation to business scope redefinition. *Sloan Management Review*, Winter 1994.

[Venkatraman 1998] N. Venkatraman, and J.C. Henderson. Real strategies for virtual organizing. *Sloan Management Review* 40(1). 1998.

[VeriSign 2003] VeriSign Inc. VeriSign digital trust services. April 2003, www.verisign.com.

[Veryard 2000] R. Veryard. Design pattern: Differentiated service. CBDi Forum, December 2000.

[Wade 1994] Wade, Andrew E. Distributed client-server databases. *Object Magazine* 4(1):47–52, April 1994.

[Ward 2002] J. Ward, J. Peppard. *Strategic Planning for Information Systems*, 3rd edition. John Wiley & Sons, 2002.

[Webber 2000] D. R. Webber. Understanding ebXML, UDDI and XML/EDI. October 2000. Available at www.xmlglobal.com/downloads/ebXML_understanding.pdf.

[Weber 1988] R. Weber. EDP *Auditing: Conceptual foundations and practice*, 2nd edition. McGraw Hill, 1988.

[Webster 1972] F. E. Webster, Jr, Y. Wind. *Organizational Buying Behavior*. Prentice Hall, 1972.

[Weick 1976] K. Weick, K. Educational organizations are loosely coupled systems. *Administrative Science Quarterly* 21, 1976.

[Weiderman 1997a] N. H. Weiderman, L. Northrop, D. Smith, S. Tilley, K. Wallnau. Implications of distributed object computing for reengineering. Software Engineering Institute, Carnegie Mellon University, 1997. Available at www.sei.cmu.edu/publications/documents/97.reports/97tr005/97tr005abstract.html.

[Weiderman 1997b] N. H. Weiderman, J. K. Bergey, D. B. Smith, S. R. Tille. Approaches to legacy system evolution. Technical Report CMU/SEI-97-TR-014, Software Engineering Institute, Carnegie MellonUniversity, 1997. Available at www.sei.cmu.edu/publications/documents/97.reports/97tn014/97tr014abstract.html.

[Weill 1998] P. Weill, M. Broadbent. Leveraging the new infrastructure: How leaders capitalize on information technology. Harvard Business School Press, Boston, 1998.

[Weiser 1984] M. Weiser. Program slicing. *IEEE Transactions on Software Engineering* SE-10(4). 1984.

[Wernerfelt 1984] B. Wernerfelt. A resource-based view of the firm. *Strategic Management Journal* 5(2). 1984.

[WfMC 1998] Workflow Management Coalition. Workflow management application programming interface (interface 2&3) specification. Document Number WFMC-TC-1009, Version 2.0. July 1998.

[WfMC 1999a] Workflow Management Coalition. Terminology & glossary. Document Number WFMC-TC-1011, February 1999.

[WfMC 1999b] Workflow Management Coalition. Interface 1 process definition interchange. Document Number WFMC-TC-1016-P, October 1999.

[WfMC 2000] Workflow Management Coalition. Interoperability Wf-XML binding. Document Number WFMC-TC-1023, May 2000.

[White 2004] S. A. White. Introduction to BPMN. Business Process Trends, July, 2004. Available at www.bptrends.com.

[Whitehead 2002] K. Whitehead. *Component-based Development*. Addison Wesley, 2002.

[Wigand 1995] R.T. Wigand, R. Benjamin. Electronic commerce: Effects on electronic markets. Journal of Computer-Mediated Communication 1(3). 1995. Available at `www.ascuse.org/jcmc/vol11/issue3/wigand.html`.

[Wigand 1997] R.T. Wigand. Electronic commerce: Definition, theory and context. The Information Society 13, 1997.

[Wilkes 1999] L. Wilkes. Application integration. Butler Group Management Guide, May 1999. Available at `www.butlergroup.com`.

[Williamson 1975] O.E. Williamson. *Markets and Hierarchies*. MacMillan, New York, 1975.

[Williamson 1979] O. Williamson. Transaction cost economics: The governance of contractual relationships. *Journal of Law and Economics* 22:233–261. 1979.

[Williamson 1981a] O.E. Williamson. The modern corporation: Origin, evolution attributes. *Journal of Economic Literature* XIX, 1981.

[Williamson 1981b] O.E. Williamson. The economics of organization: The transaction cost approach. *American Journal of Sociology* 87(3). 1981.

[Williamson 1983] O.E. Williamson. Organizational innovation: The transaction cost approach. In J. Ronen (ed.). *Entrepreneurship*. Lexington Books, Lexington, MA, 1983.

[Williamson 1991] O.E. Williamson. Comparative economics organization: The analysis of discrete structural alternatives. *Administrative Science Quarterly*, 36. 1991.

[Wilson 2000] P. Wilson. e-Business strategy. *Management*. August/September, 2000.

[Wolf 2003] C. Wolf. Value chains and business processes. *Business Process Trends* 1(11). November 2003.

[Womack 1998] J. Womack, D. Jones. *Lean Thinking*. Touchstone, Simon and Schuster, London, UK, 1998.

[WS-I 2002] S. Anderson, M. Chapman, M. Goodner, P. Mackinaw, R. Rekasius (eds). Supply chain management use case model. Working Group Draft. Web Services Interoperability Organization, Nov. 2002. Available at `www.ws-i.org/SampleApplications/SupplyChainManagement/2002-11/SCMUseCases-0.18-WGD.htm`.

[WS-Policy 2003] OASIS Cover Pages. Updated versions of web services policy (WS-Policy) specifications. June 2003, Available at `http://xml.coverpages.org/ni2003-06-04-a.html`.

[Yang 2000] J. Yang, M. P. Papazoglou. Interoperation support for electronic business. *Communications of the ACM* 43(6). June 2000.

[Yee 2001] A. Yee, A. Apte. *Integrating your e-Business enterprise*. Sams Publishing, 2001.

[Young 2002] G. Young. EIPP for financial services. Logica Payment Solutions White Paper. Logica plc, London, UK, 2002.

[Zenz 1994] G. Zenz, G.H. Thompson. *Purchasing and the Management of Materials*, 7th edition. John Wiley and Sons, NY, 1994.

[Zimmermann 2003] O. Zimmerman, M. Tomlinson, S. Preuser. *Perspectives on Web Services*. Springer-Verlag, Berlin, 2003.

[Zucker 1986] L. Zucker. Production of trust: Institutional sources of economic structure: 1840–1920. in B. Staw and L. Cummings (eds), *Research in Organizational Behaviour* 8. JAI Press, 1986.